HUMAYMA EXCAVATION PROJECT, 1
RESOURCES, HISTORY,
AND THE WATER-SUPPLY SYSTEM

AMERICAN SCHOOLS OF ORIENTAL RESEARCH
ARCHEOLOGICAL REPORTS

Kevin M. McGeough, Editor

Number 15

Humayma Excavation Project, 1
Resources, History, and the Water-Supply System

To Anna Marguerite McCann Taggart,
my mentor, patron, and dear friend,
and to her partner Robert Taggart,
who supported the work at Humayma
when help was most needed

HUMAYMA EXCAVATION PROJECT, 1

RESOURCES, HISTORY, AND THE WATER-SUPPLY SYSTEM

By

JOHN PETER OLESON

Including Technical Reports by
G. E. BROWN, M. FINNEGAN, J. D. MITCHELL,
C. NIKOLIC, AND C. T. SHAY

AMERICAN SCHOOLS OF ORIENTAL RESEARCH • BOSTON, MA

Humayma Excavation Project, 1

Resources, History, and the Water-Supply System

by

John Peter Oleson

The American Schools of Oriental Research © 2010

ISBN 978-0-89757-083-1

Library of Congress Cataloging-in-Publication Data

Oleson, John Peter.
  Humayma excavation project, 1 : resources, history, and the water-supply system / by John Peter Oleson
    ; including technical reports by G.E. Brown ... [et al.].
    p. cm. -- (Archeological reports / American Schools of Oriental Research ; no. 15)
  Includes bibliographical references and index.
  ISBN 978-0-89757-083-1 (alk. paper)
  1. Humaymat Site (Jordan) 2. Water supply--Jordan--Humaymat Site. 3. Excavations (Archaeology)-
    -Jordan--Humaymat Site. I. Title.
  DS154.9.H86O54 2010
  939'.48--dc22
                  2010040809

Printed in the United States of America on acid-free paper.

Contents

List of Illustrations

List of Tables

Preface and Acknowledgements

The Humayma Hydraulic Survey, a survey of the regional water-supply system of ancient Hawara (modern Humayma), along with numerous probes, was carried out under the author's direction in 1986, 1987, and 1989. In 1991, the author turned his attention to excavation of the settlement centre of Hawara, directing field seasons in 1991, 1992, 1993, 1995, 1996, 1998, 2000, 2002, 2004, and 2005. Co-Directors and Assistant Directors of the excavation project have been Khairieh 'Amr (1991–96), Robert Schick (1991–98), Rebecca Foote (1994–2005), M. Barbara Reeves (2000–2005), Erik de Bruijn (2000–2005), and Andrew Sherwood (2002–2005), and all remain involved in the ongoing publication programme. Reeves (2008, 2010) and Foote (2002, 2008) have also directed their own excavations at the site. This book has benefited from consultations with all of these individuals. In this volume, I report in detail only the results of the Humayma Hydraulic Survey (1986–89), but I have naturally drawn upon information gathered during the subsequent excavation seasons in the settlement centre, and I include supplementary survey information recorded as recently as 2008. I have also included reports on the botanical remains from 1989–1993 and the faunal remains from 1989–1995 as a supplement to the discussion of the environment. The final reports on the results of the excavations in 1991 and the following years will appear in subsequent volumes, along with more extensive reports on botanical and faunal remains. A detailed report on the Roman Bath (Structure E077), which was excavated in 1989, 2008, and 2010 (Oleson 1990a; Reeves 2009b), will be included in the final report on its companion structure, the Roman Fort (E116). Nevertheless, a summary description of the bath appears here in Chapter 4 as part of an evaluation of the structures served by the water-supply system. Numerous interim reports on all these seasons have appeared in print, along with preliminary analytical discussions (see the bibliography entries for Oleson, Oleson et al., Foote, Reeves, and Schick).

Transliteration from Arabic to English is always difficult and at best an approximation, and the modern name of Humayma is no exception. During the 1970s and early 1980s, "Humayma" was the most widely-accepted transliteration, and Graf, Eadie, and I adopted that version for our publications. In 1988, however, the Department of Antiquities published a General Index to ADAJ volumes 1–30 (1951–86), in which an "official" transliteration as "el-Humeima" appeared (p. 55), and I accepted this transliteration for my publications from 1989 through 2000. In 1997, the Royal Jordanian Geographic Centre once again adopted "Humayma" as the official transliteration, and I have returned to that spelling since. In the text, I use "Hawara" in discussions specific to the Nabataean settlement, "Hauarra" for discussions specific to the Roman period settlement, and "Humayma" for discussions specific to the early Islamic settlement, the modern period, or the archaeological site in general across time; it has not been possible to be completely consistent. I have not inserted diacritics in transliterated Arabic words, except in quotations from other works and in the titles of Arabic publications.

The fieldwork between 1986 and 1989 was funded by the Social Sciences and Humanities Research Council of Canada (SSHRC), with supplementary funding provided by the University of Victoria. I am very grateful for this generous support. Our survey work in Jordan was assisted in innumerable ways by the American Center of Oriental Research and its directors at that time, David McCreery and Bert De Vries, and in the years since by Pierre and Patricia Bikai, and Barbara Porter and Chris Tuttle. The support of the Department of Antiquities was also crucial, as was the kindness of its former Directors Adnan Hadidi, Ghazi Bisheh, and Fawwaz el-Khraysheh. I owe a great debt of gratitude as well to the participants in these three field seasons. In 1986, the team included only Oleson, Andrew Sherwood, and Suleiman Farajat (Department Representative). In 1987, the team consisted of

Oleson, Sherwood, Erik de Bruijn, Essam el-Hadi, and Suleiman Farajat (Department Representative). In 1989, an expanded team included Oleson, de Bruijn, el-Hadi, Robert Schick, Sylvie Blétry-Sebe, Daniel Ritsema (Architect), and Wael Rushdan (Department Representative). SSHRC continued to fund my work at Humayma from 1991 through my last field season in 2005, for which I am very grateful. Since 1991, the project has also received generous support from the Taggart Foundation, the van Berchem Foundation, the American Schools of Oriental Research, the American Center of Oriental Research, the Department of Antiquities of Jordan, and the University of Victoria, and from the many self-supporting volunteers who participated in the excavation.

I am very grateful to everyone who has taken part in the project for sharing their energy and time. I owe a particular debt of gratitude to Andrew N. Sherwood, who shared the excitement and hardships of the first two survey seasons, then rejoined the project in 2002. He remains a good friend. I also owe a great debt of gratitude to Erik de Bruijn, who has been a stalwart friend and indispensable colleague at every field season since 1987. I am also deeply grateful to M. Barbara Reeves, who took on the burden of directing a new excavation project at Humayma in 2008. This book is dedicated to two individuals who have had a great influence on my career. Most of all, however, I am grateful to my wife Martha, who put up with many long periods apart during my work at Humayma without losing faith in me.

Many scholars have assisted my research, most of all the collaborators named above. I am particularly grateful to David Graf, who brought the importance of the site to the attention of the modern scholarly world while engaged in his survey of inscriptions and the road network in Southern Jordan, for his continued interest in my work at the site and for his sage advice. John Eadie first brought me to Jordan for his project to test the archaeological potential of Humayma in 1983, at which point I became fascinated with the water-supply system. When it became clear that his research would take him elsewhere, he made no objection to my application for a permit to undertake survey in and around the site. Like so many North American scholars working in Jordan, I owe a particular debt of gratitude to Glen Bowersock, who I first encountered when I was an undergraduate at Harvard in 1966. In the 1970s, he not only defined the historical context of the area in antiquity, but also pointed out the paths fieldwork might take in the future. He also took on the selfless task of writing numerous letters of reference in support of my many grant applications, so essential to work in the field. In addition to the individuals mentioned above, many other scholars assisted my work at Humayma in its early stages and over the following years of study and excavation. I apologize if I have unwittingly omitted anyone from this list: Ian Babbit, Leigh-Ann Bedal, Ueli Bellwald, Patricia Bikai, Pierre Bikai, Ghazi Bisheh, Brendan Burke, David A. Campbell, Bert DeVries, Benjamin Dolinka, Suleiman Farajat, Tali Gini, Robbyn Gordon, Moshe Hartal, William L. Jobling, Martha S. Joukowsky, Z. Kamash, David L. Kennedy, Ludwig Koenen, Philippe Leveau, Manfred Lindner, Judy Logan, Burton MacDonald, David McCreery, Wilson Myers, Christina Nikolic, Milorad Nikolic, S. Thomas Parker, Yehuda Peleg, Megan A. Perry, Dino Politis, Kenneth W. Russell, Stefan Schmid, Devon Skinner, Jane Taylor, Laurent Tholbecq, Tsvika Tsuk, Trevor Van Damme, Mohammed Waheeb, Robert Wenning, Donald S. Whitcomb, Hector Williams, and Fawzi Zayadine. I am also very grateful to Kevin McGeough, the ASOR Archaeological Reports series editor, and two anonymous readers for their detailed comments on the manuscript of this book. Chris Mundigler has provided very skillful assistance with the maps and ceramic profiles.

Publication of this book was assisted by a generous subvention from The Joukowsky Family Foundation.

John Peter Oleson
September 2010

Abbreviations

AA	*Archäologischer Anzeiger*
AAE	*Arabian Archaeology and Epigraphy*
AASOR	*Annual of the American Schools of Oriental Research*
AB	Abbasid (750–969)
ABD	D. N. Freedman, ed., 1992. *Anchor Bible Dictionary.* 6 vols. New York: Doubleday.
ADAJ	*Annual of the Department of Antiquities of Jordan*
AJA	*American Journal of Archaeology*
ANRW	H. Temporini, W. Haase, eds., 1972–. *Aufstieg und Niedergang der römischen Welt.* Berlin: de Gruyter.
asl	above mean sea level
AY	Ayyubid (1174–1263)
BA	*Biblical Archaeologist*
BASOR	*Bulletin of the American Schools of Oriental Research*
BEFAR	*Bulletin de l'École Française d'Athènes et de Rome*
BY	Byzantine (400–550)
cum	cubic metre
CAJ	*Cambridge Archaeological Journal*
DOP	*Dumbarton Oaks Papers*
EANE	E. M. Meyers, ed., 1997. *Oxford Encyclopedia of Archaeology in the Near East.* 5 vols. Oxford: Oxford University.
EB	Early Byzantine (324–400)
EMC	*Echos du monde classique / Classical Views*
EN	Early Nabataean (4th century BC–30 BC)
ER	Early Roman (63 BC–AD 106)
ETSA	Eastern Terra Sigillata A
EZ I	A. Bignasca et al., 1996. *Petra, ez Zantur I: Ergebnisse der Schweizerisch-Liechtensteinischen Ausgrabungen 1988-1992.* Mainz: Philipp von Zabern.
EZ II	S. Schmid, B. Kolb, 2000. *Petra, ez Zantur II: Ergebnisse der Schweizerisch-Liechtensteinischen Ausgrabungen.* Mainz: Philipp von Zabern.
EZ III	D. Keller, M. Grawehr, 2006. *Petra: ez Zantur III.* Mainz: Philipp von Zabern.
FA	Fatimid (969–1171)
FgrH	F. Jacoby, 1923–. *Fragmente der griechischen Historiker.* Leiden: Brill.
IEJ	*Israel Exploration Journal*
JAS	*Journal of Archaeological Science*
JFA	*Journal of Field Archaeology*
JNES	*Journal of Near Eastern Studies*
JRA	*Journal of Roman Archaeology*
JRS	*Journal of Roman Studies*
JW	Josephus, *Jewish War*

LB	Late Byzantine (550–640)
LN	Late Nabataean (106–fourth century AD)
LR	Late Roman (235–324)
MA	Mamluk (1250–1516)
MCM	manufactured construction material (i.e., plaster or mortar)
mcm	million cubic metres
mm	millimetre
NEA	*Near Eastern Archaeology*
NEAEHL	E. Stern, A. Lewinson-Gilboa, J. Aviram, eds., 1993. *New Encyclopedia of Archaeological Excavations in the Holy Land.* 4 vols. New York: Simon & Schuster.
NFW	Nabataean fine ware
NPFW	Nabataean painted fine ware
MN	Middle Nabataean (30 BC–AD 106)
MOH	Mohs scale of mineral hardness
MPH	Maximum preserved height
MPL	Maximum preserved length
OT	Ottoman (1516–1918)
PEQ	*Palestine Exploration Quarterly*
QDAP	*Quarterly of the Department of Antiquities in Palestine*
RBib	*Revue Biblique*
RE	A. Pauly, G. Wissowa, W. Kroll, eds., 1893–1980. *Real-Encyclopädie der klassischen Altertumswissenschaft.* Munich: Druckenmüller.
RF	Roman foot, Roman feet, *pes monetalis;* equals 0.296 m.
RO	Roman (106–235)
SHAJ	*Studies in the History and Archaeology of Jordan*
StDev	Standard Deviation
Th	Thick, thickness
UM	Umayyad (640–750)
UTM	Universal Transverse Mercator
ZDPV	*Zeitschrift des deutschen Palästina-Vereins*
ZPE	*Zeitschrift für Papyrologie und Epigraphik*

Chapter 1

Introduction:
Project Objectives and Previous Field Work

1.A. OBJECTIVES OF THE HUMAYMA HYDRAULIC SURVEY

When I first visited Humayma in June 1981, the site was difficult to reach, and the local Bedouin were uncertain about the reasons for our interest in the region (fig. 1.1). Even in 2005, nearly 20 years after the start of the Humayma Hydraulic Survey, the settlement centre and the approximately 234 sq km survey area remained relatively untouched by development. In 2008, the biggest threats were the spread of open-pit silica mines in the hills of Disi sandstone east of the site and the development of a military installation and royal palace to the west. The Qa Disi to Amman water pipeline fortunately had passed well east of the site in 2005–6. Most of the cisterns around the survey region and one of the reservoirs had been cleaned out for re-use by the mid-twentieth century, and a few small Bedouin houses had been built here and there in the settlement centre out of the heaps of rubble remaining from the ancient structures. The few families that lived on or around the site at that time for the most part inhabited tents (see Russell 1993: 19); they were attracted to New Humayma (Humayma al-Jadideh) on the renovated Desert Highway in the late 1970s by facilities provided by the Canadian Government. The damage from ploughing, road construction, and modern illicit digging was relatively light in 1986, when the Humayma Survey Project began, and even though the

pace of regional development and local clandestine excavation accelerated in the late 1990s, the site and its historical landscape are essentially intact (fig. 1.2). Since 2000, the Department of Antiquities of Jordan has attempted to purchase the central portion of the site from the local landowners in order to ensure its preservation. This action was followed by the construction of a Visitors' Centre in the centre of the site by the Ministry of Tourism in 2004–5 (fig. 1.3).

Not only are the site of Humayma and its hinterland well preserved, but its identity, a foundation story, and some events of its subsequent history can be documented in ancient sources, along with its names: Hawara, Αὐάρα, Hauarra, and Humayma (see pp. 50–57). As with most Arabic place names, the transliteration of Humayma into European languages has varied enormously. The official transliteration in the early 1980s was "al-Humayma," in the late 1980s "al-Humeima," and from the mid-1990s "al-Humayma." These changes are reflected in the publications of the Humayma Excavation Project. For ease of use, the name is written here simply as "Humayma." In this book, "Humayma" is used to refer to the modern archaeological site and the Early Islamic settlement, "Hawara" in reference to the Nabataean period settlement, and "Hauarra" in reference to the Roman and Byzantine settlement. Consistency has not always been possible.

Even before excavation began in 1963, surface remains, particularly the rich scatter of potsherds,

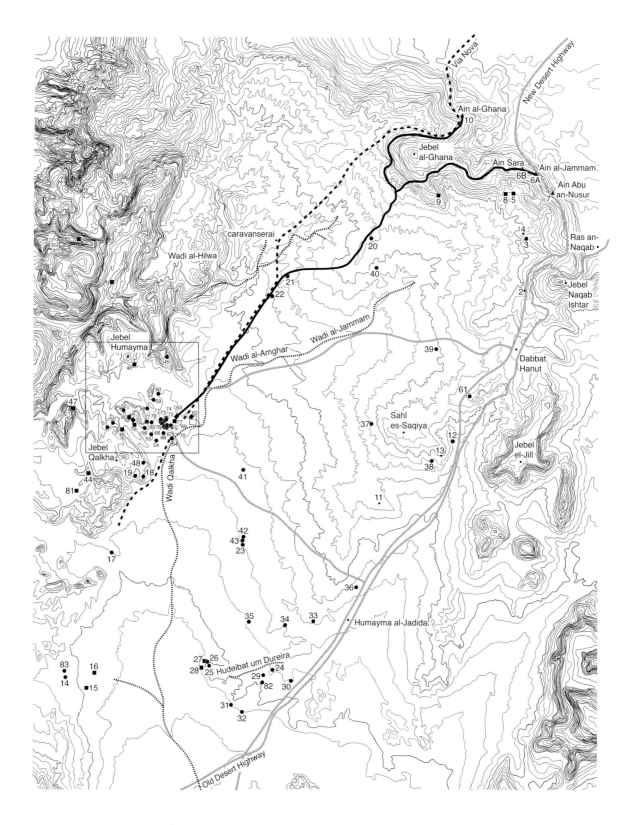

Fig. 1.1 *Topographical map of survey area. Aqueduct in dark solid line; Via Nova in dark dotted line; wadi courses in dark small dots; modern roads in light solid lines.*

FIG. 1.2 *Aerial view of Humayma from the south (Photo: Jane Taylor).*

supported historical sources indicating that the site flourished from the first century BC through the mid-eighth century AD. The relatively tight chronological range of the site and the presence of substantial remains from all four main cultural periods — Nabataean, Roman, Byzantine, and Umayyad — make Humayma an excellent subject for studies involving cultural evolution at a small desert settlement. The location and historical context suggest that ancient Humayma was intended to serve as a centre for sedentarization of the nomadic Nabataean pastoralists who occupied the region. Through proper management of the meagre water supplies, this community enjoyed a settled existence based on agriculture, stock raising, the servicing of caravans, and probably as a regional market. The architectural remains indicate that at least a modest prosperity continued through

the Roman, Byzantine, and early Islamic periods, based in part on trade moving north and south along the old King's Highway, rebuilt by Trajan as the Via Nova Traiana. Historical sources record that the Abbasid family purchased the town site in the second half of the seventh century, built a fortified house and family mosque, and plotted the overthrow of the Umayyad caliphate there. After the success of their conspiracy in the mid-eighth century and the shift of the caliphate to Baghdad, occupation of the site was thin and sporadic. There is a significant amount of Fatimid pottery on the surface around F102. Recently, Foote has uncovered evidence she feels indicates that the manor house of the Abbasid family was reoccupied and renovated in the Ottoman period (Oleson et al. 2003). Since no trace of occupation was visible when Laborde visited the site in 1828 (see pp. 9–11),

FIG. 1.3 *Humayma Visitors' Centre.*

this phase might date anywhere from the sixteenth to the eighteenth century AD.

The Humayma Hydraulic Survey was designed to document the regional water-supply system and its relationship to the settlement centre. The first few weeks of survey activity in 1986 made it clear that the water-supply system of Hawara, the original Nabataean settlement, was regional in scale and was integrated with the settlement design. In addition, the settlement location seems to have been selected with this critical consideration in mind (Oleson 1992a, 1995, 1997a, 2003a, 2007). The settlement is located at the conflux of several run-off fields that provided a reliable supply and manageable amount of water to two (possibly three) public reservoirs and numerous private, domestic cisterns. Furthermore, the site lies at the southernmost point that could conveniently be reached by a gravity flow aqueduct fed by springs on the escarpment 15 km to the north, it is near good agricultural soil, and it is on the main north–south route to ancient Aila (Aqaba). Subsidiary routes gave access southeast to Wadi Ramm and west directly to the Wadi ʿArabah. The scale of the water-supply system developed in the late first century BC or early first century AD, including public reservoirs, aqueducts, and ornamental pool, indicates some kind of central, probably royal, planning and sponsorship. Either King Aretas III or Aretas IV founded the settlement and initiated the system. Drainage of wastewater

was more casual, but it also involved some site planning and construction (Oleson 1996).

From the start, several research questions were at the forefront.

1) What kinds of structures were built to provide water to the inhabitants of the countryside around Hawara and to those of the settlement centre itself, and what was the scale of the resource provided?

2) What role did the existence of the water-supply system, or the potential for such a system, play in the location and design of the original settlement, and how did this role relate to issues of sedentarization?

3) What was the relationship between the rural water-supply system and its managers or beneficiaries and the water-supply system and population of the settlement centre?

4) When did the Roman occupation of the site begin, and how did Roman administration and influence affect the water-supply system, settlement design, and architectural development?

5) How did the strategies and structures of the overall water-supply system evolve over time, and how did any non-Nabataean techniques or structures fit in with the hydraulic technology of the ancient Near East and the Mediterranean world?

6) Do any aspects of the water-supply system reflect new needs or techniques developed during the Byzantine and Early Islamic periods?

Fortunately, the survey and probes carried out in 1986–87 and 1989, along with the 12 campaigns of excavation by the Humayma Excavation Project in the settlement centre since 1991, have made it possible to respond to all of these questions to a greater or lesser degree. Chapters 3 to 6 assemble the raw data, Chapter 7 presents a case study of the water-supply system of the small but thriving Nabataean settlement of Hawara, its evolution through eight centuries of use and adaptation, and the relation between society and technology. Chapter 8 evaluates the technological context of the Hawara system and its relationship to earlier and contemporary water-supply systems in the Near East. The analysis presented here may have to be amended as continued excavation in the settlement centre provides further information, but at this point it is possible to reconstruct a reasonably accurate picture of the water-supply system and its evolution.

The 1986–87 survey focused on the area around Humayma that was suitable for human occupation and delimited by natural boundaries, approximately 234 sq km in area (fig. 1.1). Within this survey area, special attention was paid to the topographical catchment that sends run-off water past Humayma in the Wadi Qalkha and the run-off area to the south of the settlement, 189 sq km in area. There is a smaller area, just west of the Desert Highway, 17 sq km in area, that is part of a separate catchment basin, but which sustained numerous cisterns associated with the settlement at Humeima. Run-off from a third catchment comprising 28 sq km in the northwest corner of the survey area is directed through the Wadi Hilwa west into the Wadi ‘Arabah.

Humayma is situated close to the west edge of the survey area, 13.25 km southwest of ‘Ain al-Ghana, 8 km west of the modern Desert Highway, and 12 km north of the highway bridge over the Wadi Qalkha. The survey area was essentially the drainage catchment between Humayma and the al-Shara escarpment, along with the Wadi Qalkha and its tributaries from Humayma proper as far south as the modern Ma’an–Aqaba Highway. The northern boundary was the crest of the escarpment between ‘Ain al-Ghana and the line of the new Desert Highway as it passed below Ras en-Naqb. The line of this road defined the eastern and southern border of the survey area as well. Although an artificial boundary in archaeological terms, the line of the road includes slightly more than the run-off catchment area along its northern portion, and in the south follows a natural southern boundary, the gap between Jebel Thaur and Hudeibat Um-Dureira through which the Wadi Qalkha flows. The western limit of the main survey area north of Humayma was the boundary between the Wadi al-Jammam and Wadi Hilwa watersheds. The former becomes the Wadi Amghar and Wadi Qalkha. The latter joins the Wadi al-Beida, which dives steeply through the western mountains to the Wadi ‘Arabah. We searched this area in vain for hydraulic structures but made note of the Via Nova and a Nabataean caravanserai. South of Humayma, the western boundary of the survey area was the crest of the Jebel Qalkha, which backs up against the precipitous descent to the Wadi ‘Arabah, while the lower slopes of the Jebel Thaur, which towers over the pass down the Wadi Yutum to Aqaba, formed the southern boundary.

The perceived boundaries of the territory controlled culturally or politically by the inhabitants of ancient Humayma undoubtedly varied from period to period as the settlement passed from Nabataean to Roman control, or into the possession of the Abbasid family. Furthermore, since the transition from a nomadic to a semi-sedentary way of life was relatively recent at Nabataean Hawara, individuals "settled" there undoubtedly moved with their families and flocks from time to time and maintained tribal contacts over significant distances, as do the modern Bedouin tribes. Nevertheless, the boundaries of the survey area mark a real division between a landscape intensely settled and exploited, and the more empty desert beyond. West of the site, the precipitous cliffs forming the descent to the Wadi ‘Arabah are impassable except at a few points, and Jebel Thaur forms a lofty barrier on the south. There is open desert to the south and southeast, beyond the Desert Highway, with only isolated sandstone jebels (fig. 1.4). This area was not systematically surveyed for the Humayma

FIG. 1.4 *View of al-Shara escarpment and desert east of Humayma.*

project, but repeated visits by team members since 1987 have failed to locate any undocumented ancient hydraulic installations in this area, or on Jebel al-Jill and the other offshoots of the al-Shara escarpment framing the Wadi Judaiyid. The only other clusters of ancient cisterns or other hydraulic installations in the region are found on Jebel Kharaza and Jebel Ratama, 12 km east of Quweira, and at Wadi Ramm. Both sites are well outside the survey area. Graf assumes that there was a small Nabataean settlement at Jebel Kharaza (Graf 1983: 654; cf. Kirkbride and Harding 1947: 19–20; Jobling 1983a–b: 317–23, 1983–84: 266, 1986a: 406–7), and there was both a small settlement and a sanctuary at Wadi Ramm (Graf 1983: 655; Dudley and Reeves 1997; Tholbecq 1998).

On the north, the al-Shara escarpment forms an obvious topographical barrier which was probably a cultural and political boundary as well, despite the north–south corridor formed by the old King's Highway. On the summit of the escarpment, the topography, geology, pedology, and hydrology are all dramatically different from those of the Hisma Desert 500 m below and much more favourable to human occupation (fig. 1.5). The top of the escarpment may have marked the southern limit of the Edomite kingdom (Bartlett 1989: 34; MacDonald 1992: 295; Edelman 1995: 2–3; but cf. Herr and Najjar 2001: 338–40). Beginning in the first century BC, this point probably served as the boundary between the territory controlled by Zadagatha (modern Sadaqa), or ancient Mureighah, 15 km to the north, and that controlled by ancient Humayma, equidistant to the south (see Hart 1986a–b). Nabataean Hawara reached out as far as the escarpment with its aqueduct, but this was probably the full extent of its control to the north. It may be significant that Augustopolis (Udhruh), Zadagatha, Ammatha, and other towns closer to Petra are mentioned in the sixth-century Petra

FIG. 1.5   *View of al-Shara escarpment by Jebel Ghana.*

Papyri, and even towns in the Negev (Frösén 2001: 490–91; Kaimio 2001: 721; Koenen 1996: 181–83; Lehtinen 2001: 788; Frösén, Arjava, Lehtinen et al. 2002), but not flourishing Hauarra/Humayma—as if it belonged to a separate world.

Although the survey area was large, the objective of virtually complete coverage appears to have been realised, as only two new cisterns (nos. 82–83) have been noted in the course of frequent travel through the survey area since 1987. Undoubtedly, some have been missed: possibly the three "Shereif el-Rekaib" cisterns seen by Kirkbride and Harding in 1946 somewhere near New Humayma, along with some rock-cut cisterns they mention to the southwest, near the Wadi Shubeika (Kirkbride and Harding 1947: 21–22).

The goals of the Humayma Hydraulic Survey were circumscribed and strictly defined, and the structures targeted were very characteristic in design and usually easy to spot in the barren landscape. The heaps of light-coloured silt dug out of the re-used cisterns made them particularly easy to find, a phenomenon Kirk noted in the Negev (1938). The objective was to locate and catalogue all water resources and the structures associated

with their exploitation. The final count included four springs, one aqueduct system, four reservoirs, 62 cisterns, three impoundment dams, three sets of wadi barriers, and eight sets of artificial terraces or cleared fields.

In order to work out the survey procedures and obtain a preliminary knowledge of the lay of the land and the modern network of dirt roads and tracks, the survey team began work first in areas that could be traversed relatively quickly and seemed likely from their geology or topography not to be rich in hydraulic structures. These areas included the foot of the escarpment and the upper reaches of the Wadi al-Jammam on the north, and the lower slopes of the Jebel Thaur on the south. The team travelled by four-wheel-drive vehicle to the survey areas, where the search for hydraulic installations was then carried out for the most part on foot. Once we had searched these areas, we traced and recorded the aqueduct system from 'Ain al-Jammam and 'Ain al-Ghana all the way to Humayma. The team then gradually charted the sites along Jebel Qalkha, Hadabat Sumei'a, Hadabat Um al-Adhfar, Hudeibat edh-Dhiru, and the Hudeibat Um-Dureira. The majority of our dis-

FIG. 1.6 *Aerial view of Humayma from the southwest (Photo: David Kennedy).*

coveries were made in these areas. We then criss-crossed the rolling lowland fields of the two main valleys, working towards Humayma and the hills behind the site. Survey information was entered on standard data sheets, samples of mortar and plaster were taken, and any diagnostic ceramics were collected. In fact, very little ceramic material was found around most of these structures outside the settlement centre, perhaps because leather water bags were used in the rural areas. The same paucity of ceramic finds around Nabataean cisterns has been noted in the Negev (Kloner 2001–2: 471). In 1987, we completed the recording of structures in the settlement centre and excavated probes along the aqueduct and at several of the reservoirs and cisterns. More probes were dug in 1989 and the Roman bath was excavated. In 2000–2001, all the structures (except for Cistern no. 34, which could not be re-located) were revisited, so that GPS readings could be taken and some ambiguities resolved.

1.B. PREVIOUS SURVEYS
AND EXCAVATIONS

Although the site of Humayma is relatively isolated, most of its structures are easily visible in the open desert landscape, and, until recently, traces of the paving of the Via Nova Traiana or the 'Ain Ghana aqueduct guided the stranger directly to the ruins (fig. 1.6). From the nineteenth century, and probably for at least several centuries before that, the Huweitat Bedouin have occupied the region between Aqaba and Ma'an, including Humayma (von Oppenheim 1943: vol. 2, pp. 291–95; Peake 1958: 210–14; Russell 1993: 16, 23). Although the precise boundaries were fluid, the Huweitat Ibn Djazi controlled the northern portion of this region, including the sites of Humayma and Ramm, while the 'Alâwîn, another sub-group of the Huweitat, controlled the southern portion and the Wadi al-Yutm as far as Aqaba (Jaussen 1903: 108). There was also a small group of Bedul Bedouin from Petra at Humayma by the early twentieth century (Russell 1993: 16). The tribal memory of all the regional Bedouin has continued to connect the site and its ruins with the activities of the Nabataeans, Romans, and Abbasids, and many of the personal names of the

early Abbasid heroes continue in use in the region. The precise nature of the relationship between the 'Alâwîn and the Bedul of Wadi Musa is disputed by both groups (Ohannessian-Charpin 1992). A vivid picture of the traditional patterns of life of this tribe is provided by T.E. Lawrence's account of the Arab revolt, most dramatically in his portrait of the warrior leader Sheikh Auda abu Tayi, of the Huweitat Ibn Djazi (Lawrence 1927: 92–94).

> Centuries ago the Howeitat came from Hejaz, and their nomad clans prided themselves on being true Bedu. Auda was their master type. His hospitality was sweeping; except to very hungry souls, inconvenient. His generosity kept him always poor, despite the profits of a hundred raids. He had married twenty-eight times, had been wounded thirteen times; whilst the battles he provoked had seen all his tribesmen hurt and most of his relations killed. He himself had slain seventy-five men, Arabs, with his own hand in battle… Auda raided as often as he had opportunity, and as widely as he could…, and he was careful to be at enmity with nearly all tribes in the desert, that he might have proper scope for raids. He saw life as a saga. All events in it were significant: all personages in contact with him heroic.

Several of the early European travellers to the Hisma took note of Humayma and the ruins of its structures, particularly the cisterns, reservoirs, and the walls of the Roman fort. The nineteenth-century visitors found the site unoccupied and in much the same condition that the Humayma Excavation Project found it in 1986 (fig. 1.7). On the homeward leg of the pioneering journey that took him to Petra in 1812, Burkhardt travelled as far south as Sadaqa but then turned west to Gharandal (Bartlett 1989: 16–17). Léon de Laborde and Louis Maurice Linant de Bellefonds, in contrast, after their visit to Petra in 1828, travelled south with their large camel caravan from Wadi Sabra to 'Ain al-Ghana and on through the Hisma to Aqaba. During this trip, they became the first outsiders to describe Humayma and the Ghana aqueduct system, visiting the site on Tuesday, 8 April 1828 (Laborde 1830:

FIG. 1.7   *View of Humayma from the west.*

61–62, quoted from Augé and de Bellefonds 1994:
200–1; cf. Brünnow and Domaszewski 1904–9: 1, pp.
476–78; Laborde 1836: 208). Laborde's description
is the longer of the two.

> En continuant notre route dans un large
> enfoncement qui s'élève insensiblement,
> nous arrivâmes aux sources de Qana
> ['Ain al-Ghana], près desquelles on re-
> marque des ruines considérables… C'est
> en quittant cette ville et en descendant
> la pente de la montagne, qu'on suit, avec
> étonnement, l'aqueduc ancien qui menait
> les eaux des sources de Qana et de celles
> de Guman ['Ain al-Jammam] à la ville
> d'Ameimé [Humayma], construite dans
> la plaine sur la route de Petra à Aila. Cet
> aqueduc, qui suppose une construction
> continue de plus de trois lieues, suit le
> niveau du terrain, au-dessus duquel il ne
> s'élève jamais. C'est par un soin assidu à
> étudier les mouvements du sol, par une

> science remarquable de nivellement, qu'on
> est parvenu, sur une si grande distance, à
> conserver à l'eau une pente régulière.
>
> Les ruines d'Ameimé offrent une masse
> de débris plus considérable que les ruines
> des villages que nous venions de rencon-
> trer. Cependant rien ne laisse supposer un
> grand luxe de monuments; et, quant aux
> habitations, elles semblent n'avoir eu qu'un
> but, et leur emménagement qu'une desti-
> nation, c'est-à-dire l'approvisionnement
> de vivres et d'eau pour les caravanes, qui,
> soit dans un but commercial ou pour tout
> autre motif, passaient sur cette grande
> route et s'arrêtaient dans leurs murs.
> Aussi le terrain est-il creusé partout à une
> profondeur de quelques pieds, et des mu-
> railles cimentées, des voûtes habilement
> construites, font, de cette ville, une ville
> de citernes. Chaque maison avait la sienne,
> et, en outre, des larges réservoirs publics

servaient à abreuver les animaux. On ne concevrait pas, sans l'avoir vu, mais surtout sans avoir senti ce besoin par l'aspect du pays, ce soin d'emménagement, ce but unique qui a présidé à la construction de cette ville, et l'habileté avec laquelle les eaux de l'aqueduc, pendant l'été, celles des ravins avoisinants, pendant la saison des pluies, étaient dirigées vers leur destination. — Aujourd'hui, comme tout est ruiné et abandonné, on sent encore mieux, par l'absence de l'eau qu'on désire, l'habileté et l'ingénieuse persévérance des habitants qui fondèrent ce lieu de halte.

Je cherchai, après avoir parcouru la ville et les environs, à conserver un souvenir de cette habitation factice au milieu d'une aridité bien réelle. Je trouvai moyen de dessiner sur un premier plan quelques-unes des voûtes et des citernes, et dans le fond une partie de la longue lisière de rochers qui forme l'enceinte de la plaine d'Ameimé au milieu des montagnes. Je publierai cette planche plus tard. Je relevai en même temps, avec autant d'exactitude que le permettaient mes moyens, les nombreux pitons de rochers dont les uns forment chaîne, tandis que les autres s'éparpillent dans la plaine.

Laborde's observations are perceptive. Although his decision not to include the drawings in his publication is regrettable, his description of the site was not surpassed for over a century. In the course of a short visit, he recognised both the essentially functional character of the architecture in the settlement centre and the relationship between the settlement and the ancient routes of travel. He also understood that the water-supply system was crucial to the settlement and that this system included both public reservoirs and private cisterns, aqueduct water and run-off from precipitation. It is difficult to determine whether Laborde saw more than the 13 domestic cisterns now visible at the site, but his assertion that he saw them "everywhere" and the title "City of Cisterns" may imply that some have since been obscured by debris. The lack of water at the site even in the month of April strongly

suggests that the Bedouin had not as yet put any of the cisterns back into service, and therefore that the site was uninhabited. Since the surrounding fields apparently were not under cultivation, Laborde did not realise their agricultural potential. Furthermore, without having had the opportunity to see more than a few hydraulic structures outside the settlement centre (see Chapter 3, Cistern no. 25, Dams nos. 27, 28) Laborde remained unaware of the potential for pastoral activity and of the close relationship between the settlement centre and its large catchment area.

Bellefonds' succinct account of this visit, only published in 1994 (Augé and Bellefonds 1994: 201–2), is largely descriptive, but it contains a few interesting details. He reports that both of the Nabataean reservoirs in the settlement centre retained their roofing arches, and he seems to suggest that the diversion conduit that filled the cistern in the Roman fort still survived.

On remarque encore les voûtes de deux citernes qui n'ont rien de remarquable sinon qu'elles étaient un peu plus plates que le plein-cintre… Dans l'angle nord-ouest [of the fort] est un grand basin qui a 42 pas sur 25 et qui recevait l'eau par le canal qui vient de Gana. Ce canal est bien fait, suivant le détour des collines pour conserver le niveau…

Bellefonds states explicitly that there were no traces of recent cultivation in the area of the ancient settlement, and he, too, misses the agricultural potential of the site.

On ne voit aux environs aucun reste de cultivation et on voit aussi d'après la précaution que l'on avait eue pour avoir de l'eau que les pluies étaient très rares et qu'ainsi il ne devait pas y avoir de terre cultivée. Or pour la subsistance de cette ville on tirait sans doute les provisions des montagnes qui sont dans le nord.

Subsequent visitors to Petra in the mid-nineteenth century, such as John Lloyd Stephens (1836), Lord Lindsay (1837), Comte de Bertou (1838), David Roberts (1839), and Edward Lear (1848–58) followed what had by then become the standard route up the Wadi ʿArabah from Aqaba (Bartlett 1989: 19–27), which was far easier than the route up the Wadi Yutum, across the Hisma, and over the al-Shara mountain range. Sixty years later even the redoubtable Brünnow and Domaszewski did not continue their survey past ʿAin Sadaqa and across the Hisma to Aqaba in 1897–98, relying instead on the reports of the visits by Laborde (1830), Morris (1840), Maughan (1872), Doughty (1875), and Jaussen (1902) (Brünnow and Domaszewski 1904–09: 1, pp. 470–75). Maughan comments (1874: 188; cf. Jaussen 1903: 103) on a recent tribal alliance that had re-opened the Wadi Yutum route.

> We were told that there had been no travel-
> ler to Petra for three years past, so that we
> may consider ourselves fortunate in hav-
> ing been allowed to proceed there. A much
> greater privilege was the fact of our being
> able to take the Eastern route by way of
> the Wady-el-Ithm, Laborde's route, which
> has been hardly ever traversed by any one
> since his time. A recent matrimonial alli-
> ance between Sheikh Mohammed's sister
> [of Aqaba] and the ruler of the territory
> of the Wady Ithm enabled the former to
> guarantee us a safe passage.

Both Morris and Doughty must have passed close by Humayma while following the route via the Wadi Yutum and the Hisma to Petra (Morris 1842: vol. 2, 265–67) and Maʿan (Doughty 1936: vol. 1, 84–86), but neither turned aside to visit the site. Morris' description of the Hisma provides a surprising image of fertility and pastoral activity, perhaps because his visit fell sometime in March. He describes a march from somewhere near Qu-weira to somewhere near the foot of the al-Shara escarpment (Morris 1842: vol. 2, 265–67), probably through the Wadi Judaiyid, where there were flow-ing springs in the early decades of the twentieth century (Henry et al. 1983: 10; Hassan 1995: 30).

> The second day's travel [from Aqaba] lay
> across this plain, which was covered with
> tufts of wild grass and shrubs; Bedouin
> tents, and flocks of sheep and goats scat-
> tered over it, gave it a pleasing pastoral
> appearance; in the evening of this day we

obtained good quarters in a large cave among the mountains… The next morn-ing, on rising from my rocky couch, I was surprised to see that we were again in a region of fertility; the bed of the little valley was covered with verdure, through which a rill of water flowed in a devious course, after tumbling down from the mountains in a little cascade… I heard the pleasant warbling of birds; the plaintive notes of the cuckoo, and lively whistle of the partridge, mingled with the sighing of the trees, and noise of falling waters.

Even after making allowances for narrative exag-geration, the picture suggests a larger and more active local population and a more forgiving land-scape than Laborde had seen around Humayma, 15 km to the west. Forty years later, Doughty as well refers to the verdant springtime pasturage (Doughty 1936: vol. 1, 85–86).

> …After two dark hours we found another
> of their nomad encampments pitched
> under a berg of sandstone… These were
> tents of Saidîn Howeytát, Arabs of the
> Ghor, come up hither for the better spring
> pasture in their kinsman Ibn Jad's high
> country. There seemed much nakedness
> and little welfare among them.

The landscape was empty, however, during Maughan's visit on 18 March 1872. Maughan ap-parently travelled with a copy of Laborde's report in hand, and following that account he veered west from the usual route in order to visit Humayma (Maughan 1874: 194–96).

> Proceeding on our journey we were now
> enveloped in clouds of fine dust, with a tre-
> mendous wind blowing in our faces, until
> we reached the very extensive ruins of Hu-
> meiyumeh, or, as Laborde calls it, Ameimé.
> These ruins cover a vast extent of ground,
> and we wandered for more than two miles
> amidst masses of stones. Although the re-
> mains are very extensive, yet they exhibit
> no traces of architectural splendour, and
> the dwelling-houses seem to have been

mainly constructed with a view to storing provisions and water, judging by the great numbers of cisterns to be met with. This place must have been a great rendezvous or *entrepôt* for all the caravans traversing this important commercial route. I came first upon an immense tank or pool, about 100 feet long by 60 broad [Reservoir no. 63], the walls of which enclosed it being built of large stones, most regularly placed in an unbroken line, 3 feet in height and the same in width. Half a mile farther on were the foundations of a very large building [E116, the Roman Fort], of which the outer wall could be distinctly traced. The court which it enclosed was extensive, about 250 yards across. At the north-west corner was a very distinct and complete reservoir for water [Reservoir no. 62], which is sunk 6 or 8 feet below the level of the ground and regularly cemented with mortar. At each corner of the walls is a kind of angular niche, partially covered over; in length this cistern is about 96 feet and in breadth about 45 feet. We had but little time to examine the extensive masses of stones and *débris*, or the mounds of earth scattered about, which, doubtless, covered ancient buildings, forming the ruins of this once prosperous city. On leaving the spot we could trace for nearly three miles the remains of the ancient aqueduct, which keeps exactly to the level of the ground, and conveyed the water from the wells of Gana to these great reservoirs.

Maughan's account of his short visit adds little to the report from Laborde, other than some fairly accurate dimensions, but the absence of any mention of local inhabitants or re-used cisterns suggests that the site was still abandoned. In fact, Maughan claims that his party encountered only one individual (near Petra) on the entire five-day trip from Aqaba to Petra (Maughan 1874: 193).

On 7 March 1902, Jaussen camped near the jebels southeast of Humayma. He comments on the fine view of the Jebel Qalkha to the west, which partly concealed the "Djebel Hemeïmèh,"

but he does not mention the site itself. His guide indicated that this was the boundary between the territory of the 'Alâwîn Bedouin on the south and the Huweitat Bedouin on the north (Jaussen 1903: 108); aggressive groups from both sub-tribes were encountered during the trip. Jaussen's route from Aqaba to Ma'an, which seems to follow that of the first Desert Highway, was called the "Tariq es-Sultan." The map he provides indicates "Harabeh" in a location appropriate for the Harrabat al-'Abid cistern (Chapter 3, Cistern no. 25).

Musil travelled through the region in 1910 on one of his long mapping and ethnographic expeditions and found the Bedouin still difficult to deal with. Musil had in fact passed within 7 km of Humayma during his third trip in the spring of 1898, but he did not have the opportunity to see "die Gräber und die Höhlen von el-Homejma," and he had to be content with the Harrabat al-'Abid cistern his three predecessors had visited (Musil 1907–08: 266). Musil's visit on 3 June 1910 was short, but full of incident (Musil 1926: 56–61). The party approached the site from the north.

> We rode alongside the aqueduct, which is said to lead from the copious well of al-Kena' ['Ain al-Ghana] and rises only a very little above the plain. The lower wall is 70 cm. broad, the trench [water channel?] being 15 cm. deep and 40 cm. broad. South of the aqueduct there stretches a lowland which could be transformed into fields. The remains of old field and garden walls extend as far as the ruins of al-Homejma, which we reached at 12:42 p.m. (temperature: 29.8° C).

> These ruins cover the eastern and southern foot of the elevation of Umm al-'Azâm as well as the surrounding lowland for several square kilometres; but not a single building has been preserved. The soft limestone of which they were constructed has collapsed, so that the isolated buildings are now reduced to whitish-yellow heaps of soft powdery lime… There are numerous capacious artificial reservoirs for rain water that are not more than half covered. In every building were installed

pyriform cisterns, where the 'Alâwîn conceal chaff and corn. Inasmuch as some of the buildings are constructed in a style which resembles that of the ruined houses at Wâdi Mûsa, it may be inferred with certainty that al-Homejma was also built by the Nabataeans, and for this reason I locate here the Nabataean city of Auara.

After a fruitless attempt to find the "necropolis," or "rock tomb(s)," Musil was called back to the settlement centre by a rifle shot (Musil 1926: 61).

> It was an alarm signal with which my native companions were recalling me. Running out from the rocks, I saw my companions and the camels surrounded by a crowd of the 'Alâwîn. The latter had been reaping barley southeast of al-Homejma and, hearing of our arrival, had rushed up to my baggage, where they were begging for food and presents… We should have liked to move on, but Rif'at had not yet returned. When at last he came running back, he pointed to his half-torn clothing and explained that among the rocks to the west he had been attacked by shepherds and robbed of everything he had.

Clearly, at some point between Maughan's visit in 1872 and Musil's arrival, the Bedouin had begun to exploit the fertile loessial soil around Humayma, relying on run-off water to moisten the fields. Oral tradition among the Bedouin of the Negev indicates that territorial disputes and undisciplined grazing made farming impossible in that region in the nineteenth and early twentieth century (Bailey 1980; Russell 1993). The nineteenth-century travellers quoted above all refer to similar inter-tribal hostility in the territory of southern Transjordan; perhaps the question of territorial ownership or control had finally been resolved by the end of the century. No "pyriform cisterns" are visible at the site at present, although the domed cistern or storage bin no. 72 (see Chapter 4) might fit Musil's description. Perhaps Musil observed the draw holes above several of the renovated cylindrical domestic cisterns and simply assumed that they were bottle-shaped like many rock-cut cisterns,

and that all held grain rather than water. Stein saw pits for grain and straw at the site during his visit almost 70 years later (Stein in Gregory and Kennedy 1985: 321), but the Humayma Excavation Project has not yet been able to document these. If extensive farming was going on at the time of Musil's visit, it is likely that at least some of the cisterns had been renovated to sustain the farmers and their herds.

Besides his report of the local inhabitants, Musil's main contribution is his observation that they called the site "Hawâra," leading to his conjecture that the site should be identified with the ancient Auara/Hauarra recorded in Uranius, the Peutinger Table, and the *Notitia Dignitatum* (1926: 59, n. 20; see Chapter 2.B.1). Although the relevant ancient literary sources had long been known (Benzinger 1898; Brünnow and Domaszewski 1904–9: 3, pp. 260, 262, 273, 277), and Brünnow seems to have been the first to propose this identification in 1909 (Brünnow 1909: 23–24), Musil does not cite him. In any case, for several decades the identification had been ignored or mistrusted. Clermont-Ganneau (1906: 421–22) identified "Houmeîmé" with Ammatha, and Auara with an unknown site near Sadaqa, while Thomsen (1906: 121–22) equated Auara/Hauarra with Quweira.

It is difficult to determine from the reports of these early travellers whether Humayma and its environs were in fact essentially deserted in the nineteenth century, or the Europeans simply chanced to miss a mobile Bedouin population. Perhaps the local population was concentrated to the east of the modern Desert Highway, where Morris saw them, along the favoured modern route from Quweira to Naqb Ishtar. Musil arrived during harvest time, when local activity would have been particularly visible, but Laborde and Maughan arrived during growing season, when any nearby fields would have been green with shoots. In addition, one would expect more evidence of reuse of the cisterns if there had been significant local activity. Perhaps tribal agreements or an increase in population toward the end of the century stirred an interest in the soil and water resources of Humayma.

During the period of the First World War and the Arab Revolt against the Ottoman Empire, the attention of European scholars was focused on other regions, although the *Denkmalschutzkommando* units of the German army did concern themselves with the protection and publication of some archaeological sites in Palestine and Transjordan (Wiegand 1920). The activities of T.E. Lawrence naturally were focused farther east and north, along the Hejaz Railway, but he also spent time in the Hisma and travelled the route between Quweira and Ras en-Naqb during the campaign against Aqaba (Lawrence 1927: 141–61). He makes no mention, however, of the ruins at Humayma, so he probably passed well to the east on the more direct route followed by Morris, Jaussen, and others. Nevertheless, in the itinerary of his travels in 1917, he notes leaving Aqaba and arriving at "Wadi Itm" on the 26th of August, then at "Hawara" on the 27th, before moving on to "Rumm" on the 28th (Lawrence 1927: Appendix II). Although Humayma is well out of the way if Rumm (i.e. Wadi Ramm) was his only objective, I do not know of another site between Wadi Itm and Ramm that might be called "Hawara." Musil (1926: 59 n. 20) states that the local 'Alâwîn used the name Hawwâra interchangeably with "al-Homejma" during his visit in 1910. The arrival of the automobile during World War I allowed speedier and more convenient survey work, although many areas around the Hisma, including the approaches to 'Ain al-Jammam and 'Ain al-Ghana, could still be accessed only on foot or by camel.

More professional and comprehensive surveys of the Hisma commenced in the 1930s (see Graf 1983; Henry 1995: 11), but only sporadic and superficial notice was paid to Humayma itself. Both Savignac and Glueck bypassed the site, although Glueck visited all three springs that fed the aqueduct and was "told that it follows a track leading to el-Hemeimeh, the great Nabataean-Roman centre in the Hisma valley." (Glueck 1934–35: 65). Glueck goes on to mention that the two Horsfields and Mr. Head had made an earlier, otherwise unattested, visit to the site and "picked up quantities of Nabataean sherds." These sherds, combined with the identification of Humayma as the Auara proposed by Musil, may have led Glueck to his prophetic evaluation of the site as a "great Nabataean-Roman centre."

Frank visited Humayma on 26 October 1933 in connection with his travels around the Wadi 'Arabah. He provides a good description of the Ghana spring and the aqueduct. Unlike previous visitors, he seems to have followed the entire course of the aqueduct from the 'Ain al-Ghana spring, thereby noting the off-take Cistern no. 20, the adjacent track of the Via Nova, and heaps of milestones (Frank 1934: 236–37). Frank describes briefly the Nabataean aqueduct pool (Structure no. 63), the Roman fort and reservoir, the apse of a still-unexcavated church (probably B126), and the rock-cut tombs on the western ridge. Citing Musil's visit and the description in Brünnow and Domaszewski, Frank evaluated the site as "schon ausreichend erforscht," and cut his visit short. Nevertheless, he seems to have noticed traces of the Via Nova heading south from the site towards the Wadi Yutum.

Over the course of two days during the Autumn of 1935, Frank and Alt traced the southern end of the Via Nova between Humayma and Aqaba by automobile, their time constrained by "unvorhergesehene Schwierigkeiten" that one can easily imagine (Alt 1936: 93). Alt describes the aqueduct briefly, but indicates that its termination point in the settlement of "chirbet el-ehmeme" could not be determined. The junction of the aqueduct with Reservoir no. 63, although conjectured previously, would only be revealed by the probe I made in 1983. Now that much of the Hisma had been explored in at least a cursory manner, Alt was able to appreciate for the first time the unique character of Humayma in this desert landscape and the importance of its location for trade and agriculture (Alt 1936: 94).

Das sehr ausgedehnte flache Ruinenfeld von *chirbet el-ehmeme* birgt die Reste der letzten großen Siedlung an der römischen Straße vor ihrem von hier noch fast 75 km entfernten Zielpunkt am Roten Meer, zugleich anscheinend der einzigen großen Siedlung an der *hesma*-Ebene überhaupt. Aus dieser Gunst der Verkehrslage erklärt sich die Größe der Ortschaft mindestens zum Teil; als weiterer Grund kommt hinzu, daß der Boden in ihrer näheren Umgebung nicht überall so hoch mit Sand bedeckt ist wie sonst in der Ebene und daher Möglichkeiten des Ackerbaus bietet, die noch heute von den beduinischen Besitzern genutzt werden.

Apparently the Bedouin who had troubled Musil were still farming the fields around the ruins. Alt comments on the relative absence of sand on the fields, but in fact deposits of sand appear and disappear according to short-term climatic cycles. During the drought of 1998 to 2002, large amounts of fine red sand were deposited on recently ploughed fields in the region. Alt was also the first visitor — setting aside Glueck's second-hand report — to publish his deductions concerning the history of the site based on a reading of the potsherds he found there (Alt 1936: 94): "Der Scherbenbelag des Ruinenfeldes besteht vor allem aus byzantinischer, aber auch aus nabatäisch-frührömischer Ware und beweist somit, daß die Siedlung das ganze spätere Altertum durchlebt hat."

Alt and Frank did not have time to visit the necropoleis west of the town, but they did measure the walls of the Roman fort and identify its character correctly. Alt also mentions that the Bedouin had begun to clear some of the ruins to build houses, and that three apses of a Byzantine church had been cleared "nahe dem Südostrand des Ruinenfeldes" (Alt 1936: 94–95, pl. 3b.). The only three-apse church known at Humayma until 1998 was the "Lower Church" (C101), but this structure is located at the southwest edge of the site. In 1998, the church Alt mentions was identified by the Humayma Excavation Project — through comparison of his photograph with the present remains — as the core of a Bedouin house situated near the two central Nabataean reservoirs (Structure B126; Schick in Oleson et al. 1999: 430–32). Only the central apse survives. As Alt's photograph shows, the side apses were constructed by rounding off the corners of rectangular rooms with curved blocks, and these have since been removed. At the end of his account, Alt identifies Humayma as the ancient Ammatha, passing over Hauarra because of supposed errors in the section of the Peutinger Table that illustrates Aqaba and the Hisma (Alt 1936: 106–11; cf. Aharoni 1963: 39–41, and here Chapter 2.A.2, 2.B.1).

Sir Aurel Stein visited Humayma by car on 21–22 April 1939 as part of his survey of the southern end of the "Roman Frontier." He carefully surveyed the distances separating Aqaba, Khirbet al-Khalde, and Humayma, and finding the distances to correspond closely to those between Aila, Praesidio, and Hauarra indicated on the Peutinger Table, he accepted the identification of "the large ruined site of Homeima" as Auara (Stein 1940: 437; Arden-Close 1941: 21; Stein in Gregory and Kennedy 1985: 319). Although the report published in 1940 was very brief, Stein examined the site carefully, made extensive notes, and took photographs for his *Limes Report*, only published forty years later (Kennedy 1982: 271–78, Gregory and Kennedy 1985: 317–29). Like Alt, Stein comments on the relative fertility of the soil around Humayma, appreciating the extent of ancient and modern cultivated fields (Stein in Gregory and Kennedy 1985: 319–20).

> Homaima marks a position where conditions favourable for cultivation must have invited permanent occupation from early times. Between a line of hills to the west overlooking the Wadi 'Araba and a peneplain stretching down from the Shera' range in the north-east there lies a broad trough where climatic conditions due to an elevation of more than 3,000 feet and much fertile alluvium brought down from the limestone slopes make cultivation possible. Plentiful growth of grass and scrub is to be seen on both sides of the Wadi al-Jaman which descends from the Shera' range and passes Homaima in a wide curve before running south towards the Wadi al-Yitm. It affords evidence of the amount of moisture which this trough receives during the winter rains through drainage from both hill ranges. Shapeless heaps of debris from stone built dwellings decayed into low mounds mark the ground once occupied by the ruined old settlement, broken in places by small patches of fields brought under tillage in recent times. These remains extend for fully a mile northward on the west of the wadi. Indications of ancient cultivation

could be traced much further up. Along the left bank, too, of the wadi cultivation has been resumed in patches over what apparently had been part of the former tilled area.

Stein suggests, however, that modern occupation of the site was only seasonal (Stein in Gregory and Kennedy 1985: 321).

Here and there small pits have been dug out amongst the shapeless mounds by Bedouins of the 'Alawin tribe, as noted by Musil, who now visit Homaima in the summer and autumn for grazing and intermittent cultivation. These pits are used for the storage of grain and fodder. Near the southernmost debris heaps there was seen a circular cistern closely resembling those at al-Khaldi with four arches supporting the flat roofing [Structure no. 54 or 69?]… Proceeding further north…I found a small orchard planted with young fig trees occupying a hollow in the ground.

About 120 yards to the south [*sic*; the context suggests he meant "north"] of the orchard there is exposed on a small eminence a portion of a better preserved ruin (pl. 67d) which appeared to have been recently cleared for the storage of corn and straw. It comprises one large room about 15 feet [the published text reads "125 feet (4.57 m)"] wide, ending eastwards in a semicircular apse.

Shadows cast by the small grove of fig trees he mentions can be seen in RAF aerial photographs of the site taken as early as 1926 (Kennedy cat. nos. 26:002), just northeast of Cistern no. 69. Some trees were still visible in an aerial photograph taken in 1953 (Kennedy and Riley 1990: 146, fig. 89), but no traces of them remain today. The Humayma Excavation Project also so far has not recognised the storage pits. At some time after this visit, the cleared chancel area of the church B126, also seen by Alt, was partly walled in and roofed over for housing. An Arabic inscription has been pecked into the lintel of the modern door: "There is no god

but God and Muhammad is the Messenger of God. / Muhammad Ali al-Hijazi." The modern mud and timber roof collapsed around 2005.

Stein mentions two circular cisterns apparently cleared out for re-use and holding water at the time of his visit, probably Cisterns nos. 64 and 69, along with the collapsed dome of Structure no. 72. His description also suggests that the conduit carrying the overflow from Reservoir no. 63 could be traced from the vicinity of the excavated apse of B126 northeast to the Nabataean Reservoir/Pool no. 63, and that the branch line from the Ghana aqueduct feeding Reservoir no. 62 in the Roman fort was still visible. Stein took accurate measurements of the reservoirs and the fort and describes them carefully, but he did not have time to examine the "*castellum*" wall for towers (Stein in Gregory and Kennedy 1985: 323–26). Stein's account of the settlement centre closes with an appreciation of the importance of Humayma in antiquity (p. 325). At the end of the visit, the group followed the line of the aqueduct and road as far as the valley below 'Ain al-Ghana (pp. 325–28).

Brief as this description of the surface remains of Homaima must be it may suffice to show the importance once attaching to the site. This importance was obviously increased by the fact that it served as a half-way station on the route connecting the port of Aila with Petra… Cultivation was possible here over a considerable stretch of potentially fertile ground even without irrigation. This must have attracted to the place a settled population sufficiently large to provide local supplies such as could materially aid traffic passing by this route. Only methodical excavation could furnish materials for tracing the history of Homaima. But it may be considered as certain that it existed as a settlement of some size already in Nabataean times and remained such through the Roman and Byzantine periods down to the early centuries after Islam.

Stein's account of his visit to Humayma clearly describes the archaeological potential of the site, and if the *Limes Report* had been published promptly, survey and excavation might have begun decades earlier than they actually did. The charms of Humayma were mostly lost on Kirkbride and Harding, who visited it during a rapid tour of the Hisma in 1946 (Kirkbride and Harding 1947: 21).

> Its general appearance is a dreary waste of tumbled blocks, among which a few spaces have been cleared and some attempt made to grow crops by local Bedul. The most remarkable feature of the site is its cisterns; two very large open reservoirs, and innumerable underground ones, many still roofed over, but the water no longer conducted to them. Sherds ranging from Nabataean to Early Arab were found.

It is interesting that these visitors did not see water in any of the cisterns, and their comments suggest that Bedouin occupation of the site remained seasonal at best. The party then drove south, where it saw the well-preserved Nabataean dam in the wadi just south of Jebel Qalkha (Structure no. 44), the adjacent Nabataean and Thamudic graffiti, and a large cistern at the mouth of the wadi (Cistern no. 18). They also visited some cisterns near the south edge of the survey area.

After Kirkbride and Harding's cursory report, the Hisma and Humayma more or less disappear from the literature again until the publication of Bowersock's "A Report on Arabia Provincia" in 1971, essentially a call for further archaeological activity in the region and related historical research (Bowersock 1971). Humayma is mentioned briefly (pp. 238–39). In fact, a great deal of aerial photography had taken place around this region in the 1930s and 1950s, some of the images taken explicitly to record archaeological features, and all of them of some use for this purpose. Unfortunately, the intervention of World War II and the subsequent Arab-Israeli conflict restricted access to the images for security reasons, so their publication and archaeological evaluation only began in the 1980s (Kennedy and Riley 1990; see Humayma on pp. 146–48).

Bowersock's call to action helped stimulate the resumption of survey activity across the whole Hisma by Graf and Jobling in the late 1970s and early 1980s, and Parker's survey of the eastern

military frontier in 1976, 1980, and 1982. The site briefly attracted the interest of the Jordanian Department of Antiquities, which carried out the very first archaeological excavation at Humayma in 1963. The team cleared an Umayyad-period house 100 m northwest of the Nabataean Reservoir no. 67 in the centre of the settlement and half of the nave of the Byzantine church at the southwest edge of the settlement (Field C101). Unfortunately, no report was published, and all the excavation records were destroyed in a flood at the Department of Antiquities office in Amman in 1967. The site apparently remained neglected until the indefatigable Lindner visited with his Petra survey team on a day off in April 1976. He published a short account (Lindner 1976: 90–91) describing several cisterns and reservoirs, mentioning the presence of several churches, and reflecting on the importance of the site to the Abbasids. Some Bedouin were camped nearby and tending their fields, which had been tilled "with the help of the government." Lindner for the first time proposed the need for protection and preservation of the site, and the reaction of the landowners was hostile (Lindner 1976: 91): "Nun soll das ganze Gebiet wegen seiner archäologischen Bedeutung unter Denkmalschutz gestellt werden. Die Aufregung ist groß. Alle reden durcheinander und niemand hat zum Tee eingeladen. Das ist kein gutes Zeichen." Unfortunately, strong opposition by local landowners to management or protection of the site remained firm until the end of the 1990s, when the advantages of tourist development became apparent. The attitude of the local sheikhs added enormous difficulties and significant expense to my own excavations in the 1990s, problems that even the regional Department of Antiquities office could not cope with. A few months after Lindner's visit, Parker carried out a survey of military sites in the region from Petra to Aqaba, but he bypassed Humayma (Parker 1976).

By this time it had become obvious that there was enormous archaeological potential in the Hisma region, and Graf posed some of the related historical problems in 1978 in a seminal article concerned with the role of local tribes in the organisation of the frontier (Graf 1978). Graf also carried out the first systematic archaeological survey of the Hisma in June 1978 (Graf 1979). Although the project lasted only a week, the results were significant, allowing Graf to publish a revolutionary evaluation of the extent of Nabataean occupation of the Hisma (Graf 1983), including a short account of its early explorers. The survey report only described Humayma briefly (1979: 125), but the 1983 article provided a description and historical account of the site, along with a sketch plan and an evaluation of its importance in the context of the Hisma.

> But the overwhelming impression of the ruins is that they mark the site of one of the largest Nabatean villages in southern Jordan and certainly the largest Nabatean settlement to be found in the Hisma.

> Humayma, almost certainly ancient Auara, thus represents a major obstacle to the characterization of the Hisma as basically a desolate region, marked only by an isolated temple and a few caravanserais or road stations strung across its barren landscape, during the Nabatean period. This site, with its complex water system, extensive occupational remains, and Nabatean sanctuary, demonstrates that at least one other major settlement existed in the region besides that at Wadi Ram. Whether Humayma functioned as an agricultural center, industrial complex, and/or entrepôt on the Nabatean route leading to Petra, cannot be determined without excavation and further exploration of the region, but that the settlement was of sizeable proportions and significance is indisputable (Graf 1983: 660).

Graf also reported that the Nabataean reservoir in the centre of the settlement (Structure no. 67) had been cleared out and repaired for re-use in the early 1960s, and that the Bedouin living at or around the site had been lured to New Humayma by housing and other facilities provided by Canadian development money through the UN agency CARE in 1979.

The time had come to undertake excavation at Humayma, and in 1981 Eadie and Graf organised a small team to reconnoitre the site and develop plans for substantial archaeological excavation. I was invited to join this group in order to evaluate the water-supply system. One season of excavation was carried out in 1983 (Eadie 1984), during which the site was mapped and measurements taken to produce a plan. Eadie and Graf probed the lower Byzantine church (C101) and a possible Nabataean caravanserai 6.5 km north of the site (variously called Rujm al-Shugg, Rujm Abu Hashem, Beda; Graf 1993a, 1995: 252–57), while I probed the Nabataean aqueduct (Structure no. 1) and its pool (Structure no. 63) and surveyed the aqueduct as far as the al-Shara escarpment (Eadie 1984; Eadie and Oleson 1986). During these same years, Graf continued his survey of the regional road system and recorded graffiti (Graf 1992a, 1993a–b, 1995). As it turned out, Eadie and Graf were not able to execute their plans for excavation, and in 1985 Eadie agreed that I should apply for my own permit to carry out the survey and excavation recorded in this volume, work which I continued until 2005 through the generous permission of the Department of Antiquities.

During the 1980s, the Hisma as a whole was the object of intense survey activity and some excavation by other groups as well. In 1979, Henry carried out a survey of late Pleistocene and early Holocene sites in Wadi Judaiyid below Ras en-Naqb, just outside the subsequent Humayma Survey Project area, supplemented by some excavation (Henry et al. 1981). He later went on to excavate a Lower Palaeolithic site along the Wadi Qalkha, 2 km north of Humayma (Henry 1995: 43–48), a Middle Palaeolithic rock shelter at Tor Faraj in Wadi Aghar, just south of Humayma, near the Nabataean dam (Structure no. 44; Henry 1982, 1985; Henry 1995: 49–107; 1996), and several Upper and Epi-Palaeolithic sites just south of Humayma (Henry 1995: 133–214). Henry's conclusions about the palaeo-ecology and climate of the region and the patterns of pastoral subsistence are applicable to the early historical period as well (Henry 1983, 1987, 1992; Henry 1995). In 1979, Jobling organised the 'Aqaba–Ma'an Survey, which evolved into a project designed to record cultural remains throughout Jordan's southern desert (Jobling 1981, 1983). He recorded few habitation sites, but until his premature death in 1994, Jobling's team "investigated the hydrology, surface structural remains, surface lithics, and rock art" in a region of 2,700 sq km largely unknown to outsiders (L. Jobling et al. 1997). The inscriptions and rock art they recorded revealed the intensity with which the ancient peoples used the desert, and they provided evidence for the nature of their activities there, the composition of their flocks and game animals, and climate change (Jobling 1986a–b, 1989a–b; Munro et al. 1997). Although Jobling initially visited Humayma and recorded inscriptions around the periphery of the survey area (Jobling 1983a: 188; 1983b: 317; 1983–84: 266; 1984: 40, 44), he intentionally avoided duplication of the research efforts of Graf and Eadie, and later of myself.

By this point, Humayma/Auara had entered the archaeological literature and become part of the historical analysis of ancient Arabia Petraea. Negev alludes to the site in his survey of Nabataean archaeology and history (1977: 537–38), and several of Eadie's publications concerning the Roman frontier cite evidence from Humayma (1985: 414; 1986: 247–48). The archaeological evidence is cited several times in Bowersock's synthetic study of Roman Arabia, and he notes that the question of the identification of the site with Hauarra on the Peutinger Table had been settled (1983: 94, 173–74, 185; cf. Aharoni 1963: 41). Parker's final publica-

tion of his survey of Roman military sites along the whole military frontier in Jordan is essentially a historical evaluation of a decade of archaeological research by him and others (Parker 1986); Humayma, of course, appears throughout (esp. pp. 104–5).

My survey of the water-supply system in the catchment area of ancient Humayma in 1986 and 1987, along with my probes in the settlement centre itself in 1989, convinced me of the need to undertake excavation of the habitation area — both to understand the water-supply system and to understand the historical development of the ancient settlement (see fig. 2.14). I directed ten campaigns of excavation and two seasons of geophysical survey between 1991 and 2005. Rebecca Foote, who has supervised work in the Abbasid manor house (F103) as part of the Humayma Excavation Project since 1993, directed her own excavations in F103 in 2002 and at Structure no. 72 in 2008. In 2008, M. Barbara Reeves began a new series of excavations at the site. Humayma has now become an important part of our understanding not only of the ancient Hisma, but also of the Provincia Arabia, the Roman frontier, and the early Islamic period in southern Jordan.

Chapter 2

Territory, Resources, and History

2.A. TOPOGRAPHY, GEOMORPHOLOGY, AND THE ROAD SYSTEM

2.A.1. *Topography and Geomorphology*

Humayma is located in the desert region now termed the Hisma or Wadi Hisma ("canyon land," in Arabic), approximately equidistant along a straight line between Petra, 45 km to the north, and Aqaba, 55 km to the southwest (fig. 2.1). This region is also referred to as the Disi-Rum Highlands (Bender 1974: 9) and is part of the Southern Mountain Desert (Macumber 2001: 3, 17–19). The site benchmark at the northeast corner of the rebuilt Nabataean reservoir in the centre of the settlement (Structure no. 67) is at an elevation of approximately 965 m; the coordinates are (UTM) 36R 0726183, 3315632; (Palestine Grid) 829293; (Lat./Long) N 29° 57' 01.71", E 35° 20' 37.24". The most striking topographic features in the vicinity of the site are the steep cliffs of the al-Shara or Ras en Naqb escarpment rising to 1700 m elevation 13 km to the north (figs. 1.5, 2.2), a chain of steep-sided red sandstone jebels rising to 1200 m elevation on the west, and on the east isolated, rounded white sandstone jebels with elevations up to 1300 m (fig. 2.3). The mountains on the west, particularly Jebel Humayma and Jebel Qalkha (fig. 2.4), are dissected by deep, steep-walled valleys that lead to the Wadi 'Arabah, only 7 km farther west but not visible from the site. To the south and southeast a plain composed of sandy loam or loess alternating with drifted sand descends gradually towards Quweira (17 km distant) at the upper termination of the Wadi Yutum, and then gently upwards to Wadi Ramm (43 km distant to the southeast; figs. 1.2, 1.4).

A less conspicuous ridge of white sandstone, the Hudeibat edh-Dhiru, extends southwest from the foot of the escarpment below the projecting Jebel Naqb Ishtar, forming the eastern boundary of the Humayma water catchment (fig. 1.1). A corresponding ridge extends from the escarpment below Jebel Ghana nearly as far as the site, guiding run-off from the escarpment into Wadi Jammam, which becomes Wadi Amghar, then Wadi Qalkha as it passes Humayma. Wadi Qalkha is poorly defined as it crosses the gently sloping plain south of Humayma, ultimately disappearing in a mud-flat near Quweira. The ridge below Jebel Ghana diverts the Wadi Hilwa, which drains the valley below 'Ain al-Ghana, and its tributary the Wadi Beida into the steep valley below Jebel Humayma that leads to the Wadi 'Arabah. The regional geomorphologic units include "the Ma'an-Ras en Naqb Plateau, Ras en Naqb escarpment, alluvial fans, outliers and *inselbergs*, wadi terraces, modern wadi, aeolian sand, and mud-flat" (Henry et al. 1983: 7–10).

The geology and geomorphology of this region have been well-studied (Bender 1974: 20–24, 49–53; Osborn and Duford 1981; Rabba 1991; Hassan 1995; Heinrichs and Fitzner 2000; cf. Cordova 2007:

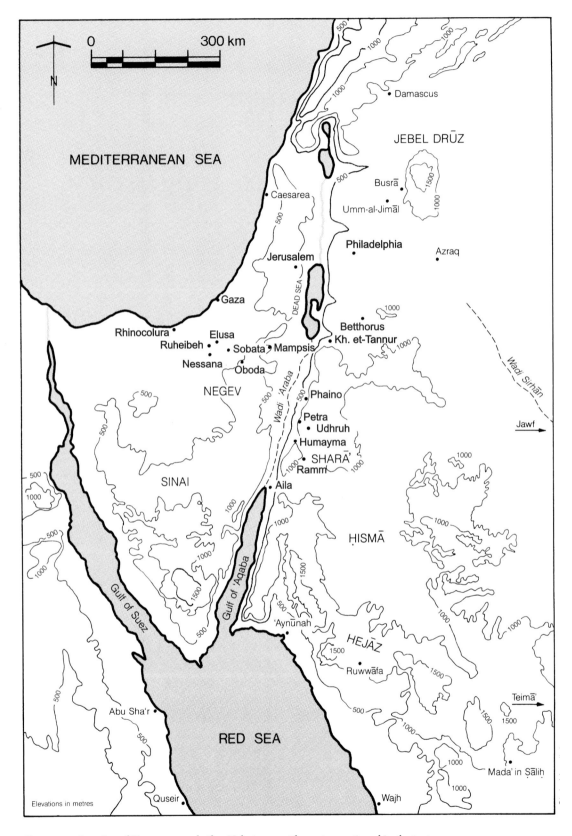

FIG. 2.1   *Location of Humayma and other Nabataean settlements mentioned in the text.*

FIG. 2.2   *View of al-Shara escarpment from the south.*

15–61). In geological terms, the region is on the edge of the Nubo-Arabian Shield, the exposed sequence consisting of Cambrian to Silurian sandstones overlying pre-Cambrian igneous rocks that slope to the north and east (Osborn and Duford 1981: 5). The aplite-granite, granodiorite, and quartz diorite forming the basement are submerged around the site, but scattered surface fragments can be found. These igneous rocks (the Aheimir Volcanic Suite) frame the deep valleys west of Humayma and form the mountains west of Quweira that mark the south end of the survey area.

The hills and *inselbergs* around the site are composed of a sequence of five distinctive sandstones. The lowest, the Cambrian Salib Arkose, consists of a reddish-brown, bedded deposit of cemented, sand-sized grains of feldspar and quartz. It is exposed only along the lowest slope of the south face of Jebel Qalkha and in a few scattered outcroppings in the southwest margin of the survey area. The stone is relatively fine-grained and impermeable, but of the ancient cisterns, only no. 18 was cut into it. The two other features recorded in this formation

(Structure nos. 17, 19) are natural potholes that may have been adapted for water storage.

The Salib Arkose Formation is overlaid by the Umm 'Ishrin Formation, consisting of massive, dark red-brown to nearly black sandstone with frequent pebble inclusions and widely-spaced vertical master joints. These joints and the massive nature of the deposit have made it the major cliff-forming unit in the area (Osborn and Duford 1981: 9), noticeable above all in the steep, sharp profiles of Jebel Qalkha and Jebel Humayma. Wind and water erosion create deep hollows below brittle shelves that ultimately break off and form small talus formations. This process is particularly far advanced on the Hudeibat Um-Dureira at the southeast edge of the survey area, adjacent to the Desert Highway. Cistern excavators generally avoided the joints, but at several locations around the Hudeibat Um-Dureira (Structure nos. 29, 30) the stone between joints that approach each other has been chiselled out to form cisterns. The stone of the Umm 'Ishrin Formation is less permeable to water than that of the Disi Formation (see below), but both provide

FIG. 2.3   *Jebels of white Disi sandstone, east of Humayma (Photo: R. Gordon).*

FIG. 2.4   *View of Jebel Qalkha from Humayma, with white camel (Photo: Ian Babbit).*

good material for rock-cut cisterns (Lloyd 1969: 89). With the exception of the Hudeibat Um-Dureira outcroppings, the Umm 'Ishrin Formation is found west of the Wadi al-Amghar and Wadi Qalkha, above the alluvium and wadi sediments of the plain, forming a dramatic backdrop to the settlement. (fig. 2.4) Because of their proximity, the deposits of Umm 'Ishrin sandstone provided most of the construction material for ancient Humayma, and quarries can be seen in the valleys south of the site and around some of the hills to the north. Most of the tombs at Petra were carved in this formation (Heinrichs and Fitzner 2000: 285; Bellwald and al-Huneidi 2003: 17–20).

The Disi Formation, composed of white Cambrian sandstone, overlies the Umm 'Ishrin Formation and forms the bedrock of the whole catchment basin east of the Wadi Qalkha (other than the Hudeibat Um-Dureira hills) and north up the face of the escarpment to an elevation of approximately 1300 m. The distinctive landscape of pillowy ridges and rounded hills north and east of Humayma, occasionally dissected by deep, narrow gullies, results from the poor cementation of this sandstone, which is particularly susceptible to wind and water erosion. (fig. 2.3) The exposed surfaces of the *inselbergs* tend to recede uniformly as the wind carries sand particles away, and talus formations are removed by the same mechanism, ultimately leaving only low domes like the Hudeibat edh-Dhiru across from the modern settlement of Dabbat Hanut. Disi sandstone is easily excavated for the construction of cisterns. Most of the formation is composed of nearly pure silica, which since 2004 has been mined for the production of glass. Although Hawara was located on slopes of red Umm 'Ishrin sandstone, the brilliant white landscape to the east may have had something to do with the choice of the ancient name (see pp. 50–53). The Nabataeans undoubtedly recognised the similarity between this landscape and the al-Hubtha hill at the centre of Petra, part of the same Disi Formation. Although the Disi sandstone is soft and weathers easily, it was used as a construction material in the settlement, particularly in the Nabataean period. Many of the Nabataean column drums, column and pilaster bases, and capitals found around the site have been cut from

this stone, probably because of its fine grain and striking whiteness.

The Disi Formation is capped by both the Ordovician Um Sahm Formation and the Cretaceous Kurnub Formation. The Um Sahm Formation, bedded brown to purple or pink sandstone that is highly fractured and poorly cemented (Osborn and Duford 1981: 12), is found high up on the escarpment and in the jebels east of the Desert Highway. Because of its location, this formation has little relevance to Humayma, although purple sandstone building blocks occasionally found at the site may have been cut from it. The Kurnub Formation consists of white and purple, massive, coarse-grained sandstone that forms rounded to sub-rounded domes. There are small residual exposures along the modern road leading north from the site, from 1 to 2 km north of Reservoir no. 63, a larger exposure 5 km north of the site by the eroded Pleistocene lake bed, and large exposures near the top of the escarpment.

The top 150 m of the al-Shara escarpment are composed of Cenomanian limestones, particularly Na'ur limestone and Wadi as Seir limestone, containing numerous fossils and nodules of chert. As the softer sandstones below erode, enormous blocks of this limestone break off and tumble hundreds of metres down to the talus slopes below. A stratum of Muwaqqar Chalk-Marl also appears, a soft, very fine-grained yellow-brown stone that weathers into regular blocks. These often tumble down the escarpment, becoming available for use on the plain below. This stone was sought out by the Nabataeans for carving the conduit blocks for the Nabataean aqueduct serving Hawara. The groundwater and geology support numerous springs and seeps around the periphery of the escarpment, at around 1450 m asl. Five small outcroppings of Na'ur Limestone also occur along the west bank of the Wadi al-Amghar, 1 to 2 km north of Humayma. The closest knoll shows signs of quarrying, perhaps to provide limestone blocks or lime for mortar. The farther knoll, which was cut to allow passage of the Via Nova, is backed by a deposit of Cenozoic Dana Conglomerate. The low hill just across the wadi east of the settlement centre is also composed of Dana Conglomerate.

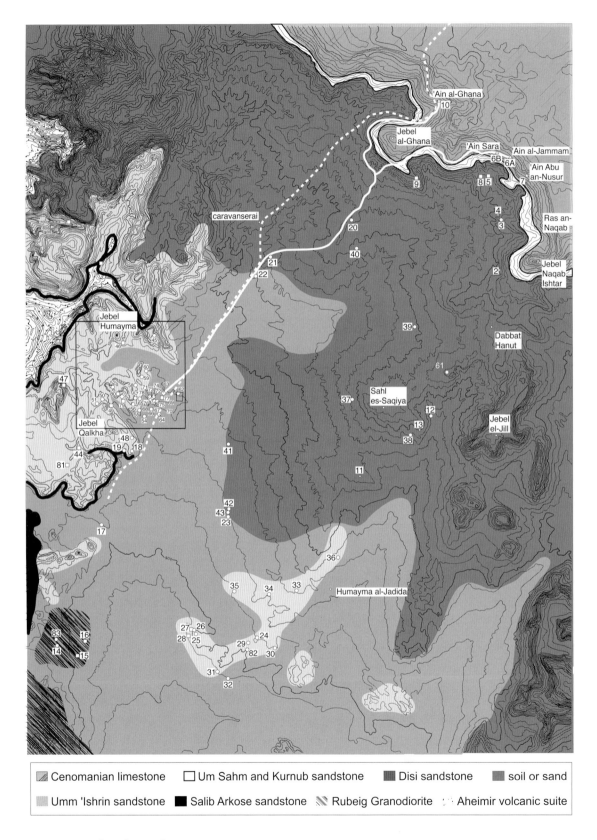

FIG. 2.5   *Geological map of survey area.*

FIG. 2.6   *View towards Humayma (upper left) from escarpment. Ghana aqueduct visible at lower left.*

Seen from the hills above Humayma, the catchment area appears as two great bowl-shaped depressions northeast and south of the settlement centre, separated from each other by the low ridge of white Disi sandstone extending west from Sahl es-Saqiya almost as far as the site itself. (figs. 2.5–6) Wadi Amghar interrupts this ridge and unites the two basins. The wandering courses of the Wadi al-Jammam and Wadi al-Amghar in the north and the larger Wadi Qalkha in the south form their respective foci. The upper slopes of the northeast basin constitute a pediplain, a complex of bedrock pediments left by the erosion of the Disi Formation *inselberg*s (Osborn and Duford 1981: 12–14). At the lower elevations, usually close to the courses of the main wadis, there are alluvial and aeolian deposits of sandy loam and loess that were cultivated in antiquity and in the recent past (Cordova 2007: 28–29). West of the Wadi al-Amghar, from 2 to 4.5 km north of the site along the course of the aqueduct, there is a large Pleistocene lake deposit that also shows signs of recent cultivation (Lloyd 1969:

27–28; Cordova 2007: 25–26). Aeolian deposits of sand form, disappear, and re-form here and there around the basin according to the topography, the season, and variations in precipitation. There was a noticeable increase in the deposit of sand during a drought that extended from 1998 to 2002. Deep excavation around the site exposes a compact pre-occupation soil that is composed largely of reddish sand with calcareous lumps.

The geomorphology of the southern basin is similar, although slopes are more gentle and the deposits of soil therefore more extensive. The fields in the immediate vicinity of the settlement centre to the north, east, and south seem to have the best-quality soil, although it is nevertheless a very light, sandy loam or loess. The proportion of sand, and of coverage by aeolian sand, increases toward the southern end of the survey area, where the Wadi Qalkha begins to wander back and forth across the plain. Here, too, the movement of surface sand has increased since 1998.

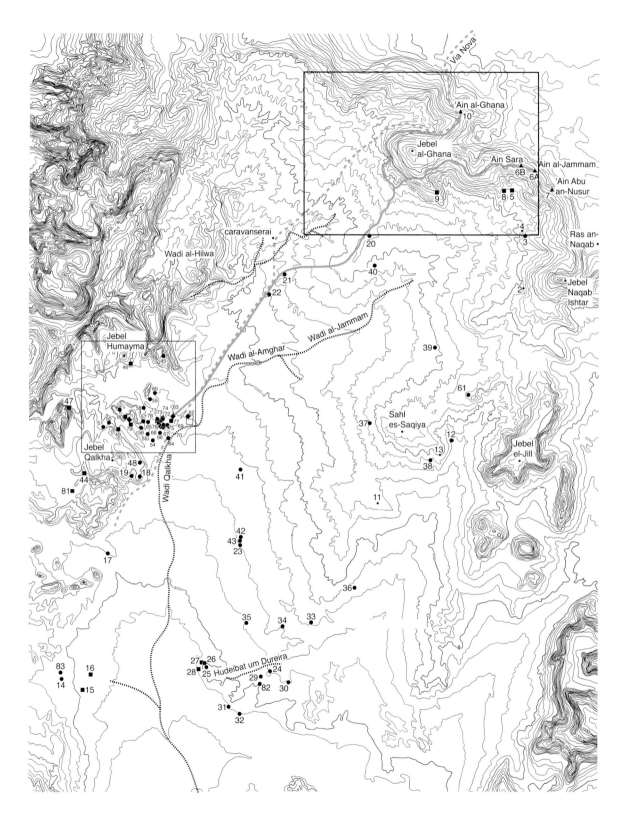

FIG. 2.7 *Map of survey area with indication of ancient roads and structures. Aqueduct, light grey solid line; Via Nova, dotted light grey line; wadi courses, dark dotted lines.*

2.A.2. *Routes of Passage*

From the settlement centre the crest of the escarpment can be attained in about five or six hours of walking (depending on the route), the eastern edge of Sahl es-Saqiya in two hours, the intersection of the Wadi Qalkha and the new highway in about three hours, and the sheer cliffs overlooking the Wadi Aheimir and Wadi 'Arabah beyond in about one hour (fig. 2.7).

The path of the Via Nova Traiana dropped over the edge of the escarpment at 'Ain al-Ghana, passed just below the present lower spring, and continued steeply down the loamy sand slopes and alluvial fans along the north slope of the Jebel Ghana (see figs. 3.1, 3.10). The Ghana aqueduct descended more gradually, but at km 2.974 from the spring, the aqueduct and road are only 50 m apart. At this point, near the mouth of the valley, the road struck off in nearly a straight line towards Humayma, passing close to a large Nabataean structure, possibly a caravanserai, 6.5 km north of the site (Rujm al-Shugg, Rujm Abu Hashem, Beda; UTM 36R 0729531, 3321321; Graf 1993a, 1995: 252–57).[1] The route taken by the road forced it to cross a fairly deep section of the Wadi Beida somewhere south of the caravanserai. Because the engineers who built the aqueduct had to both conserve height and follow a constant slope, they selected a longer route that deviates from the road, along the western slope of the ridge projecting towards Humayma from the foot of Jebel Ghana, just below the watershed between the Wadi Jammam and Wadi Hilwa. This line avoided nearly all the wadi tributaries and descended by easy stages to the relic Pleistocene lake bed along the right bank of the Wadi Amghar.

At 13.4 km from 'Ain Ghana, the aqueduct rejoined the course of the road, and both structures followed essentially a straight line, with the aqueduct on the southeast (left) side of the road, which is marked by milestones and occasional stretches of rough cobble paving with edging slabs. At a point 2.2 km north of the settlement centre, the course of the Wadi Amghar passes close to some very steep-walled gullies draining into the Wadi Hilwa and the 'Arabah. The engineers anticipated encroachment on the road and aqueduct by the gullies — which

in fact have since swallowed up several stretches of both structures. In consequence, the road was diverted over a low limestone hill, while the aqueduct followed a detour cut into its south slope (Stein in Gregory and Kennedy 1985: 327). The rest of the route to the settlement centre did not present any difficulty to the road-builders, although the aqueduct engineers had to contend with a very gentle slope (approximately one percent).

At some point between the hillock and the Roman fort, the road almost certainly crossed over the course of the aqueduct and paralleled its eastern flank as far as the settlement centre, where the aqueduct flow was distributed down-slope to the west and south. The most logical point for the crossover would be just after the two structures leave the hillock between the two wadis. Unfortunately, the ancient remains in this area have been obliterated by road building, ploughing, and erosion. The crossing probably consisted of an earth viaduct over a reinforced section of the aqueduct structure. Along the approach to the fort, the aqueduct channel has been badly damaged by ploughing, and the modern dirt road has destroyed what might have remained of the Via Nova. An aerial photograph taken during the Hunring Aerial Survey in 1953 (Aerial Photographic Archive for Archaeology in the Middle East, APA 1953/HAS 26.002), before motor vehicles — or, indeed, any kind of wheeled vehicle — were common in the region, shows faint traces of a straight road or path parallel to the east side of the aqueduct as it approaches the terminal pool (Structure no. 63) — most likely the Via Nova. What appears to be a branch road angles off from the main road about 200 m north of the fort and follows a straight line to the north gate (fig. 2.8).

The course of the Via Nova has been lost in the settlement, but a terracotta pipeline that led from Pool/Reservoir no. 63 to the shrine in E125 provides evidence for its course. Just outside the northwest corner of the E125 complex, the pipeline, excavated in 1998 and 2000, was provided with an inverted siphon that allowed it to pass beneath a feature 8 m wide, just west of the structure. This is the most suitable route for the Via Nova — west of the fort, east of the Nabataean reservoir or pool, along the slight elevation above the settlement centre (fig. 2.7). A dirt track can be seen to follow

Fig. 2.8 *Aerial photograph of site in 1953, Hunrin Aerial Survey (Aerial Photographic Archive for Archaeology in the Middle East, APA 1953/HAS 26.002).*

this route in the earliest aerial photographs and still follows it today. No traces of the Via Nova, however, have been observed recently to the south along the 18 km stretch between Humayma and Quweira (Graf 1995: 257–58). Savignac (1932: 582), however, asserts that the modern track he took in 1932 from Quweirah to Ma'an followed a less

propitious route than "la voie romaine qui passait plus à l'ouest par el-Homeimeh." The road most likely followed the right bank of the Wadi Qalkha, on the slopes above the soft sand of the wadi bed, and subsequent erosion may have destroyed all traces. From Quweira the main road followed the Wadi Yutum to Aqaba. Graf restores a road leading

Table 2.1   Mean temperatures (°C) at Quweira (*Climatic Atlas of Jordan* [1971]).

	Jan	Feb	Mar	Apr	May	Jun	Jul	Aug	Sep	Oct	Nov	Dec	Year
Mean Monthly	6	8	10	14	16	20	32	22	20	20	14	8	20
Mean daily max.	14	18	20	24	26	32	32	32	30	26	20	16	24
Mean daily range	10	10	12	13	15	16	15	15	15	15	11	13	13

east from Humayma on the basis of a milestone found halfway between the site and Dabbat Hanut on the Desert Highway (Graf 1995: 257–63). Eadie (1984: 216) uses the orientation of the road north of Humayma to reconstruct a route for the Via Nova 2 km east of the fort, but in terms of function, security, and topography, such a route makes less sense than passage through the settlement.

Unpaved, unmarked paths used by the local tribes since the foundation of Hawara must have struck out from the site across the desert in various directions. One such route probably led directly southeast to Wadi Ramm, the cisterns at Jebel Ratama providing a convenient watering point. Similarly, a route down into the Wadi ʿArabah must have existed, most likely down one of the valleys north and west of Jebel Humayma, although a convenient passage down the initial steep cliffs has not yet been identified. In 1995, with A. Smith and R. Lane, I walked from the foot of Jebel Humayma down the Wadi al-Hilwa and Wadi Nukhleila to the modern Wadi ʿArabah Highway in seven hours.

2.A.3. *Climate, Hydrology, and Pedology*

Like the geology, the climate across the Humayma catchment area varies remarkably because of the significant fall in elevation from north to south. In fact, it is likely that one attraction of the site to its Nabataean settlers was the fact it occupied an ecotone, a transitional area between two or more ecological zones, allowing exploitation of a wide variety of resources. In general terms, the overall climate involves a short, wet winter followed by a

long dry season, both characterised by relatively mild temperatures. Nevertheless, Henry defines four distinct climate zones for this region based on elevation (Henry 1995: 14–18; cf. also Lloyd 1969: 38–67; Shehadeh 1985; I. Künne in Lindner et al. 1990: 217–22):

1) upland Mediterranean Zone at the top of the escarpment (1,300–1,700 m asl), with a cool, temperate, rainy climate; average annual temperature ranging from 12-17° C; average annual precipitation ca. 300 mm.
2) semi-arid Cool Steppe Zone along the slope of the escarpment (1,000–1,300 m asl); average annual temperature 18° C or less; average annual precipitation less than 300 mm.
3) arid Cool Desert Zone on the basin floor around Humayma (900–1,100 m asl); average annual temperature 18° C or less; average annual rainfall less than 200 mm.
4) arid Warm Desert Zone toward Quweira (less than 900 m asl); average annual temperature ranging from 19–25° C; average annual rainfall less than 100 mm.

There are no annual temperature figures recorded for Humayma, but those for Quweira should be similar, although slightly warmer (Table 2.1).

Although the definition of the climatic zones is useful, Henry's figures for average annual rainfall are higher than those in the Natural Resources Authority, and the temperatures seem low. According to the latter statistics, the long-term, average precipitation around Humayma is approximately 80 mm/year; the moisture in Zones 3 and 4 arrives almost entirely as rain, nearly all of

Table 2.2   Rainfall at Ras en-Naqb, Quweira, Wadi Ramm collection stations, in mm (Natural Resources Authority 1977: III A-2.4, p. 16).

	1963 1964	1964 1965	1965 1966	1966 1967	1967 1968	1968 1969	1969 1970	1970 1971	1971 1972	1972 1973	1973 1974	1974 1975	Avg.	StD
Ras en-Naqb	139	254	121	69	120	170	70	140	141	58	304	170	143	61.5
Quweira	80	335	70	49	50	129	17	70	96	33	123	42	87	81.7
Wadi Ramm	73	176	59	14	42	65	25	77	159	23	163	97	82	44.5

Table 2.3   Precipitation and run-off yield in sub-region ED11 (National Water Master Plan).

	Precip. (mm)	Total (mcm)	Run-off (mcm)	Run-off/sq km (cum)
Dry Year	40	56.6	0.28	197.7
Avg. Year	95	134.5	2.69	1899.7
Wet Year	150	212.4	8.50	6002.8

it between November and April (Natural Resources Authority 1977: Annex IIIA-2.3, p. 4; Bender 1974: 10; Shehadeh 1985: 30–31). The total, however, can vary significantly and the rainfall distribution is erratic, as figures show for the Ras en-Naqb, Quweira, and Wadi Ramm collection posts (Table 2.2; source, Natural Resources Authority 1977: III A-2.4, p. 16; cf. Kirk 1998). The southern boundary of the 100 mm isohyet line of annual mean rainfall is at Wadi Ramm (fig. 2.9, Station ED12). From this point the profile line swings northwest between Quweira (ED4) and Ras en-Naqb (ED16) and along the mountains above the 'Arabah, and northeast past Ma'an. The average annual precipitation at Petra is 136 mm (StD 75.0).

In the National Water Master Plan Humayma is counted as part of the Wadi Yutum catchment, map area ED, an area of 4443 sq km; the specific sub-region is ED11, the Wadi Rumman catchment, an area of 1416 sq km. The plan provides rough calculations of the total precipitation and the yield from run-off for sub-region ED11 (Table 2.3).

The figure of 1,899.70 cum/sq km total rainfall for an average year assumes 2.0 percent run-off. If this calculation is approximately correct and is applicable to the sub-region of the Humayma catchment, in a year of average rainfall the 206 sq km area serving the structures of ancient Humayma would yield somewhere in the range of 391,338 cum of run-off water.[2] If this calculation of run-off yield for an average year is applied directly to the estimated total precipitation of the Humayma catchment alone (80 mm × 206 sq km = 16.48 mcm), the run-off yield is 329,600 cum. The figure of 2.0 percent may be excessively cautious for the Humayma catchment, given the high proportion of exposed bedrock slope, especially since the run-off yield from gravelly earth slopes in the Negev has been calculated at 15 percent (Kedar 1957; Hillel 1982: 97). Applying the factor of 15 percent to the estimated Humayma catchment precipitation results in a run-off yield of 2.472 mcm. Nevertheless, given the high standard deviation in average annual rainfall across the Hisma, caution is appropriate when applying the figures for one site to the entire catchment around it. Even the lower yield of 2.0 percent would be far more than needed to fill the suburban (7956.7 cum) and urban (4476.4 cum) cisterns, reservoirs, and dams that captured run-off water (regional total: 12,433.1 cum). There is further discussion of the resources available to the water-supply system of ancient Humayma in Section 7.B. According to the local Bedouin, on the relatively rare occasions that precipitation arrives as snow at the basin floor, little can be harvested for the cisterns, because the slower rate of run-off allows much of the water to be absorbed by soil, stone, or evaporation. Class A Pan Evaporation in the ED11 region is 3300–3400 mm/year (Natural Resources Authority 1977: Map SW-5), indicating the vulnerability of pooled water and of water supplies stored in unroofed cisterns. According to the UNESCO aridity index (the ratio of annual precipitation to annual evapotranspiration), Humayma, with a ratio of 0.024, is in a Hyper-Arid Zone. The lower threshold for classification as an Arid Zone is 0.03 (Bruins 1990a: 88).

The hydrogeology of the Hisma region was not particularly favourable to pre-modern human settlement (Lloyd 1969). There are occasional springs and seeps, but over most of the region the ground water is too deep to have been accessible with ancient technological resources. Qa ed-Disa is the only area in the region where the aquifer is at a depth of less than 100 m, in this case 66 m. At Station 6, a drill point 10 km southeast of Humayma, the aquifer is 258 m below ground level (Lloyd 1969: 199). The depth of the aquifer across the Humayma catchment varies from more than 300 m at the escarpment, to 200 m in the vicinity of the settlement (Lloyd 1969: 124, fig. 35). Approximately seven run-off-producing storms occur each year at Ras en-Naqb, five at Wadi Ramm (Osborn and Duford 1981: 6; cf. Lloyd 1969: 56–67). The exiguous precipitation runs off the rocky slopes, where there is seldom any soil to store it for later

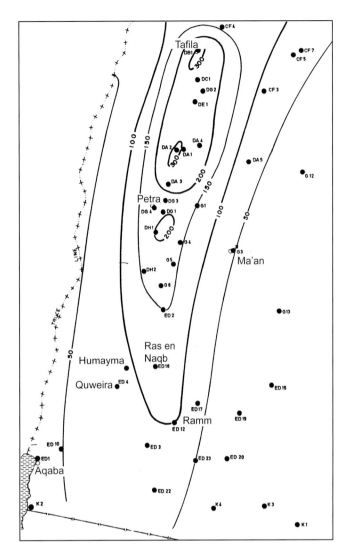

FIG. 2.9 *Rainfall isohyets for southern Jordan, normal year (adapted from National Water Master Plan of Jordan, Map SW 4.2).*

release, and disappears into the deep deposits of sand, silt, or gravel that form the valley floors. Modern drilling has revealed unconsolidated sediments as deep as 370 m below the present surface (Osborn and Duford 1981: 13). In the basins of the Humayma catchment, fields of sandy loess or loam positioned near the rocky slopes or the main wadis can frequently receive and hold enough moisture to bring a crop of grain to maturity, but most of the run-off sinks beyond reach in the deeper sediments toward the centre of the catchment. The absence of any traces of ancient or modern wells in the Humayma area indicates that pools of water

FIG. 2.10 *Distant view of Site no. 48.*

perched on buried geological features must be rare and/or too deep to exploit.

No flowing spring existed on the Hisma floor in the vicinity of Humayma in the historical period. Crusts of water-deposited carbonate cement around an opening in the side of the Jebel Qalkha, across the valley south of the settlement centre, suggest the presence of a spring at this point in the eighth or ninth millennium BC or earlier, but there is no indication the source was flowing in the Nabataean period (*pace* Farrand 1984; Eadie and Oleson 1986: 55; Graf 1992a; Henry 1995: 216) (fig. 2.10) A cistern (Structure no. 48) was cut in the rock nearby to take advantage of run-off from precipitation, not flow from the former spring (see figs. 3.89–91). The adjacent niche containing three betyls and the numerous graffiti probably reflect religious interest in the site stimulated by the conspicuous landmark of the cave in the hillside. Significant seeps can be seen today near the base of the deep Wadi Hilwa, but these are hundreds of metres below the settlement site. The only flowing water accessible to ancient Humayma came from

the springs high up on the escarpment, brought in at enormous effort by means of the Ghana and Jammam aqueducts.

The question of climate change is very important in the study of any ancient desert community. The analysis of plant and animal remains and soils from the Palaeolithic and Epi-Palaeolithic sites around Humayma has revealed variations in precipitation, but in general a climate more moist than that of today, culminating in humid periods ca. 13,000–12,500 and 9,000–7,000 BP (Emery-Barbier in Henry 1995: 380, 383–84; MacDonald 2001: 597–98), followed by an arid climatic phase around 7,000–5,500 BP (Henry et al. 1981: 123; 1983: 10). Jobling and his survey team report evidence from site occupation patterns and rock art suggesting a period of drought from ca. 2,500–800 BC, then climatic amelioration through the Early Islamic period, followed by a decline in precipitation (Jobling 1984b: 194; Munro et al. 1997: 100; MacDonald 2001). If accepted at face value, the appearance of bovines and horses in the rock art presumably dating from the first century BC to the eighth century AD suggests a grazing regime very different from the present one (Munro et al. 1997: 100; cf. Klein in Henry 1995: 410–12). Rubin, in contrast, argues that the high population of the Negev in the Roman–Byzantine period was the result of skills in water harvesting and water management rather than climatic amelioration (Rubin 1989). The evidence for climatic change in the pre-modern historical period remains subjective, particularly the very precise phasing proposed by Shehadeh on the basis of archaeological evidence for prosperity (Shehadeh 1985: 27–29). Both documentary and oral evidence suggest increasing aridity in the Hisma and throughout Jordan since the later nineteenth century (Henry et al. 1981: 123; 1983: 10; Shehadeh 1985: 28–29; Kirk 1998; MacDonald 2001: 599). The personnel of the Humayma Excavation Project witnessed growing aridity around the site during the 1990s, with some amelioration after 2004.

The array of plants and animals available to the inhabitants of ancient Humayma, as documented by the Humayma Excavation Project (Section 2.A.4), also indicates a desert climate slightly more moist than at present. Details of the construction of the aqueduct also suggest that precipitation was scant at the time of its construction and has not increased substantially since then. Along their difficult descents of the escarpment, both the Ghana and Jammam branches of the aqueduct depend here and there on viaducts built across small erosion gullies (see, e.g., figs. 3.20, 3.27, 3.32, 3.50). In some cases openings are provided for run-off water to flow through, but a significant number of these viaducts simply block gullies that appear to the modern eye to be active run-off collectors. The fact that most of these viaducts remain intact indicates both that the Nabataean engineers knew run-off would not be a problem in the climate they were familiar with, and that precipitation has not increased markedly since.

The analysis of soil samples taken from several fields around Humayma (see Chap. 6.E) revealed that the general agricultural potential of the soil is surprisingly high for a desert area. The pH and level of plant nutrients is generally suitable for grain crops, and the levels of salt and sodium are not high enough to cause problems. At present, the levels of nitrogen and phosphorus are low, but this depletion may be the result of ancient and recent agricultural activity. In addition, the application of manure may have been easier in antiquity, when there was a significant settled population in and around the site available to supervise grazing patterns closely and engage in soil improvement. The physical properties of the soil vary significantly within the north and south drainage basins, depending on location and origin. At most locations within the basins around Humayma, the soils can be classified as loam or sandy loam (a water-deposited mixture of sand and silt-sized particles, containing < 7% clay, < 50% silt, > 43% sand) or sandy loess (a wind-deposited mixture of sand and silt-sized particles). As in the Negev, most of these soil deposits probably formed during the wet climatic periods of the Late Pleistocene (Bruins 1986: 193).

It cannot be an accident that the fields the Bedouin of modern Humayma have found most suitable for grain cultivation over the past century lie within a radius of 5 km from the ancient settlement centre (see Palmer 2001 for farming techniques). It seems likely that one major reason for the foundation of Hawara at this location was the presence of deposits of good soil that could be irrigated by run-off water. The maximum distance of 5 km to agricultural fields, approximately equal to an hour's walk, can be documented by site catchment analysis of other ancient and modern Middle Eastern villages and is based on the "principle of least effort" (Simmons 1981; Beaumont et al. 1976: 164–65; Wagstaff 1985: 52–53). Tree crops can be cultivated at a greater distance, while critical hunting and gathering activities can take place up to 10 km or a two-hour walk away from the settlement. Arboriculture does not seem to have been an important part of the economy of ancient Humayma until the Umayyad period, when we hear of 500 trees in an olive grove planted by Muhammad, son of 'Ali ibn 'Abd Allah ibn 'Abbas (al-Duri and al-Mutallabi 1971: 107–8, 149, 154; al-Bakri 1945–51: 130; al-Balâdhurî 1978: iii, 75; Schick 1995a: 312–13; 1995b: 320, 2007). Such a large grove, if real, indicates production for a regional market rather than subsistence farming (Oleson 2001: 578), but the location of the plantation has not yet been determined.

2.A.4. *Native Flora and Fauna*

Despite their aridity, desert landscapes can be rich with plant and animal life. At the same time, the ecology is vulnerable to disruption and can be slow to regenerate when subjected to the pressures of excessive grazing by domesticated animals or widespread ploughing. Although the ecology was undoubtedly already affected by human activities during the Nabataean and Roman periods, the present steppe and desert ecologies of the Humayma catchment are pale reflections of the situation that existed even a century ago. At the same time that aridity was worsening, the population of locally active Bedouin increased, along with their flocks of sheep, goats, and camels, and their need for fuel. Photographs in the report by Musil appear to show the site overgrown with closely spaced, tall shrubs (Musil 1926: 58–59, figs. 16–17); these are now absent, largely used up for cooking fires. It is not clear how much of the climax forest of juniper and Atlantic pistachio remained in this region at the time the Turks occupied it, but Cordova assumes that the demands for timber to build the Hejaz railway was the "last blow" for the southern woodlands (2007: 93–94; cf. Barker et al. 2007: 38). The analysis of ancient hyrax middens at Petra suggests that extensive deforestation had already taken place before the Roman occupation, reducing the original Mediterranean forest to a *maquis* or *garigue*. By the end of the Byzantine period, continued pressure from harvesting and grazing had reduced this to a Mediterranean *batha* or steppe (Fall 1990: 277–79).

The population of wild animals has also been under pressure. T.E. Lawrence mentions meals consisting of wild gazelle or of ostrich eggs, taken farther out in the desert in 1917 (Lawrence 1927: 115, 138), but both species are now completely extinct in the Hisma, along with the mountain lion. Adult informants at New Humayma report that their grandmothers recalled seeing ostriches in the region, probably at the beginning of the twentieth century (cf. Lancaster and Lancaster 1999: 110, 167–71). Despite these losses, the observant visitor in the Humayma area even today will sooner or later spot the desert fox, hyrax, hare, hedgehog, jerboa, gerbil, and numerous species of snakes and birds, particularly chukar partridge and quail.

During the course of a hike from Humayma to the Wadi ʿArabah highway in 1995, A. Smith, R. Lane, and I found recent remains of a large ibex skull and the dehydrated corpse of a lynx in the Wadi al-Hilwa. Local informants report rare sightings of gazelles and hyenas in the same deep valley and successful hunts for ibex as recently as 2007. A recent study of the Faynan region reports an even more drastic deterioration of the flora and fauna of that region, beginning in the Bronze Age (Barker et al. 2007: 25–96).

Most of the native mammals of particular importance to humans in the historical periods already appear in the Palaeolithic sites around Humayma: small rodent (*Rodentia* gen.), hare (*Lepus capensis*), jackal (*Canis* sp.), red fox (*Vulpes vulpes*), ass/horse (*Equus* sp.), gazelle (*Gazella* sp.), bovine (Auroch? *Bos primigenius*), caprines (sheep, *Ovis* sp.; goat/ibex, *Capra* sp.), Chukar Partridge (*Alectoris chukar*), and ostrich (*Struthio camelus*) (Klein in Henry 1995: 405–16). This selection of fauna suggests a rocky, hilly, semiarid environment not necessarily much different from the recent one (Klein in Henry 1995: 416). Rock art in the Wadi Judayid includes illustrations of camels, horses, salukis, ibex, ostriches, and mountain lions (King 1988), and Jobling found representations of horses and bovines at other sites around the Hisma (Jobling 1989a–b; Munro et al. 1997: 100). It is highly unlikely that wild bovines survived into the historical period, and the horses are shown with riders. The presence of domesticated horses and cattle in the Hisma in the period the rock art was most actively produced (ca. first century BC to ca. AD 750?) indicates either a more beneficent grazing regimen, a significant focus of agricultural resources on these two species for reasons of prestige, or narration of real or imagined stories of honour and heroism. Strabo's famous description of settled Nabataeans — possibly an image of a better-watered region of the kingdom — confuses the issue (16.4.26): "The sheep are white-fleeced and the cattle are large, but the country produces no horses. Camels afford the service they require instead of horses." Neither horses nor cattle can have played a large part in the economy of the Hisma during the period ancient Humayma flourished, although the Romans maintained

Table 2.4   Abundance and frequency of uncharred seeds from Humayma.

Common Name	Family Name	Scientific Name	Abundance		Frequency (n = 40)	
			No. seeds	%	No. samples	%
Mallow Family	*Malvaceae*	Unident. *Malvaceae*	3.0	14.0	4.0	10.0
Puccoon	*Boraginaceae*	*Lithospermum sp.*	2.0	9.3	2.0	5.0
Poppy	*Papaveraceae*	*Papaver sp.*	2.0	9.3	3.0	7.5
Pink Family	*Caryophyllaceae*	Unident. *Caryophyllaceae*	1.5	7.0	2.0	5.0
Sow Thistle	*Compositae*	*Sonchus oleraceus*	1.0	4.7	1.0	2.5
Sedge Family	*Cyperaceae*	Unident. *Cyperaceae*	1.0	4.7	1.0	2.5
Borage Family	*Boraginaceae*	Unident. *Boraginaceae*	1.0	4.7	1.0	2.5
cf. Pink Family	*cf. Caryophyllaceae*	*cf. Caryophyllaceae*	1.0	4.7	1.0	2.5
Storksbill	*Geraniaceae*	*Erodium sp.*	0.5	2.3	1.0	2.5
	Compositae	*Hedypnois rhagdioloides*	0.5	2.3	1.0	2.5
unidentified seeds			8.0	37.2	7.0	17.5
Total =			21.5	100.2		

cavalry in the fort — mounted on either horses or camels. Bones of both animals have been found at Humayma, but in small numbers, and it is likely that their frequent appearance in rock art is the imagery of prestige rather than a record of daily life. There is less evidence for the original ecology of native plants in the Hisma, and domesticates, of course, do not occur in the pre-Neolithic cultures. A wide variety of domesticated and wild species have been documented in the excavated strata at Humayma (see pp. 36–49).

Although the boundaries are not distinct, the four major climate zones in the Humayma region foster the development of vegetation units belonging to several geobotanical regions (Zohary 1962; al-Eisawi 1985: 54–56; Henry 1995: 15–18; I. Künne in Lindner et al. 1990: 217–22; cf. Evenari et al. 1982: 39–75, 191–300; Zohary 1982). The plateau and top of the escarpment are characterised by *garigue* and *batha* Mediterranean vegetation, consisting of shrubs and bushes such as *Rhamnus palaestinus*, thorny broom (*Calycotome villosa*), thorny burnet (*Sarcopoterium spinosum*), grey-leaved sagebrush (*Artemisia herba-alba*), and ladanum (*cistus* spp.), along with small, isolated remnants of forest containing juniper (*Juniperus phoenicea*) and Atlantic pistachio (*Pistacia atlantica*). The lower slopes of the escarpment and the hills and ridges above Humayma form a piedmont supporting Irano-Turanian steppe vegetation, characterised by small shrubs and bushes such as sagebrush, jointed saltwood (*Haloxylon articulatum*, also named *Hammada scoparia, Hammada salicarica*), bean caper (*Zygophyllum dumasum*), white broom (*Retama raetam*), and jointed anabasis (*Anabasis articulata*). The dry basin floor is characterised by cool desert and warm desert vegetation of the Saharo-Arabian and Sudanian zones, mainly shrubs such as sagebrush, white saxual (*Haloxylon persicum*), the broom-like *Calligonum comosum*, jointed anabasis, white hammada (*Hammada salicorica*), spiny zilla (*Zilla spinosa*), and milfoil (*Achillea fragrantissima*). Sudanian tree species, such as acacia (*Acacia* sp.) and thorn (*Zizyphus spina-christi*), appear in small stands or as isolated individuals in dry locations around the basins, particularly in the talus slopes and alluvial fans around the south edge of the survey area.

2.A.5. *Analysis of Excavated Plant Remains (1989–1993) (Based on a report by C.T. Shay)*

Flotation samples from 42 excavation loci at Humayma excavated between 1989 and 1993 were

Table 2.5   Abundance and frequency of charred seeds from Humayma.

Common Name	Family Name	Scientific Name	Abundance		Frequency (n=40)	
			No. seeds	%	No. samples	%
DOMESTICATES						
Cereals						
Six-rowed Barley	*Gramineae*	*Hordeum vulgare*	24.0	3.9	5.0	12.5
Grass family	*Gramineae*	Unident. Gramineae	12.0	2.0	3.0	7.5
Bread Wheat	*Gramineae*	*Triticum aestivum*	2.5	0.4	1.0	2.5
Wheat	*Gramineae*	*Triticum sp.*	0.5	0.0	1.0	2.5
Legumes						
Chick-pea	*Leguminosae*	*Cicer arietinum*	1.0	0.2	1.0	2.5
Tree Crops and Vines						
Fig	*Moraceae*	*Ficus sp.*	14.5	2.4	5.0	12.5
Date	*Palmae*	*Phoenix dactylifera*	3.0	0.5	3.0	7.5
Olive	*Oleaceae*	*Olea europaea*	2.0	0.3	1.0	2.5
cf. Fig	*Moraceae*	*cf. Ficus*	1.0	0.2	1.0	2.5
Grape	*Vitaceae*	*Vitis vinifera*	1.0	0.2	1.0	2.5
WILD PLANTS						
White broom	*Leguminosae*	*Retama raetam*	86.0	14.1	5.0	12.5
Goosefoot family	*Chenopodiaceae*	Unident. *Chenopodiaceae*	26.0	4.3	9.0	22.5
Mouse-ear chick-weed	*Caryophyllaceae*	*Cerastium sp.*	22.5	3.7	5.0	12.5
Plantain	*Plantaginaceae*	*Plantago sp.*	21.0	3.4	7.0	17.5
Common peganum	*Zygophyllaceae*	*Peganum harmala*	17.5	2.9	1.0	2.5
Medick	*Leguminosae*	*Medicago scutellata*	17.5	2.9	5.0	12.5
Sea-Blite	*Chenopodiaceae*	*Suaeda sp.*	13.0	2.1	5.0	12.5
Legume family	*Leguminosae*	Unident. *Leguminosae*	8.0	1.3	6.0	15.0
Pink family	*Caryophyllaceae*	Unident. *Caryophyllaceae*	7.5	1.2	5.0	12.5
Trigonel	*Leguminosae*	*Trigonella sp.*	5.5	0.9	1.0	2.5
Mallow family	*Malvaceae*	Unident. *Malvaceae*	5.0	0.8	6.0	15.0
Poppy	*Papaveraceae*	*Papaver sp.*	5.0	0.8	4.0	10.0
Sedge family	*Cyperaceae*	Unident. *Cyperaceae*	4.0	0.7	2.0	5.0
Grass family	*Gramineae*	Unident. *Gramineae*	4.0	0.7	3.0	7.5
cf. Pink family	cf. *Caryophyllaceae*	cf. *Caryophyllaceae*	4.0	0.7	4.0	10.0
Scorpion vetch	Leguminosae	*Coronilla sp.*	3.5	0.6	1.0	2.5
Goosefoot	Chenopodiaceae	*Chenopodium sp.*	3.5	0.6	1.0	2.5
cf. Trigonel	Leguminosae	cf. *Trigonella sp.*	3.5	0.6	2.0	5.0
Oval-leaved Androsace	Primulaceae	*Androsace maxima*	3.0	0.5	2.0	5.0
Mustard family	Cruciferae	Unident. *Cruciferae*	3.0	0.5	3.0	7.5
Bedstraw	Rubiaceae	*Galium sp.*	2.0	0.3	2.0	5.0
Rye grass	Gramineae	*Lolium sp.*	2.0	0.3	2.0	5.0

Table 2.5   Abundance and frequency of charred seeds from Humayma (cont.)

Common Name	Family Name	Scientific Name	Abundance		Frequency (n=40)	
			No. seeds	%	No. samples	%
Alkanna	*Boraginaceae*	*Alkanna* sp.	2.0	0.3	1.0	2.5
cf. Star-of-Beth-lehem	*Liliaceae*	cf. *Ornithogalum*	1.5	0.2	1.0	2.5
Daisy family	*Compositae*	Unident. *Compositae*	1.0	0.2	1.0	2.5
Wild Watermelon	*Cucurbitaceae*	*Citrullus colocynthis*	1.0	0.2	1.0	2.5
Parsley family	*Umbelliferae*	Unident. *Umbelliferae*	1.0	0.2	1.0	2.5
Bermuda grass	*Gramineae*	*Cynodon dactylon*	1.0	0.2	1.0	2.5
Pigweed	*Amaranthaceae*	*Amaranthus* sp.	1.0	0.2	1.0	2.5
Nightshade family	*Solanaceae*	*Solanaceae*	1.0	0.2	1.0	2.5
Fumitory	*Fumariaceae*	*Fumaria* sp.	1.0	0.2	1.0	2.5
Milk-Vetch	*Leguminosae*	*Astragalus* sp.	1.0	0.2	1.0	2.5
cf. Goosefoot family	cf. *Chenopodiaceae*	cf. Chenopodiaceae	1.0	0.2	1.0	2.5
cf. Medick	*Leguminosae*	cf. *Medicago*	1.0	0.2	1.0	2.5
cf. Scorpion vetch	cf. *Leguminosae*	cf. *Coronilla*	1.0	0.2	1.0	2.5
cf. Grass family	cf. *Gramineae*	cf. *Gramineae*	0.5	0.0	1.0	2.5
cf. Pigweed	cf. *Amaranthaceae*	cf. *Amaranthus sp.*	0.5	0.0	1.0	2.5
Unidentified seeds			267.5	43.7	25.0	62.5
TOTAL =			611.5	100.4		

analysed by Shay in 1994 (cf. Oleson 1997a: 178–79). The resulting data are presented here in order to provide a picture of the botanical resources of the site along with the other resources. Many hundreds more samples are being analysed by J. Ramsay and will be presented in Volume 2. This first group of samples came from four locations: the late Roman bath building (E077); the Byzantine Lower Church (C101); an Umayyad/early Abbasid house or market complex built on top of a Byzantine church (B100); an Umayyad house built on top of a Byzantine church and a Nabataean or Roman structure adjacent to a Nabataean-type cistern (F102) (Tables 2.4–6). The samples derive from various contexts, including occupation level, fire pit, dump, midden, destruction level, collapse, and fill. They were associated with such materials as iron, copper, glass, ceramics, plaster, stone, bone, and ash. The estimated dates for the samples range from the first to the eighth century AD, with the majority spanning the seventh century.

The samples contained 633 seeds; 611.5 were charred and 21.5 were uncharred. The uncharred seeds (Table 2.4) are considered recent intrusions. Of the charred seeds (Table 2.5), 10.2% or 61.5 belonged to domesticated plants such as cereals, tree crops, vines, and other fruits. These were, in order of abundance, six-rowed barley (*Hordeum vulgare*), fig (*Ficus* sp.), unidentified grass family species (*Gramineae*), date (*Phoenix dactylifera*), bread wheat (*Triticum aestivum*), olive (*Olea europaea*), grape (*Vitis vinifera*), chick pea (*Cicer arietinum*), possible fig (cf. *Ficus* sp.), and unidentified wheat (*Triticum* sp.). Most of the domesticates were found in relatively few samples. The more frequent domesticates were barley, found in 12.5% of the samples, fig in 12.5%, unidentified grass family species in 7.5%, and date in 7.5%. Each of the remaining domesticates was found in only 2.5% of the samples (Table 2.5).

Over 30 types of wild plant seeds were identified (Table 2.6). The nine with percentages of

Table 2.6   Possible domesticated and wild plant uses at Humayma.

Common name	Scientific name	Description	Cultivated fields	Waysides, wasteland	Other locations	Use(s)
DOMESTICATES						
Six-rowed Barley	*Hordeum vulgare*	Annual grass	Yes	Yes		One of the most important grain crops
Bread Wheat	*Triticum aestivum*	Grass	Yes			Wheat normally used for making bread, etc.
Chick-pea	*Cicer arietinum*	Erect or sprawling annual herb	Yes	Yes		Seeds eaten, also made into flour, fodder
Date	*Phoenix dactylifera*	Perennial tree	Yes			Staple food and dessert
Olive	*Olea europaea*	Evergreen bush or tree	Yes	Yes	Hillsides in *garigue* or *maquis*	Fruit pickled, source of olive oil. Also used in decoration, fuel, craft, medicine and fodder
Fig	*Ficus* (*F. carica*)	Trees, shrubs and climbers	Yes			Edible fruit, also used for fodder, craft, medicine, food and poison
Grape	*Vitis vinifera*	Deciduous climber or trailer	Yes	Yes	In thickets and wooded ravines	Fruit eaten fresh or dried, seeds used to make oil, used in medicine, fodder, crafts and beverages
WILD PLANTS						
Oval-leaved Androsace	*Androsace maxima*	Herbaceous annual	Yes	Yes		
Common peganum	*Peganum harmala*	Herbaceous perennial		Yes	Roadsides	Often a relic of cultivation, used in medicine and as a condiment
Trigonel	*Trigonella* (*T. sprunerana, T. strangulata, T. spinosa, T. spiculata*)	Annual herb, rarely a perennial	Yes	Yes	Dry rocky hillsides, *garigue*	A fodder plant
Scorpion vetch	*Coronilla* (*C. securidaca, C. scorpioides*)	Annual or perennial herbs or shrubs	Yes	Yes		*C. scorpioides* purgative used for fodder

Table 2.6   Possible domesticated and wild plant uses at Humayma (cont.).

Common name	Scientific name	Description	Cultivated fields	Waysides, wasteland	Other locations	Use(s)
Mouse-eared chickweed	Cerastium (C. dubium, C. dichotomum C. brachypetalum, C. semidecandrum, C. illyricum, C. glomeratum)	Annual or perennial herbs or shrubs			Some are widely distributed; mountain slopes, river banks cultivated fields, damp ground	Consumed as a potherb
Sea blite	Suaeda (S. aegyptiaca)	Annual or perennial herbs or shrubs			Cosmopolitan, near salt marshes/lakes	Eaten cooked or raw
Milk-Vetch	Astragalus (A. asterias, A. hamosus, A. boeticus, A. lusitanicus, A. caprinus, A. echinus)	Annual, biennial and perennial herbs and subshrubs	Yes	Yes	Cosmopolitan	A. hamosus and A. boeticus used for food, A. hamosus also used medicinally
White broom	Retama raetam	shrub		Yes	Dominates large sand and gravelly areas	Medicinal, used as fuel
Fumitory	Fumaria (F. gaillardotii, F. judaica, F. macrocarpa, F. petteri, F. officinalis, F. densiflora, F. bracteosa)	Annual	Yes	Yes	Europe, Mediterranean and Western Asia	
Medick	Medicago scutellata	Annual	Yes	Yes	Mediterranea, Cultivated and fallow fields and waste ground	
Alkanna	Alkanna (A. tinctoria, A. galilaea, A. hirsutissima, A. strigosa)	Perennial herbs			Dry hillsides in garrigue, sandy and rocky places	A. tinctoria eaten as a vegetable dye derived from roots
Wild Watermelon	Citrullus colocynthis	Prostrate trailing perennial herb		Yes	Dry sandy and rocky places	Seeds are eaten, also used medicinally

Table 2.6   Possible domesticated and wild plant uses at Humayma (cont.).

Common name	Scientific name	Description	Cultivated fields	Waysides, wasteland	Other locations	Use(s)
Plantain	*Plantago* (*P. major, P. coronopus, P. lanceolata, P. lagopus, P. amplexicaulis, P. notata, P. ovata, P. loeflingii, P. cretica, P. bellardi, P. afra*)	Annual or perennial herbs or sometimes woody subshrubs	Yes	Yes	Rocky slopes	Food source; *P. cretica* and *P. afra* used medicinally
Goosefoot	*Chenopodium* (*C. botrys, C. foliosum, C. vulvaria, C. murale, C. opulifolium, C. album*)	Annual or rarely perennial herbs	Yes	Yes		Food source
Bedstraw	*Galium* (*G. canum, G. humifusum, G. setaceum, G. peplidifolium, G. aparine, G. pisiferum, G. tricornutum*)	Annual or perennial herbs or subshrubs	Yes	Yes	Rocky ground, crevices	*G. aparine* eaten and used medicinally
Pigweed	*Amaranthus* (*A. hybridus, A. retroflexus, A. albus, A. viridis, A. graezicans*)	Annual or rarely a perennial herb	Yes	Yes		Food source, *A. lividus & A. retroflexus* used medicinally
Poppy	*Papaver* (*P. rhoeas, P. minus, P. hybridum*)	Annual or perennial herbs	Yes	Yes		*P. rhoeas* used as spice, also used in craft, fodder and medicine
Rye grass	*Lolium* (*L. multiflorum, L. rigidum, L. perenne, L. loliaceum*)	Annual or perennial grasses	Yes	Yes		*L. rigidum* used for fodder
Bermuda grass	*Cynodon dactylon*	Perennial grass	Yes	Yes	Sandy areas	Cool drink is made from the root

more than 1% were white broom (*Retama raetam*), plantain (*Plantago* sp.), chickweed (*Cerastium* sp.) sea-blite (*Suaeda* sp.), common peganum (*Peganum harmala*), medick (*Medicago scutellata*), and unidentified members of the pink (*Caryophyllaceae*), legume (*Leguminosae*), and goosefoot (*Chenopodiaceae*) families. These wild seed types were more frequent in the samples (2.5 to 22.5%) than most of the domesticates.

The interpretation of past plant uses depends upon factors such as the conditions of preservation, the part of the plant used, and the methods of preparation. Some reconstructions of uses of the species identified at Humayma are summarised in Table 2.6. There is a good mix of grain foods, vegetables, herbs, and oil seeds.

The only way that plant remains can be preserved for any length of time in soils which are subject to alternating wet and dry cycles is through charring or mineralization. The probability of a plant food becoming charred is dictated by its structure and the way in which it is processed. Few plant foods are likely to become charred during preparation, other than cereal grains that are parched or roasted over a fire. With this qualification in mind it is possible to offer some insights into the ancient vegetation, agricultural economy, and uses of wild plants of the Hawara area, particularly during Byzantine times. Archaeological, geological, and botanical evidence all suggest that the local climate and vegetation of this arid area in Byzantine times was similar to that of today (see above). A number of the seed types from the site can be attributed to communities within deserts and grasslands, although many could also be found in disturbed ground.

Although the desert vegetation includes mostly annual plants, such as those belonging to the pink and legume families, it is characterised by several types of shrubs. In sandy areas, these would have included white broom, the seeds of which were numerous in the Humayma flotation samples and perhaps shrubby species of milk-vetch. Saline depressions would have supported salt-tolerant species of sea-blite. The Mesopotamian grassland steppe is represented among the seeds by grasses such as rye grass and Bermuda grass. This type of plant community would also have included annuals and scattered shrubs.

Many of the seed types belong to plants characteristic of disturbed ground, such as that found along roadsides and trails, fields and pastures, and areas within the settlement. Since ancient Humayma was located on a caravan route, and both travellers and the local pastoral inhabitants probably established temporary tent camps in the area, it is not surprising that many of the seed types belong to plants of disturbed ground. These plants include chickweed, plantain, common peganum, medick, trigonel, poppy, scorpion vetch, goosefoot, bedstraw, pigweed, and fumitory.

The domesticates found at Humayma include the traditional crops of cereals, legumes, olives, grapes, figs, and dates. These have been part of the Near Eastern crop complex since at least the Bronze Age (Hopkins 1997). It is not known whether all these crops were grown locally or imported, but Arabic sources mention a grove of 500 olive trees at the site around AD 700 (al-Dûrî and al-Mutallabi 1971: 107–8, 149, 154; al-Bakri 1945–51: 130; al-Balâdhurî 1978: iii, 75), and olive, fig, and apple trees have been cultivated with modest success by landowners at the site at least since Stein's visit in 1939. The wild watermelon seed found may have come from a plant that was cultivated locally.

The wild seeds found at Humayma may have come from several sources. They could originate from plants that grew in the settlement area itself, or they could have been brought to it along with fodder, fuel, or manure. The seeds of white broom, for example, could have been carried in on shrubs used as fuel, which was certainly an important application of local plants. The Romans even heated the hot bath with a local shrub (*Haloxylon articulatum*, also called *Hammada salicorica*, *Hammada scoparia*) still used by the Bedouin today to boil their tea water (Oleson 1990a: 305). Some of the wild plants undoubtedly were brought to the site intentionally by the early inhabitants for use as food or medicine or both (Table 2.6). Trigonel, coronilla, poppy, and lolium are today used for fodder. White broom, common peganum, milk-vetch, watermelon, plantain, bedstraw, pigweed, poppy, chickweed, medick, goosefoot, and coronilla are eaten or are useful in medicine.

Archaeological research in the region of Humayma has shown that over the long span of

Table 2.7   Humayma 1995. Number and percentage of all animal bones.

	No. of Buckets with Bones	No. of Pieces	% of Total	% of identified Species only
Archamedes	10	12	0.15	1.36
Bird	2	8	0.10	
Camel	5	5	0.06	0.57
Carnivore	3	4	0.05	
Cattle	4	4	0.05	0.45
Chicken	135	201	2.56	22.84
Clam	1	3	0.04	0.34
Clam/Oyster	6	12	0.15	1.36
Conch	1	1	0.01	
Deer	1	1	0.01	0.11
Dog	1	2	0.03	0.23
Egg Shell	2	34	0.43	
Equids	12	38	0.48	4.32
Fish	56	166	2.11	
Goat	33	36	0.46	4.09
Hare	1	1	0.01	0.11
Ostreidae	3	3	0.04	0.34
Ostrich Shell	6	10	0.13	1.14
Pig	80	175	2.23	19.89
Rodent	1	1	0.01	
Sea Urchin	1	3	0.04	0.34
Sheep	43	48	0.61	5.45
Sheep/Goat	195	269	3.43	30.57
Snail	13	39	0.50	
Trochus	13	17	0.22	1.93
Large Bird	1	1	0.01	
Large Mammal	75	267	3.40	
Medium Bird	62	90	1.15	
Medium Mammal	1188	5432	69.19	
Small Bird	6	6	0.08	
Small Mammal	47	84	1.07	
Small Rodent	5	26	0.33	
Undetermined Mammal	71	586	7.46	
Undetermined Bone	43	221	2.80	
Undetermined Marine Shell	17	45	0.57	
Total	2143	7851	99.97	
Total of Identified Species:	565	880	11.21 (of 7851)	

its existence the residents depended on a mixed regime of grain-growing and pastoralism, supplemented by trade and military activities. Analysis of the botanical remains indicates that the inhabitants made excellent use of local soil for growing domesticated grains and fruits, and that they harvested wild species as well. The main crops grown in the fields around the town were barley, wheat, and chick-peas, possibly supplemented by figs, dates, and grapes. We cannot yet tell, however, if the seeds of the last three domesticates were produced locally or imported. In the samples, barley, fig, and date predominate. In antiquity as today, there was probably significant production of wheat and barley in the fields around Humayma. During the winter, while the grain crops were growing, the livestock would be grazed in the rocky highlands surrounding the Humayma basin, where the rains had refreshed the landscape. During the summer, after the grain had been harvested, the flocks would be grazed on any stubble left in the fields, or fed on the whole uprooted grasses left after threshing. Both procedures are followed today (Lancaster and Lancaster 1999: 180–214). It is clear from analysis of flotation samples from the habitation area that there was also great reliance on wild species used for food, medicine, and fodder.

2.A.6. Analysis of Excavated Faunal Remains (1989-1995) (Based on a report by M. Finnegan)

The landscape around ancient Humayma was heavily used for grazing as well as for drought farming. Analysis of the bones found in the 1989, 1991–93, and 1995 seasons shows, as might be expected, that sheep and goat predominate among the remains of domesticated mammals, along with camel, equid, pig, cow, and dog. Chicken, dove, and raven are found, along with numerous ostrich eggs. Wild mammals include gazelle, mountain lion, hare, rodents (probably gerbils and jerboas), and possibly boar. It was interesting to discover that large quantities of fish were imported: mullet and sea bream from the Red Sea and Nile perch, probably from lagoons in the Aqaba area. Fresh oysters and conch in the shell were imported from Aqaba as well. The results presented here are still tentative, particularly with regard to changes in

use of animals over time, since the chronological information needs to be refined. The tables do not go beyond genus identification for many of the categories, and the fish species remain unidentified. The statistics below are based for the most part on material recovered in the 1995 season, summarised in Table 2.7, but with reference to a small amount of data from the 1987–1991 seasons (Tables 2.8–9). As with the plant remains, these data are presented here to provide an indication of the resources of the region. Analysis of all faunal material recovered since 1987 will appear in a homogeneous report in Volume 2.

Excavation of five areas at Humayma in 1995 yielded 7851 animal bones and bone fragments. The bones were dry brushed, washed when necessary, and separated into generalised categories such as large, medium, or small mammals, fish, birds, etc. Bones possessing diagnostic morphologic features were further identified, when possible, to family, genus, and species.[3] All bones were examined for butcher marks, spalls, rodent or carnivore gnawing, and evidence of burning. Worked bone or bone tools, separated from the assemblage, were washed, repaired, and registered.

Predominantly, the recovered bone was in a good to excellent state of preservation, but due to breakage and fragmentation, it was often in a poor condition with respect to identification. Of the recovered bones, 2.8% were so badly broken that they could not be classified, and are listed as undetermined bone (Table 2.7). Bones of a certain size and thickness, but lacking specific morphologic features, could only be classified in general categories: large, medium, and small mammals (these categories were responsible for 73.66% of all recovered bone). Bones belonging to the large mammal category (3.4% of the total assemblage) probably represent the cow (*Bos*) and the horse or donkey (*Equus*). Bones belonging to the medium mammal category (69.19% of the total assemblage) undoubtedly represent non-diagnostic fragments of sheep (*Ovis*) and goats (*Capra*), although the bones of wild ungulates may be represented as well. Bones within the non-diagnostic small mammal category (1.07% of the total assemblage) belong to rabbits, cats, and the smaller rodents. These percentages are in line with the identified mammal

Table 2.8   Humayma 1987–91, Number and percentage of all animal bones.

	1987–89	% of Total	1991	% of Total	1987–91	% of Total
Camel	1	0.54	6	0.22	7	0.24
Cattle	11	5.91	31	1.12	42	1.42
Chicken	13	6.99	97	3.45	110	3.71
Dog	4	2.15	1	0.04	5	0.17
Dove	2	1.08	—		2	0.07
Equid	2	1.08	52	1.87	54	1.82
Fish	25	13.44	848	30.51	873	29.44
Fox	—		1	0.04	1	0.03
Gazelle	—		5	0.18	5	0.17
Goat	6	3.22	57	2.05	63	2.12
Hare	—		2	0.07	2	0.07
Large Mammal	—		17	0.61	17	0.57
Marine Shell	—		220	7.92	220	7.42
Medium Mammal	—		19	0.68	19	0.64
Ostrich (egg)	1	0.54	397	14.28	398	13.42
Pig	13	6.99	4	0.14	17	0.57
Raven	2	1.08	—		2	0.07
Rodent	—		42	151	42	1.42
Sheep	5	2.69	13	0.47	18	0.61
Sheep/Goat	101	54.30	762	27.42	863	29.11
Small Egg Shell	—		56	2.02	56	1.89
Small Mammal	—		41	1.48	41	1.38
Small Ruminant	—		108	3.89	108	3.64
Total	186		2779		2965	
Unidentified	169	47.88 (of 355)	8652	75.69 (of 11431)	8821	74.84 (of 11786)

categories, where domesticated sheep and goats form the largest percentage of identified remains (30.57%), followed by domestic chicken (*Gallus*; 22.84%) and domestic pig (*Sus*; 19.89%). These trends correspond well with the initial, rough analysis data recovered from the 1992 and 1993 field seasons at Humayma. The corresponding statistics for 1987-1991 are somewhat different (Tables 2.7-8): ovicaprids 35.05% of the identified species, bird (probably mostly domestic chicken) 4.47%, and domestic pig only 0.69% (see below).

Many of the diagnostic sheep/goat, pig, and cattle bones from the 1993–1995 seasons showed evidence of spalls, or green bone fractures. These fracture types generally occur during the butchering process of the animal, when heavy blows are delivered against the shafts of long bones of the axial skeleton with a sharp tool not unlike a cleaver. The majority of sheep/goat, pig, and cattle bone fragments and spalls recovered from the site were autopodia, metapodials, phalanges, and hoof cores — bones associated with the lower, non-

Table 2.9   Humayma 1987–91. Number and percentage of all identified species from bones.

	1987–89	% of ID	1991	% of ID	1987–91	% of ID
Camel	1	0.54	6	0.26	7	0.28
Cattle	11	5.91	31	1.36	42	1.71
Chicken	13	6.99	97	4.26	110	4.47
Dog	4	2.15	1	0.04	5	0.20
Dove	2	1.08	—		2	0.08
Equid	2	1.08	52	2.28	54	2.19
Fish	25	13.44	848	37.26	873	35.46
Fox	—		1	0.04	1	0.04
Gazelle	—		5	0.22	5	0.20
Goat	6	3.22	57	2.50	63	2.56
Hare	—		2	0.08	2	0.08
Ostrich (egg)	1	0.54	397	17.44	398	16.17
Pig	13	6.99	4	0.18	17	0.69
Raven	2	1.08	—		2	0.08
Sheep	5	2.69	13	0.57	18	0.73
Sheep/Goat	101	54.30	762	33.48	863	35.05
Total	186		2276		2462	

meat-bearing portions of the legs. Very likely, one of the first steps in the process of butchering sheep and goats, pigs and cattle involved removing the lower legs in the region of the articulation between radius and tibia and their associated autopodia. These disarticulated leg bones were undoubtedly discarded as the meat bearing portions of the carcass were further processed.

In the 1995 collection, identified sheep outnumber identified goat by a slight but significant margin: 5.45% to 4.09% (13.6% and 10.2% of the sheep, goat, and ovicaprids taken together), a ratio that can be seen at some earlier sites in Jordan (Bab edh-Dhra, Finnegan 1978; Tell Nimrin, Finnegan, unpublished reports to directors). The slightly larger proportion of sheep over the hardier goats might be taken to suggest that a more lush grazing environment was available for these animals at Humayma during antiquity than today. It should be noted, however, that the preliminary statistics from the earlier seasons give a very different result (Table 2.9), the goats constituting 2.56% of all identified

species, and sheep only 0.73% (6.67% and 1.9% of the sheep, goat, and ovicaprids taken together). Discrepancies such as this can be the accidental result of the sampling or analysis, or may indicate chronological differences in herding practices, or even reflect the location of butchering areas.

The 1995 excavations indicate that the chicken (*Gallus gallus*; 22.84%) also formed an important part of the diet at Hawara (Table 2.7), particularly as compared with earlier sites in Jordan. Chicken accounts for more of the faunal remains than do pig (19.89%) and either sheep or goats singularly (but not combined) and must be counted as part of the population's meat preference along with sheep, goats, pigs, and cattle. The domesticated horse and donkey, beasts of burden and at the same time a secondary meat source, were recovered in moderate numbers (4.32% combined) during the 1995 field season. Fish bones represented 2.11% of the overall faunal inventory in 1995 (Table 2.7), and 30.46% in the earlier seasons (Table 2.8), with representation of the families *Mugilidae* (mullet), *Scaridae* (parrot fish), *Sparidae* (sea bream), *Mochokidae* (perch), and possibly *Cyprinidae* (carp) and *Bagridae* (armoured catfish). Given that they had to be imported fresh from Aqaba, marine shells represent a very impressive 6.93% of the 1995 faunal remains and 7.92% of the 1991 sample, including the families *Trochidae* (topshells), *Strombidae* (conch), *Ostreidae* (oysters), and *Tridacnidae* (clams).

Remains of pig were found in 1995 in a greater proportion (19.89%) than at a number of other Jordanian sites, suggesting that it had a prominent place in the diet alongside chicken, sheep, and goat. Pigs constitute only 0.50% of the sample in the 1991 and earlier excavations, and their increase in the 1995 material is connected with the Roman fort, where excavation began only in 1993. Spatial and chronological analysis of the material is not yet complete, nor were measurements taken to determine if the pigs associated with Humayma were wild or domesticated (cf. Flannery 1982). Pigs recovered from the Middle Bronze Age levels of nearby Jericho, because of small size and immaturity, have been called domesticated when compared to the bones of the hunted wild pigs excavated from earlier Pre-Pottery Neolithic levels of the same site (Clutton-Brock 1971). Nevertheless, it is possible that some of the fragments of pig recovered from Humayma may belong to the wild boar, which would have been an easily accessible, although formidable, quarry for the hunters of Humayma.

Overall, the 1995 faunal data are in general agreement with the faunal data from the earlier field seasons, indicating that throughout the period of occupation sheep and goat were favoured in the diet of the inhabitants of ancient Humayma, while cattle were raised in smaller numbers for their milk, meat, and skin. Cattle yield approximately six times as much edible meat as sheep or goats, making them a close second for meat production. While the inhabitants of Hawara overwhelmingly followed a subsistence pattern based on animal husbandry and agriculture, they occasionally varied their diets by means of the chase — hunting the wild hare (*Lepus*) and deer (*Cervus*) (one each), and probably the boar. Deer, represented by one bone fragment in the 1995 assemblage, prefer more forested conditions than seem to have been

current in southern Jordan in the Holocene. The smaller gazelle (*Gazella* sp.) appears in the 1987–91 material (0.20%). Although it was not identified in 1995, some of the medium mammal bones may represent this animal. Inhabiting drier climates than the red deer, the gazelle would have browsed in dry grass steppe and desert region near Humayma and could have been captured by nets or snares (Cansdale 1970; Lancaster and Lancaster 1999: 168–69). Ostriches may have been captured for their meat, but so far only fragments of egg shells have been recovered. The rodents identified in the faunal remains of every season might derive in part from burrowing by these animals into cultural deposits laid down long before. Some, however, may represent individuals caught for consumption; even today the local Bedouin catch and cook the jerboa that populate the site. The single fox (*Vulpes* sp.) that appeared in the 1991 sample and the four unidentified carnivore bones (probably lynx or mountain lion) in the 1995 sample probably represent predators whose corpses were brought back to the site for recovery of their pelts.

Entry of the material excavated since 1995 into a unified database with phasing dates will make it possible to determine trends in the use of various wild and domesticated species at Humayma over time. In any case, it is likely that — except for pigs — the domestic animals and birds were raised for more than just their meat. Equids and dogs, of course, served other purposes too. Mature animals could produce a wide variety of valuable secondary products: from sheep/goat, wool, hair and milk; from cattle, milk and work potential (e.g. pulling a plough); from camels, milk, hair, and work potential (transport); from chickens, eggs.

In conclusion, it is likely that a mixed animal farming policy was employed, involving the use of both primary and secondary products, with no single product of paramount importance. The meat demand was met almost exclusively by domestic animals, and sheep/goat in particular. It is likely that some feral species that still live in the vicinity, such as chukar partridge and quail, were hunted in antiquity as they are today (Heinzel et al. 1979: 102–3; Lancaster and Lancaster 1999: 167), but their remains simply have not yet been recovered or recognised. The dove (probably rock or stock dove)

is one species which may have either been
hunted or a domesticate. Our understanding
of the use of wild and domesticated animals in
ancient Humayma will be elucidated further
by analysis of the rest of the bone collection.

2.A.7. Summary: The Resources of Ancient Humayma

Despite the very arid environment, the ancient settlement at Humayma flourished for
800 years, probably relying more on local
resources than on the profits of trade and
passing caravans. The loessial soil in the
plains is sandy and light, but suitable for grain
production (figs. 2.11, 3.39). The precipitation,
although meagre in absolute terms, could be
concentrated by directing the run-off from
the surrounding sandstone hills into fields, or
by storing it in cisterns and reservoirs. Many
wild species of plants were available for food,
medicine, fodder, and fuel, and a significant
stock of wild species of mammals, birds, and
reptiles was subject to exploitation. The environment was also capable of supporting a variety of domesticated animals, and herds could
easily be moved around the open landscape
in search of fodder, exploiting the seasonal
opportunities offered by this ecotone. Ancient
Humayma straddled local and long-distance trade
routes, but the only imported food for which there
is significant evidence is seafood — a discretion-
ary item of diet impossible to produce locally. A
modest number of wine amphoras, particularly
the third- to fourth-century Aegean Class 47 type
(Peacock and Williams 1986: 193–95), have been
found in the Roman fort. Wine must have been a
luxury, although a small amount may have been
produced at a wine press near Hawara (see Chapter
3, Structure no. 51). The landscape provided several
types of stone suitable for construction, limestone
for producing lime, and inexhaustible quantities of
sand suitable for micro-aggregate in mortar and
plaster. The only necessity imported to the site
in bulk was pottery, particularly from Petra and
Aila, perhaps because of the absence of extensive
local deposits of clay and the scarcity of fuel. Fuel
must always have been in short supply, but the

FIG. 2.11   *Wheat growing at Humayma in 1987.*

local grasses and shrubs, along with dung from
donkeys and camels, were certainly sufficient for
the domestic needs of a sparse population.

It would be difficult to estimate the carrying
capacity of the Humayma catchment in antiquity
on the basis of the geomorphology, pedology, climate, and native flora and fauna alone, since too
many variables are involved. It is possible, however,
to calculate the minimum daily need for water on
the part of humans and domestic animals. These
statistics, combined with an analysis of the capacity
and design of the water supply system of ancient
Humayma, allow a rough estimate of the maximum
population of humans and domestic animals the
region could support (see Chapter 7.E.3; cf. Oleson
1997: 176–77): 448 persons, 300 camels or donkeys,
and 3008 ovicaprids. The resulting population
density of 1.91 inhabitants per sq km is lower than
the 3.0 inhabitants per sq km recorded for the

whole Wadi Rumman region in 1975 (National Water Master Plan, sub-region is ED11), but this is understandable given improved medical care in the modern Hisma and the availability of imported goods and services. The figure is within reason for a well-organised culture intensively exploiting the local landscape. It should be noted that the Romans managed somehow to sustain at Hawara a garrison possibly as large as 500 individuals along with some cavalry mounts, perhaps doubling the regional population at a single moment. Clearly the inhabitants of ancient Humayma cannot have been living a constrained, marginal existence.

2.B. THE HISTORY AND MONUMENTS OF ANCIENT HUMAYMA

2.B.1. *Foundation, Name, and Pre-Islamic Literary Sources*

The Upper Palaeolithic and Epi-Palaeolithic inhabitants of the Humayma region are relevant to the historical period only because of the light their occupation deposits throw on the available natural resources (see above). The only evidence for occupation of the Humayma area in the pre-Nabataean historical period consists of the badly damaged remains of two structures associated with Iron-Age, possibly Edomite, pottery (K. ʿAmr, oral communication, June 1993), 2.5 km northwest of the later settlement centre (UTM 36R 0724788, 3316694; 1003 m asl). The southern structure (ca. 20 m square), built of roughly trimmed blocks and rubble and situated on a low rise, was almost totally destroyed by a bulldozer in 2000. The northern structure, separated from the first by a gully, now consists of a line of rubble wall (L ca. 8 m). These structures enjoy a good view of the surrounding area, but the position does not seem to have any particular strategic value. Ceramics indicate that the structures were reoccupied in the Nabataean period (J. Cook, unpublished report, July 2000). It is likely that this previously unpublished structure should be associated with Edomite occupation along the edge of the plateau above the al-Shara escarpment (Hart 1986a). The long, puzzling gap between seventh-century-BC Edomite and first-century-BC Nabataean architectural expression,

may be explained by the Edomite people's return to nomadism (Hart 1986a: 57; cf. Bienkowski 2001: 348–49).

The Nabataean settlement centre was founded sometime in the first century BC by either King Aretas III or Aretas IV, at a previously unoccupied site. Although Graf (1992a: 69) mentions the presence of "late Hellenistic" sherds at Humayma, no ceramics or coins earlier than the first century BC have been recovered in the 11 seasons of excavation since 1991. Nomadic groups undoubtedly passed across the site in the centuries prior to the impulse towards sedentarization in the first century BC, but in the absence of a flowing spring, pre-agricultural Holocene communities would have found little of interest there. In any case, the pre-ceramic phase of Nabataean culture (prior to ca. 150 BC; Schmid in Stucky et al. 1996: 164; Schmidt 2001a; 2001b: 368–71) could have left few datable traces in the archaeological record. The old King's Highway (Numbers 20:17, 21:22) should have passed across or close to the site, since its reincarnation as the Via Nova Traiana passed through it (Graf 1993b: 157–59, 165–66; 1995: 256–57; Bienkowski 2001: 348; Freeman 2001: 433; Young 2001: 97–99).

A foundation story is provided in the first book of Uranius' *Arabica,* preserved in Stephanus Byzantinus, *Ethnika,* s.v. Αὔαθα and Αὔαρα (Jacoby 1958: 340 no. 1). Little is known about Uranius or why he chose to be a "Josephus" for the peoples of Arabia, but close analysis of probable fragments of his work suggests a real familiarity with the region (Bowersock 1997a; 2003: 25; cf. West 1974). He lived sometime in Late Antiquity, perhaps as late as the sixth century, and — for all it is worth — Stephanus Byzantinus (s.v. Χαράκμωβα) describes him as "reliable": ἀχιόπιστος δὲ ἀνὴρ περὶ τὰ τουαῦτα· σπουδὴν γὰρ ἔθετο ἱστορῆσαι ἀκριβῶς τὰ τῆς Ἀραβίας ("A reliable authority concerning such matters, for he took pains to give an accurate account of the matters pertaining to Arabia.").

Book 1 of Uranius' *Arabica* gave an account of all Arabia, Books 2–4 described Transjordan, Southern Arabia, and the Negev, and Book 5 presented a history of Arabia (West 1974; Bowersock 1988; some possible biographical snippets are presented in Jacoby 1958: 339–40). Presumably, at least one of his sources provided the foundation story of Hawara, both to justify the location and name of the settlement, and to record the involvement of Aretas III or IV in its foundation: Αὔαθα καὶ Αὔαρα· οὐδετέρως· συνοικία Ἀράβων, ὡς Οὐράνιος ἐν Ἀραβικῶν πρώτῃ· οἱ οἰκήτορες Αὐαθηνοί καὶ Αὐαρηνοί ("Auatha or Auara [grammatical gender: neuter]; settlement of the Arabs, according to Uranius in the first book of his *Arabica*. The inhabitants are *Auathenoi* or *Auarenoi*."). Billerbeck (2006) presents the first phrase as Αὔαθα ὡς Αὔαρα, but the meaning is the same.

> Αὔαρα· πολίς Ἀραβίας, ἀπὸ χρησμοῦ δοθεῖσα Ὀβόδᾳ κληθεῖσα ὑπὸ τοῦ υἱοῦ αὐτοῦ Ἀρέτα. ἐξώρμησε γὰρ Ἀρέτας εἰς ἀναζήτησιν τοῦ χρησμοῦ· ὁ δὲ χρησμός ἦν αὔαρα τόπον ζητεῖν, ὅ ἐστι κατὰ Ἄραβας καὶ Σύρους λευκήν· καὶ φθάσαντι τῷ Ἀρέτᾳ καὶ λοχῶντι, ἐφάνη φάσμα αὐτῷ λευκοείμων ἀνήρ ἐπὶ λευκῆς δρομάδος προϊών· ἀφανισθέντος δὲ τοῦ φάσματος σκόπελος ἀνεφάνη αὐτόματος κατὰ γῆς ἐρριζωμένος, κἀκεῖ ἔκτισε πόλιν. τὸ ἐθνικὸν Αὐαρηνός.

Auara: town in Arabia, named by Aretas from an oracular response given to his father Obodas. Aretas set out in search of the oracle's meaning, for the oracle said "to seek out a place *auara*" — which in the Arabian and Syrian languages means "white." And as he lay in wait, a vision appeared to him of a man clothed in white garments riding along on a white dromedary. But when the apparition vanished, a mountain peak appeared, quite natural and rooted in the earth; and there he founded the town. The term for an inhabitant is "Auarenos."

This account of the foundation, if correct, indicates that the original Nabataean name must have been *HWR*. The vocalisation, however, remains uncertain: possibilities include Hawar, Hawara (Graf 1992a: 73; cf. Hackl et al. 2003: 281–82, 596), and Hawra (Zayadine 1994: 38; K. 'Amr, oral communication, 17 October 2006). Based on the vocalisation and accent in the Latin version Hauarra (see below), I chose to vocalise *HWR* as Hawara in

this study, but this solution is by no means certain. The alternate Greek spelling Αὔαθα does not fit the rest of the tradition for the ancient names of Humayma, and it probably is the result of scribal error prior to Stephanus Byzantinus' compilation in the early sixth century. The variant "Hauanae" in the *Notitia Dignitatum* (*Or.* XXXIV.25) is probably the result of a similar error. Musil (1926: 59, n. 20) unaccountably transforms the mountain peak into "a portion of a tree trunk rooted in a certain place." Perhaps he read στέλεχος instead of σκόπελος, or ἐρριζωμένος ("rooted") distracted him. Daniel (2001: 334) translates σκόπελος as "tower," which theoretically is possible but less likely than "mountain peak," given the blank pre-Nabataean archaeological record at Hawara and the striking landscape. Stephanus Byzantinus (p. 237.22) identifies the al-Shara escarpment with this same term: Δουσάρη· σκόπελος καὶ κορυφή ὑψηλοτάτη Ἀραβίας. εἴρεται δὲ ἀπὸ τοῦ Δουσάρου. Although Brünnow and Domaszewski (1904–9: 1, p. 189) identify this mountain with "der heilige Berg" of Petra itself, the whole mountain chain or the high peaks just north of Hawara are just as likely.

The phrase καὶ φθάσαντι τῷ Ἀρέτᾳ καὶ λοχῶντι (translated here "as he lay in wait") is awkward, and Müller suspected it was corrupt (see Jacoby 1958: 340, *apparatus criticus*). Although Bowersock (1997a) has cast doubt on Jacoby's edition of the fragments, his overall assessment of the accuracy of the acceptable fragments is very positive. One characteristic of the historian that can be inferred from the fragments and serves as a test of their authenticity "is a philological precision in explaining the Semitic meaning of words transliterated into Greek" (Bowersock 1997a: 181). The punning story of the foundation of Hawara clearly falls into this category. If taken at face value, this passage raises a number of questions: the identity of the founder Aretas, the date of the event, the relevance of the term "white," the location of the prophetic shrine that issued the oracle, and the identification of this Αὔαρα/Auara with the site of Humayma.

Although the Nabataean king list is not certain until Obodas III (30–9 BC), most recent reconstructions indicate that the reigns of both Aretas III (85–62/61 or 60/59 BC) and Aretas IV (9/8 BC–AD 39/40) followed those of kings named Obodas

(Obodas I, 96–85 BC, and Obodas III) (Fiema and Jones 1990). Aretas IV, however, was not in fact the son of Obodas III (Josephus, *Ant* 16.9.4; Starkey 1965: 907–9, 913–14; Wenning 1993: 34), so if we interpret strictly the terms "son" and "father" used in the passage from Uranius, Aretas III should be the founder of Humayma. Recently, there has been a proposal to move the reign of Rabbel I from the mid-second century down to 85/84 BC, placing him between Obodas I and Aretas III (Wenning 1993: 30–31; Schmid in Frösén and Fiema 2002: 254). But since the reconstructed reign is only one year, this interpolation does not invalidate the dynastic link between Obodas I and Aretas III. Furthermore, Wenning assumes that Rabbel I and Aretas III were brothers, both sons of Obodas I.

A scattering of fine-ware ceramics dating to the mid-first century BC has been found at the site, along with one worn coin of Aretas III (cat. no. 1998.0484.01), but no sealed deposits that date as early as Aretas III have yet been identified. The coin was found in a surface layer, and it may easily have remained in use long after Aretas' reign. Recent excavations at Petra, however, make it clear that the context of intentional sedentarization and Hellenization of Nabataean culture fits in well with the early first century BC. According to Schmid (2001a–b; cf. Parr 1978; Young 2001: 100–12), the Nabataean kings in this period fostered sedentariza-tion, Hellenization, and an enhanced monarchy in order to stay competitive in long-distance trade, to fill the power gap left by the Seleucids, and to com-pete with the Ptolemies. Aretas III's royal epithet was "Philhellene," emphasising his connections with the Hellenistic world. Although initiatives towards sedentarization, trade, and state-building also fit the reign of Aretas IV (cf. Bowersock 1983: 60–65; 1984: 134), it seems unlikely that Obodas I or Aretas III would have overlooked this promising site in the heart of the Hisma at a time when Petra was being transformed by settlement and construction, and trade was becoming increasingly important. The Romans immediately appreciated the importance of the site in 106 AD, just as the Abbasids did in the late seventh century (Oleson 2001a; 2007a–b). Perhaps a small settlement founded by Aretas III was expanded by Aretas IV and supplied with the aqueduct and public reservoirs. The story as re-counted by Uranius fails to make clear whether the founder was still a prince at the time he followed up on the oracle given to his father, or already king. If the former, the foundation could have taken place any time between 96 and 85 BC or 30 and 9/8 BC.

As noted above, the punning value of the Nabataean name — *HWR*/Hawara, related to the root *hwr*, as with *hawar*, "white," or *hawwara*, "to whiten" (Graf 1992a: 73; cf. Hackl et al. 2003: 281–82, 596) — may have had something to do with the ridges of white Disi sandstone that are such a prom-inent part of the landscape. Although Uranius did not specify that the σκόπελος was white, the man and camel that led him there were both white, and the connection may have been felt to be implicit. A recent Bedouin name for the sandstone area north of Humayma is *Baida*, or "white" (Musil 1926: 59, n. 20). By the time the Abbasid family purchased the site, it had come to be called Humayma, which also means "white" in Arabic (*HMM*; Hackl et al. 2003: 282). The mountains of red Umm 'Ishrin sandstone that tower over Humayma and serve as a landmark across much of the Hisma may seem to the approaching visitor a more appropriate can-didate for the crag (fig. 2.4), but from the site itself, the view over the fields to the east terminates in the white Disi sandstone ridges and the domes of Jebel al-Jill, which resemble the hump of a white camel. In some of the papyri from the Cave of the Letters at Nahal Hever, the Hebrew term *ha-efer ha-lavan* ("white field") is applied to one type of agricultural field (Section 8.A.3, below; Yadin et al. 2002: 45, 50, 144) — possibly signifying crop land as opposed to orchards or vegetable plots. The term may even signify "rain-fed field," which would be very applicable to Humayma. Reeves (2009) sug-gests the related theory that "white" refers to the white blossoms produced by many of the plants documented at the site through botanical remains. Perhaps Aretas arrived after the winter rains and found the site blooming and therefore promising from the point of view of water supply. Al-Theeb (2002: 300) connects *HWR* with the Arabic word *al-hawar*, "young camel," which fits the story but misses the pun.

Benzinger (1898) suggested that Uranius' Hawara ("nicht identifiziert") was the Red Sea port of Λευκὲ Κώμη "White Village," and he was followed by Müller (1901: 997). Although it is now clear that the two sites were not the same (Kirwan 1984; Casson 1989: 61–63; Eadie 1989), Zayadine has proposed (1994) that there was in fact an intentional echo in the later foundation, in that Hawara was a desert "port" in an ocean of sand, much like Palmyra (Teixidor 1984). Derivation of the name from the Arabian *hawr* — depression, opening, canal, little stream (Hackl et al. 2003: 282, 596) — is linguistically less likely and does not fit in with either the foundation story or the later nomenclature.

The story is a typical foundation tale, involving a king, an oracle, a successful vision quest, and a topographical landmark. Although the camel Aretas saw was being ridden, it is part of a long Mediterranean and Semitic tradition of an animal serving as a divine medium to lead settlers to the site of a sanctuary or city (Frazer 1913: vol. 5, 241; Hajjar 1990: 2301–2; Dirven 1999: 84). Neither the reason Obodas sought divine advice nor the location of the shrine that provided it are specified. We have little specific information about Nabataean religion, and a recent survey makes no mention of oracular shrines (Healy 2001). The story implies that the oracular response was given in Aramaic and that the context of the quest was to be the Hisma, so an oracle within Arabia Petraea is likely — possibly at Petra, Wadi Ramm, or Hegra (Healy 2001 39–50, 53–59). The important shrine at Khirbet et-Tannur is also a possibility (Healy 2001: 59–62; McKenzie et al. 2002: 451–52). The story may also simply hark back to the traditional and archaeologically unattested use of the site by early Nabataean nomadic herders as a seasonal campsite or regional gathering point. In any case, there is no particular reason to reject the story as a fabrication by Uranius, since it fits the archaeological data, the later pun on "white" in the Arabic name Humayma, and does not carry any obvious programmatic overtones.

Subsequent references in inscriptions and pre-Islamic historical sources are much less discursive than the passage in Uranius. The only Nabataean inscription so far known at the site that possibly mentions Hawara is a graffito on a rock face adjacent to the betyl niche and Cistern no. 48, at the north foot of Jebel Qalkha (Graf 1992a; Healey

2001: 91): *slm br-tlm ʿbd ʾl-hwr*, "Peace, BR-TLM, servant of ʾAL-HWR." The inscription can be interpreted as "Peace, (personal name), servant (of the god) of Hawara." The god may have been Dushara. Hackl et al. (2003: 281) translate the inscription as "Friede! Der Sohn des Talm*, er hat gemacht die Zuleitungsrinne (?)." The conjecture "feeder-channel" is based on derivation from the Arabic *hawr* rather than the Aramaic *hwr*. At Petra, a stone-cutter's or engineer's inscription on the aqueduct channel cut across the theatre may commemorate Hawara or a personal name derived from the settlement: *dkyr hwrw*, "*hwrw* was remembered" (Knauf 1997). A "*tny*' son of *hwrw*" is mentioned in a Nabataean inscription near Medaʾin Salih (al-Theeb 2002: 299–301). A rock graffito by HWR was found in Wadi Judaiyid, just east of the Hawara catchment (King 1988: 314), and Corbett has found 17 Thamudic graffiti in the Wadi Hafir, a little farther east, that contain the theophoric *abd hwr*, "Servant of *hwr*" (personal communication, 20 November 2009; see Corbett 2009). These two last inscriptions may have some link to cult centres at Hawara. Wenning (1987: 81) interprets an inscription found at Khirbet et-Tannur as a possible mention of Hawara or a personal name derived from the place: "(The stele) which Qosmalik made for Qos, the god of Hurawa (hwrw')." Healey (2001: 61) interprets the inscription to allude to a place "Hurawa", perhaps Tannur itself. Villneuve (oral communication, December 2009) proposes that the stele was left by a visitor from Hawara.

Ptolemy mentions Auara/Hawara, but merely as one item in a list of 29 cities and towns in Arabia Petraea (*Geographia* 5.16.4): Αὐάρα, with the coordinates 66° 10', 29° 40' (ξϛ' ϛ', κθ' γο"). The list of towns finds echoes in the documents cited below: Πέτρα, Χαράκμωβα, Αὐάρα, Ζαναάθα, Ἄδρου, Ζοάρα, Θοάνα, Νέκλα, Κληθαρρώ, Μόκα. There is some confusion in modern publications about the accentuation of the Greek name for Hawara. In his edition of Ptolemy, Müller (1901: 996–97) places the accent on the penult, Αὐάρα, rejecting the reading of Αὔαρα in codices LMOP. He concludes that the city Αὔαρα praised by Stephanus Byzantinus is a different town, Leuke Kome, but correctly identifies Αὐάρα as the Hauarra of the

Peutinger Table. In his edition of Ptolemy, however, Nobbe (1913: 69) places the accent on the antepenult: Αὔαρα. Brünnow and Domaszewski (1904–9: 3, pp. 250, 262) place the accent on the penult when citing Ptolemy, but when citing Stephanus Byzantinus they fastidiously place it on the antepenult. Benzinger (1898) uses the latter accentuation. The confusion probably arose in Late Antiquity. The position of the accent on the antepenult is implied by the Latin rendition Hauarra ("Hauárra"), which most likely reflects the pronunciation of the original Nabataean name more accurately than Αὔαρα. The modern Arabic accentuation of Hawara is the same. The "u" in Hauarra most likely is a Latin consonantal "u," appearing between two vowels and pronounced quickly as English "w" together with the following vowel (Allen and Greenough 1931: 3; Allen: 1978: 40–42). Musil (1926: 59 n. 20) states that the local ʿAlâwîn used the name "Hawwâra" interchangeably with "al-Homejma" during his visit.

In fact, there seems no reason why the original Greek vocalisation should not have been Αὐάρα, with an initial rough breathing and the accent on the antepenult. This yields the vocalised form "Hawára," which — like the Latin "Hauárra" — sounds like what we presume to be the original Nabataean name.

An altar set up in a shrine in the military *vicus* at Humayma sometime in the first half of the third century provides an abbreviated form of the Latin name: *Hav(arrae),* "at Hauarra" (Oleson, Reeves, Fisher 2002: insc. no. 4). The inscription records a dedication to Jupiter Ammon by a vexillation of the Legio III Cyrenaica on behalf of two emperors. The Latin name also appears in the *Notitia Dignitatum,* under the jurisdiction of the *Dux Palestinae (Or.* xxxiv.25), probably representing the army organisation of the late fourth century: "Equites sagittarii indigenae, Hauanae" ("mounted

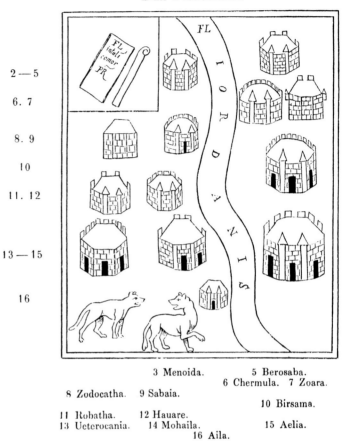

XXXIV.
Dux Palaestinae.

2 — 5
6. 7
8. 9
10
11. 12
13 — 15
16

	3 Menoida.	5 Berosaba.
		6 Chermula. 7 Zoara.
8 Zodocatha.	9 Sabaia.	
		10 Birsama.
11 Robatha.	12 Hauare.	
13 Ueterocania.	14 Mohaila.	15 Aelia.
	16 Aila.	

FIG. 2.12 *Manuscript illustration of "Hauare" and other regional sites,* Notitia Dignitatum, Or. 34.25, *as redrawn by Böcking (Seeck 1876: 72).*

native archers, at Hauarra"). The manuscript tradition has corrupted the name Hauarra, but a generic illustration of the town as a small hexagonal fort is labelled more accurately as "Hauare" (see Seeck 1876: 72; here, fig. 2.12).

24. Equites promoti indigenae, Zodocathae.

25. Equites sagittarii indigenae, Hauanae.

26. Equites sagittarii indigenae, Zoarae.

The context of Hauarra in this citation and in Ptolemy's town list provides support for an understanding of the Peutinger Table, a twelfth-century copy of a fourth-century version of a world map dating to the second century or earlier. There was

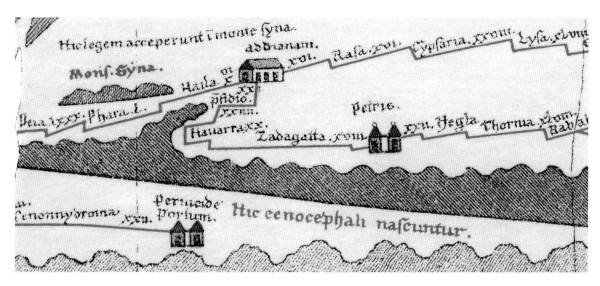

FIG. 2.13 *Southern Jordan and nearby regions on the Peutinger Table (after K. Miller 1887–88). "Hauarra" at centre.*

extensive debate in the first half of the twentieth century concerning the identification of settlements on the map with archaeological sites in Southern Jordan, but the matter is now settled (Bowersock 1983: 172–74; Graf 1995: 244). Two roads are shown leaving "Haila" (Aila/Aqaba) for the north, one up the Wadi ʿArabah, the other up the Wadi Yutum (fig. 2.13). The distances along the latter road indicate 20 Roman miles to "Praesidio" (read "Praesidium"), another 24 miles to "Hauarra," then 20 miles more to "Zadagatta." The remarkable accuracy of the mileage figures allows identification of Praesidium with the small fort at Khirbet al-Khalde, Hauarra with Humayma, and Zadagatta with Sadaqa — the Zanaatha of Ptolemy and Zodacatha of the *Notitia Dignitatum*.

The latest pre-Islamic document to mention Auara/Hauarra is the Beer Sheva Edict, which records an edict sent probably by Justinian to the *Dux Palestinae*. The inscription consisted of lists of towns in the Three Palestines, each followed by a sum of money assessed, possibly to help support the hostels and military escorts needed by pilgrims (Di Segni 2004; Kennedy 2000: 24; Isaac 1998: 451–52; Alt 1921: 8–10; cf. Mayerson 1986). Auara appears in fragment no. 2, second in a list of 18 settlements arranged in two geographical groups of southern and northern locations, and in descending order according to the size of their assessment. Many of the names also appear in the documents dis-

cussed above: Adroa, Auara, Zadacatha, Ammatha, Ariddela, Carcaria, Sobaeia, Robatha, Ellebana, Afrous, Sirtha, Fainous, Moa, Toloana, Eisiba, Praesidium, Thomaron (Thamara?), Ainauatha.

> ἀπ(ὸ) Ἀδρόων
> Ν(ομίσματα) ξεʹ καὶ τ[οῖς δούλοις Ν -]
>
> ἀπ(ὸ) Αὐάρων
> Ν(ομίσματα) μγʹ (καὶ) τ[οῖς δούλοις Ν -]
>
> ἀπ(ὸ) Ζαδακάθων
> Ν(ομίσματα) λβʹ καὶ τ[οῖς δούλοις Ν -]

From those at Adroa
  solidi 65 and to [the servants solidi ?]

From those at Auara
  solidi 43 [and to the servants solidi ?]

From those at Zadagatta
  solidi 32 [and to the servants solidi ?]

Adroa, with the highest contribution, can be equated with the large fort at modern ʿUdhruh, 21 km north of Sadaqa. Auara's contribution is second highest of all 18 in the list, indicating the significant regional importance of its garrison and civilian population. A recently discovered fragment of the inscription also mentions Mampsis, Elusa, and Zoora (Di Segni 2004: 138–39).

Stephanus Byzantinus recorded Uranius' foundation story early in the sixth century, but he

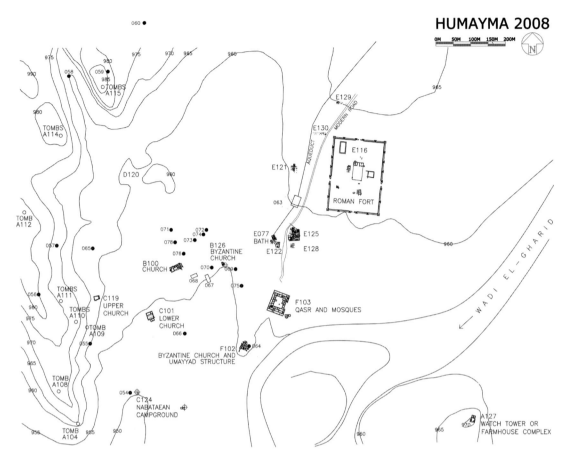

FIG. 2.14 *Plan of ancient structures at Humayma.*

added no contemporary information. In the first half of the twelfth century, Nilus Doxapatrius listed "Avarae" as one of the bishoprics of the Province of Arabia, historically under the control of the bishop of Bostra. Musil and Eadie have both proposed that this is Hauarra/Humayma (Musil 1926: 60; Eadie 1984: 219–20; Eadie and Oleson 1986: 52). Since Assemanus' text (1719–28, vol. 3, pt. 2, pp. 595–96) is often cited but never quoted, it is presented here.

> Nilus Doxapatrius Bostrenae Metropoli Ecclesias viginti attribuit, Carolus à S. Paulo septemdecim hasce enumerat: Adrae, scilicet Medavae, Gerasae, Nibe, Philadelphiae, Esbuntis, Neapolis, Philippopolis, Constantinae, Dionysiadis, Maximianopolis, Avarae, Elanae, Zerabenae, Errae, Anithae, et Parembolae. Holstenius tres addit, Canotham, Phaeno, et Bacatham seu Metrocomiam.

As might be expected, the locations are very mixed, but at least three of the names appear along with Auara in the Beer Sheva Edict: Adrae (line 1), Phaeno (line 12), and Esbuntis (line 15). Elanae is Aila/Aqaba. Schick (1995b: 320–22) doubts the identification of this Avarae with Auara/Humayma, because during the Byzantine period Auara was at first part of the province of Palaestina Salutaris, then of Palaestina Tertia, rather than of Arabia. Assemanus, however, defends the presence of Elanae/Aila on this list, because that church had historically been subject to Bostra and was shifted from its former Metropolitan "along with some other churches" to the Archiepiscopate of Petra only with the formation of Palaestina Tertia. There is no reason the same argument should not be applied to Auara/Humayma, but it remains surprising that there are no further references to such a Bishop of Auara in Early Byzantine sources. The number of churches at the site (at least five), along with Hawara/Hauarra/Humayma's continued prominence in the region from the Nabataean through the Umayyad periods, suggests that a local bishop is at least possible. Village bishoprics were common in Arabia, where the village was the normal unit of government (Watson 2001: 494). At this point, the pre-Islamic documentary sources cease.

2.B.2. *An Outline History of Hawara/ Hauarra/Humayma*

These written documents, combined with the archaeological evidence, allow reconstruction of at least the outlines of the history of Nabataean, Roman, and Byzantine Humayma (fig. 2.14; for the archaeological evidence, see esp. Oleson et al. 1999, and Oleson 2001a). Hawara, the Nabataean settlement, was founded by either Aretas III or Aretas IV on a previously unoccupied site along the King's Highway. Two public reservoirs (nos. 67–68) filled by run-off were built in the settlement centre soon after the foundation, along with an extensive aqueduct system that brought water from three springs on the escarpment to a reservoir or pool at the site (no. 63). The public water supply was most likely intended both to attract settlement to the site and to sustain the travellers moving along the King's Highway. The structures are typical of a government-sponsored trade network radiating outward from Petra (Young 2001: 115). The settlement was transformed, probably gradually, from a collection of tents to a mixture of tents and houses, some of them provided with their own cisterns. As agricultural and pastoral activity spread throughout the catchment area, cisterns were cut in the bedrock around the periphery of the arable lowland plains. The settlement flourished, and several major public buildings were constructed, of which only foundations and re-used mouldings or column drums survive (Oleson et al. 1999: 415, 417). A large slot tomb approached by steps and associated with a betyl block was cut in a prominent sandstone knoll south of the site; there were four offsets in the walls to

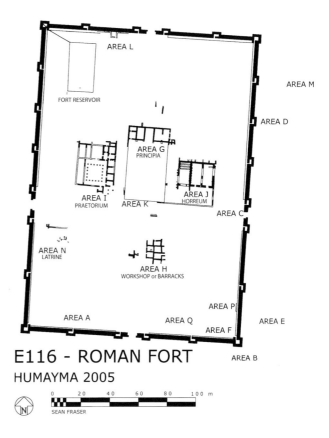

FIG. 2.15 *Plan of Roman fort, with indication of excavated areas.*

support slabs allowing five stacked burials. Smaller and usually simpler pit tombs were cut in the rocky ridges above the habitation centre on the west and south. The necropoleis will be reported on in a subsequent volume.

The Roman conquest of the Nabataean kingdom in 106 AD brought dramatic changes to Hawara. A large fort was constructed on the rise at the north edge of the settlement, adjacent to the aqueduct and the Nabataean reservoir, and the aqueduct was tapped to feed a reservoir within its walls (fig. 2.15). The frequent re-use in the fort of blocks taken from large Nabataean structures indicates that occupation of the site involved conflict and destruction. The same disruption can now be seen to have occurred at Petra, Oboda, Moje Awad, Khirbet edh-Dharih, Dhiban, and Sobata (Schmid 1997; 2001b: 401–2; Parker 2009). The fort was located at this point to watch over the largest population centre in the Hisma, its gener-

Fig. 2.16 *Aerial view of settlement centre (Photo: W. Myers, 07.21.1992, neg. H-1.9).*

ous water supply, and the old King's Highway that passed through Hawara, renovated as the Via Nova Traiana between 111 and 114 (Aharoni 1963: 39; Graf 1995: 241, 250–58; Young 2001: 115, 130). Milestones reveal that the section of the road between Aqaba and Philadelphia was renovated between 111 and 112 (Freeman 2001: 433).

The size of the fort would suit a complement of approximately 500 men (Parker 1986: 105; 2009: 145–46), and historical sources and inscriptions found in and around the fort suggest that the first unit may have been a detachment from the Legio VI Ferrata, under the command of C. Bruttius L. f. Praesens (Oleson, Reeves, Fisher 2002). At some time in the second century, this unit was replaced by a unit from the Legio III Cyrenaica. A military bath was constructed in the mid-second century, downstream from the Nabataean reservoir, and a civilian community (*vicus*), including a shrine, grew up in its vicinity. By the mid-third century, dedications to Jupiter Ammon, Zeus Serapis, and a local Nabataean divinity had been set up in this shrine. Although the garrison must have been large in comparison with the civilian population, there is little evidence that the Roman soldiers had much effect on the way of life or material culture of their Nabataean neighbours during the first century of the occupation (Oleson 2003a). For a review of the history of Arabia during this period, see Fiema 2003. There has been a long and intense scholarly debate on the strategic purpose of the Roman forts now on the territory of modern Jordan and Syria: to monitor or repel invading nomads (esp. Parker 2006: 531–52, with previous bibliography), or to administer and exploit the associated territory (Graf 1997; Isaac 1990, with previous bibliography).

A good selection of imperial coins of the mid- and later third century was found in the fort, but the series ends abruptly with the reign of Carinus in 285. No coins of Diocletian have been recovered in the fort, but numismatic evidence resumes again with Maxentius and Constantine, initiating a second period of significant but lesser activity in the fourth century AD. The phasing of the walls also indicates that the original constructions were possibly abandoned for some time, then reoccupied, accompanied by the construction of new paved floors at a higher level and the dumping of earlier

refuse in abandoned rooms (Oleson et al. 1999: 415; 2008). It is likely that Zenobia's army passed through Hauarra on its way to Egypt during her destructive revolt in 270 (Graf 1989b; Sartre 2005: 356–57). The fort may have suffered some damage at that time and the garrison subsequently may have been reduced in size. Since Diocletian engaged in an extensive reorganisation of the frontier forts in the Provincia Arabia 15 years later (Parker 1986: 135–43; Freeman 2001: 446–47), it is likely that there was a temporary withdrawal of any remaining garrison as the result of reassignment of the troops to one of the new forts. By 314, the portion of the Provincia Arabia from the Wadi Hasa south to Aila had been attached to the province of Palestine, reflecting the growing importance of trade links west across the Wadi 'Arabah (Bowersock 1983: 142–43). Around 358, the administrative designation of the territory became Palaestina Salutaris and, by 400, Palaestina Tertia (Avi-Yonah 1973: 415; Gutwein 1981; Freeman 2001: 434; Frösén et al. 2002: 2).

Numismatic and ceramic evidence suggest that a military unit was stationed in the fort once again during the reign of Constantine and his sons, possibly the *Equites sagittarii indigenae* listed for Hauarra by the *Notitia Dignitatum*. This would have been a locally recruited auxiliary force composed largely, if not entirely, of Arabs (Shahîd 1984: 51–63; Pollard 2000: 139). Around the end of the fourth or beginning of the fifth century, however, the fort was abandoned and became a source of building materials for the prosperous Byzantine settlement. It is possible that the earthquake of 19–20 May 363 that caused so much damage at Petra delivered the final blow to the Hauarra fort (*EZ* I: 51; Fiema et al. 2001: 28–29). It is not yet known how many of the 30 or so stone houses scattered around the site originated in the Byzantine period (Blétry-Sébé 1990), but ceramic surface scatters suggest that most of them were occupied at that time (fig. 2.16). The scattered, seemingly casual arrangement of houses around the settlement reflects a decentralised type of planning, which has been seen as the typical pattern of urbanisation in the Early Islamic world (Whitcomb 1996; Gawlikowski 1997). The overall prosperity of the town and its thorough Christianisation are indicated by the construction of at least five churches in the fifth and sixth centuries (figs. 2.14, 2.17; Schick

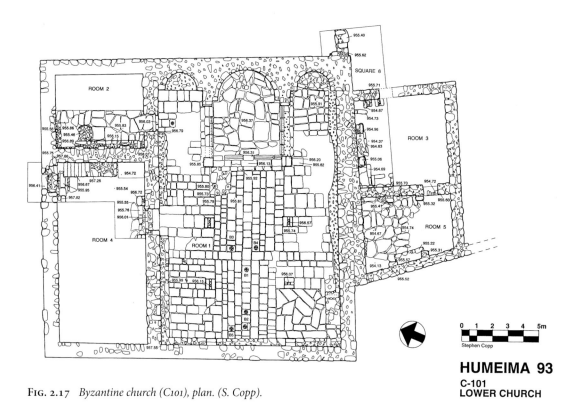

FIG. 2.17 *Byzantine church (C101), plan. (S. Copp).*

HUMEIMA 93
C-101
LOWER CHURCH

1995a: 311–13; Oleson et al. 1999: 430–36; structures B100, B126, C101, C119, F102). The pagan shrine in E125 was not reconstructed after the garrison returned in the early fourth century (Reeves 2009). It is not clear why so many churches were needed, since few sites in southern Jordan had more than one: five churches have been documented at Faynan, six or seven at Petra (Frösén 2001: 489; Bikai 2009: 25), and two at 'Udhruh. As in the Negev, the apparent oversupply of churches in small communities may simply reflect the nomadic lifestyle of their congregations, who consequently do not appear in the archaeological record (Negev 1991: 228). It is also possible that families, clans, and tribes built churches as other forms of euergetism dried up (Fiema et al. 2001: 430). There may have been a local bishop at Hauarra, reporting first to the Bishop of Bostra, then to the Bishop of Petra. The churches seem to have been abandoned gradually, without intentional destruction, during the Umayyad period or just before (Schick 1995: 340; 'Amr and Schick 2001). The B100 and F102 structures, at least, were reoccupied during that period and subdivided for reuse as habitations.

The chronology of the Islamisation of Humayma, which assumed its modern name some time in the seventh century, is still unknown. The town is not mentioned in the accounts of the Islamic conquest during the 630s, but the whole region seems to have been outside the control of the Byzantine emperor. On their way to the battle of Mu'ta in 629, Islamic forces stayed for two days at Ma'an without opposition (Watson 2001: 491), and in 630/1 the bishop or governor of Aila along with officials of Udhruh and Ma'an negotiated surrender with Muhammad at Tabuk (Kaegi 1992: 67, 82–83, 92). The purchase of Humayma by the Abbasid family in the early eighth century attracted the attention of several early Arabic historians. The history of the family is recounted in the anonymous tenth-century *Akhbâr al-Dawla al-'Abbâsiya* (*History of the Abbasid Revolution*, ed. al-Dûrî and al-Jabbâr, 1971), in the ninth century in al-Balâdhurî's *Ansâb al-Ashrâf* (*Genealogies of the Nobles*, ed. al-Dûrî, 1978), and in several other texts (Sourdel 1971; Schick 1994: 150, 1995a: 312–13, 2007).

The Abbasid family was related to the Prophet through a common ancestor, Hâshim bin 'Abd

Manâf (B. Lewis 1960: 15–16). The head of the family in the early eighth century, 'Ali ibn 'Abd Allâh ibn al-'Abbâs, moved north with his family and settled in 'Udhruh sometime after 685. Not long afterwards, he purchased the village (*qarya*) of Humayma, where he built a *qasr* (manor house) with *manazil* (apartments), a *masjid* (mosque), and a garden (al-Dûrî and al-Jabbâr 1971: 107–8, 149, 154; al-Bakrî 1945–51: 130; Schick 2007: 346). The manor house and mosque have been recognised and excavated by Foote (fig. 2.18; Oleson et al. 1999: 436–43; 2003a: 55–62; Foote 1999; 2007). 'Ali (or his son Muhammad) is said to have had an olive grove with 500 trees. He performed two sets of prayers at each tree every day, developing calluses on his forehead from all the prostrations, thus earning the honorific nickname "possessor of the calluses" (al-Balâdhurî 1978: III, 75; al-Dûrî et al. 1971: 135, 144–45; al-Tabarî 1879–1901: II, 1592). The large size of the grove — if real, rather than rhetorical — indicates a commercial scale of production, and the family history, in fact, reports that merchants and Abbasid supporters disguised as merchants stopped at the site (al-Dûrî et al. 1971: 195–96). For whatever reason, individuals travelling between Umayyad Syria and the Hejaz often stayed at Humayma.

The historical sources give the picture of a bustling rural settlement, and early Islamic pottery is found nearly everywhere on the surface at Humayma. Houses were built or rebuilt, sometimes within the derelict churches. By the time of 'Ali's death at Humayma in 735/736, his eldest son Muhammad had already begun to plot the overthrow of the Umayyad caliphate. The conspirators met in the mosque at Humayma and at the nearby village of Kudad, still not identified (al-Dûrî et al. 1971: 195, 197; Schick 2007: 347–48). After the death of Muhammad in 741/2, eight of his brothers ("The Uncles") played important roles in the revolution of 750 and in the newly established Abbasid state. Just prior to the revolution, in 749, a large group moved to the family's political power base at Qufa in Iraq. The subsequent history of the family is recounted by Cobb (2001).

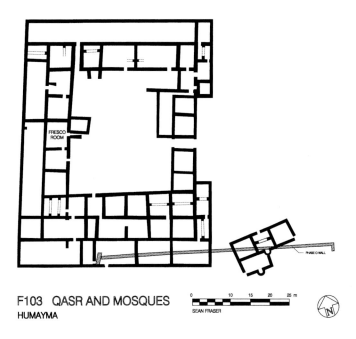

F103 QASR AND MOSQUES
HUMAYMA

SEAN FRASER

0   10   15   20   25 m

FIG. 2.18 *Abbasid manor house and mosque (F103), plan.*

Although the Abbasid family did not return to Humayma, the site continued to exist, but at a lower level of intensity. In the third/ninth century, al-Ya'qûbî recorded it in his list of place names in Arabia (al-Ya'qûbî 1892: 114), and around 985 al-Muqaddasi mentions it among the settlements in Southern Jordan: Adhruh, Ma'an, 'Arandal, Wayla, Humayma, and Ruwath. It is indicative of the changed political situation that neither Petra nor Wadi Musa are mentioned (Fiema 2002: 237). Small amounts of Fatimid to Ottoman cultural material have been found around the southern part of the site. Avni (2007) interprets the archaeological evidence from the old Nabataean cities of the Negev to show that the arrival of Islam in that region did not involve destruction of these settlements, but that they continued to flourish through the ninth and even tenth century. He sees a long period of transition from Christianity to Islam and believes that open-air mosques — such as the one at Humayma that was built next to the original Abbasid mosque — only appear a century after the conquest, after a long period of transition among the Bedouin from the worship of standing stones to the provision of simple mosques. The history of Early Islamic Humayma may have been similar.

Although the final analysis remains to be done, a raw count of the 5882 excavation buckets analysed between 1991 and 2005 provides the following statistics for numbers of buckets containing at least some material from the Islamic phases: Umayyad, 1334 buckets (22.7%); Abbasid, 850 (14.5%); Fatimid, 112 (1.9%); Ayyubid 76 (1.3%); Mamluk 75 (1.3%); Ottoman 274 (4.7%). Many of the rooms in the manor house may have been cleared out and reoccupied sometime in the Ottoman period, but given the desolation of the site at the time of Laborde's visit, this phase must have ended long before the nineteenth century. Since most of the evidence for reoccupation of the site in the Ottoman period has been found in the Abbasid family manor house, it may be that reoccupation of the site was in fact as limited then as it had been in the Fatimid through Mamluk periods. In any case, after 132/749 the importance of the site declined precipitously and never recovered.

It is possible that a combination of factors put an end to the surprisingly long florescence of this isolated desert settlement. The conquest of the whole Middle East by the Muslim armies tended to cut that region off from extensive trade with the rest of the Mediterranean world, which must have dramatically reduced the amount of trade passing through Humayma. In addition, the installation of the Abbasid caliphate in Baghdad tended to re-focus trade routes eastwards, away from the Mediterranean (Fiema 1991). It is also likely that the climate became more arid after the Umayyad period, forcing the local peoples back to a nomadic, pastoral mode of life and leaving the site abandoned but for the occasional visitor (Jobling 1983a: 194; Munro et al. 1997: 100; MacDonald 2001). The spell the site had exercised over four major regional political and cultural powers was broken.

NOTES

1   Clandestine diggers discovered a beautifully built, vaulted Nabataean tomb chamber just north of the caravanserai around 1997. I believe that the inscription of Marcus Ulpius Su'aidu (Hayajneh 2001), the existence of which was revealed by local Bedouin a few years later, refers to and belongs with this tomb.

2   The Humayma Project surveyed an area of approximately 234 sq km marked for the most part by natural boundaries. Within this area, run-off from 28 sq km in the northwest portion of the survey area runs down the Wadi Hilwa in to the Wadi 'Arabah. Run-off from the remaining area either passes by

the site or was used in other catchments to supply fields and cisterns.

3   Without the aid of a comparative collection in the field laboratory, the following sources were useful in the identification process: J. Boessneck, "Osteological Differences Between Sheep (*Ovis aries* Linné) and Goat (*Capra hircus* Linné)," pp. 331–58 in D.R. Brothwell and E. Higgs, eds., *Science in Archaeology* (New York: Praeger, 1969); E. Schmid, *Atlas of Animal Bones for Prehistorians, Archaeologists and Quaternary Geologists* (Amsterdam: Elsevier, 1972).

Chapter 3

The Regional Water-Supply System:
Catalogue of Structures Outside the Settlement

3.A. INTRODUCTION

The catalogue of the elements of the water-supply system presented in Chapters 3 and 4 is intended to document the structures observed, studied, and — occasionally — excavated during our surveys in 1983, 1986–87, and 1989. The detail with which the structures have been recorded may seem obsessive, particularly for the aqueduct, but in fact full and accurate analysis of water systems depends on careful observation of details. Such detail has very seldom been provided for Nabataean hydraulic structures, which unfortunately are singularly vulnerable to damage or total destruction. I hope that the data presented here will allow future scholars to answer questions that I have not thought to ask.

The structures were numbered consecutively during the survey, and these survey numbers have been kept (in preference to sequential catalogue numbers) for the final publication in order to avoid confusion in cross-references to earlier reports. To avoid the proliferation of numbers, the aqueduct was labelled Structure no. 1, and features along the 26,508 m of its course were recorded by their distance from 'Ain Ghana along the route to Humayma for the main branch, and for the subsidiary branch by their distance from 'Ain al-Jammam to the intersection with the 'Ain Ghana aqueduct. The distance measurements were taken by a hand-operated odometer wheel and should be very accurate. All compass bearings noted in this publication were taken with a Brunton Pocket Transit and refer to magnetic north; the magnetic deviation at Humayma in 1986 was approximately 3.5 degrees west of true north.

Since our survey of the Humayma catchment proceeded in a more or less clockwise direction around the settlement centre from the north, then entered the settlement itself, the catalogue numbers for structures in general increase as the catalogue spirals in towards the centre (fig. 1.1). For a variety of reasons, some catalogue numbers are subdivided as A and B. The initial survey work was carried out before portable GPS devices became available, and map references were calculated for the grid on the Hashemite Kingdom of Jordan Ministry of Economy/U.S.A. Operations Mission to Jordan 1:25,000 topographic Map Series (based on aerial photographs dated 1953). Individual locations were plotted by triangulation with appropriately placed natural landmarks, using the pocket transit. The figures for elevation were based on that same map series. In 2000 to 2001, however, all but two of the catalogued features were revisited (Cisterns 34 and 40 could not be relocated), previous observations verified, and GPS readings of the UTM coordinates taken with a Garmin 48 handheld Geographical Positioning System. These readings were taken just after the partial jamming of GPS accuracy was lifted on the orders of President Clinton (1 May 2000), allowing accuracy to approximately 4.0 m

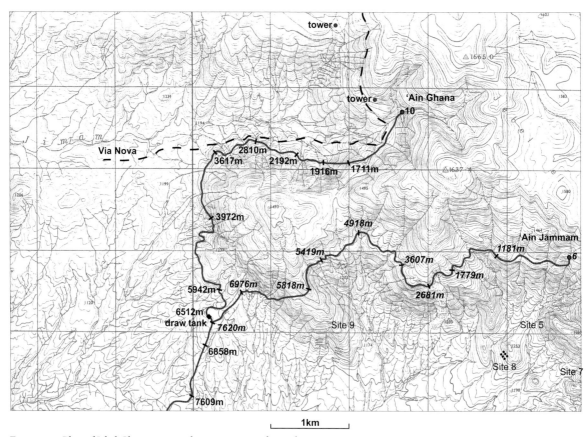

FIG. 3.1   *Plan of Jebel Ghana area and upper courses of aqueducts.*

with the instrument used. The less accurate map grid references probably became obsolete at that point, but I have included them nevertheless in this publication, since they may still be of use in some situations. The GPS elevations, although generally less accurate than the horizontal coordinates, have nevertheless in most cases been preferred to the elevations worked out from the maps. Along long stretches of the aqueduct with a low slope, the GPS elevations often were not accurate enough to give a useful indication of the fall of the channel. In these cases, the elevations taken from the map have been recorded alongside the GPS elevations, which have been put in quotation marks when they mistakenly indicate the channel is sloping "up hill." Individual structures have also been located by radial bearings from Reservoir no. 67, in order to give a more graphic idea of their relationship to the settlement centre.

The condition of archaeological remains can deteriorate even in the arid and lonely landscape around Humayma, so the catalogue also indicates the date of the first or the major observation of a structure by the author, with indication of subsequent visits if these revealed new information or — more often — noticeable degradation. I have also noted the varying degrees to which some of the larger cisterns and reservoirs were filled from visit to visit, since these data provide useful information about variations in rainfall. All dates are day–month–year. Many of these isolated structures have been damaged since the initial survey in 1986, some by vandalism and others by the clearing of a cistern by the Bedouin for re-use. The aqueduct suffered particularly extensive damage in 1988 between approximately km 10.332 and 12.481, when several kilometres were bulldozed during construction of a dirt road connecting Humayma with the top of the escarpment by way of 'Ain Ghana. Ironically, rather than following the course of the Via Nova Traiana, the modern road largely followed the course of the aqueduct, since its gentle and uninterrupted gradient is more suitable to wheeled vehicles than the less even path of the Roman road. Because of the difficulty of measuring some of the cisterns and reservoirs, particularly those that were irregular in shape, completely subterranean, or partially filled with earth, I have sometimes provided maximum and minimum calculations of capacity.

Although it was not completed as a single project, the water-supply system of Humayma was an integrated system that suited both the basically static environmental conditions and the evolving needs of the settlement (see the diagram of the system, fig. 7.1). As with all water systems, the system serving Humayma involved input, consumption, and discharge, and it incorporated structures that allowed the collection, diversion, impoundment, transport, storage, and convenient distribution of water. Although the precise character and extent of the system changed and evolved over time, the elements involved at one time or another included three springs, 26.508 km of aqueduct, five reservoirs, 57 cisterns (43 cut in the bedrock, 14 built), and three impoundment dams or barrier walls (see Table 7.2). There were also at least three sets of wadi barriers, six areas of recognisable terracing, and three fields in which stones were gathered in piles. Two off-take tanks that drew water from the Ghana Aqueduct approximately 10 km before it entered the city probably were part of the original project. They were designed to provide controlled, non-polluting access to its water outside the settlement centre. Water storage structures with a capacity of more than 450 cum were termed reservoirs; the largest cistern had a capacity of 300 cum, while the average was 97 cum. Four of the reservoirs were located in the settlement centre, and because of the geology, all were built rather than cut into the rock. The aqueduct fed two of them, while two were supplied by run-off water. The fifth reservoir was located just outside the settlement centre, cut in the bedrock, and filled by run-off water. Forty-seven of the cisterns were located outside the settlement centre, all but four of them rock-cut. Of the 13 cisterns in or adjacent to the settlement centre, only three were cut into the rock rather than built. No ancient wadi barriers have survived in the settlement centre, but four possible conduits or drains were catalogued, along with a bath building.

The catalogue cannot follow precisely the logical arrangement of the system itself, which is described and reconstructed in Chapter 7. The springs on the al-Shara escarpment appear at the head of the catalogue, as the source of input for the spectacular aqueduct system. The aqueduct system is presented second and occupies nearly half the catalogue. The cisterns located outside the settlement centre (which I define as more than 500 m from Reservoir no. 67) are listed next, followed by the dam and barrier walls, wadi barriers, terraces, and cleared run-off fields. A final section catalogues curious features termed "hillside channels" and "slides," which have no relation to the water-supply system but which might be confused with water channels. The structures within the settlement centre are catalogued in Chapter 4. Although a full description and analysis of the system is presented in Chapter 7, a brief characterisation of each type of structure is given in this chapter in order to clarify the categories and descriptions.

3.B. CATALOGUE

3.B.1. *Springs*

Site no. 6A: 'Ain al-Jammam.

Coordinates: UTM 36R 0737939, 3323626; Pal. Grid 948369. Elevation: 1418 m. 02/07/86, 07/10/95, 07/07/00, 24/03/01, 30/04/08.

The spring flows from a cave beneath a large outcropping of limestone on the southwest slope of the Jebel Jammam, 120 m below the crest of the escarpment at this point, 50 m below the Desert Highway (as rebuilt in 1998 and 2002) (figs. 3.1–2). The bearing from Reservoir no. 67 is 54 degrees and 14.2 km. A dirt road leaving the highway 1 km to the east gives access to the site, which is easily recognised by the presence of a group of large plane trees watered by the spring and an early twentieth-century (?) stone farmhouse. The farmhouse is associated with a series of modern agricultural terraces extending 500 m along the slope to the northwest as far as 'Ain Sara (no. 6B) and 50–80 m down the slope (fig. 3.3). These terraces, which for most of the 1990s supported vines, fruit trees,

Fig. 3.2   *View of 'Ain al-Jammam in 1986.*

Fig. 3.3   *View of 'Ain al-Jammam spring and farm from the west in 1986.*

FIG. 3.4   *Interior of spring chamber in 1989.*

and vegetable gardens, are designed to make use of the water from both springs conveyed to them by a mix of modern pipes and ancient conduit blocks. A new owner purchased the site in 1995, restricted access, and made some changes to the harvesting of the spring water to allow for more intensive agricultural use. By 2005, nearly all the ancient remains around the spring had been bulldozed or concealed beneath modern concrete.

In 1986, the spring water flowed from a rocky cleft at the back of a roughly square, low chamber (L 4.90 m; W 5.40 m; H 1.00–1.43 m) that had been excavated in a concreted stratum of clay and gravel underlying a more or less horizontal stratum of hard, creamy limestone (fig. 3.4). The chamber does not appear to have been altered in the modern period, although a Nabataean conduit block was placed at the mouth of the spring sometime between 1986 and 1989 to bring the discharge away from the wall. The water was then allowed simply to pool on the earth floor and trickle out of the cave into a modern concrete water-channel. By 2000, the floor of the chamber had been partly cemented to reduce water loss. The rate of flow

changes according to the season and variations in annual precipitation, and in 1986 the Jordan Irrigation Authority calculated the maximum flow at 2 cum/hour, the minimum at 0.6 cum/hour, and the average at 1.2 cum/hour (20 l/min) (oral communication by Mohammad Abu Taha, June 1986). In June 1986, a field calculation recorded a flow of 15 l/min, but in subsequent years it has generally been much less. In March 2001, however, even after three years of drought, the flow was measured as 10.6 l/min, or 0.64 cum/hour. In April 2008, the flow was measured at 6.0 l/min, or 0.36 cum/hour. None of the arrangements inside the spring chamber appear to be ancient. The enhancement or concentration of flow from an aquifer by excavating fill back to a major channel, however, was a common procedure in antiquity (Oleson 1992b: 884; Hill 1964). The arrangement at 'Ain Shellaleh in Wadi Ramm is very similar (Savignac 1933; 1934; and see fig. 8.38, this volume).

The outside face of the cave and limestone outcropping do not preserve any obvious traces of working in antiquity, but until 1986 a pair of parallel stone walls extended out several metres from the cliff face on either side of the cave opening, 2.50 m apart (fig. 3.2). At that time, bulldozing associated with road construction destroyed the western wall and disturbed the earth fill in front of the cliff face. Both walls were built of well-squared blocks of local limestone laid in even courses and chinked with stone chips and pebbles. The ancient arrangement at 'Ain Shellaleh was very similar. Although the walls are constructed of ancient blocks, they may be contemporary with the early-modern farmhouse. The eastern wall survives to a height of 1.25 m in five courses above present ground level and a total length of 2.40 m; both ends are incomplete. Although the junctions with the cliff have been lost, to judge from what remains the walls probably held back loose earth in front of the cliff face, on either side of an access and drainage route. Because of the extensive modern activity around the spring, and the deposition of large amounts of fill near the entrance to the cave, the ancient arrangements can only be guessed at. The Jammam Aqueduct, however, clearly was fed by this source (see below), probably after the water had passed through a settling tank or collecting basin. No ancient potsherds are visible in the immediate vicinity of the spring, but there are numerous Nabataean marl conduit blocks. A very rich deposit of Neolithic flint blades, scrapers, and debitage on the slope above the spring cave and grove suggest that the spring was flowing at that time (Waheeb 1996; Waheeb and Fino 1997). Reconstruction of the modern Desert Highway in 1998 and 2002 fortunately did not affect the topography of the spring, but it seems to have damaged the aquifer and reduced the flow of water.

In 1986 and as late as 1995, the run-off from the spring flowed 38 m through a combination of concrete conduits and metal pipes to a modern cistern (L 5.75 m; W 3.95 m; depth 0.96 m; cap. 21.8 cum), from which the overflow was allowed to trickle down the hill. Approximately 100 m farther down the slope there is a second modern cistern (L 7.12 m; W 6.90 m; depth 1.20 m; cap. 59 cum), built of mortared rubble, which was probably fed both by the discharge of a very weak seepage of water immediately above it and by overflow from the upper cistern. At some point in the past, water was conducted to the cistern through a very

roughly built conduit of thin, upright slabs set in the earth. This lower cistern has been dry at every visit since 1986.

In 1986, the discharge from the upper spring was channelled to the garden terraces by means of a modern conduit of concrete poured in home-made forms. This conduit, approximately 10 m lower than the spring cave, was built more or less on the course of the ancient Jammam Aqueduct, the marl conduit slabs of which can be seen tumbled down the slope or re-used in the modern re-building. For a discussion, see Site no. 1 (Jammam Aqueduct). Bibliography: Glueck 1934–35: 65; Eadie and Oleson 1986: 61–68 (with previous references); Oleson 1986, 1987a, 1988a–b, 1992a, 1995a, 1997; Waheeb 1996; Waheeb and Fino 1997.

Site no. 6B: 'Ain Sara.

Coordinates: UTM 36R 0737610, 3323111; Pal. Grid 944369. Elevation: 1425 m. 02/06/86, 27/03/01.

The water flows from a gravelly crevice immediately below a large limestone outcropping 400 m west of 'Ain al-Jammam (fig. 1.1). The bearing from Reservoir 67 is 53 degrees and 13.9 km. The topographical situation is similar to that of the Jammam spring, but no cave has been excavated back into the clay and gravel stratum below the limestone cap. There has, however, been much recent excavation in front of the spring, and none of the ancient arrangements have survived. In June 1986, a large, rectangular pool (L 18.70 m; W 16.00 m; depth 0.60–0.80 m; cap. 179.5–239.4 cum) had been excavated in the earth in front of the outcropping and the spoil left as a berm to hold the water in (fig. 3.5); not long before March 2001, this pool was rebuilt in concrete. Water flows into the northwest corner of the pool from the crevice in the vertical gravel face, but it also seems to well up inside a modern concrete box within the pool (2.7 m square). The rate of flow changes according to the season and variations in annual precipitation; in 1986, the Jordan Irrigation Authority calculated the maximum flow at 2 cum/hour, the minimum at 0.3 cum/hour, and the average at 0.75 cum/hour (12.5 l/min) (oral communication by Mohammad Abu Taha, 06/86). In June 1986, a rough calculation put the flow from the visible source at 2.0 l/

FIG. 3.5   *Pool in front of 'Ain Sara in 1986.*

min. In March 2001, the pool was half full, but no overflow was visible.

In June 1986, overflow from the pool was drawn off through a plastic hose to feed a variety of concrete and stone conduits serving the terraces below. Several ancient marl conduit blocks were observed in the gardens below the spring, some put to use once again to conduct water. No ancient potsherds were observed around the spring basin or in the adjacent fields, which were, however, covered with vegetation.

Bibliography: Glueck 1934–35: 65; Oleson 1986, 1987a, 1988a–b.

Site no. 7: 'Ain Abu an-Nusur
("Spring of the Father of Eagles")

Coordinates: UTM 36R 0738814, 3322877; Pal. Grid 954359. Elevation: 1455 m. 02/06/86, 07/07/00.

The upper spring is located on the west wall of the opening to a hanging valley near the top of the escarpment, 20 m above the modern highway, 1.15 km southeast of 'Ain al-Jammam (fig. 1.1). The bearing from Reservoir 67 is 58 degrees and 14.6

km. The valley opens on a terrace 1 ha in area, occupied by the remains of Byzantine structures, possibly farm houses, badly disturbed and partly obscured by modern structures (fig. 3.6; Waheeb 1996: 345, "Khirbat Abu an-Nusur"). No obvious hydraulic installations were observed around the ancient structures. The lower spring emerges below and 200 m north of these structures, approximately 25 m below the level of the upper spring, and well below the modern road.

The upper spring trickles from a crevice in a layer of clay and gravel below a projecting stratum of limestone. The area of earth fill around the spring has been heavily disturbed. In 1986, the water trickled into an oval basin built of earth with rubble reinforcement (fig. 3.7; D ca. 3.00 m; depth ca. 0.40 m; cap. ca. 2.1 cum), and the overflow was allowed to drain down the hill. In 1990, a concrete basin was built 2 m down the slope to capture the overflow and feed it into a conduit that led to a PVC pipeline under the modern highway conducting the water to the modern house on the site of the Byzantine structures. In 1986, a Nabataean marl conduit block (L 0.52 m; H 0.22 m; W 0.27

FIG. 3.6   *View from ʿAin Abu an-Nusur in 1989, looking south.*

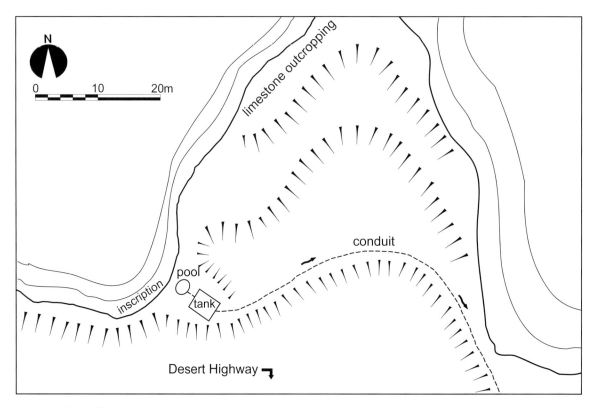

FIG. 3.7   *Plan of ʿAin Abu an-Nusur area.*

FIG. 3.8   *View of 'Ain Ghana area, from the north, with terraces and farmhouse. Lower spring at lower left.*

m; channel depth 0.14 m, W 0.10 m) was lying on the surface soil near the earth basin; fragments of two other conduit blocks were visible farther down the slope.

According to Peake (1958: 214), the Zawayda tribe of the Huweitat are traditional owners of the spring. The rate of flow changes according to the season and variations in annual precipitation. In 1986, the Jordan Irrigation Authority calculated the maximum flow at 1.42 cum/hour, the minimum at 0.5 cum/hour, and the average at 0.9 cum/hour (15 l/min) (oral communication by Mohammad Abu Taha, June 1986). In several visits to the spring since June 1986, there has never been enough overflow to measure discharge, although the pool has always contained water, and the presence of the earth channel and pipe supplying fruit trees across the highway indicates that there is sufficient overflow at some times of the year to service the needs of the modern inhabitants. A group of Thamudic inscriptions was cut into the cliff face above and to the left of the spring (unpublished; see Jobling 1983a: 188,

pl. 34.1), above an early modern shelter with rock and mud walls. Jobling made a transcription of the inscriptions, but found them "very difficult to read" (oral communication 1990). The damaged and badly weathered inscriptions were removed by the Department of Antiquities in 1995 in anticipation of the disturbance of the site by road construction. No potsherds were observed around the upper spring, probably because the recently excavated soil and sod have covered them.

The lower spring, below the modern highway, trickles from beneath an outcropping of limestone, filling a shallow earth and stone basin 3.0 m in diameter. The overflow is left simply to trickle down the slope, creating a splash of green vegetation in an otherwise barren area. No traces of conduit blocks or ancient potsherds were observed in the vicinity of this basin.

The upper spring of 'Ain Abu an-Nusur is approximately 37 m higher than the beginning of the 'Ain al-Jammam Aqueduct, allowing an overall 3.2 percent slope between the two. Careful examination of the slopes of the escarpment between 'Ain al-Jammam and both the upper and lower 'Ain Abu an-Nusur basins, however, did not reveal any traces of an aqueduct or even of isolated conduit blocks. The construction of the modern highway in the late 1970s badly disturbed a portion of the intervening area, but some traces of such an aqueduct branch should have survived, had it existed. In particular, scattered conduit blocks and fragments of yellow marl would be relatively easy to spot in the barren, brown landscape. A single well-preserved conduit block was found lying next to the modern dirt road 100 m east of 'Ain al-Jammam, but it seems to have been dumped here as part of the fill bulldozed from around the spring to serve as roadbed. It is likely that the flow of 'Ain Abu an-Nusur was too meagre to be incorporated into the Humayma aqueduct system, and that it was completely consumed in antiquity by local flocks and the inhabitants of the adjacent settlement.

Bibliography: Jobling 1983a: 188, pl. 34.1; Oleson 1986, 1987a, 1988a–b, 1992a, 1995a, 1997; Waheeb 1996: 345.

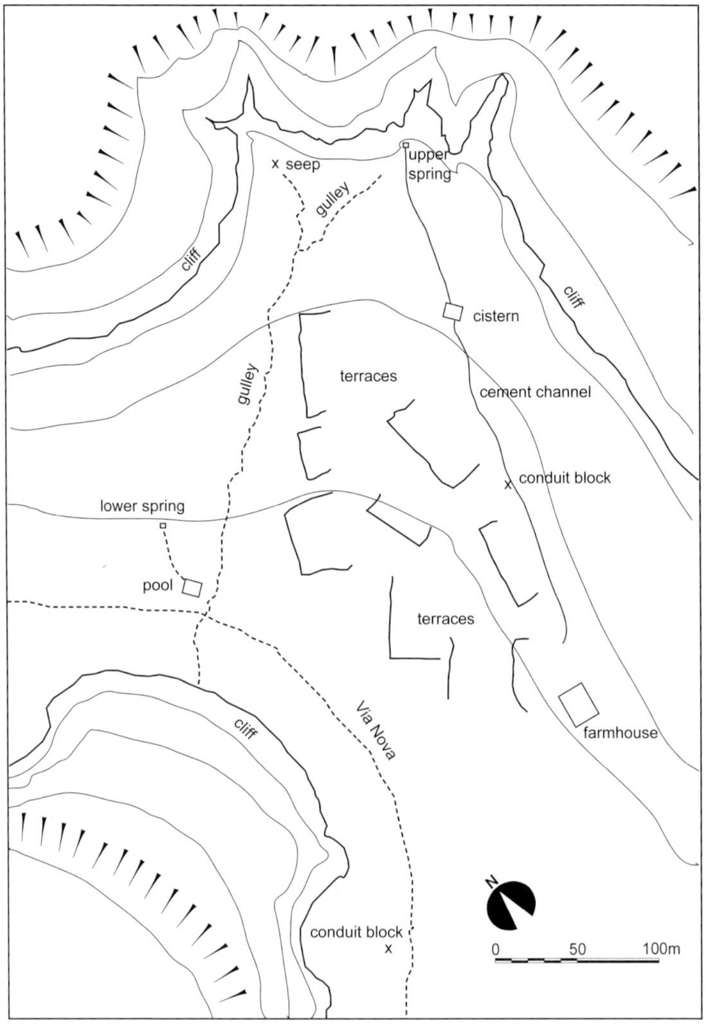

FIG. 3.9   *Plan of 'Ain Ghana area.*

Site no. 10: 'Ain Ghana ("Spring of the Conduit")

Coordinates: UTM 36R 0732327, 3325277 (lower spring); Pal. Grid 926387. Elevation: 1415–1459 m. 04/06/86, 09/07/00, 26/03/01, 30/04/08.

There are two main springs 280 m apart, set back in a wide, cliff-sided valley where the north face of Jebel al-Ghana joins the escarpment, approximately 200 m below its summit (figs. 1.5, 3.1, 3.8–10). The lower spring (elev. 1435 m), at present the most productive, is 2.84 km northwest of 'Ain Jammam; the bearing from Reservoir 67 is 43 degrees and 13.5 km. The upper spring (UTM 36R 0735787, 3324932; elev. 1459 m) trickles from a

stratum of clay and gravel below a poorly defined limestone outcropping a few metres below the cliff at the head of the valley. The soil in front of the spring has been scooped out to form a rough basin, and the entire area has been extensively disturbed in recent years. In 1986, the run-off from the basin was carried first by aluminium piping, then by a modern earth and concrete channel 80 m along the slope to the southeast to a modern rubble and mortar cistern (L 4.30 m; W 3.26 m; depth 1.20 m; cap. 16.8 cum). By March 2001, a plastic irrigation pipe had replaced the aluminium pipe. A single marl conduit block (L 0.53 m; W 0.32 m; H 0.22 m; channel W 0.08 m, depth 0.08 m) from the

FIG. 3.10 *View of 'Ain Ghana valley with springs and Via Nova Traiana (marked), in 1986.*

original Nabataean aqueduct lies on the surface next to the pipe, and a conduit constructed in the recent past of roughly-aligned stone slabs set in earth (inside W 0.15 m) runs alongside the channel now in use. Next to the cistern, there is a well-trimmed, water-worn limestone slab with a central perforation (L 0.57 m, broken; W 0.54 m; Th 0.12 m; D of hole 0.05 m), possibly used in the ancient water-system to regulate the flow of water out of a cistern or into conduits. An aluminium outflow pipe from the cistern conducted water into another slab-built conduit that extends along the east slope of the valley for 127 m to an abandoned farmhouse (36R 0735700, 3324540; elev. 1455 m), where it is lost. A second ancient marl conduit block was observed lying next to the modern channel, halfway between the cistern and the farmhouse. Traces of agricultural terraces (some of them probably rebuilt ancient terraces) extend down the east slope of the valley below the level of these channels as far as the central drainage wadi (fig. 3.8). Some of the fields on the terraces were still watered in 1986 by conduits descending from the cistern, but by 2000 they were all dry. In March 2001, some trees

were being irrigated. According to Peake (1958: 214), the al-Maraaya tribe is the traditional owner of the spring.

Some water from a seep 60 m northwest of the upper spring trickles down the wadi that drains the valley, forming a belt of green that extends to a small natural pool (D ca. 3.00 m; depth ca. 0.25 m; cap. ca. 1.4 cum) shaded by several trees (fig. 3.10). The Via Nova Traiana crossed the wadi at this point, and traces of its paving can be seen up the hill to the west, towards the crest of the escarpment, where there are remains of a small tower, fortification, or farm house. Most of the water in this pool flows from the lower spring (fig. 3.11). This spring trickles from beneath a small limestone outcropping into a basin dug into the earth and is conducted down the slope in a small channel to a modern concrete pool designed to water sheep and goats. The overflow from the lower pool flows over a wide limestone ledge at the mouth of the valley and down a cliff into one of the tributary wadis of the Wadi al-Hilwa. The first visible remains of the Ghana Aqueduct appear on the surface 150 m southeast of the lower spring, at a bearing of 150 degrees.

FIG. 3.11 *Lower spring and modern concrete basin in 2001.*

The rate of flow from these two springs changes according to the season and variations in annual precipitation; in 1986, the Jordan Irrigation Authority calculated their maximum flow at 0.4 cum/hour, the minimum at 0.0 cum/hour, and the average at 0.25 cum/hour (15 l/min) (oral communication by Mohammad Abu Taha, June 1986). In June 1986, the outflow from the cistern fed by the upper spring was calculated at roughly 10 l/min (0.6 cum/hour); in March 2001, the flow was approximately 1 l/min (0.06 cum/hour), but in April 2008, the soil was barely moist. In June 1986, July 1989, and July 2000, the lower spring was producing only a trickle of water. In March 2001, the outflow of the lower spring was measured as 5.3 l/min (0.33 cum/hour), and a significant overflow from the modern cistern was allowed to flow away down the hill. In April 2008, the discharge was about 3.6 l/min (0.216 cum/hour). In view of the effort expended to bring the water from these springs to ancient Humayma, it seems likely that their flow was somewhat greater in antiquity (see pp. 365–68). A light scattering of Nabataean and Roman common-ware sherds was observed in the area of the lower pool and the Via Nova.

Bibliography: Laborde 1830: 62; Maughan 1874: 194; Brünnow and Domaszewski 1904–9: 1, pp. 476–81; Musil 1926, II: 56–69; Glueck 1934–35: 65; Stein in Kennedy 1982: 274–77; Kirkbride and Harding 1947: 21–22; Eadie and Oleson 1986: 61–68; Oleson 1986, 1987a, 1988a–b, 1992a, 1995a, 1997.

3.B.2. *Aqueducts (Structure no. 1)*

Introduction

Three springs fed Humayma's aqueduct system (which has been catalogued collectively as Structure no. 1): 'Ain Ghana (Site no. 10), 'Ain al-Jammam (Site no. 6A), and 'Ain Sara (Site no. 6B) (fig. 1.1). Although 'Ain al-Jammam at present discharges the strongest flow, and its input into the Jammam branch of the aqueduct may have been augmented by 'Ain Sara, the archaeological and structural evidence indicates that the conduit from 'Ain Ghana to the settlement was the primary channel and was constructed first, probably toward the end of the first century BC or beginning of the first century AD. The Jammam branch may have been added later, perhaps up to a century after the original construction phase (see discussion in Sections 7.B.2, 7.D.1). In any case, the conduit connecting 'Ain Ghana to Reservoir/Pool no. 63 in Humayma is treated here as a single structure, 18.888 km long, and the Jammam branch as a later addition, 7.620 km long. The description of each branch is organised around distance measurements from their respective sources.

Although details of construction and materials vary from point to point along the structure (especially on the Jammam branch), the general design of the aqueduct is standard for the entire system. The water was conducted in typical Nabataean stone conduits: marl or sandstone blocks (L ca. 0.95 m; W ca. 0.35 m; H ca. 0.36 m) with a longitudinal gutter for the water (usually W 0.11 m; 0.12 m deep) (e.g., fig. 3.14). The conduit blocks were laid end to end in a ground-level foundation of rubble framed by heavy pieces of rubble or partly trimmed blocks. The overall width of the structure ranged around 0.90 m. A single course of fist-sized stones was laid in mortar along the upper edges of the conduit block on either side of the channel to support the roughly trimmed cover slabs (figs. 3.28–29). Where the topography demanded it, long support walls or bridges supported the substructure (fig. 3.13, 3.32), and occasionally the water channel and foundation were carved into the bedrock (fig. 3.12, 3.21). Along most of the Jammam branch, inverted terracotta tiles were set into mortar within the water channel (fig. 3.46, 3.56). Although their origin as roof tiles is likely (see pp. 328–29), they are referred to as gutter tiles in the context of the aqueduct. For a detailed discussion of the construction, see pp. 386–96.

The author carried out a preliminary reconnaissance of the aqueduct system in 1983 and excavated a few soundings across the Ghana aqueduct in the last 2.0 km before its termination at Reservoir/Pool no. 63, and one across the Jammam branch 100 m upstream from its junction with the Ghana aqueduct (Eadie and Oleson 1986). In 1986, the entire course of the aqueduct was examined metre by metre by the author and a survey team consisting of Suleiman Farajat and Andrew Sherwood. We measured its course by means of a hand-pushed odometer wheel, taking levels and calculating slopes with a telescopic hand level, and surveying bearings with a pocket transit. Absolute elevations were determined by plotting the course of the aqueduct on the 1:25,000 topographical maps. These readings were supplemented with GPS readings in 2001. In the course of the 1986 survey, several intact sections of the aqueduct and several atypical ancillary structures or features were identified. These features were cleaned or excavated in 1987 (Probes H87–01–P01 to P07, Chapter 5). Unfortunately, we were unable to leave easily-seen, permanent benchmarks in place along the aqueducts. Leaving visible markers or even cleaning for photography and drawing resulted in nearly immediate total destruction of the adjacent structure by vandals looking for "Turkish gold." I left a few small incised distance marks for my own reference in 1986, but the best references are the GPS readings taken during a walk along the aqueduct in April of 2001, combined with the descriptions given below.

Bibliography: Laborde 1830: 62; Maughan 1874: 196; Brünnow and Domaszewski 1904–9: 1, pp. 476–81; Musil 1926: II, 56–69; Glueck 1934–35: 65; Stein in Kennedy 1982: 274–77; Kirkbride and Harding 1947: 21–22; Eadie and Oleson 1986: 61–68; Oleson 1986, 1987a, 1988a–b, 1992a, 1995a, 1997.

'Ain Ghana Aqueduct

The first 500 m of the aqueduct from the upper and/or lower spring have been lost, but the present arrangement of modern cisterns and channels around the upper and lower springs and the presence of re-used conduit blocks in the intervening space suggest a possible course (see above, Site no. 10, 'Ain Ghana). Since the lower spring is smaller than the upper and there are no surviving ancient conduit blocks in its vicinity, it is possible that only the upper spring was connected to the aqueduct. Given the absence of any obvious excavated spring chambers or built boundary walls, it may be that the spring or springs used in antiquity discharged at slightly different locations than they do today. In any case, the elevation of the first surviving section of the aqueduct shows that the original source cannot have been lower than the present lower spring or pool. In the intervening space, 367 m from the upper spring, there is one possible stretch of aqueduct support wall on the valley slope, 20 m above a dirt road.

Km 0.511: The first clear traces of the aqueduct surviving *in situ* appear on a long, gentle slope south of the lower spring, 511 m from the upper spring; they consist of several marl conduit blocks (L 0.55 m; W 0.37 m; H 0.20 m; channel W 0.11 m, H 0.11 m) and traces of the framing structure. There is water-deposited concretion inside the channel to a height of 0.055 m, adhering directly to the stone. Slope back to upper cistern 7 degrees; to lower spring 3 degrees.

Km 0.840: More or less continuous remains of the aqueduct begin at this point, where a heavy stone foundation holding the rubble packing for the conduit blocks has been built up against a vertical outcropping of limestone.

Km 0.890: UTM 36R 0735298, 3324355. 1405 m asl. A bridge of slabs was built over a gully to carry the aqueduct. The channel has since been washed away, leaving the bridging slabs.

Km 0.945: The aqueduct crosses another gully on a slab bridge, immediately after which it skirts a limestone outcropping in a cutting; at this point the conduit channel has been cut into the bedrock (fig. 3.12). Beyond, the aqueduct descends at 40 degrees for 10 m; the sides and bottom of the conduit channel (again built of marl blocks) are covered with a thick layer of pillowy incrustation.

Km 0.962: UTM 36R 0735164, 3324291. A high wall (L ca. 9.0 m; W 1.0 m; H ca. 2.5 m) built of large, roughly squared limestone blocks (L ca. 0.5 m) carries the aqueduct around a limestone outcropping, buttressing it at the top of a steep slope (fig 3.13). The aqueduct descends slowly across the gently undulating slope, supported by a low, carefully built wall of roughly trimmed limestone blocks.

Km 1.088: Slope to upper spring 4.4 degrees; to lower spring 2.6 degrees; back to km 0.511, 2 degrees. The aqueduct continues descending slowly and evenly across the steep but generally unbroken hillside.

FIG. 3.12   *Ghana aqueduct km 0.945, conduit cut in bedrock.*

Km 1.311: UTM 36R 0735050, 3324091. At this point, landslips and rockslides have totally destroyed 50 m of the aqueduct, carrying the structure into the valley far below.

Km 1.366: The conduit channel (W 0.11 m; H 0.17 m) has been cut across a limestone outcropping; a thick layer of pillowy, water-deposited concretion covers the floor and sides of the channel to a height of 0.08 m. Just beyond the bedrock section, the channel (W 0.11 m; H 0.07 m) of a marl conduit block still *in situ* (L 0.75 m; W 0.34 m) is covered up to the top edge with concretions.

Km 1.436: UTM 36R 0734954, 3324083. 1395 m asl. The aqueduct crosses a support wall (L 20 m; H 2.10 m; Th ca. 1.0 m) built five courses high with roughly trimmed limestone blocks, designed to reinforce the aqueduct channel on the steep earth slope.

Fig. 3.13 *Ghana aqueduct km 0.962, high support wall.*

Km 1.458: 50 m of the aqueduct has been lost in a slide of boulders 5 m in diameter.

Km 1.503: Significant portions of the substructure in this area have been lost to land slips and rock slides. Slope back to upper cistern 3 degrees; to lower spring 2 degrees.

Km 1.561: The downhill support wall and the conduit blocks have slipped down the slope along this stretch, but the heavy blocks of the uphill framing wall have remained in position.

Km 1.638: UTM 36R 0734768, 3324073. 1397 m asl. The aqueduct has slipped down the slope, but many of the conduit blocks were accessible and several were measured: L 0.92 m, W 0.42 m, H 0.21 m, channel W 0.12 m, H 0.10 m; L 0.82 m, W 0.42 m, H >0.20 m, channel W 0.12 m, H 0.09 m (fig. 3.14). A thick layer of pillowy concretion extended up to the top of the channels on most of these blocks. Several first-century NPFW bowl sherds were found near the aqueduct.

Km 1.676: For approximately 240 m from this point the course of the aqueduct crosses an area of landslips and rock slides. Along this section, most of the conduit slabs are much shorter than those upstream (e.g. L 0.59 m, 0.52 m, 0.48 m; W ca. 0.32 m; H ca. 0.20 m, channel W 0.12 m, H 0.09 m) and are composed of the soft white sandstone typically used in the last 9 km of the aqueduct. Occasional conduit blocks of the yellow marl used for the upstream sections, however, continue to occur. It is likely that the channel had to be repaired on one or more occasions as a result of landslips that damaged the original structure, and that a suitable source of marl could not be located — most of the outcroppings of marl occur toward the top of the escarpment. Some economy of effort may also have resulted from using existing conduit blocks or nearby sandstone outcroppings. The reduction in length may have been forced by the lesser strength of the material used. Slope back to km 1.366 is 1 degree; to upper spring 3 degrees; to lower spring 2 degrees.

Km 1.711: UTM 36R 0734738, 3324130. 1389 m asl. The aqueduct plunges down the steep slope at this point (18 degrees), making a slight detour around

Fig. 3.14 *Ghana aqueduct km 1.638, displaced conduit blocks with incrustation.*

a projecting limestone crag at the bottom of the slope (fig. 3.3, 3.15).

Km 1.916: UTM 36R 0734675, 3324177. 1359 m asl. The slope levels off slightly (to 9 degrees), and the conduit blocks once more are cut from yellow marl. Bearing to the lower spring, 65 degrees. Elevation, ca. 1300 m. From this point until km 2.094, much of the course of the aqueduct has been lost in a great landslide that has exposed the subsurface bedrock, consisting of beds of red, pink, yellow, and white sandstone (Um Sahm Formation; fig. 3.16). Outcroppings of this stratum probably provided the material for the replacement conduit blocks of the previous section of the structure. The channel (W 0.11 m, H 0.12 m) cut into one of the conduit blocks preserved *in situ* (L 0.65 m; W 0.28 m; H 0.22 m) was almost completely obstructed by a pillowy water-deposit. Here, as elsewhere along the aqueduct, heavily concreted portions of the channel are interspersed with completely clear portions. This pattern might be the result of differential weathering of the concretions or the blocks on which they formed, or it may indicate clearing of portions of the structure where the flow had become obstructed, or differential rates of concretion in steeper or more level sections. Many of the marl blocks are well–preserved. Several blocks of

Fig. 3.15 *Ghana aqueduct km 1.915, view up slope to km 1.711.*

FIG. 3.16 *Ghana aqueduct km 1.500–2.200 (marked), distant view from north.*

concretion could be seen on the slope. They may have fallen from the conduits as they were knocked from position, or they may represent discards from the cleaning process. From 2.050 to 2.192 the aqueduct has a very gentle slope.

Km 2.192: UTM 36R 0734299, 3324295. 1318 m asl (fig. 3.1). The aqueduct curves around a large outcropping and ʿAin Ghana is briefly lost to sight. Bearing to ʿAin Ghana at the point of disappearance, 70 degrees. Direct line slope to the lower spring is 8.1 degrees; the average slope along the aqueduct to this point is 5.3 percent.

Km 2.249: Much of the aqueduct structure has slid down the hillside in this area, but several well-preserved sections are framed by walls built of roughly squared limestone blocks — two courses high for the uphill wall and one course for the downhill wall. From the top of the uphill wall to the base of the downhill wall the structure is 0.88 m high, with outside dimensions of ca. 1.84 m. The

conduit blocks are carefully trimmed (L 0.85–0.95 m; W ca. 0.33 m; H ca. 0.35 m; channel W 0.11 m, H 0.12 m).

Km 2.340: Approximately 60 m of the aqueduct have been lost to erosion or a landslip across a gully that now has been denuded of topsoil down to the white sandstone bedrock.

Km 2.423: A wide foundation trench was cut through an erratic limestone outcropping to support the aqueduct substructure. Slope back to km 2.192: 0.7 degrees.

Km 2.554: ʿAin Ghana reappears to view. The aqueduct substructure with framing walls is 1.4 m wide at this point.

Km 2.652: The aqueduct is well-preserved in this area, in part because it lies just above the sandstone bedrock, which provides significant support against slippage. In addition, there is a heavy substructure. The course zigzags in and out of small recesses. At

FIG. 3.17 *Ghana aqueduct km 2.652, view of conduit with course of cover-slab supports.*

FIG. 3.18 *Ghana aqueduct km 3.392, intact aqueduct structure above support wall of staggered blocks.*

several points a course of fist-sized, untrimmed pieces of sandstone (H ca. 0.05–0.10 m) survives, laid along the edges of the conduit blocks to support the cover slabs (fig. 3.17). The inside faces carry the same concretion that coats the interior of the channel, indicating that the channel was running beyond normal capacity.

Km 2.810: UTM 36R 0734102, 3324331. 1320 m asl (fig. 3.1). Bearing to 'Ain Ghana, 80 degrees; straight line slope back to lower spring, 3.5 degrees. Just after this point, 'Ain Ghana disappears from view for the last time as the aqueduct rounds a shoulder of Jebel Ghana in very broken ground. The bedrock visible where the surface soil has fallen or washed away is a white to purple soft sandstone, but enormous blocks of limestone that have eroded from higher strata lie scattered around the slope.

Km 2.974: UTM 36R 0733875, 3324304. 1320 m asl. Except for one or two short sections, approximately 60 m of the aqueduct have been lost down an enormous gully that has laid bare the purple sandstone. The Via Nova parallels the aqueduct, approximately 50 m below the landslip.

Km 3.307: The aqueduct crosses a gentler and less dissected slope, and the structure seems to be well-preserved beneath a layer of soil that has washed over it. Some possible limestone cover slabs (L ca. 0.80 m; W ca. 0.20 m; Th ca. 0.15 m) were found in the earth over the aqueduct, but none was *in situ*. A packing of small, flat stones (H 0.05–0.10 m) laid along the edges of the conduit blocks was observed at many points (UTM 3324243, 36R 0733657. 1310 m asl). In several places there were traces of a layer of mortar smoothed over the inside face of the packing stones to waterproof their joints with each other and with the conduit.

Km 3.392: UTM 36R 0733580, 3324188. 1296 m asl. A very solidly built wall supports the aqueduct as it circles the head of a gully: a levelling course of boulders supports heavy, roughly squared limestone blocks (L 0.60–1.40 m; H ca. 0.45 m) on which rests a course of thinner blocks (L 0.60–1.40 m; H ca. 0.25 m), set slightly back from the edge (fig. 3.18). The heavy framing blocks of the aqueduct (L ca. 0.60 m; H ca. 0.40 m; Th ca. 0.25 m) were laid on these slabs, set a further 0.20 m in from their

edge. The rough cover slabs seem to be in position along much of this section.

Km 3.536: Another well-preserved section of the aqueduct. Slope down to km 3.688, 4 degrees.

Km 3.617: UTM 36R 0733478, 3324188. 1298 m asl (fig. 3.1). The aqueduct turns a corner to the east, leaving the valley below the 'Ain Ghana and coming in sight of Humayma for the first time (straight-line distance to Reservoir/Pool no. 63, 11.300 km; bearing 217 degrees; slope from this point to destination ca. 3 percent. From here the aqueduct approaches the rolling, eroded floor of the plain below the al-Shara escarpment as it crosses some gentle slopes near the base of the escarpment.

Km 3.704: Along most of its course from the spring, the water channel in the aqueduct is covered with a layer of pebbly, water-deposited concretion that varies significantly in thickness, but is usually ca. 0.01–0.02 m thick. At some points, however, particularly where there are short stretches of aqueduct slightly steeper than the usual slope, the concretion nearly fills the channel cut into the conduit block. Presumably at these points the rows of small blocks along either edge of the conduit would have kept the water from overflowing. In addition, the greater velocity of the stream at these steep stretches diminished the volume per unit length, and thus the depth of the flowing stream. In these circumstances, the sinter could be allowed to build up to a greater height than on stretches of the aqueduct with a gentle slope, without causing an overflow. At km 3.704, the concretion fills the channel to the upper edges of the conduit blocks, except for a narrow runnel down the centre (fig. 3.19). The adjacent sections, however, seem to have been cleared out.

Km 3.827: Numerous flat sections of concretion were observed near the aqueduct. One had approximately 22 rings, alternating dark and light; Th 0.009 m (cf. Jammam Aqueduct km 1.779, 7.382).

Km 3.972: UTM 36R 0733290, 3323895. 1272 m asl (fig. 3.1). The course of the aqueduct begins to cross the steeper and more difficult slopes around the base of a ridge that projects from the southwest edge of Jebel Ghana. Over the next kilometre, the terrain consists of steep earthen slopes encumbered with large limestone and sandstone boulders that have fallen from the escarpment, alternating with smooth, eroded surfaces of the white sandstone bedrock. Stretches of the aqueduct footings up to 50 m long (as here) or shorter stretches of the water conduit itself are cut into bedrock.

Km 4.008: UTM 36R 0733310, 3323808. 1264 m asl. A long stretch of the aqueduct is built up on a cutting in the bedrock and carried over a small gully on a simple slab bridge with a span of 0.85 m. The limestone blocks are well squared but only roughly finished (fig. 3.20).

Km 4.212: The course of the aqueduct begins to wind in and out of the talus slopes at the foot of the escarpment and across occasional exposed faces of white sandstone bedrock (UTM 36R 0733412, 3323528. 1240 m asl). At several points there are long, tall support walls to carry the conduit, and one 50 m stretch of the aqueduct has been built on a shelf cut into the bedrock (fig. 3.21; UTM 36R 0733495, 3323436. 1225 m asl). The slope to km 4.591, at the edge of a projecting ridge, is 1.5 degrees. Between these two points, there are occasional "repair conduits" of hard red or soft white sandstone inserted in the series of marl conduit blocks; they tend to be shorter than the original marl blocks, with narrower side walls and wider,

FIG. 3.19 *Ghana aqueduct km 3.704, series of conduit blocks nearly filled with concretions.*

FIG. 3.20 *Ghana aqueduct km 4.008, bridge over gulley.*

FIG. 3.21   *Ghana aqueduct km 4.250, conduit cut in Disi sandstone bedrock; viaduct in distance.*

deeper channels (cf. fig. 3.22). One example measured L 0.69 m; W 0.33 m; H 0.25 m; channel W 0.15 m, H 0.14 m. At one point the aqueduct makes a sharp 130-degree bend, and the abutting ends of two conduit blocks have been cut to fit tightly at an angle joint.

Km 4.480: During the initial survey of the aqueduct, a well-preserved section of the conduit at this point was lightly cleaned and brushed for photography. In the course of this procedure, a small potsherd was observed incorporated into the mortar packing around a conduit block still in its original position. The sherd (Bucket 86.174.01; see fig. 5.6) was a fragment of the neck of a jug or steep-walled cup of NFW: sandy, reddish yellow (5YR 6/8) fabric with a few white inclusions and black sand temper; surface 5YR 7/6 (first or second century AD; K. Russell, personal communication, 1987; *EZ* II fig. 226, 100–25 BC, or fig. 224, 25 BC to AD 100). Since the background scatter of potsherds is very light along the aqueduct, and since this conduit seems to be in its original position, it is likely that this vessel broke during the construction process

and was incorporated in the structure at that time. The ceramic dating is not precise, but the parallels certainly allow a construction date in the late first century BC or early first century AD.

Km 4.756: UTM 36R 0733375, 3323295. 1226 m asl. A 5.0 m stretch of the aqueduct survives intact, including the cover slabs.

Km 5.048: The aqueduct is well down in the foothills, winding in and out along the gently sloping sides of the projecting ridges. Many of the marl conduit blocks are very badly fractured *in situ*, possibly either as a result of settling or of weathering. Some of the "repair conduits" of sandstone noted upstream may have been inserted to repair damage of this type. Slope back to km 4.759, 3.5 degrees. Reading at approximately km 5.400: UTM 36R 0733213, 3323225. 1229 m asl.

Km 5.547: In this area the aqueduct makes wide, smooth curves around the low ridges. One marl conduit block appeared to be larger than the typical examples in this area: L 1.07 m; W 0.29 m; H 0.25 m; channel, W 0.10 m, H 0.12 m. Reading

FIG. 3.22 *Ghana aqueduct km 5.822, possible repair conduits of red Umm Ishrin sandstone.*

FIG. 3.23 *Ghana aqueduct km 6.512, view of off-take tank and aqueduct junction structure, from the west.*

FIG. 3.24 *Ghana aqueduct km 6.512, aqueduct by-pass along southeast wall of off-take tank, from the east.*

at approximately Km 5.700: UTM 36R 0733178, 3322942, 1216 m asl.

Km 5.822: UTM 36R 0733336, 3322692. 1207 m asl. At a point 2 m downhill from the aqueduct at this point, four red sandstone conduit blocks with typical rough finish were lined up end to end parallel to the aqueduct (fig. 3.22). Since no sections of the aqueduct conduit were missing in the vicinity, these blocks may be spare repair conduits that turned out not to be needed and were left here for future use.

Km 5.942: UTM 36R 0733424, 3322594. 1207 m asl (fig. 3.1). A tall viaduct or bridge built of large, roughly squared limestone blocks carried the aqueduct across a small wadi (W 10 m); the maximum original height was over 3 m.

Km 6.072: UTM 36R 0733442, 3322435. 1205 m asl. A tall viaduct or bridge built of large, roughly squared limestone blocks carried the aqueduct across a small wadi (W 8 m); the maximum original height was over 2 m.

Km 6.512: UTM 36R 0733333, 3322822. 1202 m asl (fig. 3.1). The channel and foundations of the aqueduct have been lost 5 m upstream from the southwest wall of a large, shallow water tank (L 11.35 m; W 6.22 m; depth ca. 0.72 m; maximum water depth 0.63 m; cap. 44.5 cum) cut into the soft, white sandstone bedrock (fig. 3.23). The long axis of the tank is on a bearing of 45 degrees. At the north and south corners, the bedrock has been supplemented with two courses of carefully cut blocks of white sandstone (with diagonal surface trimming) supplemented at the base by rougher limestone blocks. Both the built and the rock-cut walls of the tank are lined with a thin layer of a hard, sandy, grey plaster. The original arrangements for filling the tank from the aqueduct have been lost, but there is no other source of water available, and a simple coincidence of location is unlikely. The aqueduct channel continued around the southeast side, built up on foundation blocks for the first 6 m, after which the marl conduit blocks were simply set into cuttings in the bedrock, 1.10 m outside the cistern (fig. 3.24). The by-pass conduit has been lost

Fig. 3.25 *Ghana aqueduct km 6.512, drain hole in northeast wall of off-take tank.*

Fig. 3.26 *Ghana aqueduct km 6.553, view of aqueduct junction.*

along the northeast wall, but the surviving down-stream portion angles toward the north corner of the tank before disappearing in a heap of earth. There is a niche (W 0.33 m, H 0.60 m, depth 0.20 m) in the centre of the northeast down-stream wall of the tank, with a drain hole (D ca. 0.07 m) cut into the base of its back wall (fig. 3.25).

The absence of both a proper run-off water catchment and settling basin make it very unlikely that this tank was excavated and used independently of the aqueduct. In addition, like the slightly larger tank at km 9.597, this one is too shallow to have been designed for long-term water storage, and it was not roofed. There must have been a sluice gate arrangement at the upstream end of the tank that allowed it to be filled from the aqueduct water as required, probably for the use of families camping in the area and their flocks. The aqueduct proper and its contents by-passed the tank on the by-pass conduit, rather than flowing through it, since the presence of an accessible open tank along the course of the aqueduct would have been an un-acceptable source of pollution and sediment. The drain hole was used to empty the tank of water to allow cleaning, or to drain out stale water before the tank was refilled. A similar off-take cistern can be seen along the Debdebah Aqueduct at Petra (al-Muheisen 1990: 208, pl. VII).

The question of whether the tank was added to the system some time after the initial construction project can no longer be answered. It is possible that the aqueduct initially passed directly across this sandstone shelf on its way to the junction and that the tank and by-pass conduit were added later, when rural groups claimed the right to draw on the flow of water. Excavation of the tank, however, would have destroyed any vestige of the original conduit. The construction technique and materials of the present by-pass conduit are identical to those of the rest of the aqueduct in this area, suggesting either a single construction phase or only a short delay between construction of the aqueduct and the addition of the tank. See the discussion of Cistern no. 20 at km 9.597.

A few sherds of NPFW bowls and NFW bowls of the first century AD were recovered from the sandy fill inside the tank. Beyond the tank, the aqueduct begins a sharp curve to the south, around the edge of a sandstone ridge. The Jammam branch joins the aqueduct 24.0 m beyond the inside down-stream face of the tank.

Km 6.553: UTM 36R 0733390, 3322293. 1201 m asl. The last 20 m of the Jammam branch descend steeply off the end of a long sandstone ridge and intersect the Ghana Aqueduct at a 90-degree angle (at km 7.620 from 'Ain al-Jammam; fig. 3.26). Unfortunately, the substantial structure originally built at the point of intersection was destroyed by vandals before 1981. The carefully cut white sandstone blocks and the rougher limestone blocks were pulled from position down to their foundation level, leaving a heap of blocks ca. 5 m across. One of the sandstone blocks carries careful diagonal surface trimming. The substantial foundation and framing courses of limestone blocks enter and leave this heap without any change in level, but the conduit blocks themselves have not survived in position. No provision for increased flow in the Ghana channel is discernible downstream of the junction.

In a situation such as this, where two gravity-flow channels intersect, the usual arrangement in the ancient world was to provide a small tank at the intersection, with an overflow relief outlet at a level slightly lower than the maximum level within the downstream conduit (Hodge 1992: 119–23). The overflow would simply have poured off into the sand to the southwest. The combined discharge of the three springs that were tapped is unlikely to have overloaded the aqueduct very often, but the potential for damage would have made caution essential.

No remains of such a basin can be identified at present, but the limestone blocks had been thickly smeared with a mortar, otherwise atypical of the aqueduct, that seems to contain ground-up potsherds as a pozzolanic admixture (Bucket 87.026). Visual inspection on site did not detect the potsherd admixture, but microscopic analysis in the laboratory revealed its presence (see Section 6.D.4). The mortar is very hard, medium weight, light grey in colour and heavily tempered with well-sorted, rounded sand micro-aggregate mixed with small, angular, poorly-sorted but well-mixed fragments of red terracotta; there are frequent large

FIG. 3.27   *Ghana aqueduct km 6.591, viaduct.*

FIG. 3.28   *Ghana aqueduct km 6.858, Probe 6. Aqueduct from the northeast after cleaning.*

lime lumps and bits of carbon and sandstone. This type of mortar, which is associated with Roman period remains in the settlement centre (see Section 6.D), may have had excellent hydraulic properties. Another sample of mortar from the structure (Bucket 87.025) did not contain any ceramic admixture, suggesting there may have been some differentiation of mortars within it. No large slabs of this material survive to suggest that it was used to line a water basin at the junction. Nevertheless, the quantity of blocks scattered around the site indicate that some sort of structure with a mass greater than the combined cross-section of the two aqueducts was built at this point. It may well have been a small basin of blocks lined with plaster that was inserted across the Ghana channel with an overflow out the downhill (right-hand) side; the foundation, walls, and roof could have produced the tumbled rubble seen today. No ceramics were observed in the area.

The overall slope to this point along the Ghana Aqueduct is 3.57 percent (234 m over 6.553 km). The aqueduct descends another 204 or 224 m in elevation (depending on the reliability of the GPS data) over the remaining 12.335 km of its length, for a slope of 1.65–1.82 percent; for the whole aqueduct from spring to reservoir, the slope is between 2.31–2.42 percent (436–458 m over 18.888 km). The slope of the Jammam branch is 2.85 percent (217 m over 7.620 km). The approximate equivalence in slope is striking, considering the very gradual descent along the last 6 km of the aqueduct system.

Km 6.591: The aqueduct crosses a gully on a viaduct of limestone blocks five courses high at the centre (fig. 3.27; max. H 1.65 m; W 0.75 m), but for the most part its course runs along gentle earth and bedrock slopes just below the top of the rolling ridges that descend toward the plain. The water-deposited concretion inside the channel adheres directly to the stone; there is no trace of the gutter tiles used in the Jammam branch. From this point on, until its termination at Reservoir/Pool no. 63, the aqueduct follows closely the divide between the watershed feeding the Wadi al-Gharid system that passes by Humayma and that feeding the Wadi al-Beida, which descends into the Wadi 'Arabah (fig. 1.1). The selection of this course was slightly

less direct than a straight line, but it avoided the heavily dissected slopes farther down each watershed — which would have required bridging — and ensured a constant, manageable slope down to the settlement. When the Bedouin decided in 1988 to bulldoze a road from Humayma up the escarpment past 'Ain al-Ghana, they followed the course of the aqueduct for the same reasons, occasionally destroying sections of it in the process.

Km 6.706: For the next 150 m, as the aqueduct descends the gentle slope near the top of the ridge, its structure is for the most part intact, including cover slabs.

Km 6.858: UTM: 36R 0733388, 3322044. 1191 m asl (fig. 3.1). Probe H87–01–P06 (Section 5.B.6) exposed the aqueduct and its interior (figs. 3.28–29). The total width of the structure, including the foundation blocks, is 0.98 m. The foundation and framing blocks together were only 0.17 m high. The conduit channel itself was 0.13 m wide and 0.12 m deep; a row of small blocks along both edges of the conduit added another 0.03 m to the depth. A thin (0.003 m) layer of a very sandy, white to grey mortar with occasional air bubbles and flecks of carbon (Bucket 87.27) was laid over the interior of the channel and up over the top of the subsidiary row of blocks. There was no evidence for the use of plaster to seal the roughly-trimmed cover slabs to the water channel. In cross-section, the thin (0.01 m) layer of concretion in the channel revealed only three "rings." No artefacts were recovered in the probe.

Km 6.937: Several of the marl conduit blocks are exposed (channel W 0.11 m; H 0.12 m). The water-deposited concretion is 0.006 m thick here, and it reaches 0.07 m up the sides of the channel.

Km 7.070: UTM 36R 0733329, 3321834. 1187 m asl. A box-like feature (L 0.47 m; W 0.35 m) was built of stone slabs against the east side of the aqueduct (fig. 3.30). Excavation of Probe H87–01–P07 (Section 5.B.7) indicated that it probably was constructed after the aqueduct had gone out of use, of materials salvaged from it. One body sherd from a NPFW bowl was recovered in the surface fill (Bucket 87.23.01; late 1st–early 2nd century). The slope back up the adjacent long, straight run of the aqueduct (bearing 210 degrees) is 3 degrees; the down-stream

FIG. 3.29   *Ghana aqueduct km 6.858, Probe 6. Aqueduct from the northwest after removal of cover slabs.*

FIG. 3.30   *Ghana aqueduct km 7.070, Probe 7. Box-like feature.*

FIG. 3.31 *Ghana aqueduct km 8.443, sharp curve.*

slope is 3 degrees; the slope along line of sight back to the point where the Jammam Aqueduct passes over the top of the escarpment is 7.5 degrees.

Km 7.609: UTM 36R 0733217, 3321319. 1164 asl (fig. 3.1). The aqueduct continues its slow descent, winding in and out of the heads of the gullies along the west side of the ridge, for the most part just below the crest. The slope back to the junction cistern by line of sight is 2.5 degrees; along the course of the aqueduct, the average slope back to the cistern is approximately 2.4 percent.

Km 8.035: UTM 36R 0733052, 3321234. 1160 m asl. The ridge between the two watersheds narrows, and the slope of the aqueduct decreases to ca. 1 percent. At this point, conduit slabs cut into the local white sandstone bedrock begin to predominate in the structure, probably because the marl beds along the escarpment were now too far away for economical transport of all the needed materials. Since some marl conduit blocks continue to appear as well, it is likely that work parties were sent in both directions. The sandstone conduit blocks seem on average to be 0.15–0.20 m shorter than

the marl blocks, probably because of the lesser strength of the material (e.g. L 0.76 m; W 0.40 m; H 0.38 m; channel W 0.12 m, H 0.11 m). The water-deposited concretion in the channel rises 0.08 m up the sides. One conduit block carved in very porous limestone was also observed in this area (L 0.55 m; W 0.34 m; H 0.28 m; channel W 0.12 m, H 0.13 m), with concretion rising 0.09 m up the sides of the channel. The discrepancies in material and proportions suggest that this may be some sort of repair block inserted in the aqueduct. A modern dirt road runs parallel to much of the aqueduct's course after this point.

Km 8.168: After a few smooth, wide curves, the aqueduct makes a long detour around a ridge. Much of the structure has been covered with blown sand in this area.

Km 8.443: The aqueduct makes a sharp (ca. 70 degrees) turn to the west to follow the ridge (fig. 3.31). The slope is very low here (ca. 1 percent), and the engineers obviously had to be careful not to lose height unnecessarily.

FIG. 3.32   *Ghana aqueduct km 8.534, remains of viaduct.*

FIG. 3.33   *Ghana aqueduct km 9.144, possible survey marks on conduit block.*

Km 8.534: UTM 36R 0732863, 3321053. 1154 m asl.
A long, tall viaduct (L 30.5 m; max. H ca. 4.0 m)
carried the aqueduct over a gully (fig. 3.32). Since
the gully drains a significant area, there was probably an opening in the central section of the wall
(which has been totally destroyed) to allow the flow
to pass through. It is conceivable that the opening was arched, but no voussoirs were observed
downstream from the structure.

Km 9.144: UTM 36R 0732509, 3320921. 1151 m asl.
Erosion has exposed a well-preserved cross-section
of the aqueduct at the head of a small gully. A
rough foundation of flat stones set in a very sandy,
crumbly grey mortar (Bucket 86.012) was laid directly on the sandy soil; this supported the conduit
slabs and conduit blocks, which are set very close
together without any extensive rubble packing. The
marl conduit blocks (L 1.0 m; W 0.36 m; H 0.21 m;
channel W 0.10 m, H 0.13 m) were very carefully
smoothed along their upper surfaces, which carried
a crowning course (H 0.07 m) of small, flat stones
set in a very sandy white mortar. Roughly-trimmed
cover slabs were laid over the crowning course. The
interior of the channel was lined with a sandy grey
plaster containing many carbon bits. A sample of
humates from the mortar provided a C14 date of 542
± 117 (see pp. 360–61). A thin (Th 0.006 m) layer of
water-deposited concretion extended up the sides
of the channel to the level of the crowning course.

Two geometric marks had been chiselled carefully into the west (downhill) edge of one of the
exposed conduit blocks before mortar was smeared
over it to hold the crowning course in place: a lozenge with two sharp ends and rounded sides (L 0.16
m; W 0.08 m) and an equal-armed cross (W 0.08
m; H 0.08 m) (fig. 3.33). Both marks are oriented
side-by-side along the direction of the channel. The
only other marks carved in this manner on conduit
blocks were found on the overflow conduit from
Reservoir/Pool no. 63, in Probes H87–63–P3, P11, and
P12, and those were of a different design. Although
the cross looks like a survey point, this stretch of the
aqueduct is tucked away at the head of a gully, with a
very restricted view. The marks may have indicated a
reference point along the course of the channel used
while laying out and levelling the conduit blocks,
subsequently covered by the packing stones and

cover slabs. Obviously, there may be many more
such marks along the aqueduct still concealed.

Km 9.597: UTM 36R 0732327, 3321143. 1151 m asl.
After a wide bend around a northward projecting
spur of the ridge, the aqueduct passes just below a
complex of cuttings and a large rock-cut tank (fig.
3.34). The entry and exit points of this system have
been disturbed, but the well-constructed by-pass
conduit of the aqueduct proper survives. This tank,
like the smaller version at km 6.512, was excavated
beside the aqueduct, and filled with water as necessary by means of a sluice gate system at the head of
the intake channels. The connection to the aqueduct was not recognised during the initial survey,
so the cistern and its feeder channel were given a
separate catalogue number (Structure no. 20). The
description, however, appears here.

The ridge is composed of white Disi sandstone,
with a light covering of sand and loess at the crest
and on the more gentle slopes. At a point 76.5 m
north (upstream) of the cistern intake (along the
rock-cut intake channel), a step 0.75 m wide has
been cut back into the gently sloping bedrock at
approximately the level of the aqueduct conduit (fig.
3.35). Unfortunately, only the aqueduct foundation
survives at this junction. From the back of the step,
which should be the footing for a block-built basin,
a rock-cut channel (W 0.11 m) zigzags for 9 m to
the south, then follows a straight course for 24 m
across the low ridge, its walls rising to a height of
ca. 0.30 m at the centre of the ridge as it slopes very
slightly towards the cistern. At the far side of this
cut, the intake conduit curves to the east along the
side of the hill, its channel still cut partially into the
bedrock along the base of a long shelf excavated
in the rock to accommodate added framing blocks
and cover slabs. The added structure around the diversion conduit has been completely lost from the
junction to a point 15 m north of the cistern; here, at
least the upper portion of the conduit channel and
the outside aqueduct framing blocks are composed
of sandstone blocks (W 0.80 m; channel W ca. 0.25
m, H >0.12 m) for a distance of 7 m. At a point 8.54
m north of the cistern, the channel is once again
completely cut into the bedrock, narrowing slightly
to 0.20 m as it approaches a sluice gate set into
two vertical slots 0.20 m outside the cistern wall

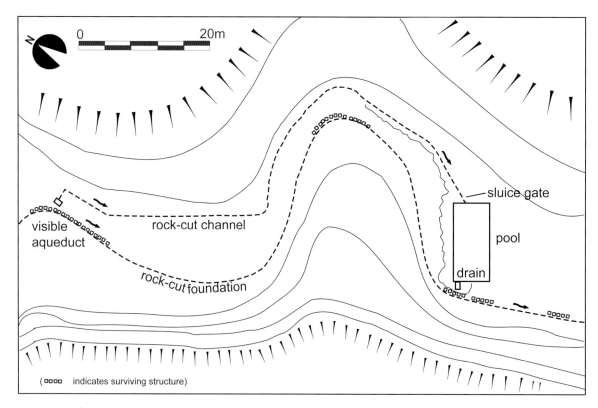

FIG. 3.34 *Ghana aqueduct km 9.597, off-take tank (Structure no. 20), plan of area.*

FIG. 3.35 *Ghana aqueduct km 9.597, off-take tank (Structure no. 20), view of diversion channel and general topography from the north.*

FIG. 3.36 *Ghana aqueduct km 9.597, off-take tank (Structure no. 20), view of feeder channel and tank from the north.*

(fig. 3.36). The sandstone sluice-gate block, which survives in position, has been cut through roughly with a chisel. It was probably intended to prevent run-off water intercepted by the long channel from entering the cistern. The channel enters the cistern at its northeast corner through a short cylindrical passage. There is another, roughly-cut and very eroded intake in the centre of the east cistern wall, possibly intended to funnel into the cistern run-off from the rock hillside that rises above it. Given the higher quality of the aqueduct water, this intake should date to some period after the aqueduct had ceased to flow.

The cistern (L 11.43 m; W 4.45 m; depth to bottom of intake channel 0.80 m; cap. 40.7 cum) has been cut neatly into the soft, white sandstone and lined with a very hard, sandy grey plaster containing a heavy admixture of sub-rounded quartz pebbles and possibly bits of pumice (Th 0.01 m). A small sherd of a NPFW bowl of Phase 3a (1st century) was found embedded in the plaster. Because of the slope, the south and east cistern walls are higher than the north and west walls, but the plaster extended to the top of the cutting on all four sides, well above possible water level.

The overflow or drain, at the northwest corner, unfortunately has been modified by ancient and recent activity (fig. 3.37). At the north end of the west wall an area of ca. 1 m square has been levelled. Below the levelled area, a square conduit (W 0.45 m; H 0.45 m) tunnels through 1 m of bedrock to emerge in a long, deep cutting (L 2.0 m; W 0.67 m), the floor of which has been excavated along the east/west centre line to form a water conduit (W 0.16 m; H 0.30 m). The floor of the cistern, of the passage through the cistern wall, and of the conduit are at the same level. At some later period, a square basin 0.20 m deep was cut across the floor of the outer passage, just outside the cistern exit, and lined with a plaster somewhat less pebbly than that inside the cistern itself. A single wide, deep, vertical slot was also cut into the south wall above the basin. The character of the tool marks clearly sets the basin and slot apart from the original building period. Finally, a mortared rubble wall was built across the outer part of the outer cutting not long before 1986.

Although it is badly damaged, the aqueduct can be traced along a path just below this system of cuttings and tank, following wide curves along the hillside. Short preserved sections can be seen just past the first junction, just below the entrance to the tank, and just past the outlet cutting. Along most of this line, the structure has been built on a narrow cutting in the bedrock. The aqueduct conduit passes immediately outside the west end of the discharge cutting, but its floor is 0.54 m higher than the floor of the adjacent rock-cut conduit carrying the tank outflow. Any water discharged from the tank must have flowed below the aqueduct channel.

It is clear that this cistern or tank, like that at km 6.512, was excavated as part of the original Ghana Aqueduct system or soon afterwards. There is no other viable source of water for the tank, there is no settling basin to clarify run-off water, and the tank is too shallow with respect to its length and width to have functioned effectively for long-term storage. The lack of a roof is also completely atypical for a storage cistern. Although the local Bedouin cleared out most of the silt and cemented up the outlet not long before the 1986 survey, and arranged some earth run-off conduits, it has not been observed holding any water whatsoever since then. Like the tank 3 km upstream, this one must have been constructed to allow access to the aqueduct water by groups living or pasturing flocks in the countryside. The sluice gate allowed filling from the aqueduct flow as needed, and the drain allowed stale water to be drained from the tank. As with the tank at km 6.512, it is no longer possible to determine whether the complex was excavated as part of the original phase of aqueduct construction or soon afterwards. At the point where the aqueduct and the discharge conduit of the tank would have intersected, the aqueduct conduit blocks meet at an awkward angle instead of as part of a smooth curve, suggesting that the present course of the aqueduct is not the original one. But this is not conclusive evidence. The construction technique and materials of the by-pass conduit itself are the same as those of the rest of the aqueduct in this area. Since the length and depth of this tank (L 11.43 m, W 4.45 m, depth 0.80 m) are close to those of the tank at km 6.512 (L 11.35 m, W 6.22 m, depth ca. 0.72 m) and the design is very similar, it is possible that both tanks are part of the same construction phase. Their capacities differ by less than 10 percent: 40.7 and 44.5 cum.

FIG. 3.37   Ghana aqueduct km 9.597, off-take tank (Structure no. 20), tank outlet with sluice gate from above. Tank is outside the bottom of the photo.

A small number of first-century and fifth/sixth-century cooking wares were recovered on the surface in the vicinity of the complex. Bucket 1990.07: 5 rim, 28 body; 10 MN, 22 LR or BY (oral communication, 1991, K. Russell, K. ʿAmr). Fifteen of the body sherds belong to a single fifth- to sixth-century cooking pot. At least four of the other sherds belong to the first century AD.

Km 9.798: Beyond Cistern no. 20, the aqueduct continues to descend very gradually as it winds in and out of depressions along the gently sloping north side of the ridge. At this point, a roughly semicircular feature (L 2.50 m; W 2.0 m) composed of one course of partly trimmed limestone rubble was visible adjacent to the uphill (east) side of the aqueduct structure. It serves no obvious hydraulic purpose, and cleaning in 1987 showed that it is simply a heap of rubble salvaged from the aqueduct, probably long after it ceased to function. It may be a collapsed cairn or the floor or base for some activity associated with a Bedouin encampment.

Km 10.333: A circular (D ca. 1.20 m) rubble feature similar to that at km 9.798 was built on the surface 1 m south of the aqueduct. The aqueduct structure is 0.88 m wide at this point; water-deposited concretions reach to the top of the surviving conduit blocks. Just past the circular feature, a well-preserved viaduct built of partially trimmed limestone blocks carries the aqueduct over a shallow gully (UTM: 36R 0732226, 3320366. 1170 m asl). A wide central opening was left for drainage.

Km 10.363: The slope by line of sight back to Cistern no. 20 is 0.5 degrees; the slope downhill to a point where the channel disappears around a ridge is approximately the same. The slope is very gradual along this portion of the aqueduct, since the engineers were trying to keep as close as possible to the high ground along the sinuous crest of the ridge.

Km 10.424: A fragment of a first- or early second-century NPFW bowl was found on the surface next to the aqueduct at this point. In this area a few sections of the aqueduct are intact, including the cover slabs.

Km 10.830: The aqueduct passes through fields of sandy loessial soil. In the late 1980s, they were planted with wheat or barley.

Km 10.881: UTM 36R 0731829, 3320206. 1163 m asl. The slope continues to be very gentle. Slope along the line of sight back to Cistern no. 20, ca. 1.5 degrees; back to 'Ain al-Jammam 3 degrees.

Km 11.107: UTM 36R 0731572, 3320364. 1148 m asl. As the aqueduct passes around a low rise, Humayma once again becomes visible, 7.51 km distant at a bearing of 224 degrees. The aqueduct makes an abrupt 45-degree bend to the west to avoid a deep gully. Although the angle is sharp, there is no extra buttressing at this point.

Km 11.526: UTM: 36R 0731142, 3320318. 1134 m asl. The aqueduct leaves the west end of the crest of the ridge and begins a series of zigzags down the

steeper slope in the direction of Humayma. The course continues to follow the watershed between the two main wadi systems, although the divide here is less well-defined than along the crest of the ridge. The slope of the first section down the ridge is 8 degrees; the slope to the centre of Humayma is approximately 1 degree.

Km 11.744: The aqueduct bends around an earth-filled hollow (L ca. 12 m; W ca. 10 m) in the sandstone bedrock. The nature of this feature is obscured by wind-blown sand, but several blocks were observed on the surface. Although these may have rolled down from the aqueduct structure, it is at least possible that there was a rock-cut cistern at this point supplemented by blocks. The fact that the Bedouin have not dug the soil out to expose a cistern for reuse, however, suggests that this depression is natural in origin.

Km 11.902: UTM 36R 0730861, 3320118. 1107 m asl. The aqueduct crosses a gully ca. 20 m across and ca. 8 m deep at its deepest point; there must have been a very solid bridging structure to carry the conduit, but it has completely collapsed and the blocks have been scattered down the slope by run-off in the wadi. The aqueduct then winds gradually down the gentle slope where the fringes of the ridge begin to meet the loessial plain around Humayma, often paralleled by the modern dirt road (which has destroyed several sections of it).

Km 12.473: UTM 36R 0730163, 3319931. 1089 m asl. The aqueduct bends slightly to the northwest to follow the line of the watershed, which brings it within 20 m of the steep-walled wadis at the head of the Wadi Jammam. The modern dirt road continues to parallel the aqueduct, and in 1989 a bulldozer destroyed approximately 500 m of the structure during roadwork.

Km 13.309: UTM 36R 0729526, 3319426. 1062 m asl. At this point the aqueduct leaves the stony badlands along the foot of the escarpment and enters the area of recent and probably ancient agricultural cultivation. The sandstone bedrock is buried more deeply here beneath sandy loessial soils that formed in an ancient lake bed. These deposits erode quickly in the vicinity of the main drainage channels, but elsewhere they form level fields that are today used

FIG. 3.38 *Ghana aqueduct km 13.400, elevated foundation; al-Shara escarpment in background.*

for grain cultivation when rainfall permits. From this point until the aqueduct reaches Humayma, it follows an extremely gentle gradient through mainly level fields, for the most part built on top of an earth or stone foundation ca. 1–2 m high (fig. 3.38). This slight elevation protected the conduit from ancient and modern traffic and agricultural activity, but its primary function probably was to level the course and thus preserve as much elevation as possible across a nearly level plain. The entire elevation seems to have been produced by a rubble support wall, but sand and earth have blown up against the structure, giving it the appearance of a long, narrow mound.

Km 13.411: The modern dirt road crosses the aqueduct and remains on its west side for 3.6 km, as far as the modern Wadi Gharid crossing 1.885 km north of Reservoir/Pool no. 63. Traces of the Via Nova paving can be seen 10 m northwest of the aqueduct, paralleling its course.

Km 13.472: Traces of the Via Nova are also visible here, 16 m northwest of the aqueduct. Cistern no. 21 is located midway between the two ancient structures.

Km 13.716: In the vicinity of a recent Bedouin cemetery, the aqueduct and the Via Nova approach within 3 m of each other.

Km 13.912: UTM 36R 0728604, 3318041. 1044 m asl. The steep earth slopes of the wadis feeding the Wadi al-Hilwa reach within 20 m of the aqueduct. The course seems to bend away slightly to avoid the wadi, but the danger was probably much less imminent at the time of construction.

Km 13.985: UTM 36R 0729141, 3319637. 1034 m asl. Cistern no. 22 is located 1 m southeast of the aqueduct (see p. 125).

Km 14.478: The slope continues to be very gentle, and from this point onward, the GPS readings of elevation (generally less accurate than the X and Y coordinates) are not accurate enough to allow calculation of the aqueduct slope on their own. They are given nevertheless, for the sake of reference, but in quotation marks. The structure of the aqueduct proper remains the same, although conduit blocks of white sandstone occasionally replace those of yellow marl. Although the sandstone has almost always disintegrated badly, one moderately well-preserved block was found (L 1.06 m; W 0.31 m; H n/a; conduit W 0.09 m, H n/a). On these blocks, the conduit channel seems to have been coated with a crumbly grey plaster, probably intended as waterproofing. The foundation of the conduit and framing blocks is very well-preserved in this area. It was built with a facing of partly trimmed limestone blocks framing a rubble core (W 0.80 m).

Km 15.410: A columnar Roman milestone with square base was dug out of the field northwest of the aqueduct at some time before it was noticed by D. Graf in 1983 and set upright near the modern dirt road. The paving of the Via Nova itself, however, has disappeared. No traces of an inscription (which may have been painted on) could be seen on the milestone, which had itself disappeared by March 2001.

Km 16.378: The aqueduct is lost in a steep-sided tributary of the Wadi al-Hilwa, 25 m wide. The Nabataean engineers apparently anticipated trouble from erosion in this area, because the aqueduct deviated sharply to the south, attempting to avoid the unstable area by passing around the east and south sides of a low limestone hill adjacent to the Wadi al-Amghar. Beginning of deviation, UTM 36R 0727841, 3317057. 1020 m asl.

Km 16.593: UTM 36R 0727789, 3317597. The aqueduct foundation is cut into the limestone bedrock of the steep east slope of the hill, 2.5 m above the present sandy wadi bed. Stein felt that the Roman road passed through a slight cutting in the top of this hill (Stein in Gregory and Kennedy 1985: 327). In the late 1990s, a modern road was bulldozed over the top.

Km 16.688: The remains of a circular lime kiln cut into the limestone can be seen just below the course of the aqueduct (D 2.5 m). In Eadie and Oleson

1986: 70 this feature was identified as a well-head, but clearing subsequently revealed burn marks and a stone floor.

Km 16.892: The aqueduct swings around the south end of the hill and heads WSW towards Humayma, steering dangerously close to the Wadi al-Hilwa feeders in an attempt both to keep to higher ground and to avoid the Wadi al-Amghar.

Km 17.005: Approximately 25 m of the aqueduct have been swallowed up by a steep-sided gully feeding the Wadi al-Hilwa. An additional 50 m of the channel have been lost to ploughing on the far side of the gully. At this point, the low earth ridge separating the gullies feeding the Wadi al-Hilwa and the main course of the Wadi al-Amghar is only 32 m across and is being actively eroded from both sides. Once the ridge is breached, the Wadi al-Amghar will be diverted into the other watershed, significantly altering the hydrology of the lower half of the Humayma catchment.

Km 17.154: UTM 36R 0727538, 3317129. "995 m," "1014 m" asl. From this point until 81 m before it reaches Reservoir/Pool no. 63, the aqueduct follows a bearing of 225 degrees and is built on a low rise, with grain fields to its west and the modern dirt road to its east (fig. 3.39). Most of the conduit blocks have been carved from white sandstone and have nearly disappeared through weathering. From this point until it reaches the reservoir, the slope of the aqueduct channel is very shallow, approximately 1 percent.

Km 18.064: UTM 36R 0726926, 3316492. "992 m," "1009 m" asl. The aqueduct crossed a depression on a viaduct built of large, partly trimmed limestone blocks, which have since been washed down the gully.

Km 18.273: UTM 36R 0726797, 3316351. "984 m" asl. The structure has been completely destroyed by ploughing in this area, including the point (somewhere around km 18.489) where a branch conduit diverted some of its flow to Reservoir no. 62 in the Roman fort. Laborde (1830) saw the branch in 1828, and Stein's account may suggest that part of this branch line was still visible during his visit in 1939 (Stein in Gregory and Kennedy 1985: 325).

FIG. 3.39 *Ghana aqueduct km 17.500, view of aqueduct foundation and Jebel Qalkha in background. Wheat grows in the field to right.*

Km 18.674: UTM 36R 0726545, 3316027. "978 m asl." The aqueduct makes its closest approach to the northwest corner of the fort (fig. 2.14).

Km 18.784: Site of Probe H83–01–P01 (see Eadie and Oleson 1986: 66, fig. 23).

Km 18.837: UTM 36R 0726445, 3315942. "979 m," "999 m" asl. A heap of blocks found scattered on the surface at this point in 1983 revealed the presence of a major structure on the course of the aqueduct that had recently been destroyed by treasure hunters. Tipped over in the centre of these blocks were the remains of a large sandstone basin with traces of several water channels cut through its walls (fig. 3.40), originally built out of four blocks. The one surviving block (L 0.72 m, W 0.32 m, H 0.58 m) preserves one-quarter of the flat-bottomed central basin (D ca. 0.30 m) and two channels. An upper channel (W ca. 0.12 m) conducted water into the basin 0.20 m above its floor; a lower channel with a threshold 0.08 m above the floor of the block

FIG. 3.40 *Ghana aqueduct km 18.837, remains of a distribution basin.*

FIG. 3.41   *Ghana aqueduct km 18.888, junction with Reservoir/Pool no. 63.*

conducted water away from the basin. There is a thin, water-deposited layer of calcium carbonate on the wall of the basin between the two conduits. Parallels elsewhere in the region — particularly on the ʿAin Brak aqueduct at Petra (fig. 8.5) — suggest that this was a water distribution basin, what the Romans termed a *castellum aquae* or *dividiculum*. The term *castellum divisorium*, frequently used in modern discussions, has no basis in ancient literature. Presumably, the upper channel received the flow of the aqueduct, a portion of which could then be distributed among several conduits, while the remainder continued on to Reservoir/Pool no. 63 (see the discussion in Section 7.D.2). This location on the edge of a bluff, just before the aqueduct emptied into Reservoir/Pool no. 63, would have been an appropriate spot for diverting water to channels of pipes leading elsewhere in the site. At this point, the aqueduct bearing changes from 225 degrees to 190 degrees, which it follows until reaching the reservoir.

Km 18.847: Clandestine digging has exposed the foundation of the aqueduct, built of carefully shaped blocks of red sandstone with fine diagonal surface trimming. The foundation is 0.85 m wide.

Just below the level of the aqueduct, 10 m to the west of this point, clandestine diggers have totally destroyed some sort of hydraulic structure, probably a cistern. There is now only a heap (ca. 5 × 5 m) of red sandstone blocks, most of which have on one side a coating (Th 0.03 m) of a very hard, sandy, pink plaster containing ground-up potsherds.

Km 18.888: UTM 36R 0726433, 3315856. "977 m" asl. 965 m asl. The aqueduct passes over the centre of the north lip of Reservoir/Pool no. 63. The last two metres of the structure fortunately were quite well-preserved at the time of excavation in 1983 (fig. 3.41; Eadie and Oleson 1986: 59–61). Carefully trimmed blocks of white sandstone framed the typical marl conduit blocks. Fist-sized pieces of white sandstone rubble were set in a bedding of a friable grey mortar along either side of the conduits to carry the cover slabs. One cover slab was preserved at this point, a flat slab of white sandstone possibly salvaged from a conduit block. The bearing from the reservoir junction direct to ʿAin al-Jammam is 54 degrees, the straight line distance 14.2 km, the slope over that line 3.1 percent. Given the length of the winding course between the Jammam spring and the reservoir, the overall slope of the water channel itself is only 2.2 percent. The overall slope along the water channel from ʿAin Ghana, which is not visible from this point but is at a bearing of 43 degrees, is nearly identical at 2.3 percent. The straight line distance, 13.5 km, is slightly less than the distance to ʿAin al-Jammam, but the slope over that line, too, is nearly identical at 3.2 percent.

Excavation at the outlet of Reservoir/Pool no. 63 (Section 5.E) revealed that the aqueduct continued at least 100 m to the south, perhaps providing water to a possible Nabataean bath building and definitely supplying the Roman Bath (E077). Stein states that during his visit in 1939 he was able to trace the conduit for another "300 yards" to a cistern smaller and more poorly constructed than no. 63 and beyond it into a field (Stein in Gregory and Kennedy 1985: 325). This second cistern may be Reservoir no. 67, but the description is ambiguous.

ʿAin al-Jammam Aqueduct

Km 0.000: UTM 36R 0737939, 3323626. 1418 m asl. ʿAin al-Jammam (figs. 3.1–4). The arrangements for pooling water in the spring cave (see pp. 65–68) have been lost, along with the first 0.582 km of the aqueduct. Ancient marl conduit blocks can be seen scattered on the ground along the probable course of the aqueduct through the modern gardens, and some are even reused in the modern irrigation system. Judging from the topography, the course of the main modern irrigation channel probably follows the same line as the ancient aqueduct.

Km 0.091: Several complete and broken ancient marl conduit blocks could be seen in 1986 tumbled down the slope below the modern conduit. Sample dimensions: L 0.74 m, W 0.34 m, H 0.20 m, channel W 0.12 m, H 0.12 m; L 0.69 m, W 0.36 m, H 0.30 m, conduit W 0.12 m, H 0.11 m.

Km 0.116: Six to ten broken conduit blocks can be seen in the vicinity of the modern channel.

Km 0.185: Several conduit blocks have been reused as part of a branch of the modern system.

Km 0.282: The modern cement conduit curves downhill to the east, to the level of the ʿAin Sara, where it becomes an earth channel.

Km 0.385: A gully has been eroded in the hillside across the probable course of the aqueduct, but no trace of it appears in the section.

Km 0.489: UTM 36R 0737610, 3323111. 1425 m asl. The outflow of the ʿAin Sara (see pp. 68–69) is carried to the garden in an earth channel. The earth channel gives out at km 0.527.

Km 0.585: The first short preserved section of the ancient conduit and foundation wall appears on the southwest edge of a ploughed field.

Km 0.650: Occasional short sections of the aqueduct are preserved across a sloping earth field, just above the limestone ledge that caps the precipitous slopes of Jebel Ghana. At one point, where the whole foundation appears to be preserved, the total width of the structure is 0.80 m; farther on, a well-preserved section is 1.10 m wide.

Km 0.773: The structure is well-preserved in this area, revealing for the first time that gutter tiles (similar to cover tiles for roofing) had been set into the channel. The tiles carry a very heavy layer of water-deposited calcium carbonate, 0.015 m thick at their upper edges, much thicker below. In some cases, the tiles are almost completely filled with concretion. The marl conduit blocks were set in a packing of small sandstone, limestone, and marl rubble mixed with a white mortar, which was also smeared around and above the flat stones used as a capping course. A small potsherd, possibly first- or second-century NFW, was found set in the mortar.

Km 0.790: UTM 36R 0737383, 3323180. 1417 m asl. The structure has been destroyed by an erosion gully.

Km 0.823: At this point the structure once again disappears in a gully, and on the far side it has been reinforced by a foundation course of large limestone blocks forming a platform 1.34 m wide, on which the framing blocks (H 0.32) for the conduit were set.

Km 0.934: UTM 36R 0737304, 3323120. 1415 m asl. The aqueduct plunges through a natural crevice in the limestone outcrop (directly below the modern electric transmission lines) and descends 2.5 m to its base, at a slope of 20 degrees. From this point

FIG. 3.42 *Jammam aqueduct, km 1.181, Probe 5. Support wall for aqueduct and settling tank.*

the line of sight slope back to 'Ain al-Jammam is 1.2 degrees.

Km 0.993: The aqueduct continues along just below the limestone outcropping, built on a solid foundation of blocks. The marl conduit blocks have been exposed, and in most cases the gutter tiles set into them have been removed, but the mortar packing in which they were set reveals their presence. Sample conduit block dimensions: L 0.70 m, W 0.33 m, H 0.21 m, channel W 0.12 m, H 0.11 m; L 0.82 m, H 0.22 m, W 0.33 m, channel W 0.115 m, H 0.12 m.

Km 1.118: UTM 3323113, 36R 0737110. 1415 m asl. In this area, the aqueduct runs just above another limestone outcropping, and the conduit channel is occasionally cut into the bedrock. The framing blocks and rubble were set into a loose grey mortar containing many carbon specks.

Km 1.177: The conduit runs just below the upper edge of the outcropping; the foundations for the conduit channel occasionally were cut into the bedrock and elsewhere were carried on dry-stone support walls.

Km 1.181: UTM 36R 0737090, 3323125. 1419 m asl (fig. 3.1). At this point, a 3.5 m high support wall of partly trimmed rubble set in a very powdery grey mortar supported the aqueduct channel and a basin or settling tank built of large, partly trimmed limestone slabs. The high support wall, which fills in a gap in the limestone outcropping, was provided with a large drain (H 0.45 m; W 0.42 m) to allow the release of water behind it (fig. 3.42). The aqueduct has itself fallen away at this point, but a portion of the tank survives on the north (uphill) side. The area was cleaned and drawn (figs. 3.43–44; see Probe H87–01–P05; Section 5.B.5). A circular retaining wall or curb (D 1.80 m), carefully built of partly trimmed limestone slabs, framed a rectangular basin built of limestone slabs. Half of the basin has been lost, but it was 0.76 m long and more than 0.50 m wide; the depth below the conduit was at least 0.30 m (cap. >114 l). The curb and basin slabs were set in a packing of cobbles with a small amount of lime mortar or mud. The basin itself was reinforced and waterproofed with the same grey mortar and white plaster found in the other probes along this stretch of aqueduct. No potsherds were recovered in the scant surface fill. The highly inconvenient

Fig. 3.43 *Jammam aqueduct, km 1.181, Probe 5. View of aqueduct and tank from southeast.*

Fig. 3.44 *Jammam aqueduct, km 1.181, Probe 5. View of tank from above.*

Fig. 3.45 *Jammam aqueduct, km 1.768. Probe 1 after surface cleaning.*

location reinforces the interpretation of this feature as a settling tank rather than a draw basin. See below km 1.779, 1.951, 2.259, and 2.497.

From this point, the slope to where the aqueduct disappears around a bend several hundred metres away is very slight, approximately 1 degree.

Km 1.359: UTM 36R 0736988, 3323241. 1418 m asl. The aqueduct passes around the head of a gully, just above the cliff, carried on a bridge constructed of three limestone slabs placed end-to-end supported on upright blocks; each span is approximately 0.70 m. The width of the aqueduct structure at this point is 0.90 m, and the conduit slabs are 0.89 m long.

Km 1.402: At this point, a short stretch of the conduit is cut into the limestone bedrock.

Km 1.484: A very neatly built substructure of mortared limestone blocks supports the aqueduct. Soon afterward, the topography begins to level off, as the aqueduct descends gradually across a gently sloping hillside of earth and sandstone scree, winding in and out of wide, shallow gullies. At several points the structure has been entirely covered with

earth washed down the slope, ensuring excellent preservation.

Km 1.768: UTM 36R 0736705, 3323181. 1415 m asl. A probe was dug (see H87–01–P01, Section 5.B.1) across a completely preserved section of the aqueduct, located on a wide, gentle earth slope (figs. 3.45, 5.1). The probe was intended to clarify the design and construction of the aqueduct and to provide ceramic evidence for the date of construction. As expected, the probe revealed that the aqueduct was composed of the typical marl conduit blocks (L ca. 0.95 m; W 0.34 m; H 0.36 m) set in a packing of rubble mortared with a soft, grey mortar and framed on either side by larger, but only partly trimmed blocks of limestone (fig. 3.45). These blocks were laid directly on the undisturbed soil, with only a few cobbles to assist levelling. A line of fist-sized cobbles packed in the same grey mortar was laid along both top edges of each conduit block, framing a terracotta gutter tile set in mortar in the channel itself (fig. 3.46). For a discussion of these tiles, see pp. 328–30, 1986.001.01–02. The narrow downstream end of each tile was set into the wide

Fig. 3.46 *Jammam aqueduct, km 1.768. Probe 1 after removal of two cover slabs.*

Fig. 3.47 *Jammam aqueduct, km 1.779, Probe 2. Settling tank after excavation, from the east.*

upstream end of the tile next in line. A coating of hard, white plaster was applied to the interior surface of the tiles and smoothed over the transition to the rubble packing above and to either side of the conduit blocks. The V-shaped water channel is 0.20 m deep, but water-deposited concretions extend only 0.08–0.10 m up the sides. The capping slabs, for the most part minimally trimmed slabs of limestone and sandstone with one flat surface, placed face-down over the channel, were set on the upper plaster surface. Their outer edges were sealed with a hard white plaster with very little sand temper.

The surface loci contained a rich collection of Middle Nabataean, Roman, and Byzantine coarse wares, while the foundation loci, including sherds imbedded in the mortared rubble, contained only Middle Nabataean wares, consistent with a construction date in the first century BC or AD. Even the surface collection suggests that the aqueduct was already in place by the Middle Nabataean period, since there is no other structure in the vicinity, and no stimulus for the concentration of sherds in this area other than the presence of the aqueduct. The slopes above and below the channel are devoid of pottery. Although there were apparently no off-take basins along this stretch of the aqueduct, individuals who had drawn water at the springs, or who were simply walking toward Humayma or the lower slopes of the escarpment, may have followed a convenient path along the gently sloping course of the aqueduct.

Km 1.779: UTM 36R 0736682, 3323171. 1413 m asl (fig. 3.1). The aqueduct follows the slope around to the southwest and at km 1.779 crosses a settling tank surrounded by a circular limestone curb. The intact structure was swept for photography in 1986, apparently exciting the interest of vandals, who dug into the centre of the installation during the following winter, everting many of the basin wall blocks and totally destroying the stratigraphy. Despite this damage, a probe (H87–01–P02, Section 5.B.2) clarified the design (figs. 3.46–47, 5.3). The structure consists of a well-built circular (D 2.15 m) curb constructed of regular limestone blocks framing a central tank built of limestone slabs, 0.80 m square and about 0.60 m deep below the incoming

conduit channel (cap. ca. 384 l). This is the largest and most heavily built of the settling tanks. See above, km 1.181; below, km 1.951, 2.259, 2.494.

The space between the curb and the outside of the basin walls was filled with cobbles set in a very soft, dark grey mortar filled with lumps of unslaked lime and flecks of carbon. A carbonised twig in the mortar provided a C14 date of 171 ± 39 (see pp. 360–61). The outflow channel, although badly disturbed, seems to have been set at the same level as the intake channel. Where it passes under the curb and into the tank, the intake channel lacked the inset tiles typical of the Jammam Aqueduct, but there was a very thin (0.004 m) layer of white mortar around the surface of the water channel (fig. 3.48). At this point, the conduit was almost completely obstructed by calcium carbonate deposit, which had formed in long, undulating strands, similar to spaghetti, oriented in the direction of the current. A close inspection of a cross-section of these deposits revealed that they had formed around tiny strands of grass or algae growing inside the conduit at this point, leaving behind central holes approximately the diameter of a human hair. The deposits had built up to a thickness of 0.03–0.04 m by the time the conduit stopped functioning, leaving only a cross-section of 15 square centimetres for water to pass (fig. 5.3). No stones suitable as cover slabs were identified, and the presence of algae growing in the conduit suggests that — at the last stage of aqueduct use, at least — the basin was open to light and air. No intact deposits were excavated, but the sherds scattered on the surface around the structure all dated to the Middle Nabataean, Roman, and Byzantine periods. A piece of tile found on the surface near the tank carried a layer of concretion 0.015 m thick; approximately 22–25 alternating dark and light layers could be counted (cf. Jammam km 7.382; Ghana Aqueduct km 3.827). For the function of this structure, see the discussion in Section 7.D.

Km 1.808: The aqueduct continues to wind in and out along the hillside in gentle curves and at this point crosses a gully on a viaduct (L 13.7 m, H 4.0 m) built of courses of limestone blocks 0.50 m square, arranged as headers about 1.5 m downhill from the channel. Some time around 1995, the viaduct was

FIG. 3.48 *Jammam aqueduct, km 1.779, Probe 2. Interior of settling tank from southwest.*

FIG. 3.49: *Jammam aqueduct, km 1.951, Probe 3. Settling tank after excavation and removal of cover stone, from the southeast.*

Fig. 3.50 *Jammam aqueduct, km 2.394, viaduct.*

covered with spoil from road construction. From this location back to the tank at km 1.779, there is no trace of tiles in the conduit, and sinter appears directly on some of the conduit blocks. Beyond this gully, the aqueduct passes along a gently sloping hillside, slightly higher and well away from the cliffs at the edge of the escarpment.

Km 1.951: At this point, the channel again crosses what appears to have been a small settling basin built of limestone slabs (L 0.52 m; W 0.33 m; depth below intake 0.30 m; cap. 51 l) set in a grey mortar and water-proofed with a hard white plaster (fig. 3.49). The conduit blocks originally were built into the east and west walls of the tank, but this connection has been damaged and lost. Only a few Middle Nabataean or Early Roman sherds were recovered from the fill in the tank (H87–01–P03, p. 238), along with a limestone slab that might have served as the cover. The strata around the exterior have been lost to erosion. This installation clearly is much smaller in scale and far more flimsy than the basins at km 1.181 and 1.779, but its function may have been much the same. There are similar basins at km 2.259 and 2.494. This basin could not

be relocated in March 2001 and may have been destroyed by road construction around 1995.

Km 2.118: A slab bridge carries the aqueduct across the head of a gully.

Km 2.181: On a section of the slope where much of the conduit has disappeared because of erosion, several white sandstone conduit blocks have been substituted for the typical marl conduits. The sandstone could have been quarried at a slightly lower level along the hillside and may have been used to repair sections damaged in antiquity. One well-preserved example measured L 0.83 m; W 0.42 m; H 0.23 m; conduit W 0.11 m, H 0.11 m.

Km 2.259: UTM 36R 0736470, 3322946. 1411 m asl. A heap of flat stone slabs 1.5 m in diameter lies across the course of the aqueduct, possibly marking the site of another settling tank or draw basin. The feature is positioned at the very centre of a spur of the jebel, at the edge of the bluff.

Km 2.394: UTM 36R 0736360, 3322979. 1409 m asl. At this point a massive viaduct (L 21 m; W 0.80 m; max. H > 2.0 m) carried the aqueduct across a gully (fig. 3.50).

FIG. 3.51 *Jammam aqueduct, km 2.494, Probe 4. Settling tank after cleaning, from the east.*

FIG. 3.52 *Jammam aqueduct, km 4.918, channel in rough terrain.*

Km 2.494: UTM 36R 0736289, 3322938. 1410 m asl. Several marl conduit blocks have been torn out of the aqueduct and lie scattered across the slope, revealing that they vary significantly in length: L 0.71 m, 0.81 m, 0.85 m, 0.93 m. The width of the channel, however, is always 0.11–0.12 m. Just beyond is a group of large slabs 1.8 m across, roughly circular on the exterior and framing a rectangular, plaster-lined settling basin (0.50 × 0.44 × > 0.20 m, cap. > 44 l) with a heavy limestone cover slab (0.78 × 0.50 × 0.15 m) tipped inside (fig. 3.51). Cleaning and partial excavation (H87–01–P04, Section 5.B.4) revealed that the tank was constructed of partly trimmed slabs of limestone set in a soft grey mortar. A few Middle Nabataean and Roman sherds were recovered from the fill. Although smaller and not as carefully built, this feature appears to be similar to the settling basin excavated at km 1.779, for it straddles the channel and some of the slabs still in position seem to have been trimmed to a circle on the exterior. It is located where the conduit makes a sharp outward bend around a low ridge.

The cover slab, if correctly identified, is far too heavy to have been intended for frequent, routine removal to access the water, reinforcing the interpretation of these features as settling tanks. Although this tank is smaller than the one exposed in Probe 2, the heavy framing is similar and suggests that it too belongs to the original phase of construction. Compare the tanks at km 1.181, 1.951, 2.259. The curbing around the basin at km 1.181 has the same diameter.

Km 2.681: UTM 36R 0736200, 3322796. 1413 m asl (fig. 3.1). The bearing to the Jammam spring is 79 degrees, 1.80 km, and the cumulative slope along the conduit just under 2 percent.

Km 2.899: UTM 36R 0735991, 3322787. 1410 m asl. The conduit turns inward and crosses the foot of a gentle valley that leads up to the col on the ridge leading to Jebel Ghana. There are a few sherds of gutter tiles along this stretch of the aqueduct, but none in position in the conduit.

Km 3.051: UTM 36R 0735957, 3322856. 1403 m asl. The soil is a very unstable yellow clay that has slipped and carried the conduit channel out of position. At this point, there is a well-built viaduct

(L 10.5 m, H 0.80 m) with three or four slab bridges that left openings for water to pass through, possibly because the engineers suspected the instability of the soil during periods of run-off. Along this stretch of aqueduct, gutter tiles have been placed in the conduit and carefully plastered over along the top edge.

Km 3.300: UTM 36R 0735949, 3323119. 1403 m asl. A viaduct 10 m long with two slab bridges to allow drainage carried the conduit across a depression 4 m deep.

Km 3.607: UTM 36R 0735862, 3323292. "1417" m asl (fig. 3.1). A viaduct 30.5 m long and 1.60 m wide carried the conduit across a depression 8 m deep. Only the footings at either end are left, but the structure must have been at least 8 m high.

Km 3.982: UTM 36R 0735480, 3323385. 1410 m asl. The conduit in this area is very badly damaged and in some places entirely lost, possibly through erosion.

Km 4.100: UTM 36R 0735296, 3323436. 1409 m asl. The aqueduct winds in and out of little ridges, and many sections have been destroyed through erosion or landslips. Complete and fragmentary gutter tiles are scattered everywhere.

Km 4.267: UTM 36R 0735246, 3323365. 1407 m asl. Very rough terrain with scattered boulders. A 50 m section of the conduit has been lost into a gully through erosion or landslips. Gutter tiles were set into the conduit.

Km 4.542: The conduit passed across the head of a steep valley, but all traces have been lost to erosion.

Km 4.918: UTM 36R 0735076, 3323294. 1410 m asl (fig. 3.1). The conduit weaves in and out among huge blocks of limestone that have tumbled down the slope (fig. 3.52). The landscape clearly had its present rough character even before the aqueduct was built.

Km 5.182: The slope becomes very slight (1 degree) as the conduit turns in around another valley. At the head of the valley (km 5.216) the conduit has been lost to erosion, which has cut through some of the sandstone bedrock as well. Where the conduit channel survives, the gutter tiles are very well preserved.

FIG. 3.53 *Jammam aqueduct, km 5.930, view up escarpment to initial descent. Conduit blocks appear as a light line.*

Km 5.240: UTM 36R 0734847, 3323168. 1410 m asl. A small slab bridge carried the conduit over a gully.

Km 5.419: A complete gutter tile (1986.001.01; pp. 328–29) was collected from the conduit channel at this point (fig. 3.1). Other gutter tiles were recovered from km 7.340 and 7.529.

Km 5.818: UTM 36R 0734548, 3322888. 1415 m asl (fig. 3.1). The conduit skirts some projecting bedrock, then follows a straight course down the shoulder at the west side of the valley, at a slope of 6 degrees (fig. 3.53).

Km 5.933: UTM 36R 0734559, 3322739. 1395 m asl. At the end of this straight stretch, the channel makes a 90-degree turn to the right, drops over the edge of a projecting face of limestone 2 m high, and heads directly down the steep slope towards the foot of the mountain. From here, the bearing to Humayma (11.3 km distant) is 226 degrees. The initial slope to a low crest above the steeper slope is 12 degrees.

Km 6.228: UTM 36R 0734327, 3322670. 1355 m asl. At the low ridge halfway down the precipitous descent, the conduit bends 90 degrees to the right and begins to wind down the hill among large boulders at a slope of 30–45 degrees (fig. 3.54). There are gutter tiles in the first section of the conduit, obstructed with considerable concretion, then no tiles and a relatively thin layer (Th 0.01 m) of concretion deposited directly on the conduit stone.

Km 6.492: UTM 36R 0734192, 3322665. 1287 m asl. Here the aqueduct encountered the stratum of Disi sandstone below the Cretaceous limestone capping the escarpment, and the engineers began to cut footings for the aqueduct into the soft bedrock. The cliff starts at 6.521 km (UTM 36R 0734079, 3322662. 1256 m asl). The cutting in the rock shows a drop of 4 m over a run of 3 m, but the channel then levelled off and left the cliff face at km 6.621 (UTM 3322697, 36R 0734048. 1236 m asl) to continue along the top of a rubble and soil

FIG. 3.54 *Jammam aqueduct, km 6.232, view uphill along steepest portion of channel.*

FIG. 3.55 *Jammam aqueduct, km 6.976, view downhill towards junction.*

talus at the foot of the cliff, among some fallen limestone masses the size of houses. The aqueduct makes many sharp bends in this area. There are no gutter tiles in the conduit, and there is a layer of concretion directly on the stone.

Km 6.784: UTM 36R 0733925, 3322726. 1246 m asl. A small slab bridge carried the aqueduct over a gully, after which the conduit has been built on a narrow ledge cut directly into the vertical sandstone cliff face for 100 m. A fragment of support wall, supplementing a hollow in the bedrock, has survived at one point. From approximately km 6.621 to km 6.884, no gutter tiles survive in the conduit, and a thin layer of concretion appears inside the conduit blocks to their upper edges.

Km 6.884: UTM 36R 0733883, 3322761. 1243 m asl. A small slab bridge carried the aqueduct over a gully, after which the conduit has been built on a narrow ledge cut directly into the vertical sand-

stone cliff face for 100 m. A fragment of support wall supplementing a hollow in the bedrock has survived at one point.

Km 6.976: UTM 36R 0733811, 3322702. 1239 m asl (fig. 3.1). After weaving in and out to follow the top of the talus, the channel turns directly downhill at this point to follow a straight line towards the junction with the Ghana Aqueduct at km 7.620 (fig. 3.55). The slope is 5 degrees along this section. Halfway down this slope, gutter tiles begin to appear in the conduit and continue to the junction with the Ghana branch. In addition, from this point to the junction, the mortared support structure framing the conduit blocks and tiles is buttressed on either side by a row of stones that increases the width of the overall structure from the usual 0.88–0.90 m to 1.35 m. It is difficult to say whether this detail reflects a rebuilding of this portion of the channel or an attempt to counteract land slippage.

FIG. 3.56 *Jammam aqueduct, km 7.543, site of surface clearing in 1983.*

FIG. 3.57 *View from Jammam aqueduct km 7.550 back towards the escarpment. Aqueduct marked with arrows.*

Km 7.340: A gutter tile was removed from the aqueduct here (1992.0613; see pp. 329–30). Other tiles were recovered at km 5.419 and 7.529. Layering is not very marked, but nine divisions can be counted. The pillowy concretions extend up to the top of the tile and left free an irregular channel only 0.01–0.03 m wide. Soft, light grey bedding mortar adheres to the exterior, containing numerous lime nodules, voids, and occasional flecks of ash.

Km 7.382: A fragment of gutter tile was recovered from the conduit. It carried a very thin (0.005 m) layer of calcium carbonate encrustation around its interior. A horizontal projecting lip 0.035 m above the interior base of the tile shows the water level at the time the aqueduct went out of use. Although the layer of concretion was thin, approximately 25 alternating dark and light rings could be counted (cf. Jammam Aqueduct km 1.779, Ghana Aqueduct km 3.827).

Km 7.529: A complete gutter tile (1986.002.01; Section 6.B.2) was collected from the conduit. Other tiles were recovered from km 5.419 and km 7.340.

Km 7.543: UTM 36R 0733490, 3322366. 1209 m asl. Site of the surface clearing by Oleson in 1983 (Eadie and Oleson 1986: 66–67 (fig. 3.56). Width of the structure is 1.35 m.

Km 7.620: UTM 36R 0733390, 3322293. 1201 m asl. Junction with Ghana branch (fig. 3.26; see above, Ghana Aqueduct km 6.553). The slope of the Jammam branch back to the spring is 2.85 percent (217 m over 7.620 km; fig. 3.57).

3.B.3. *Reservoir*

Structure no. 53. Rock-cut Reservoir: "Harrabat Kudarri" ("Pool of Kudarri")

Coordinates: UTM 36R 0725202, 3315835; Pal. Grid 819293. Elevation: 995 m. 24/06/86, 20/06/00.

The single reservoir constructed outside the settlement centre of Humayma (i.e, more than 500 m from Reservoir no. 67) has been assigned to this class because of its similarity in design and capacity to the built Reservoirs nos. 67 and 68 in the settlement. The reservoir was cut into the red Umm Ishrin sandstone bedrock near the west end

of the valley where most of Humayma's quarries were located (radial from Reservoir 67: 280 degrees, 1.00 km; fig. 1.1). It was excavated on a slight shelf between two gullies that drain the semicircular head of the valley, positioned so as to benefit from the run-off from the northern section, a hillside of mixed soil and bedrock slopes with little vegetation, approximately 12 ha in area (fig. 3.106). There are traces of three low walls in the southern section that may have supported terraces (Structure no. 80). Since wadi barriers were built just below the reservoir as well (Structure no. 79), the three structures may have been part of a single agricultural and pastoral complex. The large capacity of the reservoir, however, should signal the presence of a tent settlement nearby, since there are no remains of habitation structures in the vicinity. A low diversion wall (L 18 m; W 0.70 m; max. H 1.70 m) was built across the northern drainage gully to divert water into the reservoir. The wall has been rebuilt recently, but several of the lower courses, composed of roughly-trimmed sandstone blocks set in a soft, light grey mortar with frequent carbon flecks (only traces remain), appear to be in their original position. The wall raised the water high enough for it to flow into the tank through a rock-cut channel (W 0.40 m; H 0.50 m) at its northeast corner. There is a similar intake channel at the southwest corner, apparently intended to receive water diverted from the hillside directly above by channelling walls of stone slabs and earth that no longer survive.

The rectangular reservoir tank (L 17.53 m; W 6.54 m; depth 4.50 m; cap. 515.9 cum) was cut into the bedrock at a bearing of 225 degrees and roofed by stone slabs carried on 15 transverse arches set into imposts in the bedrock 2.60 m above the floor (figs. 3.58, 7.7). The last five imposts at the south end of the west wall and the last seven at the south end of the east wall are slightly smaller and finer than the others, and there is a slight unevenness in the wall surface and change in tool patterns at the point where the sections meet. These irregularities may indicate that the reservoir was originally built on a smaller scale (ca. 66 percent of the final size) and then expanded as demand increased or the potential resources of the catchment became clear. It is impossible to determine which end of the tank may have been excavated first; the north

FIG. 3.58 *Reservoir no. 53, view from the north.*

FIG. 3.59 *Reservoir no. 53, view of stairs and trough.*

end is closer to the main catchment, but the south end is provided with a substantial access stair and drinking trough.

The staircase, which is very carefully executed, is nearly unique at Humayma. A set of steps descends part of the way into the large Cistern no. 25; three steps provide access to the tiny Cistern no. 50; there may have been steps in Cisterns nos. 12 and 37. These other examples, however, are all uncertain or on a much smaller scale. Five steps (W 0.90–1.0 m) descend from the southwest corner of the reservoir to a landing projecting into the tank, from which point 14 steps descend along the south wall to the floor (fig. 3.59). A shallow trough (L 2.50 m; W 0.45 m; depth 0.10 m; cap. 0.11 cum) has been carved into the rock at the edge of the west wall just above the landing, but it is too high to have been filled conveniently by someone standing there. The interior of the tank was waterproofed with a very hard, sandy white plaster with a heavy admixture of pebbles (see Section 6.D). During visits in July 1983 and June 1986, the reservoir contained approximately 2 m of water. In October 1990, there was only moist sediment 0.50 m thick on the floor, in which tomatoes had been planted. In July 2000, the tank was dry. There is a light sherd scatter in the vicinity of the complex. Bucket 1990.04: 7 rims, 1 handle, 2 base, 42 body; 21 Nabataean, 13 Roman, 4 Byzantine. At least one of the Nabataean sherds is first century in date.

3.B.4. *Cisterns and Run-Off Fields*

Introduction

The 57 ancient cisterns scattered around the watershed of Humayma vary significantly in size and design, but they all incorporate a similar array of features: a catchment area to supply water, sometimes modified with cuttings and walls, an intake hole (which might serve as the draw hole as well), a roof, and a layer of water-proof plaster lining the storage area. The intake channel often passes across a settling tank. Although many of the cisterns originally had roofs built of stone blocks, usually long slabs held by transverse arches, only 14 were built of blocks rather than cut into the bedrock. Although rock-cut construction ensured stability, and prob-

ably economy of effort, it was also a by-product of necessity. The light, sandy soil forming the lowland area of the Humayma catchment absorbs water quickly, while the sandstone bedrock sheds nearly all the precipitation that falls on it, particularly where it has weathered into smooth shapes unencumbered by surface debris. The gentle slopes in the lowland area also restrict the amount of run-off available for collection. In order to ensure a reliable supply of water, the builders simply had to use the steeper bedrock slopes around the agricultural area as catchments. Most of the cisterns, however, are located close to the interface of the bedrock and soil, indicating that the arable land was the focus of interest (see discussion in Section 7.C.4). As a result of their irregular shapes, it was very difficult to calculate the size of the run-off field for each cistern, but an attempt was made to provide at least an approximate figure.

Before entering a cistern, run-off water usually was conducted through a small, shallow square or rectangular tank, where the current slowed sufficiently to allow much of the sediment to settle out before the water passed on through an overflow conduit into the cistern proper. These settling tanks were often unroofed to allow convenient, frequent cleaning.

Only two of the cisterns (nos. 34 and 39) may qualify as rock-cut bottle cisterns of the old Nabataean type described by Diodorus (19.94.7–8; p. 418) — a deep, cylindrical tank tapering to an access hole at the surface — but neither could be properly documented because of modern roofing. Some cisterns, such as nos. 3 and 40, have roofs of bedrock but are rectangular in plan. In Diodorus' arrangement, the access hole served as the intake hole as well. On most of the cisterns around Humayma, however, the intake hole was separate: a small hole located where it best suited the topography of the run-off field and the design of the cistern. The access hole had to be larger and more conveniently positioned to allow convenient dipping with skin bags and occasional entrance for cleaning. Where the roof has been preserved, the access hole usually appears as a square or circular opening toward one edge, sometimes with a low stone well-head to protect and reinforce it. Many of the cisterns that have been put back into use have access holes closed by home-made steel doors, often secured with padlocks. The roofs, of course, protected the contents of the cisterns from pollution by debris, particularly the dung of animals being watered nearby, from evaporation, and from the proliferation of plant, insect, and animal life fostered by sunlight. Despite the use of settling tanks, significant amounts of sand and mud accumulate in the cisterns over time. When the Bedouin decide to put a cistern back into use, their first job is excavation of the fill that has accumulated since the installation was last in use. This fill is dumped nearby, often forming a light-coloured mound that served the survey team as an easily spotted indication of the presence of an otherwise almost invisible structure (cf. G.E. Kirk 1938; Mayerson 1961: 36). Unfortunately, the presence of these mounds and of further ancient and modern excavation debris around the cisterns in most cases completely covered whatever sherd material may have accumulated around the cisterns in antiquity. As a result, little sherd material was available to help determine the chronology of construction and use — although deductions made on the basis of surface material would be very tentative in any case.

Some of the cisterns were provided with rock-cut watering troughs, sometimes a few metres away from the draw hole but connected to it by a rock-cut conduit. With such an arrangement, the herder could water the flock at a convenient position and distance without having to carry a water container. Modern Bedouin often use conduits fashioned from sheets of corrugated steel to conduct cistern water from the draw hole to a rock-cut or cement trough.

Most of the derelict cisterns preserve traces of waterproofing plaster inside the water tank. This plaster, sometimes laid on in several layers approximately 0.01 m thick, is very sandy and hard, sometimes almost pebbly in texture, varying from a creamy white colour to pink, depending on the colour of the sand and pebbles used in the mix (see the technical analysis in Section 6.D). Pulverised potsherds were used as a pozzolanic additive in five structures, but the non-hydraulic plaster used in the majority of cases obviously functioned sufficiently well, perhaps because of the careful compac-tion and polishing of the surface. Although close inspection was not always possible, most of the cisterns reused by the Bedouin have been patched or re-lined with Portland cement.

The cisterns are arranged consecutively by survey number, which does not always correspond to a coherent geographical sequence. Nevertheless, this approach was felt to be less confusing than assigning new catalogue number or allowing an apparently haphazard numerical sequence (see fig. 1.1).

Structure no. 3. Rock-cut cistern

Coordinates: UTM 36R 0737614, 3320652; Pal. Grid 945339. Elevation: 1249 m. 01/06/86, 19/07/00.

The cistern has been cut into a sloping field of sandstone bedrock at the foot of a ridge below the escarpment, just above the loessial soil of the plain (radial from Reservoir 67: 65 degrees, 12.50 km). The catchment field, approximately 4 ha in area, is composed of the rolling bedrock hillside, defined at the top by a low ridge and along the two sides by a combination of rock-cut channels, low rubble walls, and earthen channels. The rock-cut channels terminate in a rectangular settling tank cut into the rock above the cistern draw hole (fig. 3.60). All these cuttings appear to be ancient, but the rubble walls and earth channels are recent repairs of the ancient system. From the centre of the settling tank a smooth, round-bottomed, rock-cut channel (L 2.0 m; W 0.45 m) leads straight down the slope at a bearing of 310 degrees to a small opening built into the side of the draw-hole door frame. The cistern is rectangular (L ca. 4.0 m; W ca. 3.0 m; depth >3.27 m; cap. >39.24 cum), its smooth walls covered with a layer of polished, greyish plaster. In 1986, there was only a trace of moisture inside; in 2000, the cistern clearly had been dry for a long time. The cistern is partially roofed with bedrock, cut away to leave a central opening ca. 2 m long and 1.25 m wide. The present draw hole has recently been re-built with mortar and stones and fitted with a metal door frame, but the rest of the opening is roofed with two roughly-trimmed stone slabs (L 1.57 m; W 0.20–0.25 m; Th 0.20 m). The slabs appear to be original, and the present draw hole is probably at the site of the original one. No ancient ceramics were observed in the area of the cistern.

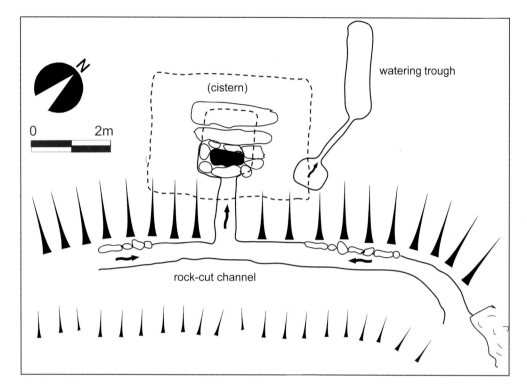

Fig. 3.60 *Cistern no. 3, plan.*

There is a shallow, basin-like cutting in the rock surface 1.5 m to the northeast of the draw hole, connected by means of the 1.5 m long channel to a rock-cut trough (L 2.2 m; W 0.35 m; depth undetermined). Presumably, water drawn from the cistern would be emptied into the basin, then flow through the channel to the trough, which is more conveniently positioned for watering animals than the vicinity of the access hole.

Structure no. 12. Rock-cut cistern (Harrabat al-Hanut)

Coordinates: UTM 36R 0735305, 3314910; Pal. Grid 920283. Elevation: 1060 m. 04/06/86, 06/07/00.

The cistern has been cut back into a high, smooth, vertical bedrock face on the east side of the Sahl es-Saqiya, approximately 80 m west of the Desert Highway (radial from Reservoir 67: 273 degrees, 9.14 km; fig. 3.61). Alluvium and recent building activity have concealed any ceramics. The catchment consisted of a section of the undulating surface of the sandstone ridge approximately 400 × 200 m square (8 ha), totally devoid of soil or shrubs. The run-off followed a series of gullies that were occasionally trimmed down to facilitate flow and converged just above the cistern at an unroofed settling tank (L 3.5 m; W 2.55 m; depth >0.20 m; cap. >1.8 cum; fig. 3.62). The overflow from this tank was guided over the edge of the cliff in a water-worn groove (W 0.70 m; depth 0.50 m) that extends down to the upper edge of a large, rectangular niche cut back into the rock (H to present level of sand 3.6 m; W 2.2 m; depth 1.5 m). The lower portion of the niche (for 1.8 m above present sand level) contains an opening (W 1.2 m) leading back into the cistern chamber, now sheltered by a modern cinderblock shed with concrete slab roof. The shed's roof conceals the join between the door and niche. The cistern (L 6.7 m; W 7.15 m) is now filled with moist sand to within 2.4 m of its flat roof. There are a shallow niche inside the chamber just to the right of the door as one enters and possible traces of rock-cut steps below, but no other features, or any remains of plaster, are visible.

The water spilling out of the settling tank probably fell into a catch basin projecting slightly from the niche and from there flowed into the cistern. The capacity of the cistern cannot be calculated without removing some of the sand, but it is likely to have been significant, in view of the substantial effort involved in excavating the complex. A depth of 5 m below the present door sill would give a capacity of 240 cum.

This is probably the "Harabet el Hanut" mentioned by Kirkbride and Harding. They mention that "a little to the south [of Harabet el Hanut] the military have cleared out three large cisterns, called Shereif el Rekaib; they are of the same type as those at Khalde [i.e., roofed with slabs carried on transverse arches]." This description does not seem to fit the double cistern no. 36, which is 5 km to the south, so perhaps these cisterns remain to be discovered. The missing cisterns may be somewhere in the vicinity of Cistern no. 30, which was cut into the foot of a hill where there was a military watch post in the 1980s and possibly earlier. Cistern no. 25 (Harrabat al-ʿAbîd) is said to be "a short distance to the south west of this point," which fits the location of no. 30.

Bibliography: Kirkbride and Harding 1947: 21.

Structure no. 14. Rock-cut cistern

Coordinates: UTM 36R 0723279, 3307742, (1:50,000): 232080. The site is just west of the last available 1:25,000 map sheet, but if that sheet existed, the coordinates would be approximately 799291. Elevation: 934 m. 05/06/86, 14/07/00.

The cistern is cut into the soft, white sandstone bedrock on the left bank of the Wadi Shubeika at the mouth of the valley, 60 m south of a low hill next to the main dirt road between Humayma and Quweira (radial from Reservoir 67: 198 degrees, 8.44 km). A few Nabataean and Roman commonware body sherds were observed in the general area. The badly disturbed remains of an ancient structure with rock-cut foundations can be seen on top of the hill, immediately above Cistern no. 83. At present, run-off from a large (ca. 25 ha), gently sloping field to the north and west fills the cistern through a roughly square notch in its northwest corner. There are a few scattered blocks around the entrance hole,

Fig. 3.61 *Cistern no. 12, façade with modern enclosure.*

but the original sluice arrangement was lost when a modern concrete wall was laid around the lip of the cistern. The cistern (L 8.65 m; W 3.88 m; depth >3.32 m; cap. >111.4 cum), excavated on a bearing of 310 degrees, was roofed by stone slabs carried on eight transverse arches (ca. 0.55 m apart) set on imposts cut into the bedrock (fig. 3.63). The arches have all fallen, but the scattered red sandstone voussoirs measure approximately L 0.53 m × W 0.26 m. The roofing slabs have disappeared. Below the arch imposts, there are traces of three layers of granular, white plaster with an admixture of red granite pebbles. Traces of a small betyl block can be seen cut in relief on the west cistern wall, above the impost level.

Kirkbride and Harding may allude to the existence of this cistern, along with some as yet uncatalogued cisterns farther up the Wadi

FIG. 3.62   *Cistern no. 12, catchment channel and settling tank.*

FIG. 3.63   *Cistern no. 14, view from southeast.*

FIG. 3.64 *Cistern no. 17, view.*

FIG. 3.65 *Cistern no. 18, view from the south.*

Shubeika towards Tulul er-Rubeiq: "Farther south [from Cistern no. 18], at Rubeik, are more rock-cut cisterns in a valley to the west…, and some amorphous piles of stones. We were told of another large cistern in an isolated hill to the south, but did not visit it."

Bibliography: Kirkbride and Harding 1947: 21.

Structure no. 17. Rock-cut cistern?

Coordinates: UTM36R 0724590, 3311544; Pal. Grid 812251. Elevation: 943 m. 09/06/86, 14/07/00.

The cistern has been excavated in sloping sandstone bedrock at the opening of a small gully, just below the cliff face along the south edge of the Jebel Qalkha (radial from Reservoir 67: 200 degrees, 4.40 km). A few scattered Nabataean and Roman common-ware sherds were found in the vicinity, but there is no intact soil deposit. The catchment area includes several hectares of the jebel slope, but the cistern is small; it may simply have been a natural fissure in the stone that was enlarged to store water (fig. 3.64). An oval opening (1.93 m × 1.15 m) provides access to a roughly spherical storage chamber with a diameter of ca. 3 m (cap. ca. 10.6 cum). Fresh tool marks on the interior and a pile of freshly broken rubble nearby show that the cistern has recently been cleared out and possibly enlarged. Probably at the same time, a small wall of fieldstones set in mortar was built around the uphill portion of the draw hole to allow some control over the intake. It is in fact even possible that the wall was intended to keep water out, so that the tank could be used for storage of grain. The same arrangement may have been used in antiquity.

Structure no. 18. Rock-cut cistern

Coordinates: UTM36R 0725548, 33134075; Pal. Grid 822276. Elevation: 980 m. 09/06/86, 22/06/00.

The cistern has been cut into the red sandstone bedrock at the mouth of a hanging valley facing south, near the east end of the Jebel Qalkha (radial from Reservoir 67: 200 degrees, 1.69 km). The whole area has been very badly disturbed, but a few characteristic Nabataean and Roman common-ware sherds were found in the general area. The catchment may include as much as 1 sq km of the surface of the jebel. The bedrock surface into which the cistern (L 10.95 m; W 5.70 m; depth >2.75 m; cap. >171.6 cum) was cut slopes to the south (fig. 3.65). In consequence, a levelled surface was excavated around the northern half of the cistern, and the walls around the southern half were built up with blocks. Many of these blocks, and some of the blocks in the rebuilt modern barrier wall, show typical Nabataean diagonal trimming; this barrier wall obscures the original arrangement of the intake hole. The cistern was roofed with slabs carried on seven transverse arches set into imposts cut into the bedrock at more or less equal intervals along the side walls, 1.75 m above the present floor level. At the time of the first visit, the cistern was full to the brim with water, obscuring any surviving ancient plastering; at the second visit, the cistern was dry.

Bibliography: Kirkbride and Harding 1947: 21.

Structure no. 19. Pothole cisterns?

Coordinates: UTM 36R 0725238, 3314116; Pal. Grid 820278. Elevation: 960–1000 m. 09/06/86, 22/06/00.

The site consists of a series of seven potholes that appear to have been worn naturally into the red sandstone bedrock of a long, wide valley that drains much of the top of Jebel Qalkha (radial from Reservoir 67: 210 degrees, 1.79 km; fig. 3.66). The potholes, several of which contained water or moist sediments at the time of the first visit, occur along a 300 m stretch of the valley, with a 40 m difference in elevation between the first and the last. Two of them are approximately L 3 × W 2 × depth 1 m (cap. ca. 6 cum) and may preserve traces of trimming or enlargement. The last pothole (L 5 m; W 4 m; depth 2 m; cap. ca. 17.9 cum), near the mouth of the valley, is larger and more regular than the rest, and no typical cisterns were found in the immediate vicinity. These features could hold a significant amount of water (ca. 35 cum in all?) and may have been modified to increase their capacity, but no attempt was made to plaster their interiors, to roof them, or to provide settling tanks. As a result, the water would have been of very poor quality. Similar slightly adapted natural pools have been identified on Jebel Haroun (Lavento et al. 2007a: 296).

FIG. 3.66 *Pothole cisterns no. 19, view of area from above.*

FIG. 3.67 *Cistern or Tank no. 21, from northeast.*

There are at present two very minor seeps of water along seams in the bedrock in this valley, but there are no traces of ancient or modern attempts to enhance or collect the flow.

Structure no. 20. Rock-cut settling tank, reservoir or cistern

Coordinates: UTM 36R 0732327, 3321143; Pal. Grid 895348. Elevation: 1151 m. 12/06/86.

This off-take tank is part of the Ghana Aqueduct system (radial from Reservoir 67: 46 degrees, 8.26 km). For a description, see the discussion of the aqueduct at km 9.597 (pp. 93–96; figs. 3.34–38). Frank (1934: 236) is the first traveller to mention this cistern, but he provides inaccurate dimensions ("5 m × 8 m").

Structure no. 21. Built cistern

Coordinates: UTM 36R 0729512, 3319974; Pal. Grid 866336. Elevation: 1034 m. 14/06/86, 28/06/00.

This small cistern or tank is located in the undulating loessial plain north of Humayma, 10 m southwest of the Ghana Aqueduct at km 13.472 and 6 m northeast of the Via Nova. It is visible just east of the modern dirt road that follows the aqueduct (radial from Reservoir 67: 36 degrees, 5.48 km; fig. 3.67). There is no evidence for any branch line to the aqueduct, and it may have been designed to hold run-off water from the sloping field to the north. A small number of probable Roman common-ware sherds was observed in the general area of the structure. The cistern (L 1.28 m; W 1.25 m; depth 0.40 m; cap. 0.64 cum) was constructed of large, regular blocks of red sandstone, two on each side, the surfaces of which show traces of very rough diagonal trimming. The floor, concealed by plaster, was probably constructed in the same manner. The interior surfaces were covered and water-proofed and the corners rounded off with a 1 cm thick layer of a hard, white plaster containing a high proportion of large pebbles. Since this plaster, the rounded corners, and the construction technique are all paralleled in reservoir no. 62, this structure too may be Roman in date. There is no evidence for any roof. Cistern no. 82 is similar in dimensions, but cut in the bedrock.

Structure no. 22. Built cistern?

Coordinates: UTM 36R 0729141, 3319637; Pal. Grid 861332. Elevation: 1034 m. 14/06/86, 28/06/00.

The cistern is located in the loessial plain north of Humayma, adjacent to the east side of the aqueduct at km 13.985, which at this point is closely paralleled by the modern dirt road (radial from Reservoir 67: 35 degrees, 4.98 km). A row of sheet metal and rubble-built modern storage huts was built nearby in the 1980s, and a few houses and a school were added in 1998–99. The cistern (L 2.98 m; W 1.28 m; depth 0.94 m; cap. 3.6 cum) is constructed of rubble and roughly squared stones set in a small amount of mortar. The inclusion of a few fragments of marl conduit blocks and the absence of any connection with the aqueduct suggest that the aqueduct was derelict at the time the cistern was built. The construction technique and the absence of any ancient potsherds suggest a modern origin. Since no intake arrangements can be seen and there are no traces of plastering on the interior of the porous walls, it is possible that the structure was used for storing something other than water. There is no sign of any roofing system. The proximity of the structure to the aqueduct may reflect the desire of the builders to make use of the aqueduct as a source for building materials rather than for water. A large proportion of the superstructure of the aqueduct has been lost along this stretch.

Structure no. 23. Rock-cut cistern

Coordinates: UTM 36R 0729662, 3311276; Pal. Grid 855254. Elevation: 966 m. 14/06/86, 19/07/00.

The cistern, oriented at 180 degrees, has been cut into the first visible deposits of soft, white sandstone that slope gently upward from the fields of loessial soil on the east bank of the Wadi Qalkha, adjacent to some modern agricultural fields (radial from Reservoir 67: 140 degrees, 5.59 km; fig. 3.68). One of the dirt roads leading from Old Humayma to New Humayma passes close by. Run-off water from a sloping area of bare bedrock several hectares in extent is channelled into the cistern by recent earth barriers through a rebuilt intake hole. Three very small sherds of NPFW bowls were recovered in the area of the structure. The cistern (L 4.62 m; W

FIG. 3.68 *Cistern no. 23, interior.*

FIG. 3.69 *Cistern no. 24, interior.*

FIG. 3.70 *Cistern no. 24, exterior superstructure from east, with intake hole.*

4.63 m; depth >3.83 m; cap. >81.9 cum), has been cut deep into the bedrock, which was supplemented around the upper edge with two to three courses of carefully cut blocks with diagonal trimming. These blocks appear to be in their original positions, in contrast to the blocks placed carelessly into a rebuilt wall set slightly back from the edge. The cistern originally was roofed with stone slabs carried by three very heavy transverse (east/west) arches set on imposts cut into the wall 2.25 m above the present floor. This roofing has disappeared, the arches and filler walls leaving impressions in the thick layer of white plaster filled with pebbles that still covers most of the interior. Tree trunks were laid across the opening long before 1986 to support some kind of roof, probably galvanised steel sheeting, which had also disappeared by the time of the initial survey.

Structure no. 24. Rock-cut cistern

Coordinates: UTM 36R 0729631, 3308166; Pal. Grid 862215. Elevation: 937 m. 15/07/86, 07/07/00.

The cistern has been cut into the soft white sandstone bedrock forming the west slope of the Hudeibat Um-Dureira, just northwest of an isolated jebel topped by a large balanced rock (radial from Reservoir 67: 154 degrees, 8.25 km). No ceramics were observed in the vicinity. Run-off water from a large sloping area of smooth bedrock to the north and east, approximately 5 to 6 ha in extent, was channelled by a small gully into a stone conduit leading over the northwest corner of the cistern (L 11.20 m; W 6.20 m; depth >4.0 m; cap. >277.8 cum; fig. 3.69). The long walls of the cistern are oriented to 65/245 degrees. The intake appears to have been rebuilt recently, obscuring any ancient settling tank originally associated with it. The upper edge of the rock was supplemented with two courses of substantial, carefully squared blocks of sandstone with diagonal trimming, the upper course serving as the foundation for a barrier wall around the complex — now largely rebuilt (fig. 3.70). Individuals standing on the ledge inside the south wall could draw water and pour it into stone conduit blocks, which carried it through the wall

FIG. 3.71 *Cistern no. 24, west wall and trough.*

→ **FIG. 3.72**   *Cistern no. 25, interior from the west, with intake channel.*

into a long, block-built stone trough (L 4.60 m; W 0.45 m) immediately outside (fig. 3.71). This may be the original arrangement, rather than a modern rebuild, since the open seams between the trough blocks have not had their mortar replaced.

The cistern was roofed by sandstone slabs carried on 10 close-set transverse arches, of which four survive, along with a few of their roofing slabs. The arches rested on imposts cut into the bedrock walls 2.50 m above the present floor. There are traces on the cistern walls of a 0.01 m thick layer of a hard white plaster containing many pebbles. There were signs that some water had been drawn from the cistern not long before the first survey visit, and the soil on the floor inside was moist. The presence of several large shrubs and trees growing inside, however, indicates that the cistern has not been filled to anywhere near its capacity in recent years. In July of 2000 the cistern was dry, and the tree was alive but stressed.

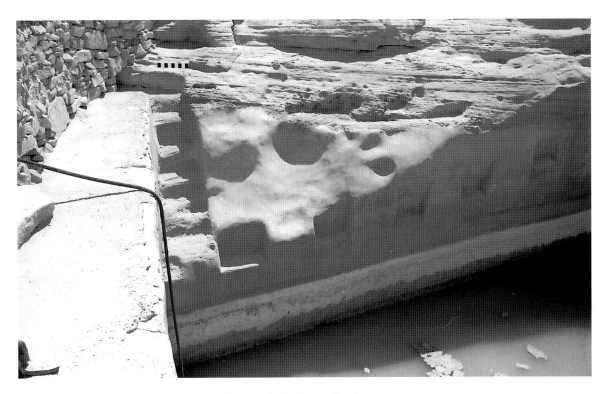

FIG. 3.73 *Cistern no. 25, northwest corner of tank, with blocking wall and access stairs.*

Structure no. 25. Rock-cut cistern:
"Harrabat el-'Abîd" ("Pool of the Blacks")

Coordinates: UTM 36R 0727548, 3308132; Pal. Grid 842216. Elevation: 900 m. 15/06/86, 07/07/00.

The cistern was created by enlarging and blocking the end of an enormous fissure at the west end of a spur of the Hudeibat Um-Dureira. L 13.70 m (north wall), 11.15 m (south wall); W 3.65 m (east wall), 5.40 m (west wall); depth >4.24 m; cap. >237.9 cum (radial from Reservoir 67: 168 degrees, 7.65 km; figs. 3.72–74).

Laborde visited the cistern in 1828 and describes it as a reliable water source. He states that the hill was called "Macbert el Abid" (probably "maqbarat," "Tomb of the Blacks") as a result of the following incident:

> Nous partîmes d'Améimé et nous arrivâmes, après une bonne heure de marche, à un rocher de grès que ces citernes comme la tradition que s'y rattache rendent intéressant.

Elle porte qu'autrefois le roi des noirs vint ravager ce pays avec des troupes innombrables; il avait déjà chassé devant lui tous les habitants, lorsque arrivé dans la plaine d'Ameimé [Humayma] il voulut se désaltérer dans cette citerne, et se penchant à la surface de l'eau pour boire à la manière des Arabs, il tomba; un de ses gardes accourut pour lui porter secours et tomba de même; un autre, voulant secourir ce dernier, le suivit également. De cette manière toute l'armée fut engloutie, et ce rocher reçut le nom de Macbert el Abid.

The variant name Harrabat el-'Abîd, alluded to by Maughan ("Harabah," 1874: 194) and reported by Musil (1926: 266) and present-day local Bedouin, is similar and constitutes important evidence for the continuity of oral tradition in this sparsely inhabited area. It is interesting that the story implies that the roofing slabs had already disappeared by the time the "King of the Blacks" arrived on the scene.

FIG. 3.74 *Cistern no. 25, west blocking wall from outside.*

Run-off water was gathered from nearly the whole surface of the ridge, an area of approximately 400 × 500 m (ca. 20 ha), by building low rubble and earth walls around its circumference. These guide the flow towards rock-cut channels close to the west end of the ridge, which conduct it into the narrow east end of the fissure and into the cistern through an opening built into the modern barrier wall. The cistern itself has a roughly rectangular plan with walls that bulge outward slightly in plan and curve inward slightly in elevation. It is likely that a large crevice was enlarged to create the cistern, or perhaps a narrow dike of sandstone isolated by seams of carbonate deposits (*nari*, see Henry 1996: 37–38). No attempt has been made to level the sloping surface, except towards the west end, where footings were prepared for the west blocking wall and a flight of stone steps was cut to give access to the interior, down to the level of the imposts (fig. 3.73). Stairs providing access to cisterns are infrequent at Humayma (cf. Reservoir no. 53 and Cisterns nos. 12, 25, 37, and 50). The stairs at this cistern, however, do not provide access to the floor of the tank. The blocking wall is constructed

of eight courses of large sandstone blocks, several of which carry careful diagonal trimming (fig. 3.74). Two block-built outlets at the southwest corner of the cistern were used to conduct drawn water to basins at ground level, 3 m below. The slab roof was carried on eight transverse arches that sprang from imposts cut into the rock 2.24 m above the present floor at the west end of the cistern. Since the imposts were all at the same height, but the spans of the arches varied according to their location, the curvature must have varied significantly from span to span, raising interesting questions about the technique of construction. The interior of the cistern has been covered with modern cement, and the complex was in use at the time of the initial survey. In June 1986 the cistern was nearly full; in July 2000, the soil inside it was still moist, after a long drought had completely dried nearly all the other cisterns in the region.

Bibliography: Laborde 1830: 63; Maughan 1874: 194; Brünnow and Domaszewski 1904–9: 1, pp. 476–77, fig. 546 no. c; Musil 1907–08: 266; Kirkbride and Harding 1947: 21.

Structure no. 26. Rock-cut cistern

Coordinates: UTM 36R 0727305, 3308096; Pal. Grid 839215. Elevation: 900 m. 15/06/86, 07/07/00.

The cistern is located in a recess in a sandstone jebel at the west end of the Hudeibat Um-Dureira, into which drains most of the northeast quadrant of the jebel, approximately 4 hectares in area (radial from Reservoir 67: 170 degrees, 7.65 km). Brünnow and Domaszewski equate this jebel with the "Harabah" of Maughan (1874: 194), presumably echoing the more recent name of the Harrabat el-'Abîd cistern. Maughan's description suggests a large, rock-cut cistern with stepped dromos and a central draw hole in the roof.

> The entrance is by a steep groove chiselled in the rock, with distinct remains of steps cut across it, and is partially covered over by a large slab of stone. The slope of the passage is about 7 or 8 feet in length, and the chamber measures 30 feet by 18, the bottom being covered with sand. The upper portion of the rock-hewn walls is covered with a coarse surface of plaster, deep pick marks indent the face of the stone. Light is admitted by a circular hole in the roof, where the rock is between 2 and 3 feet thick. The height of this curious chamber is about 6 feet, but the sand had evidently also accumulated to nearly that extent in the interior. Near the hole in the roof is a channel half a foot deep, apparently to prevent the rainwater from flowing into the chamber, and after a course of about 20 feet the water is discharged into a small open cistern. On both sides of the entrance to the cave are inscriptions of the Sinaitic character [i.e. similar to Nabataean or Thamudic inscriptions Maughan had seen in the Sinai?], but much worn and defaced, the stone being very soft. It is difficult to say whether this chamber has been a tomb, a cistern, or a hermit's cave…

Musil saw the same features during his visit in 1898 (Musil 1907–08: 266), but recognised the large chamber as a cistern. The surface arrangements above the cistern described by these two authors sound similar to what can be seen today above Cistern no. 26: a large circular opening (now walled up), a shallow water trough cut into the rock, diversion channels to catch run-off, and an open settling basin (figs. 3.75–76). Furthermore, there is no other structure in the area corresponding to these descriptions. The stepped dromos has been filled with earth, but its outline is visible extending north towards the edge of the hill. Perhaps the Bedouin sometime since 1898 renovated the cistern by walling up the entrance door, filling in the dromos to prevent falls, and preparing a smaller draw hole. If this is the case, the capacity would be approximately 153 cum (assuming a height of 10 ft., 3.05 m), explaining why this cistern held water in July 2000, after a long drought had dried nearly all the other cisterns in the region. The interior could not be examined, but surface indications suggest that the cistern length is at least 7.5 m, which is close enough to Maughan's figure of 30 ft (9.14 m).

The loessial soil of the plain — here particularly sandy and light — slopes off to the north and west immediately below the cistern opening. Run-off pouring down the bare rock slopes of the gully was intercepted by a shallow rock-cut channel cut across the line of flow (L 8.5 m; W 0.40 m; depth ca. 0.20 m) that guided the water to a small settling basin (L 2.30 m; W 1.26 m; depth 0.60 m; cap. 1.7 cum). A second rock-cut channel extended from the settling basin west up the opposite slope for 19 m to intercept run-off from that portion of the hill; the last 7 m of the downhill side of this channel were built up with small field stones set in mortar not long before the 1986 visit. An overflow channel (L 2.30 m; W 0.40 m; depth 0.20 m) 0.25 m above the floor of the settling basin conducted water east through a small intake hole and into the cistern. The area of the intake hole and the downhill side of the intake channel have recently been rebuilt with one course of small field stones set in mortar, and a square area approximately the same size as the settling basin has been built adjacent to it in the same manner. The area around the present draw hole, 3 m to the east, has been rebuilt as well and fitted with the small steel door typical of the region. Since this door was locked, the configuration and depth of the cistern could not be measured. The cistern obviously is roofed with bedrock, but some short

FIG. 3.75 *Cistern no. 26, view of area from northeast. Backfilled dromos at bottom left.*

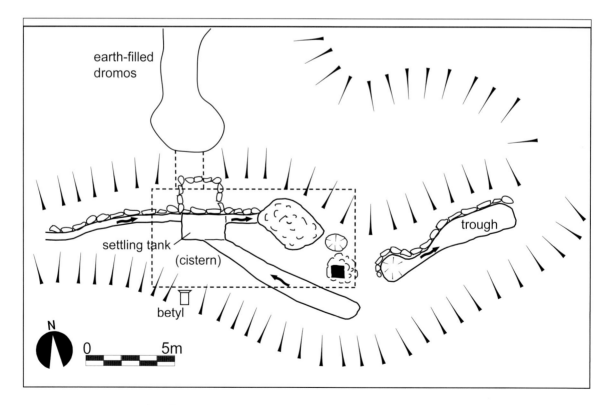

FIG. 3.76 *Cistern no. 26, plan of area.*

slabs may have been used to cover the area around the draw hole, now obscured by modern mortar. A small conduit, partly cut into the rock and partly built up with stones, conducted water from just southeast of the draw hole to a long drinking trough built in the same technique (L 7.50 m; W 0.40 m; depth 0.20 m; cap. 0.6 cum). There are traces of a small, circular basin (D ca. 0.50 m) cut into the rock just north of the draw hole. A small betyl was carved in relief 3 m above the settling basin, and a few ridged body sherds of Byzantine common ware were found in the soil at the foot of the hill. Bibliography: Maughan 1874: 194–95; Brünnow and Domaszewski 1904–9: 1, pp. 476–77, fig. 546 no. c; Musil 1907–08: 266.

Structure no. 29. Rock-cut cistern

Coordinates: UTM 36R 0729303, 3307510; Pal. Grid 859213. Elevation: 920 m. 15/06/86, 07/07/00.

The cistern has been cut into the slope at the foot of the west side of the main mass of the Hudeibat Um-Dureira, which is composed of friable red Umm 'Ishrin sandstone (radial from Reservoir 67: 157 degrees, 8.73 km). A natural gully channelled run-off water into the cistern from several hectares of the adjacent slopes. The cistern (L 11.55 m; W 2.02 m; depth 2.70 m; cap. 63 cum) was formed by enlarging a natural cleft; its long sides appear to have been defined by two narrow, vertical seams of carbonate deposits (*nari*, see Henry 1996: 37–38) that run down this portion of the slope (fig. 3.77). The sandstone between the seams was quarried away, and the north and south short sides were filled in with stones set in mortar. There is no evidence of any attempt at roofing. The present filling walls are modern, but some of the quarry marks in the rock-cut section appear to be weathered and ancient. No potsherds were observed, since the ground surface around the cistern is covered with sediment dredged from the interior.

Structure no. 30. Rock-cut cistern

Coordinates: UTM 36R 0729590, 3307093; Pal. Grid 864209. Elevation: 927 m. 15/06/86, 07/07/00.

The cistern has been cut into a natural cleft in the south side of a small sandstone jebel near the

FIG. 3.77 *Cistern no. 29, interior from east.*

southeast edge of Hudeibat Um-Dureira, several hundred metres west of the Desert Highway (radial from Reservoir 67: 157 degrees, 9.22 km). It was designed to collect the run-off from a bare stone surface ca. 1 ha in extent. The water is guided into the cistern (L 10 m; W 1.55 m; depth 2.1 m; cap. 32.6 cum) by a catchment channel that is partly cut into the rock and has recently been supplemented with fieldstones set in the soil. The natural cleft was enlarged by excavating either side; both ends were closed with walls of mortared rubble. There were water marks on the interior at the time of the visit, but no plaster lining. The walls are modern, but some of the cuttings in the bedrock, especially in the catchment channel, are weathered and have an ancient appearance. No potsherds were observed in the area.

Fig. 3.78 *Cistern no. 31, view.*

Structure no. 31. Rock-cut cistern

Coordinates: UTM 36R 0728649, 3307070; Pal. Grid 850202. Elevation: 917 m. 15/06/86, 07/07/00.

The cistern has been cut into a large natural cleft in the sloping red sandstone at the south end of the Hudeibat Um-Dureira, several hundred metres west of the Desert Highway (radial from Reservoir 67: 162 degrees, 8.94 km). Run-off from the slope (ca. 50 m × 200 m) and the adjacent hillside was captured and guided towards the upper end of the cleft by a wall of upright slabs and field stones set in earth (L 32 m). The cistern itself (L 19 m; W 0.85–2.5 m; depth 4.4 m; cap. ca. 140 cum) was carved out of the fissure and blocked at either end by walls of rubble set in mortar. The upper half of the cistern was roofed with roughly trimmed slabs of sandstone from the hillside (fig. 3.78). The conduit channel, blocking walls, and cement lining inside appear to be modern, but the method of roofing and the visible rock-cut surfaces have a weathered and ancient appearance. No ancient ceramics were observed in the area.

Structure no. 32. Rock-cut cistern

Coordinates: UTM 36R 0731018, 3308665; Pal. Grid 875221. Elevation: 922 m. 16/06/00, 07/07/00.

The cistern has been cut into the east edge of a sloping surface of red sandstone (ca. 75 m square) toward the north end of Hudeibat Um-Dureira, just above the loessial soil that slopes gently toward the Desert Highway 100 m to the east (radial from Reservoir 67: 144 degrees, 8.50 km). A wall of roughly-trimmed slabs of sandstone set in earth and mortar guides run-off from this area and from the sandstone slopes behind it into a rock-cut conduit channel that intersects the southwest corner of the cistern. The cistern itself (L 5.65 m; W 3.35 m; depth 4.0 m; cap. 75.7 cum) seems to have been excavated by enlarging a natural fissure in the rock; it is now lined on the interior with modern cement (fig. 3.79). The heaps of spoil from the excavation are still visible around the cistern, but the fractures do not appear to be recent. At present, the cistern is roofed with corrugated iron sheets carried on transverse wooden poles, but the depth of water inside at the time of the visits (3.5 m) did not allow examination of the walls for rock-cut imposts for arches that may have carried an ancient roof. The collection channel clearly has been rebuilt recently, but the cistern may possibly be ancient in origin. No ancient ceramics were observed in the vicinity of the cistern.

Structure no. 33. Rock-cut cisterns (Group of 7)

Coordinates: UTM 36R 0731051, 3309429; Pal. Grid 875230. Elevation: 974 m. 16/06/86, 07/07/00.

The cisterns have been cut into a sloping sandstone hillside at the north end of the Hudeibat Um-Dureira, within 20 to 70 m of one another (radial from Reservoir 67: 140 degrees, 7.90 km). All seven cisterns have the same design: the soft, white sandstone bedrock has been removed between two vertical seams of calcium carbonate deposit and the ends of the excavation blocked by walls of field stones set in modern mortar. The calcium carbonate is left as a kind of natural plaster. Since several of the cisterns show recent tool marks or fresh breaks in the spoil from their excavation, and there is a modern sandstone quarry and farmer's shelter nearby, it is possible that some or all of the cisterns are modern or have been extensively enlarged. All the blocking walls are modern. Two of the cisterns (33.2, 33.6), however, are still partly filled with earth and sand, suggesting that some time has passed since their excavation, and no. 33.5 may originally have extended 6 m beyond one of the modern blocking walls. The cisterns are all positioned in such a way that water can flow into them as it runs off the bare hillside, which provides a catchment of 20–25 ha, but no water was observed in them at the time of either visit. During the second visit, it was observed that several of the cisterns had been finished neatly on the interior with cement. The cisterns are numbered from north to south. Total capacity of the group is 738.6 cum.

no. 33.1:   L 9.95 m; W 3.90 m; depth 4.0 m;
             cap. 155 cum.
no. 33.2:   L 7.30 m; W 3.10 m; depth >1.5 m;
             cap. >34 cum.
no. 33.3:   L 10.35 m; W 2.90 m; depth 4.40 m;
             cap. 123.1 cum.

FIG. 3.79 *Cistern no. 32, view.*

no. 33.4:   L 8.90 m (E), 10.18 m (W); W 2.53 m (S),
             3.70 m (N); depth 3.50 m;
             cap. ca. 104.5 cum.
no. 33.5:   L 7.59 m; W 3.67 m; depth 3.64 m;
             cap. 101.4 cum.
no. 33.6:   L 12.17 m; W 1.97 m; depth >1.0 m;
             cap. >24 cum.
no. 33.7:   L 6.61 m; W 6.70 m; depth 4.44 m;
             cap. 196.6 cum.

Structure no. 34. Rock-cut cistern

Coordinates: (Pal. Grid) 862228. Elevation: 935 m. 16/06/86.

The cistern has been cut into the white sandstone bedrock of a gentle slope next to a small gully, in a dip between the two north peaks of the Hudeibat Um-Dureira (radial from Reservoir 67: 142 degrees, 7.2 km). At the time of the visit,

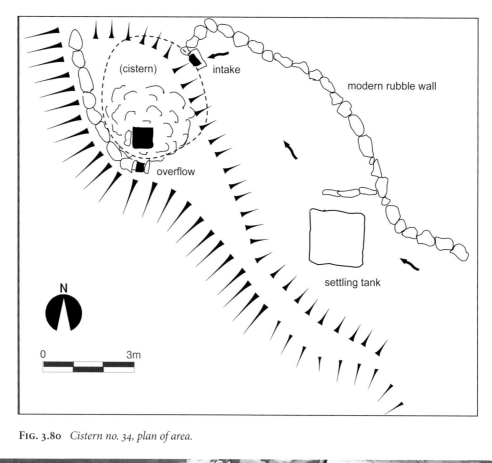

FIG. 3.80 *Cistern no. 34, plan of area.*

FIG. 3.81 *Cistern no. 36, interior of northern tank.*

there was a small modern storage shack nearby. The cistern could not be relocated in July 2000 or March 2001. The gully drains an area of six or seven hectares. At present, a barrier of stone slabs set in mortar diverts water from the gully across the bare rock towards the rock-cut settling tank (L 1.6 m; W 1.6 m; depth 0.25 m; cap. 0.64 cum) 5 m to the south (fig. 3.80). A low modern barrier wall of one course of field stones set in mortar guides the water into the settling tank and then on to the intake for the cistern proper. Since there are no visible traces of rock-cut channels across this surface, a similar arrangement must have been used in antiquity. The intake has been reinforced with modern cement, but it appears to have been a simple hole cut through the bedrock cistern roof. A rebuilding with stones and mortar has obscured the original arrangements for the draw hole and overflow conduit. The overflow, partly cut into the bedrock and partly built of stone slabs, pours excess water back into the gully as it curves around the low knoll into which the cistern has been cut. The draw hole has been fitted with a small iron door and frame, set into plaster on a shaky roof of mud plaster carried on beams. The cistern proper appears to be circular (D ca. 3.0 m; depth 4.0 m; cap. 28.3 cum) and seems to be lined with ancient or modern plaster. The modern roof obscures the original roofing system but seems to be almost as wide as the cistern itself; the cistern may have been left unroofed, or — more likely — roofed with slabs carried on transverse arches. Alternatively, the original bedrock roof may have fallen in the post-classical period, requiring replacement. No ancient ceramics were observed in the vicinity of the cistern. There is a modern earthen wadi barrier below the cistern, designed to capture water from the same gully and allow it to infiltrate a small agricultural field.

Structure no. 35. Rock-cut cistern

Coordinates: UTM 36R 0729251, 3309441; Pal. Grid 851228. Elevation: 941 m. 16/06/86, 19/07/00.

The cistern has been cut into the floor of a gully at the edge of the loessial soil of the plain, near some modern agricultural fields at the northwest edge of the Hudeibat Um-Dureira (radial from Reservoir 67: 152 degrees, 6.93 km). It was formed (L >4.0 m; W 2.0 m; depth undetermined; cap. >16 cum ?) by enlarging a small fissure. Closing walls probably were built at either end, but a dump of soil recently dug out of the cistern proper now obscures these. No artefacts were observed nearby.

Structure no. 36. Rock-cut double cistern

Coordinates: UTM 36R 0732188, 3311273; Pal. Grid 890243. Elevation: 1008 m. 16/06/86, 07/07/00.

The cisterns have been cut into the white sandstone bedrock several hundred metres below the crest of a ridge overlooking the Desert Highway 500 m to the east, approximately 1 km NNW of New Humayma, adjacent to a dirt road leading to Old Humayma (radial from Reservoir 67: 124 degrees, 7.43 km). A high cinderblock wall was built around the northern cistern not long before 1986, using as a foundation a roughly-built wall incorporating a number of ancient blocks. No potsherds were observed in the area. Both of the cisterns have been cut into the bedrock across a small, relatively shallow gully that drains 20–25 ha of the bare rock slope above; they are oriented at right angles to each other and join through an archway at one end to form an L. The northern-most cistern, oriented east/west, is the larger of the two (L 7.40 m; W 5.0 m; depth >3.20 m; cap. >118.4 cum; fig. 3.81). The intake conduit, close to the southwest corner, has been cut into the bedrock of the gully and roofed with stone slabs where it passes through the lower barrier wall. The overflow conduit close to the southeast corner has been built in the same fashion. The cistern proper was roofed by stone slabs set on five transverse arches, which rested on imposts cut into the rock walls 1.3 m above the present floor. Only the easternmost arch and a few stone slabs have survived, and the cistern was dry at the time of the visit. The walls carry the remains of two layers of very pebbly grey stucco.

An arched, rock-cut doorway (blocked with a modern stone wall) at the west end of the south wall of the east/west cistern leads into the second, which is oriented north/south. The arch-supported stone slab roof over this second cistern is intact. Because the connecting door was blocked and the door of the present draw hole (near the north end of the cistern) was locked at the time of the visit, the interior could not be inspected. The roofing slabs, however, although partly obscured by a layer of modern cement, occupy an area of 7.30 × 2.55 m, probably slightly larger than the cistern itself. Given the other similarities in design with the adjacent cistern, it is likely that there are five transverse arches supporting the roof. The intake conduit, cut into the rock floor of a very shallow gully intersected by the north end of the cistern, was roofed with stone slabs. The depth to the level of the slab-built overflow conduit, located just to the east of the present draw hole, is 3.50 m (cap. 61.7 cum). In June 1986, the water in this cistern was 2.8 m deep; in July 2000, the cistern was dry. This structure may be the "Nabataean roofed cistern" mentioned in Bisheh et al. 1993: 125, with slightly different UTM coordinates: "7313 33112."

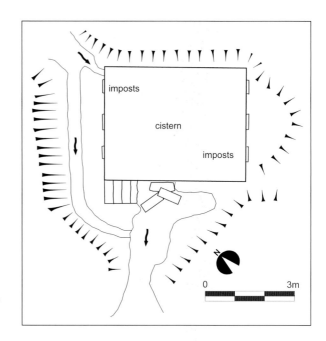

Fig. 3.82 *Cistern no. 37, plan.*

Structure no. 37. Rock-cut cistern

Coordinates: UTM 36R 0732225, 3315604; Pal. Grid 889291. Elevation: 1060 m. 17/06/86, 22/07/00.

The cistern has been cut into the bed of a small gully that drains 5–10 ha of bare white sandstone on the west slope of the Hudeibat edh-Dhiru, at a point where the gully expands slightly just before emptying into the soil of the plain (radial from Reservoir 67: 89 degrees, 6.04 km). Run-off water flowing down the gully poured directly into the cistern (oriented 135 degrees) at its north corner, without passing through a settling tank (fig. 3.82). Erosion has obscured the original form of the intake, but there are slight traces of vertical grooves for a sluice gate to allow closing of the opening once the cistern had filled. The central portion of the downstream wall was built with well-trimmed stone blocks set into step-like settings in the rock, but the rest of the cistern (L 4.95 m; W 3.85 m; depth 2.60 m; cap. 49.6 cum) has been cut down into the soft, white sandstone. There are traces of rock-cut stairs (W 1.6 m) leading down into the cistern at its south corner to give access to the water, but re-cutting and erosion have obscured the original arrangement. A slab roof was carried on three arches oriented with the long axis of the cistern, across the bed of the gully. All that remains

Fig. 3.83 *Cistern no. 38, intake channel on jebel.*

FIG. 3.84 *Cistern no. 38, exterior, with intake channel wall above.*

are traces of the imposts cut into the rock 1.8 m above the floor (W 0.60 m; 0.77 m apart). The small block-like outline of a betyl was cut into the northeast cistern wall, but the plaster waterproofing probably would have obscured it. The hard, white, sandy bedding plaster was covered by a very pebbly grey plaster that survives at only one or two points. It seems unlikely that the cistern was located in such a position that the watercourse had to flow directly over the roof once it was filled, but the original arrangement cannot be restored with complete confidence. There is a narrow shelf (W ca. 1 m) along the northwest side of the cistern, extending from the intake behind the stairs to the edge of the gully below the complex. Although erosion has damaged the surface extensively, there are traces of a depression along this shelf, indicating that it may have served as an overflow channel. If this was the case, a sluice gate or well-placed block could have been used to divert water flow around the cistern once it had filled. No potsherds were observed in the area.

Structure no. 38. Rock-cut cistern

Coordinates: UTM 36R 0734927, 3313716; Pal. Grid 911275. Elevation: 1093 m. 17/06/86, 06/07/00.

The cistern is cut back into a large natural fissure in the south end of the Hudeibat edh-Dhiru, 200 m west of the Desert Highway (radial from Reservoir 67: 97 degrees, 8.81 km). Run-off was collected from the entire south end of the pillowed, bare, white sandstone ridge behind it, an area of approximately 25 ha. This water was channelled down a natural gully into a settling tank cut into the rock (L 5.60 m; W 1.57 m; depth 1.0 m; cap. 8.8 cum) 50 m north of the cistern. The settling tank fed a deep, wide, rock-cut channel (W 0.28–0.42 m; depth 0.25–0.96 m) that wound around the east edge of the ridge for 54.5 m before emptying into the top of the cleft, 8 m above ground level (figs. 3.83–84). The settling tank is waterproofed with a very hard pebbly grey plaster. At several points, the outside edge of the channel has been built up with field stones set in modern mortar, probably a reconstruction of the original arrangement.

The fissure, which was enlarged to allow water storage, is approximately 13 m high, expands in width from 0.10 m at the top to 1.57 m at present ground level, and now extends approximately 25 m back into the ridge. Tool marks on the interior show that the side walls of the lower half of the fissure were excavated to increase the storage capacity of the space, which is nevertheless still remarkably narrow in comparison to its length and depth. The south end, at the outside cliff face, was closed with a wall of blocks that now survives only to present ground level. Originally, it must have been built 1.5 m higher to the level of the pebbly grey plaster waterproofing that still survives on the walls. The water storage area proper would have been 25 m long, ca. 1.70 m wide, and 6 m deep (cap. ca. 255 cum). Several square cuttings can be seen in the wall close to the south end, above the original water level, but they do not appear to be angled properly to have served as imposts for arches to carry a roof. In any case, the water storage area is well protected by the natural bedrock roof. Beams may have been laid across the cistern on these cuttings to support a walkway for water-drawers. No potsherds were observed in the sandy area outside the cistern.

This may be one of the cisterns mentioned by Kirkbride and Harding.
Bibliography: Kirkbride and Harding 1947: 21.

Structure no. 39. Rock-cut cistern

Coordinates: UTM 36R 0734508, 3318654; Pal. Grid 913316. Elevation: 1112 m. 18/06/86, 22/07/00.

The cistern has been cut into the sloping white sandstone bedrock next to a small gully at the extreme western edge of the Hudeibat edh-Dhiru,

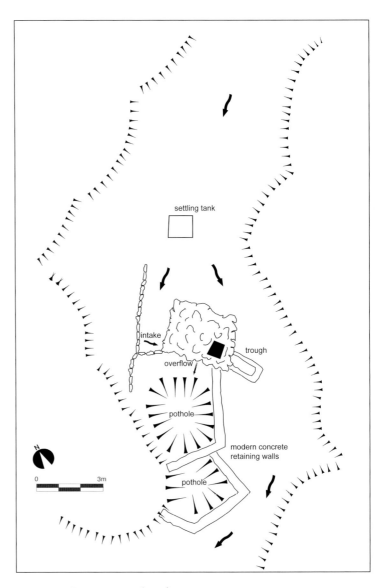

FIG. 3.85 *Cistern no. 39, plan of area.*

adjacent to the loessial soil of the plain and some modern agricultural fields (radial from Reservoir 67: 68 degrees, 8.85 km). The gully drains an ill-defined area of the bare rock slope, approximately 20–30 ha in extent. Of the original arrangements for intake, only the settling tank survives (L 1.47 m; W 1.31 m; depth 0.22 m; cap. 0.42 cum), cut into the bedrock at the middle of the wide, smooth watercourse 3.5 m upstream from the cistern (fig. 3.85). Since there are no traces of rock-cut channels, it seems likely that flow was diverted into the settling tank by means of a wall of blocks or field stones set in earth or mortar, and from the settling tank to the cistern intake in the same fashion. At present, a low modern wall of one course of fieldstones set in mortar captures and channels the water to the intake hole, leaving the settling tank completely dysfunctional. One attraction of this site was probably the presence of two natural, round potholes (D 2.60 m; depth >1.0 m; cap. >5.3 cum. D 2.10 m; depth >1.0 m; cap. >3.5 cum) just below the small knoll selected for the cistern. These natural features probably were used for water storage in antiquity, and they now have been supplied with high concrete walls to increase their capacity. The modern stone wall that diverts water to the cistern also directs it over the ledge behind the cistern into these potholes, with overflow from the upper one pouring naturally into the lower. At present, the cistern is covered by a roof of brush and mud plaster 3.4 m on a side, set on cross-beams and edged on the slope toward the gully by a low wall of roughly trimmed stones that seems to be in part ancient. The modern intake hole (ca. 0.20 m square) has been built of flat fieldstones, and a modern draw hole and drinking trough have been built at the south corner. The access door was locked during our visits, preventing examination of the cistern, but the surface outline appears to be circular in plan, with a diameter of at least 3 m. This diameter and a depth of 4 m would give a capacity of 28.27 cum. An overflow conduit built of roughly trimmed slabs set into the mortared wall was positioned so as to discharge into the upper of the two potholes. Any surplus water ultimately drained back into the gully. No potsherds were observed in the vicinity.

Structure no. 40. Rock-cut cistern

Coordinates: UTM 36R 07333470, 3320180; Pal. Grid 900335. Elevation: 1075 m. 18/06/86.

The cistern has been cut into the bedrock of a white sandstone hillside in the south slope of the foothills of the Jebel Ghana, 1 km southeast of the aqueduct at km 9.943, just above the loessial soil of the plain (radial from Reservoir 67: 56 degrees, 8.59 km). The cistern was filled by the run-off from an area of the foothills approximately 25 ha in extent,

drawing the water from an adjacent shallow gully. A row of roughly shaped blocks set in modern mortar now diverts water into a long irregular opening (L 3.0 m; W 1.5 m) in the bedrock roof, which has been partly rebuilt with irregular stones set in mortar on wooden supports. The original intake and draw hole probably was much smaller. The cistern itself is roughly square (L 3.20 m; W 3.20 m; depth 2.5 m; cap. 25.6 cum) and appears never to have been plastered. A natural depression just above the opening has been deepened slightly to serve as a drinking trough. No ancient ceramics were observed in this area, but the adjacent fields have good soil and a natural catchment, and at the time of the first visit, they were planted with grain. The cistern could not be relocated in July 2000, but a GPS reading was taken in the approximate vicinity.

Structure no. 41. Rock-cut cistern

Coordinates: UTM 36R 0730205, 3313186; Pal. Grid 855271. Elevation: 1001 m. 21/06/86, 19/07/00.

The cistern has been cut into one of the most westerly exposures of white sandstone across the Wadi al-Amghar from Humayma, adjacent to some of the best grain-growing land in the basin (radial from Reservoir 67: 120 degrees, 4.71 km). It was filled with run-off from an ill-defined area of sloping rock and soil approximately 15 ha in extent. The cistern (L 5.70 m; W 3.23 m; depth 3.90 m; cap. 71.8 cum) is surrounded by a modern concrete wall and in 1986 was provided with a roof of corrugated iron carried on wooden beams. No potsherds were observed, and there is nothing about the cistern that marks it out as ancient, but the absence of any heaps of stone rubble suggests that it was excavated in antiquity. When fractured, the soft, white sandstone decays fairly quickly into a light silica sand that blows away, but it is likely that some traces of spoil heaps would be visible if the cistern had been constructed in the modern period.

Structure no. 42. Rock-cut cistern

Coordinates: UTM 36R 0729603, 3311806; Pal. Grid 853259. Elevation: 967 m. 21/06/86, 19/07/00.

The cistern was cut into the same geological feature as Cistern no. 41, but 1.5 km farther

FIG. 3.86 *Cistern no. 45, view of site from above.*

FIG. 3.87 *Cistern no. 45, cistern roof from northeast.*

south (radial from Reservoir 67: 137 degrees, 5.14 km). The catchment area is approximately 10 ha, and the adjacent fields are now in use for growing grain. The modern draw hole with iron door occurs towards one end of a large mortared area approximately 6 m long and 3 m wide, probably the upper surface of the rebuilt or resealed cistern roof. The roughly square draw shaft (W 0.79 m; depth 0.90 m) provides access to a cistern that is 4 m deep to the present floor. The walls could not be examined through the draw hole, but the echo from a pebble dropped into the cistern suggests that it is substantial in size. If the mortared area represents the extent of the roof, the cistern would have a capacity of approximately 72 cum. Although the sides of the draw hole were covered with modern mortar, the mortared area on the surface suggests that this cistern is a rectangular rock-cut design with slab roof supported by transverse arches, rather than a completely rock-cut bottle cistern. Given the length of the tank, it is likely that there are 3 arches (cf. no. 59). The mortar serves no apparent purpose other than as a sealant for a slab roof below, and the depth of the draw hole is typical of this type of roofing system (see Cistern no. 69). The absence of spoil heaps and the presence of a permanent roof are both features that set this cistern apart from other obviously completely modern cisterns in the valley. No potsherds were observed in the area.

Structure no. 43. Rock-cut cistern

Coordinates: UTM 36R 0729676, 3311488; Pal. Grid 853257. Elevation: 967 m. 21/06/86, 19/07/00.

The cistern has been cut into the same geological feature as Cistern no. 42, but 300 m to the southeast (radial from Reservoir 67: 137 degrees, 5.43 km). It was filled by run-off diverted from a shallow gully that drains approximately 15 ha of the slopes above, and it is adjacent to agricultural fields. Corrugated steel sheets have been laid over beams to roof the cistern cut (L 3.76 m; W 2.80 m; depth 2.44 m; cap. 25.7 cum). A modern cement draw hole, probably built over a recess in the wall at one end of the cistern, allows access to the water supply. It was not possible to examine the cistern walls for traces of arch imposts, but in view of its dimensions, it is likely that the roof was composed of slabs car-

ried on two transverse arches (cf. Cistern nos. 57, 83). No potsherds were observed, but the absence of any spoil from recent excavation suggests that this cistern is ancient.

Structure no. 45. Rock-cut cistern

Coordinates: UTM 36R 0726470, 3317594; Pal. Grid 832311. Elevation: 949 m. 23/06/86, 05/07/88, 10/10/90, 19/06/00.

The cistern has been cut into a narrow shelf of fine red sandstone on the north side of a long ridge of Disi sandstone projecting from the loessial plain N of the settlement centre (radial from Reservoir 67: 7 degrees, 1.99 km; fig. 3.86). The sloping plain, formed in an ancient lake, constitutes the major catchment for the reservoirs and cisterns in the centre of Humayma. The ridge, connected to the plain only by an earth isthmus 3 m wide, is surrounded by deep canyons that drain into the Wadi 'Araba. The cistern catchment is formed by a natural gully that drains an area of bedrock along the side of the ridge approximately 15 ha in extent. The cistern is oriented almost due east/west; at present, water enters at the middle of the west end, but the original arrangements for intake and overflow have been lost (fig. 3.87). A wall of carefully trimmed sandstone blocks up to two courses high supplemented the rim of the cistern where the bedrock slopes off toward the east. The cistern (L 7.90 m; W 4.0 m; depth 3.90 m; cap. 123.2 cum) was roofed by long, roughly trimmed slabs of limestone (avg. L 1.10 m; W 0.43 m; Th 0.10 m) carried on five transverse arches that spring from cuttings 2.20 m above the floor (fig. 3.88). Some of the sandstone voussoirs have been carefully cut to a wedge shape and finished with diagonal trimming, while others were only roughly shaped and chinked with small stones and pebbles along their outer edges. Four of the arches and most of the roof survive. The spandrels have been filled with packing walls composed of fieldstones, rubble, and reused blocks. There is a marked offset in the north wall, 4 m from the west end of the cistern, suggesting that the original plan called for an almost square cistern with three arches and that the excavation was extended toward the west either before or after the roof had been built. The offset has no obvious

FIG. 3.88   *Cistern no. 45, interior from the east.*

FIG. 3.89   *Cistern no. 48, solution hole and niche with betyls.*

function, unless it was felt desirable to lessen the span of the last two arches slightly. If some time passed between the two stages of the project, it may be that the owner either noticed that the catchment was capable of filling a larger cistern, or his water requirements had increased markedly. Traces of a sandy grey plaster survive on the interior, in some places heavily tempered with pebbles. The small pockets of soil in the vicinity of the cistern yielded only two ancient potsherds (Bucket 1990.05): one Nabataean of the second to third century, the other either first-century Nabataean common ware or fifth- to sixth-century Byzantine common ware (K. Russell, oral communication). The cistern was half full of water at the time of the first survey visit, slightly less full at the time of a second visit in July 1988, and nearly empty in late October 1990. In June 2000, during a prolonged drought that had left nearly all the cisterns in the region dry, this cistern still contained water to a depth of ca. 0.20 m.

Structure no. 48. Rock-cut cistern

Coordinates: UTM 36R 0725509, 3314764; Pal. Grid 823283. Elevation: 988 m. 24/06/86, 22/06/00.

The cistern has been cut into the red sandstone bedrock to the left of a deep cleft in the north face of the Jebel Qalkha, approximately 500 m from its western tip (radial from Reservoir 67: 216 degrees, 1.10 km; fig. 2.10). The prominent tomb with stepped approach at the south edge of the settlement (T1, A104) is just across the valley. The cleft is part of a natural fault line that has been eroded up the hillside into a great cirque that funnels run-off from a large area of the steep rock hillside, cliff, and tableland above, approximately 15 ha in extent. In places the cleft is nearly filled with *nari*, a caliche or travertine-like water-deposited carbonate cement (see Henry 1996: 37–38). Just above the cistern — immediately above the intersection between the bedrock of the jebel and the earth talus below — the cleft expands slightly around a horizontal solution tunnel (ca. H 1.40 m; W 1.15 m; L 5.90 m; fig. 3.89). This geological feature has the superficial appearance of a spring, but the geology and topography indicate that there was no flowing spring in the historical period (G. Baker, oral communication, June 2002; *pace* Farrand 1984; Henry

1995: 216). The character of the cistern also contradicts the hypothesis of a flowing spring (*pace* Eadie and Oleson 1986: 55). There is evidence for heavy occupation along both sides of the Jebel Qalkha by Palaeolithic and Epi-Palaeolithic cultures, at a time of greater rainfall, and the water deposits and tunnel formation probably date to those periods (Henry 1987; Henry 1995).

Nevertheless, the prominent location of this curious feature high on the hillside south of the settlement, surrounded in antiquity as today by vegetation nurtured by the run-off water, must have attracted attention early in the history of Hawara. A large aedicula niche (H 0.90 m; W 0.65 m) containing three block-like betyls, or a block framed by two altars, has been carefully carved into the rock just to the left of the tunnel opening (fig. 3.89). Attached columns with bases and blocked-out Nabataean Corinthian capitals frame the niche and support a flat architrave with simple projecting crowning moulding. All three blocks are carved in relief at the back of the niche, separated from each other by grooves, the central block taller than the others. Although weathering has badly affected the blocks, the central one may have had a rounded top (Wenning 2001: 85, Type A.2), while the two shorter blocks appear to have had horns and thus may represent altars. Petroglyphs illustrating archers hunting gazelles cover the surface of a rounded projection of the bedrock to the right of the opening, along with a few Thamudic and Nabataean graffiti, one of which is dedicated to "the God of Hawara" (Graf 1992a; Healey 2001: 91; cf. Hackl et al. 2003: 281): *slm br-tlm 'bd 'l-hwr*, "Peace, BR-TLM, servant of 'AL-HWR." The inscription can be interpreted as "Peace, (personal name), servant (of the god) of Hawara." The god may have been Dushara (see discussion in Section 2.B.1). The combination of cleft, water-supply system, and betyl resembles the situation of a small "water sanctuary" identified by Parr at the foot of Jebel Haroun at Petra (Parr 1962).

Although the site has been badly disturbed and is still in use, the original arrangements can be reconstructed with some confidence (fig. 3.90). The cistern was carved entirely within a projection of the bedrock to the left of the cleft, 12 m east of the betyl niche and across from the pictographs

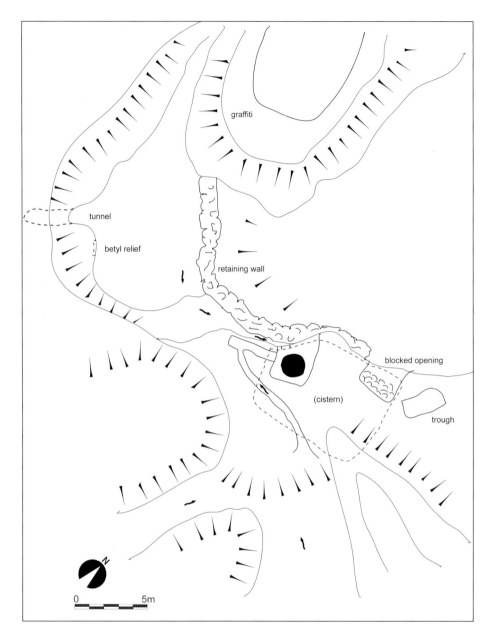

FIG. 3.90   *Cistern no. 48, plan of area.*

(fig. 3.91). The overall arrangement is similar to that of Cistern no. 55, just above the settlement centre (see Chapter 4). Run-off descending along the line of the cleft and a few adjacent feeder channels collected behind a wall built in a curving course across the debris-filled wadi below the solution tunnel. The present, largely modern, wall (H 1.15 m; Th 0.80 m) is built of un-mortared fieldstones. The upstream face of the wall does not appear to have been plastered to make it waterproof, but

waterproofing is not absolutely essential, since the space it defines is almost completely filled with sand. The wall was designed mainly to hold the water at a level high enough to allow it to flow into the cistern through a rock-cut intake hole in its roof; it may also have served as a settling tank. Run-off from a subsidiary gully that opens out just above the cistern was collected in a rock-cut channel (L 8.0 m; W 0.16 m; depth 0.15 m) that snakes down the hillside to a shelf (L 3.40 m; W

0.40 m) 1.20 m above the level of the intake hole. The outside edge of this shelf probably carried a low stone wall that channelled the water to the northeast and into the intake; at present, this water simply pours off the edge and mingles with the water behind the built retaining wall. The circular intake hole (D 0.90 m; depth 0.85 m) is cut into the horizontal floor of a recess (W 1.70 m) set back into the cliff face. It gives access to a roughly rectangular cistern (L ca. 8.0 m; W ca. 5.0 m; depth >4.0 m; cap. >160 cum). At some time, a second recess (L 1.95 m; W 1.22 m) was cut into the rock face 4 m farther along the hillside to give access to the water; this draw hole has recently been walled up with mortared rubble. A betyl has been carved in low relief on one of the side walls. An individual could stand on the floor of this recess (1.90 m below the intake hole), draw water with a bucket and rope, and pour it into a portable trough or container directly below or into the small trough (L 1.47 m; W 0.55 m; depth 0.30 m) cut into the rock to the left of the recess. Water was present in this cistern during survey visits in 1986, 1987, and 1989, but it was dry in October 1990, July 2000, and July 2004.

No ancient potsherds were visible in the vicinity of the cistern and adjacent rock-cut features, but a small number were collected from the wadi 15 m below the cistern, and there is a significant surface scatter along the earth talus leading up to the cistern. Bucket 1990.03: 3 rims, 2 handles, 1 base; 24 Nabataean (at least four of the first century), 22 Roman, 4 Byzantine.
Bibliography: Eadie and Oleson 1986: 55; Graf 1992a.

Structure no. 50. Rock-cut cistern

Coordinates: UTM 36R 0724500, 3315725; Pal. Grid 812292. Elevation: 1035 m. 24/06/86, 21/06/00.

The small basin or cistern has been cut into the surface of a red sandstone shelf at the mouth of a wide valley in the north face of Jebel Qalkha, just above the loessial soil of the sloping valley floor (radial from Reservoir 67: 271 degrees, 1.68 km; fig. 3.92). The catchment consists of the slopes of the Jebel Qalkha immediately above, along with some

FIG. 3.91 *Cistern no. 48, intake channels and cistern cuttings.*

of the cliff face and jebel summit; altogether the area is approximately 10–15 ha in size. There are traces of a low rubble diversion wall at the level of the cistern lip. The cistern itself (L 2.98 m; W 2.45 m; depth 1.05 m; cap. 7.7 cum), oriented east/west, is not much larger than a settling tank, but there are no traces of any larger water-storage structure nearby. Three rock-cut steps (W 0.77 m), cut into the southwest corner, descend to 0.70 m above the level floor. Some regular cuttings along the north and east sides of the basin suggest that blocks may have been used to supplement the bedrock at those points. There are patches of a thin layer of white, water-deposited calcium carbonate at several places within the basin, but no artificial waterproofing. A light scatter of first- and second-century NFW sherds was observed in the area.

FIG. 3.92 *Cistern no. 50, from the northeast.*

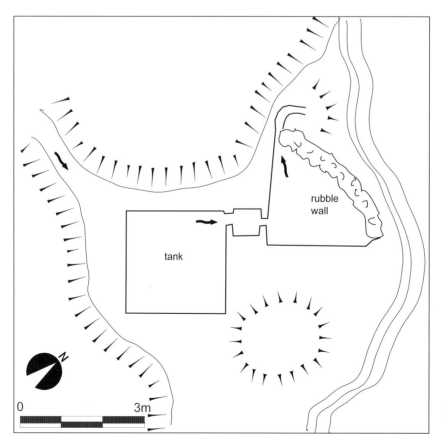

tank

rubble
wall

0   3m

FIG. 3.93 *Structure no. 51,*
plan of area.

Structure no. 51. Rock-cut cistern or wine press?

Coordinates: UTM 36R 0724388, 3315599; Pal. Grid 811291. Elevation: 1046 m. 24/06/86, 21/06/00.

The two basins — either a settling tank and cistern or a wine press — have been cut into a shelf of red sandstone 170 m southwest of Cistern no. 50, just above the soil level at the end of a ridge separating the main valley and a tributary (radial from Reservoir 67: 267 degrees, 1.79 km; fig. 3.93). A natural gully channels water into the first tank from an area of approximately 7 ha along the north slope of the ridge. This roughly square tank (L 2.36 m; W 2.30 m; depth 0.50 m; cap. 2.7 cum) seems too large in relation to the size of the second cistern to have served simply as a settling tank, but it is also too shallow to have served for effective long-term storage (fig. 3.94). All the interior surfaces in the entire complex have been plastered with a hard, very sandy grey plaster containing many small pebbles. In addition, the first tank has been paved with irregular pieces of purple-grey slate (D ca. 0.15 m) set into a slightly whiter mortar without the admixture of pebbles. From the first tank, water flowed over or through a partition wall (Th 0.28 m) at its north corner into a smaller tank (L 0.88 m; W 0.75 m; depth 0.75 m; cap. 0.50 cum), the floor of which is 0.25 m lower than the first. The central portion of this wall has been broken through, but a second flow barrier on the opposite wall has both a central overflow notch and a small hole (D 0.13 m) at the level of the floor. This hole, however, has the appearance of a careless later addition to the small intermediate tank, which would serve no apparent function if water were allowed to flow directly through it at floor level. It is more likely that (if this is a cistern complex) the original arrangement involved overflow across a central notch at the top of each partition wall. Water flowing out of the intermediate tank spilled into the south corner of a third tank. This tank has two perpendicular rock-cut walls and a third, outer wall built of mortared rubble that follows the edge of the outcrop into which the complex has been carved — forming a curving barrier wall with a radius of approximately 2.05 m. The resulting tank has the shape of a quarter cylinder (radius 2.05 m; depth 2.0 m; cap. 26.4 cum), with a long,

FIG. 3.94 *Structure no. 51, view from the south.*

narrow, rock-cut overflow conduit at the northwest corner that discharges over the cliff after making a right-angle bend. The curved blocking wall seems to have been built recently, and at first glance it looks as if it was intended to replace an original rock-cut outer wall that has been lost to erosion or collapse. There is no rubble nearby that might have resulted from such a collapse, however, and the rather awkward arrangement for overflow suggests that there never was sufficient bedrock along the outside face to allow rock-cut walls. A light scatter of Middle Nabataean and Roman common-ware sherds was observed in the soil of the valley below the complex.

This complex, if designed for water capture and storage, would be a very atypical and inefficient arrangement. There are several large cuttings in the same ridge, 20 m to the west — a narrow platform (L 5.0 m; W 0.80 m) and a rock-cut channel (L 4.0 m; W 0.80 m) — which seem to represent projects abandoned when faults or a hard, brittle stratum of

Umm Ishrin sandstone (typical of this part of the Jebel Qalkha) were encountered. It is possible that the original design of this complex had to be altered or truncated when similar problems occurred. The paving on the floor of the first tank in particular may conceal imperfections encountered in the stone. Nevertheless, this explanation does not take account of the presence of the intermediary tank.

Parallels around Petra suggest that this feature was a wine press, the only one so far recognised in the Humayma region. Except for the large lower tank, which has been rebuilt, the arrangement resembles some of the many rock cut pressing installations in and around Petra (al-Muheisen 1990: 210, pls. x–xiii; Bienert, Lamprichts, and Vieweger 2000: 134, fig. 21; Lindner and Gunsam 2002: 228–30) and Beidha (P. M. Bikai 2003: 3; Salameen 2005). These installations generally include a large, shallow upper tank (for treading), a small intermediate filtration tank, and a slightly larger tank for the must. The 36 installations at Beidha are associated with a walled irrigated field appropriate for wine growing; this whole complex seems to pre-date the second century. Similar grape-treading installations built of blocks can be seen around many of the Nabataean through Byzantine sites in the Negev (Evenari et al. 1982: 206–7; Shereshevski 1991: 48, 82, 89–90). Although we have no other evidence to suggest the cultivation of grapes for wine production at Humayma other than a few charred grape seeds from the settlement (Section 2.A.5; Oleson et al. 1997), it is possible that some attempt was made to produce wine locally, perhaps in the Byzantine period, when wine production was at its height in Gaza. If this was the case, the shallow upper tank at Site 51 would have been used for treading grapes, the intermediary tank for filtration, and the lowest shelf used either as a collection tank or to hold jars. Such a primary application, of course, would not have prevented the secondary use of the tanks as cisterns during the rainy season, after the vintage. The absence of sockets for poles or beams in the installations at Petra and Humayma indicate that olives, which require heavy presses and weights, were not being processed at these installations.

Structure no. 52. Rock-cut cistern

Coordinates: UTM 36R 0724788, 3316371; Pal. Grid 817297. Elevation: 1018 m. 24/06/86, 21/06/00.

The cistern, which is unfinished, was cut into the red sandstone bedrock below a natural funnel-shaped valley near the top of the west side of the main ridge behind Humayma (radial from Reservoir 67: 298 degrees, 1.49 km). The catchment is approximately 12 ha in size, and long earth channels reinforced with field stone slabs were built in the recent past to conduct water into the tank. The cistern, however, has always been dry when visited. Several details suggest that the tank (L 8.42 m; W 5.64 m; depth 4.28 m; cap. 203.3 cum) was never finished: the southeast corner has not been squared off, bedrock was still being removed by the trench-and-wedge system at the southwest corner, and there are no impost cuttings for arches or plaster waterproofing. The location, depth, and absence of an access ramp or stairs indicate that this feature was intended as cistern rather than simply a quarry pit. A light scattering of first- to early second-century NFW and NPFW bowl fragments was observed in the vicinity of the cistern.

Structure no. 58. Built cistern?

Coordinates: UTM 36R 0725677, 3316304; Pal. Grid 824297. Elevation: 991 m. 24/06/86, 21/06/00.

The possible cistern is located in a natural catchment near the head of a valley, in a pass between the settlement centre and the Jebel Humayma area (radial from Reservoir 67: 321 degrees, 0.84 km). The soil appears to have been scooped out, leaving a central depression surrounded by a berm (L 26.8 m; W 23 m), just below an outcropping of red sandstone. Erosion and clandestine excavation have not revealed any traces of a cistern beneath the spoil, but the location and character of the site make it possible that there was one here. An elderly shepherd interested in my research asserted that there was once a cistern on this spot. Any such cistern would have had to be largely built of blocks. On 21 June 2000, the broken remains of a rectangular basin carved out of sandstone were found in a recent erosion gully on the edge of the berm (L 1.30 m, W 0.75 m, H uncertain). A background scatter of

FIG. 3.95 *Cistern no. 59, view of settling tank and cistern.*

typical Nabataean and Roman potsherds suggests some sort of activity here in antiquity.

Structure no. 59. Rock-cut cistern

Coordinates: UTM 36R 0725927, 3316247; Pal. Grid 826299. Elevation: 995 m. 24/06/86, 19/06/00.

The cistern has been cut into a shelf of red sandstone bedrock on the edge of the ridge northwest of the settlement centre, next to a modern dirt road (radial from Reservoir 67: 336 degrees, 0.67 km). The catchment is an ill-defined area of the sloping upper surface of the ridge, possibly 4 ha in extent. The run-off follows the natural slope of the hill. Two rubble walls 10 m W of the cistern channel run-off into a rock-cut settling tank (L 1.90 m; W 1.01 m; depth 0.40 m; cap. 0.77 cum), separated from the cistern lip by a thin rock-cut partition (Th 0.20 m) with a channel for the over-flow (fig. 3.95). The channel (W 0.18 m) leading from the settling tank to the cistern is grooved to allow the insertion of a sluice gate used to cut off

the flow of water into the cistern when it reached its capacity. The cistern (L 5.20 m; W 5.0 m; depth 3.75 m; cap. 97.5 cum) was roofed with stone slabs carried by three north/south transverse arches set on imposts cut into the side walls 1.10 m above the cistern floor. The irregular upper edge of the bedrock has been supplemented with mortared rubble and blocks on the lower, south and east, sides. Most of this supplementary construction is a rebuild, but there are surviving ancient filler walls of roughly-trimmed natural sandstone slabs set in copious amounts of a soft, light grey mortar with numerous pebbles and carbon specks. At ground level, they were topped with at least one course of carefully shaped sandstone blocks. The same type of blocks frames the settling tank. The interior of the cistern has been waterproofed with modern cement, but an offset can be seen at the base of the south wall. A light scatter of Nabataean, Roman, and Byzantine potsherds was observed around this entire area of the site.

FIG. 3.96 *Cistern no. 60, view from east.*

FIG. 3.97 *Cistern no. 61, interior from west.*

Structure no. 60. Rock-cut and built cistern?

Coordinates: UTM 36R 0726044, 3316371; Pal. Grid 826304. Elevation: 976 m. 25/06/86, 18/06/00.

The structure has been built in the corner of a sandstone quarry near the foot of an isolated jebel northwest of the settlement centre (radial from Reservoir 67: 348 degrees, 0.76 km). The adjacent hillside (area ca. 3 ha), which slopes down gently from three nearby sandstone domes, could have served as a catchment field, but no intake channel is visible. The construction technique would be very atypical for a cistern. The north and west sides (L 4.75 m; W 2.34 m; depth 1.65 m; cap. 18.3 cum) are formed by the quarry face, while the south and east sides are formed by a wall (Th 1.10 m) built of two facings of heavy, partly trimmed blocks of rubble chinked with smaller stones set in mortar, around a mortar and rubble core (fig. 3.96). A large recess (L 2.32 m; H 1.33 m; depth 0.95 m; cap. 2.9 cum), possibly a pre-existing tomb niche, occupies most of the north wall, increasing the interior capacity to 21.2 cum. The floor and lowest 0.10 m of the built and rock-cut walls were covered with two layers of a very friable, sandy grey plaster heavily tempered with pebbles; the joint between floor and walls is carefully rounded off. No obvious traces of plaster remain at present on the upper surfaces of the walls, but some must have been applied if the structure functioned as a cistern. Since the plaster is relatively soft, its loss here is not surprising. The height of the built walls and the absence of a doorway make it unlikely that the plastered basin was used for processing grain or wine, although storage of grain is possible. The method of construction is similar to that of the Roman reservoir in the fort (no. 62). The whole quarry area yielded a light scatter of Nabataean, Roman, and Byzantine potsherds.

Structure no. 61. Rock-cut cistern

Coordinates: UTM 36R 0735611, 3316305; Pal. Grid 927298. Elevation: 1170 m. 25/06/86, 07/07/00.

The cistern (L 5.90 m; W 5.40 m; depth 4.30 m; cap. 137 cum) was cut into a slope on the southwest side of a large hill of white Disi sandstone 150 m east of the Desert Highway, 1.75 km south of the hamlet of Dabbat Hanut (radial from Reservoir 67: 84 degrees, 9.44 km). The run-off from a large portion (ca. 5 ha) of the adjacent hillside passed close to the cistern in a natural gully, from which it was conducted into the cistern through a rock-cut channel (L 5.5 m; W 0.26 m; depth 0.08 m), supplemented at several points with rubble set in mortar. The eastern, up-hill third of the cistern was roofed by the remnants of the original bedrock surface, while the rest was roofed with stone slabs set on two transverse arches (now fallen; fig. 3.97). The imposts were cut into the cistern walls 2.40 m above the floor. The interior was waterproofed with two layers of a hard, white, sandy plaster containing a heavy admixture of pebbles. No artefacts were observed in the vicinity. During roadwork in 1999, the cistern and surrounding area were completely covered with an enormous excavation dump. The UTM coordinates given above were taken at its estimated original position.

Structure no. 82. Rock-cut cistern?

Coordinates: UTM 36R 0729288, 3307430; Pal. Grid 927298. Elevation: 917 m. 07/07/00.

The small cistern or tank has been cut into the slightly sloping white sandstone extending from the west side of the main mass of the Hudeibat Um Dureira, 80 m south of Cistern no. 29 (radial from Reservoir 67: 158 degrees, 8.80 km; fig. 3.98). Run-off water was channelled into the cistern from several hectares of the adjacent slopes by a natural gully, but the cistern itself is very small (L 1.30 m, W 0.83 m, depth > 0.30 m, cap. > 0.324 cum; oriented approximately E/W). It consists of a simple rectangular cutting, neatly finished with a chisel, with a narrow flat margin around the upper edge. No settling tank, overflow channel, or roof slabs are visible, but a groove has been worn into the centre of the downhill end by rope abrasion. It is not clear what practical purpose such a small tank could have served, other than a settling tank for a large cistern that was planned but not completed. Cistern no. 22 is similar in dimensions, but built of blocks.

FIG. 3.98 *Cistern no. 82, from the east.*

FIG. 3.99 *Cistern no. 83.*

Structure no. 83. Rock-cut cistern

Coordinates: UTM 36R 0723313, 3307921; Pal. Grid 800213. Elevation: 942 m. 14/07/00.

The cistern has been cut into the west side of a low, isolated jebel of Disi sandstone, adjacent to a small wadi (radial from Reservoir 67: 199 degrees, 8.26 km). A few Nabataean and Roman common-ware body sherds were observed in the general area. The badly disturbed remains of an ancient structure can be seen on top of the hill, and Cistern no. 14 is 180 m south. A line of unworked sandstone blocks 10 m long may have channelled the wadi waters into the settling tank at the southwest corner of the main tank. A conduit cut into the bedrock opens on the southwest corner of the settling tank (L 1.82 m, W 1.06 m, depth > 0.30 m, cap. > 0.58 cum), but a modern rubble wall built around the cistern obscures the connection with the cistern (fig. 3.99). The cistern (L 3.94 m, W 3.50 m, depth > 3.60 m, cap. 49.6 cum, orientation 180 degrees) was roofed with slabs carried on two arches oriented N/S (now lost). The interior of the cistern has been cemented in the modern period.

3.B.5. *Barrier Walls, Dam, and Wadi Barriers*

Introduction

Dams, barrier walls, and wadi barriers are similar in that they all are designed to obstruct the flow of water along a natural route of drainage; in consequence, they have been catalogued together here. Dams are substantial structures designed to impound a large pool of water, while wadi barriers are designed to slow the stream as it flows over their walls, forcing the water to deposit earth behind the low barrier and to moisten it by infiltration. I have made a further distinction for barrier walls, which I take to be relatively small constructions designed to enhance the holding capacity of a natural pool. All these structures can be found at other Nabataean sites (see Chapter 8).

Barrier Walls and Dam

Because of the character of the water regime, rapid evaporation of standing water, and the permeability of much of the bedrock, impoundment dams are relatively rare throughout the entire Nabataean cultural region (see pp. 460–78). There is either not enough water to justify impoundment in a standing pool, or the run-off comes in such volume and with such force that the barrier walls and spillways cannot handle it, or the basin is soon filled with sediment. The Umm Ishrin sandstone typical of much of the landscape west and south of Humayma is often too fractured to form large natural basins capable of holding water, but some homogeneous strata do occur (Osborn and Duford 1981: 6–11). The dam and barrier walls catalogued below were associated with strata of such a type. The Disi sandstone formation is typically more uniform than the Ishrin formation, but it also seems more absorbent. In any case, the pillowy formations of the Humayma region generally do not favour the creation of large, enclosed basins with bedrock floors. At least one of the large natural stone basins along the Muqawwar (or Mughur) cascades, 29 km east of Humayma, was adapted for the impoundment of water, although not by means of a barrier wall (Jobling 1989a; Corbett 2009: 344). Barrier Walls nos. 27 and 28 deal with the potential problem of excessive water flow by tapping fairly restricted catchment areas; Dam no. 44 solves the same problem through massive construction and the use of a rock-cut spillway.

Structure no. 27. Barrier wall

Coordinates: UTM 36R 0717167, 3308124; Pal. Grid 838216. Elevation: 908 m. 15/06/86, 07/07/00.

The wall was built across the opening of a short, narrow recess in the very western tip of the crumbly red sandstone of the Hudeibat Um-Dureira, at the conjunction of several gullies that drain approximately 3.5 ha of the hilltop (radial from Reservoir 67: 170 degrees, 7.60 km). A modern wall of rubble set in cement (L 7.88 m; H 2.60 m; Th 1.15 m) has been built across the opening, which is at the present ground level, to impound an irregular pool otherwise walled completely by the bedrock (ca. 20 × 20 m, 2.5 m deep; cap. ca. 1000 cum; fig. 3.100). The pool was dry at the time of both survey visits, but water marks on the walls show that it had recently held water to a depth of approximately 1

FIG. 3.100   *Barrier wall no. 27.*

FIG. 3.101   *Barrier wall no. 28 and pool.*

m. Although the impoundment wall is completely modern in construction and no ancient foundation cuttings are visible at either end, Laborde seems to have seen a blocking wall during his visit in 1828, very likely an ancient one. Several carefully squared sandstone blocks with diagonal surface trimming have been reused in the present wall. These blocks may have been recycled from the original barrier wall, or they may have been taken from the small Nabataean tower on top of the jebel (see Cook 2004: 220–21). There are signs of intensive Nabataean occupation in the immediate area: the tower, Cistern no. 26 just around the corner of the jebel to the east, and a Nabataean inscription (badly weathered) cut into the rock of an isolated jebel 50 m to the northwest. The nearby Cistern no. 25 and Barrier Wall no. 28 are very similar in design. No ancient potsherds were observed in the immediate area of the dam.

Bibliography: Laborde 1830: 63; Brünnow and Domaszewski 1904–9: 1, 476–77, fig. 546 no. D.

Structure no. 28. Barrier wall

Coordinates: UTM 36R 0727278, 3307919; Pal. Grid 839215. Elevation: 906 m. 15/06/86, 07/07/00.

The wall was built across the narrow opening of a large (D ca. 26 m) natural circular basin eroded into the crumbly red sandstone on the south face of the very western tip of the Hudeibat Um-Dureira, directly south of Cistern no. 26 across a narrow ridge (radial from Reservoir 67: 171 degrees, 7.82 km; fig. 3.101). A modern cement barrier wall (L 2.82 m at base, 8.70 m at top; H 2.30 m; Th 0.64 m) has been built across the opening, which is approximately 5 m above present ground level; a thinner capping wall has been built for 10 m along the top of the natural outside sandstone barrier to divert overflow over the cement barrier wall and to keep animals out of the basin. The pool (cap. ca. 1069 cum) was dry at the time of the both survey visits, but marks on the walls seen during the first visit indicated that it had recently held a significant quantity of water. It is difficult to estimate the size of the catchment area provided by the slopes of the jebel, but it is probably in the order of 3–4 ha. No trace survives of an ancient wall across this basin, other than some possibly ancient trimming

of the bedrock next to the modern wall. Laborde, however, seems to have seen a blocking wall at this point, too, during his visit in 1828, very likely an ancient one. In addition, the spectacular potential of the basin, combined with the proximity of the watchtower mentioned above (cf. Structure no. 27), suggest that there may well have been a barrier wall here in antiquity. No artefacts were noted in the basin area other than a few sandstone blocks with diagonally trimmed faces that probably had tumbled down from the watchtower on the summit.

Bibliography: Laborde 1830: 63; Brünnow and Domaszewski 1904–9: 1, pp. 476–77, fig. 546 no. A.

Structure no. 44. Dam

Coordinates: UTM 36R 0723459, 3314168; Pal. Grid 801278. Elevation: 964 m. 22/06/86, 22/06/00.

The dam was built near the head of the Wadi Aghar, across a narrow, vertical-walled canyon that drains most of the western half of Jebel Qalkha (radial from Reservoir 67: 240 degrees, 3.09 km). Below this point, 350 m upstream from its junction with two other valleys draining from the north and south, the canyon begins to widen significantly. The catchment area, a barren plateau composed almost entirely of sandstone, is approximately 3 sq km (300 ha) in extent. The dam (L 9.70 m; W 4.36 m; max. H 3.65 m), which has survived virtually intact, is built of roughly-trimmed, approximately rectangular blocks of the local red sandstone, chinked with river stones and set in a very sandy grey mortar containing frequent charcoal specks (figs. 3.102–3). It is oriented perpendicular to the two adjoining cliff walls, at a bearing of 15 degrees. A small probe at the south end of the upstream face of the dam revealed that this surface was faced with a layer (Th 0.02 m) of medium hard white plaster (Bucket 87.032; see p. 241, Probe 1; analysis in Section 6.D.), heavily tempered with rounded, poorly-sorted red sand and pebbles, containing occasional lime nodules and infrequent flecks of carbon. The surface was very carefully smoothed, then apparently coloured with a brownish red wash. This same colour can be seen on dams in the Siq at Petra, possibly as part of an attempt to make these engineering interventions blend in with the land-

FIG. 3.102 *Dam no. 44, view from above to north.*

scape (Bellwald and al-Huneidi 2003: 61, 71). There are no traces of plaster on the downstream face of the dam, perhaps because it has been exposed to the elements since construction. The wide crest of the dam was finished with an even surface of more or less regular rectangular blocks and slabs. There traces of two layers (each Th 0.03 m) of very hard white plaster with pebbles and numerous poorly-sorted sand particles on the upper surface around the west side of the altar (Bucket 87.030, 87.031). This paving may have originally extended over the whole crest.

The upper and downstream faces reveal that occasional blocks were laid end-on to either face of the wall to serve as tie-blocks binding the facing to the core. A similar technique was used on the dam at Safir in the Negev (Kloner 1973: pl. 4). A particularly long, narrow block near the centre of the upstream side (4.70 m south of the north end), carries the inscription "VII" pecked into its west end, oriented with the apex of the V toward the west (upstream; L 0.195 m; H 0.07 m; see below). The crest of the dam may originally have been sealed with two layers (each Th 0.03 m) of a

hard, light grey plaster very heavily tempered with poorly-sorted, rounded grains of clear and reddish quartz sand, and containing occasional flecks of charcoal. Patches of this paving survive at the south end of the dam, on either side of a large altar or betyl block (W 1.90 m; H 0.60 m; Th 0.50 m) cut into the bedrock of the canyon wall (fig. 3.104). This block, the top of which carries five shallow depressions, projects from the centre of the wide, deep slot into which the south end of the dam has been built for watertightness and support. The north end of the dam was also built into a wide slot in the bedrock. The north recess, however, angles back into the cliff just below the upper level of the dam to accommodate a wide, shallow spillway (W 1.20 m; D 0.10 m; fig 3.102). A bedrock curb (H 0.35 m; W 0.23 m) separates the floor of the spillway (ca. 0.10 m deep) from the dam; a narrow channel (W 0.12 m; depth 0.12 m) was cut down into the outside edge of the downstream half of the spillway. The total length of the dam complex, including the spillway and altar, is 11.40 m. Two rock-cut steps directly below the spillway were probably designed to break the force of the discharge.

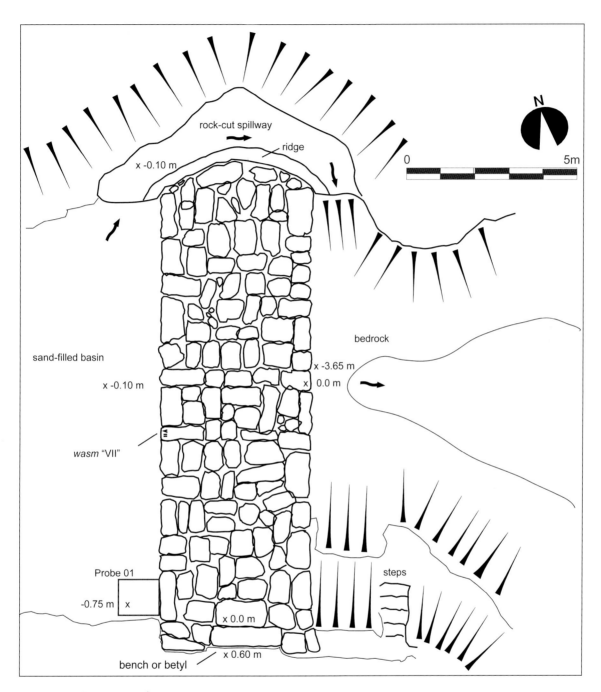

Fig. 3.103 *Dam no. 44, plan.*

The original V-shaped canyon floor at the site of the dam was levelled in several stepped cuttings (W 1–3 m) before the impoundment wall was built. Steps and a short walkway, cut into the rock at the south end of the dam to give access to the altar and pool from the downstream side, are probably part of the original construction phase.

In view of the absence of any other means of access, individuals would have had to dip water out of the impoundment pool while standing on the broad crest of the dam.

The downstream face of the dam is encrusted with a lime deposit left by water percolating through the fabric of the wall. The basin upstream

Fig. 3.104 *Dam no. 44, upper surface, possible altar or bench, and steps.*

is filled with red sand to the level of the spillway, concealing the profile of the canyon floor in this area. The width of the canyon tapers from 11 m at the dam to 8.6 m at a point 40 m upstream where the canyon makes a bend to the north, then to 7 m at a ledge and pool 78 m north of the dam. If a uniform rise in the canyon floor is assumed, and the depth of entrained water decreased from ca. 3 m at the dam to ca. 1.5 m at the 40 m mark and 0.50 m at the 78 m mark, the maximum capacity of the reservoir would have been approximately 1,400 cum.

Numerous Nabataean inscriptions have been carved into the canyon wall 10 to 20 m upstream from the dam, from 1 to 2 m above the sand. Individuals probably reached this area by scrambling along the sides of the reservoir when it was only partly full. A ledge for walking may be preserved below the level of the present sand fill. There are traces of a Thamudic inscription cut into the rock above the ledge and natural stone basin 78 m upstream from the dam. A narrow flight of rock-cut steps goes around the left side of that ledge, leading

to a further 20 m stretch of the canyon terminating in another pool and ledge. Beyond this point, the canyon narrows to 1 m and winds steeply into the mountain. There are also three natural bowl-shaped basins downstream from the dam, one of which may have been altered to an approximately rectangular shape. They all seem too large, however, to have been used efficiently as drinking troughs filled from the reservoir with buckets.

No ancient potsherds were observed in the vicinity of the dam, but the presence of a betyl indicates a Nabataean cultural origin. The technique of insetting each end of the dam into the bedrock, the use of alternating header and stretcher blocks, and the application of red plaster on the faces of the structure all find parallels in the detention dams constructed at Petra in the first century (see Chapter 8 and Bellwald and al-Huneidi 2003). The inscribed "VII" resembles the Roman numeral "seven," but it can also be compared with Bedouin *wusum* (sing. *wasm*) — tribal camel brands also used to mark grazing land or water sources. The local Huweitat, in fact, use a shape like an in-

verted V, called *'afayhij*, "having the legs apart," and vertical lines (*mitraq*, "stick") often appear as modifiers (King 1992: 880). Interpretation of the sign as a *wasm* seems the most likely reading, since the Roman numeral VII (= 7) does not correspond with the activity of any legions known from historical sources to have been active in the region. Other than a unit of the Legio III Cyrenaica stationed at Hawara itself, and possibly a unit of the Legio VI Ferrata (Oleson, Reeves, Fisher 2002), the only legions stationed close by were the Legio X Fretensis at Aila and possibly the Legio VI Ferrata at Adrou (Udhruh) (Speidel 1977; Parker 1986: 98; Kennedy 2008).
Bibliography: Kirkbride and Harding 1947: 22; Oleson 1991d.

Wadi Barriers

As noted above, wadi barriers were low walls intended to slow the flow of water down an earthen run-off route — usually a valley bottom or a hillside erosion gully — long enough to allow the water to drop its load of soil and to infiltrate the soil already deposited behind and below the barrier wall. This moistened soil can then be used to nurture a grain crop, planted only after the owner of the field judges the moisture to be sufficient to bring the crop to maturity. Because of their location across watercourses and on soil rather than bedrock, wadi barriers are seldom well-preserved in the Humayma catchment. In addition, because of the simplicity of their construction, it is usually very difficult to determine the age of a set of wadi barriers. Those identified below as ancient were selected because of their ruinous condition, proximity to other ancient structures, or location far from recent habitation areas. It is likely that there were many more such barriers in the lower reaches of the Wadi al-Gharid and Wadi al-Qalkha, where the annual flow of water and soil was virtually guaranteed, but where the structural remains would have lasted only a few years without maintenance before being buried or completely scattered.

Structure no. 5. Wadi barriers

Coordinates: UTM 36R 0737467, 3322901; Pal. Grid 942360. Elevation: 1254 m. 01/06/86, 24/07/00.

The barriers were built across the Seyl 'Ain Jammam over a stretch of 200 m where the slope of the escarpment levels out in a wide shelf just above the edge of the plain (radial from Reservoir 67: 55 degrees, 13.40 km; fig. 3.1). Run-off from the spring on the escarpment above has produced green traces of vegetation down the slope to approximately 200 m above the highest barrier, but the barriers were designed to intercept the run-off and eroded soil from a wide adjoining area of the escarpment, approximately 50 ha in area. Five barriers are clearly defined, although in varying degrees of ruin, and two possible barriers consist of alignments of boulders scattered across the wadi bed (fig. 3.105). The remaining barriers vary significantly in size (L 10–20 m; H 0.50–1.20 m; Th 0.05–1.0 m) and degree of preservation. Of the very damaged examples, mostly the facing or core of large boulders (D 0.50–0.75 m) survives, shifted slightly from their original alignment and now stripped of the original packing stones and the soil they held back. Several well-preserved examples, in which the core is still covered with fist-sized fieldstones, seem to have been rebuilt recently. These barriers are still effective in collecting and preserving the light, loessial soil carried down by the wadi, which elsewhere is very stony and barren. Recent tent rings and a Bedouin cemetery can be seen several hundred metres away to the south and west, indicating a possible source for the renovation. When all seven barriers were functioning, they would have provided approximately 4 ha of deep soil, watered by the run-off that soaked into them. No ceramics were observed in this area, but there was a light scatter of flint tools and debitage on either bank of the wadi.

Structure no. 16. Wadi barriers

Coordinates: UTM 36R 0724100, 3308134; Pal. Grid 807216. Elevation: 925 m. 09/06/86, 14/07/00.

The barriers were built across the course of a slight depression that drains an area of gently sloping loessial fields approximately 13 ha in extent,

Fig. 3.105   *Wadi barriers no. 5, from south.*

Fig. 3.106   *Wadi barriers no. 79, from east. Reservoir no. 53 in background.*

at the foot of a low sandstone jebel (radial from Reservoir 67: 194 degrees, 7.81 km). The six barriers visible at present (L 10–15 m; W ca. 1.0 m; H ca. 0.60 m) were laid out approximately 20 m apart and built up of small stones (D 0.10–0.25 m) heaped up with the soil. The barriers were designed to hold back run-off water temporarily, to allow some of it to soak into the soil that piled up behind them, while the surplus flowed over or through them. The nature of the construction, the erosion patterns, and the presence of agricultural activity indicate that these barriers may be modern or at the very least extensively rebuilt in the modern period, but the presence of large Jointed Saltwood shrubs on several indicate that they are not ephemeral in character. Furthermore, several ancient structures on the adjacent jebel (possibly a watch-tower, a farmhouse, and a cist grave) indicate ancient activity in the general area. Nabataean and Roman common-ware potsherds were observed on the surface of the jebel.

Structure no. 79. Wadi barriers

Coordinates: UTM 36R 0725290, 3315708; Pal. Grid 820292. Elevation: 980 m. 26/06/90, 28/06/00.

The three barriers have been built across the small wadi that drains the valley formed by the Jebel Qalkha and the ridge west of the settlement centre, 100 m below Reservoir no. 53 (radial from Reservoir 67: 273 degrees, 0.90 km; fig. 3.106). The catchment is approximately 14 ha in area. The uppermost of the barriers (L 9.60 m; H ca. 0.60 m; Th 0.60 m) is the best preserved, although the central section and the upper courses of the wall have been lost. The surviving portion has been constructed of untrimmed but regular sandstone slabs (L ca. 0.30–0.70 m), chinked and supplemented with a few smaller fieldstones; it extends well into the embankment on either side. The wall survives to only two visible courses and its present profile follows that of the V-shaped wadi bed, so it is likely that several courses have been lost toward the central part of the wall in the direct path of the run-off. The two lower barriers, 50 and 100 m downstream, survive only as faint traces, but they appear to have been constructed in the same manner and to essentially the same dimensions. Because gaps

have appeared, none of the barriers now retain any significant terraced ground. No ancient potsherds were observed in the area of the barriers.

3.B.6. *Terraces and Stone Piles*

The distinction between terraces and wadi barriers is not always clear, since both types of structure served as barriers to the flow of water and the movement of soil. In general, barrier walls are classified as terraces if they are located high up on hillsides rather than low in a valley and do not obstruct a well-developed, distinct watercourse. The technique and its objectives are obvious, and this type of water harvesting in the Near East goes back at least to the Middle Bronze Age (Levy and Alon 1987: 56). There are numerous parallels at other Nabataean sites (see Chapter 8). I have catalogued terraces and stone piles together, because they often appear together and because the construction technique often is very similar. Few of the terraces in the Humayma catchment appear to have been carefully built or monumental in design or construction, and as a result of weathering and structural decay only the terrace walls at Structure no. 81 remain well-defined. Most of the terrace walls are simply long heaps of stones oriented across a slope, and the stone piles are roughly circular heaps. While the terraces should have functioned as barriers to hold soil and moisture on a sloping field, the function of the stone piles is less clear. Several of the ancient desert cities in the Negev are surrounded by large areas in which the hillsides have been cleared of stones, leaving patterns of long down-slope heaps of stones or carefully arranged circular heaps. Removal of the stones increased run-off by speeding up flow and by fostering the formation during rainfall of a natural crust impervious to water (see the discussion in Evenari, Shanan and Tadmor 1982: 127–47). The chronology of this technique also is uncertain, but it probably originated during the Middle Nabataean period and reached a peak of application during the Byzantine period.

In any case, the function of the stone piles at Humayma is not at all clear. Only the fields of stone piles at Sites nos. 8 and 47 are extensive enough to have generated appreciable extra run-off, and

FIG. 3.107   *Terraced area no. 9, partial view.*

neither site is associated with a field or cistern that might have benefited from the improvement. Since the other fields of stone piles are all quite restricted in area and are associated with terraces, it is likely that they represent simply a strategy for ridding the surface of a terraced plot of impediments to cultivation. Interpretation of all these features is made more difficult by the deflation or erosion of the soil exposed by the stone piles and once held by the terraces. Given the very stony ground that serves as pastureland around Humayma today, it seems unlikely that any desire to improve grazing opportunities alone would have justified construction of stone piles. Given their rarity, these terraces and stone piles may represent failed experiments.

Structure no. 9. Terraces and Stone piles (?)

Coordinates: UTM 36R 0735011, 3322849; Pal. Grid 919361. Elevation: 1277–1300 m. 03/06/86, 25/07/00.

The terraces cover an area of approximately 6 ha high on the shoulder of a spur projecting south from Jebel Ghana, 500 m southeast of the closest

stretch of the Jammam Aqueduct and 75 m below it (radial from Reservoir 67: 49 degrees, 11.40 km; fig. 3.1). The terrace walls (L 10–25 m; H ca. 1.0 m), built for the most part of angular boulders of limestone (D 0.25–0.55 m) gathered from the surface, are scattered at wide intervals across the slope (fig. 3.107). There is no apparent regular pattern to their location, but they are staggered rather than in rows, possibly to catch the run-off better, and some are built at the focus of a slight natural drainage channel. The surface of the slope behind and between the walls is very stony, indicating that any soil exposed or collected by the terrace walls has washed or blown away. Some of these features lack any linear definition, suggesting that they were in fact simply heaps of stones collected from the surface of the slope. Judging from the piles of stones behind them, even some of the well-defined cross-slope walls may have been intended simply as retaining walls to keep stone heaps from collapsing down the hill. At least some of the walls, however, still retain soil. Perhaps each small terrace was intended to accommodate and nurture a single tree. No ancient potsherds were observed in the vicinity of the terraces, but the loss of soil from the fields suggests that the arrangement is ancient.

There are a few isolated clusters of possible terrace walls here and there around the deep valley northeast of this spur and a few groups of terraces approximately 5 ha in area close to the base of the escarpment, just to the south and southwest, between 1175 and 1200 m elevation. These terraces (and stone piles?) are similar in character to the group of terraces near the top of the slope, but somewhat less monumental and less well-preserved.

Structure no. 15. Terrace

Coordinates: UTM 36R 0723760, 3307400; Pal. Grid 803210. Elevation: 944 m. 09/06/86, 14/07/00.

The terrace extends along the front of a natural, theatre-shaped catchment on the northwest slope of a low sandstone jebel on the left bank of the Wadi esh-Shubeita (radial from Reservoir 67: 195 degrees, 8.61 km). The curved retaining wall (L ca. 20 m; H 0.30–0.35 m) was constructed of one to two courses of large, untrimmed but regular slabs of the local red sandstone; it still holds back the earth of the hillside. Most of the flat upper surface of the hill drains into the theatre-shaped catchment slope, but the total area is still only about 0.75 ha. The terrace should probably be associated with a roughly square structure (ca. 20 m square) the re-mains of which can be seen at the foot of the north slope of the jebel. The doorjambs are very carefully squared and were finished with typically Nabataean diagonal trimming. There is no trace of a cistern near this hill; the inhabitants may have made use of Cisterns no. 14 and 83, 600 m to the northwest. A cistern and settling tank built into excavations in the alluvial soil 300 m to the northwest (UTM 3307447, 36R 0723287) are probably modern, since the modern cement lining seems to cover cement blocks rather than stone.

Structure no. 46. Terraces (?) and Stone piles

Coordinates: UTM 36R 0725219, 3317671; Pal. Grid 819312. Elevation: 1016 m. 23/06/86, 20/06/00.

The terraces and associated stone piles were built along a relatively small (L 200 m; W 125 m;

2.5 ha) and steep (40 degrees) patch of rocky soil on the east shoulder of Jebel Humayma, just below the sandstone peak (radial from Reservoir 67: 333 degrees, 2.26 km; fig. 3.108). The four terrace walls (L ca. 120 m; W ca. 2.5 m; H ca. 0.50 m) are now simply long, scattered heaps of field stones laid across the slope at even intervals. Since there is no apparent vertical downhill face and very little build-up of soil on the uphill side, these features may in fact simply be the result of field clearing, the stones being laid in long piles across the slope to slow the run-off of water and soil. Nevertheless, the piles may have been intentioned to function in more or less the same way as proper terraces, without having the same architectural definition. Circular heaps of stones (D ca. 2.5–3.0 m) appear at uneven intervals in the spaces between the long piles, as well as on the adjacent, slightly larger (ca. 200 × 200 m; 4 ha) south slope of the jebel. No other arrangements for water-harvesting or water storage were found in the vicinity of these slopes. Although no ancient potsherds were found in these fields, the fuzzy outlines of the stone piles and the deflation of the soil exposed between them indicate that they are not recent. In the absence of any sig-nificant run-off catchment field, it is unclear what sort of agriculture could have been carried out on this steep slope.

Structure no. 49. Terraces

Coordinates: UTM 36R 0724739, 3315723; Pal. Grid 815291. Elevation: 1017 m. 24/06/86, 21/06/00.

Five short terraces have been built of hard, black sandstone rubble across a run-off gully between two earth and rubble talus slopes on the north side of Jebel Qalkha (radial from Reservoir 67: 272 degrees, 1.44 km). They are located at the foot of the sandstone cliff below the highest peak, directly below a long, narrow crevice that extends up the entire cliff face and directs all run-off to this point; at present, the five terrace walls are cut by the narrow gully, which continued to grow after maintenance of the walls ceased. The two upper walls are the longest (L 70 m; W ca. 4 m; H ca. 1 m), the lower walls becoming rapidly shorter as they follow the profile of the original gully. Traces of the neatly laid vertical wall faces are visible, but

FIG. 3.108 *Area of terraces and stone piles no. 46, telephoto view from east.*

the walls now have the appearance of long stone piles rather than proper terrace walls. Nevertheless, a significant amount of soil has accumulated above them, resulting in a terraced effect. Although the soil is now covered once again with fieldstones, it is likely that the original intent of the arrangement was the provision of protected, nearly horizontal agricultural fields that could store run-off water from the large catchment area. No ancient potsherds were observed in the vicinity, but there were numerous flint blades, scrapers, and debitage.

Structure no. 80. Terraces

Coordinates: UTM 36R 0725018, 3316052; Pal. Grid 818295. Elevation: 1000–1010 m. 24/06/86, 21/06/00.

Three terraces have been built across a slight run-off depression on a theatre-shaped slope approximately 12 ha in area, at the head of the valley containing most of Humayma's quarries, just above and west of Reservoir no. 53 (radial from Reservoir

67: 288 degrees, 1.24 km). The terrace walls (L ca. 15 m; W ca. 2 m; H ca. 0.75 m) have been constructed by heaping up the small (D 0.1–0.15 m) fieldstones that cover the surface of the hill in parallel lines, roughly 10 m apart. The barriers are relatively lightweight structures, but the run-off apparently is not violent at this point, since they show little apparent damage and earth has collected behind them. No ancient potsherds were observed in the vicinity, and there is no decisive evidence to date these walls, but given the occupation history of the region, they are most likely ancient.

Structure no. 81. Terraces

Coordinates: UTM 36R 0723453, 3313577; Pal. Grid 808287. Elevation: 1040–1055 m. 20/06/86.

The four terraces have been built of red sandstone rubble just below the summit of the pass between the south and north slopes of the Jebel Qalkha, in the gently sloping upper reaches of a narrow valley (radial from Reservoir 67: 231 de-

FIG. 3.109 *Valley with terraces, no. 81.*

grees, 3.42 km; fig. 3.109). The valley joins Wadi Aghar just below Dam no. 44. The terraces were built approximately 10 m apart down the slope and vary in length from 8 to 12 m. The maximum height is approximately 1.5 m. The downhill walls have neat, vertical faces, although the stones are not trimmed, and the upper surfaces dip slightly toward the centre. The lowest wall in the series has been breached at one point by erosion, but the rest are intact and hold back large pockets of a light soil on an otherwise very stony slope. There are no signs of recent cultivation. No artefacts were observed in the vicinity of the walls.

Structure no. 8. Stone piles

Coordinates: UTM 36R 0737173, 3322720; Pal. Grid 939379. Elevation: 1250 m. 03/06/86, 24/07/00.

The stone piles appear on the gentle southwest slope (area ca. 2.5 ha) of a low jebel adjacent to the wadi in which the wadi barriers of Structure no. 5

were built (radial from Reservoir 67: 55 degrees, 13.10 km). The piles (D ca. 1–2 m; H 0.25–0.60 m) appear more or less at random across the slope, their location defined most likely by variations in the degree of surface cover and the size — and thus the maximum tossing distance — of the stones (D 0.10–0.30 m; fig. 3.110). The stones are angular fieldstones with weathered surfaces, generated by the jebel on which they were found. There are traces of relatively recent Bedouin settlement on the northeast end of this jebel, but the stone piles may be ancient, since the soil exposed by gathering up the stones has been deflated and the present desert pavement appears undisturbed. From a distance, however, the hillside appears slightly less rough than the surrounding territory, since the larger stones have been gathered up. No potsherds were observed in the vicinity of the mounds. At the foot of the jebel there are traces of two possible terrace walls perpendicular to the slope (L ca. 15 m), but they are not placed at any natural focus of

FIG. 3.110   *Field with stone piles, no. 8.*

FIG. 3.111   *Field with stone piles, no. 47, from the north.*

the run-off. Since there are no cisterns or marked fields that would have benefited from the enhanced run-off that might have resulted from construction of these piles, they are more likely to have been set up simply to expose soil for agricultural use or grazing. There are occasional groups of two or three less well-defined stone piles on some of the other slopes around the Seyl 'Ain al-Jammam at this elevation. These may represent attempts to determine the depth or character of the soil at sites selected for agriculture but then abandoned.

Structure no. 47. Stone piles

Coordinates: UTM 36R 0723811, 3316327; Pal. Grid 805297. Elevation: 1029–1050 m. 23/06/86, 20/06/00.

The stone piles have been built across two talus slopes (ca. 450 × 200 m; ca. 9 ha) curving around from an easterly to a northerly exposure, below a steep sandstone ridge projecting from the northwest corner of the Jebel Qalkha (radial from Reservoir 67: 285 degrees, 2.47 km; fig. 3.111). A few of the piles on the east-facing slope meld together to form a ragged line, but most of them (D 5–8 m; H ca. 1 m) are scattered evenly across the slopes in an approximate quincunx pattern. The downhill side of some of the piles is supported by a low retaining wall built of field stone slabs against which stones were heaped from above, but it is clear that many of the piles have spread beyond their original dimensions. Since there are no fields or cisterns below the slopes that would have benefited from any increased run-off, it seems likely that the piles were constructed in the course of clearing land for cultivation. The soil exposed by the clearing, however, has now been lost to wind and water erosion. No ancient potsherds were observed in the fields, but the absence of any traces of modern cultivation and the scattering of the stone piles suggests that the features are ancient in origin.

3.B.7 *Hillside Channels and Slides*

Introduction

By the coincidence of their location, several hillside channels and slides came to my attention at the beginning of the Humayma catchment survey in 1986. At the time, it seemed to me unlikely that these features had anything to do with water management, and several of the slides also seemed likely to be recent in date. Nevertheless, I recorded all the hillside channels as we came across them, along with a sample of the slides, as a precaution. It soon became clear that slides were recreational sites created by Bedouin children at play. They consist simply of grooves worn in steep, low slopes of the soft white sandstone of the Disi Formation by the stones or flattened jerry cans used by the children as sleds. Occasionally, footholds are carved or worn in the rock alongside a particularly successful slide to facilitate a quick return to the top.

Careful recording and analysis also made it clear that the hillside channels, while not modern in date, can have had nothing to do with water. Nevertheless, they are impressive in scale, spectacularly located, and — as far as I can tell — not paralleled elsewhere in Arabia Petraea. They consist of sets of shallow, wide, flat-bottomed slots cut in a sandstone slope, usually carrying a shallow, round-bottomed central groove. The slots range around 0.50 m wide, 0.05–0.08 m deep, and 1.5 to 31 m long; the central grooves are around 0.08–0.10 m wide and 0.05–0.13 m deep. Series of these channels are cut vertically in the pillowy hillocks of white Disi sandstone in such a way that one channel leaves off at the same level where another begins, but separated horizontally by several metres. The visual effect is that of a giant "Snakes and Ladders" game. Most of the channels were oriented somewhere between southeast and southwest, but this may be in part an accident of the topography. K. Russell (oral communication, October 1990) reported seeing similar channels cut into the mountains "around Petra," but lacking the central groove.

The hillside channels serve no obvious practical function, suggesting some sort of cultic significance. Given the absence of any obvious Greco-Roman, Christian, or Islamic parallels, it is likely that their origin lies in the less well-documented Nabataean period and religion. The only interpretation that comes immediately to mind, given the pillowy forms in which most of the channels have been cut, is that they constitute abstract representations of the female genitalia. The striking monumentality

FIG. 3.112   *Area of hillside channels, no. 2.*

FIG. 3.113   *Hillside channel, no. 11.*

of these channels, however, combined with the absence of parallels for such a symbol elsewhere in Nabataean art, counts against this hypothesis.

Site no. 2. Hillside channels

Coordinates: UTM 3336R 0737564, 19903; Pal. Grid 944327. Base elev.: 1234 m. 01/06/86, 19/07/00.

Eight channels have been cut vertically in the pillowy sandstone slopes on both sides of a wadi at the foot of the rocky slope of Jebel Naqb Istar, just below the modern highway (radial from Reservoir 67: 68 degrees, 12.10 km). Five of the cuttings, which vary from one another somewhat in width and depth, have a longitudinal central groove, while the rest are flat. They are all carefully laid out, but their surfaces have been only roughly finished, leaving the marks of the pick or punch with which they were

executed. The most spectacular of the group begins on a flat, natural bedrock platform on the spur of a sandstone ridge (L 30.0 m; W 0.43 m; gutter W 0.055 m; depth 0.01–0.05 m; fig. 3.112). The feature extends for 30 m in a southerly direction, descending 10 vertical metres down the stepped face of the ridge to an abrupt, undifferentiated termination at ground level. A second cutting, 30 m southwest of the first (L 8.5 m; W 0.49 m; depth 0.14 m), had no central channel. Six more cuttings were observed on both sides of the wadi for 60 m to the south, four of them with central grooves. The two longest of these cuttings (L 11.9 m, W 0.42–49 m, central channel W 0.05–0.08 m, depth 0.08–0.13 m; L 9.26 m, W 0.50 m, central channel W 0.12–0.14 m, depth 0.13–0.14 m) both begin like the first at natural platforms, and terminate at ground level after a steep and undulating, but straight, course. The rest of the cuttings are shorter, tend to lack central channels, and extend from ground level to 1.5–2.0 m up the pillowy bedrock face. There does not appear to be any special orientation, but because of the topography, the longest cuttings face more or less south. No artefacts were observed in the vicinity of the cuttings.

Site no. 11. Hillside channels

Coordinates: UTM 36R 0734898, 3314228; Pal. Grid 898266. Base elev.: 1053 m. 04/06/86, 09/07/00.

Seven channels have been cut into the southeast face of a pillowy formation of white sandstone toward the south end of Hudeibat edh-Dhiru, 500 m west of the Desert Highway (radial from Reservoir 67: 98 degrees, 8.82 km). The channels are straight, uniform in width, and carry a central longitudinal groove (W 0.34 m; depth 0.02 m; central groove W 0.08 m; fig. 3.113). They vary in length from 2 to ca. 10 m and are arranged in a disconnected series beginning at ground level, each unit starting at the same horizontal level where the previous one leaves off, but often separated from it laterally by several metres (fig. 3.114). There is a separate series of three channels close to the top of the ridge. No ancient potsherds were observed in the vicinity of the channels.

Site no. 13. Hillside channels

Coordinates: UTM 36R 0735074, 3314400; Pal. Grid 915278. Elevation: 1057 m. 04/06/86, 11/07/00.

A series of nine "slides" has been cut into the southeast face of a pillowy formation of white sandstone on the east side of the Hudeibat edh-Dhiru, 500 m west of the Desert Highway (radial from Reservoir 67: 96 degrees, 8.97 km). The channels are straight — but less uniform in width than those of Site no. 11 — and carry a central longitudinal groove (W ca. 0.3 m 0; depth 0.02 m; central groove W 0.05 m). They vary in length from 2 to ca. 8 m and are arranged in a disconnected series like that at Site no. 11.

Site no. 4. Slides

Coordinates: UTM 36R 0737388, 3320725; Pal. Grid 943340. Elevation: 1231 m. 01/06/86, 19/07/00.

FIG. 3.114 *Area of hillside channels, no. 11.*

The sliding grooves have been worn in the face of an outcropping of white sandstone 3 m high, sloping at ca. 40 degrees, 100 m southwest of Site no. 3 and below the modern power lines (radial from Reservoir 67: 64 degrees, 12.30 km). The grooves range in width from 0.05 to 0.12 m and in length from 4 to 6 m. There are indented toeholds in the rock to one side of the widest channel. Several abraded rocks were observed at the base of the slope. Grooves of this type can be found throughout this region, on almost every manageable slope of Disi sandstone. Flattened, abraded jerry cans, abraded stones, and old shoes frequently are found near the base of the grooves. Observation showed that Bedouin children formed the grooves by sliding down the soft sandstone slopes seated on the stones or cans.

Chapter 4

The Water-Supply System in the Settlement Centre: Catalogue of Structures

4.A. INTRODUCTION

This chapter presents a catalogue of the elements of Hawara's water-supply system found in the settlement centre proper or in its immediate vicinity (within 500 m of Reservoir no. 67). Although the aqueduct enters the settlement, it is described in Chapter 3. The reservoir in the Roman fort (no. 62) is 510 m from Reservoir no. 67, but it is included in this chapter because the fort is clearly part of the settlement centre. This catalogue is organised as far as possible according to the hierarchy of the system itself: major reservoirs or pools fed by the aqueduct and by run-off, then cisterns, conduits, and finally drains. The Bath Building E077 is also catalogued here, because of its relevance to the water-supply system, although full description and analysis are reserved for a later volume. The dates of first examination are not given for these urban structures, since, unlike many of the extra-urban structures, they have been observed or examined frequently and in some cases excavated long after the initial examination. GPS coordinates and elevations are provided for these structures in addition to the Palestine grid coordinates. Compass directions and distances from Reservoir no. 67 in the centre of the settlement (based on GPS data) are provided as well to give the reader a more graphic idea of the spatial relationship of the structures. In addition to GPS elevations, some of the structures in the settlement centre also have elevations surveyed with an EDM in 1989. At this time, the northeast corner of Reservoir no. 67 was taken as the base point, and its elevation was calculated as 955.00 m asl — an estimate based on elevations in the 1:25,000 map series. Based on the GPS reading, it now seems likely that the actual elevation of the base point is closer to 965.00 m asl. The discrepancy does not have any real significance, but the EDM survey probably provides more accurate readings of the relative elevations of the various structures than the GPS readings, so both figures are given where they are available.

In summary, the water-supply system is straightforward (see fig. 7.1). The aqueduct (Structure no. 1) brought exogenous spring water into the settlement, where it flowed through the shallow, unroofed Reservoir/Pool no. 63. The original outflow channel from this reservoir or pool (Conduit no. 63) can be traced for only 100 m towards the settlement centre, so its intended termination or the final use of any overflow cannot be determined. The flow, probably not very large in quantity but steady, may have been consumed entirely by activities in a solidly built Nabataean structure adjacent to the conduit, later reused for the Roman bath building. If this early building was in fact not a bath or other consumer of water, the overflow may have continued either to the public Reservoirs nos. 67 and 68 in the settlement centre, or to irrigated fields and groves south of it. After construction of the Roman fort at the beginning of the second

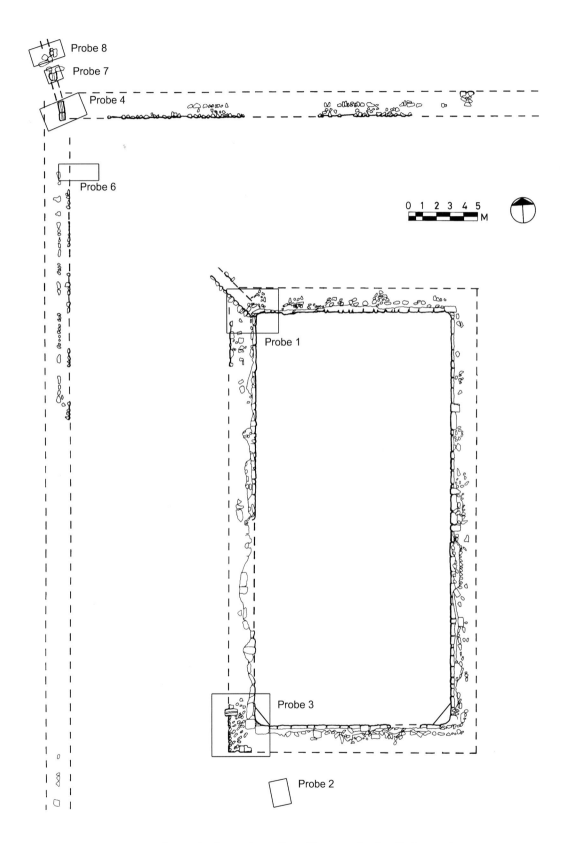

FIG. 4.1　*Reservoir no. 62, plan, with adjacent fort walls and location of probes (D. Ritsema)*

century, the main aqueduct was tapped north of Reservoir/Pool no. 63 by a branch course that fed Reservoir no. 62, an open-air storage reservoir inside the walls of the fort, which seems to have fed a pipeline serving the occupants. Not long afterwards, Reservoir/Pool no. 63 was transformed into a holding tank for a bath constructed inside the Nabataean structure 100 m to the south, adjacent to the line of the overflow conduit. At this time, the overflow conduit was replaced by a pressurised pipe system set into the conduit channel, while a small conduit of terracotta pipe sections carried the remaining flow of the aqueduct from a point just north of the reservoir around its west flank and to the south. The intended termination of this alternative overflow is also undetermined, but it may be connected with a pipeline feeding a Late Roman shrine and habitation area nearby in area E125.

The remainder of the water-supply system at ancient Hawara depended on run-off water. Because of the geology of the area, no aquifers surfaced near the site as springs or were accessible to wells. The only nearby springs emerge from the walls of Wadi Aheimir, 300 m below the settlement and several kilometres to the north, on the route to the Wadi 'Arabah. Two large public reservoirs — Reservoirs nos. 67 and 68 — identical in size and design, were constructed just to the west of the major run-off route that traversed the settlement centre, draining the large (ca. 1 km square) gently sloping field just to the north. The run-off was tapped by means of two long intake channels, clarified in settling tanks, and stored in reservoirs that were roofed and sealed against evaporation and pollution. While their capacities make it likely that these reservoirs served public water needs, at least seven (possibly nine) smaller, private cisterns were built subsequently to tap the same run-off regimen: Cisterns nos. 54, 64, 66, 69, 70, 71, 72?, 73?, and 74. All but one of these (Cistern no. 54) are associated with the ruins of a substantial structure, probably a house. Cisterns nos. 54 and 64 tapped different run-off catchments than the rest of the group. Four other cisterns were cut into the bedrock (Cisterns nos. 55, 56, 57) or built (Cistern no. 65) on the hillside at the western fringes of the settlement, drawing their run-off from the hill itself.

Other than the run-off conduit from Reservoir/Pool no. 63, the only convincing ancient conduit in the settlement centre (Conduit no. 76) seems to be associated with the collection of urban run-off — perhaps from house roofs or courtyards — for conveyance to an unidentified cistern or, possibly, as wastewater. Given the proximity of public and private structures and the quantity of water coming into the system from run-off and aqueduct flow, drainage must have been an important consideration within Hawara itself. Nevertheless, the sandy character of the soil seems to have made organised provision for the disposal of domestic "grey water" or sewerage unnecessary. Even the wastewater from Bath E077 seems to have simply flowed out a waste hole onto the adjoining sandy slope. Conduit no. 76 is the only possible wastewater drain recognised at the site so far (see Oleson 1996), although others probably await discovery.

4.B. CATALOGUE

4.B.1. *Reservoirs*

The four reservoirs catalogued here are distinguished from cisterns by their size and the sources of water that fed them. Reservoirs nos. 62 and 63 are not only the largest water storage structures at the site, but both were designed to receive water from the aqueduct rather than through run-off. The remaining two, Reservoirs nos. 67 and 68, were fed by a large run-off field, but they hold four to six times more water than the typical cistern inside or outside the settlement area. In addition, they were built as a matched pair, increasing the intended total capacity and indicating some application beyond an individual family's needs. All but Reservoir no. 62 seem to belong to the early years of Hawara's development, indicating that the need for mass public storage was addressed during the first phase of occupation. Reservoir no. 62 was added later on mainly for strategic reasons, to secure a supply of water within the Roman fort.

Structure no. 62. Fort Reservoir

Coordinates: (UTM) 36R 0726555, 3315976, (Pal. Grid) 833295. Elevation: 984 m (GPS 972 m).

FIG. 4.2   *Reservoir no. 62, view from southeast.*

FIG. 4.3   *Reservoir no. 62, northwest corner after excavation.*

The reservoir was constructed inside the northwest corner of the Roman fort, nearly equidistant from the inside faces of the north (14.67 m) and west (14.37 m) walls (figs. 2.15, 4.1–2). The intended distance was probably 50 Roman feet (14.78 m). The bearing from Reservoir no. 67 is 45 degrees, 510 m. The present ground level slopes down gradually for 2 m from the stubs of the fortification walls to the reservoir lip on these two sides; at the time of construction, it was a level walkway. There are traces of a pavement of sandstone slabs extending out 1.90 m from the rim of the reservoir at either end of the west wall. On the east and south sides, the reservoir is bounded by a berm of soil and rubble composed of either the spoil from the excavation of the reservoir or the remains of a retaining wall and walkway around the reservoir at this point (or both). At its midpoint, the crest of the east berm extends 6.25 m east and 0.47 m higher than the top inside edge of the east reservoir wall. The reservoir was located at the highest point in the fort both for proximity to the Nabataean aqueduct that fed it and to allow a gravity flow water-supply system within the walls. A short section of a pressurised terracotta piping system was found within the fort in 2000 in Area J02, running east/west under the sidewalk along the north side of the *via principalis sinistra* (Oleson et al. 2003). Further evidence for a system of pressurised pipes was found in 2005 beneath the *via principalis dextra*, in the *Praetorium*, and at the latrine in the southwest quadrant of the fort (Oleson et al. 2008). The extent and purpose of this system and the manner in which it was fed by the reservoir remain undetermined. A detailed discussion of the reservoir and the water-supply system in the fort will appear in a subsequent volume.

The reservoir was planned with internal dimensions in even numbers of Roman feet: L 100 RF, W 50 RF, depth 10 RF at the north end (29.40 × 14.20 × 3.05 m; cap. 1273.3 cum). A sounding at the centre of the south end of the reservoir revealed a floor at 3.87 m below the rim (see below). The error in execution of the hypothetical modules varies from 1 to 4 percent. The intended dimensions for wall thickness are less clear, probably because the structure was built into an excavated hole. At various points where the wall has been cleaned and can be measured, the thickness varies between 1.35 and

1.50 m, 4.5–5 RF. The fort itself has outside dimensions of 700 by 500 Roman feet (206.32 × 148.32 m), and its major sub-divisions correspond to regular numbers of Roman feet (Oleson et al. 1995b: 321–30, 1999: 414–16; Oleson 2009; fig. 2.15). Like the fort itself, the reservoir is oriented just east of north, the long walls at a bearing between 5 and 10 degrees magnetic. The fort walls are oriented approximately 4 degrees magnetic. Since compass deviation here is 3.5 degrees west, all these structures are oriented very close to True North.

The reservoir cannot have been roofed. It was far too wide for transverse arches, and there are no traces of internal supports or roofing slabs. The interior wall was faced with large, carefully squared blocks of red sandstone (H ca. 0.40–0.48 m; L ca. 0.95–1.10 m; Th ca. 0.40 m), laid in eight courses that vary slightly in height. There are occasional tie blocks in the eighth, top course. The four corners are rounded off neatly and capped at course seven with a long, thin sandstone slab (L 1.17 m; Th 0.20 m) that follows the interior quarter circle (fig. 4.3). Except at the northwest corner (see below), these blocks formed the transition to heavy, square sandstone blocks that reinforced the corners at course eight, best preserved at the southwest corner. This construction detail seems to have attracted the attention of Maughan during his visit to the site in 1872 (1874: 196): "At each corner of the walls is a kind of angular niche, partially covered over..."

The interior facing blocks were laid in a crumbly white mortar with a moderate temper of rounded quartz sand and pebbles, containing frequent large bubbles and nodules of lime. This mortar was packed into the seams and smeared over most of the surfaces of the adjoining blocks as waterproofing (Buckets 86.013, 87.173). The floor was paved with heavy, irregular slabs of sandstone set in same white mortar, which also appears as a heavy, rounded seam waterproofing the joint between floor and walls (exposed in Probe 1). A probe executed at the midpoint of the south wall in 2004 (Probe 3) revealed a different arrangement. At a point 2.4 m below the top of course six, 3.6 m below the top of the wall, the joint between wall and floor was filled with plaster, the smooth face of which slopes at 24 degrees and levels off at a depth of 3.87 m (13 RF?). There may have been a sump at this point, to facilitate cleaning, or the whole floor of the cistern may have sloped from north to south. If the whole floor sloped to the south at an even rate, the volume would be 1615.3 cum instead of the 1273.30 cum calculated on the basis of a flat floor at the level seen in the northwest corner. Until the entire reservoir has been cleared, we will accept the lower figure.

Most of the interior facing has been lost on the south and west wall, exposing the rubble core. The body of the wall was constructed of sandstone rubble and field stones set in a crumbly, light grey mortar containing a small proportion of well-sorted, rounded grains of quartz sand and occasional small nodules of lime and flecks of carbon (Bucket 87.173). At the southwest and northeast corners, where the capping blocks of course eight have been preserved, their interior surfaces and the adjoining top surface of the capping slab of course seven are plastered with a very hard white plaster similar to that found on the lower surface of the walls, but containing a very heavy admixture of rounded granite pebbles (Bucket 86.015). Probe 3, at the southwest corner, revealed that the reservoir was built in an excavated foundation hole, only its rim standing free above the level of the ground (Section 5.D.3). The rubble wall packing and mortar were laid in this excavation without any apparent exterior facing.

The reservoir was filled by a special branch line built from the aqueduct, now lost outside the fort walls, but commented on (or possibly just assumed) by several previous travellers (Stein in Kennedy 1982: 275; Gregory and Kennedy 1985: 323). The course restored by Kennedy from aerial photographs taken in 1953 (1990: 145) results from a misinterpretation of a footpath that entered the gap formed by the north gate of the fort. There was no trace of any conduit or substructure on the ground in 1983, and an elderly Bedouin man told me in 1987 that the last of the visible conduit blocks had been salvaged for construction material many years before. In 1987, probes traced the conduit in the projecting northwest corner tower (Probes 4–5, 7–8), its course zigzagging between 10 degrees and 350 degrees (see pp. 249–50, 253–54; Oleson 1988a: 161–62). A projection of this approximate bearing to the line of the Ghana aqueduct passes close

to a low heap of rubble (D 2.25 m; H 0.75 m) on the course of the aqueduct 215 m before it enters Reservoir/Pool no. 63, 100 m northwest of the northwest corner of the fort. Within the fort, the conduit blocks were framed by rubble and earth fill and covered by stone slabs carried on low side walls built of reused building materials.

Just inside the line of the inside face of the western wall of the fort, the southernmost conduit slab found *in situ* was oriented on a bearing of 179 degrees, which could have taken it either along the inside face of this wall or diagonally across the space between the wall and the reservoir's southwest corner. Probes 2 and 6 failed to uncover any traces of the conduit in this intervening space, but clearing of surface debris around the southwest corner of the reservoir revealed a sandstone conduit block set into the top of the rubble packing behind the great blocks of its western wall (fig. 5.10). This conduit, identical to those at the corner of the fort, was oriented east/west in a position that would have served to carry water into the reservoir. Unfortunately, the surface context was disturbed, and the block cannot be said with certainty to be resting in its original position. No conduit slabs survive at the northwest corner of the reservoir, but several untrimmed stones may form a line 4.2 m long leading to the corner; two stones may constitute the remains of a second, parallel wall 0.88 m away (see Probe 1, figs. 5.7–8). In their original state, the two walls may have framed the last few metres of the aqueduct course before it emptied over the corner capping stone of course seven. The large corner blocks of course eight seen at the other corners of the reservoir were absent here, suggesting some sort of unique arrangement at this corner.

Although it would have made sense to have the branch aqueduct discharge into the reservoir at its closest corner, the hypothetical framing stones rest only on earth several centimetres above the sandstone pavement, and they may be the product of later activity around the reservoir. The northwest corner is the logical entry point, unless the southwest corner was selected to allow some of the discharge to be diverted from time to time into the pipe system within the fort. The latter arrangement would have had the advantage of maintaining a strategic reserve of low-quality water in the reservoir, while at the same time supplying the soldiers (and possibly their mounts) with fresh water on some sort of scheduled delivery (see below). If the aqueduct discharged at the southwest corner, the conduit must have passed along the top of the west wall of the reservoir, since Probe 6 failed to locate it just inside the west curtain wall of the fort. The point at which the aqueduct discharged can no longer be determined with certainty.

No obvious arrangements for the discharge of water from the reservoir were found in the probes executed in 1987, 2004, and 2005 (for details of the latter campaigns, see Oleson et al. 2008). A narrow, irregular conduit (L >4.20 m; W 0.30–0.45 m), very roughly built of thin, irregular stone slabs, was traced on the surface of the berm along the south wall of the reservoir, beginning about 1.20 m south of the reservoir lip (Probe 2; Section 5.D.2). This feature, however, has been built on the present surface of the soil, and it slopes slightly toward the reservoir rather than away from it. It is far too lightly built and irregular to have been intended to serve as the overflow for such a large structure, and it more likely represents some recent attempt to channel surface run-off into the reservoir at this point.

There is no evidence along the south or east wall of the reservoir for a properly reinforced overflow conduit. A probe was dug inside the reservoir at the centre of the south wall in 2004 both to find the level of the floor at that point and to determine whether there was a drain pipe through the south wall with an exterior stopcock serving a piped water system — like the arrangement in the Roman reworking of Reservoir/Pool no. 63. No trace of any outlet pipe was found.

A probe in the southeast corner of the reservoir in 2004 revealed the same arrangement: vertical walls, then a downward slope on both the east and south to the level floor. This probe also revealed that at some point after the reservoir had been lined with its tough hydraulic plaster, the southeast corner was filled in with a solidly constructed masonry platform, triangular in plan, extending 2.5 m out from the corner to the north and west, its level upper surface at 1.95 m above the lowest reservoir floor (fig. 4.3). A similar platform,

FIG. 4.4   *Reservoir no. 62, southeast corner after excavation.*

badly damaged, was subsequently discovered in the southwest corner of the reservoir at the same level, but none existed at the northeast or northwest corners. The purpose of these platforms is unclear. Since none was built at the northwest corner, where water probably flowed into the reservoir, or at the northeast corner, which is far from the water-consuming areas of the fort, they may have had something to do with removal of water. They could have functioned as platforms for individuals working *shadufs* (counter-weighted tip beams with buckets) that lifted water to troughs on the reservoir wall. The corners may have been chosen because they help brace the installation, but it is possible that other platforms exist along the walls of the reservoir.

Excavation along the outside face of the entire south wall of the reservoir in 2004 and 2005 did not reveal any architectural features obviously associated with removing water and distributing it to the rest of the fort. In 2005, however, a pressurised terracotta pipeline was found entering the north wall of the *praetorium* 36 m south of the reservoir, and a series of conduit blocks farther east probably served a heated room or small bath in the northeast corner of that structure. The conduit and pipe systems diverged at a point 26 m south of the reservoir, but the details or any distribution basin have been lost to ploughing or some other disturbance. No pipelines survive between this intersection point and the fort. In the absence of more positive evidence, it can only be conjectured that water was lifted from the reservoirs by means of *shadufs* operating at its southeast and southwest corners. These might have dumped water into low masonry or wooden troughs on the south reservoir wall, from which terracotta pipes and conduits made with trough blocks carried the water elsewhere in the fort through the system mentioned above.

Since the aqueduct continued to fill Reservoir/Pool no. 63, which supplied the contemporary Roman Bath and some associated pipelines, water may have been diverted from the aqueduct by a sluice-gate system only when the fort reservoir needed topping-up, perhaps during the night. Unlike the cisterns outside the settlement centre that were designed to be filled by run-off water and consequently could be restored to use, Reservoirs nos. 62 and 63 have remained derelict since the aqueduct stopped functioning in the Late Byzantine or Umayyad period.

If Reservoir no. 62 was in fact a dead-end storage tank from which water could be obtained only by dipping personal containers or by use of a *shaduf*, the lack of significant flow-through would have dramatically lowered the quality of the water held there. Reservoir/Pool no. 63, although also unroofed, was designed to allow flow-through, while Reservoirs nos. 67 and 68 — although dead-end tanks — were roofed. Unless the contents of Reservoir no. 62 were constantly depleted and frequently topped up from the aqueduct, the water

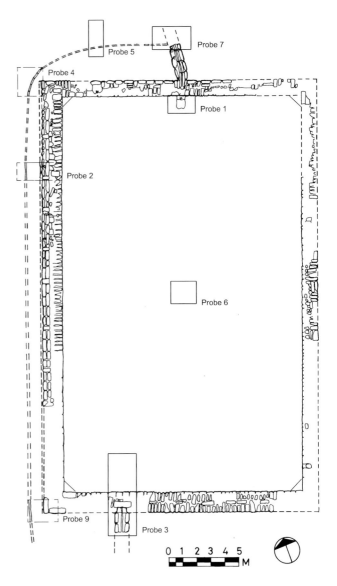

FIG. 4.5   *Reservoir/Pool no. 63, plan with indication of probe locations. (D. Ritsema).*

would have been suitable only for animals or as an emergency supply for the soldiers.

The probes excavated around the reservoir yielded only a small amount of Nabataean ceramics, and most of the deposits were Early Roman to Late Roman or Early Byzantine in character. Although no deposit was reliable enough to provide a firm date for the construction of the reservoir, logically, it should belong to the first phase of the fort, the early second century AD (Oleson et al. 1999: 414–15; Oleson et al. 2008). In this climate, a fortification would have been virtually indefensible without an

FIG. 4.6   *Reservoir/Pool no. 63, view from south after clearing and reconstruction in 2002.*

internal water supply system. Reservoir/Pool no. 63 was close by, but still outside the walls, and itself fed by an easily disrupted aqueduct. The existence of a piped water-supply system in the fort suggests that there was continuous removal of water, although the absence of an overflow conduit suggests that filling and emptying the reservoir were intermittent activities. If the reservoir was kept at least partly full, it would have constituted a significant emergency reserve in the event of interdiction of the aqueduct by hostile forces. A coin of Elagabalus (H87–057–01), found in the mortar sealing of the aqueduct channel beneath the rubble of the northwest corner of the fort, provides a *terminus post quem* of 222 for a re-construction of the intake. Bibliography: Maughan 1874: 195–96; Stein in Kennedy 1982: 275; Eadie and Oleson 1986: 57–58; Gregory and Kennedy 1985: 323; Oleson 1988: 160–62; 1991a; 1992a; 1997a: 176; Oleson et al. 1993; 2008.

Structure no. 63. Nabataean Reservoir or Pool

Coordinates: (UTM) 36R 0726435, 3315861, (Pal. Grid) 832293. Elevation: 977 m (GPS 970 m).

The reservoir or pool was constructed at the termination of the cross-country section of the Nabataean aqueduct, on the west edge of the low rise 340 m from Reservoir no. 67 at a bearing of 46 degrees, 77 m west of the southwest corner of the fort (fig. 4.5–6). It was designed from the start to be filled only by the aqueduct, which was built into the fabric at the centre of the north wall (fig. 3.41). It is not completely clear whether the structure should be regarded as a reservoir or as a pool, but for the sake of simplicity it will be referred to as a "reservoir." The reservoir was a regular rectangle in shape, its long axis on a bearing of 25 degrees; the aqueduct, with a final bearing of 190 degrees, consequently intersects the north wall at an angle of 75 degrees (fig. 5.25). The reservoir curb is nearly flush with the surrounding soil on its north and east sides, but on the west and south the modern surface slopes gently downward. Soundings revealed that on the north and west sides, at least, the original ground level sloped downward gradually from the point of the aqueduct's intersection. The original surface is approximately 0.65 m below the reservoir rim at the northwest corner (Probe

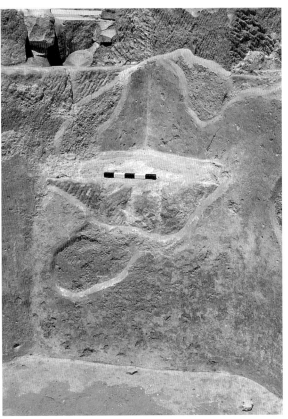

FIG. 4.7 *Reservoir/Pool no. 63, Probe 1, reservoir wall at aqueduct junction.*

FIG. 4.8 *Reservoir/Pool no. 63, infill in northeast corner.*

4), 0.75 m below at a point 4.5 m south of this corner (Probe 2), 0.70 m at the southwest corner (Probe 9), and 1 m at the outflow in the south wall (Probe 3). To judge from the present topography, the slope along the east side was less marked. The structure was probed in 1987, and in 2001–2002 it was completely cleared out and consolidated by the Department of Antiquities.

The reservoir (interior L 27.60 m; W 17.0 m; depth 1.75 m below intake channel, ca. 1.35 m below overflow channel; cap. 633.4 cum) was built of carefully finished rectangular blocks of sandstone (figs. 4.7, 5.29, 5.34); the four lower courses consist of large blocks, although along the midpoint of the west wall the coursing changes and two courses of smaller blocks replace one course of large ones. A course of blocks arranged as headers rests on a slab pavement. The joints were filled with small amounts of a very hard, sandy grey cement. Most of the visible faces have been finished with neat

diagonal trimming. The lower portions of the walls were constructed of red sandstone, while the upper courses were constructed of soft, white sandstone that has weathered badly. The blocks vary in dimensions. Samples (L × W × H): 0.54 × 0.30 × 0.26 m; 0.69 × 0.33 × 0.27 m; 0.70 × 0.24 × 0.32 m; 0.68 × 0.30 × 0.33 m; 0.68 × 0.27 × 0.28 m; 0.57 × 0.28 × 0.32 m; 0.52 × 0.33 × 0.23 m; 0.70 × 0.38 × 0.23 m; 0.82 × 0.22 × (n/a) m; 0.88 × 0.23 × (n/a) m. The floor was paved with heavy slabs of stone set in mortar then plastered over. Large patches of plaster are missing near the centre of the tank; the gaps were patched with thin, flat pieces of sandstone set in mortar.

The interior corners of the pool were filled in with mortar and blocks from the floor to a height of ca. 1 m (fig. 4.8). These infills, which share the same final layer of plaster as the rest of the pool, vary in dimensions: northwest corner, W 1.10 m, extending 0.48 m out from corner; northeast

FIG. 4.9   *Reservoir/Pool no. 63, remains of walkway along west wall.*

corner, W 0.93 m, 0.41 m out; southeast corner, W 0.90 m, 0.41 m out; southwest corner, W 1.37 m, 0.64 m out. This detail also appears in the renovated Reservoir no. 67 and, on a larger scale, on the two southern corners of Reservoir no. 62. The reservoir at Qatrana and the well at Nessana show the same detail. These structures were renovated in the Ottoman period, but the infill may be ancient. In Reservoir/Pool no. 63 the infill must belong to one of the ancient phases of use, since there is no evidence for renovation after the Byzantine period, and the aqueduct certainly was abandoned long before the Ottoman period. The southeast and southwest corners of Reservoir no. 62 were filled in during the Roman period, possibly as part of the water pumping system. The corner steps in no. 63 may have served as supports for individuals working *shadufs*, as in the fort, but it would have been easier to divert the aqueduct discharge directly to low basins or troughs adjacent to the pool. A more likely interpretation is that the small platforms served as steps to assist individuals in entering or leaving the pool for bathing (see below).

The reservoir is very shallow in relation to its length and width. From floor to curb on the interior there are eight courses of blocks of approximately the same height. Along the west wall, course seven is topped by a course of paving slabs of white sandstone (L 0.99 m; W 0.39 m; Th 0.08 m) backed by course eight, which is set back 0.99 m and caps the wall with single headers alternating with two or three pairs of stretchers (fig. 4.9). The resulting walkway seems to be absent along the north wall, and the corresponding courses are missing along the east and south walls. The west and south walls are thicker (Th 1.65 m, not counting the foundation offsets) than the north and east walls (Th 1.20 m), possibly to buttress the reservoir along the two sides where the surrounding soil did not support it to as great a height. The heavier infill at the northwest and southwest corners may be a response to the same situation. The base of the west wall was found in Probe 2 (for the probes, see pp. 255–89). A mortar and rubble footing had been laid in a shallow trench dug in sterile soil, 2.65 m below the crest of the wall (figs. 5.28–29). There was an offset (W 0.12 m) along the outside face of the wall 0.65 m below the crown, just above ancient ground level at this point. The interior of the reservoir up to the top of course seven was waterproofed with a very hard, pale brown plaster heavily tempered with poorly-sorted rounded sand and some small, angular pebbles, containing occasional very small flecks of carbon and nodules of lime (Bucket 87.151). This plaster varied in thickness from 0.01–0.03 m along the flat surfaces and was up to 0.13 m thick at the corners.

Although the termination of the final conduit block of the aqueduct was missing, it probably ended flush with the interior face of the north reservoir wall. Two limestone slabs below the spout (total L 0.95 m; W 0.66 m) project 0.07 m above the level of the rest of the floor. A smooth, irregular depression (0.12 × 0.09 m) has been eroded in the upper surface of the north slab, directly in line with the conduit and 0.12 m out from the face of the wall (fig. 4.7). Assuming that this depression was caused by water flowing into the reservoir when the water level was very low, it would have formed much farther out from the wall if the aqueduct had overhung the interior or the velocity of flow been high. For calculation of the maximum discharge of the aqueduct, see pp. 367–68. The two slabs undoubtedly were inserted here to prevent erosion of the floor of the reservoir. It is unlikely, however, that the water level in the original phase, when the aqueduct water simply flowed through this reservoir, would have been low enough with enough frequency to require such reinforcement below the intake. The slabs may in consequence belong to Phase 2, when installation of the pipe allowed complete draining of the contents. The engineers of Phase 1 may have been worried enough about erosion of the floor that they included the slabs in the original design. The third-century (?) reservoir at Mampsis was provided with a similar slab below the intake spout, even though the intake was an erratic supply possibly carried in by porters, and the pool could be emptied only by dipping (Negev 1988a: 186).

In the initial arrangement, the overflow from the reservoir passed over its south wall in a channel (W 0.12 m; depth 0.11 m) cut into a block built into course six, set into the wall 4.18 m east of the inside southwest corner. The off-centre location probably was determined by the local topography and the projected destination of the out-flow channel. The overflow block survives but has been pulled from its original position. The water poured into a niche (H 1.16 m; W 0.53 m; depth 0.42 m) built into the south face of the wall (figs. 4.6, 4.10, 5.38). In the Phase 1 arrangement, the water was probably caught in a small basin that fed an aqueduct channel — similar to the arrangement seen in monolithic catch basins at Avdat and Nessana (Colt 1962: 28). The aqueduct, identical in design and dimensions to the Ghana branch (W 0.92 m; conduit channel W ca. 0.10 m, depth ca. 0.12 m) was built of sandstone conduit blocks framed by heavy, roughly-trimmed blocks. The fact that in its initial phase the aqueduct flowed through the tank rather than around it, with a branch conduit to allow filling, sets it apart from the two intermediate tanks at km 6.516 and 9.604 of the Ghana Aqueduct. Once the flow of water had been exposed to pollution in an easily accessible pool, the overflow can only have been used for bathing and industrial or agricultural purposes.

The aqueduct was traced in Probes 8 to 12 (Sections 5.E.8–12) and on the surface for 85 m to the south at a bearing of 205 degrees — perpendicular to the south reservoir wall. Stein (in Kennedy 1982: 275; Gregory and Kennedy 1985: 323) reports that he could trace the course of this conduit for 100 m beyond the Nabataean reservoir to another "poorly built reservoir" before it faded out in a field. This second "reservoir" was most likely the ruins of the Roman Bath (Structure E077; Section 4.B.4), which is 100 m south of Reservoir/Pool no. 63. In 2010, Reeves found remains of the aqueduct leading to a small cistern in the bath complex. It is not clear whether the original aqueduct fed by the discharge from the pool was designed to convey water to the substantial Nabataean building that preceded the Roman bath or was intended to carry water past it into the settlement centre. If the Nabataean building was itself a bath, it is likely the aqueduct was intended to serve it too. Since the water flowing from Reservoir/Pool no. 63 would have been suspect in quality, its use for bathing would have been appropriate.

During Phase 2, the overflow catch basin was removed and the overflow channel replaced by a bronze pipe (D 0.053 m; wall Th 0.005 m) installed in a hole cut through the wall 0.10 m above the level of the interior floor (Probe no. 3; Section 5.E.3; fig. 5.34). The hole was irregular and roughly cut, and the extra space was filled with rubble packing set in very hard, sandy white cement. Three bronze lugs projecting from cuttings in the wall 0.11–0.12 m away from the pipe probably held a perforated bronze screen over the opening to keep debris from entering the pipeline. Such screens are common in Roman water systems (Oleson 1987b: 119). Removal of the wall and floor plaster around the pipe opening (north extension of Probe 3) revealed that the original waterproofing was a layer (Th 0.01 m) of the same hard, sandy and pebbly, pale brown plaster found elsewhere around the reservoir. After insertion of the pipe, a bulging lens of soft, grey mortar (Th 0.02 m) was laid over the original plaster and covered with a thin layer of hard, sandy white plaster. In Phase 3, after the pipe had gone out of use, the screen was torn away, the pipe filled with stones and mortar, and another layer of grey mortar (Th 0.012 m) with numerous flecks of carbon was applied and covered with a final layer of hard, sandy white mortar (Th 0.013 m). Only a slight bulge in the wall plaster indicated the location of the pipe. The floor plaster was 0.17 m thick in front of the pipe.

As part of the Phase 2 renovations, a large, bronze stopcock (L 0.296; weight 3.350 kg; H87–6332–01, Section 6.C, figs. 6.5–6.6) was soldered firmly to the end of the drainpipe inside the niche in the south reservoir wall. When discovered, the valve-plug was missing, the open body of the stopcock was plugged with rubble set in cement, and the stopcock was surrounded by mortared rubble packing (Probe 3, south; Section 5.E.3, fig. 5.36). The stopcock connected the reservoir drain to a crude lead pipe laid in a hard white mortar in the conduit channel. Although stopcocks were common in the Roman west (Oleson 1988b: 163, pl. 30; Fassitelli and Fassitelli 1990; Drack 1997), this seems to be only the third Roman stopcock so far found in the entire Near East, and by far the largest. Its dimensions (precisely 1 Roman Foot long) are large even by the standards of Italian sites (see pp. 332–34, 1987.106.01.). All but the final section of pipe adjacent to the valve had been robbed

out at some point prior to abandonment of the site (given the depth of fill over the channel), but the impression left by the pipe can be seen in the surviving sections of the aqueduct. The surviving piece of pipe (outside D 0.044–0.055 m; inside D 0.038–0.049 m; H87–6332–02, Section 6.C, fig. 6.7) was manufactured by rolling sheets of lead ca. 0.003 m thick around a mandrel and soldering the outside seam of the overlap. The entire circumference was then encased in plaster wrapped while wet in heavy woollen cloth, which has left its impression on the exterior (fig. 6.8). Given the typical Roman character of the stopcock and pipe, the reworking of the outflow aqueduct into a piped water system can be associated with provision of a pressurised water system for the nearby bath building (E077). In the second or third century, a lead pipe was installed in a stone drain at Gadara to carry pressurised water to nearby water installations (al-Daire 2004: 220, fig. 4).

In the course of the Phase 2 renovation, after the original overflow channel had been put out of use by filling it with rubble set in mortar, the niche into which it had poured was roofed with two long sandstone slabs (fig. 4.10). Four notches cut at the front corners of the niche probably held lugs that anchored a door or grating designed to control access. Since the original overflow channel could have been accessed freely, the provision of a system for — presumably — locking the niche makes sense only in connection with the addition of the stopcock, which controlled the supply of water to the bath. In the final phase of use (Phase 3), the pipe was ripped out, the valve stopper was removed, and the valve and its intake pipe stuffed with stones and mortar. Since the pipe intake was carefully plastered over on the interior of the reservoir, the aqueduct must still have been providing water. Since there was no longer any outlet from the reservoir, some other by-pass system was required at least by this time — and possibly earlier, given the presence of a stopcock to shut off the outflow.

Excavation outside the reservoir in Probes 2, 4–5, 7, 9–11 (Sections 5.E.2, 4–5, 7, 9–11) exposed a pipeline built of neat terracotta pipe sections. This conduit diverted water from the Ghana aqueduct 3 m north of its termination at the reservoir (the join unfortunately has been destroyed), and carried

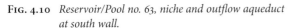

FIG. 4.10 *Reservoir/Pool no. 63, niche and outflow aqueduct at south wall.*

FIG. 4.11 *Reservoir/Pool no. 63, conduit along east wall.*

it around the west side of the reservoir just below ancient ground level, 1.10 m out from the wall (fig. 5.48). The pipe sections (L ca. 0.30 m; exterior D 0.06–0.082 m; max interior D 0.046–0.068 m; see pp. 330–31, 1987.114.01 and 02) were flanged to fit into one another. Nearly every pipe section carried a small oval hole (D ca. 0.04 m) broken though the upper surface halfway down its length, covered by a potsherd set in a very fine, soft, white gypsum plaster lacking any sand temper or carbon specks. This feature is very common in ancient terracotta pipelines and probably served to allow the removal of debris that accumulated during use (Fahlbusch 1982: 34–43; Hodge 1992: 114; Jansen 2000: 106–8). In some situations, the capped holes may have been intended to relieve air pressure (Tölle-Kastenbein 1991). Although the seams between the pipe sections were heavily smeared with the same plaster before and after joining, the cleaning holes make it unlikely that this conduit was intended for pressurised service. The pipeline continued south of

the reservoir at a bearing (180 degrees) that should have brought it across the course of the outflow conduit discussed above, 15 m south of the reservoir's south wall. Since it did not appear in our Probe 12, the pipeline either veered off on another course or has been lost to ploughing or salvage at this point. The terracotta pipeline was laid at a level 0.50 m higher than the outflow aqueduct. It is possible that this second pipeline was associated with the renovation of the Bath Building E077 in the Byzantine period. It should also be contemporary with the renovation of the reservoir that put the stopcock and its pipe out of service, since the terracotta pipeline diverts water from a reservoir without any obvious arrangement for overflow or drainage.

Clearing of the interior and immediate proximity of the reservoir by the Department of Antiquities in 2001 revealed another diversion channel just outside the east wall, composed of conduit blocks similar to those in the aqueduct (fig. 4.11).

The surviving blocks extend 4.84 m north from the southeast corner of the reservoir. After a gap of 6.12 m, there is another 1.64 m of conduit. No evidence survives for the link with the aqueduct or the destination, but since this conduit was laid on a thin layer of soil rather than built into the wall of the reservoir and bends away from the reservoir wall at its northern termination, it should belong to a late phase of use. The conduit may have been laid to irrigate a garden around the pool, as at Petra, and re-laid from time to time on loose earth fill as the plantings changed. Two of the conduit blocks in the southern stretch are deeply eroded at their upstream ends. On one block the hole has eroded completely through the stone, while the other has been partly filled with grey mortar. Mortar was used to level the base of the channel along most of the southern series of blocks, and the same mortar was applied to the joints between the blocks. There were traces of mortar along the upper edges of the conduits, used to seal the joint with the lost cover slabs.

Unfortunately, the cultural material and stratigraphy were not of much help in providing absolute dates for the changes to the water-supply system at Reservoir/Pool no. 63 (see Sections 5.E, 7.C.6). The foundations of the west wall were laid on sterile soil, and the deposit immediately above contained only a single Early Roman potsherd, which may in fact be contamination from the baulk above. The upper layers of fill all yielded a rich variety of pottery dating from the Nabataean to the Umayyad periods. The latest pottery in the hard-packed surface into which the terracotta pipeline was laid, however, was Byzantine. The loci around the bronze stopcock in the recess had been badly disturbed by the obstruction of the valve and removal of the pipe, and the potsherds ranged from Middle Nabataean to Umayyad in date. Most of the sherds, however, seem to have washed in over time. The soil packed around the valve housing itself, in contrast, contained only Roman and Byzantine pottery, and the soil beneath the valve only a few Middle Nabataean and Early Roman wares.

The quantity and wide chronological spread of the pottery found in the upper levels of fill around the reservoir reveal that the structure was a hub of activity throughout the entire history of

the settlement. In contrast, the near absence of potsherds from the foundation levels suggests that the reservoir was constructed in the early decades of Hawara's existence. The reservoir was an integral part of the aqueduct system, designed to make a quantity of water available for use in this part of the settlement, and to provide a conduit to carry the overflow farther along the ridge or into the settlement centre. Given the wide and shallow design of the reservoir and the apparent lack of facilities for making the water easily available except by dipping, the reservoir may in fact have been part of a royal prestige project, possibly a swimming pool, with some practical side benefits. If this interpretation is correct, the Hawara pool is unlikely to have been constructed before the similar pool at Petra, which was built early in the reign of Aretas IV (see pp. 383, 439–43).

Sometime in the second century, this gravity flow discharge was replaced by a pressurised pipe system, which could tap the whole reservoir, laid directly in the aqueduct channel. Later still, probably in the early third century, arrangements were made to intercept the flow into the reservoir with a terracotta pipeline, which carried water to a destination farther along the ridge, more or less in the same direction as the previous pipeline. This renovation may be contemporary with the removal from service of the stopcock and associated pipes. Excavation in E125 has shown that the terracotta pipeline carried water to a shrine associated with the Roman *vicus*. The presence of numerous Umayyad sherds around the reservoir suggests that there was water in it through the early Islamic period and, thus, that the aqueduct remained in service until then.

Structure no. 67. Nabataean Reservoir

Coordinates: (UTM) 36R 0726183, 3315632, (Pal. Grid) 829293. Elevation: benchmark at northeast corner assumed to be 955 m (GPS 966 m).

The structure was built on the right (west) bank of a natural, narrow run-off channel for a large, gently sloping field of loessial soil (area ca. 1 sq km) at the focus of what later became the settlement centre of Hawara. Reservoir no. 68 is 19 m to the northwest. Given their proximity, identical

FIG. 4.12 *Reservoirs nos. 67 and 68, aerial. (Photo: W. Myers, 07.21.1992, neg. H-2.1).*

FIG. 4.13 *Reservoir no. 67, view from south.*

dimensions and design, and conformity to the same orientation grid, these two reservoirs were very likely built as a pair, possibly at the time of Hawara's foundation (fig. 4.12). Although the intake channel and settling tank were rebuilt and the interior of the reservoir cleared out and lined with cement in the 1960s as part of a foreign aid project, the character of the structure remains clear. Until about 2000, the reservoir still received run-off water during most winters, and after a good season it constituted the major public water source in the area until the water had been consumed by July or August (fig. 4.13). The reservoir remained dry from 2000 to 2005 because of a drought, but in 2006 and 2007 it was once again nearly filled by run-off. In May 2009, the reservoir was full to the very brim as a result of a single heavy rainstorm in March of that year. In 2003–2004, the Department of Antiquities cleared out much of the silt in the tank.

At present, water is forced by a modern barrier of earth and rubble to pool in front of the east/west intake channel (L 34.40 m; W 0.81 m), through which it flows into a settling tank (L 4.37 m; W 4.29 m; depth 1.14 m below intake and outflow channels; cap. 21.4 cum). Both the intake channel and settling tank appear to have been completely rebuilt in the 1960s, with further consolidation in 2003. A channel (L 3.05 m; W 0.81 m; also rebuilt) carries the overflow from the settling tank into the reservoir at its northeast corner. As reconstructed, the reservoir is surrounded by a concrete block wall (W 0.51 m; H 0.57 m) built on the outer edge of the reservoir wall, leaving a walkway (W 0.92–0.96 m) around the unroofed interior (cf. Reservoir/Pool no. 63). The long axis is oriented approximately north/south (164/344 degrees). A low, wide conduit (L > 2.0 m; W 1.98 m) built into the north wall of the intake channel between the settling tank and the reservoir carries the overflow away to the northwest when the tank is full. Excavation showed that this arrangement does not correspond with the ancient one and that the overflow channel on Reservoir no. 67 is a modern feature. (no. 68 Probe 8; Section 5.F.8). A separate intake channel filled Reservoir no. 68, and the intakes for both reservoirs were simply closed when they had been filled. There is no overflow channel on the better-preserved no. 68. Although the absence of an outlet

for overflow seems odd to modern eyes, it accords well with the original character of the settlement of Hawara. Since at least a small population was settled at the site year around, and a larger number during the cooler winter months, some sort of guardian would have regulated the sluice gates at the head of the intake channels for these public reservoirs. The intakes could be quickly blocked when the reservoirs had filled.

It is not clear how much of the reservoir structure was rebuilt during the modern refurbishment, but its length and width (L 19.74 m; W 7.04 m) are virtually identical to those of Reservoir no. 68 (L 20.05 m, W 6.95–7.05 m). Since it was not possible to excavate the hard clay deposit in Reservoir no. 68, the elevation of the floor was measured by pounding a pointed broomstick into the sediment several metres out from the reservoir wall until it struck a hard surface. In this manner the depth was measured as 3.83 m. Excavation of the sediment in no. 67 by the Department of Antiquities in 2004 revealed a previously hidden offset (W 0.25 m) at a depth of 3.75 m below the top of the restored wall. The wall continued below the offset for 1.20 m, at which point the joint between floor and wall was filled with plaster infill sloping at 45 degrees to the level reservoir floor at 5.45 m (fig. 4.14). It seems unlikely that the similarity in level of the offset in Reservoir no. 67 and the depth measured in Reservoir no. 68 is accidental. It is possible that the original floor of Reservoir no. 67 was at the level of 3.75 m below the top of the wall, and that it was extended downward either in antiquity or during the modern renovation. If so, the original volume would have been 451.65 cum (assuming a depth of 3.50 m below the intake channel), while the present volume is 661.35 cum. Given the possibility that the central depression is a modern alteration, I have used the figure of 451.65 cum in my calculations of the capacity of the Hawara water system.

The reservoir originally was roofed by stone slabs carried on 16 transverse arches, of which only two remain, at the north and south ends (W 0.57 m; distance from wall 0.55 m and 0.57 m). Although the seams between the fallen arches and the walls were concealed with cement when the tank was cleared out and re-lined, the many similarities with the better-preserved no. 68 suggest that no. 67 also had 16 arches. As in Reservoir no. 68, the arches probably were not placed at precise intervals from one another. The dimensions of the intake channel and settling tank of no. 67 are different from those of no. 68 and probably were altered during their rebuilding. The corners of the renovated reservoir have been squared off with modern cement, presumably to improve waterproofing. Since this buttressing does not appear in Reservoir no. 68, it probably belongs to the modern restoration. The squared corners in Reservoirs no. 62 and 63 are ancient, but most likely served a different purpose (see above). Reservoirs and wells at Nessana and Qatrana that were built or renovated during the Ottoman period show courses of stones laid across the corners at regular intervals, either for reinforcement or to provide scaffolding supports during construction.

In the recent past, Bedouin standing on the inside edge drew water from the reservoir using buckets or water bags on ropes (fig. 4.15). The water was poured into a long, low concrete drinking trough (L 10 m) 5 m south of the north reservoir wall. In its original state no. 67, like no. 68, would have resembled a rectangular platform paved with large blocks and surrounded by a walkway (the top of the reservoir wall) raised slightly above the

FIG. 4.14 *Reservoir no. 67, offset and floor along west wall.*

FIG. 4.15 *Reservoir no. 67, Bedouin woman drawing water.*

FIG. 4.16 *Reservoir no. 68, view from west in 2005.*

level of the adjacent soil. Since the roof was sturdy and its joints sealed against seepage, a barrier wall to keep animals off would not have been essential, although advisable. One or more well-heads or slightly raised draw holes and troughs probably provided access to those drawing the water.

Because the reservoir was in constant use during most excavation seasons, it was not possible to lay out any soundings adjacent to its walls. The probe made on the line of the overflow channel (Probe H89–67–P01) revealed that this feature was modern, but the fill yielded numerous small, worn sherds. Understandably, the ceramics reflected the long history of activity at the reservoir, with a more or less even distribution among the Nabataean, Roman, and Byzantine periods. Historical factors and the date of Reservoir no. 68 suggest that this reservoir, too, was constructed not long after Hawara was founded (see Sections 5.F, 7.C.6).

Structure no. 68. Nabataean Reservoir

Coordinates: (UTM) 36R 0726135, 3315647, (Pal. Grid) 829293. Elevation: 954 m (GPS 964 m).

The structure was built at nearly a right angle to Reservoir no. 67, 19 m to the northwest (bearing of 285 degrees; figs. 4.12, 4.16). A line projected from the lower edge of the settling tank of no. 68 would pass 6.25 m north of the north wall of no. 67. The east and west (short) walls of the reservoir are on a bearing of 160 degrees (as opposed to 164 degrees for the long walls of no. 67); the north and south walls are at 340 degrees. Unlike its twin, no. 68 was not renovated for reuse in the 1960s, although two of the arches were knocked down and some of the roofing slabs removed during an attempt to clear it out. Until 2004, heaps of earth spoil from this activity surrounded the western end of the reservoir, which remained half full of earth. During 2004–2005, the surface of the reservoir and settling tank was cleared and consolidated by the Department of Antiquities, some of the heaps of soil were removed, and the site was regularised. During the 1980s and 1990s, the reservoir often contained a pool of water 0.50–1 m deep in early June, funnelled into it by a low earth wall at its northwest corner. The water was soon fouled by goats and birds, so the Bedouin made no apparent effort to use it. In April of 2007, after the clearance of the site, and again in March 2009, a single heavy winter downpour nearly filled the cistern.

After the 1987 survey, it was suggested that Reservoir no. 68 was filled by the overflow from no. 67, through an ancient overflow channel beneath the modern one. It would have been a needlessly risky strategy, however, to wait for one reservoir to fill before beginning to fill the second, and soundings made in 1989 revealed that Reservoir no. 68 was provided with a separate intake system (fig. 5.62). Probe H89–68–P08 was located at the intersection of the projected lines of the modern overflow for no. 67 and the ancient intake for no. 68 (see pp. 301–5). A trench 1 × 2 m was excavated to a depth of 1 m below the modern soil surface without revealing the presence of any connecting conduit. Subsequently, Probe H89–68–P01 was excavated 5 m east of the last visible section of the intake for no. 68, on line with its bearing (70 degrees). This probe uncovered the well-preserved remains of the intake channel just below the modern surface: the top surfaces of the walls at a depth of 0.20 m, the channel floor at a depth of 0.80 m. The channel curved off to the northeast, at a bearing of 50 degrees. Extension of the probe along the course of the channel revealed a continued curve to a bearing of 45 degrees. A third probe, H89–68–P02, was located 10 m northeast of H89–68–P01, on the projected line of the channel. Excavation of a trench 1 m wide for 1.5 m on either side of the projected course, to a depth of 1 m, revealed no trace of it. The channel did, however, appear in a fourth probe (H89–68–P03), located 3.5 m beyond the section revealed in Probe H89–68–P01 (see pp. 291–99). At this point, the channel continued to swing around to the north to a bearing of approximately 32 degrees. It is unlikely that the channel subsequently curved back to the northeast sufficiently to have been missed by Probe H89–68–P02, since there are no topographical or architectural features that would have enforced such a sinuous course. The channel may have continued curving towards the north, outside the reach of Probe H89–68–P02, but this bearing would have carried it slightly uphill and out of the catchment. It seems more likely that the channel either terminated at a reinforced intake

somewhere between Probe 2 and Probe 3, or that it has been lost at this point due to water damage or salvage of the blocks.

In any case, it is clear that at least at its last stage of development, Reservoir no. 68 had an intake system independent of that of no. 67. This makes sense in the context of the Nabataean habit of alleviating the risk of complete failure to intercept sufficient run-off water by using multiple water-catching and water-storage structures with independent catchment areas. The large public Reservoirs nos. 67 and 68 diverted their water from the same basic wadi system, fed by the large, protected run-off field to the north of the settlement. Their intakes were not built side-by-side or in series, but were designed to intercept run-off from two opposite sides of a low rise near the apex of the run-off field. Today, the stronger flow runs past the intake for no. 67, and the general topography of the area suggests that the same was true in antiquity. If this was in fact the case, Reservoir no. 68 may have been intended as a back-up to no. 67. It may not have filled as quickly as its neighbour or have filled to capacity as consistently, but the intake system may also not have been as susceptible to damage when the wadi carried a greater than usual flow of water.

Excavation of the fill outside the channel walls down to the level of the channel floor yielded a large amount of ceramic material dating from the Nabataean through the Umayyad periods, incorporated in a uniform fill consisting of a packed, sandy yellow earth. Since the channel walls are built of only partially trimmed stones and are only one course thick, the upper surfaces of the side walls must have been flush with the ground surface or only slightly above it. They could not have been built free-standing. No traces of cover slabs were found, but they probably were placed over at least the last 10 m of the intake channel to avoid the inconvenience and hazard of an open conduit. Removal of the slabs would have been necessary during maintenance, and the mix of ceramic material — all of which consists of small, very worn fragments — indicates that the channel was rebuilt at least once, late in the history of the structure. There is no evidence for the course followed by the original intake channel of the early Nabataean period, but the character of the topog-

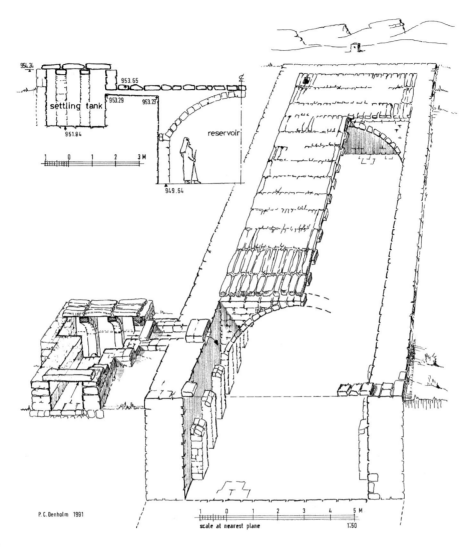

settling tank

reservoir

P.C.Denholm 1991

scale at nearest plane

FIG. 4.17 *Reservoir no. 68, reconstruction (P. Denholm).*

raphy, and the considerations of risk-management noted above, suggest that intake arrangements remained essentially unchanged throughout the structure's history.

Where it enters the settling tank, the intake channel is wide (W 0.96 m; H >0.64 m) and built of substantial, well-trimmed and carefully laid sandstone blocks and slabs capable of withstanding a heavy flow of water (fig. 4.19). The flooring slabs are particularly heavy and carefully laid. The survival of heavy roofing slabs on the settling tank outflow channel suggests that the intake was roofed as well. The channel opens into the middle of the east wall of the deep settling tank (L 3.18 m; W 2.34–2.58 m; depth below floor of intake 1.60

m, below floor of discharge to reservoir tank, 1.35 m; cap. 10.6 cum) between two transverse (east/west) arches that carried the roof slabs, several of which survive *in situ*. The arches, which spread slightly in plan in order to accommodate the intake channel, spring from spur walls built up against the walls of the tank. The one surviving arch was built of roughly-shaped and poorly laid voussoirs that have settled to an ogival rather than a circular curve. Since settling tanks for large reservoirs are subject to a great deal of wear and tear and must frequently be cleaned out, the present arches may be the product of several rebuildings. The surfaces of the walls and arches were waterproofed with a hard, white to grey plaster heavily tempered with

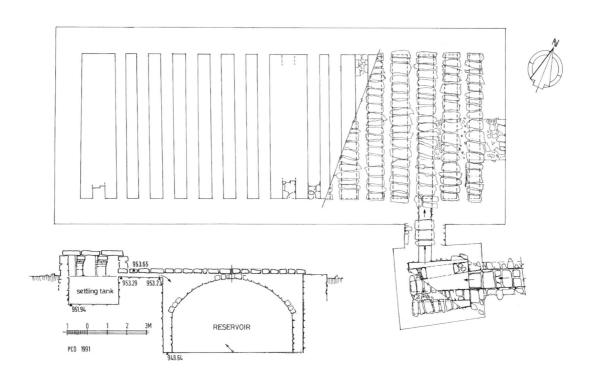

FIG. 4.18 *Reservoir no. 68, plan and section (P. Denholm).*

FIG. 4.19 *Reservoir no. 68, view of intake channel (above) and settling tank.*

Fig. 4.20 *Reservoir no. 68, interior of tank.*

poorly-sorted, rounded quartz sand and pebbles and ground-up potsherds, containing many lime nodules, bubbles, and fissures (Bucket 87.192).

At the northwest corner of the settling tank, an overflow conduit (L 3.02 m; W 0.64 m; H 0.35 m) built of well-trimmed sandstone blocks and slabs carried water north into the reservoir, discharging it at the top of its south wall, between the second and third arches from the east end (figs. 4.17–19). The wall blocks that can be seen have neat diagonal trimming. The conduit is roofed with large stone slabs, supplemented at either side by a cobble paving laid on the earth fill.

The reservoir itself (interior L 20.05 m; W 6.95–7.05 m; depth below top of wall 3.83 m, below bottom of intake channel, 3.47 m; cap. 488.42 cum) is built of large, carefully shaped sandstone blocks with neat diagonal trimming on the visible surfaces. It was roofed with large stone slabs carried on 16 transverse arches that spring from low spur walls built up against the faces of the north and south walls (fig. 4.20). The height of the arches varies slightly from one to the next, because the voussoirs,

although carefully trimmed in the same manner as the wall blocks, have not been given a wedge-shape but have been angled by means of chinking the seams between them with small stones. The arches also vary slightly in width and spacing. The measurements in Table 4.1 were taken along the south wall, measuring from east to west.

Two of the arches (nos. 8 and 16) are missing, most likely knocked down to facilitate excavation of the fill in the 1960s. Removal of approximately 40% of the roofing slabs — probably at the same time — has caused the exposed and un-reinforced arches to lean slightly to one side or the other towards the centre of their spans. The filler walls above the extrados were built of blocks and small rubble set in a soft, light grey mortar (Bucket 87.178) tempered with a moderate amount of well-sorted, rounded quartz sand, including a few rounded pebbles, very small lime nodules, very small flecks of charcoal, and frequent small bubbles. The walls of the reservoir and the sides of the arches have been plastered with a plaster very similar in composition to the mortar, but harder, and containing

Table 4.1   Arch widths and intervals, Reservoir no. 68.

	Arch width	Interval to next
E wall	—	0.58 m
Arch 1	0.61 m	0.66 m
Arch 2	0.54 m	0.69 m
Arch 3	0.55 m	0.71 m
Arch 4	0.54 m	0.66 m
Arch 5	0.62 m	0.73 m
Arch 6	0.62 m	0.47 m
Arch 7	0.63 m	0.61 m
Arch 8	0.66 m	0.61 m
Arch 9	0.60 m	0.57 m
Arch 10	0.58 m	0.64 m
Arch 11	0.54 m	0.67 m
Arch 12	0.63 m	0.64 m
Arch 13	0.59 m	0.65 m
Arch 14	0.59 m	0.60 m
Arch 15	0.52 m	0.62 m
Arch 16	0.61 m	0.62 m to W wall
Min	0.54 m	0.47 m
Max	0.63 m	0.73 m
Avg	0.59 m	0.63 m
StD	0.04 m	0.06 m

a larger proportion of small pebbles (Bucket 87.177). The surface is even, but not polished. Excavation of a probe outside the east wall of the reservoir yielded numerous samples of the mortar into which the wall blocks were laid (Bucket 90.77, 93); it is a crumbly white mortar with a very high proportion of well-sorted, rounded quartz sand, containing occasional chunks of sandstone, lumps of lime, and large flecks of charcoal.

Where the two arches and their impost walls have fallen, the smooth masonry of the tank wall reveals that neither had been bonded to it. Apparently, the reservoir box was constructed first, then the impost walls and the arches, before the structure was waterproofed with plaster. The roofing slabs are roughly rectangular sandstone slabs (L ca. 1.00–1.25 m; W ca. 0.25–0.59 m; Th ca. 0.30 m) set side-by-side to span the gaps between the arches (figs. 4.16, 4.21). They are chinked at either end and along their sides with small stones set in a very heavy bedding of the same mortar used in the walls. Part of a draw hole slab with central rectangular opening (L >0.11 m; W 0.43 m) is *in situ* close to the southwest corner of the tank. Adjacent to it, a reused slab with two rectangular recesses framing a larger central recess with arched roof has been laid face down as part of the roofing. The niches probably contained betyls (fig. 4.22; Wenning 2001: 85–87). Outside the reservoir, not far from the preserved draw hole, a large slab of sandstone was found lying on the modern heap of fill (L 1.13 m; W 0.63 m; Th 0.20 m); a recess in one surface suggests that it is the remains of a monolithic water basin, possibly one used in conjunction with the draw hole.

An east/west trench excavated over the eastern half of the reservoir in 1987 and 1989 exposed the east edge of the roof (fig. 4.21; Probe 2; Section 5.F.2). The heavily plastered roofing slabs terminated in a neat edge, 0.20 m high, above the large, flat, irregular slabs of sandstone and limestone forming the upper surface of the thick east wall of the reservoir; excavation ultimately showed that the wall was 2.15 m thick at this point. It was framed on the exterior by irregular sandstone blocks up to 0.80 m long, with well-trimmed, flat exterior faces that often carried the fine diagonal trimming typical of Nabataean stone-working. The interior of the wall was composed of irregular, fist-sized rubble and small pebbles set in a crumbly grey mortar that contained numerous nodules of lime and a very high proportion of charcoal particles. Five small potsherds were recovered from the mortar within the wall (Locus 5); three certainly were from first-century AD NFW cups and two from coarse-ware vessels probably of the same period (Bucket 89.50). An east extension of this trench was excavated for 2.25 m below the upper surface of the wall, exposing the foundation trench within which the wall had been constructed (figs. 5.65–66). The fill was composed of four major strata of sand and gravel mixed with a packing of fist-sized pieces

FIG. 4.21 *Reservoir no. 68, Probe 2. Top of east wall and roofing slabs.*

FIG. 4.22 *Reservoir no. 68, slab with niches for betyls.*

of sandstone and limestone rubble. These strata (comprising Loci nos. 10–17) had been deposited into a foundation trench cut into the sterile, coarse, red-brown sand that constitutes the original soil at this point in the site. The fill had been poured into the trench after construction of the wall, and the strata consequently sloped downwards slightly towards the wall-face and terminated on it without a break.

In section, the profile of the trench could be seen, making it clear that an enormous rectangular east/west hole with slightly sloping sides had been excavated for the reservoir, probably 26 × 13 m. The lowest 1.3 m of the inner face of the wall were built of regular, carefully trimmed blocks of sandstone (inside dimensions of 20.05 × 6.95 m). This facing then served as a retaining wall for a solid packing of rubble mixed with mortar thrown into and completely filling the approximately 1 m wide trench between the wall and the boundary of the excavation. Above this point, the rubble packing was faced with relatively large limestone and sandstone blocks (up to 0.75 × 0.25 × 0.25 m) that were not, however, laid as isodomic ashlar courses. Between this solid outer facing and the carefully built inner wall of the tank, the packing probably consisted of the mortared rubble seen in the sounding into the upper part of the wall. From a point 1.3 m above the level of the tank floor it was possible to build the outer face of the wall more carefully, because from this point up to the roof level, the hole into which the structure was built sloped outwards slightly, allowing the masons room to manoeuvre.

The profile of this trench could be seen in the north and south baulks of this sounding (figs. 5.65–66). The floor of the trench meets the outer face of the wall at a point 2.60 m below its upper surface (1.3 m above the floor of the tank). The excavation then slopes outward to a distance of 0.75 m from the wall, where it terminates in what seems to be the ancient ground level (0.30 m below the top of the wall). At a point 0.10 m below this possible ground surface, the wall is offset to the west 0.50 m, reducing the thickness of the top 0.45 m of the wall to 1.15 m. It may not be coincidence that the north and east walls of Reservoir/Pool no. 63 are 1.16 m thick, and this dimension may be the approximate equivalent of 2 cubits of 0.57 m

(see pp. 399–401). The offset along the west wall of Reservoir/Pool no. 63 is also similar in design and location, although narrower (W 0.12 m). It is clear that the masons who built this wall took no chances concerning its stability. Even though the surrounding soil would have helped buttress it against the weight of the water contained inside, the wall was built to a thickness of 1.15–2.15 m.

The loci in the foundation trench yielded only Nabataean sherds, with the exception of two possible Late Byzantine body sherds in Locus 11 (the fill just east of the curb) and Locus 14 (fill from –2.73 to –2.98 m below datum). The possible late sherds, however, are very worn, small in size, and carry no "definers." In combination with the controversies concerning the identification and chronology of Nabataean coarse wares, these factors cast doubt on the late date. Several of the more characteristic sherds in the foundation levels are clearly first century AD in date, and several probably belong to the first century BC. Comparison with the sherds found in the mixed surface fill above the foundation suggests strongly that construction was completed by the first half of the first century AD. Loci 1–2 and 6–8 all yielded enormous amounts of ceramic material of the Middle Nabataean, Roman, Byzantine, and Umayyad periods. This material was not found in successive occupation levels, but occurred in the form of small, worn sherds mixed uniformly in thin, alternating layers of water and wind-deposited sand, silt, and clay that slope downwards from east to west over the reservoir wall and the roof beyond. This deposit, which is typical of most of the site, represents the mixing and spreading of cultural material typical of the centre of a busy habitation area over a long period of time. If the reservoir had been built subsequent to the early first century AD, much clearer ceramic evidence of the Roman or Byzantine period could be expected in the lower loci.

Bibliography: Oleson 1986: 57, 1988a: 164–65; 1990a: 288–92, 1991a.

4.B.2. *Cisterns and Run-Off Fields*

Thirteen ancient structures within or on the fringes of the settlement centre of Hawara have been identified as cisterns, although two of these (nos. 72 and

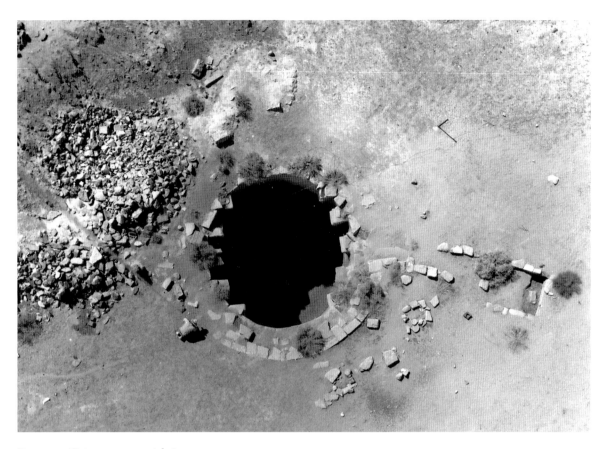

FIG. 4.23 *Cistern no. 54, aerial view.*

73) may have served some other purpose, such as grain storage (see the maps, figs. 2.7, 2.14). Since most of the settlement was built on the sandy loess of the lowlands, it is not surprising that 10 of these cisterns were constructed of blocks rather than cut into bedrock. The seven positively identified built cisterns in the settlement centre all follow a similar design. They are deep masonry cylinders roofed by slabs carried on cross-arches that spring directly from the interior walls, and are fed by individual intake channels provided with a small settling basin. With the exception of Cisterns nos. 54 and 64, these circular cisterns cluster in a group around the run-off system that fed the public reservoirs. Given the similarity in design, they may form a chronologically distinct group as well, probably of the pre-Roman, Nabataean period. Cistern no. 65 is isolated from the rest of the group by location and design. It was built on a soil talus of the hillside above the settlement centre and is rectangular in plan, with a roof carried on cross-arches. All but

one of the built cisterns are associated with ancient structures, probably houses. The exception, Cistern no. 54, is adjacent to a probable Nabataean campground.

Structure no. 54. Built cistern

Coordinates: (UTM) 36R 0725936, 3315338, (Pal. Grid) 827289. Elevation: 968 m (GPS), 951.98 m (survey).

The circular cistern was built of well-trimmed blocks of hard white sandstone, at the focus of a theatre-shaped hill (area ca. 4 ha) between the south edge of the settlement centre and the tomb with stepped approach at A104 (figs. 4.23–25). The distance from Reservoir no. 67 is 380 m at a bearing of 218 degrees. In contrast to the other circular cisterns in the settlement centre, there are no remains of structures around this cistern. Excavation in 1996 revealed the presence of a possible Nabataean campground in the adjacent field

FIG. 4.24   *Cistern no. 54, view from southwest.*

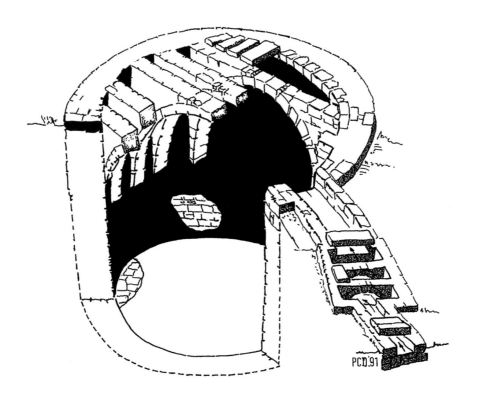

FIG. 4.25   *Cistern no. 54, reconstruction (P. Denholm).*

that may have been served by this cistern (Area C124; Oleson et al. 1999: 411–14). This area will be discussed in a subsequent volume. This arrangement reflects the character of the early settlement at Hawara, when hydraulic structures supported a still semi-nomadic culture. In the settlement centre, substantial stone structures gradually replaced the original camping areas.

Run-off from the hillside was channelled into the cistern through a long, slab-built conduit channel (L 8.12 m; W 0.68 m) that enters the cistern from the southwest at a bearing of 40 degrees (fig. 4.26). Sections of the intake structure have been damaged and a small portion rebuilt, but in the original configuration the water very likely poured directly into a settling tank (L 2.19 m; W 1.58 m; depth >1.20 m; cap. ca. 2.77 cum) constructed of blocks of sandstone carefully trimmed and set. The interior of the settling tank was lined with a hard, light grey plaster containing much poorly-sorted sand, granite pebbles, and small fragments of ground-up potsherds (Bucket 87.55). The floor was paved with irregular, flat fieldstones set in plaster, and the corners were rounded off with a thick layer of plaster laid over small stones. A sill raised ca. 0.80 m over the level of the floor allowed water to pour into a wide channel (W 0.68 m) floored with large, regular stone slabs and framed by partially trimmed blocks, laid on the same orientation as the long axis of the settling tank (65 degrees). This conduit, which has been partly destroyed, extended for 5.7 m to the cistern. The solid construction resembles the execution of the intake for Reservoir no. 68. At present, water bypasses the settling tank, entering the intake conduit at a point halfway along its length.

The cistern (D 5.80–5.83 m; depth 6.25 m; cap. 166 cum) was roofed with stone slabs carried on five arches, which sprang from impost blocks set into the wall 4.65 m above the floor and crossed the cistern at a bearing of 40 degrees, clearly coordinated with the location of the intake channel (figs. 4.24–25). In this arrangement, the spans of the arches decrease toward either side. The slabs and arches have all been lost; they are probably buried beneath the sediment recently dredged out of the cistern and piled up to the north. The interior has been lined with modern mortar, which covers all

FIG. 4.26 *Cistern no. 54, view of intake channel from the north (Probe 2).*

the coursing of the wall and the arch imposts. In June of 1986, the cistern was nearly full of water; in June of 1983, 1987, and 1989, it contained approximately 3 m of water. In October of 1990, it was nearly empty; in June and October 2000, and in June 2004 and 2005, it was dry. In May 2009, this, like many other cisterns in the settlement centre, was full, as the result of a single heavy rainstorm in March.

A sounding dug across and down the outside of the cistern wall in 1987 (Section 5.G, Probe 1; figs. 4.24, 5.75) revealed the original top surface of the cistern wall (Th 1.20 m), consisting of flat, tightly placed slabs. There are occasional gaps where the roofing slabs have been torn away. The course of blocks forming the interior cistern lip is slightly higher than the outer courses, perhaps to form a support for the roofing slabs. While the topmost course of the exterior wall was very carefully laid and trimmed, the lower courses on the exterior were composed of more irregular blocks that in some cases projected slightly from the surface of the wall. The upper 0.20 m of soil in this probe, like the ground surface for 10–20 m around the cistern, contained a rich collection of Nabataean, Roman, and Byzantine ceramics (Bucket 87.28). The compact sandy soil below, between –0.20 and –0.30 m, contained only one (possibly Roman) potsherd (Bucket 87.21). The compact sandy fill against the wall down to 1.06 m yielded only two small potsherds (Bucket 87.36), one of which can be identified as first-century Nabataean. At this level, the cistern wall exposed in the probe recedes inward. The thicker and more carefully constructed topmost metre of the ring wall was intended to reinforce the cistern at ground level. Excavation in the settling basin yielded a mix of ancient ceramics and modern artefacts.

Bibliography: Oleson 1988: 165.

Structure no. 55. Rock-cut cistern: "Birkat al-Kufr" ("Cistern of the Infidels")

Coordinates: (UTM) 36R 0725827, 3315487, (Pal. Grid) 825290. Elevation: 987 m (GPS), 969.87 m (survey).

The cistern was cut into a knoll in the southeast end of the red sandstone ridge that rises west of the habitation area. The distance from Reservoir no. 67 is 380 m at a bearing of 246 degrees. The remains of the Upper Church (C119) and surrounding structures lie 20 m to the north of the cistern intake, most of them at a slightly lower level. Two very long rock-cut and earth-and-slab channels wind along the east and west sides of the ridge and transform virtually the entire hill above the cistern into a catchment field (area ca. 5 ha). Like the nearby habitation area, the surface around the cistern is covered with potsherds dating from the Nabataean through the early Islamic periods.

At present, the north conduit begins as a channel built of earth and fieldstone slabs 250 m northwest of the intake hole, just 50 m east across

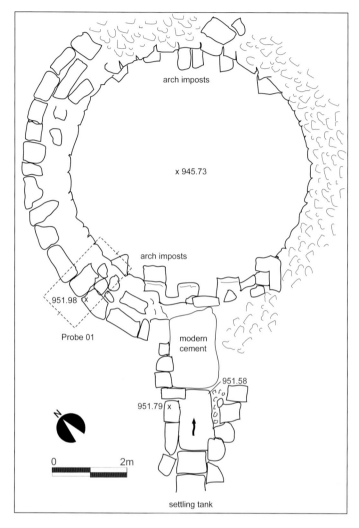

FIG. 4.27 *Cistern no. 54, plan.*

the ridge from the termination of the present south channel. The south channel winds for 367.5 m along the ridge to the intake hole. Significant portions of both of these channels have been rebuilt in recent years with earth and slabs of red sandstone, but their courses follow the lowest possible contours along the slope (and thus incorporate the largest possible catchment), and they tie in smoothly with the ancient rock-cut channels that survive at various points along their courses. Furthermore, along several rebuilt sections of the channel where shallow modern trenches now conduct the water, traces of what seem to be the ancient slab walls can be seen slightly lower down the slope. It is likely that the present channels more or less approximate

FIG. 4.28 *Cistern no. 55, view from north.*

the ancient ones. At the moment, the south channel is in better repair and seems to constitute the main source of water for the cistern. The cistern contained water every year that excavation took place at Humayma through 1998. Since 2000, however, it has been dry.

The north channel is built of earth and field stones up to a point 45.8 m northwest of the cistern intake; from here on, it joins a large rock-cut channel (W ca. 0.35 m; depth ca. 0.20 m) that winds around the hill to a settling tank (L 4.60 m; W 3.0–6.0 m; depth >0.50 m; cap. >6.9–13.8 cum; figs. 4.28–29). The tank, now completely filled with earth, was cut 3 m back into the bedrock, and the outside opening is at present blocked by a dry-stone wall of roughly-trimmed stone blocks of which only one course is visible above ground level. There may, in fact, be an outside bedrock wall below ground level. A long, straight, rock-cut intake channel (L 6.0 m; W 0.48 m; depth 0.30 m), the floor of which is 0.25 m above the present ground level in the tank, leads from a point near its southwest corner to the cistern intake hole, now obscured by modern mortared rubble. The

cistern is an irregular rectangular chamber (L ca. 8 to 10 m; W 5.20 m; depth 6.65 m; cap. 276.6–345.8 cum, catalogued as 300 cum) cut entirely within the sandstone knoll so that approximately the top third of the interior is above ground level. Three window-like openings have been cut through the eastern side wall and subsequently walled up, two of them not long before 1986. The present draw hole (D 0.52 m) was cut in the centre of a small platform (L 1.5 m; W 1.3 m) excavated into the side of the knoll at a level 1 m above the last stretch of intake channel; it was framed with roughly-trimmed stone slabs. The west intake channel (cut in the rock; W 0.35 m; depth 0.20 m) now empties on the west corner of this platform, but in antiquity it probably continued in a conduit built on a narrow ledge that winds 8 m down the slope to the south corner of the settling tank

The present southern run-off interception channel begins 368 m from the draw hole, just across the ridge from the beginning of the northern channel. It is built of untrimmed stone slabs set in earth, even across some areas of bedrock that may have been judged unsuitable for a carved channel

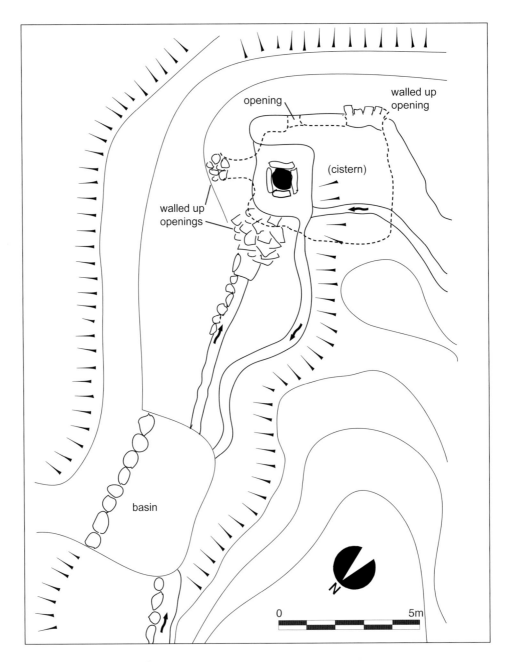

Fig. 4.29 *Cistern no. 55, plan.*

because of frequent fissures and irregularities. From a point 72.6 m upstream from the intake hole, the channel is cut into the rock (W 0.40–0.55 m; depth 0.45–0.75 m), gradually contracting in width as it slopes gently downward and around the knoll to the southeast. The last 10 m of the channel curve sharply and slope downward steeply (45–60 degrees) into the draw hole (fig. 4.29).

Structure no. 56. Rock-cut cistern

Coordinates: (UTM) 36R 0725688, 3315631, (Pal. Grid) 823292. Elevation: 999 m (GPS), 992.02 m (survey).

The cistern was cut into the red sandstone bedrock just below the crest of the ridge west of the habitation centre, 220 m north of Cistern no.

FIG. 4.30 *Cistern no. 56, view from south.*

55 and slightly higher up the slope. The distance from Reservoir no. 67 is 490 m at a bearing of 268 degrees. Run-off from the east slope of the ridge north of and above the catchment for no. 55 was channelled to the cistern in conduits made of earth backed with roughly-trimmed stone slabs. These collectors are recent in date, but the topography indicates that the arrangement must have been the same in antiquity. The cistern proper (L 6.50 m; W 5.95 m; depth 1.60 m; cap. 61.9 cum) may not have been completed (fig. 4.30). The shape is irregular, the walls are only roughly finished with gouges and picks, the depth is much shallower than usual, and there are no traces of plaster on the walls. It would have been difficult to span a cistern of this width with cross-arches. There is now a significant amount of rubble in the cistern, including a fragment of a marl conduit block (channel W 0.10 m, H >0.10 m) with traces of water-deposited calcium carbonate inside. Like the nearby habitation area, the surface around the cistern is covered with potsherds dating from the Nabataean through the Early Islamic periods.

Structure no. 57. Rock-cut cistern

Coordinates: (UTM) 36R 0725748, 3315766, (Pal. Grid) 824293. Elevation: 991 m (GPS), 973.95 m (survey).

The cistern was cut into a shelf in the red sandstone bedrock forming the ridge west of the habitation centre, approximately 150 m north of Cistern no. 56. The distance from Reservoir no. 67 is 450 m at a bearing of 285 degrees. Run-off from the adjacent slope (area approximately 4 ha) is funnelled into the cistern by a natural gully. The upper edge of the bedrock was supplemented by two courses of carefully cut blocks to bring the rim of the cistern up to the present ground level (fig. 4.31). While most of these blocks show neat Nabataean trimming, the

FIG. 4.31 *Cistern no. 57, view from east.*

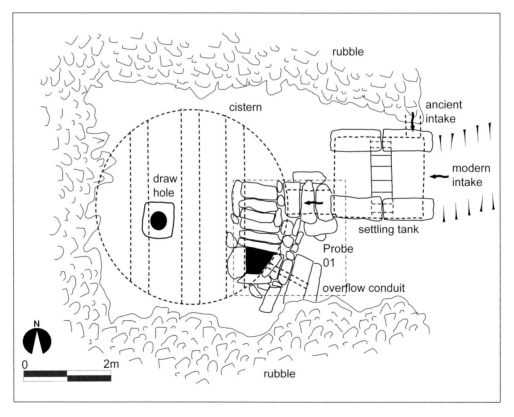

FIG. 4.32 *Cistern no. 64, plan.*

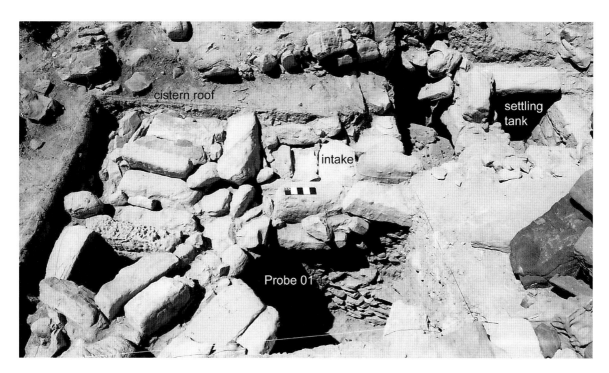

FIG. 4.33 *Cistern no. 64, view from south after partial excavation.*

coursing of the wall is irregular, suggesting that it was re-laid in the mid-twentieth century. The cistern (L 4.0 m; W 3.95 m; depth >3.50 m; cap. 55.3 cum) was roofed by stone slabs carried on two arches that spanned it along its slightly longer east/west axis. The arches, which have now disappeared, were set into imposts cut back into the bedrock. The interior was waterproofed by a layer of hard, grey stucco. A few Middle Nabataean and Roman common-ware potsherds were observed in the vicinity of the cistern. In June 1986 the cistern was nearly full, while in June 1987 it contained only 1.2 m of water.

Structure no. 64. Built cistern

Coordinates: (UTM) 336R 0726320, 315433, (Pal. Grid) 832289. Elevation: 962 m (GPS), 954.25 m (survey).

The cistern was constructed in isolation at the southeast edge of the habitation area and was later framed by Byzantine and Early Islamic structures. The distance from Reservoir no. 67 is 150 m at a bearing of 144 degrees. The cistern probably was filled by diverting water from a major, south-flowing wadi branch 20 m east of the intake channel.

Although only the outlines of the structure can be seen, the cistern and its settling tank appear to be located in a courtyard opening off the east side of the adjacent structure. Excavation of much of this structure as F102 in 1991–95 revealed traces of a house of the Nabataean and Roman periods underlying a Byzantine church, which in turn was subdivided for occupation in the early Islamic period. The immediate area has been badly disturbed in the modern period, and the fill over the cistern has been carried away, leaving a depression roughly 18 m long (east/west) and 7 m wide (north/south), exposing the cistern roof.

In recent times (although not since 1981), water was brought to the cistern by an earth trench dug from the wadi to the edge of the settling tank (L 2.08 m; W 1.84 m; depth 0.98 m; cap. 3.8 cum). The original intake, however, was a block-built channel (W 0.32 m; H 0.26 m) at the northwest corner of the tank (fig. 4.32). The settling tank was roofed with stone slabs carried on a single transverse arch (W 0.50 m) that still survives in place (fig. 4.33). The interior was waterproofed with a very thick (Th 0.13–0.22 m), very hard, pale brown plaster heavily tempered with poorly-sorted, rounded sand and

FIG. 4.34 *Cistern no. 64, view of overflow conduit from inside tank.*

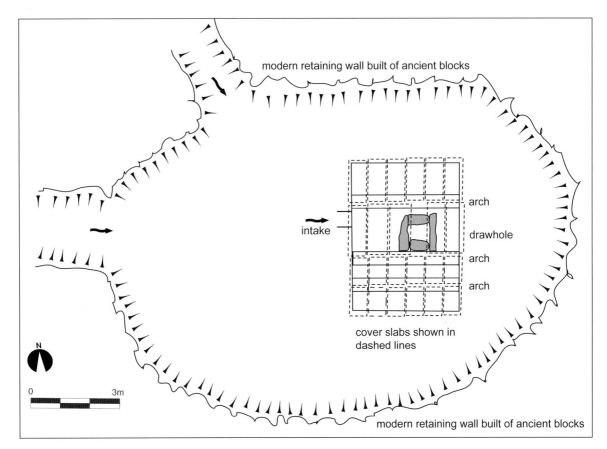

FIG. 4.35 *Cistern no. 65, plan.*

pebbles (Bucket 87.76). The roofing arch was held together with a crumbly white mortar lightly tempered with ill-sorted sand and pebbles, and containing frequent carbon bits, lime nodules, and bubbles (Bucket 87.76). A block-built channel (W 0.41 m; H 0.27 m) roofed with slabs leads from the top of the south end of the west wall of the settling tank 1.20 m west into the circular cistern (D ca. 3.8 m; depth >4.50 m, >3.80 m below overflow; cap. >43 cum). The cistern roof, built of sandstone slabs carried by three (?) transverse arches, survives intact, except for the removal of a portion of one slab near the east edge to open a new draw hole. The original draw hole consisted of a circular opening (D 0.34 m) cut through a sandstone roofing slab (Th 0.40 m); there is a slight inset around the mouth in which a lid could sit. The small size of the draw holes makes determination of the exact dimensions and design of the cistern impossible. The circular cistern wall was constructed of blocks and waterproofed with a sandy white plaster containing numerous pebbles. Two marl conduit blocks laid edge to edge to form a sort of pipe (opening W 0.12 m; H 0.28 m) have been built into the cistern wall close to the modern draw hole to serve as an overflow pipe; the floor of the channel is 0.70 m below the slab roof, 3.80 m above the present floor level (fig. 4.34). A sounding on the exterior (H89–64–P01) revealed that this conduit emptied into a larger drain built of stone slabs (W 0.21 m; H 0.30 m) that survives for a length of 0.80 m. Excavation of the upper layers of fill outside the cistern wall yielded a rich selection of Nabataean, Roman, Byzantine, and a few Umayyad potsherds. The lowest occupation level above what seems to be sterile soil (Locus 6) yielded only Middle Nabataean and Roman ceramics (see pp. 307–9).

Structure no. 65. Built cistern

Coordinates: (UTM) 36R 0725847, 3315757, (Pal. Grid) 826293. Elevation: 966 m (GPS), 963.85 m (survey).

The cistern was built on a small level area of the hillside west of the habitation centre, 150 m below Cistern no. 57, in the soil talus below the sandstone core of the ridge. The distance from Reservoir no. 67 is 360 m at a bearing of 288 degrees. The adjacent hillside (area ca. 6 ha), which drains naturally in the direction of the cistern, served as the run-off catchment. A modern intake channel (L 7.0 m; W ca. 1.30 m; depth 1.0 m), cut down into the soil and lined with reused Nabataean blocks, leads to a large oval depression (L 12 m; W 8 m; depth ca. 1 m) where the soil over the cistern has been cleared out (fig. 4.35). The berm around the depression has been reinforced in the modern period with ancient blocks. There is a second, less well-defined intake channel on the northwest. Many of the blocks reused in these walls are carefully shaped, with diagonal surface trimming. The spoil from modern activity at the site conceals the ancient ground level, but the approximately rectangular shape of the berm may indicate the presence of a structure surrounding the cistern. The site is slightly outside the main rubble field constituting the remains of Hawara, but the scatter of Nabataean to Early Islamic potsherds found around the centre can be seen here as well. The small cistern (L 4.12 m; W 3.87 m; depth >1.3 m; cap. >20.7 cum), oriented almost exactly north/south, is roofed with stone slabs carried on three transverse (east/west) arches. The roof is intact, although the frame of slabs surrounding the draw hole in the centre of the roof appears to have been rebuilt. At present, water is channelled through this opening. The original intake conduit is concealed below ground level, but its opening can be seen from inside the cistern, in the centre of the west cistern wall (W 0.23 m; H >10 m). No ancient or modern settling basin is visible around the cistern, which is now filled to within 1.3 m of the roof with soil. The three arches, 0.57 m wide and set 0.57 m apart, are built of carefully shaped and laid voussoirs. Both the arches and the interior surfaces of the cistern were waterproofed with a hard, white, sandy plaster, which has fallen away in places to reveal the carefully cut masonry of the walls.

Structure no. 66. Built cistern

Coordinates: (UTM) 36R 0726106, 3315503, (Pal. Grid) 829292. Elevation: 964 m (GPS), 952.39 m (survey).

The cistern was built toward the south edge of the settlement centre; the distance from Reservoir no. 67 is 150 m at a bearing of 209 degrees. The present run-off catchment field is the hillside and sloping field of ruins to the west (area approximately 5 ha), but the location of the ancient settling basin indicates that the cistern originally received water from the wadi that flowed through the centre of Hawara 30–40 m to the east. Removal of some of the recent fill above the cistern revealed a circular curb of carefully laid sandstone blocks, with a diameter of 7.40 m (fig. 4.36). A course of blocks intersects the south edge of this circle, at a slightly lower level (–0.60 m), forming the north wall (L 4.0 m) of an east/west intake channel or long settling basin. At the west end of this feature, an intake conduit built of blocks and slabs (H 0.50 m; W 0.40 m; L ca. 1.8 m) runs due north through the cistern wall. The present draw hole, slightly off-centre from the geometric centre of the circular curb walls, is a modern construction of cement fitted with a steel door and supplied with an adjacent cement trough; it may stand on the site of the ancient draw hole. A hole has broken through the roof near the northwest portion of the curb, revealing the presence of an east/west support arch below. Given the probable diameter of the cistern, it is likely there are six arches. The interior of the cistern could not be examined, but the line of the curb may correspond with the line of the cistern wall below. Assuming a diameter of 7.4 m and a depth of at least 5 m, the capacity of the cistern would be at least 215 cum. The ground around the cistern is covered with the same scattering of Nabataean through Umayyad potsherds seen around the entire settlement centre.

Structure no. 69. Built cistern

Coordinates: (UTM) 36R 0726266, 3315667, (Pal. Grid) 830293. Elevation: 962 m (GPS), 954.93 m (survey).

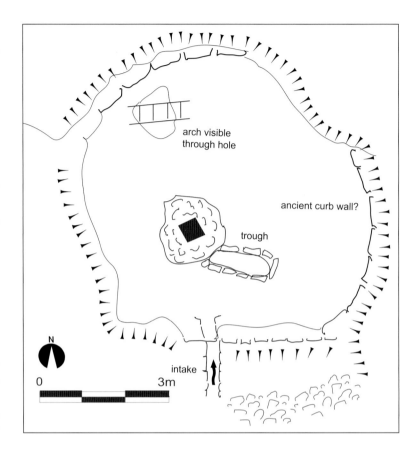

FIG. 4.36 *Cistern no. 66, plan.*

The cistern was built in the courtyard of a structure 90 m from the northeast corner of Reservoir no. 67, at a bearing of 65 degrees, just west of the channel of the present watercourse through the settlement centre. The run-off catchment was probably the general catchment field for the whole settlement, which spreads out directly to the north (area ca. 100 ha). The surrounding structure has been badly disturbed in attempts to renovate the cistern and clear the general area of debris, but the cistern appears to have been built in the centre of a square courtyard approximately 7 m on a side. Excavation of the northwest corner of this court (Probe H89–69–P01; Section 5.I) revealed a low bench or curb projecting 0.37 m from a surrounding wall or walkway, 0.41 m above the upper surface of the cistern roof. The construction material was the local red sandstone. There may originally have been a slab pavement at the level of the offset, but in the final stage of the structure's use the pavement was raised to 0.85 m above the surface of the roof (figs. 4.37, 5.78).

FIG. 4.37   *Cistern no. 69, Probe 1. Northwest corner of courtyard.*

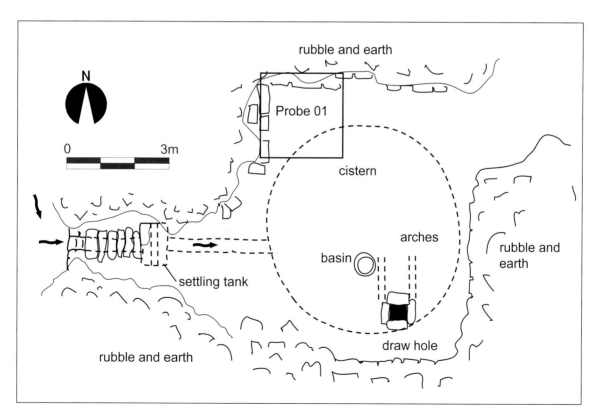

FIG. 4.38   *Cistern no. 69, plan.*

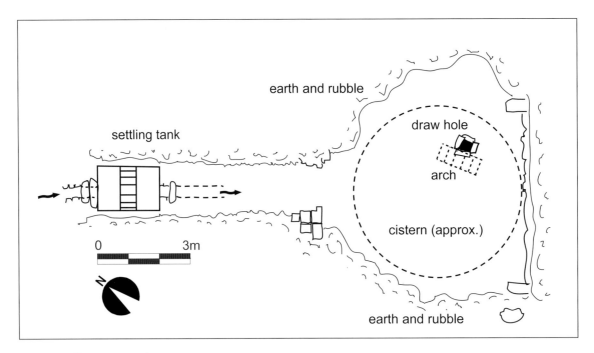

FIG. 4.39 *Cistern no. 70, plan.*

An intake conduit (W 0.40 m; H 0.69 m) built of carefully trimmed sandstone slabs extends west 4 m from the west edge of the interior cistern wall (fig. 4.38). No settling tank can be seen at this point now, but there may have been one there originally from which the intake channel would have extended north into the run-off catchment field. At present, water running off the field is directed into the surviving portion of the intake channel by earth conduits. The cistern is circular (D ca. 7.0 m; depth >5.92 m; cap. >227.8 cum), with a draw hole (0.65 m square) near its southeast edge framed by worn stone blocks. In 1989, a local shepherd stated that this draw hole was opened up only a "few years" before, and that the "original" one was on the west side of the cistern. The present ground level is approximately 1.3 m above the cistern roof, built of roughly-trimmed stone slabs set on transverse arches oriented north/south. The two arches visible through the draw hole are 0.57 m apart; if the arches themselves are approximately the same width, six of them would be sufficient to support the roof. The cistern walls could not be examined. Every year between 1989 and 1998 the cistern provided water for human and animal consumption; the water quality was considered excellent. In June

2000, June 2002, and October 2003 the cistern was dry, both as a result of drought and of alterations to the catchment field. The sounding in 1989 was restricted in area in deference to the fear of local herders that camels would fall in the excavation square and be injured while being watered. The ceramics found in the probe between the pavement and the cistern roof were a mix of Nabataean through Late Byzantine types, but most were Middle Nabataean and Roman (Section 5.I).

Structure no. 70. Built cistern

Coordinates: (UTM) 36R 0726200, 3315680, (Pal. Grid) 829293. Elevation: 970 m (GPS), 954.54 (survey).

The cistern was built in the courtyard of a structure adjacent to the south edge of the catchment field that served the whole settlement. The distance from Reservoir no. 67 is 50 m at a bearing of 18 degrees. The structure surrounding the cistern has been badly disturbed, and only the stubs of short, unconnected stretches of wall can be seen here and there in the heaps of rubble around the roughly circular (D ca. 7.0 m) depression excavated over the cistern by the Bedouin (fig. 4.39). The longest wall (L 6.5 m; H ca. 1.0 m) extends along the south side of the depression at a bearing of 250 degrees and is defined at either end by what seem to be the original corners. A long intake channel (L ca. 6.0 m; H 0.26 m; W 0.36 m), built of well-trimmed blocks and roofed with sandstone slabs, extends northwest from the north edge of the cistern area to a settling tank. The settling tank (L 1.96 m; W 1.47 m; depth > 0.80 m; cap. >2.3 cum) is located on the very edge of the present rubble field. A 1 m stretch of the upstream intake channel is visible beneath the fill at the north end of the tank, into which run-off from the catchment field is now directed by an earth channel. The tank originally was roofed with stone slabs carried on a single transverse (east/west) arch. Modern rubble retaining walls hold back the heaps of rubble along the course of the intake channel and around the cistern roof. A door-jamb (H 1.30 m; Th 0.75 m) built of substantial, carefully squared blocks has survived on the west side of the intake at approximately the point where it intersects the cistern wall. It is likely that Cistern no. 70, like Cisterns nos. 64 and 69, was set in the centre of a square courtyard, at the core of a large square or rectangular structure. The long intake channel was probably intended to allow placement of the settling tank outside the boundaries of this structure, where cleaning would be easier. The circular, block-built cistern (D >5.0 m; depth >4.02 m; cap. >78.9 cum) was roofed with stone slabs set on transverse (north/south) arches The visible portion of the present draw hole (0.40 m square) is a modern re-build using ancient blocks, set over the southeast edge of the cistern. The area around the cistern is covered with the same scatter of Nabataean through Early Islamic potsherds seen throughout the ancient habitation area.

Structure no. 71. Built cistern

Coordinates: (UTM) 36R 0726088, 3315786, (Pal. Grid) 829294. Elevation: 975 m (GPS), 956.12 m (survey).

The cistern was built in a structure or group of structures near the northwest edge of the northern cluster of structural remains and adjacent to the general catchment field that served the whole settlement. The distance from Reservoir no. 67 is 180

m at a bearing of 326 degrees. The visible portion of the structure surrounding this cistern has been very badly disturbed, and the rest seems still to be buried beneath a thick layer of silt. Only heaps of rubble and a few very shaken stubs of walls can be seen around the roughly rectangular (L ca. 6 m; W ca. 5 m) depression excavated over the cistern by the Bedouin. Two fragments of marl conduit blocks were observed in the rubble 10 m west of the cistern area (L >0.35 m; H 0.19 m; W 0.20 m; channel H 0.08 m, W 0.10 m). At present, water enters the cistern depression from the northwest and flows directly into a short intake channel (L 0.89 m; H 0.23 m; W 0.23 m) that carries it over the southwest lip of the cistern at a bearing of 70 degrees (fig. 4.40). Although it is no longer visible, there may be a settling tank below the silt in the area where the water now pools before flowing through the intake channel. The cistern is roofed with stone slabs carried on transverse arches (bearing of 335 degrees). The two arches that can be glimpsed through the draw hole are set 0.55 m apart, suggesting that there are probably four in all. Only a very small patch of the cistern wall can be seen, but the plan appears to be circular (D >5.0 m; depth >4.25 m; cap. >83.5 cum). The visible portion of the draw hole (ca. 0.45 m square) is a modern rebuild using ancient blocks; there is a modern rubble and mortar basin (D 0.75 m) near it. The area around the cistern is covered with the same scatter of Nabataean through Early Islamic potsherds seen throughout the ancient habitation area.

Structure no. 72. Built cistern?

Coordinates: (UTM) 36R 0726187, 3315781, (Pal. Grid) 829294. Elevation: 973 m (GPS), 955.96 m (survey).

The possible cistern was built in a structure or group of structures near the east edge of the northern cluster of structural remains, adjacent to the general catchment field that served the whole settlement. The distance from Reservoir no. 67 is 150 m at a bearing of 0 degrees. The visible portion of the structure surrounding it has been very badly disturbed, except for the walls framing the feature itself, leaving only heaps of rubble and a few wall stubs. The circular, domed structure is

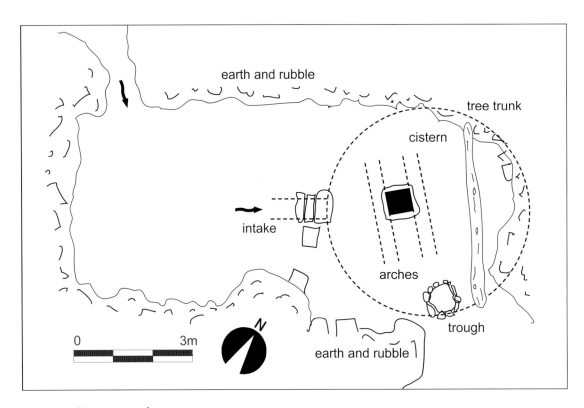

FIG. 4.40 *Cistern no. 71, plan.*

FIG. 4.41 *Structure no. 72, view from west.*

FIG. 4.42 *Structure no. 72, east interior wall.*

framed by a room 7 m square formed by walls (Th 0.82 m; bearing of east wall, 160 degrees) built of well-laid, partly trimmed slabs of red sandstone (fig. 4.41). The upper surfaces of these walls, rising approximately 2.5 m above the level of the adjacent run-off field to the east, are even and level, suggesting that they originally terminated at this point or were built of mudbrick above it. There are traces of a cobble paving 0.40 m below the preserved upper edge of the east wall and possible remains of stone steps at the southeast corner. No traces of an intake channel can be seen. The draw hole or entrance hole must have been built into the top of the dome, level with the paving at the centre of the room; the upper portion of the dome has collapsed into the cistern (D 5.50 m; depth >3.90 m; cap. >92.7 cum). The dome and cistern walls were built of roughly trimmed natural slabs of red Umm Ishrin sandstone (avg. L 0.44 m; W 0.18 m; Th 0.05 m) set in a soft, light grey, sandy mortar containing numerous carbon specks and nodules

of lime (Bucket 87.86). The plaster that originally lined the interior (see below) has disappeared from the visible portions of the wall and dome, and the mortar between the blocks has receded several centimetres from the surface. The blocks are laid horizontally in the vertical walls, then in tipped courses in the dome (fig. 4.42). At its upper preserved edge, 1.40 m below the top of the east framing wall, the preserved inside diameter of the dome is 4.50 m; the full diameter is 5.50 m.

Probe 1 was dug down the interior face of the cistern wall at a point on the southeast where the rubble fill had been partly removed by the Bedouin. The fill was composed of undifferentiated rubble and water-deposited silt, mixed with significant numbers of Nabataean, Roman, Byzantine, and Umayyad potsherds (Buckets 87.144, 149, 150, 165; Section 5.J; fig. 5.82) Because of the danger of collapse, it was not possible to excavate as far as the floor. The probe stopped at a point 3.90 m below the surviving upper level of the dome (5.30 m below the top of the east wall). At this point a layer of soft, pale brown plaster (Th 0.02 m), heavily tempered with poorly-sorted rounded sand and pebbles, and containing occasional small lumps of lime, adhered to the exposed wall surface (Bucket 87.179).

This structure and the much less well-preserved Structure no. 73 do not resemble any of the other cisterns at Humayma or in the surrounding countryside, and so far they have no close parallels elsewhere in Jordan (see below). The design resembles that of a domed domestic cistern, and the plaster found on the interior may have provided a modicum of waterproofing, but it is much softer than the ancient plaster in other cisterns. In addition, the structure is too high to have been filled from the adjacent run-off field on the east. Run-off may have been diverted from the catchment field at a point higher up the slope and brought to the cistern in a conduit now lost or concealed by rubble, or brought across the north rubble area from the hills to the west of the settlement, but either of these alternatives would have been difficult to arrange. It is possible that the structure was intended for the storage of grain or fodder, rather than water, and that it was built up high to avoid the danger of occasional flooding. The area around the cistern is covered with the same scatter of Nabataean through Early Islamic potsherds seen throughout the ancient habitation area. In April 2008, R.M. Foote carried out cleaning and limited excavation of the walls above and surrounding the domed structure. The walls were found to be associated with Byzantine occupation levels, but may possibly be earlier in date. Foote did not probe the interior of the domed structure.

The construction technique, atypical for Humayma, may indicate an Early Islamic date, but there are a few partial parallels of Byzantine date elsewhere. A smaller cistern in the atrium of the fourth-century West Church at Mampsis has

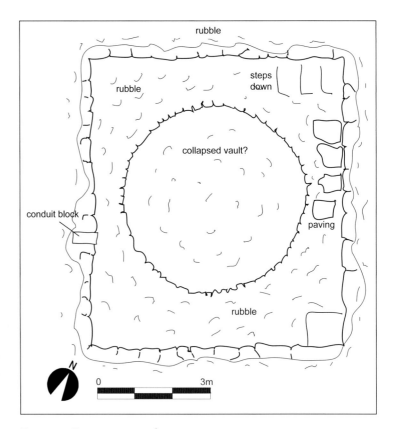

FIG. 4.43 *Structure no. 73, plan.*

a similar type of cupola roof constructed of small, irregular slabs of stone, and the walls are lined with a crumbly red plaster laid over a soft grey mortar (Negev 1988b: 57–59). While the stonework of the walls is actually a lining meant to waterproof the porous bedrock into which the cistern was cut, the cupola with central opening for the well-head is a mortared construction similar to that of Cistern no. 72. A similar cistern in the seventh-century North Church at Nessana was built completely of mortared rubble (Colt 1962: 27). The cistern in the courtyard of the Petra Church shows some generic similarities with this cistern, but it was much less carefully constructed (Fiema et al. 2001: 71–72).

Structure no. 73. Built cistern?

Coordinates: (UTM) 36R 0726149, 3315753, (Pal. Grid) 829294. Elevation: 980 m (GPS), 956.76 m (survey).

This feature is part of a structure or group of structures in a field of rubble 25 m from the southwest corner of Structure no. 72 (at a bearing of 60 degrees). The distance from Reservoir no. 67 is 130 m at a bearing of 342 degrees. Although the visible portion of the possible cistern and the structure surrounding it has been very badly disturbed, the arrangement is similar to that of no. 72: a circular space below a square room (fig. 4.43). The construction materials, however, are different, consisting of roughly-trimmed and carelessly laid yellow and black sandstone blocks rather than slabs. The dimensions, too, differ from those of no. 72. The circular structure (D 4.90) is framed by a roughly square room (east and west walls, L 7.72 m, on a bearing of 160 degrees; north and south walls L 7.03 m; thickness undetermined). The upper surfaces of these walls are broken and irregular, but there are traces of a pavement of large slabs of red sandstone inside the east wall, 1.42 m below the highest surviving portion of the framing walls. Traces can also be seen of a stone staircase at the northeast corner, descending through the level of the paving along the north wall. An overturned marl conduit block (L 0.38 m; W 0.30 m; H 0.19 m; conduit W 0.11 m, depth 0.12 m) has been built into the west wall at the level of the paving; at present it leads only to rubble fill, but the coincidence of level with the paving suggests that it may originally have had something to do with intake or drainage. The upper edge of the circular wall within the room, only partly visible, lies 0.35 m below the surface of the paving. Since there is no tilt to the upper courses of this wall and little room between the vertical wall and the pavement, it seems unlikely that the central feature can have been roofed with a dome like that on no. 72. The space between the exterior of the circular wall and the interior of the walls forming the room is filled with tumbled rubble. The interior of the circular feature is filled with rubble to a level of 1.42 m below the paving. No plaster lining is visible, and only traces of a soft, chalky, light grey mortar containing specks of carbon and frequent nodules of lime can be seen deep in the crevices between the blocks. This structure looks less like a cistern than no. 72, but the coincidence of general design and location strongly suggests that both it and no. 72 are roughly contemporary and served similar functions. If a depth of >3.90 m is assumed, the capacity would have been > 73.5

cum. If no. 73 was designed as a cistern, it probably drew run-off from the catchment field to the west of the settlement centre, using the overturned conduit block as part of the intake channel. In this case, the cistern itself may have been left unroofed, utilising the protection of the roof of the structure around it. The area around the structure is covered with the same scatter of Nabataean through Early Islamic potsherds seen throughout the ancient habitation area.

Structure no. 74. Built cistern

Coordinates: (UTM) 36R 0726174, 3315774, (Pal. Grid) 829294. Elevation: 976 m (GPS), 955.19 (survey).

The cistern was built within a structure now largely concealed beneath silt. It is 13 m southwest of Cistern no. 72 on the edge of the run-off field that serves the entire settlement. The distance from Reservoir no. 67 is 140 m at a bearing of 354 degrees. At present, water diverted from this field by an enhanced natural gully is guided over the east corner of a settling tank (L 2.0 m; W 1.6 m; depth >0.77 m; cap. >2.5 cum) built of carefully trimmed sandstone blocks, now almost entirely filled by silt (fig. 4.44). An intake channel (L 1.0 m; H 0.20 m; W 0.25 m) built of blocks and roofed with slabs extends from the centre of the west wall at a bearing of 325 degrees over the southeast edge of the cistern wall. A curb of neat blocks projecting through the surface fill outlines the circumference of the cistern (D 5.1 m; depth >4.54 m; cap. >92.7 cum), which is roofed with stone slabs carried on transverse arches. There is a draw hole (0.50 m square) framed by long blocks laid in modern mortar at approximately the centre of the cistern roof, through which three arches can be seen (0.58 m apart; bearing of 325 degrees). Four arches would be sufficient to carry the roof. It could not be determined whether there was ancient or modern plaster on the interior. No potsherds were observed in the vicinity.

4.B.3. *Conduits and Drains*

Because Hawara was built on porous, sandy soil, impermeable conduits were needed for the transport of water to locations where it would be used

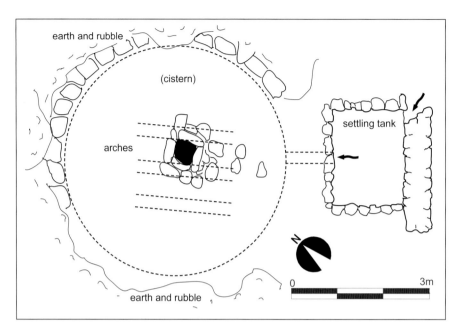

Fig. 4.44 *Cistern no. 74, plan.*

or stored, while drains seem to have been unnecessary — or at least rare. Only two convincing ancient
conduits have been identified in the settlement centre (the overflow from Reservoir/Pool no. 63 and
Conduit no. 76), both part of the input regime. In
contrast, the Roman fort was served by a systematic
network of drains that guided run-off water out the
south gate. The fort, however, probably contained a
much higher proportion of roofed or paved surface
area than did the settlement centre. Furthermore,
the Roman engineers who built the fort undoubtedly were reluctant to abandon or were required to
follow design details that had proven their worth
elsewhere in the eastern provinces. At the Roman
bath, in contrast, waste water simply ran out a hole
in the west wall.

Structure no. 63. Overflow conduit

Coordinates: (UTM) 36R 0726433, 3315856, (Pal.
Grid) 832292. Elevation: 975 m.

In the original arrangement, the overflow
from Reservoir/Pool no. 63 was carried away by
a conduit built on the same design as the Ghana
aqueduct, which fed the reservoir. This conduit
leaves the reservoir at a bearing of 205 degrees
(perpendicular to the south reservoir wall), and

well-preserved stretches were traced for 21 m in
Probes 3, 8, 11, and 12 (figs. 4.10, 5.54). In Probe
12, the conduit was only 0.68 m below the present
surface, and it was next traced in the form of isolated stretches of foundation stones 62.2 m, 70–74
m, and 84.1 m south of the reservoir. The rest of the
conduit in this area seems to have been destroyed
by ploughing or stone robbing. A large fragment
of a marl conduit block was found on the line
of the conduit 78.8 m south of the reservoir. No
remains of the conduit that can be identified with
any confidence were found more than 84 m south
of the pool. Continuation of the structure on the
same bearing of 205 degrees would have taken it 10
m east of the Roman bath (E077), across the course
of the present dirt road at a distance of 104 m from
the reservoir. Just beyond this point, at 110 m, a very
rough linear feature (W ca. 0.80 m) of sandstone
rubble curves for 60 m around the east edge of a
slight west-facing depression. The feature is not
coherent, but its approximate correspondence with
the line and the dimensions of the aqueduct, and
the fact that it curves around a depression, make it
at least possible that it served as part of the foundations for the conduit. At a point 164 m south of
the reservoir, at the south end of the depression,
there begins a better preserved stretch of wall or

FIG. 4.45   *Conduit no. 75, view from south.*

foundation (W 0.80) built of sandstone slabs and rubble; the bearing is 215 degrees. Eleven meters farther on, this feature, which is here essentially a long, slightly elevated heap of rubble and earth, curves westward to a bearing of 225 degrees, and at 222 m (near the modern school house) it shifts to a bearing of 275 degrees. This last bearing would have taken the conduit down the slope of the low ridge directly to Reservoir no. 67, 385 m to the west. Unfortunately, no further traces of the rubble feature or a conduit could be found, either on the course to Reservoir no. 67 or farther south along the edge of the ridge. All of the features beyond the 84.1 m point have only a tenuous possible relevance to the outflow conduit.

Structure no. 75. Conduit

Coordinates: (UTM) 36R 0726280, 3315618, (Pal. Grid) 831291. Elevation: 973 m (GPS), 954.97 m (survey).

A short stretch of conduit blocks has eroded out of the present ground level on the gentle westerly slope above the wadi course through the settlement.

The distance from Reservoir no. 67 is 100 m at a bearing of 96 degrees. The eight blocks, identical to the marl and sandstone blocks of the Ghana Aqueduct and Conduit no. 74, are lined up for 5 m down the slope, curving gradually from a bearing of 290 degrees to 320 degrees, and dropping 0.15 m in elevation from east to west (fig. 4.45). They do not link up with any water supply above or any receptacle below, and the structure has the appearance of a re-application of ancient conduit blocks salvaged from around the site. The blocks are laid very carelessly, without the bedding or the framing blocks typical of the Nabataean aqueducts, and one sandstone conduit block appears among the marl blocks. In addition, the water-deposited calcium carbonate in the channels of the marl conduit blocks is discontinuous across the joints, and the sandstone block does not show any deposits at all. A probe across the course of the blocks (Probe 1, Section 5.K) revealed that they were laid on and surrounded by loose undifferentiated rubble that contained a few very worn potsherds ranging in date from the Nabataean to the Byzantine periods (Buckets 87.93, 102–103). It is possible that the conduit was laid out

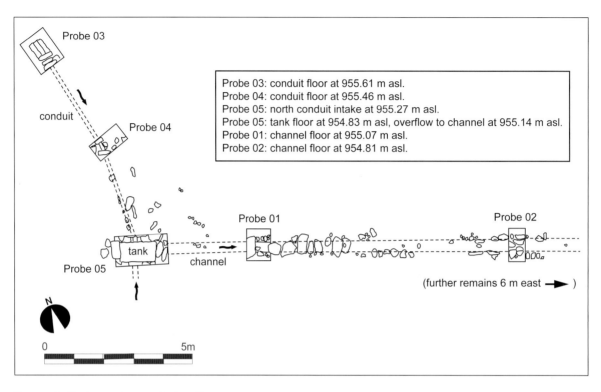

Probe 03: conduit floor at 955.61 m asl.
Probe 04: conduit floor at 955.46 m asl.
Probe 05: north conduit intake at 955.27 m asl.
Probe 05: tank floor at 954.83 m asl, overflow to channel at 955.14 m asl.
Probe 01: channel floor at 955.07 m asl.
Probe 02: channel floor at 954.81 m asl.

(further remains 6 m east ➤)

0   5m

FIG. 4.46 *Drain complex no. 76, plan of area.*

FIG. 4.47 *Drain complex no. 76, view of settling tank and drain to east.*

FIG. 4.48 *Drain complex no. 76, view of settling tank from southwest.*

in the Late Byzantine or Umayyad period, but the reuse of so many conduit blocks suggests a date after the aqueduct had ceased to function, perhaps in the early modern period. The intended function of the feature remains undetermined.

Structure no. 76. Complex of drains or conduits

Coordinates: (UTM) 36R 0726117, 3315717, (Pal. Grid) 829294. Elevation: 974 m (GPS), 955.77 m (survey).

The complex of drains or conduits was built down the length of an unpaved road or passage for the flow of floodwater (W ca. 10 m), 110 m from Reservoir no. 67 at a bearing of 320 degrees (fig. 4.46). This passage separates the main northern cluster of structural remains in the settlement centre from the main cluster around Reservoirs nos. 67–68. The central feature is a settling tank (L 0.86–0.98 m; W 0.61–0.66 m; depth 0.94 m from top of walls, 0.36 m from sill of discharge opening; cap. 0.21 cum) built of carefully trimmed blocks of sandstone (figs. 4.47–48). The tank is lined with a hard, very pale brown plaster heav-

ily tempered with poorly-sorted rounded quartz sand and pebbles, and containing frequent carbon bits and lime nodules (see pp. 344–45). The plaster was brought to a smooth finish, but not polished. Probe 5 revealed that the structure had been rebuilt at least once (pp. 324–25). In the final arrangement, a drain discharged into the tank through a rectangular opening in the centre of the (longer) north wall (sill 0.47 m above floor), and the overflow exited through a corresponding opening in the centre of the south wall (sill 0.36 m above floor). The north opening was reinforced by a trimmed-down fragment of the central portion of the hourglass-shaped runner stone from a "Pompeian type" grain mill (fig. 4.48). The shorter, slightly higher (uphill) west wall showed no sign of an opening (although plaster still covers most of its surface). There was originally a wide opening in the east (downhill) wall (sill 0.42 m above floor) that was later in-filled with carefully laid rubble and probably plastered over (fig. 4.47). The intake drain on the north, built carelessly of reused marl conduit blocks covered by stone slabs, was traced over a winding course northwards for 11 m to the remains of what appears to have been a courtyard in front of a small house (Probes 3–4; Section 5.L.3–4). At this point the drain is lost, but it is interesting to note that the upright doorjambs of the house were also built of reused marl conduit blocks. The drain drops 0.36 m from its present beginning to the tank, a slope of 2.8%. Because of the presence of heaps of rubble, the drain south of the tank could not be excavated.

The house associated with the drain was excavated by the Department of Antiquities in the 1960s, but the results were not published. The ceramics recovered during the excavation and piled nearby are mostly Early Islamic in date, and the location of the house within the uppermost rubble level in this part of the site also suggests an Early Islamic date for its construction. If this chronology is correct, the second phase of use of the drain and conduit may be Early Islamic in date as well.

The tank is on line with a much larger drain (W 0.28–0.32 m; H 0.34 m) that could be traced for 17.2 m to the east on a bearing of 105 degrees (Probes 1–2; Section 5.L.1–2; figs. 4.46–47). The walls of this drain were built of large, carefully laid field stones, the inner faces of which were trimmed to a neat surface, laid on a floor of irregular sandstone slabs (fig. 5.90). It was roofed with larger, rectangular stone slabs (L ca. 0.57 m; W ca. 0.45 m; Th ca. 0.10 m) resting at either end on a course of smaller pieces of rubble (D 0.12–0.25 m). This type of transitional course of small stones also appears on the Ghana Aqueduct. There were no traces of plaster on the interior. The presumed sill in the east wall of the tank in Probe 5 is 0.09 m above the floor of this drain in Probe 1, 3.20 m to the east, and the drop from the sill to the floor in Probe 2, 17.2 m away, is 0.35 m (a slope of 2.8% and 2.0%, respectively). The drop in the floor of the drain from Probe 1 to Probe 2 is 0.26 m over 8.5 m, a slope of 3.0%. At a point 17.2 m east of the tank, this drain disappears below fill and recent silt in a natural hollow where some run-off water now collects, 70 m NNW of Reservoir no. 67.

The function of this complex can only be guessed at. To judge from the similarity in orientation, levels, and construction technique, the large east/west drain and the tank should be contemporary. If this is the case, the tank can be interpreted as a settling tank in which run-off water from the road or the roofs of the surrounding houses, or both, was collected and clarified before continuing east in the drain. This drain may have carried it beneath the path or road to a cistern or reservoir, possibly Reservoir no. 67. The sturdy construction and roofing of all the drains suggests that they were built at or close to ancient ground level, possibly along a passageway between houses. In this sandy location, household wastewater would not have required either a settling tank or such a large capacity drain. Water may have entered the tank through an opening in the roof, an opening in the west wall now concealed by the plaster, or through the present opening in the north wall — the only one higher than the presumed sill of the large east drain. At some later period, the large drain went out of use, and the tank was put to use in a system fed by the roof (?) of the house at the end of the north conduit system.

The precise chronology of the system is also uncertain. The fill inside all the drains and the tank contained small, very worn potsherds dating from the Nabataean through the Umayyad periods — the last category being very small in number. The fill outside the north conduit and large east/west drain contained a rich mix of small fragments of pottery dating from the Nabataean through the Byzantine periods. The complex seems, therefore, to have been constructed in the Byzantine period, and to have remained in use through the beginning of the Umayyad period.

Structure no. 78. Conduit or drain?

Coordinates: (UTM) 36R 0726077, 3315747, (Pal. Grid) 829294. Elevation: 975 m.

The possible conduit or drain can be traced for 15 m along the surface of the low-lying silt-covered ground 50 m NW of the west end of Drain no. 76. The distance from Reservoir no. 67 is 160 m at a bearing of 315 degrees. It skirts the remains of the adjacent house as it proceeds at a bearing of 230 degrees. The construction is very rough (W 0.68 m); side walls and a floor built carelessly of very irregular rubble isolate a channel 0.25 m wide and 0.20 m deep. There are no traces of interior plastering or cover slabs. The feature may in fact be a partly robbed-out wall stub rather than a drain or conduit. The surface around the feature yielded the same mix of Nabataean through Umayyad potsherds found elsewhere on the site. In July 2000, this feature was covered with blown sand and could not be precisely relocated, but UTM coordinates were taken for the approximate location.

4.B.4. *Roman Bath*

The Bath (E077) was first built in association with the Roman fort (E116), probably in the course of the second century AD. The complete architectural description, probe reports, and analysis of the historical and technological context will appear with the full report on the fort and associated structures in a subsequent volume. Nevertheless, a brief introduction to the Bath must be presented here, since its construction had an impact on the water-supply system. The Bath differs markedly from the structures catalogued above in that it was a consumer of water rather than a conduit, barrier, or pool. Only an outline of the design and chronology of the structure is provided in this volume, with emphasis on its relationship to the water-supply system. The Bath was first designated by the survey number 77, then, subsequent to excavation, by the field designation E077.

Structure no. 77. Bath (E077)

Coordinates: (UTM) 36R 0726357, 3315740, (Pal. Grid) 832292. Elevation: 975 m.

The Bath building is located 100 m SSW of the south end of Reservoir/Pool no. 63, slightly below it on the very edge of the low, flat-topped ridge above the settlement centre, 200 m northeast of Reservoir no. 67 (fig. 2.14). The only other visible structural remains in the immediate vicinity are the Nabataean and Late Roman structures at E122, E125, and E128, to the east. A line projected along the last preserved stretch of the overflow conduit from Reservoir/Pool no. 63 (45 m northeast of the Bath) passes just 10 m east of the building. The terracotta pipeline found in 1987 running outside the west wall of the Nabataean reservoir or pool also was traced in this direction. It is likely that the bath was constructed at this point to make use of aque-

duct outflow from the reservoir, possibly replaced later by the terracotta pipeline. The central portion of the Roman Bath was constructed on top of the walls of a solidly built Nabataean building dated by ceramic evidence to no later than the first or early second century AD. Given the juxtaposition of the Nabataean outflow conduit and this Nabataean structure, the earlier structure may also have been a bath building.

Excavation of the Roman bath in 1989 revealed a roughly rectangular structure (10.3 m E/W, 13.8 m N/S) enclosing seven relatively small rooms (labelled Rooms A to G; figs. 4.49–50). Unfortunately, the fill above the plaster floor in all these rooms was a secondary deposit containing a modest assortment of sherds dating from the Nabataean to the Umayyad periods, along with thousands of fragments of flue tiles. According to local informants, much of the interior had been cleared out between 1948 and the mid-1960s by a "Moroccan wizard" who built the small stone hut that adjoined the northeast corner of the bath (removed in 1995). The intact *calidarium* floor was broken up by the local landowner Abu Salameh and his family in the Winter of 1986. Nevertheless, it was possible to determine the plan of the bath building, and several probes in undisturbed deposits beneath the floors and outside the walls of the structure have provided a tentative history of its construction and development. M. B. Reeves carried out further excavation in and around the structure in 2005, 2008, and 2010 (Reeves et al. 2009). The structure will be described room by room, proceeding logically from the entrance area to the furnace, rather than in the order in which the rooms were excavated.

The Bath went through three phases of development that can be dated tentatively to the Middle Nabataean (Phase 1; first century BC or AD), Roman (Phase 2; later second century?), and Late Roman (Phase 3) periods. The Phase 1 structure was well-built with ashlar blocks and probably connected with Reservoir/Pool no. 63 by means of the outflow conduit. It may well have been a bath, but the structure has not been sufficiently exposed to confirm its function. In Phase 2, the Bath consisted of five rooms: a reception and undressing room (*apodyterium*; Room B) that probably contained two (or possibly three) benches for sitting or reclining; a

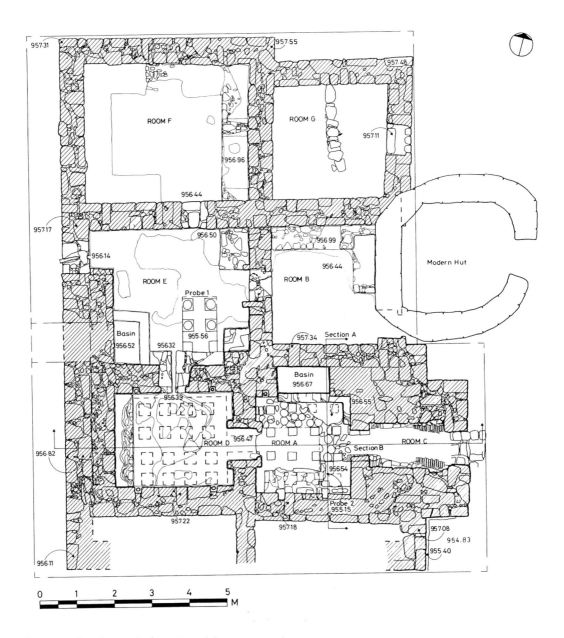

FIG. 4.49 *Late Roman Bath, no. E077 (Plan: D. Ritsema).*

bathing room (*frigidarium*, Room E) with a basin for cold water and a heated floor (*hypocauston*; fig. 4.51); a sweat room (*laconicum*; Room D), with a bench for sitting, and heated floor and walls; and a hot bath room (*calidarium*; Room A), with a heated floor and walls and a basin for heated water (fig. 4.52). As usual with Roman baths, the furnace room (*praefurnium*; Room C) adjoined the *calidarium*. In Phase 3, a second, larger *apodyterium* with six benches was added (Room F), the hypocaust floor

in the *frigidarium* was filled in, and the hypocaust heating system serving Rooms C, A, and D was rebuilt. The relationship of Room G to this complex is unclear, but it cannot be earlier than Phase 2. The walls are less well-built than those elsewhere in the Bath, they do not bond with the walls of Rooms B or F, and the only door opens outside the building. The interior of this room was cleared out to the foundation level sometime in the post-classical period, and no interior features remain to provide

FIG. 4.50 *Late Roman Bath no. E077, aerial view in 1992, before removal of recent hut walls (Photo: Wilson Myers, 21.07.1992, neg. H-4.1).*

a clue to its original function. It is possible that it served as a public toilet (*latrina*), a facility typically associated with Roman public baths, but it may also be a modern addition.

Room B, the reception room in Phase 2, contained two plastered benches built of flat stones and fired bricks set in a hard white mortar and finished with the same hard, sandy white plaster that was used for the floor and walls. Each bench has a plaster pillow or fulcrum at one end. The damage to the south side of the room has made it impossible to discern whether or not a third bench was located at this point, but there seems to be room

for it. A door in the middle of the west wall opened outward toward Room E, the *frigidarium*. The benches seen at present probably belong to Phase 3, but there should have been some arrangement for seating in this room in Phase 2 as well. Neither this room nor Room F, the Phase 3 reception room, contained any hydraulic installations.

The entrance door to Room F, the largest room in the Bath and at a slightly higher elevation than the other rooms, is in the centre of the north wall. Two benches built of bricks, stones, and mortar, as in Room B, occupy the entire east wall. Marks in the hard, sandy white plaster that covers the floor

Fig. 4.51 *Late Roman Bath no. E077, basin in Room E.*

and the benches reveal that there were originally two more benches along the north wall, two along the west wall, and one at the west end of the south wall — all cut away to floor level, most likely in the modern reoccupation period. A door and step in the middle of the south wall lead into Room E.

Construction details strongly suggest that Room F was a Phase 2 addition to the Bath complex. It seems likely that the Phase 2 reception facilities in Room B were found to be inadequate for the needs of the bath, so a larger *apodyterium* was added. It is possible that at this same time the door in the east wall of Room B fell out of use or was blocked up and that the north door in Room F became the principal entrance to the Bath. Patrons could enter through this door, undress here or in Room B, then begin the process of bathing with a cold splash from the basin in Room E. From this point onward, the process of bathing was fixed by the plan of the structure, which follows the typical Roman bathing

liturgy of progressively warmer rooms, followed by a return along the same route.

Room E, the cold bath room, or *frigidarium*, is a roughly square space at the centre of the Bath, with doors providing access to both the dressing rooms and the heated bathing areas, and possibly an exit door or service entrance. The fittings consisted of square tables or benches built into the northeast and southeast corners and a basin built into the southwest corner (fig. 4.51). The table in the northeast corner was torn out, leaving only the outline of its intersection with the plaster floor, but the southeast table survives. The small portion of the upper surface that is preserved does not show any signs of fittings or recesses, and it seems likely that the table was simply intended as an elevated support for a water jar or some other equipment required for bathing.

The focus of the room was the basin built into the southwest corner: a simple bench with basin

FIG. 4.52 *Late Roman Bath no. E.077, basin and hypocaust in Room A.*

on top, constructed of fired brick and flat stones in the same manner as the table opposite (outside L 1.32 m, W 0.93 m; preserved height 0.60 m). The plaster inside the basin (inside dimensions: 1.04 × 0.67 × 0.44 m) is the same type as that used for the floors and walls of the room (Bucket 89.62). The basin walls (Th 0.27 m) probably were built to a height of about 0.70 m above the floor. As preserved, the basin has a capacity of 307 litres. There is a drain hole approximately in the middle of the north basin wall (D 0.025 m) at the level of the basin floor, apparently composed of the neck of a thin-walled NFW juglet. The drain slopes downward markedly towards the floor of the room. The wastewater apparently was simply allowed to drain off across the floor toward the west door, which has a drain built into its door-sill. The floor of the room slopes markedly from the southeast to the northwest to facilitate evacuation of the water from this basin and from the basin in Room A — which

entered through a similar drain in the door-sill of the door in the south wall of Room E, after passing through Room D. The red plaster used for the floor and walls of this room and of Rooms A and D probably was designed to resist the effect of this water and the resulting humidity. Both this basin and the basin in Room A are too small and too inconveniently placed to have allowed bathing by immersion. Instead, the bathers would have dipped water out of the basins with cups and splashed themselves with it, leaving great puddles that ran off across the floor. The drain opening in the west wall was roofed with bricks; outside, there was a flat area of small pieces of rubble set in brown, sandy surface soil, concreted by the presence of water.

A step in the south wall of Room E leads to a door opening into Room D, the *laconicum*, or sweat room. An open drain channel built into the threshold allowed water draining from Room A across the sloping floor of Room D to pass through the raised threshold and flow across the floor of Room E and out the west drain. There were benches and a heated floor in this room, but no basins. Evaporation of the water flowing across the floor from the basin in Room A would have provided a moist atmosphere. The bench is built in the same manner as the tables and benches in Rooms B, E, and F. The floor pavement is supported on sixteen brick hypocaust pillars in the same manner as the floor of Room A (see below). The heat from the furnace in Room C passed below the floor of Room A and into the sub-floor level of Room D by means of an opening corresponding to the east door. There is a similar opening beneath the north door in Room D that — in Phase 2 of the Bath — allowed hot air to enter the hypocaust of Room E. Heat and smoke could also escape from the Room D hypocaust by means of four vents in the walls.

A door in the east wall led into Room A, a slightly smaller, approximately square room with a basin built into its north wall (fig. 4.52). This room and Room C (the *praefurnium*) were built into a larger room within the earlier Nabataean structure, making use of its north and east walls, but inserting a new wall on the west to separate Rooms A and D, and adding an enormous amount of rubble and mortar packing to isolate the furnace structure. In consequence, the basin (1.35 × 0.67 × >0.47 m) appears to be set into the wall of the room. The basin floor is 0.12 m above the pavement in the room, but the original upper edge of its wall has been lost. The capacity at present is 425 litres, 39% more than the basin in Room E, but it was drained by means of the same sort of thin terracotta pipe set into the western end of its southern wall. The water then was allowed to run across the floor, which is not preserved, through Rooms D and E and out the drain in the west wall of Room E. The basin is waterproofed with the same light red plaster used for the floor and walls of this room and Room D.

Four vertical recesses for flue tiles were built into the east and west ends of the north and south walls of the room in the same manner as those of Room D, but arranged less symmetrically. The two north recesses had to be moved closer to either end of this wall in order to avoid the basin. As in Room D, these vents were designed to heat the walls of the room, provide a draft for the furnace,

and carry off smoke. The south wall of this room, however, was provided with a further heating facility, preserved at the time of excavation only at the southeast corner. The entire south wall was covered with a layer of medium-hard white plaster 0.135 m thick, which encased a layer of upright flue tiles set side-by-side to carry heat up through the wall. These tiles, in contrast to the circular tiles set into the walls of this room and of Room D, had a slightly rounded rectangular section (outside D 0.085 × 0.15 m).

The heating system in Room A was exposed and made accessible through the destruction of the floor by clandestine diggers. The pillars, built of square bricks (0.21 m square; Th 0.03 m), rest on a pavement composed for the most part of the circular bricks used for the hypocaust pillars of Phase 2, chinked with fragments of rectangular bricks. There were 16 pillars (H ca. 0.80 m) in the room, carrying a complex paving (Th 0.35 m) composed of bricks, flat stones, and mortar. The interior stone faces of the walls of the room were enclosed by brick walls built up to the level of the paving. Insets were built into this brick lining corresponding to the vertical flues built into the walls above, and an opening 0.57 m wide extending back as far as the party wall between Rooms A and B allowed heated air to circulate beneath the water basin. The floor of the basin was supported at this point on large slabs of red sandstone. Another gap in the west wall allowed heated air to enter the space below Room D and — in Phase 2 — to continue on to the hypocaust below Room E. Along the south wall, a gap was left between the floor pavement and the wall to allow hot air to enter the vents in the plaster heating layer.

Room C, the furnace area, is totally different in design, but it shows much the same building history and materials as the rest of the Bath. The furnace was built into a slightly projecting foyer or reception area for the Phase 1 Nabataean structure — possibly the main entrance to that building. The room was drastically remodelled in Phase 2 of the Bath, during its transformation into a furnace. Two east/west walls 1.10 m apart were built across Room C to delineate the furnace area, and the spaces behind them to the north and south were filled with earth covered by an enormous volume of rubble set in a crumbly, light grey mortar. These blocking walls, and the paving on the floor of the room, were constructed of red sandstone blocks. Several courses of bricks (0.22 m square) were built up along either side of this paving, against the side walls, to a height of 0.10 m. The original floor — now visible only at the east and west ends of the room, below the Phase 3 furnace floor, extends out at least 0.50 m east of the east door of the building. The extension of the pavement probably was intended to facilitate introduction of fuel into the building and the scraping out of the ashes. It is no longer possible to determine how the Phase 2 furnace was roofed.

After a period of use, evidenced by the marks of burning on the sandstone walls and floor and several thin lenses of ash, the furnace was completely rebuilt, probably at the time of the Phase 3 renovation. Well-cut, reused sandstone blocks were set against the side walls of the furnace and across the east entrance, and the space inside above the original floor was filled with a packing of sandstone and limestone rubble 0.24 m thick, set in a hard, orange clay and capped with a smooth layer of clay 0.05 m thick. The ceramics found in this filling date from the Middle Nabataean to the Late Byzantine periods. The furnace box was built of fired bricks above this new floor. Just inside the east entrance, a pitched brick vault, 0.81 m long and approximately 0.85 m high, was built of coarse, dark red bricks set in a crumbly, grey mortar possibly mixed with clay. West of this vaulted entrance there was an oval, domed fire box 0.85 m long, built of the same type of bricks, but laid flat rather than on their edges. A shorter pitched brick vault (L 0.25 m) abutted two brick piers (0.55 × 0.23 m) that framed the opening (W 0.52 m) into the hypocaust below Room A. A large amount of ash was recovered from the floor of this later furnace, including some large pieces of charcoal. Several large pieces of stem reveal that at least one of the fuels used was jointed saltwood (*Haloxylon articulatum* or *Hammada scoparia*), a bush that can be found everywhere around Humayma today, and which the Bedouin still use for cooking. It produces a very hot flame, but for only a short time, so enormous quantities must have been needed to heat the Bath building. One carbonised twig from this deposit yielded a calibrated C14 date of 416 ± 83 (see pp. 360–61), which works out well in the context.

Two important questions that were not settled by the excavation of the Bath are the arrangement of the water-supply and the type of roofing. Since the upper portion of the building has been lost, both these problems can be answered only hypothetically. The overflow channel from Reservoir/Pool no. 63 can last be traced to approximately 20 m north of the Bath, but it follows a consistent bearing up to this point, one which would have carried it approximately 10 m east of the Bath's east façade. In the original arrangement, this run-off channel probably conducted the overflow water either to the Nabataean building, to the cisterns in the settlement centre, or to small gardens below the settlement. Sometime in the Roman period, however, the free overflow was replaced by a lead pipe system laid in the conduit, and the flow of water was controlled by a bronze stopcock installed behind a grating or door outside the south wall of the reservoir. This lead pipe system may well be contemporary with Phase 2 of the Bath, since the pipe could have left the aqueduct channel at the point of its closest passage by the building and entered it below ground level. It may have carried the water directly to all the basins in the building (one in each of Rooms A and E) by means of pipes in the walls, for the slope is sufficient to provide the necessary pressure. Alternatively, the pipeline may have filled a holding reservoir for both tanks, perhaps built into the masonry packing over Room C, from which the cold water tank could have been filled by means of a separate pipe or by jars. There may also have been a metal reservoir over the furnace in Room C, from which a pipe could have conducted heated water to the basin in Room A. The water in this basin was also heated from below, by the air in the hypocaust.

Two separate pipelines drew water from the Nabataean Reservoir. The lead pipe fed through the stopcock has already been noted, but there was also a line of terracotta pipes that bypassed the reservoir altogether. This pipeline drew the water from the aqueduct at a point 5 m north of its intersection with the reservoir, carried it around the west side of the reservoir, and can last be traced to 20 m south of its south wall, on a bearing slightly east of that of the aqueduct. The lead pipeline should be associated with Phase 2 of the Bath, while the terracotta pipeline carried water to a shrine on the south side of the mudbrick *vicus* building in E125.

Restoration of the roof is also a difficult problem. The walls do not seem sturdy enough to have supported mortared or stone-built barrel vaults, and the large masses of masonry one would expect as the result of the ruin of either type of roof are absent. Transverse arches could have been built in the rooms to support slab roofs, as in the cisterns and houses of the Nabataean to Byzantine periods found throughout this region, but no traces of the imposts survive on the plaster floors or walls. As a result, it seems more likely that wooden beams were used as the major rafters for flat roofs of brush, reeds, and stucco. The absence of roof-tiles in the excavation area indicates that the roofs were flat and probably waterproofed with stucco.

Bibliography: Oleson 1990a: 152–61; 1990b: 294–306; Reeves 1996; Reeves and Oleson 1997; Reeves et al. 2009.

Chapter 5

Descriptions of Probes: 1986–1987, 1989

5.A. INTRODUCTION

During the 1986 survey, several sites along the aqueduct and at major reservoirs and cisterns within the settlement centre were selected for the excavation of probes in 1987. Particular emphasis was placed on probes that might clarify the design, chronology, and function of the aqueduct (Structure no. 1), reservoir in the fort (Reservoir no. 62), pool at the end of the aqueduct (Reservoir no. 63), two major covered reservoirs in the settlement centre (Reservoirs nos. 67 and 68), one cylindrical and one domed domestic cistern (Cisterns nos. 54 and 72), and the dam (Structure no. 44) south of the habitation area. As work progressed in 1987, several conduits and drains associated with water management were identified and probed as well (Sites nos. 75, 76). Finally, in 1989, further probes were carried out around Reservoirs nos. 67 and 68, at domestic Cisterns nos. 64 and 69, and at the Bath Building (Structure no. 77). In all, 43 probes were executed at 10 distinct structures in 1987 and 1989. The probes were designated by year, structure number, and probe number. A brief account of the excavation of the Bath Building has been given in Chapter 4, but the full account including probes since 1989 by M. B. Reeves has been reserved for a subsequent volume concerned with the Roman fort and related structures.

As noted above, the absolute levels above sea level provided in this chapter for the structures in the settlement centre are based on EDM readings taken from the northeast corner of the rebuilt Reservoir no. 67 in the settlement centre, assuming an elevation of 955.00 m asl for this location. Subsequently, GPS readings suggested that the true elevation may be closer to 966 m asl, but I have continued to use the figure of 955.00 as the benchmark elevation for the sake of consistency. In any case, the discrepancy does not affect the interpretation of the archaeological remains. Elevations for the probes along the aqueduct are given in reference to an arbitrary point selected at the probe, since the probes are small, unrelated to each other, and the GPS elevation readings along the aqueduct not particularly accurate.

The relevance of the data provided by these probes to the essential design and chronology of the structures has been presented above in the catalogues in Chapters 3 and 4. Although some introduction and interpretation have been necessary, unnecessary repetition has been avoided, and this chapter provides essentially the raw archaeological data, including ceramic profiles and mention of other finds. An overall analysis of the ceramics, along with catalogues of registered ceramic and non-ceramic finds, appears in Chapter 6. Only loci that yielded artefacts appear in the locus lists that follow each probe report. Profiles have not been provided for handle sections, body sherds, or very poorly preserved potsherds. To facilitate sorting in the database, all bucket numbers consist of the last two digits of the year, a decimal point, and a three digit bucket number. Sherds within a bucket description are catalogued by the last two digits of the bucket number and the sherd number within the bucket. All too often the rim sherds were too small to allow an accurate determination of the rim diameter. In such cases I have indicated the uncertainty or simply illustrated the rim profile. Where diameters could be closely determined, I have provided them; unless otherwise stated, "D" refers to rim diameter. In the bucket lists, dates are given as, for example, "1C–ea. 2C," instead of "first century to early second century." Dates are AD unless designated as BC.

J. P. Oleson, S. Farajat. A. N. Sherwood, E. de Bruijn, and E. al-Hadi carried out the field readings of the ceramics. After counting and removing the diagnostic sherds for study and drawing, we attempted to sort the non-diagnostic sherds by the chronological/cultural periods noted above. With a few exceptions, I have decided not to present the results of this sorting here, since our identifications were very problematic, given our meagre experience and the generally poor understanding of the ceramics of southern Jordan at that time. Even in the early twenty-first century, ceramic experts still find it difficult to identify non-diagnostic common-ware sherds from southern Jordan (cf. Gerber 2000: 410; 2001a; 2001d: 378). Later on, advice concerning the ceramics from particularly important loci was kindly provided by K. 'Amr, K. Russell, and S. T. Parker. Their readings are attributed in the bucket lists. I re-read the definers in 2006 and have added citations of published parallels from recent excavations and of Gerber's unpublished dating of ceramics excavated at Humayma since 1998. The pottery profiles are reproduced here at fifty percent.

5.B. THE AQUEDUCT SYSTEM (STRUCTURE NO. 1)

Seven probes were dug along the aqueduct system leading to Humayma, five toward the beginning of the Jammam branch (km 1.181, 1.768, 1.779, 1.951, and 2.494), and two on the main Ghana line just down-stream from its junction with the Jammam

branch (km 6.858 and 7.070; fig. 3.1). The points for excavation were selected on the basis of either particularly good preservation or the presence of structural features out of the ordinary and clearly associated with the design or function of the aqueduct. Another goal was the recovery of ceramics or other cultural material that might help date the construction and development of the system. In all, three probes were made across the aqueduct itself (H87-01–P01 and P06; here, Probe 1 and 6), and five at basins or suspected basins associated with it (H87-01–P02, P03, P04, P05, and P07; here Probes 2, 3, 4, 5, and 7).

5.B.1. *Aqueduct Probe no. 1*

This probe was laid out at km 1.768 of the Jammam branch (1415 m asl), at a point where the fabric of the aqueduct — including the cover stones — appeared to be particularly well-preserved and some plastering was visible along the upper surface of blocks framing the water channel (fig. 3.45). In this area, the aqueduct bends to the south around a gently sloping ridge; the orientation of the channel at the probe is 212 degrees. The probe, 1.25 m along the aqueduct and 2 m wide across it, provided a glimpse of the structure at the final stage of its development and in essentially undamaged condition. The ceramic evidence unfortunately is ambiguous, but it indicates at least that there was activity in the area in the first century BC or AD, and possibly some sort of reconstruction of this portion of the aqueduct sometime in the second or third century AD.

Removal of the 0.10 m of topsoil over the entire square (Locus 00) exposed the framing blocks and cover slabs of the aqueduct (Locus 01; fig. 3.45) and scattered rubble and cobbles set in hard, red earth to west (Locus 02) and east (Locus 03). There were numerous very small sherds in these surface loci. The Locus 02 ceramics dated from the first to the third century (K. Russell, oral communication). Locus 03, a packing of cobbles set in a hard red earth (Th 0.12 m), extended out 0.30 m from the face of the aqueduct framing blocks; many of the cobbles had been pushed up against the mortar of the aqueduct foundation while it was still wet (fig. 5.1). Only two small sherds were recovered

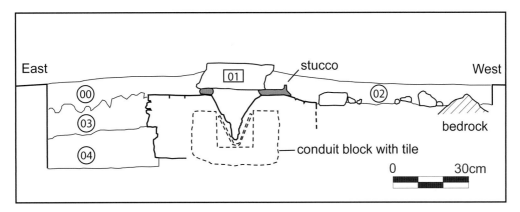

Fig. 5.1 *Jammam aqueduct Probe 1, cross-section.*

from this locus, possibly second or third century (T. Parker, personal communication; K. Russell could not identify). At this point, 0.12 m below the top surface of the channel, the foundation was recessed 0.04 m. Locus 04, composed of hard red earth with a smaller proportion of cobbles than in Locus 03, was laid up against it, immediately above undisturbed soil. The 11 very small, non-diagnostic sherds found in the earth and adhering to the mortar were very tentatively identified as second or third century, but one rim may be as early as the first century BC.

The conduit structure, built of irregular sandstone blocks and cobbles, is 0.60–0.615 m wide to the outside of the packing and 0.24 m high from the foundation base to the mortared upper surface. Partly trimmed, irregular, red sandstone slabs (ca. L 0.20–0.70 m, W 0.31 m, Th 0.10–0.15 m) were laid along the centre line of the structure to cover the water channel. Along their outside edges, the joint between the blocks and the upper surface of the aqueduct was thickly smeared with a fine, chalky, white plaster containing infrequent grains of quartz sand and frequent badly-sorted lumps of lime, small flecks of carbon, and frequent large air bubbles (Bucket 87.016). This sealing plaster had been applied on top of a harder, sandier white plaster that covered the small, flat stones forming the upper surface of the framing structure. This mortar surface came to a fairly sharp tooled edge 0.20 m from the west side of the aqueduct and 0.22 m from the east, edging the deep, V-shaped trough that carried the water (W 0.195 m, 0.185 m deep; fig.

3.46). Although the plaster lining of the water channel was not removed in this probe, observation of less well-preserved sections farther downstream revealed that the channel was formed by a series of tapering tiles with a V-shaped cross-section (fig. 3.56). These were overlapped end to end, plastered on the interior, and topped on either side by a row of low flat stones. The tiles had been inserted into the original water channel built of marl gutter blocks. The lower 0.12 m of the plastered interior of the channel carried a pebbly calcium carbonate deposit.

Locus 00 (surface soil to –0.10 m)
Bucket 87.001. 56 body, 2 rim.
Bucket 87.016. Sample of plaster used to seal cover slabs. White, chalky in appearance, with infrequent particles of quartz sand and frequent badly-sorted lumps of lime. Occasional small flecks of charcoal and frequent large air bubbles.

Locus 01 (aqueduct structure)

Locus 02 (fill above packing rubble, west of conduit, –0.10 to –0.20 m)
Bucket 87.004. 5 body, 1 rim. K. Russell tentatively dated rim 1st–2nd C, group 1st–3rd C.
4.1. Pot (?): medium fine, slightly sandy, red (2.5YR 5/6) fabric.

Locus 03 (northeast corner of square, dirt-packed stones to second layer of stones, 0.12 m below top of framing wall).
Bucket 87.012. 2 body.

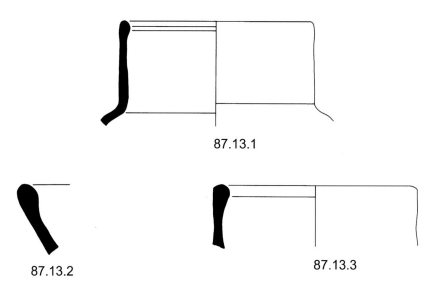

87.13.1

87.13.2

87.13.3

FIG. 5.2   *Jammam aqueduct Probe 1, ceramics from Locus 4 (scale 1:2).*

Locus 04 (northeast corner, foundation deposit, stones in mortar, from 0.12 m below top of conduit wall; fig. 5.2)

Bucket 87.013. 8 body, 3 rim. Very small sherds; rim diameters could not be determined. Identification of 13.2 as second-century BC is very tentative. Jars would be appropriate to carrying or drawing water in the immediate neighbourhood.

13.1. Jar: hard, sandy, red (2.5YR 4/8) fabric with some soft white inclusions and black sand temper. Reddish yellow (5YR 7/6) surface. D 0.10 m.

13.2. Bowl (?): slightly sandy, light red (2.5YR 6/8) fabric. Cf. *EZ* II fig. 146, Phase 1 (2C–mid 1C BC).

13.3. Jar (?): hard, slightly laminar, sandy red (2.5YR 5/8) fabric with black sand and a few white inclusions. Reddish yellow (5YR 7/6) surface. D 0.10 m.

5.B.2. *Aqueduct Probe no. 2*

This probe was laid out across a circular feature with central square tank straddling the aqueduct at km 1.779 (1413 m asl). The surface of the structure was cleaned for photography in June 1986, attracting the attention of local clandestine diggers who dug out much of the interior over the following winter. Although part of the inner tank was lost and the stratigraphy irreparably damaged, the general plan and elevation of the structure could be determined. The structure consisted of a well-built, circular limestone curb (outside D 2.15 m) framing a central settling tank (ca. 0.70 m square; fig. 3.46). The conduit blocks passed under the circular curb wall in line with each other both upstream and downstream, and the whole installation was carefully designed and well built. No stratified ceramics were excavated inside the structure, but body and rim sherds from first- and second-century vessels were recovered from the robber dump and surface (Locus 01; Bucket 87.002). A surprising discovery was a fragment of a used flue tile similar to those found in the Roman Bath at E077; it may have been broken in half and used to line the conduit channel in place of a roof tile. The undisturbed earth packed against the outside northeast quadrant of the curb was excavated to 0.20 m below the surface, yielding a few ceramics that are not distinctive but might well be first- to second-century in date (Locus 02, Bucket 87.005).

The curb was built of large, irregular limestone slabs (L ca. 0.40–0.60 m; W ca. 0.20–0.28 m; H 0.25–0.40 m) trimmed to a curve on the outside edges and chinked with marl and limestone cobbles. Inside this curb, the spaces north and south of the outside edge of the conduit (which

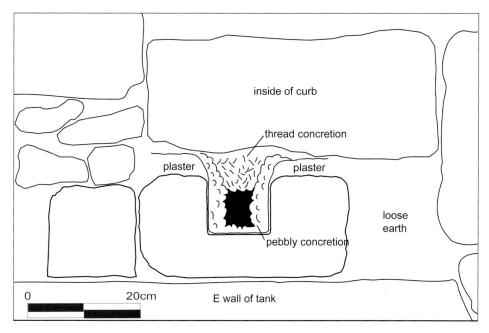

FIG. 5.3 *Jammam aqueduct Probe 2, elevation drawing of intake conduit.*

has a bearing of 89 degrees) were each occupied by a large semicircular limestone slab that faced and reinforced the adjacent walls of the central tank. This arrangement created a solid surface for support of the cover slabs.

The tank itself (0.70 m square; 0.49 m deep below the floor of the upstream intake channel; cap. 0.24 cum) was constructed of five large slabs of sandstone (L ca. 0.80 m; W ca. 0.41 m; Th 0.15 m) backed by a packing of boulders and cobbles (fig. 3.47). This packing served as the foundation for the curb as well. The foundation pit had been dug 1.10 m into the hard sandy red soil. Four upright slabs formed the walls of the tank, their lower edges resting on the horizontal floor slab. Two corner slabs and a small fragment of the floor slab were all that remained *in situ* at the time of excavation. The packing immediately adjacent to the tank slabs (Locus 05) consisted largely of a soft, very dark grey mortar containing much rounded quartz sand and poorly-sorted pebbles, as well as infrequent small nodules of lime; it was thick with flecks of carbon and some carbonised twigs. There were numerous bubbles and air holes, resulting from poor compaction. Carbon 14 analysis of a carbonised twig recovered from the mortar adjacent to the outlet conduit block (Locus 04; Bucket 87.014) provided

a calibrated date of AD 171 ±39 (Section 6.F). The tank was lined with a crumbly, light grey plaster (Th ca. 0.02 m) containing frequent sub-rounded sand grains and occasional small pebbles, infrequent very small nodules of lime, and flecks of carbon (Buckets 87.03, 07). The seams and corners between the lining slabs were filled in with this mortar, which was tooled to a flat surface meeting each adjoining slab at 135 degrees. This treatment of the corners, intended to make the seams watertight, can be seen on a larger scale in Reservoir/Pool no. 63, into which the aqueduct emptied, and around the base of Reservoir no. 67 (as reconstructed). The seams around the bottom of the south wall of Reservoir no. 62 in the Roman fort have the same angle reinforcement, and the corners are built to a curve. Water-deposited calcium carbonate concretions can be seen on the tank walls up to 0.015 m above the original level of the intake conduit.

The upstream intake conduit block (L unknown, W 0.32 m, H 0.21 m) crossed under the curb but stopped 0.10 m short of the inner face of the tank. The water channel (W 0.11 m, H 0.10 m) was almost completely blocked by calcium carbonate concretions at the time the aqueduct went out of use (fig. 5.3). Although no roof tile insert remained in the conduit at the time of its abandonment, a thin layer of mortar (Th 0.004 m) beneath the concretion, along with the same plaster topping seen in Probe 1, strongly suggests that a tile was present at some point. It is likely that the tile was removed when the channel first became occluded at this point, allowing new concretion to form on the remaining bedding plaster. There clearly was some sort of problem either with levelling or with the volume of flow, since the final pillowy concretion layers extend up the entire height of the conduit and over the capping plaster on the upper surface as far as the base of the curb block. The concretion hanging from the base of the curb block is very different in character from that on the sides and base of the conduit, consisting of a tangle of small, string-like strands. Each strand has a small (<0.001) central hollow, indicating the concretion formed around the very fine strands of water weed or algae that grew in the channel at this point. This type of plant can still be seen in the modern water channels fed by 'Ain Jammam. By the time the flow of water stopped, the intake opening had been reduced to approximately one centimetre square.

Unfortunately, the downstream overflow conduit was torn out of position by the clandestine diggers and badly damaged. Nevertheless, it was possible to determine that at least part of this conduit contained roof tile inserts and that only a modest amount of concretion was present. The original conduit floor of the upstream channel and the first surviving conduit slab of the downstream channel are at the same level, reflecting the very slight slope of the aqueduct at this point. The C14 date may indicate that the settling tank was renovated at the time the gutter tiles were added to the conduit.

The presence of plants in the aqueduct channel indicates that the tank was unroofed in its final stage of use. The structure was probably intended as a settling basin, but some sort of cover must have been supplied to keep pollutants out of the water. A wooden door would have been easier to remove than stone slabs, and no slabs of the appropriate size were found nearby. Loss of this cover and the build-up of concretions are indications of serious problems with maintenance of the aqueduct just before its abandonment. The very solid construc-

tion of this feature seems excessive for a settling tank, but the purity of the aqueduct water would have been compromised by the presence of a draw tank of this design, and the 'Ain Sara is quite close. The heavy curb may have allowed the structure to serve as an overflow point to reduce the pressure on the aqueduct structure at times of unexpected increases in the flow from the springs. There are similar basins, probably serving the same function, at km 1.181, 1.951, 2.259, and 2.497.

Locus 01 (surface soil and spoil from clandestine excavation of tank; fig. 5.4)

Bucket 87.002. 20 body, 3 rim. The material appears to date 1–2C.

2.1. Cooking pot: hard, sandy, light red (2.5YR 6/8) fabric with numerous white inclusions. Spots of smoke darkening on exterior. D 0.17 m. Gerber 1994: fig. 15A (late 1–2C). This type is common at Humayma.

2.2. Rib-necked jar: hard, sandy, light red (2.5YR 6/8) fabric with occasional white inclusions. Surface reddish yellow (5YR 7/8). D 0.08 m. Cf. Dolinka 2003: 128 no. 20 (late 1–ea. 2C).

2.3. Flue tile, rounded rectangle in cross-section: hard, sandy, slightly laminar light red (2.5YR 6/8) fabric with occasional white inclusions. Interior surface stained dark grey (5YR 4/1). D 0.09 m. Given the parallels at the Late Roman bath (E077) in the town centre, this should date late 2C.

Bucket 87.003. Mortar sample. Light grey, very crumbly mortar, containing frequent rounded sand particles and occasional pebbles, infrequent very small nodules of lime and flecks of carbon. Found in surface spoil from clandestine digging; probably from tank lining.

Bucket 87.007. Mortar sample. Lining of tank. As sample in Bucket 87.003.

Bucket 87.010. Roof tile channel liner, with water deposit on interior.

Locus 02 (packed earth against outside northwest quadrant of curb, to –0.20 m; fig. 5.5)

Bucket 87.005. 2 body, 3 rim. Although nondescript, the group appears to be 1–2C.

5.1. Lid: hard, slightly sandy, light red (2.5YR 6/4) fabric with numerous white inclusions.

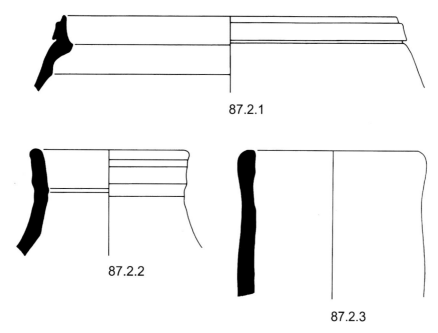

FIG. 5.4   *Jammam aqueduct Probe 2, ceramics from Locus 1 (scale 1:2).*

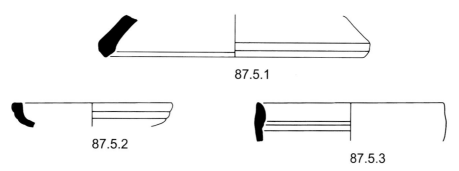

FIG. 5.5   *Jammam aqueduct Probe 2, ceramics from Locus 2 (scale 1:2).*

Surfaces burned dark grey (2.5YR 4/0). D 0.14 m?

5.2. Cup: very fine, red (2.5YR 4/8) fabric. D 0.08 m.

5.3. Bowl: sandy, red (2.5YR 5/8) fabric with numerous white inclusions. D 0.10 m?

Locus 03 (concretion within intake conduit)

Bucket 87.006. Wormy concretions, formed in concentric layers around a very small central hole (D < 0.001 m), as if around a small stalk of grass or algae.

Locus 04 (mortar packing along south face of discharge conduit)

Bucket 87.014. Carbonised stick. L 0.03 m; W 0.007 m. C14 date (TO-1150): 1,840 ±30 years BP (c.i. 68.3% for AD 123–224; c.i. 95.5% for AD 84–242).

Locus 05 (mortar packing around intake conduit)

Bucket 87.015. Mortar sample. Crumbly grey mortar containing frequent particles of clear, rounded quartz sand and poorly sorted pebbles, lumps of lime, frequent flecks of ash, and numerous holes and air bubbles. Poorly compacted and very friable.

5.B.3. *Aqueduct Probe no. 3*

The probe was laid out across a feature resembling a small settling tank, built into the course of the Jammam aqueduct at km 1.951. Clearing of the surface debris revealed a small tank built of marl slabs and blocks (L 0.52 m, W 0.33 m, depth below intake 0.30 m, cap. 0.051 cum) sealed with grey mortar and waterproofed with a hard white plaster. The side walls and the waterproofing plaster have been weathered down to stubs. A single stone slab set in mortar formed nearly the entire floor (L 0.48 m, W 0.34 m; fig. 3.49). Large limestone blocks on the uphill slope (north side) provided protection. One of these blocks preserves some water-deposited calcium carbonate. It seems very likely that the conduit blocks of the aqueduct were built into the east and west walls of the tank, but the context has been disturbed; the closest conduit block is 1.5 m to the east. Projection of the surviving course of the aqueduct passes directly over the tank. Only a few sherds were recovered from the fill in the tank. The soil on the exterior was badly disturbed by erosion.

Although the tank is smaller and more lightly built than the settling basin at km 1.779, the design is similar and suggests that this tank, too, served the same purpose — probably removal of sediments from the aqueduct channel. The similarities in design suggest that these two tanks belong to the same construction period.

Locus 01 (surface cleaning)
> Bucket 87.008. 2 body. Both sherds are from coarse-ware vessels, of a pink fabric with dark sand.

Locus 03 (Plaster lining of basin)
> Bucket 87.020. Soft, very pale brown plaster moderately tempered with well-sorted, rounded sand and pebbles; occasional lime nodules. The seams and bubbles of the outer layer are filled with water-deposited calcium carbonate. There was a moderately hard, greyish-brown (10YR 5/2) backing mortar heavily tempered with rounded sand and containing frequent flecks of carbon.

5.B.4. *Aqueduct Probe no. 4*

The probe was laid out across a feature resembling a small settling tank, built into the course of the Jammam aqueduct at km 2.494 (1410 m asl), where the aqueduct crosses a slope. Clearing of the surface debris revealed a small basin very similar in scale and construction to that in Probe 3 (L 0.50 m, W 0.44 m, depth below intake >0.20 m, cap. > 0.044 cum; fig. 3.51). The west end of the structure had been disturbed at some time in the past. The basin was constructed of slabs fixed in a soft, grey mortar, and the interior was waterproofed with white plaster. Roughly trimmed limestone blocks framed and reinforced the feature at ground level on all four sides, as with the basin at km. 1.779. The aqueduct conduits passed under the east and west framing blocks. The original cover slab, a roughly flat piece of limestone (L 0.78 m, W 0.50 m, Th ca. 0.15 m), was found tipped into the tank. Although this feature is smaller than the tank exposed in Probe 2, the heavy framing is similar and suggests that it, too, belongs to the original phase of construction. A few first- and second-century sherds were recovered from the fill.

Locus 01 (surface cleaning)
> Bucket 87.009. 5 body. A Nabataean roulette-decorated, red slip body sherd dates 1C.
> Bucket 87.017. Mortar from lining of basin. Soft, light grey (10YR 8/1) mortar moderately tempered with poorly sorted quartz sand and pebbles, containing large lime nodules and large carbon bits.

5.B.5. *Aqueduct Probe no. 5*

The probe involved extensive surface clearing of a settling tank built across the course of the Jammam aqueduct at km 1.181 (1410 m asl). This feature appears at a point where a section of the aqueduct had to be built along the edge of a vertical limestone scarp 5 to 10 m high. The foundation of the aqueduct was partly cut into the bedrock and partly supported on occasional substructures of high rubble walls filling gaps in the bedrock. At the location of the probe, the aqueduct was carried across a gap in the cliff on a neat dry-stone wall

3.5 m high (fig. 3.42). The aqueduct structure and half the tank have been lost down the cliff, but the support wall and aqueduct footings survived. The aqueduct passed across a circular retaining wall or curb (exterior D 1.80 m), carefully built of heavy limestone and marl blocks set in a soft, dark grey mortar with numerous inclusions of ash and lime. The curb, which resembles the curbs around the basins in Probes 2 and 4, framed a slab-built basin, half of which has been lost (L 0.76 m, W > 0.50 m, depth below conduit > 0.30 m, cap. > 0.114 cum; figs. 3.43–44). The basin was reinforced with the same grey mortar as the other tanks, and it was waterproofed with a hard white plaster with ash flecks, lime nodules, and pebbles. The plaster could be traced for 0.26 m above the surviving fragment of basin floor. The mortar and plaster are similar to that found in the other probes in this area. No sherds were recovered from the scanty surface fill.

The inconvenient location of this feature on a precipitous slope at the edge of a drop-off indicates that it cannot have been intended to serve as a draw basin. It may have served as a settling tank or overflow basin.

Locus 01 (surface cleaning)

Bucket 87.018. Plaster lining of settling basin. Very irregular outer surface. Very hard, sandy, off-white plaster, containing frequent specks of carbon and much poorly-sorted, clear, rounded quartz sand. Attached to it is the mortar backing on which it was laid, a soft, grey (2.5YR 5/0) mortar with a few lime inclusions.

Bucket 87.019. Mortar from support wall. Medium soft, friable, light grey (10YR 7/1) mortar containing a moderate amount of well sorted, rounded sand, frequent large nodules of lime, and occasional large carbon bits.

5.B.6. *Aqueduct Probe no. 6*

This probe (1 m north/south, 1.60 m east/west) was laid out across what appeared to be an intact section of the Ghana aqueduct at km 6.858, 300 m downstream from the junction with the Jammam branch (1191 m asl). The purpose was clarification of the design and chronology of the Ghana branch of the aqueduct system. The Jammam aqueduct is essentially identical in design and construction to the Ghana aqueduct, except that roof tiles were set into its conduit channel.

Clearing of windblown sand and loose cobbles (Locus 01) revealed carefully squared limestone blocks framing the conduit, forming a structure 0.98 m wide (fig. 3.28). The packing between the framing and the conduit blocks consisted of soil and cobbles. Flat stones (Th ca. 0.03 m) were laid along the upper edges of each marl conduit block, framing the channel and supporting the cover slabs. The cover slabs were only roughly trimmed, although the edges adjoining other slabs were approximately straight. Two cover slabs at the north end of the probe were removed and the earth fill in the conduit cleared (Locus 02; fig. 3.29). A very thin (Th 0.003 m) layer of whitish grey plaster had been applied to the inside surface of the channel (W 0.11 m, H 0.12 m) and extended up over the inside and top surfaces of the thin framing stones supporting the cover slabs and out over the flat rubble surface framing the structure (sample, Bucket 87.027). The deposit of calcium carbonate (Th 0.005 m) on the lower portion of the channel showed three distinct layers in cross-section. The cover slabs were laid directly on the mortared surface. No trace of plaster sealing was observed around the cover slabs, but it may have been lost to weathering. The probe was carried down to the foundation of the aqueduct outside the east framing wall (Locus 03), 0.25 m below the present surface and 0.10 m below the base of the aqueduct, but no sherds were recovered.

Locus 02 (cleaning inside channel)

Bucket 87.027. Plaster.

5.B.7. *Aqueduct Probe no. 7*

At km 7.070 of the Ghana branch (1187 m asl), a box-like structure built of stone slabs was observed abutting the left (southeast) side of the aqueduct structure (fig. 3.30). A probe was laid out (1.30 m × 1.25 m) around the feature. Clearing of the loose, brown, sandy surface soil (Locus 01) revealed numerous insect burrows, snail shells, and one

late first- to early second-century potsherd, above
a roughly rectangular arrangement of stone slabs.
Removal of similar soil within the feature, to a
depth of 0.18 m below the surface (Locus 02),
showed that it was poorly defined and lacked a
floor. This feature is apparently a casual arrangement of slabs removed from above the conduit,
possibly for a Bedouin tea fire.

Locus 01 (surface clearing)
> Bucket 87.023. 1 body. 1 NPFW bowl fragment,
> phase 3b (1–ea. 2C).
> Bucket 87.024 Snail shells.

5.B.8. *Aqueduct Probe no. 8*

During the initial survey of the Ghana aqueduct
in 1986, a well-preserved section of the conduit
at km 4.480 was cleaned and brushed for photography. The cleaning revealed a small potsherd
incorporated into the mortar packing around a
conduit block still in its original position. The
sherd (Bucket 86.174.01) could date to the late first
century BC or early first century AD, but a precise
dating is not possible. Since the background scatter
of potsherds is very light along this stretch of the
aqueduct, it is possible that this vessel broke during
the construction process and was incorporated in
the structure at that time.

Locus 01 (surface clearing; fig. 5.6)
> Bucket 86.174. 1 rim.
>> 174.1. NFW cup: sandy, reddish yellow (5YR
>> 6/8) fabric with a few white inclusions and
>> black sand temper. Surface 5YR 7/6. D 0.08
>> m? *EZ* II fig. 226, 100–25 BC, or fig. 224, 25
>> BC to AD 100; K. Russell, personal com-
>> munication, 1987 (1C–2C).

5.B.9. *Summary of the Aqueduct Probes*

The probes excavated along the aqueduct system
have clarified its design and construction. The small
amount of ceramic material recovered reinforces
the impression derived from close parallels with
the design of Nabataean aqueducts at Petra that at
least the Ghana Aqueduct was built by Nabataean
engineers at some point early in the history of
Hawara, in the later first century BC or the early

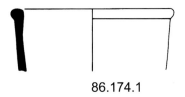

86.174.1

FIG. 5.6   *Ghana aqueduct Probe 8, sherd
from Locus 1 (scale 1:2).*

first century AD. This chronology is confirmed
by the ceramics recovered in the probes at Pool/
Reservoir no. 63, an integral part of the aqueduct
system (see below), and by other considerations
discussed in Chapter 7.

The character of the junction between the
Ghana Aqueduct and the Jammam Branch strongly
suggests that the Jammam Branch was added after
the Ghana Aqueduct had been built. The small
amount of pottery from closed contexts in the
probes along the Jammam Branch tends to suggest a construction date in the later first or early
second century AD. The pottery found along the
Jammam branch shows that at least the first three
kilometres of channel attracted significant attention
in the Roman period. The C14 date of AD 138 (or AD
84–242) obtained for the basin at km 1.779 could
refer to either the original construction phase or
a reconstruction phase associated with the insertion of the roof tiles. The insertion of tiles in the
channel along most of the course of this aqueduct
still cannot be completely explained. The so-called
settling tanks examined in Probes 2 to 5 do not appear elsewhere along either aqueduct, so both tiles
and tanks may have been intended to solve related
problems. Possibly either or both the 'Ain Jammam
and 'Ain Sara threw a particularly heavy sediment,
and the hyperbolic curve of the cross-section of
the tiles was designed to speed up the water during
periods of low flow so that the sediment would be
carried to the tanks for removal. In addition, along
occasional stretches of the aqueduct, the tiles have
been roughly removed for 10 or 20 m (for example,
just upstream from the tank in Probe 4). Possibly
the insertion of tiles in the aqueduct had raised its
level to such an extent that some sections became
inoperable as a result of even slight settling. It is
unlikely, in view of the uniqueness of this feature

among Nabataean aqueducts, that the Jammam branch was designed from the start to use tile inserts. There is at present no water deposit on the stone conduit channels that carry tiles, but this deposit — if it had reached the problem stage — may have been removed before the tiles were inserted as a solution. It is possible that the tiles were meant to make the periodic elimination of carbonate deposits easier, perhaps by removal of the tiles and giving them a hard tap. See the analysis in Section 7.D.1.

5.C. DAM (STRUCTURE NO. 44)

5.C.1. *Dam Probe no. 1*

After survey of the dam proper, a probe (1 × 1 m) was excavated in the sand fill against the south end of the upstream face, in order to to examine the structure and waterproofing (fig. 3.103). The coarse, red sand fill, carried down from the catchment area by winter floods, was level with the top of the dam. Below the surface, the fill remained moist even in June. No artefacts were recovered. At a depth of 0.50 m below the crest, a layer of hard, light red plaster (Th 0.02 m) was found adhering to the face of the dam (Bucket 87.032); it was full of poorly-sorted grains of quartz sand and small pebbles of clear quartz and other stones, with infrequent flecks of carbon (see the analysis in Section 6.D.2, 4). The surface was carefully smoothed, possibly polished. The light red colour was at first interpreted as stain left by the sand, but it has recently been shown that a similar colour was intentionally added to the plaster surfacing the dams that control the flow of water into the Siq at Petra (Bellwald and al-Huneidi 2003: 71). It is likely that the colour was selected to make the structures blend in better with the sandstone landscape. The probe terminated in sterile sand at a depth of 0.75 m.

There were two thin layers of a very hard, pebbly plaster around the rock-cut altar or betyl at the south end of the dam (Bucket 87.030). The entire upper surface of the dam may have originally been surfaced with this material.

Locus 01 (sand fill against upstream face of dam)
Bucket 87.032. 1 base. Plaster from upstream face of dam.

5.D. RESERVOIR IN THE ROMAN FORT (STRUCTURE NO. 62)

Excavation since 1993 has shown that the fort was built early in the second century AD, probably abandoned during the reign of Diocletian, reoccupied under Constantine, and abandoned for good around 400 (Oleson et al. 1995, 1999, 2003, 2008; Oleson 2001a, 2003; figs. 2.14–15). Eight probes were excavated in 1987 around the reservoir in the northwest corner of the fort in order to clarify its dimensions and method of construction, the location and design of any intake and discharge conduits, and its connection with the Nabataean aqueduct (fig. 4.1). As elsewhere in the fort, the ceramics in nearly all the loci consist of a mix of first- through fourth-century wares (Oleson et al. 1999: 414–21; 2003). The three bronze coins found on the surface around the reservoir are also typical of surface finds elsewhere in the fort: cat. nos. 1987.194.01 (House of Constantine), 1987.104.02 (House of Constantine), 1987.193.01 (second half of third century?) (Section 6.C.3).

Sixteen more probes were excavated in and around the reservoir in 2004 and 2005 (Oleson et al. 2008: Hydraulic Probes nos. 9–24). Although Probes 1 to 8 could logically be described along with the later probes in a subsequent volume, they will be presented here because they provide documentation of the reservoir's integration into the water-supply system of Hawara.

5.D.1 *Reservoir no. 62, Probe no. 1*

A square was laid out inside the northwest corner of the reservoir (1.5 m north/south, 2 m east/west), where the blocks forming the reservoir wall seemed particularly well preserved (top surface 963.42 m asl; figs. 4.1, 4.3, 5.7). In addition, it was assumed that some trace would be found at this point of the intake from the aqueduct, so the probe included clearing of the adjacent rim of the reservoir to the northwest. The fill inside the cistern was a largely uniform mix of large rubble and blocks from the walls of the fort and reservoir, cobbles, and sandy soil, with a small amount of ceramic material dating from the first to the seventh century (fig. 5.8). There was very little to distinguish Loci 01 to

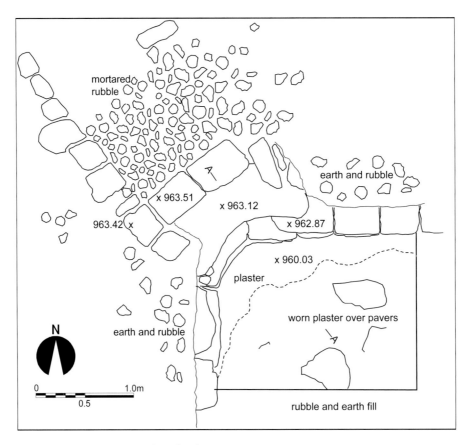

FIG. 5.7   *Reservoir no. 62, plan of Probe 1.*

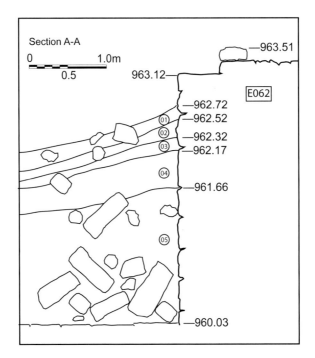

FIG. 5.8   *Reservoir no. 62, section across Probe 1.*

03 from one another, except slight changes in the density of the fill. Locus 04 was made up of slightly darker soil, possibly in part because of increased dampness.

Locus 05 consisted of a softer brownish yellow soil surrounding large blocks and rubble that extended down to floor level (960.03 m asl), probably the result of the initial collapse of the structure. Unfortunately, no ceramics were recovered from this stratum. The seams between the blocks of the walls and the pavers of the floor were smeared with a crumbly white mortar moderately tempered with rounded quartz sand and pebbles, containing frequent bubbles and nodules of lime. This probe revealed that the reservoir had been constructed of eight courses of blocks, varying in height but continuing more or less evenly around the entire interior of the structure.

Surface clearing above the cistern curb revealed a row of roughly rectangular blocks leading towards the northwest corner of the fort at a bearing of 325 degrees. There are traces of a parallel row of blocks ca. 1 m to the northeast. These blocks rested on a rough paving of small, irregular sandstone slabs set into a light grey mortar containing numerous flecks of charcoal. The two rows of blocks probably represent the framing courses for the extension of the Nabataean aqueduct, from between which the conduit blocks have been taken for reuse.

Locus 01 (surface soil and rubble to –0.20 m, 962.72 to 962.52 m asl)

    Bucket 87.033. 20 body, 2 rim, 1 handle. Very heavy coarse wares and storage wares.

Locus 02 (light brown soil and rubble, 962.52 to 962.32 m asl)

    Bucket 87.034. 9 body, 2 rim, 2 handle.

Locus 03 (light brown soil, 962.32 to 962.17 m asl)

    Bucket 87.049. 7 body, 1 handle.

Locus 04 (brown-yellow soil, 962.17 to 961.66 m asl)

    Bucket 87.050. 3 body, 1 handle.

    Bucket 87.052. 2 body, 1 rim. 1 NFW bowl sherd.

    Bucket 87.068. 2 body. Thick-walled Aqaba ware amphora, possibly Umayyad; cf. 'Amr and Schick 2001: 111, no. 13 (mid-7C).

Locus 05 (brown-yellow soil and blocks to floor, 961.66 to 960.03 m asl)

    Bucket 87.066. Mortar from near base of wall.

5.D.2. *Reservoir no. 62, Probe no. 2*

Probe 2 was excavated to clarify the design of a possible channel built of sandstone slabs, 3.10 m east of the southwest corner of the reservoir and 3 m south of its south wall. Thin upright slabs of sandstone form a rough channel (W 0.20 m, 0.14 m deep; 963.55 m asl) that slopes gently up over the rubble surface for 4.10 m to the southeast. Only 0.10 m of soil had accumulated over this feature, which is too fragile to have served to conduct water. No sherds were recovered during the clearing. Given its location and fragility, this feature is probably recent.

5.D.3. *Reservoir no. 62, Probe no. 3*

Probe 3 was laid out around the southwest corner of the reservoir (W 3.50 m, L 3.50 m) to clarify the character of a possible pavement, to determine whether or not steps led down into the reservoir at this point, to explore the function of the single visible conduit block, and to define the chronology and structure of the reservoir wall. Surface clearing revealed that the large sandstone slabs (963.22 m asl) were part of the wall construction rather than a pavement and that there were no steps down into the interior. The interior of the reservoir at this corner was excavated in 2004 (Probe 14), revealing the presence of a triangular platform built into the corner after completion of the reservoir. A similar platform was found in the southeast corner (fig. 4.4). It is possible that pumpers stood on these platforms to operate *shadufs* that raised water to troughs or basins feeding a pressurised pipe system that distributed water around the fort. Since the large blocks forming the upper surface of the southwest corner of the reservoir wall are more monumental than those at the other corners, it is possible that they served as the footings for the *shaduf* or a main collection basin. Unfortunately, the context of the conduit block was disturbed, and it could not be determined whether or not it remains in its original position.

FIG. 5.9   *Reservoir no. 62, view of southwest corner after clearing (1989).*

The southern end of the reservoir has been more badly damaged than the rest of the structure. Courses 7 and 8 (of the 8 courses of wall blocks) have been lost along the whole south wall, and courses 6, 7, and 8 along the southern half of the west wall. What remains at the southwest corner are several sandstone blocks of the south wall and a poorly-defined mass of mortared rubble and tumbled rubble around the corner itself (fig. 5.9). A north/south seam, ca. 0.60 m west of the inside facing of the west reservoir wall, seems to separate the mortared from the un-mortared rubble. The un-mortared rubble ends in a fairly neat face ca. 0.60 m west of the mortared edge, and this line is carried on by walls that continue south and west of the probe. It is possible that the intended thickness of the built and mortared reservoir wall was 2 Roman feet, backed by a surface packing of stones and earth 2 Roman feet wide. The conduit block (L 0.99 m, W 0.45 m, H 0.24 m; channel W 0.11 m, H

0.10 m), although oriented neatly with the adjacent reservoir walls, was not firmly encased in mortared rubble or blocks, but was set in the mix of rubble and earth west of the mortared area.

Cleaning of the surface soil and rubble to a depth of ca. 0.10 m (Locus 01, 03) clarified the structural remains around the edge of the southwest corner and produced a mix largely composed of storage and kitchen wares, probably first- to early second-century in date, although the only definers date to the first century. Removal of 0.30 m of fill inside the cistern against the southwest corner (Locus 02, no artefacts) revealed that the blocks visible at that point had fallen from the wall.

A trench (1 m east/west, 3.5 m north/south) was laid out at the west edge of the cleaned area, outside the area of mortared rubble, to investigate the fill behind the wall and the context of the conduit block (figs. 5.10–11). The fill down to –0.25 m (963.08 m asl, Locus 04) was very loose brown soil

FIG. 5.10 *Reservoir no. 62, view of Probe 3.*

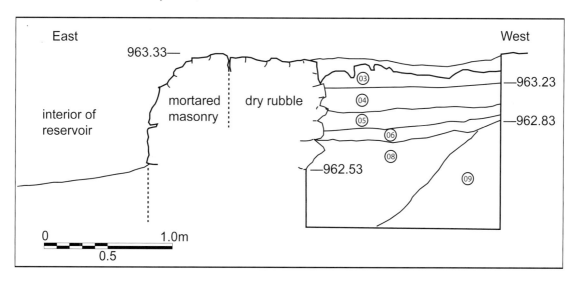

FIG. 5.11 *Reservoir no. 62, section across Probe 3.*

stained grey with ash, mixed with loose rubble, and containing sherds dating from the first to fourth century. None of the dateable ceramics below this locus are later than the second century. Beneath was a stratum of soft, reddish brown soil with loose rubble (Locus 05) containing the same mix of ceramics but with very few definers, extending down to 962.96 m asl. Locus 06 (to 962.83 m asl)

was similar, but seems a stronger brown colour. All these strata were poorly defined and appeared either disturbed by digging or the result of dumping. Locus 07 was similar, consisting of loose, ashy brown soil and cobbles sloping up against the rubble reservoir packing around and beneath the conduit block. It contained a rich assortment of first- and second-century ceramics. The original

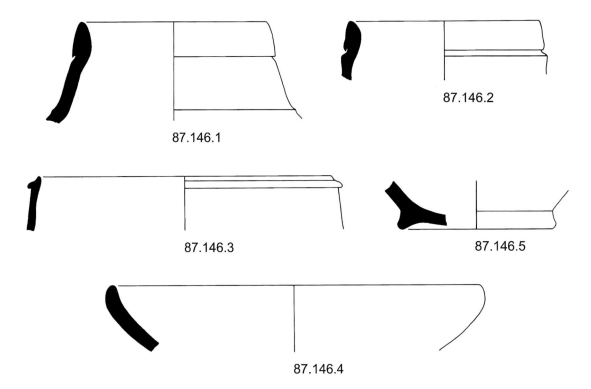

87.146.1

87.146.2

87.146.3

87.146.5

87.146.4

FIG. 5.12 *Reservoir no. 62, ceramics from Probe 3, Locus 4 (scale 1:2).*

backfill around the cistern may be represented by Locus 08, a stratum of more compact, light brown soil containing much sandstone rubble and some late first- to early second-century ceramics (962.83 to 962.11 m asl).

Excavation had to be stopped at this level because of the danger of undermining the structure of the wall and lack of time. Nevertheless, it is clear that a large hole with sloping sides was excavated for the reservoir, then backfilled after the floor and walls had been constructed. The only dateable ceramics in this backfill belong to the first and early second centuries, confirming that the reservoir belongs to the first phase of the fort's development.

Locus 01 (surface fill inside conduit slab, 963.10 m asl)

Bucket 87.035. 1 Nabataean string-cut base and wall of juglet (1C).

Locus 03 (surface soil over whole square, to –0.10 m, 963.23 m asl)

Bucket 87.137. 34 body, 8 rim, 10 handle. Mix of storage and kitchen wares, especially very

heavy handles. 1 fragment Nabataean rosette lamp (1C). Heavy bowl with pie-crust rim, Gerber, Humayma catalogue 98.0365 (3–4C); casserole, *EZ* I fig. 775 no. 48 (4C); cook pot, Gerber 2001a: fig. 3c (2–3C); cook pot, Gerber 2001b: fig. 1.18 (2–3C).

Locus 04 (greyish brown soil outside reservoir wall, 963.23 to 963.08 m asl; fig. 5.12)

Bucket 87.146. 34 body. 6 rim, 1 base, 4 handle.

146.1. Jar: medium coarse, hard, sandy, pink (5YR 7/4) fabric with frequent white inclusions, some bubbles. Slightly lighter outer surface. *EZ* I fig. 760 no. 33 (300–363).

146.2. Jar: fabric as 146.01, but core white (10YR 8/2) toward interior, light red (2.5YR 6/6) toward exterior with grey exterior surface (2.5YR N5). *EZ* I fig. 761 no. 34 (300–363).

146.3. Bowl: fabric as 146.01, but light red (2.5YR 6/6). *EZ* I fig. 738 no. 11 (300–363). Cf. Gerber 1997: fig. 7 (2nd half 1–ea. 2C).

146.4. Flat-bottomed pan: hard, slightly sandy, reddish yellow fabric (5YR 7/6) with a few white specks and bubbles. Grey (5YR 6/1) core comes to surface near inside base. Interior surface burnished or possibly slipped. D 0.20 m. Possibly Pompeian red ware. *EZ* I no. fig. 575 no. 115 (1C).

146.5. Bowl: fabric as 146.1. Base D 0.08 m?

Locus 05 (reddish brown soil outside reservoir wall, 963.08 to 962.96 m asl; fig. 5.13)

Bucket 87.147. 39 body, 4 handle, 1 rim.

147.1. Basin (?): hard, sandy, red (2.5YR 5/8) fabric with many white and brown inclusions and bubbles. Burned grey (2.5YR 5/0) on exterior.

147.2. NFW juglet: string cut base: soft, sandy, reddish yellow (5YR 6/6) fabric (1C).

Locus 06 (brown soil, 962.96 to 962.83 m asl; fig. 5.14)

Bucket 87.162. 15 body, 2 rim. Very worn sherds.

162.1. Jug (?): fine, light red (2.5YR 6/8) clay. Pocked red (2.5YR 5/6) slip on surface. Although the fragment is very small, the fabric and slip resemble that of ETSA; *EZ* I: 133 (1C–1st half 2nd C).

162.2. Nabataean jar with grooved strap handle: fine, hard, slightly sandy, red fabric (2.5YR 5/8) with a few bubbles and white inclusions. Bikai and Perry 2001: fig. 9 no. 15 (1C); Villeneuve 1990: pl. II. 2 (100–150).

Locus 07 (ashy brown soil sloping up to conduit block; fig. 5.15)

Bucket 87.163. 72 body, 5 rim, 4 handle, 3 base. Parker (oral communication) says this is a very homogeneous group; ribbed body sherds are second- to third-century in date.

163.1. Cooking pot: hard, medium fine, light red (2.5YR 6/6) fabric with a few white inclusions and bubbles. Pink surface (7.5YR 7/4). D 0.15 m. Gerber 2001b: fig. 1.12 (2nd half 1C–ea. 2C); ʿAmr et al. 1998: fig. 4.12 (2C).

163.2. As 163.1.

163.3. As 163.01, but red (2.5YR 5/6) fabric. Gerber, Humayma 98.0336 (1C).

FIG. 5.13 *Reservoir no. 62, ceramics from Probe 3, Locus 5 (scale 1:2).*

FIG. 5.14 *Reservoir no. 62, ceramics from Probe 3, Locus 6 (scale 1:2).*

163.4. Cooking pot: hard, medium fine, light red (2.5YR 6/6) fabric with a few white inclusions and bubbles. D 0.13 m.

163.5. Saucepan: fabric as 163.1. Exterior fire-blackened very dark grey (2.5YR 3/0). D 0.17 m. Cf. Gerber 1994: fig. 16H (ea. 2C).

163.8. Jug: slightly sandy, grey (2.5YR 5/0) fabric. Pink interior surface (5YR 7/3) (1–2C). Base D 0.03 m.

163.9. Bowl: fine hard, pink (5YR 7/4) fabric with a few white inclusions (1C).

163.10. Bowl: very fine, slightly soft, reddish brown (5YR 5/4) fabric. Surface burnished?

Locus 08 (compact, light brown soil around and below rubble wall, 962.83 to 962.11 m asl; fig. 5.16)

Bucket 87.148. 19 body, 2 rim, 1 handle, 2 base.

148.1. Jar (?): very fine, hard, very pale brown (10YR 7/3) fabric. Surface possibly slipped. Burned? D 0.08 m? Cf. *EZ* II figs. 342, 351, Phase 3b (70–100).

148.2. NPFW bowl: very fine, hard, light red (2.5YR 6/6) fabric. Interior surface painted red (2.5YR 4/6), solid colour except for dots

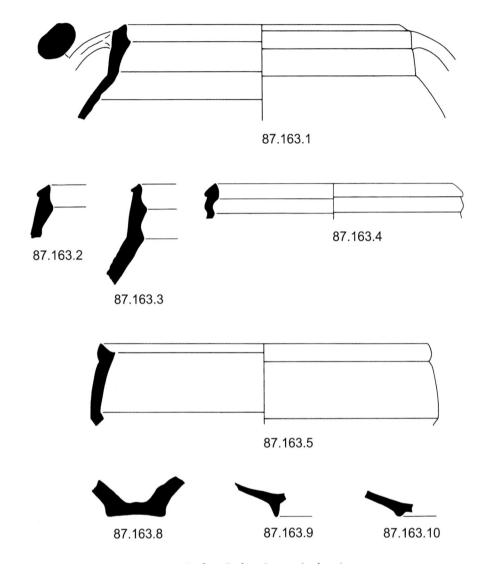

FIG. 5.15   *Reservoir no. 62, ceramics from Probe 3, Locus 7 (scale 1:2).*

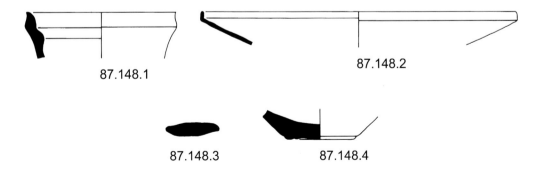

FIG. 5.16   *Reservoir no. 62, ceramics from Probe 3, Locus 8 (scale 1:2).*

around rim. D.0.17 m. *EZ* II no. 91, Phase 3b (70–100).

148.3. NFW strap handle: slightly laminar, sandy, red (2.5YR 5/8) fabric (1–ea. 2C).

148.4. Nabataean lamp: very fine, slightly chalky, very pale brown, (10YR 8/3) fabric. Interior has traces of very dark grey slip (10YR 3/1). Base D 0.034 m. *EZ* III no. 208 (1C).

Locus 09 (compact, sandy red soil, sloping from 962.83 m asl. Sterile?)

5.D.4. *Reservoir no. 62, Probe no. 4*

Probes 4 to 8 were laid out within and outside the northwest corner tower of the fort in an attempt to define the design and the course of the aqueduct branch that served the reservoir (fig. 4.1). The aqueduct channel was found in Probes 4, 7, and 8. The tower itself was poorly preserved: the exterior faces were completely lost, and the interior was filled with tumbled rubble and soil. Only a short stretch of the east wall of the interior room could be defined during the excavation. Although the design of the corner towers was unknown in 1987, excavations in the better-preserved southeast tower in 1993 revealed that the towers were ca. 6 m (20 Roman Feet) square, projected 1.80 m (6 RF) from the curtain walls, and contained a room 2.98 m (10 RF) square (Oleson et al. 1995: 325–27). The entrance corridor to the room inside the northwest tower ran north/south, framed on the east by the end of the access walk inside the north curtain wall and on the west by the inside face of the west curtain wall. Probe 4 (L 3.70, W 1.0 m) was laid out diagonally across the entrance corridor, more or less northeast to southwest and perpendicular to the hypothetical direct course of the aqueduct. The northwest corner of the reservoir is 19.40 m to the southeast.

Clearing of 0.20 m of surface soil and rubble (Locus 00) produced no ceramics. The stratum of brown soil and rubble below (Locus 02, from 964.51 to 963.74 m asl) is essentially the same deposit as Locus 00 but slightly more compact. The ceramics are the mix of first- to fourth-century wares typical of all the destruction and abandonment

FIG. 5.17 *Reservoir no. 62, Probe 4 from southwest.*

levels in the fort. A stratum of still more compact, reddish-brown soil containing nodules of lime (Locus 03) represents a floor level, which slopes down slightly from the east corridor wall, over the aqueduct channel, and disappears under a heap of very heavy blocks and rubble at the southwest end of the trench. A shallow trench had been cut into this floor along the east wall of the entrance corridor to accommodate the aqueduct (Locus 04), composed of the standard conduit blocks framed by mortared flagstones and cobbles (fig. 5.17). A thick layer of mortar was smeared over the edges of the conduit blocks and framing, and the cover slabs were laid on this surface. When excavated, the cover slabs were covered by a sloping stratum of reddish soil identical to that of Locus 03 but incorporating rubble from the decay of the tower. This material may represent decayed mudbrick

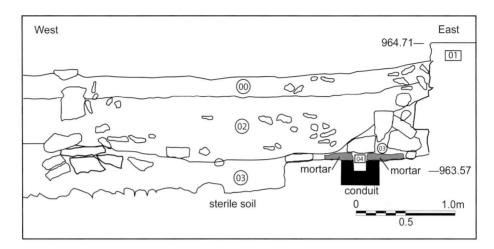

West   East

                                                    964.71—

                                                                    [01]

                          ⓪⓪

                    ⓪②

                                              ⓪③
                                         [04]
                              mortar   mortar —963.57

                         ⓪③   conduit
                                              0   1.0m
          sterile soil
                                                   0.5

FIG. 5.18 *Reservoir no. 62, section across Probe 4.*

or mud plaster applied to the walls. South of the conduit and below the floor level, the Locus 03 fill (Th 0.25 m) contained numerous cobbles and a few first-century ceramics. This material rests on a level stratum of reddish brown sand that probably represents the original soil surface (Locus 05, 963.31 m asl; fig. 5.18).

The white sandstone conduit blocks (L > 0.67 m, W 0.42 m, H 0.20 m; channel W 0.10 m, H 0.09 m) of the aqueduct were framed by small, irregular sandstone slabs set in a crumbly, grey mortar containing frequent specks of white lime nodules and charcoal (Locus 04). This packing extended over the top edges of the conduit, where it held a packing of flat stones (Th 0.06 m) in position. These, in turn, were covered with a thin layer of hard, white plaster (963.70 m asl). There were no traces of plaster or water concretions in the conduit channel. An irregular cover slab rested on top of the packing. A coin of Elagabalus struck at Petra was found resting on top of the plaster topping the conduit channel at the north face of the probe (AD 221–222; cat. no. 1987.057.01; p. 335).

Because of the tumble of very heavy blocks visible in the northwest baulk, the southeast baulk was extended 0.90 m farther south to expose more of the conduit. The aqueduct, however, ended abruptly just south of the original south baulk. The conduit blocks had been pulled out, and in their place was a stratum of soft, ashy brown soil with rubble (Locus 07), unfortunately without any artefacts. The adjacent corridor wall had also been

pulled down at this point, probably when the fort was mined for construction materials in the Late Byzantine and Umayyad periods.

Locus 02 (brown soil and rubble fill, 964.51 to 963.74 m asl)
> Bucket 87.069. 15 body, 1 rim, 2 handle. Nabataean cream ware jug (1–ea. 2C). Cook pot, Gerber 2001a: fig. 2G (4C).

Locus 03 (compact brown soil with cobbles and lime nodules, 963.74 to 963.31 m asl)
> Bucket 87.056. 8 body, 1 handle, 1 base. String-cut juglet base (1C). Fragment of pipe.
> Bucket 87.057. 1 bronze coin of Elagabalus, struck at Petra (cat. no 1987.057.01; fig. 6.9a). Found on top of mortar packing on conduit slab.
> Bucket 87.094. 5 body, 2 rim, 1 handle.
> Bucket 87.126*bis*. 6 body, 1 rim.
> 126*bis*.1. Jug: hard, slightly sandy, light red (2.5YR 6/6) fabric with a few small white inclusions. Grey core (2.5YR N5/) and exterior blackened to same colour. D 0.10 m. *EZ* II no. 350; Phase 3a (mid–1C).

5.D.5. *Reservoir no. 62, Probe no. 5*

Probe 5 (L 4.5 m, W 0.75 m) was laid out on a northeast to southwest orientation perpendicular to the projected course of the aqueduct branch revealed in Probe 4, 15 m north of Probe 4, 2 m north of what appeared to be spill from the fallen

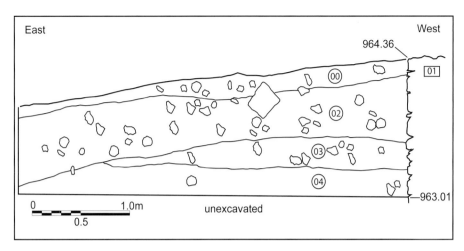

FIG. 5.19 *Reservoir no. 62, section along Probe 6.*

north wall of the tower. Clearing of the loose top-soil to ca. −0.25 below the present surface (Locus 01, 964.21 to 963.96 m asl), exposed Locus 02, a layer of compact brown soil containing cobbles, occasional larger pieces of rubble or blocks, and potsherds of the first and probably fourth century. This locus rested on a level surface of sandy reddish brown soil (Locus 03, 963.31 m asl) that appears to be the original ancient ground level. In any case, this surface is 0.50 m below the top of the conduit blocks in Probe 5 and at almost precisely the same level as the original ground surface in Probe 5. The conduit was either entirely robbed away outside the tower, or it made a sharp turn to the west to join the Ghana aqueduct farther south than anticipated. Probes nos. 7 and 8 inside the tower showed that the aqueduct was on a course to intercept Probe 5 (see below).

Locus 02 (compact brown soil, 963.96 to 963.31 m asl)

    Bucket 87.082. 11 body, 1 rim, 2 handle.
    Bucket 87.112. 14 body.
    Bucket 87.125. 7 body, 2 handle.

5.D.6. *Reservoir no. 62, Probe no. 6*

Probe 6 was laid out 10 m south of Probe 4, extending 5 m out from the inside face of the western curtain wall at a point where it seemed to be well-preserved (top of wall at 964.36 m asl). It was thought that if the aqueduct branch revealed in

Probe 4 had carried water to the southwest rather than the northwest corner of the reservoir, its course might have followed the wall face as it did inside the corner tower, out of the way of traffic. Such a route seemed illogical, but worth testing.

The bulk of the fill against the wall consisted of dumped rubbish, forming poorly-defined strata of soft, brown to grey, ashy soils, sloping slightly away from the wall and containing large amounts of rubble and significant numbers of potsherds (Locus 00, 02–04; fig. 5.19). Locus 04 consisted of loose, pink, sandy soil without rubble, but the chronology of the ceramics is still mixed: largely cooking and storage wares, first- to fourth-century in date. Unfortunately, time did not allow excavation below this stratum (963.01 m asl), which is 1.35 m below the surviving top of the wall and 0.30 m below the original ancient ground level in Probe 4. No trace of the water channel was found in this trench, and it has either been salvaged at this point, as possibly in Probe 5, or — more likely — it took a different course, directly into the northwest corner of the reservoir.

Locus 00 (loose, brown-grey topsoil, 0.0 to −0.15, 964.36 to 964.21 m asl)

Locus 02 (loose, grey-brown soil, −0.15 to −0.80, 964.21 to 963.56 m asl; fig. 5.20)

    Bucket 87.081. 48 body, 3 handle, 2 base. Several sherds of an Aqaba amphora; 'Amr and Schick 2001: fig. 3 no. 1 (mid to late 7C).

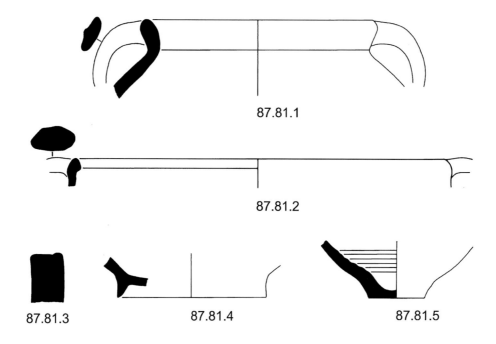

87.81.1

87.81.2

87.81.3   87.81.4   87.81.5

FIG. 5.20   *Reservoir no. 62, ceramics from Probe 6, Locus 2 (scale 1:2).*

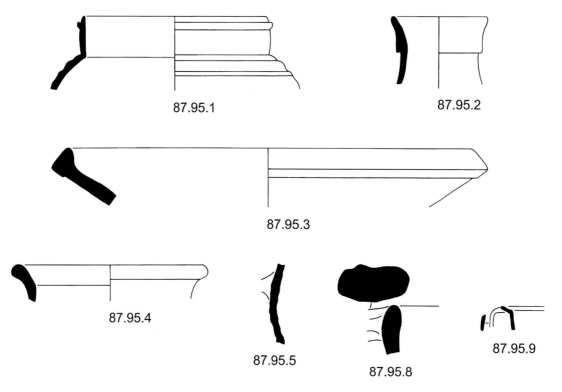

87.95.1   87.95.2

87.95.3

87.95.4

87.95.5   87.95.8   87.95.9

FIG. 5.21   *Reservoir no. 62, ceramics from Probe 6, Locus 3 (scale 1:2).*

81.1. Cooking pot: hard, sandy, light reddish brown (2.5YR 6/4) fabric. Slightly lighter surface. D 0.12 m. *EZ* I fig. 744, no. 17 (last quarter 4C–ea. 5C).

81.2. Casserole: hard, coarse, sandy, reddish yellow (5YR 6/6) fabric with white inclusions. Light grey 5YR 7/1) core. Exterior surface burned grey (10YR 6/1). *EZ* I fig. 773–74, nos. 46–7 (4C–ea. 5C).

81.3. Roof tile flange: hard, flaky, light red (2.5YR 6/6) clay with quartz sand. Th 0.017 m. (ea. 2C).

81.4. NFW bowl or jug: hard, sandy, light red (2.5YR 6/6) fabric. Pinkish white (7.5YR 8/2) surface (1–2C). Base D 0.08 m.

81.5. Jug: hard, sandy, light red (10R 6/6) fabric with numerous white inclusions. Pale red (10R 6/2) core. String-cut base; base D 0.03 m. (1C).

Locus 03 (loose grey-brown soil with cobbles, 963.56 to 963.31 m asl; fig. 5.21)
Bucket 87.095. 41 body, 4 rim, 6 handle.

95.1. Cooking pot: very sandy, hard, laminar, red (10R 4/8) fabric with white specks and bubbles. D 0.10 m. Gerber 2001a: fig. 3B (2–3C); ʿAmr et al. 1998: fig. 6.14 (4C); Parker 1987: fig. 100.82 (284–363).

95.2. Jar (?): medium fine, light red (10R 6/8) fabric. Pink (7.5YR 7/4) outer surface. D 0.05 m.

95.3. Nabataean cream ware (?) bowl: very hard, sandy, pale yellow (2.5YR 7/4) fabric with clear quartz sand and white specks. Very pale brown (10YR 8/4) core. D 0.22 m? ʿAmr 1992: fig. 5 (1C–ea. 2C).

95.4. Jar (?): sandy, hard, reddish yellow (5YR 6/6) fabric. Exterior burned very dark grey (5YR 3/1). D 0.10 m? *EZ* I fig. 762, no. 35 (300–363); Gerber 2001b: fig. 1.24 (2–3C).

95.5. NFW jug: very fine, light reddish brown (5YR 6/3) fabric. Reddish yellow (7.5YR 7/6) exterior (1C).

95.8. Jar (?): very hard, sandy, grey (10YR 5/1) fabric with numerous white specks and small bubbles. Pink (7.5YR 7/4) exterior surface. D 0.12 m.

95.9. NFW jar: slightly sandy, light red (2.5YR 6/6) fabric. Dark grey (2.5YR 4/0) exterior surface. *EZ* II fig. 249; Phase 3b–3c (1–2C).

Bucket 87.099. 44 body, 5 rim, 6 handle. NPFW bowl (Phase 3b, 1C); Nabataean cream ware jug (late 1–ea. 2C); jar, *EZ* I fig. 761 (4C).

Locus 04 (loose, greyish pink sand, 965.31 to 963.01 m asl; fig. 5.22)
Bucket 87.111. 21 body, 6 rim, 6 handle, 1 base.

111.1. Slot rim jug: coarse, sandy, hard, light reddish brown (5YR 6/4) fabric with a few white inclusions. Fabric shades to reddish grey (5YR 5/2) on interior surface, and pinkish grey (7.5YR 7/2) on exterior. Gerber 2001a: fig. 2P (4C–5C); *EZ* I fig. 761, no. 34 (300–363).

111.2. Cooking pot: hard, sandy, light red (2.5YR 6/6) fabric with white inclusions and a few bubbles. Grey (2.5YR 5/0) exterior surface. Gerber 2001b: fig. 1.12–13 (2nd half 1C–ea. 2C); Gerber 1997: fig. 4.A (mid to 2nd half 1C).

111.3. NFW bowl: very fine, hard, light red (2.5YR 6/6) fabric. No paint visible. D 0.08 m? *EZ* II no. 57; Phase 3b (70–100).

111.4. Bowl: fine, slightly soft, light reddish brown (5YR 6/4) fabric, with a few white specks. *EZ* II no. 370; Phase 3b (70–100); Schmid 2003: fig. 61.19; Phase 3 (1C).

111.5. Lid: hard, slightly sandy, yellowish red (5YR 5/8) fabric. Burned dark reddish grey (5YR 4/2) toward exterior. D 0.13 m? Parker 1987: 528 no. 121 (late 4C–5C); Dolinka 2003: 124 nos. 11–12 (1–2C).

111.10. Nabataean cream ware jug base: slightly sandy, rough, pink (7.5YR 8/4) fabric. Very pale brown (10YR 8/4) surface. Base D 0.06 m? (1C–ea. 2C).

5.D.7. *Reservoir no. 62, Probe no. 7*

When Probes 5 and 6 failed to locate the aqueduct outside the northwest tower or inside the curtain wall, Probes 7 and 8 were opened to document its course inside the tower. Probe 7 (1.0 m east/west, 0.75 m north/south) was laid out 2 m northwest of

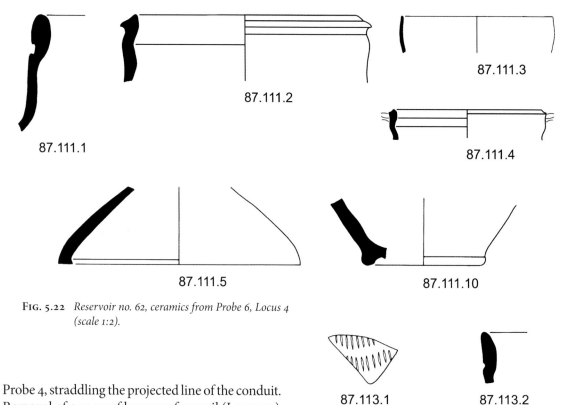

87.111.1

87.111.2

87.111.3

87.111.4

87.111.5

87.111.10

FIG. 5.22 *Reservoir no. 62, ceramics from Probe 6, Locus 4 (scale 1:2).*

87.113.1   87.113.2

FIG. 5.23 *Reservoir no. 62, ceramics from Probe 7, Locus 2 (scale 1:2).*

Probe 4, straddling the projected line of the conduit. Removal of 0.10 m of loose surface soil (Locus 01) revealed the same mixture of rubble and compact brown soil (Locus 02) seen in Probe 4. This soil rested directly on the mortared upper surfaces of the small flat stones laid along either side of the sandstone conduit blocks (Locus 03, at 963.84 m asl) and filled the channel (channel floor at 963.69 m asl). The junction of two conduit blocks was exposed in the small sounding, but no cover slabs were found in position. The bearing of the conduit channel was almost exactly magnetic north, and the fall to the conduit floor in Probe 4 is a surpris-ing 0.12 m, 8 percent or 1:12.5. The ceramic material dated to the first and fourth century.

Locus 02 (compact brown soil and rubble, 0.10 m below surface to –0.80 m, 964.54 to 963.84 m asl; fig. 5.23)

Bucket 87.113. 24 body, 1 rim, 1 handle, 1 base.
113.1. NFW bowl: very hard, fine, red (10R 5/8) fabric. Rocker-decorated surface. *EZ* II no. 103 (late 1–2C).
113.2. Jar with grooved rim: fine, hard, very pale brown (10YR 7/3) fabric with a few white specks and bubbles. *EZ* I fig. 761 no. 34 (300–363).

5.D.8. *Reservoir no. 62, Probe no. 8*

Probe 8 (2.0 m east/west, 1.5 m north/south) was laid out 1.2 m northwest of Probe 7, 2 m south of Probe 5, straddling the projected line of the conduit. Removal of the loose surface soil (Locus 01) to –0.15 m (964.34 m asl) revealed the same mixture of rubble and compact brown soil (Locus 02) seen in Probes 4 and 7 (964.34 to 964.22 m asl). This locus rested on a stratum of softer, light brown soil and rubble sloping from east to west (Locus 3, 964.22 to 963.80 m asl). Locus 03 had been de-posited directly on the mortared upper surfaces of the small flat stones laid along either side of the sandstone conduit blocks (Locus 04, 963.81 m asl) and filled the channel. The exposed conduit block was 0.41 m wide (fig. 5.24). The channel (W 0.11 m, 0.10 m deep) showed no traces of plaster or water-deposited concretion. A heavy cover slab (L 0.54 m, W 0.35 m, Th 0.11 m) was found in position over the southern part of the block. Most of the sandstone blocks used to raise the side walls of the conduit block carried typical Nabataean diagonal trimming. One of these slabs (H87–6283–01) preserved a portion of an inscription in either Nabataean or Greek (cat. no. 1987.164.01; pp. 336–37; fig. 6.11). The bearing of the conduit channel was almost exactly magnetic north. The small amount of ceramic material dated first- and fourth-century.

Locus 02 (compact, brown soil, 964.34 to 964.22)
    Bucket 87.128. 1 rim with handle.
    Bucket 87.128A. 3 body.
    Bucket 87.145. 1 Nabataean cream ware body sherd (1C–ea. 2C).

5.E. RESERVOIR/POOL FED BY NABATAEAN AQUEDUCT (STRUCTURE NO. 63)

The central location, unique design, and dimensions of Reservoir no. 63 indicate that this structure was a very important part of the aqueduct system serving Humayma, possibly the focus of the entire system (figs. 2.14, 4.5–11). In addition, the design and construction techniques showed that the aqueduct and reservoir belonged to the same construction phase. In consequence, it was considered important to probe this large structure sufficiently to reveal its design, chronology, and phasing. Probes were laid out around the periphery and interior, revealing a variety of features that led to the excavation of 12 probes in all (figs. 4.5, 5.25). Since the long axis of the reservoir is oriented 25 degrees east of N, the probes laid out perpendicular or parallel to its features follow the same orientation. These probes confirmed that the pool was constructed during the late first century BC or the early first century AD.

During 2001, Dr. Sausan Fahkri, Director of Antiquities office for the Aqaba region, directed the complete clearing of the interior of the reservoir and consolidation of its structure. This clearing revealed several new structural features (see the description in Section 4.B.1), and the fill yielded the carved foot of a stone basin of Umayyad date, indicating that the pool was not allowed to fill with soil prior to the late seventh or eighth century.

Fig. 5.24 *Reservoir no. 62, view of Probe 8.*

5.E.1. *Reservoir/Pool no. 63, Probe no. 1*

Probe 1 was excavated in 1983 and 1987 against the inside face of the north wall of the reservoir, directly below the point where the aqueduct discharged (at 960.41 m asl), to reveal the depth of the reservoir and any features associated with the discharge (2.0 m east/west, 1.5 m north/south; fig. 4.7). Numerous blocks fallen from the wall lay on the light brown loess which filled the entire reservoir to approximately 0.50 m below the top of the walls. The upper stratum (Locus 01, Th 0.65 m), slightly sandy, much less compacted than the lower levels, and devoid of sherds, probably was deposited by the wind. The lower stratum (Locus 02, Th 0.80 m) is very uniform and hard and less sandy than Locus 01, suggesting that much of it was water-deposited or compacted by precipitation

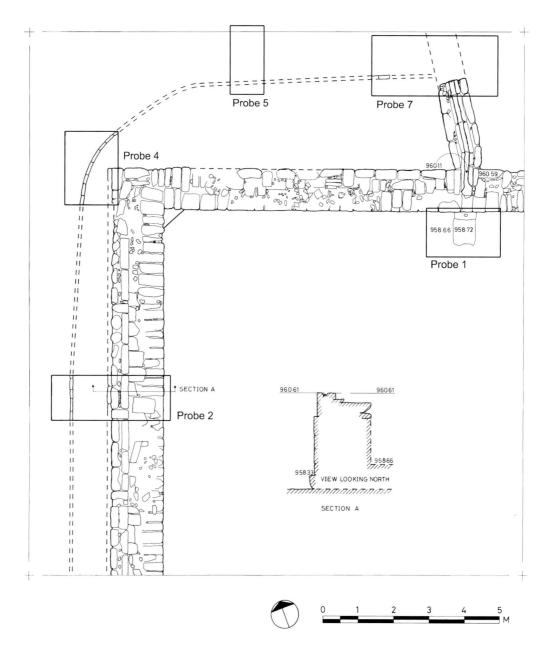

FIG. 5.25 *Reservoir/Pool no. 63, plan of northwest corner with indication of Probes 1, 2, 4, 5, and 7 (D. Ritsema).*

caught by the reservoir. No consistent pattern of layering in the fill was found in any of the probes within the reservoir. The scanty ceramic material from Probe 1 contained one dateable sherd from the first or early second century. Some ceramics and a few stone artefacts were found during the complete clearing of the fill in the pool in 2001, dating from the first to the eighth century.

The floor of the cistern, consisting of large, flat field stones set into and covered over with a very hard white plaster, was exposed at a level 1.93 m below the aqueduct channel (at 958.48 m asl). Two flat, partly trimmed sandstone blocks were set into this plaster floor, forming an approximately rectangular base (0.95 north/south, 0.66 east/west) that rises 0.07 m above the floor directly below the aqueduct. The joint between the north block and the reservoir wall was smoothed over with the hard white plaster (Th 0.04 m) that covers the wall. There is a smooth, roughly oval depression (ca. 0.12 m × 0.09 m, depth 0.04 m) in this block directly beneath the line of the aqueduct conduit, 0.12 m out from the wall. This depression appears to have been eroded over a significant period of time by water pouring from the spout while the reservoir was nearly empty, suggesting that it belongs to the Roman reworking of the reservoir that allowed the water to be completely drained through a pipe and stopcock.

Locus 02 (hard packed, light brown sandy soil below spout, 959.28 to 958.48 m asl; fig. 5.26)

    Bucket 87.041. 1 base.

        41.1. Nabataean cream ware jug: soft, fine, chalky, pale yellow (5Y 8/3) clay. Base D 0.07 m. 'Amr 1992: fig. 3.W (1–ea. 2C).

    Bucket 87.046. 1 body, 1 handle.

5.E.2. *Reservoir/Pool no. 63, Probe no. 2*

Probe 2 was laid out against the outside of the west wall of the reservoir, 5.70 m south of the northwest exterior corner, at a point where the structure of the wall and the deposit of fill against the exterior appeared well-preserved (1.25 m north/south, 2.30 m east/west; figs. 4.5, 5.25). This seemed a good

location at which to reach the foundation of the reservoir walls and obtain a cross-section of the cultural deposits surrounding it. Excavation revealed that the wall was 2.65 m high from the mortared rubble footing (957.89 m asl) to what seems to be the original capping course (960.01 m asl) and 1.50 m thick (figs. 5.27–29). There is an offset 0.15 m wide at the top of the fourth course of blocks, more or less at the ancient ground level (959.86 m asl); the top of the foundation footing, composed of mortared rubble laid in a shallow trench 0.40 m deep, projects an additional 0.12 m (at 958.41 m asl).

The surface soil (Locus 00) consisted of a stratum of sandy brown soil (Th 0.12 m) contain-

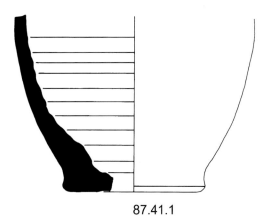

87.41.1

FIG. 5.26 *Reservoir/Pool no. 63, ceramics from Probe 1, Locus 2 (scale 1:2).*

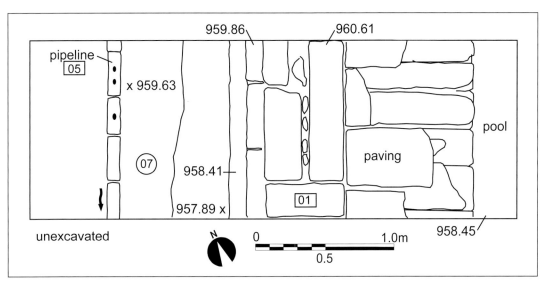

FIG. 5.27 *Reservoir/Pool no. 63, Plan of Probe 2.*

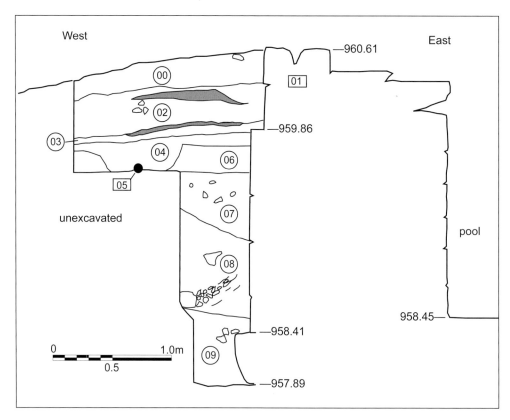

Fig. 5.28 *Reservoir/Pool no. 63, Section across Probe 2.*

ing numerous cobbles, sherds that appear to date from the first to sixth or seventh century, and an early fourth-century coin (cat. no. 1987.042.01; pp. 334–35). This layer slopes gently downhill, away from the reservoir wall above Locus 02, composed of the same soil but with fewer cobbles, and a similar but larger selection of sherds. Below it, Locus 03 consisted of loose, reddish brown sand mixed with ash, its bottom level coinciding with the top of the upper wall offset at 959.86 m asl. A similar offset more of less coincident with the original ground level can be seen on Reservoir no. 68. The sherds were very small and worn, but several provided dates from the first to the third century. Locus 04, composed of the same type of sand but without the ash, abutted the wall face on top of the original ground level (Locus 06). The sand of Locus 04 also filled a shallow trench (W 0.70 m, 0.20 deep m) dug into the compact, silty soil of Locus 06 in order to allow installation of a terracotta pipeline (Locus 05; fig. 5.30). The dateable ceramics recovered from Locus 04 may range

as late as the third century, suggesting the pipeline was installed sometime in the Late Roman or Early Byzantine period. The pipeline, 1.20 m west of the reservoir and 1 m below the top of the west wall, consisted of well-fired, wheel-turned pipe sections (L 0.30 m, outer D 0.082 m, inner D 0.068 m) with inset downstream ends (D 0.06 m) that fit tightly into the wide end of the adjacent pipe. The joints were heavily smeared with a soft, white mortar. Roughly circular holes had been pecked into the upper surface of two pipe sections, then covered over with curved potsherds mortared into position. The pipeline sloped to the south.

The compacted soil of Locus 06 (Th 0.23 m) contained a large number of body sherds from utilitarian wares. The few definers that could be dated belong to the first or early second century, but Parker identified two or three sherds as possibly Byzantine. Since no artefacts were recovered from the loci below Locus 06, extending a further 1.97 m to the base of the foundation footings, the ceramics in Locus 06 should reflect the period of

FIG. 5.30 *Reservoir/Pool no. 63, view of Probe 2, Locus 6 and pipeline.*

FIG. 5.29 *Reservoir/Pool no. 63, view of Probe 2 to foundation.*

construction and early use. The lower loci (Locus 07–09) consist of sterile, light brown or reddish sand excavated to allow construction of the reservoir wall, then returned as backfill. The absence of any background ceramics from the backfill furthermore suggests that the pool and the aqueduct that filled it were constructed early in the occupational history of the site.

Locus 00 (surface soil to –0.12 m, 960.61 to 960.49 m asl)

> Bucket 87.042. 5 body, 1 rim. Bronze coin of Maximian (cat. no. 1987.042.01).

Locus 02 (light brown, sandy soil, 960.49 to 960.21 m asl)

> Bucket 87.058. 54 body, 2 rim, 3 handle, 5 base.
>
> > 58.1. Nabataean cream ware ribbed body sherd (1C–ea. 2C).

Locus 03 (soft brown sand mixed with ash by upper offset, 960.21 to 959.86 m asl; fig. 5.31)

> Bucket 87.059. 98 body, 5 rim, 11 handle, 4 base.
>
> > 59.1. Cooking pot: hard, slightly sandy, light red (2.5YR 6/8) fabric with some bubbles. Red (2.5YR 4/8) exterior surface. Gerber 1997: fig. 4.E (mid to 2nd half 1C); cf. 'Amr and Momani 1999: fig. 14.16 (2nd half 1C–ea. 2C).
> >
> > 59.2. Jar: hard, sandy, weak red (2.5YR 4/2) fabric with a few white inclusions and bubbles. Grey exterior (2.5YR 5/0). Tholbecq and Durand 2005: fig. 13.E (1C); Gerber, Humayma 98.0305 (2C–3C).
> >
> > 59.3. Cooking pot: fabric as 59.01, but exterior grey (2.5YR 5/0). *EZ* I fig. 738 no. 11 (300–363), or Gerber 1997: fig. 7 (2nd half 1C–ea. 2C); Gerber 2001b: fig. 1.12 (2nd half 1C–ea. 2C).
> >
> > 59.4. NFW jar: fine, red (2.5YR 5/6) fabric. cf. *EZ* II nos. 251–52; Phase 3b (70–100); Schmid 2003: fig. 61.19; Phase 3 (20–100).

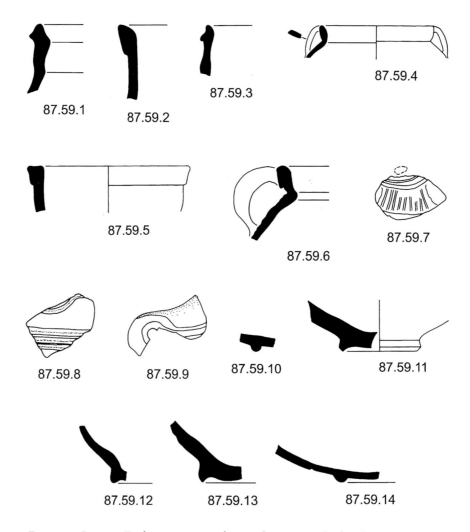

FIG. 5.31 *Reservoir/Pool no. 63, ceramics from Probe 2, Locus 3 (scale 1:2).*

59.5. Jar: slightly sandy, red (2.5YR 5.6) fabric with a few black inclusions. D 0.08 m. Gerber, Humayma bucket 98.0532 (2C–3C).

59.6. Storage jar (?): hard, sandy, very dark grey (2.5YR 3/0) fabric with white sand inclusions. Tholbecq and Durand 2005: fig. 16 (late 1C–ea. 2C)?

59.7. Lamp: portion of disk and shoulder, with raised line decoration: fine, slightly sandy, reddish yellow (5YR 6/6) fabric. *EZ* III *Typentafel* II.L (325–520).

59.8. Body sherd: sandy, yellowish red (5YR 5/6) fabric. Incised surface decoration. Gerber 2002: fig. 5 (6C–7C), 2008: no. 32, 35 (Early Islamic).

59.9. Lamp: part of nozzle and wick hole: very fine, pink (5YR 7/4) fabric. Possibly with a light reddish brown slip (5YR 6/4). Burning around nozzle. (1C?).

59.10. Base: hard, slightly sandy, yellowish red (5YR 5/6) fabric with a few white inclusions.

59.11. NFW jar or jug: very fine, hard, light red (2.5YR 6/8) fabric.

59.12. Jug base (?): hard, slightly sandy, light reddish brown (5YR 6/4) fabric. Dark grey (7.5YR 4/0) surface.

59.13. Bowl or jug: fine, hard, slightly sandy, red (2.5YR 5/8) fabric (1C–2C).

59.14. Bowl (?): slightly sandy, yellowish red (5YR 5/6) fabric with numerous large white

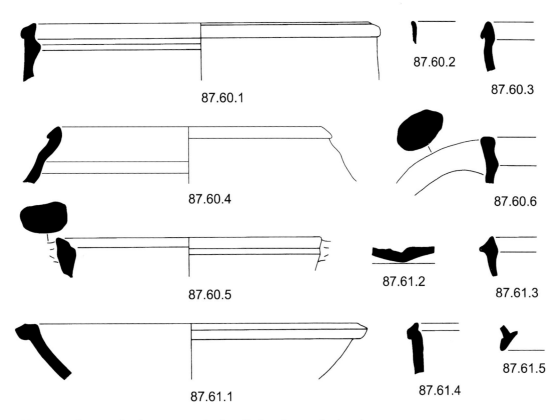

FIG. 5.32 *Reservoir/Pool no. 63, ceramics from Probe 2, Locus 4 (scale 1:2).*

inclusions. Outer surface scored by debris during throwing (1C).

Locus 04 (soft, reddish sand, level with offset on wall, 959.86 m asl, and above terracotta pipe 05, 959.60 m asl; fig. 5.32)

Bucket 87.060. 55 body, 4 rim, 6 handle.

60.1. Cooking pot: hard, sandy, light red (2.5YR 6/8) fabric with a few white specks and bubbles. Red (2.5YR 5/6) outer surface. D 0.18 m. 'Amr and Momani 1999: fig. 14.16 (106–150)?

60.2. NFW bowl: hard, very fine, red (2.5YR 5/8) fabric. Low ridges on exterior. *EZ* II nos. 181, Phase 3a–b (20–100).

60.3. Cooking pot: fabric as 60.1, but exterior grey (2.5YR 5/0). (2C?).

60.4. Cooking pot: fabric as 60.3. D 0.14 m? *EZ* II no. 345, Phase 3b (70–100); Gerber 2001b: fig. 1.25 (2C–3C)?

60.5. Jar (?): hard, slightly sandy, red (2.5YR 5/6) fabric. Light grey (2.5Y 7/0) core containing white specks. Flaky white (2.5Y 8/2)

surface slip. D 0.14 m? *EZ* II no. 342, Phase 3b (70–100)?

60.6. Jar (?): fabric as 60.5, but no dark core.

Bucket 87.061. 25 body, 4 rim, 1 base, 1 handle. Mainly well-made coarse and kitchen wares.

61.1. Saucepan: hard, sandy, yellowish red (5YR 5/6) fabric with numerous white inclusions. Dark grey (5YR 4/1) surface. D 0.18 m. Cf. Parker 1987: fig. 99.78 (284–363).

61.2. NFW bottle: fine, hard, red (10YR 4/8) fabric. Pinkish grey (7.5YR 7/2) outside surface; dimple base. (1C).

61.3. Cooking pot: sandy yellowish red (5YR 5/6) fabric with white inclusions.

61.4. Cooking pot: hard, sandy, reddish yellow (5YR 6/8) fabric with white inclusions.

61.5. NFW bowl: very fine, hard, reddish yellow (5YR 6/6) fabric. Carefully tooled shape (1C)

Locus 06 (compact sandy earth below offset, 959.82 to 959.63 m asl; fig. 5.33)

FIG. 5.33 *Reservoir/Pool no. 63, ceramics from Probe 2, Locus 6 (scale 1:2).*

Bucket 87.078. 68 body. 9 rims. 8 handles. 3 bases. Mainly cook wares and storage wares. T. Parker (oral communication) evaluates this group as mostly first-century, with a couple of possible fourth-century sherds. The definers all date to the first or possibly early second century.

78.1. Cooking pot: very sandy, grey (5YR 5/1) fabric with white inclusions and bubbles. Gerber 1997: fig. 4B (mid to 2nd half 1st C); cf. Bikai and Perry 2001: fig. 9.14 (20–100).

78.2. Pitcher: very fine, reddish yellow (5YR 7/6) fabric. Light grey (5YR 6/1) exterior. Villeneuve 1990: pl. V.5 (100–150).

78.3. NFW bowl: fabric as 78.2, but reddish yellow (5YR 6/6). Pink (7.5YR 8/4) surface. (1C).

78.6. NFW bowl or plate: fine, hard, reddish yellow (5YR 7/6) fabric. Base D 0.05 m. (1C).

5.E.3. *Reservoir/Pool no. 63, Probe no. 3*

Since the Ghana Aqueduct emptied directly into the reservoir and there was no diversion channel in the first phase of use, it was clear that there must have been some sort of arrangement for release of overflow from the reservoir once it was filled. No overflow conduit could be seen along the surviving wall tops, but at a point 5.10 m east of the south-west corner of the reservoir, two long sandstone blocks (L ca. 1.25 m, W ca. 0.45 m) oriented east/west interrupted the normal sequence of smaller blocks arranged as headers along the outer face of the wall (fig. 4.10). The top surface of these blocks (960.00 m asl) corresponds very closely to the top surface of course 6 of the blocks along the interior of the cistern. Unfortunately, the course 6 blocks did not survive in position in the area of

FIG. 5.34 *Reservoir/Pool no. 63, pipe in south wall in Probe 3 north, after removal of plaster.*

this probe. Probe 3 (1.5 m east/west, 6.25 m north/south) was laid out over these blocks, extending 3 m into the reservoir and 1.75 m south of its south wall (fig. 4.5). Excavation of the probe revealed that although there was an overflow conduit at this point in Phase I, rebuilding and renovation had taken place in two further phases of use. The Phase I overflow conduit spilled into a basin in a niche in the south wall and fed an outflow aqueduct identical in design and dimensions to the Ghana aqueduct (fig. 4.10). This aqueduct flowed south at a bearing of 205 degrees and was traced in Probes 8, 11, 12, and on the surface for a total of 100 m, to

FIG. 5.35 *Reservoir/Pool no. 63, niche in south wall in Probe 3 south, with pipe and stopcock* in situ.

→ **FIG. 5.36** *Reservoir/Pool no. 63, niche in south wall in*
Probe 3 south, detail of pipe and stopcock.

within 15 m of structure E077. The aqueduct may have carried water to a Nabataean bath below the Roman bath in E077 or it may have continued on into the settlement centre.

In Phase II, the overflow conduit was torn out, the niche roofed with sandstone slabs, and a bronze drain pipe with metal filter at its intake was installed in a hole hacked through the south wall near the floor of the reservoir (fig. 5.34). At the south end of the pipe, a large bronze stopcock (1987.106.01; Section 6.C.2) controlled the flow of water from the reservoir into a lead pipe (1987.106.02) laid in a thick deposit of mortar in the outflow aqueduct (figs. 5.35–36). The pipe was crudely constructed by wrapping lead sheeting around a mandrel, and the mortar may have been intended as much to waterproof the conduit as to protect it or hold it in position. At the same time, some sort of gate or grill, probably with a locked latch, was installed over the face of the niche to control access to the stopcock and thus the outflow water. The pipeline very likely carried water to the Roman bath (E077).

Fig. 5.37 *Reservoir/Pool no. 63, possible original overflow conduit.*

In Phase III, the filter was torn out of position at the head of the pipeline inside the reservoir, the adjacent outflow pipe packed with stones and mortar, and the pipe stub plastered over. Since the stopcock was found in its original position, it is possible that the lead pipe was torn out of the aqueduct long after the reservoir had fallen out of use and the stopcock had been covered with debris.

Probe no. 3, North of Reservoir Wall

After removal of loose surface debris across the entire extent of the probe and cleaning of the top of the reservoir wall, the north end of Probe 3 (1.50 m east/west, 3.0 m north/south) was laid out against the inside face of the south wall of the reservoir (Locus 03). A few blocks fallen from the wall and scattered field stones were embedded in the light brown loess that filled the entire reservoir to approximately 0.50 m below the top of the walls (in this probe, at 959.60 m asl).

What may have been the original overflow conduit was found in the fill adjacent to the wall

(fig. 5.37). To judge from its dimensions (H 0.32 m, W 0.40 m, L > 0.47 m), this sandstone block was dislodged from the sixth course in the south wall. A water channel of the same dimensions as those in the intake and outflow aqueducts (W 0.12 m, 0.11 m deep) was cut into the upper surface of the block from one short side to the other. One end of the block has been lost, but the diagonal trimming across the opposite end, along with the rough finish of the other two sides, suggests that this surface faced the interior of the reservoir. If placed back on the wall in course 6, above a layer of bedding mortar, the overflow channel stands at 959.86 m asl, 1.32 m above the original stone paved reservoir floor at this point, approximately 0.55 m below the level of the intake from the Ghana aqueduct. If replaced in course 7, it would stand at 960.18 m asl, 1.64 m above the original floor and 0.23 m below the intake conduit. Given the use in course 7 of pairs of long, narrow blocks arranged as headers and stretchers, installation of this block in course 6 seems more likely, despite the resulting shallow depth of water retained. At some subsequent period, probably during the Phase II renovations, the conduit channel was blocked with cobbles set in mortar.

Locus 01, the upper stratum of fill in the reservoir (959.60 to 959.34 m asl), consisted of a soft, slightly sandy, light brown loessial soil deposited by the wind. Approximately 0.25 m below the present surface, the fill became more uniform and compact and less sandy (Locus 02), suggesting that much of it was water-deposited or compacted by precipitation held in the reservoir. The scanty ceramic material probably extends from the first to sixth or seventh century and included one fragment of a flue tile from the bath building fed by the Phase II arrangements. The seventh-century sherd may or may not have been correctly identified, but the carved foot of an Umayyad marl tripod basin found in the reservoir during the clearing in 2003 reveals that the pool was not allowed to fill with earth before the Umayyad period. Destruction of the bath had commenced at least by the time the reservoir was half full of earth.

As in Probe 1, the floor of the reservoir in Probe 3 (958.54 m asl) was constructed of sandstone blocks and slabs set in a hard white mortar. The original floor level here is close to its level in Probe 1 (958.48 m asl), but during Phase II or III a thick layer of mortar topped with small cobbles and waterproofed with a surface of hard white plaster (Locus 04, see below) was laid on top of the stone paving. The cobbles were exposed in several large areas in Probe 3, and it appears as if patching was attempted with a pebbly mortar. The mortar/plaster layer is thickest against the south reservoir wall (Th 0.17 m) and slopes downward gently toward the north as it tapers off (from 958.71 to 958.54 m asl at a point 2 m N). The original floor level is nearly the same in Probes 1, 3, and 6, and complete clearing of the pool in 2003 revealed a basically level floor.

Once the bronze stopcock and lead pipeline had been uncovered in the niche south of the reservoir wall (see below), it was clear that the bronze pipe feeding the stopcock somehow had to tap the reservoir water. Examination of the plaster inside the reservoir revealed a slight bulge at the appropriate point, and a strip of plaster 0.50 m wide (Locus 03) was removed from the reservoir lip to floor to examine the arrangements (fig. 5.34). The north end of the pipe (D 0.058 m, L ca. 0.92 m, wall Th 0.005 m, centre at 958.81 m asl) was revealed nearly flush with the wall face at a point 0.12 m above the floor. In order to insert the pipe, a rough hole (D ca. 0.17 m) had been hacked from south to north along the seam between two blocks in the lowest wall course. Since this hole entered the reservoir slightly below floor level, a slot (0.11 × 0.11 m) was cut in its upper surface to accommodate the feeder pipe. The pipe was set in a fine, white, chalky plaster, and the original hole was packed with sandstone rubble set in a crumbly grey mortar. Thick, roughly rectangular flanges project from the upper and lower segments of the pipe, 0.01 m in from its termination. Three small, shallow settings were cut into the wall face 0.10 m away from the pipe, at the 4:00, 8:00 and 12:00 o'clock positions, most likely to hold a perforated bronze sheet intended to prevent debris from entering the pipe. A fragment of one of the mounting lugs (Th 0.003 m) projects from the setting at 4:00 o'clock. The filter was torn away as part of the Phase III renovations, and the pipe was packed with a hard white mortar.

A square 0.35 m on a side was excavated into the plaster waterproofing on the cistern floor directly below the pipe (Locus 04). The hard white floor plaster (Th 0.01 m) was applied to a thick layer of very hard, grey, pebbly mortar (Th 0.17 m) above a floor of carefully finished red sandstone blocks. The wall plaster shows signs of several renovations associated with Phases II and III. The original layer of very hard, grey pebbly mortar (Th 0.01 m) with a thin covering of white plaster (Th 0.05 m) can be seen around the whole reservoir. After installation of the pipe, the wall around it and the floor for nearly 2 m north were repaired with a bulging lens of grey mortar (Th 0.12 m) covered with white plaster. After the pipe was taken out of service, the wall was repaired once again with a layer of grey mortar containing numerous carbon flecks (Th 0.012 m) and covered with white plaster (Th 0.013 m). The thick layer of mortar and plaster probably was applied to avoid leaks damaging the wall fabric where the pipe had been inserted.

Locus 01 (slightly sandy, loose light brown loess in north end probe, 959.60 to 958.94 m asl)

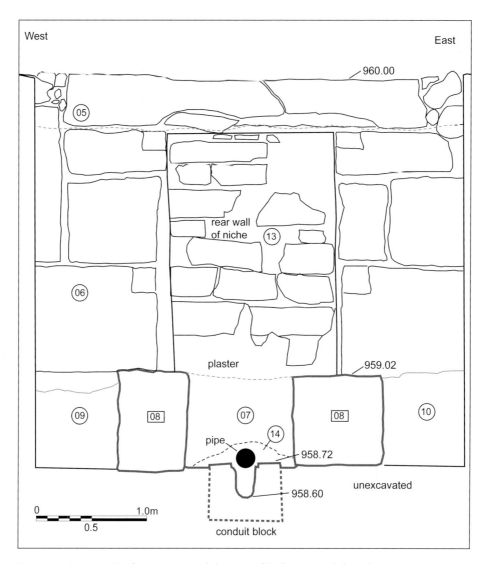

FIG. 5.38 *Reservoir/Pool no. 63, sectional elevation of Probe 3 at south face of reservoir.*

Bucket 87.047. 4 body, 1 base.
Bucket 87.048. 1 body.
Bucket 87.074. 1 body, 1 rim. Fragment of a flue
  tile pipe, oval in section, with heavy, projecting rim; mortar on exterior.

Locus 02 (compact light brown soil in north end
probe, to floor, 958.94 to 958.54 m asl)
  Bucket 87.075. 5 body, 1 rim, 1 base.

Probe no. 3, South of Reservoir Wall

After removal of loose surface debris (Locus 05),
the south end of Probe 3 (1.50 m east/west) was

laid out, extending 1.75 m south of the south face
of the reservoir. A long conduit block of white
sandstone lay on the surface at this point. The
loose, light brown, sandy loess below the surface
soil constituted a uniform deposit (Locus 06, from
959.72 to 959.08 m asl) containing numerous fragments of plaster and mortar, blocks tumbled from
the reservoir wall, and a large number of potsherds
dating from the first to the fifth century. The earth
fill extended into the niche in the south wall, but
the opening was concealed by rubble. Removal
of Locus 07, tumbled blocks surrounded by loose,
sandy soil, exposed two parallel, north/south lines
of neatly cut blocks (upper surface at 959.02 m asl;

Th 0.22–0.31 m, 0.40 m apart) that framed the out-flow aqueduct (Locus 08) and originally supported its cover slabs (figs. 4.10, 5.38). One thick stone slab (L 0.72 m, W 0.32 m, Th 0.20 m) had been tipped up on one edge and leaned against the face of the niche, perhaps at the time the pipe was salvaged. The sandy soil of Locus 07 extended down between the framing blocks to the marl conduit blocks of the aqueduct (upper edge 958.72 m asl), which were partly filled with a hard white mortar bearing the impression of the lead water pipe of Phase II (impression of pipe at 958.60 m asl). The coincidence of level between the outflow aqueduct and the reservoir floor (at 958.54 m asl) is another indication that the reservoir and outflow conduit belong to the same construction phase. The space between the conduit blocks and the framing blocks was sealed with mortar. A sandstone covering slab was found in position at the south end of the probe, with four similar slabs stacked on top of it. The slabs were probably disturbed at the time the lead pipe was torn out. Two virtually identical markings had been cut into the west edge of the conduit, one on the conduit block just outside the niche and the second on the conduit block at the south end of the probe (see fig. 5.61, inset box). The mark or symbol resembles the letter M with a crossbar joining the feet and central angle, the crossbar towards the channel, the peaks oriented to the west. The sign most likely represents a horned altar or an abbreviated betyl. It is less likely but at least possible that the marks are schematised representations of a *chorobates*, used to level the aqueduct outflow conduit. This device, carefully described by Vitruvius (8.5.1–3) as a tool for level-ling water channels, consisted of a long plank with central groove used as a water level and four legs supported by diagonal bracers, in front of which swung plumb bobs (Adam 1994: 17–19; Dilke 1971: 74–76). Perhaps the marks indicated the point at which the surveyor placed the feet of the *chorobates* to calculate the downhill slope.

The blocks framing the aqueduct held back a stratum of loose, light brown, sandy loess contain-ing numerous cobbles — possibly constituting a cobble pavement, although another cobbled sur-face appeared below at the base of the west course of framing stones. The fill west of the west curb

(Locus 09) consisted of a soft, sandy soil containing first- through possibly third- or fourth-century ce-ramics. The harder, light brown soil packed around the upper edge of the east framing slabs (Locus 10) contained ceramics of the later first century BC to the later first century AD.

At the south end of the probe, a stratum of much harder, pebbly, brown soil originally ex-tended across the last visible 1 m of the aqueduct; it seems to have been cut through at the time the pipe was salvaged. The upper portion of this deposit (Locus 11, 959.40 to 959.01 m asl) has a relatively flat upper surface and may represent a surviving ancient surface level, since it is coincident with the boundary between weathered and unweathered stones along the south wall of the reservoir. The deposit contained first- through fourth-century ceramics. Below it, a similar deposit of hard pebbly soil (Locus 12, 959.01 to 958.84 m asl) extends down to the level of cobbles framing the west side of the aqueduct, adjacent to the stacked cover slabs. This locus contained a small amount of first-century ceramics.

Removal of the rubble and fill in the upper levels of the southern half of Probe 3 allowed excavation of the fill in the niche built into the south reservoir wall (W 0.64 m, H 1.06 m, depth ca. 0.68 m). From the bottom surface of the two east/west roofing slabs (959.84 m asl) to the hard clay packing around the bronze stopcock (958.77 m asl), the niche was filled with a loose, light brown, sandy loess (Locus 13), apparently part of the same deposit as Locus 06 and containing a rich deposit of first- through fourth-century sherds, as well as possibly some of the seventh century. Numerous sandstone cobbles were piled on top of the stop-cock. Four notches (0.08 × 0.08 × 0.08 m) were cut into the upper, outside corner of the highest and lowest blocks framing the niche opening, probably to mount a hinged, locked grating that restricted access to the stopcock in Phase II (figs. 4.10, 5.38). A tethering hole has been cut through the corner of one block on the west side of the niche. Perhaps in Phase I animals were tied up here while the owners filled containers in their panniers with water from the overflow conduit. The side and back walls of the niche were plastered with a crumbly, grey plaster, which has fallen away in large patches, exposing the smaller, partly trimmed blocks (H 0.065–0.09 m) forming the north wall. This back wall is slightly concave.

Removal of the loose cobbles at the bottom of Locus 13 revealed the top of the bronze stopcock and the last surviving section of lead pipe, connected to the stopcock pipe by a lead collar reinforced with a fine, hard, white plaster (figs. 5.35–36). The stopcock (1987.106.01 ; L 0.296 m, H 0.118 m, valve D 0.088–0.074 m; pp. 332–33; figs. 6.5–6) was cast in bronze. The pipe (1987.106.02; L 0.325 m, outside D 0.055–0.044 m), which only abutted the stopcock pipe, was made of a narrow lead sheet rolled around a mandrel and soldered along the 0.008 m overlap (1987.106.02; p. 334, figs. 6.7–6.8). Either as part of the waterproofing of the joint with the stopcock or as reinforcement for the very rough longitudinal seam, the pipe was surrounded with a layer of the same hard white plaster, wrapped or shaped with roughly woven woollen cloth that has left its impression on the plaster. The valve plug (now lost) had been removed from the stopcock when the lead pipe was put out of service in Phase III, the plug socket filled with small stones and mortar, and the stopcock surrounded by a packing of cobbles set in a very hard, red-brown clay soil (Locus 14, 958.77 to 958.62 m asl). There was a scatter of very small sherds in this packing, mostly coarse wares; the dateable material belongs to the first and early second century.

Removal of the stopcock and pipe revealed that a sandstone conduit block with a channel slightly wider than normal (W ca. 0.14 m) had been installed on the floor of the niche (conduit channel at 958.62 m asl). This mounting block may have been installed during the Phase II alterations, since the north end is incorporated in the packing filling the hole hacked through the reservoir wall. If this conduit block belonged to Phase I, it would have served to catch the overflow from the reservoir and conduct it to the outflow aqueduct. A small, high-walled basin would have served this purpose better, however, and perhaps such a basin was removed during excavation of the hole for the pipe, then the conduit block installed and trimmed to hold the stopcock in position. The small amount of clay-like fill on which the stopcock was installed (Locus 15) produced first- and second-century ceramics. A

soil sample (Bucket 87.161) was taken from inside the pipe through the reservoir wall (Locus 16); it consisted of lenses of a fine grey clay with bubbles and a few sand inclusions.

Locus 05 (light brown, loessial soil from surface, 960.00 to 959.72 m asl)

Bucket 87.062. 7 body. 1 rim.
Bucket 87.063. 1 body.

Locus 06 (light brown sandy loess, 959.72 to 959.08 m asl; fig. 5.39)

Bucket 87.064. 259 body, 15 rim, 40 handle, 11 base. A varied assortment of wares.

64.1. NFW rocker-decorated bowl: fine, hard, slightly sandy, red (2.5YR 5/6) fabric with a few white inclusions. D 0.14 m? *EZ* II fig. 62, Phase 3b (70–100).

64.2. Cooking pot: hard, sandy, red (2.5YR 4/8) fabric with white grits. Exterior fire blackened to very dark grey (2.5YR 3/0). Gerber 2001a: fig. 3c; *EZ* I fig. 733 no. 6, fig. 739 no. 12 (300–363).

64.3. Cooking pot: fine, hard red (2.5YR 6/8) clay with a few white inclusions. *EZ* I fig. 733 no. 6 (last quarter 4C–ea. 5C).

64.4. Lid: hard, granular, reddish yellow (5YR 7/6) clay with numerous white grits and bubbles. Exterior of rim fire blackened to dark grey (5YR 4/1). D 0.12 m?

64.5. Cooking pot: hard, sandy, very pale brown (10YR 7/3) fabric with black and white grits and bubbles. Brown (7.5YR 5/4) exterior surface. *EZ* I fig. 732 no. 5 (last quarter 4C–ea. 5C); Parker 1987: fig. 100 no. 82 (284–363), fig. 94 no. 33 (ea. 4C).

64.6. Jug (?): hard, slightly sandy, red (2.5YR 5/8) fabric with a few white grits and bubbles.

64.7. Jar rim with handle: hard, sandy, light red (2.5YR 6/6) fabric with many bubbles and white grits. Light grey (5YR 6/1) surface. Gerber, Humayma: bucket 98.0105, 98.0532 (2C–3C).

64.8. Nabataean cream ware jug: very fine, soft, white (5Y 8/2) fabric with a few dark grits. 'Amr 1992: fig. 4 (1C–ea. 2C).

64.9. Jug?: hard, fairly fine, light grey (2.5Y 6/0) fabric with a few large black and white

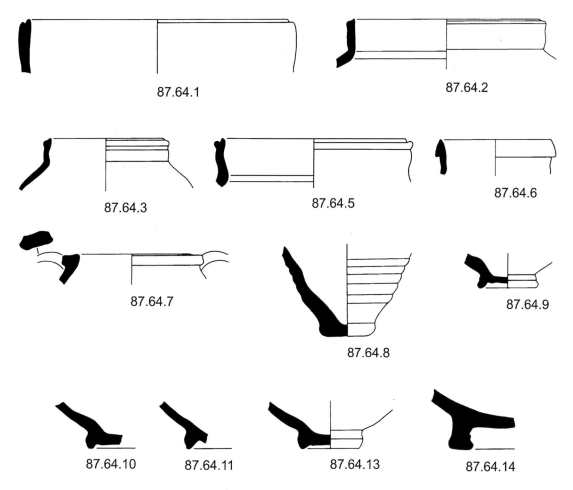

FIG. 5.39 *Reservoir/Pool no. 63, ceramics from Probe 3, Locus 6 (scale 1:2).*

grits. Reddish brown (2.5YR 5/4) surfaces. Base D 0.03 m. (1C– ea. 2C?).

64.10. NFW jug: hard, sandy, red (2.5YR 5/6) fabric with many white grits and bubbles. Grey (2.5YR 6/0) core and light grey (2.5Y 7/2) exterior surface. Bikai and Perry 2001: fig. 8.9 (20–100).

64.11. Jug (?): fabric as 64.10, but exterior grey (10YR 5/1).

64.12. Jug (?): hard, sandy, dark grey (10YR 4/1) fabric with many white grits.

64.13. Jug (?): joins 64.10. Base D 0.03 m.

64.14. Jar (?): medium soft, slightly sandy, light red (2.5YR 6/8) fabric with many bubbles and white grits. Pale red (2.5YR 6/2) core.

Locus 07 (loose, sandy soil above and between conduit framing blocks, 959.08 to 958.60 m asl; fig. 5.40)

Bucket 87.065. 42 body, 2 rim, 1 handle, 1 base. NFW bowls (1–ea. 2C); jars (Gerber 2008a: fig. 22.7, 50–150; fig. 23.25, 2–3C).

Bucket 87.073. 35 body, 2 rim, 1 handle, 1 base, 1 pipe fragment. Fragments too small for convincing dating.

73.1. Cooking pot (?): hard, fairly fine, light reddish brown (5YR 6/4) fabric with occasional white inclusions. Dark grey (5YR 4/1) surface.

73.2. Pot (?): very fine, slightly chalky, light red (2.5YR 4/1) fabric.

73.3. Strap handle: very hard, sandy, light red (2.5YR 6/6) fabric. Grey (2.5YR N6/) core and surface.

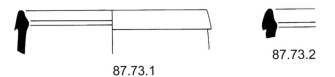

87.73.1

87.73.2

FIG. 5.40 *Reservoir/Pool no. 63, ceramics from Probe 3, Locus 7 (scale 1:2).*

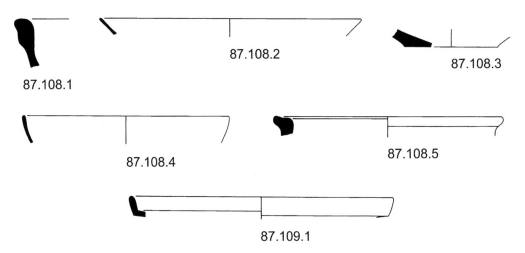

87.108.1

87.108.2

87.108.3

87.108.4

87.108.5

87.109.1

FIG. 5.41 *Reservoir/Pool no. 63, ceramics from Probe 3, Locus 9 (scale 1:2).*

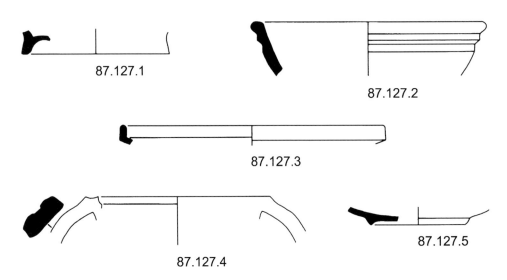

87.127.1

87.127.2

87.127.3

87.127.4

87.127.5

FIG. 5.42 *Reservoir/Pool no. 63, ceramics from Probe 3, Locus 10 (scale 1:2).*

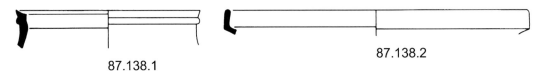

87.138.1

87.138.2

FIG. 5.43 *Reservoir/Pool no. 63, ceramics from Probe 3, Locus 12 (scale 1:2).*

Locus 09 (soft, sandy soil west of conduit framing blocks, 958.95 to 958.70 m asl; fig. 5.41)

Bucket 87.108 67 body, 5 rim, 1 handle, 1 base. Very small sherds. T. Parker (oral communication) identified all the definers as first-century, except 1 possible fourth-century rim (108.01).

108.1. Jar: hard, sandy, grey (5YR 5/1) fabric with frequent white inclusions. Reddish yellow (5YR 6/6) core. Gerber 2001b: fig. 1.19 (2–3C); 2008: no. 32 (Byzantine).

108.2. NFW bowl: hard, slightly sandy, red (2.5YR 5/8) fabric. Light reddish brown (2.5YR 6/4) surface.

108.3. NFW bowl: hard, light red (2.5YR 6/6) fabric with a few white inclusions and bubbles. Base D 0.05 m.

108.4. NFW bowl: very hard, fine, light red (2.5YR 6/6) fabric with some very small bubbles. Light grey exterior surface (5YR 6/1). D 0.11 m?

108.5. Bowl (?): very hard, fine, reddish yellow (5YR 6/6) fabric. D 0.12 m?

Bucket 87.109. 43 body, 1 rim, 1 handle. Very small sherds, mostly first-century NFW bowls. 1 Nabataean cream ware sherd with graffito decoration, white slip (1C–ea. 2C).

109.1. NFW bowl: very fine, reddish yellow (5YR 7/6) fabric with light red (2.5YR 6/6) surface. D 0.14 m. *EZ* I fig. 654, Phase 3 (1C).

Locus 10 (light brown, compact soil around cobbles east of conduit framing blocks, 959.04 to 958.92 m asl)

Bucket 87.127. 22 body, 3 rim, 1 handle, 2 base. All seem to be first-century (fig. 5.42)

127.1. Small jug (?) or bowl: fine, chalky, reddish yellow (5YR 7/6) fabric; ring base. Base D 0.08 m. Cf. Bikai and Perry 2001: figs. 5.1, 6.3 (20 BC–AD 80).

127.2. Bowl, with sharp V-grooves below rim on exterior: slightly sandy, reddish yellow (7.5YR 6/6) fabric. Very pale brown (10YR 7/3) surface. D 0.12 m. *EZ* II fig. 109, Phases 1 (100–50 BC) and 2a (50 BC–AD 20)

127.3. NFW bowl: very fine, red (2.5YR 5/8) fabric. Light reddish brown (2.5YR 6/4) core. (1C). D 0.14 m.

127.4. NFW jar or pot: strap handle and part of rim. Fine, reddish yellow (5YR 6/6) fabric. Light red (10R 6/8) surface. D 0.10 m. (1C).

127.5. NFW bowl: very fine, reddish yellow (5YR 7/6) fabric with smudge of grey at core. Bikai and Perry 2001: fig. 9.4 (20–100).

Locus 11 (hard packed brown soil in southwest corner of probe, 959.40 to 959.01 m asl)

Bucket 87.130. 81 body, 3 rim, 3 handle. 20 sherds of NFW bowls, Phase 2a–2b (20 BC–AD 20). 1 Nabataean cream ware jug (1–ea. 2C).

Locus 12 (hard packed, pebbly brown soil in southwest corner of probe, 959.01 to 958.69 m asl; fig. 5.43)

Bucket 87.138. 43 body. 2 rim. 1 handle. 2 base. Nothing looks later than first century.

138.1. Cup or pot: very fine, hard, pink (5YR 7/4) fabric. Light red (2.5YR 6/6) surface. D 0.10 m.

138.2. NFW bowl: very fine, hard, light red (2.5YR 6/8) fabric. Light reddish brown surface. D 0.16 m. *EZ* I fig. 654; Phase 3 (20–100).

138.3. Handle: hard, slightly sandy red (2.5YR 5/6) fabric. Reddish brown (2.5YR 3/4) surface.

Bucket 87.140. 22 body, 1 rim, 2 base. According to K. Russell (oral communication) the latest sherd in the group is second-century.

Locus 13 (loose, light brown sandy soil in niche in south reservoir wall, 959.84 to 958.77 m asl; fig. 5.44)

Bucket 87.083. 61 body, 4 rim, 4 handle, 3 base.

Bucket 87.084. 156 body, 14 rim, 22 handle, 6 base. Bone fragments, 1 shell fragment, 2 pieces of a polished slab of shelly Ma'an limestone.

84.1. Jar: hard, sandy, red (2.5YR 4/8) fabric with numerous holes, soft red and white inclusions. Pink (7.5YR 4/8) exterior surface. D 0.12 m. Cf. 'Amr et al. 1998: fig. 32.8, Early Islamic (7C).

84.2. Flue tile rim (?): hard, slightly sandy,

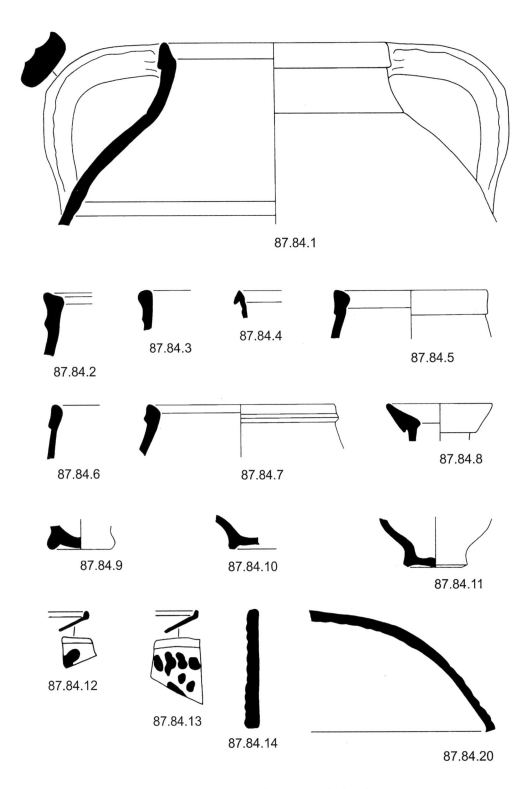

FIG. 5.44 *Reservoir/Pool no. 63, ceramics from Probe 3, Locus 13 (scale 1:2).*

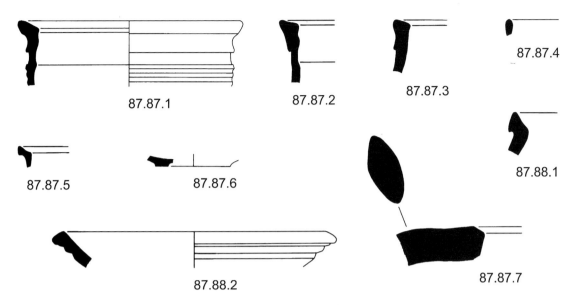

FIG. 5.45 *Reservoir/Pool no. 63, ceramics from Probe 3, Locus 14 (scale 1:2).*

yellowish red (5YR 5/8) fabric. Outer surface possibly slipped white (10YR 8/2).

84.3. Nabataean cream ware jug: fine, light yellowish brown (10YR 6/4) fabric shading to very pale brown (10YR 8/3) on exterior surface (1C–1st half 2C).

84.4. Cooking pot: hard, sandy, dark brown (7.5YR 4/2) fabric with some white inclusions. Dark grey (7.5YR 4/0) surfaces.

84.5. Jar: sandy, laminar, brown (7.5YR 5/4) fabric with white specks. Light red (2.5YR 6/8) core. Gerber, Humayma 98.0305, 98.0532 (2C–3C).

84.6. Jar: fabric as 84.5.

84.7. Jar: sandy, red (2.5YR 5/8) fabric with a few white inclusions. Very pale brown (10YR 8/3) exterior surface.

84.8. NFW jug: very fine, medium hard, strong brown (7.5YR 5/6) fabric. D 0.055 m. *EZ* II, fig. 330–332; Phases 3b–c (1C–ea. 2C).

84.9. Base: fabric as 84.5. Exterior possibly slipped pink (7.5YR 8/4). Base D 0.038 m.

84.10. Base: sandy, hard, grey (7.5YR 5/0) fabric. Outer edge yellowish red (5YR 5/6). Base D 0.03 m.

84.11. Base: hard, coarse, sandy, reddish brown (5YR 4/4) fabric with numerous white specks and bubbles. Base D 0.035 m.

84.12. NPFW bowl: very fine, red (2.5YR 5/6) fabric. Dark reddish brown (2.5YR 2.5/4) paint. *EZ* II fig. 92–94; Phases 3c–4 (100–4C).

84.13. NPFW bowl: fabric as 84.12, but dark grey core (2.5YR 3/0). The 8 other bowl sherds could be from this or other vessels. *EZ* II fig. 94; Phase 4 (2C–4C).

84.14. NFW vertically grooved strap handle: sandy, yellowish red (5YR 5/8) fabric with a few white inclusions and bubbles. *EZ* II fig. 314 (20–100); Bikai and Perry 2001: fig. 8.14 (20–100).

84.20. Cooking pot lid, or casserole: hard, sandy, pink (7.5YR 8/4) fabric with many bubbles. Pale yellowish (5Y 8/3) slipped surface. 'Amr and Schick 2001: no. 24 (casserole)(mid-7C); Dolinka 2003: 124 no. 13 (lid)(ea. 2C); Parker 1987: fig. 96.52, fig. 97.55–62 (casseroles and lids)(4C).

Locus 14 (compact red-brown soil around pipe and valve, 958.77 to 958.62 m asl; fig. 5.45)

Bucket 87.087. 44 body, 5 rim, 3 handle, 1 base.

87.1. NFW jar: hard, gritty, red (2.5YR 5/8) fabric. D 0.12 m. *EZ* II fig. 310; Phase 3b (70–100); Bikai and Perry 2001: fig. 8.14 (20–100)

87.2. Bowl or jar: coarse, sandy, light red (2.5YR 6/6) fabric containing much white sand, white inclusions, and bubbles. Interior surface pale red (2.5YR 6/2). D 0.14 m?

87.3. Flue tile (?) rim: coarse, sandy, light red (2.5YR 6/6) fabric containing much white sand, white inclusions, and bubbles. D 0.11 m?

87.4. NFW bowl: very fine, light red (2.5YR 6/6) fabric. Very pale brown (10YR 8/3) slip on outside of rim (1–2C).

87.5. NFW jar: fabric as 87.4. *EZ* II fig. 344; Phase 3b (70–100).

87.6. NFW bowl: very fine, reddish yellow (5YR 7/6) fabric (1C).

87.7. Handle: very sandy, laminar, yellowish red (5YR 5/8) fabric with clear sand grains. Dark brown (7.5YR 4/2) surface.

Bucket 87.088. 30 body, 3 rim, 1 handle. Mostly storage and cooking wares.

88.1. Jug: hard, sandy, light red (2.5YR 6/6) fabric with a few small white inclusions. Reddish brown (2.5YR 5/4) surface. Cf. *EZ* II, fig. 314 (20–100).

88.2. Nabataean cream ware jug, with sharply tooled grooves and ridges on exterior below rim: slightly sandy, light reddish brown (5YR 6/4) fabric with pink (5YR 7/4) surface. D 0.14 m? 'Amr 1992: fig. 1 (1C–ea. 2C).

88.3. Strap handle: very sandy, rough, light red (2.5YR 6/6) fabric with numerous cavities and white inclusions. Surface dark grey (2.5YR 4/0).

Locus 15 (compact red-brown soil below stopcock, 958.65 to 958.57 m asl)

Bucket 87.106. 4 body. Parker (oral communication) identifies as MN and ER wares; K. Russell (oral communication) assigns to first/second century.

Locus 16 (plaster from joint between stopcock and lead pipe)

Bucket 87.180. Very light brown (less than 10YR 8/2), friable, light-weight plaster containing a moderate amount of well-sorted, sub-rounded sand, frequent bubbles, large nodules of lime, and the casts of vegetable temper.

5.E.4. *Reservoir/Pool no. 63, Probe no. 4*

Probes 4 and 5 were laid out to trace the course of the terracotta pipeline found in Probe 2, Probe 4 around the northwest corner of the reservoir, and Probe 5 adjacent to the north wall halfway between the northwest corner and the aqueduct (fig. 5.25). Probe 4 (1.50 m east/west, 2.0 m north/south) also exposed a portion of the northwest corner (0.30 × 1.0 m) of the structure. The brown, sandy soil forming the present surface, more or less even with the top of the reservoir wall (top of course 7, at 960.21 m asl), slopes away from the corner to the north and west. Removal of the surface soil (Locus 01) revealed a layer of compacted brown soil mixed with cobbles (Locus 02), which represents the same deposit as Locus 06 in Probe 2 to the south, including first- through fourth-century wares and some metal corrosion products. The soil of Locus 02, compacted by traffic and water spills during use of the reservoir, extends from 0.26 to 0.92 m below the top of the wall (959.95 to 959.29 m asl), enveloping the upper offset of the west reservoir wall also revealed in Probe 2 (at 959.87 m asl). Only the upper portion of this locus was removed. The terracotta pipeline (Locus 04) was uncovered 1 m west of the reservoir wall, curving neatly around the northwest corner, 0.58 m below the top of the reservoir wall, sloping markedly toward the south (959.63 to 959.56 m asl; fig. 5.46). The pipe appears to have been laid in a trench cut into Locus 02, then — unlike the situation in Probe 2 — backfilled with the same material and well compacted (cf. fig. 5.50). Although the trench was poorly defined, the soil within 0.15 m of the pipe was isolated as Locus 03. The only dateable sherd recovered belongs to the first or early second century. The six completely exposed and two partly exposed pipe sections were the same design as those in Probe 2, varying between 0.25 to 0.28 m in length, joint to joint (north to south: L > 0.10, 0.25, 0.26, 0.25, 0.28, 0.25, 0.28, > 0.19 m). Cleaning holes had been pecked into the third and sixth pipe sections from the north and sealed with body sherds set in mortar.

Locus 00 (brown, sandy surface soil, 960.15 to 960.12 m asl)

FIG. 5.46 *Reservoir/Pool no. 63, pipeline in Probe 4.*

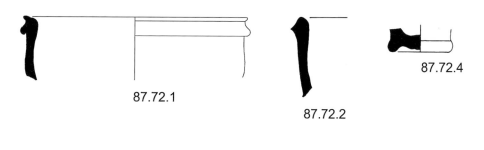

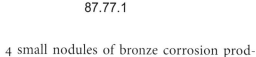

FIG. 5.47 *Reservoir/Pool no. 63, ceramics from Probe
4, Locus 2 (nos. 72.1-4) and Locus 3 (no. 77.1)
(scale 1:2).*

Bucket 87.070. body. 3 rim, 1 handle, 1 base. Nabataean cream ware jug with filter neck (1–ea. 2C); NFW bowls (1–ea. 2C); mortarium with very heavy black temper (2C?).

Locus 01 (slightly harder, brown soil, 960.12 to 959.92 m asl)

Locus 02 (compact brown soil with frequent cobbles, 959.92 to 959.29 m asl; fig. 5.47)

Bucket 87.071. 73 body, 4 rim, 8 handle, 4 base. Fragments of juglets with string-cut bases (1C), jar (Gerber 2008a: fig. 22.4, 50–150).

4 small nodules of bronze corrosion products.

Bucket 87.072. 34 body, 2 rim, 3 handle, 1 base. Many ridged cooking pot sherds. K. 'Amr (oral communication) dates a yellowish sherd fifth- to sixth-century. 7 small (D 0.005–0.01 m) nodules of iron and bronze corrosion products. 1 shell fragment.

72.1. Cooking pot: fine, hard, slightly sandy, light red (10R 6/6) fabric shading to pink (7.5YR 8/4) on interior surface. A few bubbles. Exterior surface pinkish grey

FIG. 5.48 *Reservoir/Pool no. 63, pipeline in Probe 5.*

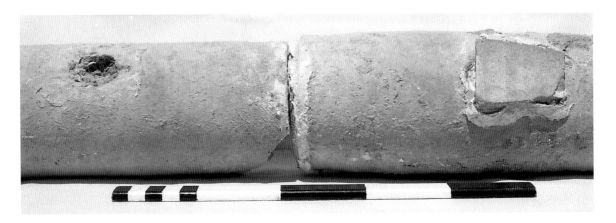

FIG. 5.49 *Reservoir/Pool no. 63: pipes in Probe 5, view of cleaning holes with and without covering sherds.*

(7.5YR 7/2). D 0.12 m. Gerber 2008a: no. 25 (Byzantine); cf. *EZ* I fig. 729 (last quarter 4C–ea. 5C).

72.2. Cooking pot (?): fabric as 72.1. Gerber 1997: fig. 7 (2nd half 1C–ea. 2C).

72.3. ETSA body sherd (very small): very fine, light red (2.5YR 6/6) fabric with slightly glossy, red (2.5YR 5/8) slip. *EZ* I: 133 (1C–1st half 2nd C).

72.4. Small jug or bottle base: fine, hard, pinkish grey (7.5YR 7/2) fabric. Base D 0.03 m. (1C).

Locus 03 (compact brown soil around terracotta pipe, 959.63 to 959.56 m asl; fig. 5.47)

Bucket 87.077. 27 body, 1 rim, 1 handle. 1 iron hobnail head (D 0.01 m, L 0.015 m), 1 fragment bronze finial (L 0.015 m). The sherds were mostly NFW bowl fragments.

77.1. NFW pot: very fine, light red (2.5YR 6/6) fabric; surface slipped pink (7.5YR 8/4). D 0.09 m. *EZ* II fig. 271, Phases 3b–3c (70–2C).

Bucket 87.133. 2 body. The 2 sherds were used as covers on the access holes in the pipes.

5.E.5. *Reservoir/Pool no. 63, Probe no. 5*

Probe 5 (1.25 m east/west, 1.0 m north/south) was laid out approximately midway between the northwest corner of the reservoir and the west wall of the aqueduct, 1.30 to 2.30 m north of the north reservoir wall, to trace the course of the terracotta pipeline found in Probe 4 (figs. 5.25, 5.48). The brown sandy topsoil (Locus 01) sloped gently to the north. Locus 02 below it, like Locus 02 in Probe 4, consisted of a compacted brown soil containing numerous sherds dating from the first to the fourth century, representing the working surface during use of the reservoir. A trench approximately 0.10 m deep was cut into this deposit, and untrimmed field stones were packed roughly as protection above the terracotta pipeline (Locus 04), which is aligned east/west at this point (top surface at 959.78 m asl; figs. 5.48, 5.50). The soil filling the trench (Locus 03) is backfill from its excavation, but containing numerous sherds from pipe sections that apparently had been broken and replaced. Locus 02 was excavated slightly below the level of the pipeline and two pipe sections were removed and catalogued (1987.114.01, 02; L 0.30

m, D 0.082 m; see pp. 330–31, fig. 6.4). The pipes, most of which had cleaning holes covered with potsherds (fig. 5.49), seem to date to the second century AD.

Locus 01 (brown, sandy surface soil, 960.37 to 959.95 m asl)

Bucket 87.090. 50 body, 8 rim, 1 base, 1 handle. NPFW bowl (Phase 3b, 1C); NFW bowls (1C); pipe fragments. 2 bronze and 2 iron tacks. Glass bowl rim. Bronze clipping.

Locus 02 (compact brown soil with occasional cobbles, 959.95 to 959.70 m asl; fig. 5.51)

Bucket 87.092. 80 body, 4 rim, 1 base. Numerous sherds of NPFW bowls. Iron hobnail.

92.1. Offset pipe rim: coarse, granular, reddish yellow (5YR 6/8) fabric. Very pale brown (10YR 7/3) surface. D 0.10 m. Cf. 87.114 (2C).

92.2. Bowl: fine, reddish yellow (5YR 6/8) fabric. D 0.07 m. *EZ* II fig. 157, Phase 3b–c (late 1C–2C).

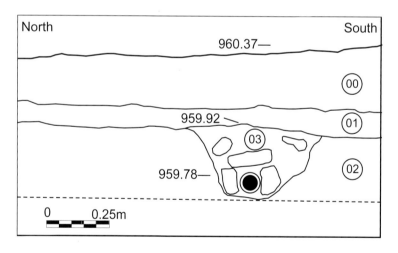

FIG. 5.50 *Reservoir/Pool no. 63, section across pipeline in Probe 5.*

FIG. 5.51 *Reservoir/Pool no. 63, ceramics from Probe 5, Locus 2 (scale 1:2).*

FIG. 5.52 *Reservoir/Pool no. 63, Probe 7 from the north.*

92.3. Jug: gritty, yellowish red (5YR 5/6) fabric with white specks. Reddish brown (5YR 5/3) core. *EZ* II, fig. 343, Phase 3b (70–100l).

92.4. NFW bowl: fine, yellowish red (5YR 5/8) fabric with a few very small white specks (1C).

92.5. NPFW bowl body sherd: slightly granular, grey (5YR 6/1) fabric. Reddish yellow (5YR 7/6) exterior surface, with palmette in reddish grey (5YR 5/2) slip paint. *EZ* II, fig. 185, Phase 3a (20–70).

Locus 03 (brown soil and stone packing around pipe 04, 959.92 to 959.78 m asl; fig. 6.4)

Bucket 87.104. 23 body (mostly pipe), 4 rim (incl. 3 pipe).

Bucket 87.114. 2 terracotta pipe sections.

114.1. Pipe: hard, slightly sandy, red (10YR 5/8) fabric containing much clear quartz sand and a few white specks. Pp. 330–31, cat. no. 1987.114.01. Cf. ʿAmr and al-Momani 2001: 270, fig. 24 (2C).

114.2. Pipe: fabric as 114.1. Pp. 330–31, cat. no. 1987.114.02.

Locus 04 (brown soil inside pipe 1987.114.01)

Bucket 87.115. Soil sample (see pp. 358–59).

5.E.6. *Reservoir/Pool no. 63, Probe no. 6*

Probe 6 (1.5 × 1.5 m) was laid out approximately in the centre of the reservoir to determine whether the floor extended across the whole structure at the same level revealed in Probes 1 and 3 (fig. 4.5). The surface soil (Locus 01) consisted of sterile, light brown sandy loess with pebbles (surface to –0.20 m, 959.37 to 959.17 m asl). Locus 02 was a very compact, silty light brown soil containing only 3 sherds. The reservoir floor was exposed at 958.50 m asl, the same level as in Probes 1 (958.48 m asl) and 3 (958.54 m asl). Here, too, the floor was constructed of flat fieldstones set in mortar and covered with a hard, sandy, white plaster. In 2001, the Department of Antiquities cleared all remaining fill from the reservoir and consolidated the entire structure.

Locus 02 (earth fill from 959.17 m to floor, 959.50)

Bucket 87.085. 2 body, 1 handle, 1 sherd possibly red-gloss ware (2C).

5.E.7. *Reservoir/Pool no. 63, Probe no. 7*

Probe 7 (3.0 m east/west × 2.5 m north/south) was laid out over and west of the aqueduct, at its projected intersection with the pipeline exposed in Probe 5 (ca. 2.8 m north of north reservoir wall; fig. 5.25). Unfortunately, the area of intersection had been badly disturbed by ploughing and stone robbing, but traces of a plaster-lined tank were found, mediating between the aqueduct and the pipeline (fig. 5.52). The aqueduct structure itself has been lost to ploughing at the north end of the probe. One conduit block was found apparently dislodged 0.50 m from its original position and rotated to an east/west orientation. It is possible that this conduit in fact was at the head of the conduit diversion channel found outside the east wall of the pool, but the context is too disturbed to allow any clear interpretation. The light brown sandy surface soil was mixed with stones and roots, but contained numerous sherds of a large variety of wares.

The harder, more compact and darker brown soil below the surface was excavated as Locus 02. It contained essentially the same ceramic sample as Locus 01 and constituted the fill built up around the aqueduct and associated features as they were in use. A deposit of reddish brown sand exposed in the southeast corner of the probe (960.22 m asl) was labelled Locus 03, but left unexcavated. Clearing of Locus 02 west of the aqueduct channel, at the point where it has been lost to robbing and at the projected intersection with the pipeline, revealed a packing or fall of rubble labelled Locus 04. Removal of Locus 04 exposed a deposit of loose, reddish brown sandy fill (Locus 05) containing fragments of broken pipe sections. Two intact pipe sections (Locus 06, top at 960.04 m asl) were found in position at the west edge of the probe. The disturbance in this area may be quite recent, since a fragment of plastic was found in the fill. Unfortunately, the pipeline is lost between this point and the aqueduct channel (1.60 m W); the only features possibly in their original position in the intervening area are two untrimmed, flat field stones 0.21 m lower than the level of the adjacent surviving conduit block (channel at 960.41 m asl). These slabs may represent the floor of a small tank that fed the pipeline, connected to the aqueduct

87.105.1   87.105.2

FIG. 5.53 *Reservoir/Pool no. 63, ceramics from Probe 7, Locus 4 (scale 1:2).*

flow by a simple sluice gate. The context is too damaged to allow any certainty about the design or the chronology of the connection.

Locus 01 (light brown sandy soil, surface to −0.22 m, 960.29 m asl)

    Bucket 87.098. 73 body, 5 rim, 2 handle. Cook pot, *EZ* I fig. 755 no. 28 (4C). 1 oyster shell. 1 iron tack. 1 brick.

    Bucket 87.116. 19 body.

    Bucket 87.117. 37 body, 6 rim, 8 handle. Mostly very heavy wares, some NFW bowls and juglets (1C).

    Bucket 87.119. 47 body, 2 rim, 4 handle, 3 base. Base of Aqaba amphora (7C).

Locus 02 (compact brown soil, 960.29 to 960.13 m asl)

    Bucket 87.096. 58 body, 7 rim, 15 handle, 2 base. NFW bowl (1C); horn from ibex figurine, curved with serrated front edge; cf. *EZ* I fig. 874 (4–5C), ʿAmr and Momani 1999: fig. 7.2 (2C?). 2 bones. 1 iron tack. 1 lump bronze. 1 fragment glass.

    Bucket 87.120. 57 body, 7 handle, 3 base. Very small, worn sherds.

Locus 04 (disturbed stone packing around east end of pipeline, 960.06 m asl; fig. 5.53)

    Bucket 87.105. 5 body, 2 rim. 1 body sherd of Nabataean cream ware (1C–ea. 2C).

    105.1. NFW jar: hard, slightly sandy, red (2.5YR 5/6) fabric. Gerber 1994: fig. 16.G (ea. 2C).

    105.2. NFW unguentarium: very fine, slightly chalky, light red (2.5YR 6/8) fabric. *EZ* II fig. 316, Phase 3a–b (20–100).

Locus 05 (loose reddish sand fill around pipe, 960.13 to 959.92 m asl)

    Bucket 87.118. 55 body, 3 rim, 14 handle, 2 base. 8 sherds most likely from broken pipe sec-

FIG. 5.54 *Reservoir/Pool no. 63, conduit in Probe 8.*

tions 1 lump of iron corrosion. Very coarse wares.

5.E.8. *Reservoir/Pool no. 63, Probe no. 8*

Probes 8 through 12 were laid out around the south end of the reservoir, along the projected courses of the outflow aqueduct identified in Probe 3 and the terracotta pipeline identified in Probe 02 (fig. 4.5). The objective was documentation of their courses, design, and any possible intersection or interrelationship. The aqueduct was exposed in Probes 8, 11, and 12, the pipeline in Probes 9 and 10.

Probe 8 (1.5 m east/west, 1.0 m north/south) was laid out 6.2 m south of the south face of the reservoir, straddling the projected line of the outflow channel identified in Probe 3. The fill from the surface (at 959.53 m asl) to the top of the conduit blocks (958.62 m asl) was composed of a compact light brown soil with occasional pebbles and the typical mix of small, worn potsherds dating from the first through at least the late fourth century, and possibly as late as the seventh century. No stratigraphy could be distinguished, but the top 0.20 m

of soil were separated out as Locus 01 in order to isolate any recent surface contamination. Locus 02 terminated at 958.63 m asl on a slightly sandier deposit (Locus 03) that surrounded the remains of the conduit (Locus 04; fig. 5.54). Portions of two neatly-cut marl conduit blocks were exposed in the probe, surrounded on either side by rubble packing laid in the loose, reddish brown sandy soil of the original surface (Locus 05, at 958.67 m asl). The conduit blocks were 0.29 m wide, the packing visible on the west 0.29 m wide. The central water channel (W 0.10 m, 0.11 m deep) was lined with the hard, white, sandy mortar bedding for the water pipe of Phase II. The plaster extended up the sides of the channel but does not seem to have been applied systematically to the top of the block on either side. The thick layer of mortar at the bottom of the channel carries the impression of the lead pipe, torn out for salvage; one fragment was recovered (Bucket 87.128). The base of the pipe setting (958.50 m asl) is 0.10 m below the level of the pipe setting in Probe 3.

FIG. 5.55 *Reservoir/Pool no. 63, southwest corner of Reservoir and pipeline in Probe 9.*

Locus 01 (compact light brown soil with occasional pebbles, surface to –0.20 m, 959.53 to 959.33 m asl)

> Bucket 87.107. 40 body, 5 rim, 3 handle, 1 base. NFW bowls (1C); lamp.

Locus 02 (compact light brown soil with occasional pebbles, 959.33 to 958.63 m asl)

> Bucket 87.126*bis.* 169 body, 12 rim, 17 handle, 4 base. 9 oyster shells, 1 fragment glass jar base, 1 scrap bronze, 1 rodent skull. Many fragments of NFW bowls (1–2C); Nabataean juglet with string-cut peg foot (1C); ledge rim casserole (Gerber 1994: fig. 16.1, 100); jug (*EZ* I fig. 822 no. 95, 100–150); small lamp fragment (probably *EZ* III pl. I no. 1.5, 100–150).

Locus 03 (slightly sandy light brown soil, 958.63 to 958.60 m asl)

> Bucket 87.128. 92 body, 7 rim, 4 handle, 4 base. NPFW bowl (Phase 3a, 20 BC–AD 20); many fragments NFW bowls (1C). Nabataean cream ware jug (1–ea. 2C). 5 oyster shells. 1 fragment lead sheet.

5.E.9. *Reservoir/Pool no. 63, Probe no. 9*

Probe 9 (2.20 m east/west, 1.5 m north/south) was laid out over the southwest corner of the reservoir in order to document the construction of the corner and to determine whether the terracotta pipeline traced in Probes 2, 4, 5, and 7 continued south along the west side of the reservoir (fig. 4.5). The loose, pebbly, light brown surface soil (Locus 01) extended up to the top of the wall, which is preserved to course 6 at this point. Below the larger rubble, a sloping stratum of slightly darker brown, loose soil was designated Locus 02. Removal of this stratum exposed the compact, reddish brown sandy soil forming the original ground level (Locus 03) sloping gently away from the reservoir wall (top surface 959.33 to 959.25 m asl). Scraping of this level at the west end of the probe exposed the pipeline (Locus 04, top surface at 959.23 m asl), which had been laid in an irregular shallow trench cut into Locus 03 and backfilled with the same soil (fig. 5.55). Six pipe sections (L ca. 0.30 m) were exposed, following an irregular bearing of approximately 200 degrees, 0.88 m west of the west reservoir wall, their

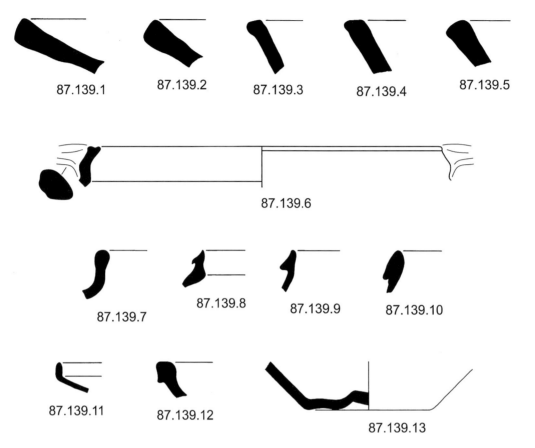

FIG. 5.56 *Reservoir/Pool no. 63, ceramics from Probe 9, Locus 2 (scale 1:2).*

joints heavily smeared with a hard, sandy, white mortar. The top surface of the two northernmost pipes had been almost completely broken away, but no access holes with mortared covers could be observed. Two courses of heavy, carefully finished red sandstone blocks were exposed at the corner of the reservoir, but since Locus 03 was left undisturbed, we did not expose the upper offset seen in Probes 2 and 4. A large block (Locus 06; 0.63 × 0.26 × 0.26 m) of the same material and finish had been installed up against the west wall at the corner, sitting on top of Locus 03, and chinked on its east side with small flat stones. The upper surface of the installation, which may have served as a step or seat, is at 959.67 m asl.

The many ceramic fragments found in Loci 02–03 appear to range over the whole period of Hawara's history, but with a strong concentration on the second through fifth centuries. Most of the vessels were cooking or coarse wares. Unfortunately, only a few diagnostic sherds were recovered.

Locus 01 (light brown soil with pebbles and cobbles, surface to 959.38 m asl)

Bucket 87.129. 195 body, 11 rim, 2 base. Mostly coarse wares; some large and joining sherds. String-cut juglet base (1C); NFW jug with fine zig-zag combing. 3 slot rim jars, Gerber 2001a: fig. 2P (4C–5C); *EZ* I fig. 761, no. 34 (300–363). Ledge rim saucepan, Gerber 1994: fig. 16.I (100); cook pot rim, Gerber 1994: fig. 15.T (2nd half 1C).

Locus 02 (light brown soil with pebbles, 959.38 to 959.25 m asl; fig. 5.56)

Bucket 87.139. 64 body, 10 rim, 6 handle, 1 base.

139.1. Bowl: hard, slightly sandy, yellowish red (5YR 5/8) fabric with black and white grits.
139.2. Bowl: fabric as 139.1.
139.3. Bowl: fabric as 139.1.
139.4. Bowl: fabric as 139.1.
139.5. Bowl: fabric as 139.1.

139.6. Cooking pot (?): medium hard, slightly sandy, yellowish red (5YR 5/8) fabric with some white grits. Pinkish grey core (5YR 6/2) and surface. D 0.18 m. Cf. *EZ* I fig. 732, no. 5 (last quarter 4C–ea. 5C).

139.7. Jar (?): fabric as 139.1.

139.8. Cooking pot: medium hard, sandy, light red (2.5YR 6/8) fabric with white grits. Very pale brown surface (10YR 8/3). Gerber 2008a: no. 8 (2nd half 1–1st half 2C); Bikai and Perry 2001: fig. 9.14 (20–100).

139.9. Cooking pot: hard, sandy, laminar, red (2.5YR 4/6) fabric with white grits and bubbles. Grey (2.5YR 6/0) surface. Cf. Gerber 2001a: fig. 2F (4C).

139.10. Jar (?): sandy, reddish yellow (5YR 6/6) fabric with many white and grey grits. Outside surface pinkish white (7.5YR 8/2).

139.11. NFW bowl: very fine, hard, reddish yellow (5YR 6/8) fabric. Outside surface of rim and adjacent wall dark grey (5YR 4/1); possibly slipped. *EZ* II no. 46, Phase 2a (late 1C BC).

139.12. Bowl (?): very sandy, brown (7.5YR 5/2) fabric with large white grits.

139.13. Jug (?): medium hard, sandy, yellowish red (5YR 5/8) fabric with many white grits. Base D 0.07 m. Cf. *EZ* I fig. 762, no. 35 (300–363).

5.E.10. *Reservoir/Pool no. 63, Probe no. 10*

Probe 10 (2.0 m east/west, 1.0 m north/south) was laid out west of Probe 8, 6.5 m south of the southwest corner of the reservoir, on the projected course of the terracotta pipeline exposed in Probe 9. Locus 01, extending from the surface (at 959.46 m asl) to a depth of approximately –0.92 m, consisted of a compact light brown soil with pebbles, a few cobbles, and a large amount of sherd material dating from the first through at least the third century; the definers are nearly all first- and early second-century in date. The large fragments, mix of wares, and appearance of bones and glass in a uniform soil deposit suggest that this is occupation debris carried here from elsewhere and dumped. The soil in Locus 02 (959.06 to 958.80 m asl), which also extended across the whole probe, was sandier,

light reddish brown in colour, and devoid of ceramics. Below it, the original ground level (Locus 03, at 958.80 m asl) was composed of a hard-packed sandy, reddish brown soil (not excavated). Removal of Locus 02 exposed the pipeline (Locus 04) running nearly due north/south along the east edge of the probe. The pipe sections (top level, 959.06 m asl) were set into a very shallow trench cut into Locus 03, but surrounded and protected with a packing of flat fieldstones and cobbles rather than with backfilled soil. The packing extended in a fairly regular line 0.26 m west of the pipes, and was built up 0.06 m above their top surface, where it supported fieldstones covering the pipes. The pipes were set in a hard, white, sandy mortar.

Since the pipe would have been better protected against damage by complete burial, it is likely that the engineer simply had run out of slope at this point and had to bring the pipe to the surface. Certainly there is no appreciable slope between the pipeline in Probe 10 and in Probe 11, 8.2 m farther south. Since traffic would have been a problem, the pipes were reinforced by being set in mortar and surrounded by a rough housing of stones. The housing either was immediately covered with sterile fill to protect it from traffic, or its slight elevation above the surface quickly attracted windblown soil.

Locus 01 (compact light brown soil with pebbles and cobbles, surface to 959.06 m asl; fig. 5.57a–b)

Bucket 87.141. 102 body, 17 rim, 1 handle, 5 base. Numerous large fragments of finer wares and kitchen wares, Nabataean cream ware sherds; bones and the base of a blown glass vessel.

141.1. Cooking pot: hard, sandy, red (2.5YR 4/8) fabric with a few white specks and bubbles. Fire-blackened surface. D 0.14 m. Gerber 1994: fig. 16B (100); Gerber 2001a: fig. 2B (1C).

141.2. Pot: hard, sandy, reddish brown (2.5YR 4/4) fabric with many white specks and bubbles. Grey (2.5YR 5/0) core and surface. D 0.12 m. Cf. Gerber 2001b: fig. 1.25 (2–3C).

141.3. Pot: hard, sandy, light red (2.5YR 6/6) fabric with a few white specks. Grey (2.5YR 5/0) surface.

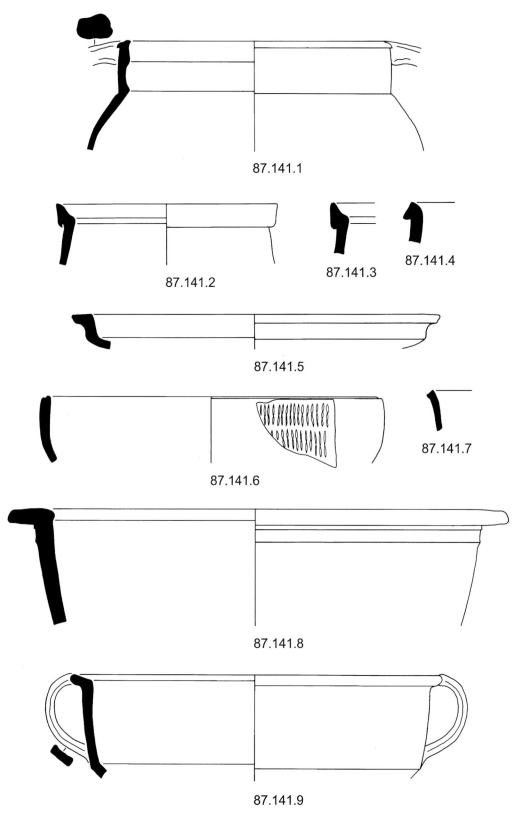

FIG. 5.57A *Reservoir/Pool no. 63, ceramics from Probe 10, Locus 1 (scale 1:2).*

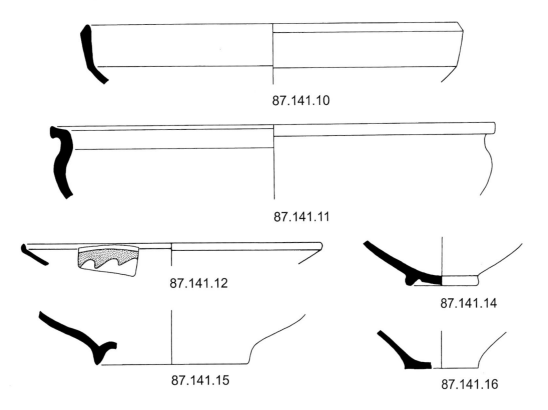

FIG. 5.57B *Reservoir/Pool no. 63, ceramics from Probe 10, Locus 1 (scale 1:2).*

141.4. Pot: fabric as 141.3.

141.5. Bowl: fine, hard, light brown (7.5YR 6/4) fabric. Very pale brown (10YR 8/3) surfaces, possibly a decayed slip. D 0.19 m? Cf. Hayes 1985: pl. 18.8 (1C), Cypriote sigillata or an imitation of it; Tushingham 1985: pl. 51.3 (late 1C BC), ETSA or an imitation of if.

141.6. NFW bowl: very fine, hard light red (2.5YR 6/6) fabric with a few bubbles. Rocker decoration on exterior. D 0.18 m. *EZ* I fig. 667 (20–100); *EZ* II no. 65, late 1C.

141.7. NFW cup: fabric as 141.6. *EZ* II fig. 235, Phase 3b (70–100).

141.8. Bowl or basin: heavy, fairly fine, light red (2.5YR 6/6) fabric with a few white inclusions and numerous bubbles. Grey (2.5YR 6/0) core. D 0.24 m.

141.9. Saucepan: fabric as 141.8. D 0.20 m. Gerber 1994: fig. 16I (late 1C–ea. 2C).

141.10. NFW bowl: fine, medium hard, red (2.5YR 5/8) fabric with a few large white and grey inclusions. D 0.20 m. Gerber 1994: fig. 16N (ea. 2C).

141.11. Bowl: slightly sandy, hard, red (2.5YR 5/8) ware with frequent white inclusions and bubbles. D 0.24 m. 'Amr and Momani 1999: fig. 10.16 (2C?).

141.12. NPFW bowl: very fine, hard, red (2.5YR 5/8) fabric with dark red (2.5YR 3/6) painted decoration. D 0.16 m. *EZ* II no. 93, phase 3c (100–106).

141.14. NFW bowl or jug: fabric as 141.10. Base D 0.04 m. Bikai and Perry 2001: fig. 8.11 (20–100).

141.15. NFW pot: fabric as 141.10. Base D 0.08 m. Bikai and Perry 2001: fig. 8.12 (20–100).

141.16. NFW jug: same fabric as 141.10, but cruder workmanship. Base D 0.04 m. (1C).

Bucket 87.142. 16 body, 3 handles. Mostly heavy wares.

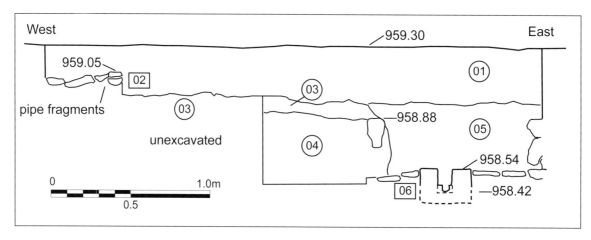

FIG. 5.58 *Reservoir/Pool no. 63, section across Probe 11 facing north.*

5.E.11. *Reservoir/Pool no. 63, Probe no. 11*

Probe 11 (2.75 m east/west, 1.0 m north/south) was laid out 7.5 m south of Probe 8, 14.70 m south of the south wall of the reservoir, across the projected lines of the overflow conduit and the terracotta pipeline, to determine their relationship and possible junction. The present ground surface at this point is at 959.30 m asl. Excavation of Locus 01, consisting of compact light brown soil with pebbles and the usual mix of badly broken potsherds, exposed the protective stone structure around the pipeline (Locus 02) at the west end of the probe, only 0.15 m below the surface (at 959.05 m asl; fig. 5.58). Partly trimmed fieldstones framed a central recess in which the pipes had been installed (bearing: ca. 185 degrees), but only fragments remained. This structure (W 0.55 m) has been disturbed, possibly through light ploughing. No ancient ground level could be discerned around the pipeline structure, but the compact, light brown pebbly soil below 959.00 m asl seems to pass beneath the packing stones. This stratum was isolated as Locus 03 and removed in the east half of the probe. The sandy, reddish brown soil forming the original Nabataean period ground level (Locus 04) was encountered just below Locus 03 (at 958.88 m asl), west of a north/south line of upright stones. East of this feature, as far as several field stones at the same level in the east baulk of the probe, the soil was dark brown in colour and softer (Locus 05). Locus 04 was removed to the level of the blocks framing the overflow aqueduct (at 958.49 m asl)

FIG. 5.59 *Reservoir/Pool no. 63, view of aqueduct and pipeline in Probe 11.*

and proved to be sterile. The soil of Locus 05, apparently backfill in a trench excavated between the two rows of stones, contained numerous first-

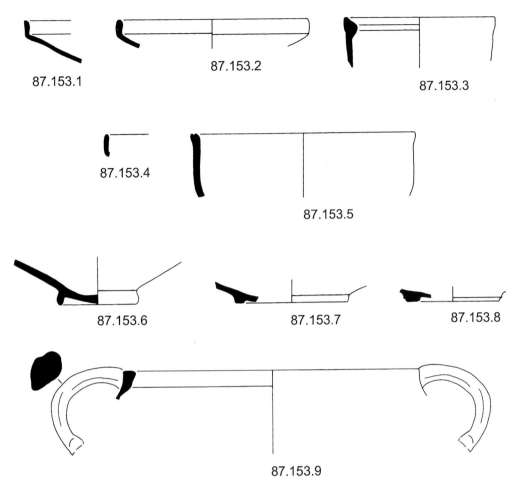

FIG. 5.60 *Reservoir/Pool no. 63, ceramics from Probe 11, Locus 5 (scale 1:2).*

century potsherds. The design and construction of the aqueduct was the same as in Probes 3 and 8: W ca. 0.53 m; conduit block W 0.29 m; channel W 0.10 m, 0.12 m deep (fig. 5.59). The joints between the neatly cut marl blocks were sealed with sandy white mortar, and the conduit was partly filled with a sandy white mortar that bore the impression of the lead pipeline, now lost. A quarry mark or survey mark — resembling a square with the lines of one side extended past the corners — is visible on the west upper edge of the conduit block at the north baulk (cf. Probes 3 and 12; fig. 5.61, inset).

It appears that the outflow conduit at this point was either built into a trench cut into the original, undisturbed ground level, leaving the soil of Locus 04 undisturbed, or it was constructed on the original surface, roofed with the usual arrangement of cobbles and slabs, and then covered quickly with

a dump of sterile soil or windblown soil. At some later period the aqueduct was uncovered, the roofing material piled on either side, and the lead pipe installed. The soil of Locus 05 may have been thrown in at this point or later on, when the pipe was torn out. Although the context is disturbed, the terracotta pipeline appears to have been built on top of a thin layer of soil (Locus 03) deposited after construction of the aqueduct. This pipeline is 0.57 m higher than the aqueduct pipeline, but it could nevertheless flow because it was fed from the level of the reservoir intake, which is 1.81 m higher than the level of the original outflow aqueduct, and 1.60 m above the drain feeding the lead pipeline.

Locus 01 (compact light brown soil with pebbles, from surface at to –0.95 m, 959.30 to 959.05 m asl)

Bucket 87.152. 25 body, 7 rim, 2 handle, 3 base. Mostly fine Nabataean wares and coarse Roman wares and pipe fragments. NFW bowls, Phase 2c (1C). 1 rim of glass beaker.

Locus 05 (brown soil with pebbles above aqueduct, from 958.88 to 958.49 m asl; fig. 5.60)

Bucket 87.153. 28 body, 4 rim, 2 handles, 3 base.

153.1. NFW bowl: hard, slightly sandy, light red (2.5YR 6/6) fabric with white grits. Slightly grey (2.5YR 6/0) core in body wall. *EZ* II fig. 49 (1C); Bikai and Perry 2001: fig. 9.1 (20–100).

153.2. NFW bowl: fabric as 153.1, but no grey core. Bubbles. D 0.10 m. *EZ* II fig. 46 (1C); Bikai and Perry 2001: fig. 5.1 (20 BC–AD 80).

153.3. NFW jar or jug: hard, slightly sandy, light red (10R 6/6) fabric with a few white grits and bubbles. Slightly reddish grey (10R 6/1) core. D 0.08 m. *EZ* II fig. 342 (70–100); cf. Bikai and Perry 2001: fig. 5.14, 5.16 20 BC–AD 80).

153.4. NFW bowl: fabric as 153.1, but no core. (1C).

153.5. NFW bowl: fine, hard, red (2.5YR 4/6) fabric with a few white grits. D 0.12 m? *EZ* II no. 162 (1C–2C), fig. 163 (1–2C?).

153.6. NFW bowl: hard, slightly sandy, light red (10R 6/6) fabric with a few white grits and bubbles. Slightly reddish grey (10R 6/1) core. Base D 0.04 m. Bikai and Perry 2001: fig. 9.2 (20–100).

153.7. NFW bowl: fabric as 153.3, but no core. Base D 0.06 m. *EZ* II fig. 50 (1C); Bikai and Perry 2001: fig. 5.5 (20 BC–AD 80).

153.8. NFW bowl: fine, hard, red (2.5YR 5/8) fabric with a few white inclusions. Base D 0.05 m.

153.9. Cooking pot (?): coarse, hard, sandy, light red (2.5YR 6/6) fabric with numerous bubbles and white grits. Pale red (10R 6/2) core. Surface shades to pale red where burnt.

5.E.12. *Reservoir/Pool no. 63, Probe no. 12*

Since the two water conduits were found to be still 2.04 m apart in Probe 11, Probe 12 (1.0 m east/west, 1.5 m north/south) was laid out 3.35 m south of Probe 8, 19.45 m south of the south wall of the reservoir, at the projected point of their intersection. The light brown, pebbly fill of Locus 01, from the present ground surface (at 959.12 m asl) to the level of the outflow aqueduct (958.44 m asl), seems to form a single deposit (fig. 5.61). It contained a small amount of worn potsherds, first- to probably third-century in date. The outflow aqueduct, which probably ran along the ancient ground surface at this point, was constructed in the same manner seen closer to the reservoir, but much of the external packing was missing. Mortar inside the water channel bore the impression of the salvaged pipe. At a point exactly 21 m south of the south reservoir wall, two large T-shaped marks (L 0.12 m, W 0.08 m) had been cut deeply into the upper edges of the southernmost conduit block in the probe. The crossbars face the cistern and are aligned with each other. The west edge of this block also carries six shallower parallel lines (L 0.07 m), oriented approximately perpendicular to the conduit, upstream from the T. The next upstream block has similar lines, nine parallel and three at an angle on the west edge, six parallel and one at an angle on the east edge. A square 0.04 m on a side has been cut into the south end of the west edge of the next conduit block. Given the depth and precision of the cutting and orientation, the T-shaped marks probably served as survey markers, allowing calculation of slope or the amount of work completed by a team of construction or repair workers. Division of 21 m by a cubit of 0.525 m yields 40 cubits, but this is not definitive proof of the use of such a module (cf. Section 7.E.2 for a discussion of modules). Comparable marks were found in Probe 3 and on a block along the Ghana Aqueduct at km 9.144. The base of the mortar setting for the pipe (at 958.33 m asl) is 0.27 m below the equivalent point at the south wall of the reservoir, yielding a slope of 1.3 percent, which is close to the slope of the last few kilometres of the Ghana Aqueduct

No trace of the terracotta pipeline was found in this probe. Since the present ground level is 0.18

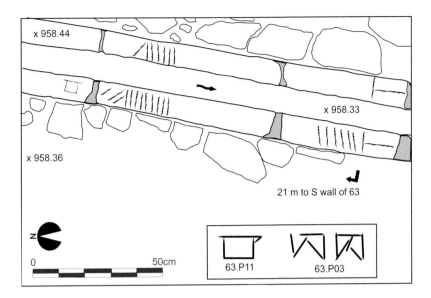

FIG. 5.61 *Reservoir/Pool no. 63, plan of Probe 12. Inset shows markings in Probes 3 and 11.*

m lower at this point than at Probe 11, where the pipeline had already been disturbed at a depth of 0.15 m, it is possible that the structure has been completely lost to weathering or ploughing here. Alternatively, the terracotta pipeline may have made a sharp turn in the area between Probes 11 and 12 to take advantage of the burial and relative low level of the outflow aqueduct in order to cross its course on the way towards the E125 complex.

Locus 01 (surface to conduit, at 958.44 m asl)
Bucket 87.154. 12 body, 2 rim, 3 handle, 3 base.
Bucket 87.159. 6 body, 1 rim. Cook pot, *EZ* I fig. 755 no. 28 (4C).

5.F. NABATAEAN RUN-OFF RESERVOIR (STRUCTURE NO. 68)

The four probes carried out in 1987 (Probes 1–4) for the most part involved removal of soil that had washed into the reservoir and the adjacent settling tank after the attempt to clear out the structure for reuse in the 1960s (fig. 5.62). The probes were designed to determine the relationship of the settling tank to the reservoir (Probes 1, 4), the design of the reservoir roof (Probe 2), and the depth of the reservoir (Probe 3). Probe 2 was expanded in 1989 to clarify the construction and dimensions

of the east end of the reservoir roof. In addition, the east end of the east/west trench was extended down outside the east wall of the reservoir to its foundation level to obtain data on construction technique and the date of construction.

Four new probes were excavated in 1989 (Probes 5–8) in order to document the design and course of the intake channel leading to the settling tank, and thus to clarify the relationship between Reservoir no. 67 and Reservoir no. 68. The survey in 1987 noted the presence of an overflow channel for Reservoir no. 67 that seemed to direct its surplus to no. 68. This overflow channel, which, like the top courses of the whole complex of no. 67, was totally rebuilt in the 1960s, is located on the north edge of the short channel between the settling basin and the cistern proper (fig. 4.13). It extends to the northwest for 3 m before disappearing beneath recently deposited silt. Once Reservoir no. 67 has completely filled, the water backs up into the last section of the intake channel and spills out at this point, flowing west toward Reservoir no. 68 and south between the two structures. Excavation of the settling basin for no. 68 in 1987 revealed that the intake channel for that cistern extended eastward for at least 3 m — up to the east baulk of the excavation area. It was consequently assumed that no. 68 was filled with the overflow from no. 67, a

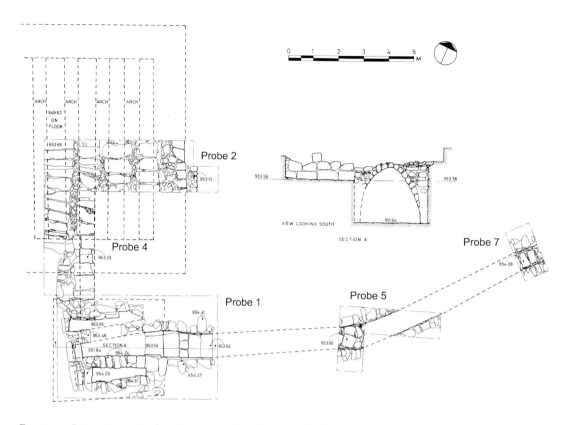

FIG. 5.62 *Reservoir no. 68, Plan of east end with indication of Probes 1, 2, 4, 5, 7. (D. Ritsema).*

relationship indicating the unified character of the complex. It was recognised, however, that there were several problems with this hypothesis. One was the presence of the settling basin associated with no. 68. If the water entering Reservoir no. 68 had already been allowed to settle in the basin associated with the no. 67 intake, the second settling basin was redundant. Furthermore, in view of the short duration of run-off in this region, it seemed a risky strategy to wait for one reservoir to fill before beginning to fill a second one.

In fact, Probes 5 to 8 revealed that Reservoir no. 68 did make use of a separate intake system that curved northeast for at least 17 m. Although the original entrance was not found, there most likely was a reinforced intake near this point, oriented to receive flow from the large catchment north of the settlement. Although Reservoir no. 67 diverted its water from the same field, the intakes were not built side-by-side but were designed to intercept run-off from two opposite sides of a low rise near the apex of the run-off field. Today, the stronger flow runs

past the intake for no. 67, and the general topography of the area suggests that the same was true in antiquity. If this was in fact the case, Reservoir no. 68 may have been intended to serve as a back-up to no. 67; it might not have filled as quickly as its neighbouring counterpart or have filled to capacity as consistently, but the intake system may also not have been as susceptible to damage by the full force of particularly heavy run-off.

The ceramic material recovered from the probes along the intake channel to Reservoir no. 68 reveal the vulnerability of this part of the structure. Intake channels of this type were built flush with the ground level. Excavation of the fill outside the channel walls down to the level of the channel floor yielded a large amount of ceramic material dating from the Nabataean through the Umayyad periods, incorporated in a homogenous fill of packed, sandy, yellow earth. Clearly, the relatively fragile intake channel had to be rebuilt frequently.

In view of all these factors, it seems likely that the overflow channel from Cistern no. 67 is com-

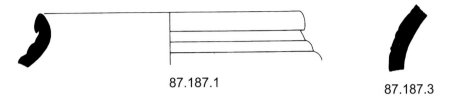

87.187.1

87.187.3

FIG. 5.63 *Reservoir no. 68, ceramics from Probe 1, Locus 4 (scale 1:2).*

pletely modern in character. This accords with the absence of an overflow channel associated with the better-preserved Cistern no. 68. Although the absence of a controlled outlet for overflow may seem risky to modern eyes, it accords well with the original character of the settlement of Hawara. At least a small settled population was living on the site year around and particularly during the cooler winter months, when pasturage was better, travel easier, and water supplies would be rejuvenated. The maintenance, filling, and use of the two major, probably public reservoirs in the centre of the habitation area were carefully regulated — and particular vigilance must have been exercised during the rainy season, when the opportunity to fill the cisterns could come at any moment. In these circumstances, some sort of guardians would have been put in control of the sluice gates or earth and stone blocking walls at the head of the intake channels for these two reservoirs. These individuals would have overseen the filling of the reservoirs and could easily have stopped the intake of water with a sluice gate or earth barrier once the cisterns were filled to capacity. In such a circumstance, the presence of an overflow channel is redundant. In the case of modern Humayma, the smaller and more transient population cannot supervise the reservoir closely, so an overflow channel is necessary to prevent overfilling from damaging the structure. In 2004–5, the entire roof and circumference of the reservoir were cleared and stabilised by the Department of Antiquities (fig. 4.16).

5.F.1. *Reservoir no. 68, Probe no. 1*

The soil throughout this probe, which encompassed the entire settling basin and the last 1.50 m of the intake channel (6.0 m east/west, 3.60 m north/south), consisted of compact, very light brown loessial soil with occasional lenses of water-deposited silt and cobbles or rubble fallen from the walls of the structure (figs. 4.18, 5.62). Most of this material seems to have been washed in recently, after the clearing in the 1960s, and the ceramic material did not suggest any differentiation in the chronology of the fill. Clearing of the surface deposit to the floor of the intake channel (953.56 m asl, Locus 01, 02) did not produce any ceramics. Removal of fill in the centre of the tank (Locus 03, 04, 05), between the two roofing arches, revealed a floor of large slabs mortared around their edges (951.94 m asl), and remains of plaster on the west wall (fig. 4.19). The plaster (Bucket 87.192) was hard, white to grey in colour, heavily tempered with poorly-mixed rounded sand and pebbles and angular fragments of terracotta; there were numerous lime nodules, bubbles, and fissures. The absence of Middle Nabataean wares from the worn potsherds found in the loci inside the tank is surprising, given their ubiquity in virtually all post-Nabataean deposits around the site. The absence of early ceramic material and presence of late ceramics, including some Mamluk or Ottoman handmade wares, suggest some small-scale cleaning and use of Reservoirs 67 and 68 after the Abbasid family left Humayma in the mid-eighth century.

Locus 03 (fill in settling tank)
   Bucket 87.169. 3 body.

Locus 04 (fill in settling tank; fig. 5.63)
   Bucket 87.187. 11 body, 1 rim, 2 handle. R. Brown (oral communication, 1991) identifies 1 handmade, straw-tempered sherd as probably Mamluk or Ottoman, from late 12th to late 19th century.
   187.1. Storage jar: fine, chalky, pink (7.5YR 7/4) fabric. D 0.14 m. Cf. Gerber 2008a: fig. 22.13 (2nd half 1C–1st half 2nd C, or later).

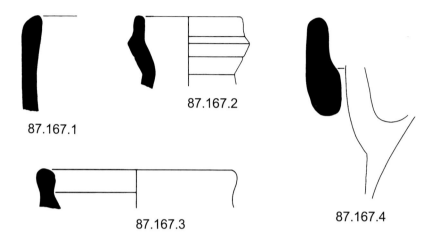

87.167.1

87.167.2

87.167.3

87.167.4

FIG. 5.64 *Reservoir no. 68, ceramics from Probe 1, Locus 5 (scale 1:2).*

187.3. Pot body sherd with flat-topped groove decoration: fine, very pale brown (10YR 8/3) fabric. Gerber, Humayma bucket 98.075, F103.78.18 (7–8C); 2008: fig. 24.35 (late 7–8C).

Locus 05 (fill in settling tank; fig. 5.64)

Bucket 87.167. 25 body, 3 rim, 1 handle. 2 handmade, straw tempered sherds as in Locus 04.

167.1. Rim of rectangular flue tile: hard, reddish yellow (7.5YR 8/6) fabric with black sand. (2C).

167.2. Amphora or jug (?): soft, fine, reddish yellow (5YR 7/6) fabric. Exterior ridged. Aqaba ware? D 0.055 m. (7C?).

167.3. Amphora (?): fine pink (5YR 7/4) fabric with a slightly grey core. Aqaba ware? D 0.10 m. Cf. 'Amr and Schick 2001: fig. 3.1 (mid-7C).

167.4. Handle and body fragment of large jar: fabric as 167.3. Cf. 'Amr and Schick 2001: fig. 6.9 (mid-7C).

Bucket 87.192. Plaster from west wall of settling tank.

5.F.2. *Reservoir no. 68, Probe no. 2*

In 1987, a trench (5.0 east/west, 1.0 north/south) was laid out approximately in the middle of the east end of the reservoir to expose the roof and the east edge of the structure (figs. 4.21, 5.62). The

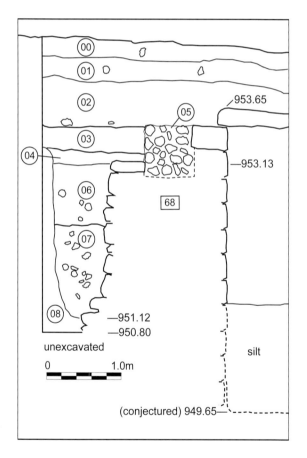

FIG. 5.65 *Reservoir no. 68, section across Probe 2.*

fill below the surface Locus 00 consisted of layers of water-deposited silt with occasional lenses of gravel or ash (Loci 01–02). The sherds were all very worn and included fewer first-century wares

Fig. 5.66 *Reservoir no. 68, view of Probe 2 sounding to foundation.*

than usual and a higher proportion of later wares. The eastern termination of the roofing slabs (top 953.65 m asl) and the top of the east reservoir wall (953.45 m asl) was found at the east end of the sounding. In 1989, Probe 2 was widened to 2 m, extended 1 m further to the east, and excavated to below the foundation level outside the reservoir (figs. 5.65–66).

The top of the east wall, constructed of large, flat, irregular slabs of sandstone and limestone, extended 0.90 m east of the edge of the roofing slabs (fig. 4.21). Excavation revealed that the upper part of the wall was 1.15 m thick, increasing to 1.60 m thick below an offset, then gradually sloping out to 2.14 m thick near the base. A probe was cut 0.30 m into the top of the wall at this point to determine the construction technique and to attempt the recovery of dateable potsherds (Locus 05). The outer face of the wall was built of irregular sandstone blocks up to 0.80 m long, with well-trimmed, flat exterior faces that often carried the fine diagonal trimming typical of Nabataean stone-working. The core of the wall consisted of irregular, fist-sized rubble and small pebbles set in a crumbly, grey

mortar containing numerous nodules of lime and a very high proportion of ash particles (probably resulting from the process of burning the lime). Five small potsherds were recovered from the mortar (Bucket 89.050). Three certainly were derived from first-century Nabataean fine ware bowls, and two very probably from Nabataean coarse-ware vessels possibly first-century in date.

The extension of this trench east of the cistern wall was excavated for 2.65 m below the wall's upper surface (953.45 to 950.80 m asl). Removal of the uppermost strata, consisting of alternating, water-deposited layers and lenses of sand, silt, stones, and gravel containing first- and second-century ceramics (Loci 01–03), exposed an offset 0.48 m wide (at 953.13 m) just below what appears to have been the original ground level (Locus 04, at 953.30 m asl), consisting of a very hard stratum of coarse red-brown sand (figs. 5.65–66). A similar arrangement can be seen on Reservoir/Pool no. 63. The foundation trench within which the cistern walls were constructed had been dug into the sterile sand (Locus 08) from this level down to 951.12 m asl, sloping gradually inward toward the structure. The profile of the trench could be seen in the north and south baulks; it meets the face of the outer wall at a point 2.33 m below its upper surface (1.47 m above the cistern floor), then slopes outward to a distance of 0.75 m from the wall, where it terminates at the ancient ground level (0.35 m below the top of the wall). The backfill within this foundation trench consisted of two major strata of sand and gravel mixed with a packing of fist-sized pieces of sandstone and limestone rubble (Loci 06 and 07). Since the fill had been poured into the trench after construction of the wall, the deposits sloped slightly downwards towards the wall face and terminated on it without a break.

The masons who built this wall took no chances concerning its stability. The upper 0.50 m of the wall, above the ground and water levels, was 1.15 m thick. Below ground level, however, it was built to a thickness of 1.60–2.15 m, even though the surrounding soil would have helped buttress it against the weight of the water contained inside. The profile of the foundation trench shows that an enormous rectangular east/west hole with slightly sloping sides had been excavated for the cistern, probably 26 × 13 m on its sides and 4.25 m deep. The floor (surface at 949.62 m asl) and lowest 1.3 m of the inner face of the wall were then built of regular, carefully trimmed blocks of sandstone (inside dimensions of 20.05 × 6.95 m). This facing served as a retaining wall for a solid packing of rubble mixed with mortar thrown into and completely filling the approximately 1 m wide trench between the wall and the boundary of the excavation. Above this point, the rubble packing was faced with relatively large limestone and sandstone blocks (up to 0.75 × 0.25 × 0.25 m) that were not, however, laid in regular courses. Between this solid outer facing and the carefully built inner cistern wall, the packing probably consisted of the mortared rubble seen in the sounding into the upper part of the wall. From a point approximately 1.3 m above the cistern floor it was possible to build the outer wall face more carefully, because from this point up to the roof, the face of the excavation into which the structure was built sloped outwards slightly, allowing the masons room to manoeuvre.

The loci in the foundation trench (Loci 06–07) contained sherds for which the proposed dating

extends from the later first century BC to the first century AD, with the exception of two coarse-ware body sherds in Locus 06 identified as possibly Byzantine in date. Identification of these two sherds is not certain, and the otherwise Nabataean character of the ceramic material from Loci 04, 06, and 07 strongly suggests that construction was completed sometime in the first century AD. Loci 01–03 all yielded an enormous amount of first- through sixth-century ceramic material. This material was not found in successive occupation levels, but occurred in the form of small, worn sherds mixed uniformly in thin, alternating layers of water and wind-deposited sand, silt, and clay that slope downwards from east to west over the cistern wall and the roof beyond. This deposit, which is typical of most of the site, represents the mixing and spreading of cultural material typical of the centre of a busy habitation area over a long period of time. If the reservoir had been built or even renovated in the Byzantine period, much clearer evidence for Byzantine ceramics would be found in the foundation levels. A construction date in the first half of the first century AD is most likely.

Locus 00 (surface to –0.25 m)
>   Bucket 87.168. 27 body, 2 rim, 2 base.
>   Bucket 87.189. 42 body, 1 rim, 3 handle.

Locus 01 (hard yellow silt, –0.25 to –0.50 m)
>   Bucket 87.188. 85 body, 3 rim, 3 handle, 5 base. Casserole, *EZ* I fig. 772–776 (4C). Slot rim jar, *EZ* I fig. 761 (4C). Nabataean cream ware jug (1).

Locus 02 (water-deposited layers of silt and sand, –0.50 m to roofing slabs at –0.60 m and east wall at –0.80 m, 953.45 m asl)
>   Bucket 87.191. 7 body, 1 rim, 1 handle.
>   Bucket 89.059. 24 body, 2 handle.
>   Bucket 89.069. 4 body.

Locus 03 (alternating layers of fine silt and sand east of cistern wall, 953.45 to 953.30 m asl; fig. 5.67)
>   Bucket 89.076. 29 body, 3 rim, 3 handle, 1 base. 1 very small bone frag. 1 fragment marble chancel screen (white with grey streaks; 5–6C). K. 'Amr (oral communication, 1989) most of the material is first- or early second-century.

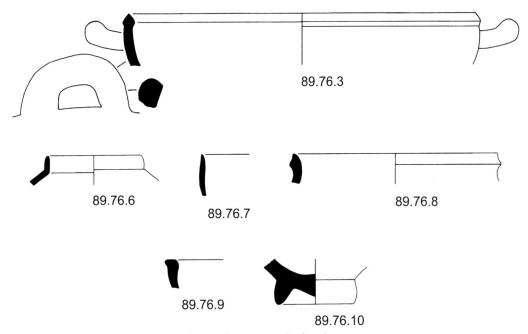

Fig. 5.67 *Reservoir no. 68, ceramics from Probe 2, Locus 3 (scale 1:2).*

76.1. NPFW bowl body sherd: fine, thin, red (2.5YR 5/8) fabric with a few white specks. Reddish brown (2.5YR 4/4) painting (large brown spot, several parallel and 1 oblique lines) on interior. Phase 3b (late 1st C to ea. 2nd C).

76.2. NPFW bowl body sherd: as 76.01, red (2.5YR 5/6) fabric. Dark grey (10YR 4/1) core, very pale brown (10YR 8/3) slip.

76.3. Saucepan: medium fine dark greyish brown (10YR 4/2) fabric with a few white specks; yellowish red (5YR 5/8) core. *EZ I* fig. 775, no. 48 (late 4C–ea. 5C).

76.6. NFW pot: very fine, light red (2.5YR 6/8) fabric. *EZ II* fig. 275, Phase 3b (70–100).

76.7. NFW bowl: slightly sandy red (2.5YR 5/8) fabric. *EZ II* fig. 182, Phase 3a–b (20–100).

76.8. Bowl: medium fine yellowish red (5YR 5/8) fabric with some white specks; outer surface pink (7.5YR 8/4). Cf. *EZ II* fig. 235, Phase 2a? 3b? (50 BC–AD 100).

76.9. Pot: sandy, dark greyish brown (2.5Y 4/2) fabric with white inclusions. Brown (7.5YR 4/4) shades in core.

76.10. ETSA cup: very fine, light brown (7.5YR 6/4) fabric; runny red (2.5YR 4/8) slip. Hayes 1985: pl. 6.19, Form 51 (70–120).

Locus 04 (coarse red sand and gravel east of wall above offset, 953.30 to 953.13 m asl; fig. 5.68)

Bucket 89.077. 5 body, 1 handle, 1 rim. Very small fragments. Mortar sample.

77.1. Handle: medium coarse, red (2.5YR 4/8) fabric with white inclusions. Light olive grey (5Y 6/2) surface.

77.2. NFW bowl body sherd: fine, hard, red (2.5YR 5/8) fabric with a few small white specks.

77.3. NPFW bowl body sherd: slightly sandy red (2.5YR 4/6) fabric. Thick, dark grey (5YR 4/1) core; reddish brown (2.5YR 5/4) paint on interior. *EZ II* fig. 89, *Farbtafel* 2.4, Phase 3a (20–70/80).

77.4. NPFW bowl body sherd: very fine, red (2.5YR 5/8) fabric; red (2.5YR 4/6) paint.

77.5. NFW bowl body sherd: light red (2.5YR 6/8) fabric.

77.6. NFW bowl: very fine, dark grey (2.5YR 4/0) fabric (burned).

Bucket 89.086. 16 body, 1 base, 1 handle. Some flint microliths and debitage. K. 'Amr (oral communication, 1989) dates the ceramic assemblage to the first century.

86.1. NFW cup: fine, light red (10R 6/6) fabric; light grey (7.5YR N6) core; reddish brown

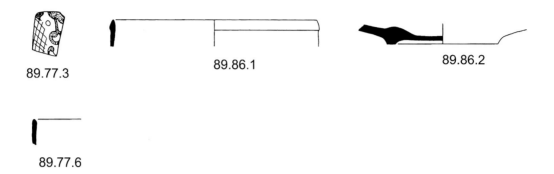

FIG. 5.68 *Reservoir no. 68, ceramics from Probe 2, Locus 4 (scale 1:2).*

FIG. 5.69 *Reservoir no. 68, ceramics from Probe 2, Locus 5 (scale 1:2).*

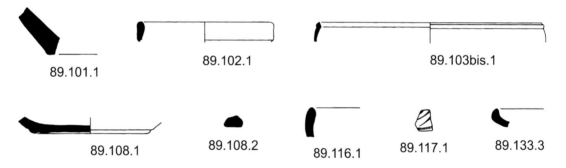

FIG. 5.70 *Reservoir no. 68, ceramics from Probe 2, Loci 6 and 7 (scale 1:2).*

(2.5YR 5/4) paint. *EZ* II fig. 235, Phase 3b? (20–70/80).

86.2. NFW bowl: hard, red (2.5YR 5/8) fabric with some white specks and bubbles; dark grey (2.5YR N4) core.

86.3. Handle: slightly laminar, reddish yellow (5YR 7/6) fabric with a few white specks; white (5Y 8/2) slip.

86.4. NFW bowl: very fine, hard, red (10R 5/6) fabric.

86.5. NFW bowl: slightly sandy, red (2.5YR 5/8) fabric; grey (2.5YR N5) core; stripes of a pinkish white (7.5YR 8/2) slip on exterior.

86.6. NPFW bowl: very fine yellowish red (5YR 5/6) fabric; grey (5YR 5/1) core; 2

reddish brown (5YR 4/4) painted dots on interior surface. Very small sherd. Phase 3a or 3b? (20–100?).

Bucket 89.085. 3 body. 5 microliths, and flint debitage.

85.1. NFW bowl: medium fine, light red (2.5YR 6/8) fabric with a few white specks. Dark grey (10YR 4/1) core.

85.2. NFW bowl: slightly sandy, light red (2.5YR 5/8) fabric. Surface dark grey (10YR 4/2).

85.3. Grooved body sherd: coarse, sandy light red (2.5YR 5/8) fabric with numerous white specks and inclusions. Light grey (5YR 6/1) core, white (10YR 8/2) exterior slip.

Bucket 89.093. Soft mortar with abundant carbon bits.

Locus 05 (mortared rubble wall fabric from 953.45 to 953.00 m asl; fig. 5.69)

Bucket 89.050. 1 rim, 4 body. K. ʿAmr (oral communication, 1989) suggests that the NPFW bowl fragment dates to the first century, the rest possibly to the first or second century.

50.1. NFW bowl body sherd: fine but sandy, yellowish-red (5YR 5/8) fabric with a few white specks. Slight reddish brown (5YR 5/3) core.

50.2. NFW bowl: burned, fine dark grey (7.5YR N4/0) fabric. Light reddish brown (5YR 6/6) surfaces. *EZ* II fig. 182, Phase 3a–3b (20–100).

50.3. coarse-ware body sherd: sandy, hard fabric with grooved surfaces. Brown (7.5YR 5/2) exterior, yellowish red (5YR 5/6) inner surface. Th 0.005 m.

50.4. Cooking pot (?), ridged body sherd: sandy red (2.5YR 5/8) fabric. Very pale brown slip on exterior surface. Th 0.004 m.

50.5. NPFW bowl: fine red (2.5YR 5/8) fabric. Slightly reddish brown (2.5YR 5/4) core and reddish brown (2.5YR 4/4) paint. *EZ* II fig. 89, *Farbtafel* 1.3, Phase 3a (20–70/80); Schmid 2003: fig. 64, Phase 3a (20–70/80); Bikai and Perry 2001: fig. 4.6 (20 BC–80).

Locus 06 (sloping lenses of brown sand, pebbles, and cobbles in foundation trench, 953.13 to 951.93 m asl; fig. 5.70)

Bucket 89.101. 1 base, 1 rim. 1 flint microlith or debitage. K. ʿAmr (oral communication, 1989) dates assemblage to first century.

101.1. Juglet with string-cut base: thick, slightly sandy, light red (2.5YR 5/6) fabric. Reddish yellow (5YR 7/6) core. (1C).

101.2. NFW bowl: fine, light red (2.5YR 5/8) fabric. (1C).

Bucket 89.102. 9 body, 1 rim. K. ʿAmr (oral communication, 1989) dates assemblage to first or early second century, with exception of 102.03, which may possibly be fifth-century in date.

102.1. NFW bowl: fine, sandy, yellowish red (5YR 5/8) fabric with a few very small

bubbles. *EZ* II fig. 49, Phase 2b–3b (25 BC–AD 100).

102.2. Bowl (6 body sherds): very fine, hard, reddish yellow (5YR 6/8) fabric. Th 0.004 m.

102.3. Body sherd (very small): coarse, sandy, hard red (2.5YR 5/8) fabric with a few white specks. Greyish brown (2.5Y 5/2) outside surface. Th 0.035 m.

102.4. Body sherd (very small): fine, hard, yellowish red (5YR 5/8) fabric. Dark grey (10YR 4/1) surface.

102.5. Body sherd: very sandy, pale yellow (2.5Y 8/4) fabric with a few bubbles. Th 0.005 m.

Bucket 89.103*bis*. 1 rim, 1 body. K. ʿAmr (oral communication, 1989) dates assemblage to late first century BC or early first AD.

103*bis*.1. NFW pot: fine, light red (2.5YR 6/8) fabric. Faint white (10YR 8/1) core. Rolled, grooved lip and handle stub. *EZ* II no. 268, Phase 3b–3c (70/80–106).

103*bis*.2. Bowl body sherd: sandy, laminar, light red (2.5YR 6/8) fabric. Red (2.5YR 5/6) matte slip on exterior. Th 0.005 m.

Bucket 89.108. 9 body, 1 handle, 1 base. Small blobs of mortar. Very small sherds. K. ʿAmr (oral communication, 1989) dates the NFW bowl sherds to the first century, but the dark-slipped wares could be earlier.

108.1. NFW bowl: very fine red (2.5YR 5/8) fabric. *EZ* II fig. 52, Phase 3a–3b (20–100); Bikai and Perry 2001: fig. 9.2 (20–100).

108.2. NFW pot (handle): fine red (2.5YR 4/8) fabric with a few white particles. *EZ* II fig. 370, Phase 3 (20–100).

108.3. Plate: coarse, hard, sandy red (2.5YR 5/8) fabric with a few bubbles and white specks. Very light wash of weak red (2.5YR 5/2) slip. Th 0.007 m.

108.4. NFW bowl: light red (2.5YR 6/6) fabric with a few white specks. Light grey (10YR 7/2) core.

108.5. Bowl (body sherd): sandy, slightly laminar red (2.5YR 5/8) fabric. Ridged. Th 0.003 m.

108.6. Bowl (body sherd): red (2.5YR 6/8) fabric. Very light traces of red (2.5YR 5/6) paint on ridged exterior. Th 0.003 m.

108.7. Bowl (body sherd): very sandy, light reddish brown (5YR 6/3) fabric. Th 0.005 m.

108.8. Bowl (body sherd): slightly laminar light red (2.5YR 6/8) fabric with a few white specks. Traces of weak red (2.5YR 4/2) paint on exterior. Th 0.004 m.

108.9. Bowl (very small body sherd): sandy red (2.5YR 5/8) fabric. Occasional traces of weak red (2.5YR 5/2) paint. Th 0.005 m.

108.10. NFW bowl: very fine, light red (2.5YR 6/8) fabric. Traces of wide stripe of red (2.5YR 4/6) paint on shaved exterior.

108.11. NFW bowl: fine, light red (2.5YR 6/6) fabric.

Bucket 89.116. 1 rim. Probably a cup/bowl; slip looks black, but shape is Nabataean. K. ʿAmr (oral communication, 1989) dates to probably before 40/50 BC, part of a Late Hellenistic tradition. K. Russell (oral communication, 1989) dates first century BC or AD. Blobs of mortar.

116.1. NFW bowl: fine, light red (2.5YR 6/6) fabric. Pink (5YR 7/3) core, traces of dark grey (2.5YR N4) slip. Cf. *EZ* II fig. 12, 15 (1C BC)

Bucket 89.117. 2 body. K. ʿAmr (oral communication, 1989) dates to first century BC, but could be as late as first century AD, based on the light colour paint and fabric, and the freehand brush strokes.

117.1. NPFW bowl: very fine light red (2.5YR 6/8) fabric. Slight, light red (2.5YR 6/6) core. Interior surface has lines painted in red (2.5YR 5/8) slip. Possibly Phase 2c: *EZ* II *Farbtafel* 1.1–3 (20).

Bucket 89.118. 3 body. K. ʿAmr (oral communication, 1989) dates 118.01 to early first century AD, the burned body sherd 118.02 to the fourth or sixth century. K. Russell (oral communication, 1989), however, stated that 118.02 could also be first century.

118.1. NFW bowl: very fine red (2.5YR 5/6) fabric. Pale red (2.5YR 6/2) core.

118.2. Body sherd: very coarse, sandy, laminar fabric. Inside surface red (2.5YR 4/6); slightly ridged, dark grey (7.5YR 4/0) exterior surface. Th 0.035 m.

118.3. Body sherd (very small): medium fine, reddish yellow (5YR 6/6) fabric. Pink (7.5YR 8/4) slip on exterior. Th 0.006 m.

Locus 07 (sloping lenses of light brown sandy soil and cobbles in foundation trench, 951.93 to 951.12 m asl; fig. 5.70)

Bucket 89.119. 3 body.

119.1. Body sherd: hard, sandy, light red (2.5YR 6/6) fabric with many white specks. Pale red (2.5YR 6/2) core, exterior slipped white (10YR 8/2). Th 0.008 m.

119.2. Body sherd: sandy, light red (2.5YR 6/6) fabric. Weak red (2.5YR 5/2) exterior slip. Th 0.003 m.

119.3. Body sherd: gritty, light red (2.5YR 6/8) fabric.

Bucket 89.120. 1 body.

Bucket 89.129. 1 body. 1 large lump of mortar with a smooth, rounded form (L 0.12 m, W 0.08 m) reflecting the bowl or sherd in which it was mixed.

129.1. Body sherd: hard, yellowish red (5YR 5/8) fabric. Drag line on surface. Th 0.003 m.

Bucket 89.133. 4 body, 1 rim. 1 fragment of alabaster revetment plaque.

133.1. NPFW bowl (very small body sherd): light red (2.5YR 6/8) fabric, with very small pink (5YR 7/3) inclusions. Traces of brown (7.5YR 5/4) slip-paint on exterior.

133.2. Body sherd: hard, sandy, laminar, reddish yellow (5YR 5/8) fabric with very small inclusions of sand or mica and a few white specks and bubbles. Pink (5YR 8/4) slip on ridged exterior. Th 0.006 m.

133.3. NPFW bowl: fine reddish yellow (5YR 7/6) fabric, with a few white specks and sand grains. Grey (5YR 5/1) slip on lower part of exterior. *EZ* I fig. 613, Phase 1 (2nd half 2C–50 BC); *EZ* II fig. 11, Phase 1 (50 BC).

133.4. NFW bowl: hard, gritty, light red (2.5YR 5/8) fabric. Drag marks on exterior.

133.5. Body sherd: sandy, reddish yellow (5YR 7/8) fabric with a few white specks. Light strokes of reddish yellow (5YR 6/6) slip paint on exterior. Th 0.004 m.

5.F.3. *Reservoir no. 68, Probe no. 3*

A square (1.50 north/south, 1.0 east/west) was laid out near the southwest corner of the interior of the reservoir, in an area where the hard silt fill was at a lower level than elsewhere, in order to probe for the original floor. The first 0.45 m of the compact, clay-like fill were excavated only with great difficulty. It was devoid of artefacts. We then probed the fill by driving a wooden shovel handle into it with a sledge hammer, reaching a solid surface 3.83 m below the lower surface of the ceiling slabs at this point (949.62 m asl). Since this dimension is very close to the depth of the interior offset of Reservoir no. 67 (floor 3.75 m below present rim of reservoir), it is accepted as correct.

5.F.4. *Reservoir no. 68, Probe no. 4*

A trench (2.75 north/south, 0.75 east/west) was laid out between the west end of Probe 2 and the north side of Probe 1 in order to clarify the structure of the roof over the intake channel leading into the reservoir from the settling tank. The fill was identical to that in Probe 2, uniform, compact loess, with occasional lenses of slightly darker, water-deposited silt, containing ceramics probably dating from the first to the seventh century. The roof was built of roughly-squared sandstone slabs set on top of the mortared slabs forming the top of the reservoir wall and roof.

Locus 01 (surface soil)
> Bucket 87.190. 35 body, 1 rim, 1 handle, 1 base.

5.F.5. *Reservoir no. 68, Probe no. 5*

Probe 5 (1.0 m east/west, 2.5 m north/south) was laid out 5 m east of the east baulk of Probe 1, on the projected line of the intake channel to the settling tank (fig. 5.62). The side walls of the channel were exposed only ca. 0.10 beneath the surface, surviving ca. 0.60 m above the heavy, partly trimmed slabs forming the floor (at 953.95 m asl). The side walls (Th ca. 0.30 m) were constructed of a mix of unshaped and partly trimmed fieldstones held in place mainly by the soil behind them. They frame a conduit ca. 0.92 m wide, on a bearing of 60 degrees. No cover slabs survived. The north 1 m of the probe was extended 3 m east to expose more of the channel, which narrows slightly (W 0.75 m) and bends north to a bearing of 40 degrees. The fill in the channel (Locus 01) was a homogenous, sandy, light brown soil with a few scrappy first- through seventh-century ceramics and Umayyad steatite vessel fragments.

Since the channel walls were built only one course thick, with partially trimmed stones, they could not have projected much above the original ground level. The upper surfaces of the side walls most likely were flush with the ground surface and covered with slabs to prevent injury to humans and animals, as well as damage or obstruction of the conduit. This is the typical arrangement for other ancient cisterns around the site. Actual burial of the conduits is unlikely, since this would have made repairs and cleaning difficult.

Locus 01 (light brown, sandy soil, from surface to floor of channel, 954.65 to 953.95 m asl)
> Bucket 89.051. 16 body, 1 base. Nabataean cream ware jug (1–mid 2C). 3 pieces of steatite vessel.
> Bucket 89.058. 7 body, 1 handle. 1 very heavy jar or dolium rim.
> Bucket 89.060. 9 body, 1 base.
> Bucket 89.070. 12 body, 1 handle.

5.F.6. *Reservoir no. 68, Probe no. 6*

Probe 6 (3.0 m east/west, 1.0 m north/south) was laid out 10 m north of the northeast corner of Probe 5, on the projected line of the intake channel. Excavation of the light brown, sandy soil to a depth of –0.70 m (954.30 m asl) revealed no trace of the intake, which may either have terminated south of this point or had been destroyed here. The fill contained badly broken and weathered sherds dating first through seventh century.

Locus 01 (light brown sandy soil, to 0.70 below surface (954.30 m asl)
> Bucket 89.071. 13 body, 1 base, 1 handle. 1 fragment of thin-walled glass vessel.
> Bucket 89.078. 42 body, 5 handle.

FIG. 5.71 *Reservoir no. 68, Probe 7 from south.*

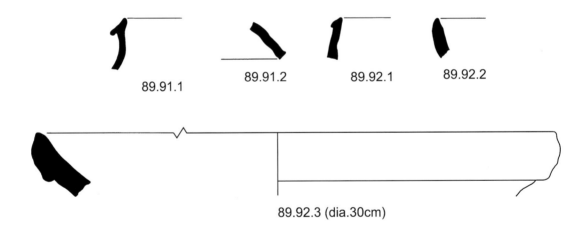

FIG. 5.72 *Reservoir no. 68, ceramics from Probe 7, Loci 4 and 5 (scale 1:2).*

5.F.7. *Reservoir no. 68, Probe no. 7*

Probe 7 (2.0 m northwest/southeast, 1.0 m north-east/southwest) was laid out 3.5 m north of the northeast corner of Probe 5, on the projected line of the intake channel. Removal of the compact, light brown surface soil (Locus 01) to a depth of –0.10 m to –0.15 m (954.93 to 954.88 m asl) exposed the side walls of the channel, constructed in the same manner as in Probe 5, but slightly narrower (W 0.63 m). Removal of the light brown, sandy soil inside the channel exposed the slab-built floor at 954.08 m (fig. 5.71). The channel slope from Probe 7 to the settling tank is 1:32. The course of the channel has turned slightly farther north, to approximately 34 degrees. The ceramic material inside the channel fill dated from the first to the sixth or seventh century.

The fill west of the west channel wall was excavated in order to clarify the construction method and obtain datable ceramics. The fill below the level of the channel contained ceramics dating from the first to the eighth centuries AD, indicating rebuilding of the channel at least once in the late period, but probably on several occasions when the channel walls were damaged by excessive run-off.

Locus 01 (light brown sandy soil, surface to top of channel framing walls, 954.93 to 954.88 m asl)
Bucket 89.082. 1 body, 1 rim, 1 handle.

Locus 02 (light brown sandy soil inside water channel, 954.88 to 954.08 m asl)
Bucket 89.083. 45 body, 1 handle. Very small worn fragments. 1 piece of brick. 2 fragments of a very thick-walled vessel.

Locus 03 (light brown sandy soil behind west channel wall, 954.88 to 954.71 m asl)
Bucket 89.084. 80 body, 2 rim, 1 handle. The pottery fragments are very small and worn. A few bone fragments, rim of glass bowl.

Locus 04 (light brown sandy soil behind west channel wall, 954.71 to 954.08 m asl; fig. 5.72)
Bucket 89.091. 13 body, 2 rim. Very small fragments of coarse and kitchen wares.
91.1. Cooking pot: sandy, slightly laminar, light reddish brown (5YR 6/4) fabric with much white sand. D uncertain. Gerber 2001a: fig. 2C (2–3C); 2008: fig. 23.26 (2–3C).
91.2. Cooking pot lid: sandy, reddish yellow (5YR 7/6) fabric shading to light reddish brown (5YR 6/4) at rim, with much white sand and bubbles. D uncertain. Gerber 1998: fig. 16F (4C); *EZ* I fig. 841, no. 114 (4C).

Locus 05 (light brown sandy soil west of west channel wall, below level of channel, 954.08 to 953.93 m asl; fig. 5.72)
Bucket 89.092. 47 body, 1 rim. K. ʿAmr (oral communication, 1989) dates the assemblage from the first to the eighth century. 92.01 is

an Early Byzantine shape; 92.03 is Umayyad or early Abbasid, of a type common in Aqaba; 92.04 is a first-century Nabataean cream ware.
92.1. Cooking pot: medium coarse red (2.5YR 4/8) fabric with numerous brown specks and some bubbles. Weak red (4/2) core. Gerber 2001a: fig. 2C (2–3C); 2008: fig. 23.27 (2–3C).
92.2. Bowl: sandy red (2.5YR 5/8) fabric with a few white specks and one white inclusion. Reddish grey (5YR 5/2) slip.
92.3. Basin: light grey (5Y 7/2) fabric containing much clear sand. Pink (7.5YR 7/4) surface. Melkawi, ʿAmr, Whitcomb 1994: fig. 8F (7–8C).
92.4. Nabataean cream ware jug: slightly sandy, laminar, reddish yellow (5YR 7/6) fabric. Very pale brown (10YR 8/3) slip on ridged exterior.

5.F.8. *Reservoir no. 68, Probe no. 8*

Probe 8 (1.0 m east/west, 3.0 m north/south) was laid out at the intersection of the projected lines of the modern overflow for no. 67 and the ancient intake for no. 68, 5 m east of Probe 7. The compact light brown earth (Locus 01) was excavated to a depth of 1 m below the modern soil surface (953.80 m asl) without exposing any connecting conduit. A rich collection of very small and worn sherds of first- through sixth-century ceramics was recovered from this locus. Some modern debris was found in Bucket 89.053, suggesting that all this fill was mixed or deposited at the time Reservoir no. 67 was renovated in the 1960s. Although of no stratigraphic value, the ceramics are reported here as comparative material.

Locus 01 (compact light brown soil, surface to –1.0 m, 953.80 m asl; figs. 5.73a–b)
Bucket 89.036. 75 body, 10 base, 2 rim, 18 handle. 1 lamp. K. ʿAmr (oral communication, 1989): dark surfaced material is fourth century, and darker with sand grit may be also; sherds with very crisp, angular ribbing are sixth-century; no obvious Islamic ceramics. 1 glass bowl rim with pinched decoration.

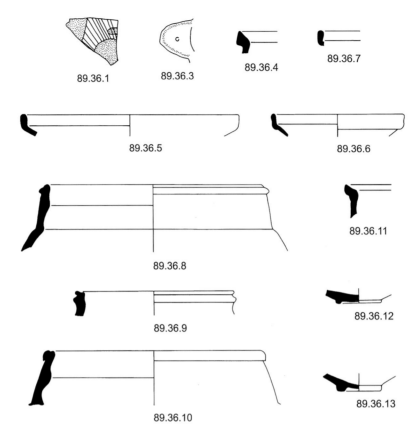

Fig. 5.73A *Reservoir no. 68, ceramics from Probe 8, Locus 1 (scale 1:2).*

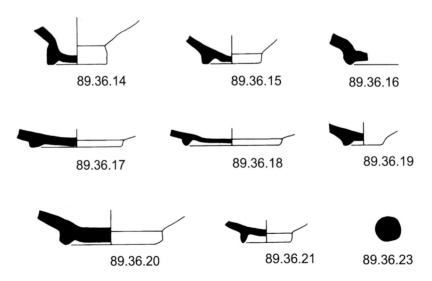

Fig. 5.73B *Reservoir no. 68, ceramics from Probe 8, Locus 1 (scale 1:2).*

36.1. NPFW bowl: red (2.5YR 5/8) fabric, very fine line motif in red (2.5YR 4/6) paint. *EZ II Farbtafel* 3, Phase 3b (70/80–100).

36.2. ETSA body sherd of a closed shape: very fine, reddish yellow (7.5YR 6/6) fabric. Red (10R 4/8) outer surface. (1C–2C?).

36.3. Lamp handle: slightly sandy and laminar reddish yellow (7.5YR 7/6) fabric. Grey (10YR 5/1) outer surface. Possibly *EZ III Tafel I* Class I1, I5 (80–200) or *Tafel II* Class K4, K5, or K6 (280–350).

36.4. NFW cup: very fine red (2.5YR 5/8) fabric with some white specks and bubbles. Very pale brown (10YR 8/3) surface. Cf. *EZ II* fig. 235, probably Phase 3b (70/80–100).

36.5. NFW bowl: slightly sandy, red (2.5YR 5/8) fabric with a few white specks. Dark reddish grey (5YR 4/2) outer surface. *EZ II* fig. 45 (late 1C BC).

36.6. NFW bowl: very fine, red (2.5YR 5/6) fabric with a few white specks. Very pale brown (10YR 8/3) surface. *EZ II* fig. 49 (1C).

36.7. NFW bowl: red (2.5YR 5/6) fabric with a few white specks. Light yellowish brown (10YR 6/4) surface. *EZ II* fig. 46, Phase 2c (1st half 1C).

36.8. Cooking pot: medium fine, red (2.5YR 5/8) fabric containing white sand. Pink (7.5YR 8/4) surface. Cf. Gerber 2001a: fig. 3F (4C); *EZ I* fig. 732 no. 5 (last quarter 4C–ea. 5C).

36.9. Jar: very fine red (2.5YR 5/8) fabric. Very dark grey (5YR 3/1) slip. Gerber 2001b: fig. 1.18 (2C–3C); 2008: fig. 23.25 (2C–3C).

36.10. Cooking pot (?): medium fine red (2.5YR 5/6) fabric with a few white specks. Pink (7.5YR 8/4) slip. Dolinka 2003: 121 no. 6 (ea. 2C).

36.11. Jug (?): sandy red (2.5YR 5/6) fabric with a few white specks. Very pale brown (10YR 8/4) slip. *EZ II* fig. 351, 70/80–100?).

36.12. NFW bowl: medium coarse, light red (2.5YR 6/6) fabric with a few bubbles. (Probably 1C).

36.13. NFW bowl: red (2.5YR 5/8) fabric with numerous dark specks and small bubbles. Drag marks on exterior. (Probably 1C)

36.14. NFW jug (?): very fine red (2.5YR 5/6) fabric with a few white specks and bubbles. (Probably 1C).

36.15. NFW bowl: very fine red (2.5YR 5/6) fabric. Very light brown (7.5YR 6/4) inside slip. (Probably 1C).

36.16. NFW jug (?): very fine, red (2.5YR 5/6) fabric, with some white specks and a few bubbles. Brown (7.5YR 5/4) inside slip.

36.17. NFW bowl: red (2.5YR 5/6) fabric with a few large bubbles. (Probably 1C).

36.18. NFW bowl: very fine, light red (2.5YR 6/6) fabric. Reddish brown (5YR 5/4) slip. Cf. Bikai and Perry 2001: fig. 9.4 (20–100).

36.19. NFW bowl: very fine, red (2.5YR 4/6) fabric with some white sand. (Probably 1C).

36.20. NFW bowl or jug: very fine, soft, light red (2.5YR 6/8) fabric. White sand and bubble.

36.21. NFW bowl: very fine red (2.5YR 5/6) fabric.

36.23. Handle: very fine, soft, pale yellow (5Y 8/3) fabric. Possibly Nabataean cream ware (1C).

Bucket 89.047. 7 rim, 3 base, 3 handle, 82 body. 1 lamp. Many sherds of NPFW bowls of Phase 3a (20–75; fig. 5.74)

47.1. NFW Juglet: sandy, red (2.5YR 5/8) fabric with black sand. (Probably 1C).

47.2. NFW Juglet (?): fine, light red (2.5YR 6/8) fabric. White (2.5Y 8/2) exterior surface. Base D 0.03 m. (Probably 1C).

47.3. NFW bowl: very fine, red (2.5YR 5/8) fabric. Remnants of white (2.5Y 8/2) slip around exterior of rim. Bikai and Perry 2001: fig. 9.1 (20–100).

47.4. NFW jug: very fine, light red (2.5YR 6/6) fabric. Grey (10YR 5/1) core. (Probably 1C).

47.5. Cooking pot: slightly sandy, red (2.5YR 5/8) fabric with occasional white specks and bubbles. White (2.5YR 8/2) exterior. Gerber 2001a: fig. 2F (4C).

47.6. Cooking pot: laminar, red (2.5YR 5/8) fabric with frequent white sand. Gerber 2001a: fig. 2C (2C–3C).

47.7. NFW bowl: slightly sandy, red (2.5YR 5/8) fabric. White sand.

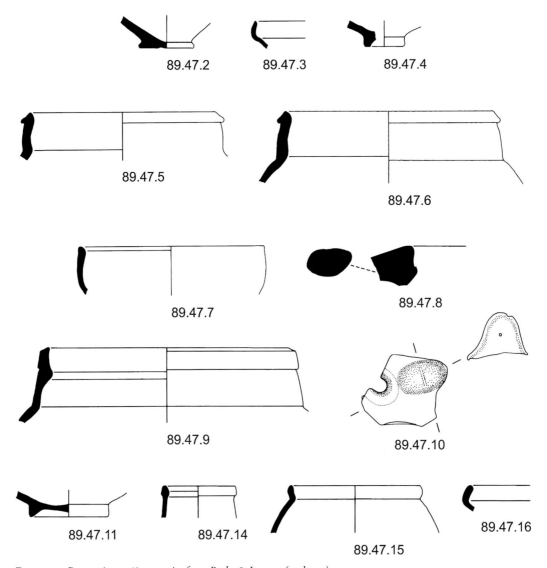

FIG. 5.74 *Reservoir no. 68, ceramics from Probe 8, Locus 1 (scale 1:2).*

47.8. Handle and rim of very heavy storage jar: hard, sandy, yellowish brown (10YR 5/4) fabric, with white inclusions. Possibly an early Islamic Aqaba ware?

47.9. Jar: sandy, light red (2.5YR 6/8) fabric with white sand and white inclusions. Remnants of white (5Y 8/2) slip on exterior surface. Gerber 1994: fig. 16A (ea. 2C); 2008: fig. 22.5 (2nd half 1C–1st half 2C).

47.10. Lamp: perforated vertical lug handle, fill hole, dot decoration on shoulder. Very fine, yellowish brown (10YR 5/6) fabric. *EZ* III *Typentafel* 2, Class J3 (225–300).

47.11. NFW bowl: very fine, slightly soft, light red (2.5YR 6/8) fabric with occasional grains of white sand. (Probably 1C).

47.14. Juglet (?): very fine, light red (2.5YR 6/8) fabric with occasional white sand grains. Rim D 0.04 m. *EZ* II fig. 286 (50 BC–AD 106).

47.15. NFW pot: very fine fabric as no. 14. *EZ* II fig. 251 (3rd quarter 1C).

47.16. NFW bowl: very fine, light red (2.5YR 6/8) fabric, with occasional white sand. White (5Y 8/2) exterior surface. Rim D 0.13 m. *EZ* II fig. 46, Phase 2c (1st half 1C).

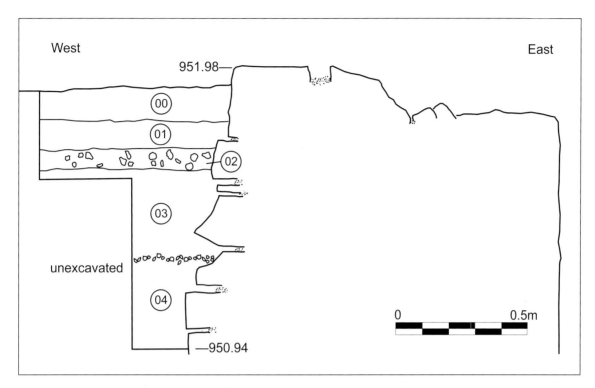

FIG. 5.75 *Cistern no. 54, section across Probe 1.*

Bucket 89.053. 67 body, 2 base, 7 rim. 2 pieces of glass, 1 possibly modern. Half a bronze ring, possibly a modern grommet.

5.G. CYLINDRICAL CISTERN (STRUCTURE NO. 54)

Since erosion, ploughing, and roadwork near this cistern made it clear that there was no other structure in the vicinity, probing in 1987 was focused on clarification of the design and chronology of the cistern itself. In 1996, several excavation squares were laid out in the adjacent field to the east (Field C124), where numerous complete or nearly complete first-century BC to first-century AD bowls and other ceramics had been exposed by ploughing (Oleson et al. 1999: 411–14). Extensive ceramic evidence for Early Nabataean and Middle Nabataean occupation was recovered, but no evidence for any structures other than Cistern no. 54. Given the absence of habitation structures in the area, it seems likely that the ceramics were deposited by individuals living here from time to time in tents, possibly drawing their water from

the adjacent cistern. This may have been a camping ground for the family that owned the cistern and occasionally participated in the events at Hawara or tended crops in the adjacent fields, which were relatively well-watered by the outflow of the wadi that passed through the settlement.

5.G.1. *Cistern 54, Probe no. 1*

Probe 1 was laid out over a well-defined section of the cistern wall along its west edge (1.30 m north/ south, 1.50 m east/west), extending 0.70 m into the hard-packed silt and soil outside the wall (figs. 4.24, 4.27, 5.75). The top of the wall (951.98 m asl, Th 1.20 m) and adjoining area of the probe were cleared of loose soil (Locus 00), exposing the structure. The upper courses of facing on the exterior and interior were composed of large, regular sandstone blocks carefully trimmed to the structure's circular plan. The core was filled with rubble packing and soil. Like Locus 00, Locus 01, designated arbitrarily at 0.10 m below the surface (950.74 m asl), consisted of compact silty soil that had washed down the catchment hill or been dredged from the cistern.

As might be expected for a structure that remained in use for centuries, the ceramics in Loci 00 and 01 dated from the first to seventh century.

A layer of sandstone cobbles and soil that contained nodules of mortar (Locus 02, Th 0.08 m) extended across the probe 0.30 m below the top of the wall. Since the surface does not seem regular enough to have constituted paving, the cobbles may simply represent construction debris or backfill. Below this point, the exterior facing of the cistern becomes irregular and projects up to 0.16 m beyond the neat face of the uppermost course. Locus 03 and 04 consist of compact brown sand, differentiated only by a lens of pebbles at 951.29 m asl. At 950.98 m asl, the outer facing of the cistern disappears or recedes markedly inward.

Locus 00 (surface clearing to –0.20 m, 951.78 m asl)

Bucket 87.028. 52 body, 1 rim, 1 handle, 2 base. All very small and worn.

Locus 01 (compact, sandy soil, 951.78 to 951.68 m asl)

Bucket 87.021. 1 body.

21.1. Jar (?) body sherd: very sandy, slightly laminar, red (2.5YR 5/8) fabric with much white sand and numerous bubbles; grey (2.5YR 5/0) core.

Locus 02 (sandstone cobbles, mortar, soil, 951.68 to 951.60 m asl)

Bucket 87.022. Sandstone cobbles.
Bucket 87.029. Nodules of fine, chalky, light grey mortar with very little sand, occasional flecks of carbon and air bubbles.

Locus 03 (sandy fill, 951.60 to 950.29 m asl)

Locus 04 (compact, sandy fill, 951.29 to 950.94 m asl; fig. 5.76)

Bucket 87.036. 1 base, 1 body.

36.1. NFW bowl; slightly gritty, red (2.5YR 5/6) fabric weak red (2.5YR 5/2) core (1C).

5.G.2. Cistern 54, Probe no. 2.

Probe 2 was executed inside a settling tank that served the cistern, exposed by surface cleaning of two lines of blocks 6 m southwest of the cis-

87.36.1

FIG. 5.76 *Cistern no. 54, ceramics from Probe 1 (scale 1:2).*

tern (figs. 4.26–27). The fill inside the tank was removed in two separate areas at the southwest end and northeast corner in largely arbitrary loci (for a description of the structural remains, see pp. 199–202). The presence of modern artefacts, such as foil from cigarette packets, in the lowest levels indicate that the fill was deposited in the modern period. Nevertheless, recovery of ceramics from the whole span of Hawara's history reveal the cistern's long period of use.

Locus 01 (surface)

Bucket 87.037. 15 body, 2 handle, 1 base. Very small and worn.

Locus 02 (loose, sandy soil, –0.23 to –0.50 m; disturbed surface fill)

Bucket 87.039. 38 body, 4 rim, 3 base. Very small and worn. NFW bowl and jug bases (1C); cook pot (Gerber 2008a: fig. 22.4, 50–150).

Locus 03 (loose, sandy soil, –0.50 to –0.95 m; disturbed surface fill)

Bucket 87.040. 38 body, 3 rim, 1 handle, 3 base. Very small, mostly very worn sherds, a mixture of fine and coarse wares. NPFW bow, Phase 3b (1C).

Bucket 87.053. 43 body, 5 rim, 1 handle, 3 base. Very small, mostly worn sherds. NFW bowl (*EZ* I fig. 666, second half 1C).

Locus 04 (fill in settling basin; disturbed)

Bucket 87.054. 5 body. One body sherd from a very large, heavy, hand-made jar is probably Ottoman in date; dark grey fabric, with white specks.

Bucket 87.055. Mortar or bedding plaster from wall of settling basin. Hard, light grey (10YR 7/1) mortar or plaster containing much poorly-sorted sand, pebbles, and angular fragments of terracotta. No visible charcoal flecks.

Locus 05 (fill in cistern intake channel; disturbed)
Bucket 87.067. 6 body, 1 rim, 1 base. Body sherd
of ESTA bowl (1–2C?).

5.H. CYLINDRICAL CISTERN
(STRUCTURE NO. 64)

One objective of the soundings in the habitation
area was determination of the original construction period of the seven built, cylindrical cisterns
with arch-supported roofs found around the site,
all but no. 54 associated with what appeared to
be domestic structures. In view of the difficulty
encountered in excavating to undisturbed deposits
around Cistern no. 69, Cistern no. 64 was selected
for investigation in 1989. This built, cylindrical
cistern at the southeast edge of the settlement was
most likely associated with a large adjacent structure excavated from 1991–95 under the designation
F102 (fig. 2.14). This complex (to be reported on in
Volume 2) seems to have been a domestic structure
during the Roman or Late Roman period, which
was later transformed into a Byzantine church.
The whole complex was then rebuilt as a domestic
structure in the Early Islamic period. Extensive
first-century Nabataean ceramic deposits were
found in strata below the later walls, along with
traces of mudbrick constructions. No other cisterns
are visible in Area F on the southeast fringe of the
habitation area of Hawara.

5.H.1. *Cistern 64, Probe no. 1.*

The cistern, its intake channel, and the associated
settling basin are all well-preserved, and the roof is
intact. Because of the presence of large numbers of
poisonous snakes, the interior of the cistern could
not be entered for close examination, but the diameter is 3.80 m, the depth 4.5 m to the present level
of the fill inside, and three arches supported the
slab roof. At present, the roof is surrounded on the
north, west, and south by 1.5 m high heaps of blocks
and rubble fallen from the F102 structures and piled
up by modern Bedouin when the cistern was put
back into use (figs. 4.32–33). This rubble obscures
the likely connection between the cistern and the
earlier stages of the F102 complex. The cistern was
observed in use in 1983, but it has remained derelict

since that time, probably because the gully from
which it drew water has eroded below the level of
the intake. In addition, the landowner is said to live
elsewhere. Only the southeast corner of what may
have been a courtyard with stepped curb around
and above the cistern is free of the rubble. At this
point, adjacent to the intake channel, Probe no.1
(2.0 m east/west, 2.0 m north/south) was excavated
in the hope of uncovering some sealed foundation
deposits outside the cistern wall.

Loci 01 to 03 consisted of strata of light brown
loessial soil containing numerous cobbles and a
mix of ceramics probably washed down over the
cistern since its modern renovation. Removal of
this late deposit uncovered the slab roof of the
intake channel (at 953.86 m asl) and a packing of
small rubble (Locus 04) occupying the rest of the
square (953.85 to 953.74 m asl). The more compact
brown soil surrounding the rubble, which seemed
to serve as a packing between the outside of the
cistern wall and the exterior face of the south wall
of the intake channel, contained numerous worn
sherds that date from the first to the fourth century.
Removal of the packing revealed the cistern's overflow conduit (Locus 05), built into the circular wall
at a bearing of 111 degrees. Two aqueduct conduit
blocks placed edge-to-edge formed the passage
through the cistern wall (fig. 4.34), and the drain
continued into the fill around the upper edge of the
cistern as a slab-built conduit (W 0.44 m; H 0.40
m, floor level 953.37 m asl). The floor of the intake
channel, naturally, is slightly higher, at 953.51 m asl.
Beneath the floor slabs of the overflow channel, a
compact, darker brown, sandy soil with an admixture of clay (Locus 06) occupied the entire square
between the exterior of the cistern wall and the
lower portion of the intake channel. This deposit,
which should form the backfill from the original
construction period, contained ceramics dating
from 50 BC to AD 20. The lower levels (excavated
down to 952.34 m asl) were sterile.

The probe revealed that Cistern no. 64 was
constructed on an unoccupied site probably in the
late first century BC or the beginning of the first
century AD. The intake channel, settling basin, and
water reservoir were constructed simultaneously of
carefully cut blocks on the interior, faced on the
outside with large, irregular pieces of limestone and

Fig. 5.77 *Cistern no. 64, ceramics from Probe 1, Locus 6 (scale 1:2).*

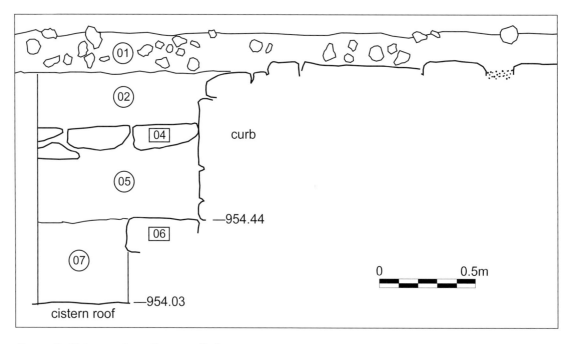

Fig. 5.78 *Cistern no. 69, section across Probe 1.*

sandstone rubble set in a grey mortar with flecks of ash. At a later time, probably in the Early Byzantine period, the upper levels of the foundation deposit were disturbed, possibly in connection with the repair of the cistern roof and the insertion of an overflow conduit. The overflow channel is the only one documented so far in the cisterns examined in the Humayma region, although this feature may well have been common when the cisterns were first built.

Locus 01 (light brown loessial soil and cobbles, surface to –0.20 m, 954.52 to 954.32 m asl)
> Bucket 89.079. 29 body, 2 rim, 2 base, 2 handle. NFW bowls, including 1 of Phase 2c (20 BC–AD 20). Numerous ovicaprid bones and a modern glass bottle.
> Bucket 89.104. 6 body, 1 rim, 2 handle.

Locus 2 (compact clay layer with ash, beneath Locus 01, 954.32 to 954.16 m asl)
> Bucket 89.080. 40 body, 4 handle, 2 rim. 1 lamp. Many amphora and cooking pot sherds. NPFW bowl, Phase 3b (1C). Nabataean cream ware jug. Jar: Gerber 2001a: fig. 2.Q (4C). Lamp with lug handle: *EZ* III, pl. 2, J.2 (3C). Many bone and seashell fragments.

Locus 3 (soft, brown sandy layer, beneath Locus 02, 954.26 to 953.78 m asl)
> Bucket 89.065. 23 body, 4 handle. Many cook pot sherds and handles. 1 Nabataean unguentarium, Johnson 1990: fig. 2, VII (1C). A few bone and seashell fragments.
> Bucket 89.099. 55 body, 9 rim.
> Bucket 89.100. 8 body, 2 base, 3 rim.
> Bucket 89.105. 3 rim, 1 body. 1 NFW bowl, Phase 2c (ea. 1C).

Locus 04 (brown soil and rubble packing, 953.78 to 953.30 m asl)

> Bucket 89.106. 55 body, 4 rim, 2 handle, 1 base. Sherds very small and worn. A few very weathered bone fragments.
>
> Bucket 89.110. 25 body. NPFW bowl (Phase 3C, 100); NFW bowl black painted motif on exterior (Phase 4; *EZ* II fig. 212, 2–3C).
>
> Bucket 89.126. 36 body, 3 rim, 1 base. Fragments of bone and teeth.

Locus 06 (compact, light brown, clay-like soil below level of overflow channel, 953.30 to 952.34 m asl; fig. 5.77)

> Bucket 89.124. 48 body, 1 rim, 1 base, 1 bronze clipping.
>
> > 124.1. NFW bowl: very fine grey (10YR 6/1) fabric with light reddish brown (5YR 6/4) slip. Burned? (50 BC–AD 20?).
> >
> > 124.2. NFW bowl: fabric as 124.01, possibly from the same vessel; outside of rim white (10YR 8/2). *EZ* II fig. 49, Phase 2 (50 BC — AD 20).
> >
> > 124.3. NFW bowl: fine red (2.5YR 5/6) fabric with a few white specks.
> >
> > 124.4. NFW bowl: fabric as no. 1 and 2, possibly from the same vessel. Streak of weak red (2.5YR 5/2) paint on exterior (50 BC–AD 20?).
>
> Bucket 89.125. 7 body, 2 rim.
>
> > 125.1. NFW Bowl: very fine red (2.5YR 5/8) fabric. *EZ* II fig. 49, Phase 2 (50 BC–AD 20).
> >
> > 125.2. Cooking pot: hard, sandy, light red (2.5YR 6/8) fabric, with numerous white specks. Light grey (7.5YR N7) core.

5.I. CYLINDRICAL CISTERN (STRUCTURE NO. 69)

One objective of the soundings in the habitation area was determination of the original construction period of the seven built, cylindrical cisterns with arch-supported roofs found around the site, all but no. 54 associated with what appeared to be domestic structures. Cistern no. 69 was selected as one of the priorities for probing during the 1989 season, because even before clearing, it appeared

to be associated with a domestic structure close to the centre of the habitation area. The cistern tank was cylindrical (D ca. 7.0 m, 5.92 m deep), with five transverse arches supporting a slab roof. The area immediately above the slab roof had been cleared of blocks at some point in the modern period, when the cistern was cleaned out for use as a source of water for humans and animals. During the 1990s, the Bedouin considered the water from this cistern as the best available in the ancient habitation area. A square shaft (0.65 m square) built of blocks provides access to the water through the 1.10 m of earth fill that has accumulated on top of the cistern roof. According to local Bedouin, this shaft was built recently to replace an original (?) opening several metres to the northwest.

The courtyard in which the cistern was located (ca. 8 × 8 m) can be traced as a regular depression in the tumbled remains of the house built up around it (fig. 4.37–38). The south and east sides of this square have been covered with heaps of rubble removed from the square in recent times, and the west side seems to have been lost to stone robbing and erosion, but in 1989 the northwest corner appeared to be virtually intact. It was assumed that a sounding at this point might reveal both the relationship between the cistern and the courtyard and yield some sealed foundation deposits behind the cistern walls. Probe no. 1 (2.40 m east/west, 2.40 m north/south) was laid out across both the corner of the court and portions of the surrounding pavement and walls on the west and north. The size of the probe was restricted by the need to leave safe access to the cistern for the local Bedouin and their animals, and by their concerns about destabilising the roof.

5.I.1. *Cistern 69, Probe no. 1.*

Removal of the surface debris over the square and for 1 m to the north (Loci 01–03) revealed a stepped arrangement of walls above a curb wall that retained 0.88 m of earth fill (Loci 05, 07) over the cistern roof (Locus 08, at 954.03 m asl; figs. 4.37, 5.78). There was a paving of sandstone slabs over the earth fill (Locus 04, at 954.90 m asl). The curb wall was built of carefully squared sandstone blocks with diagonal trimming, laid as

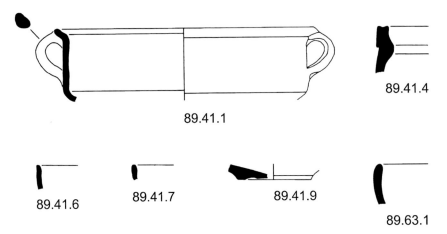

FIG. 5.79 *Cistern no. 69, ceramics from Probe 1, Locus 5 (scale 1:2).*

stretchers with an occasional header block. Traces were found of a second level of sandstone paving 0.50 m below the first (Locus 06, at 954.44 m asl), 0.40 m above the long, roughly-trimmed blocks roofing the cistern.

The loci above the upper paving (Loci 01–03), a series of sloping layers of light brown loess, sand, and ash with occasional cobbles, contained a rich assortment of ceramic material dating from the first to the seventh centuries, along with ovicaprid and bird bones and numerous small fragments of glass vessels. Although the context probably has been disturbed, or at best is a dump from elsewhere at the site, it is interesting to contrast the wide variety of shapes, including saucepans and cooking pots, with the coarse-ware storage and transport vessels found in the upper layers of fill around Reservoirs 67 and 68. The appearance of bones and glass also suggests a domestic context.

Excavation of ashy fill beneath the upper paving (Locus 05) yielded a large number of badly worn sherds from the first and second centuries, along with a few possibly Byzantine wares that may reflect the occupational history of the house. The ashy fill (Locus 07) between the lower paving (Locus 06) and the cistern roof contained sherds of the first to second century, possibly as late as the third. This deposit may date to the time of construction of the cistern.

Unfortunately, due to the danger of destabilising the roof and putting at risk the people and animals using the cistern, the landowner would

not allow excavation into the deposits behind the cistern wall. Since no sealed structural loci were excavated, the pottery recovered in this probe cannot be used to date the construction of the cistern. Nevertheless, the predominance of first- and second-century wares beneath the lowest surviving paving indicates that an early date for the construction of the complex is possible. Documentation of the courtyard curb and paving, combined with the character of the wares in Loci 05 and 07, suggest the domestic character of the complex.

Locus 01 (surface cleaning of light brown sandy soil and rubble to –0.20 m, ca. 955.16 m asl)

> Bucket 89.037. 40 body, 4 rim, 2 handle, 1 base. Several cooking pots; several pieces of green glass (modern?); 1 fish vertebra. Cook pot: see ʿAmr and Momani 1999: fig. 11.24 (2nd half 1C).

Locus 02 (compacted sandy soil and ash below Locus 01 and above Locus 04 paving, 955.16 to 954.90)

> Bucket 89.038. 2 rim, 1 base, 35 body. NPFW bowl, Phase 3b (late 1–ea. 2C); NFW bowls (1C). Heavy amphora sherds. Bird and ovicaprid bones. 2 fragments of glass.

Locus 03 (cleaning between blocks and rubble around square)

> Bucket 89.039. 1 rim, 25 body. 1 dolium wall fragment, 1 cook pot rim and handle, fragments of glass bottle.

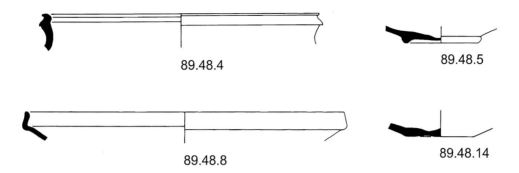

Fig. 5.80 *Cistern no. 69, ceramics from Probe 1, Locus 7 (scale 1:2).*

Bucket 89.049. 4 body, 1 base. 1 NFW bowl sherd (1C); base of NFW juglet, cf. Bikai and Perry 2001: no. 16 (20 BC–AD 80).

Locus 05 (sand and ash below Locus 04 pavement, 954.80 to 954.44 m asl)

Bucket 89.041. 2 rim, 1 handle, 29 body, 1 base. Bone fragments, fragments of thin-walled glass bottle. K. ʿAmr (oral communication 1989) dates the assemblage first to second century (fig. 5.79).

41.1. Bowl or saucepan: fine red (2.5YR 5/8) fabric with occasional white sand grains. Cf. Gerber 1994: fig. 161 (ea. 2C); 2008: fig. 22.12 (2nd half 1 to 1st half 2C). D 0.14 m.

41.2. Body sherd: gritty red (2.5YR 5/8) fabric with occasional white specks and bubbles. Exterior surface partially painted pale yellow (2.5Y 8/2).

41.3. Handle: sandy, laminar, yellowish red (5YR 5/8) fabric with occasional white specks. Exterior surface grey (10YR 6/1).

41.4. Cooking pot: slightly sandy, light red (2.5YR 6/8) fabric with frequent white sand grains. White (2.5Y 8/2) exterior surface. D 0.10 m. Dolinka 2003: 120 no 5 (ea. 2C); Gerber 1994: fig. 16A (ea. 2C); 2008: fig. 22.5 (2nd half 1 to 1st half 2C).

41.5. Body sherd: slightly sandy, light red (2.5YR 6/8) fabric, with frequent white sand grains. White (2.5Y 8/2) exterior surface.

41.6. NFW Cup: very fine, red (2.5YR 5/8) fabric with occasional white sand grains. D 0.09 m? (1C).

41.7. NFW bowl: fabric as 41.6. (1C?).

41.8. Cup: fabric as 41.6.

41.9. NFW bowl: fabric as 41.6. Cf. *EZ* II fig. 50 (ea 1C).

Bucket 89.063. 8 body, 1 handle, 1 rim. K. ʿAmr (oral communication 1989) dates this assemblage mostly first to second century, with some fifth- or early sixth-century sherds.

63.1. NFW bowl: sandy, light red (2.5YR 6/8) fabric with a few white specks. Red (2.5YR 5/6) core. D 0.13 m. (1C?).

63.2. Bowl body sherd: hard, light red (2.5YR 6/6) fabric with a few white specks and bubbles. Grey (7.5YR 5/0) core. Drag marks on exterior. (probably 1C).

63.3. Bowl body sherd: hard, slightly sandy, reddish yellow (5YR 6/6) fabric. Dull red (10R 5/6) slip on both surfaces. Th 0.007 m.

63.5. NFW bowl: slightly sandy, red (2.5YR 5/8) fabric. Very pale brown (10YR 7/3) slip paint on interior surface. Th 0.002 m.

63.6. NFW bowl: very fine, light red (2.5YR 6/8) fabric with occasional white sand grains. Grey (10YR 5/1) core, very pale brown (10YR 7/3) surfaces.

63.7. Body sherd: hard red (2.5YR 5/8) fabric. Drag marks on exterior. (probably 1C).

63.9. Body sherd: hard, laminar, light red (2.5YR 6/8) fabric. Very pale brown (10YR 7/4) exterior surface with sharp-ridged comb pattern. (5C?).

Locus 07 (compact, reddish orange sand and ash, below Locus 05, 954.44 to 954.03 m asl; fig. 5.80)

Bucket 89.048. 3 rim, 1 handle, 2 base, 76 body. Ovicaprid bones.

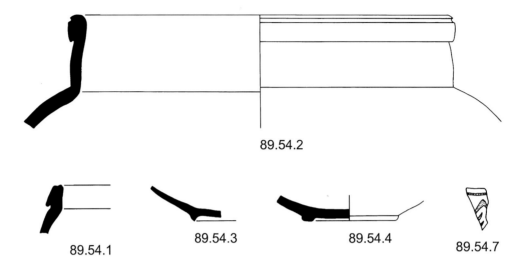

89.54.2

89.54.1   89.54.3   89.54.4   89.54.7

FIG. 5.81 *Cistern no. 69, ceramics from Probe 1, Locus 7 (scale 1:2).*

48.2. Nabataean cream ware jug: soft, pale yellow (5Y 8/3) fabric with occasional white sand grains. (1–ea. 2C).

48.3. Handle: hard, sandy, laminar red (2.5YR 5/8) fabric with occasional bubbles and white specks. Dark brown (7.5YR 4/2) core, weak red (10R 5/4) surfaces.

48.4. Pot or jar: slightly sandy, red (2.5YR 5/8) fabric with bubbles and white sand grains. Very pale brown (10YR 7/3) exterior surfaces. Cf. Gerber, Humayma bucket 98.0137 (1–2C); 2001b: fig. 1.21 (2–3C).

48.5. NFW bowl: fine, hard, light red (2.5YR 6/6) fabric with some bubbles. Bikai and Perry 2001: fig. 9.4 (20–100).

48.6. Ribbed body sherd: fine, hard, light red (2.5YR 6/8) fabric.

48.8. NFW bowl: slightly sandy, light red (2.5YR 6/8) fabric with occasional white sand grains. Occasional remnants of very pale brown (10YR 7/3) exterior surface slip. *EZ* II fig. 49 (ea. 1C); Bikai and Perry 2001: fig. 9.1 (20–100).

48.14. NFW jug (?): string-cut base: slightly sandy, red (2.5YR 5/8) fabric with occasional white specks. (1C).

Bucket 89.054. 40 body, 2 base, 2 rim. K. ʿAmr (oral communication, 1989) says that all the definers are first to second century, and most

of the material appears to be second-century in date (fig. 5.81).

54.1. Cooking pot: red (2.5YR 4/8) fabric with many white specks, white pebbles, and a few bubbles. Light brown (7.5YR 6/4) wash on exterior. Dolinka 2003: 121 no. 6 (ea. 2C).

54.2. Cook pot: dark greyish brown (10YR 4/2) fabric with white sand grains. Thin red (2.5YR 4/8) core. Cf. Gerber 1994: fig. 16A (ea. 2C).

54.3. NFW bowl: light red (2.5YR 6/8) fabric with very small white specks and a few bubbles. Traces of light, very pale brown (10YR 8/3) slip on interior. Dragging on outside surface.

54.4. NFW bowl or jug: hard, medium fine, yellowish red (5YR 5/8) fabric with a few white specks. Reddish grey (5YR 5/2) slip on exterior. (1C).

54.5. Ridged body sherd: red (2.5YR 5/6) fabric. White (10YR 8/2) slip. Th 0.003.

54.6. NFW bowl: yellowish red (5YR 5/8) fabric. Pinkish grey (7.5YR 7/2) core. Th 0.003.

54.7. NFW cup or juglet: arrow-shaped incision on exterior; very fine, red (2.5YR 5/8) fabric. *EZ* II fig. 368 (70/80–100); Bikai and Perry 2001: fig. 7.6 (20–100).

54.8. NFW bowl: red (2.5YR 5/6) fabric. Dark grey (2.5YR N4/) core, weak red (2.5YR 4/2) slip on both surfaces.

54.9. Body sherd from large pot: coarse, dark grey (10YR 4/1) fabric. Thin red (2.5YR 4/6) outer core, greyish brown (10YR 5/2) surface.

54.10. Handle: slightly sandy, red (2.5YR 5/6) fabric with a few white specks. Light brownish grey (10YR 6/2) surfaces.

54.11. Handle: red (2.5YR 5/6) fabric with white sand and bubbles. Red (10YR 5/1) slip.

5.J. DOMED CISTERN OR GRANARY (STRUCTURE NO. 72)

Since the design of this possible domed cistern seemed very different from that of the other cisterns visible around Humayma (figs. 4.41–42), a probe was excavated in its interior in order to find the floor and to document any surviving plaster that would prove it was used to hold water. Surface ceramics found around the structure appear to date from the first century BC through the Umayyad period, but the ceramic definers found in the fill within the structure cluster around the first and second century. Sealed contexts are needed to date this structure.

5.J.1. *Cistern no. 72, Probe no. 1*

A point was selected along the east wall where the level of the fallen rubble filling the cistern was lower than elsewhere, and a probe was laid out extending 1.5 m out from the wall and 2 m along it (fig. 5.82). The surface clearing (Locus 01) to −0.25 m (953.96 m asl) removed loose soil and stones and some modern rubbish. Below this level, down to −1.80 m (952.41 m asl), the fill was essentially uniform, consisting of light sandy soil containing numerous fallen sandstone blocks from the dome and walls. The ceramics were the usual mix of small fragments of Nabataean through Byzantine or possibly Umayyad wares found everywhere on the surface and in the upper depositional levels at Humayma, along with a few bird and ovicaprid bones suggesting the deposit of refuse. At 952.41 m asl, a deposit of a fine,

white, powdery material mixed with pebbles and ash or decayed plaster (Locus 04) was observed extending out 0.25 m from the wall surface. Because of the presence of large blocks of rubble, this locus could be removed only in a small portion of the south corner of the square (0.40 × 0.35 m). The deposit tapered inward toward the wall, until at 952.11 m asl it abutted a plastered surface; up to this point, there were no traces of plaster on the walls. No ceramics were recovered. The plaster (Bucket 87.179) was soft, very pale brown (10YR 8/3), heavily tempered with poorly-sorted, rounded sand and pebbles, and contained occasional small lumps of lime. It does not appear to be a suitable hydraulic plaster, but possibly this upper edge has been softened by weathering or burning. Unfortunately, the peril of structural collapse and the presence of large pieces of rubble made it impossible to follow this plaster down to a floor level.

Locus 00 (random surface finds outside of cistern)
Bucket 87.166. 5 body, 1 rim, Pestle of very pale brown marl (fig. 5.83).

166.1. NPFW bowl: very fine, pink (5YR 8/3) fabric with a dull but even, light red (2.5YR 6/8) slip on interior and exterior. D 0.16 m. *EZ* II fig. 17 (1C BC). The shape is very close to ETSA (cf. Hayes 1985: pl. III.8, Form 20, 2nd half 2nd C BC), but the slip does not seem glossy enough, and the ceramic date is too early for the site.

166.3. Body sherd of jar (?): soft, sandy, very pale brown (10YR 8/4) fabric; dark emerald green glazed exterior, with two darker green horizontal stripes; possibly Parthian Ware. This ware appears very rarely at Petra and Humayma; cf. *EZ* I: 138 (100 BC–AD 150).

Locus 01 (surface soil and rubble to −0.25, 953.96)
Bucket 87.143. 69 body, 5 rim, 3 handle, 1 base. 1 body sherd of ETSA (1C?).

Locus 02 (sand and stone fill, 953.96 to 953.41 m asl; fig. 5.83)
Bucket 87.144. 14 body, 1 handle.
Bucket 87.149. 63 body, 9 rim, 3 handle, 6 base.

149.1. NFW bowl: granular, laminar, light red (2.5YR 6/8) fabric with white grits and bubbles. D 0.12 m. *EZ* II no. 135 (100–50 BC).

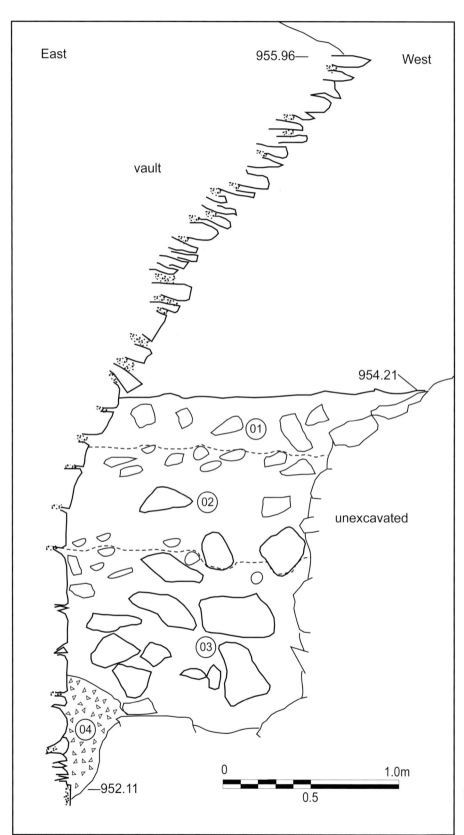

East   955.96—   West

vault

954.21—

01

02   unexcavated

03

04

—952.11

0   1.0m

0.5

Fig. 5.82 *Cistern no. 72, section across Probe 1.*

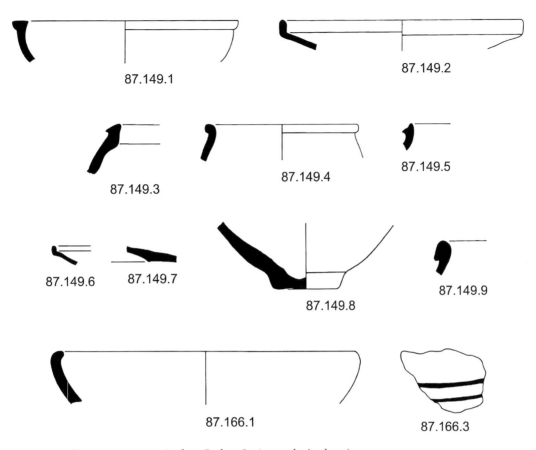

FIG. 5.83 *Cistern no. 72, ceramics from Probe 1, Loci 00 and 2 (scale 1:2).*

149.2. NFW bowl: medium fine, red (2.5YR 5/8) fabric with a few white grits. D 0.13 m. Cf. *EZ* II fig 49, Phase 2c (0–20).

149.3. Cooking pot: fabric as 149.1. Gerber 2001b: 1.13 (2nd half 1–ea. 2C); Gerber 2008a: fig. 22.8 (2nd half 1–ea. 2C).

149.4. Pot: medium fine, hard, weak red (2.5YR 4/2) fabric with white grits. Possible light reddish brown (2.5YR 6/4) stripe on rim and just below. D 0.08 m? *EZ* II fig. 224 (1C).

149.5. Cooking pot: sandy, dark grey (2.5YR 4/0), fabric with white grits and bubbles.

149.6. NPFW bowl: fine red (2.5YR 5/8) fabric; reddish brown (2.5YR 4/4) paint on interior. *EZ* II fig. 379, Phase 3c (100–106).

149.7. Juglet (?): fabric as 149.2. String-cut foot. (1st C).

149.8. Jug: hard, sandy, weak red (2.5YR 5/2) fabric with numerous white and black in-

clusions and bubbles. Pale red (2.5YR 6/2) surfaces. Base D 0.036 m.

149.9. Jar or cooking pot: hard, sandy, dark reddish grey (5YR 4/2) fabric with numerous white grits.

Locus 03 (sand and stone fill, 953.41 to 952.41 m asl; fig. 5.84)

Bucket 87.150. 12 body, 1 rim, 2 handle, 1 base. Includes first-century Nabataean "honey pot" and NFW bowl.

Bucket 87.165. 60 body, 13 rim, 1 handle, 2 base.

165.1. Jar: hard, sandy, reddish brown (5YR 5/4) fabric with frequent white grits and a few bubbles. Pink (7.5YR 8/4) surface.

165.2. Jar: medium hard, sandy, light red (2.5YR 6/8) fabric with numerous white grits, inclusions, and bubbles. D 0.14 m. Cf. Gerber 2001c: fig. 12U (1C).

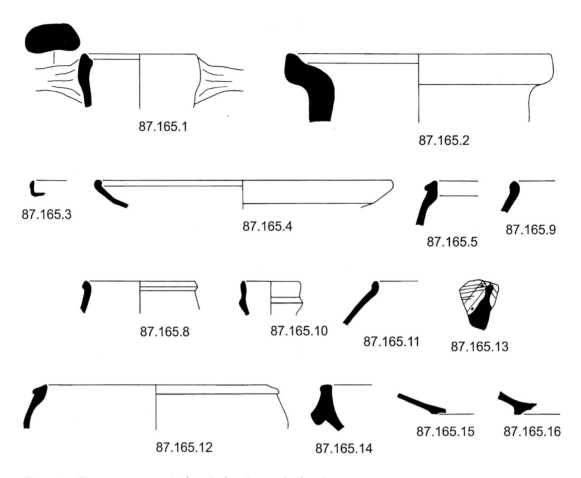

87.165.1

87.165.2

87.165.3

87.165.4

87.165.5

87.165.9

87.165.8

87.165.10

87.165.11

87.165.13

87.165.12

87.165.14

87.165.15

87.165.16

Fig. 5.84 *Cistern no. 72, ceramics from Probe 1, Locus 3 (scale 1:2).*

165.3. NFW bowl: fine, hard, red (10R 5/6) fabric. Outside surface reddish grey (10R 5/1). *EZ* II fig. 55, Phase 3b (70/80–100).

165.4. NFW bowl: fine, hard, red (2.5YR 5/6) fabric. D 0.15 m. Cf. *EZ* II fig. 93, Phase 3c (100–106).

165.5. Cooking pot: hard, sandy, yellowish red (5YR 5/8) fabric with a few white inclusions. Cf. Gerber 2001b: fig. 1.14 (2nd half 1–ea. 2C).

165.8. Pot: medium hard, sandy, yellowish red (5YR 5/6) fabric with a few white specks. *EZ* II fig. 228, Phase 3b–c (70/80–106).

165.9. Pot: hard, sandy, reddish yellow (5YR 6/8) fabric with numerous white specks. *EZ* II fig. 225, Phase 3b (70/80–100).

165.10. Jug: hard, sandy, reddish yellow (5YR 6/6) fabric with white specks. Dark grey (5YR 4/1) surface. *EZ* II fig. 323, Phase 3b (70/80–100).

165.11. Jar: hard, fine, strong brown (7.5YR 5/6) fabric with a few white specks. Light grey (7.5YR 7/0) surfaces. *EZ* II fig. 225, Phase 3b (70/80–100).

165.12. Cooking pot: hard, sandy, yellowish red (5YR 5/8) fabric with numerous white specks and bubbles. Very pale brown (10YR 7/3) outer surface and grey (10YR 6/1) core. D 0.12 m. Gerber 2001c: fig. 12G (mid to 2nd half 1C).

165.13. NPFW bowl: fine, hard, yellowish red (5YR 5/8) fabric. Red (2.5YR 4/6) slip paint. Phase 3b (late 1C).

165.14. Plate: very fine, red (2.5YR 5/6) fabric. Slightly flaky red (2.5YR 4/8) slip. Possibly ETSB: Hayes 1985: pl. XV.12, Form 77 (1st half 2C).

165.15. NFW bowl: fine, hard, red (2.5YR 5/6) fabric. Burnished surface? (1C).

165.16. NFW bowl: fine, hard, yellowish red (5YR 5/8) fabric. (1C).

Bucket 87.179. Soft, very pale brown (10YR 8/3) plaster heavily tempered with poorly-sorted, rounded sand and pebbles, and containing occasional small lumps of lime.

5.K. CONDUIT BLOCKS (STRUCTURE NO. 75)

In the search for surface remains of the continuation of the aqueduct (Structure no. 1) beyond the Roman bath (Site E077) and into the settlement centre, a 5 m stretch of 7 marl and 1 sandstone conduit blocks identical to those used in the aqueduct was observed at present ground level 100 m east of Reservoir no. 67 (fig. 4.45). Although the conduits had been laid carelessly on the soil, without the heavy foundation typical of the aqueduct, they represented the only possible trace of the aqueduct in this area and were high enough to allow flow into the reservoir. In consequence, a probe was laid out across the channel around the middle of its course (1.0 × 1.25 m) to search for a foundation.

5.K.1. *Conduit Blocks (Structure no. 75), Probe no. 1*

Clearing of 0.05 m of loose surface soil to 955.90 m asl (Locus 01) revealed that the conduits had been laid without much care, leaving small gaps between each block that were filled with sand and pebbles. Some of the blocks carried traces of concretion but most did not, and there was no continuity of concretion across the joints. The rubble and soil in the southwest corner was cleared to the base of the fourth and fifth conduit blocks (counting from the top of the slope; Locus 02), revealing the same deposit of sandy soil, cobbles, and very worn sherds found in Locus 01. The same soil was found 0.10 m beneath and 0.50 m west of the conduit blocks (Locus 03, to 955.51 m asl), along with the same cultural material.

The sloppy construction of this feature and the absence of any foundation strongly suggest that the conduit blocks found here were in secondary use. Given their exposure on the surface in an area that has been heavily altered by the Bedouin over the last century, it is likely that the feature was constructed in the recent past with conduit blocks salvaged from the aqueduct and other structures around the site. The intended function is not clear.

Locus 01 (surface clearing to 955.81)
Bucket 87.093. 7 body, 2 handle, 1 base.

Locus 02 (rubble and soil in southwest corner to 955.61)
Bucket 87.102. 22 body, 1 base, 1 handle.

Locus 03 (rubble and soil below base of conduit blocks 4 and 5, 955.61 to 955.51 m asl)
Bucket 87.103. 6 body.

5.L. SETTLING TANK AND ASSOCIATED DRAINS (STRUCTURE NO. 76)

During survey of the settlement centre in 1987, a series of cover slabs was noted at ground level in an area of house remains 30 m northwest of Reservoir no. 67. Surface cleaning revealed the presence of a subterranean channel or drain built of slabs, at least 16 m long, draining eastward at a gentle slope (figs. 4.46–48). Probes 1 and 2 revealed the design of this feature. Probes 3 and 4 uncovered a channel of conduit blocks sloping from north to south, intersecting the line of the drain at a settling or storage tank, explored in Probe 5. Water originally flowed out of the tank through an overflow opening into the east/west conduit. It is unclear what the original arrangements were for filling the tank, but in a late phase water entered the tank through the north conduit and the western overflow was closed up.

5.L.1. *Drain no. 76, Probe no. 1*

A probe (L 0.75 m east/west, W 1.0 m north/south) was laid out across the apparent drain, which appeared to be about 0.60 m wide (figs. 5.85–86). Clearing of the surface soil (Locus 01) to −0.14 m revealed flat, roughly-trimmed sandstone slabs (L ca. 0.60 m, W ca. 0.40 m, Th ca. 0.10 m). Removal of one slab revealed that these were cover slabs

FIG. 5.85   *Drain no. 76, Probe 1 from east.*

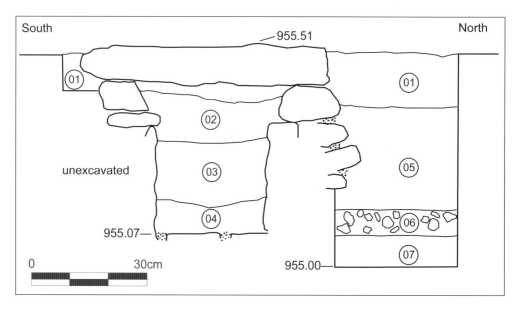

FIG. 5.86   *Drain no. 76, section across Probe 1.*

87.124.1   87.124.2   87.124.3   87.124.4

FIG. 5.87   *Drain no. 76, ceramics from Probe 1, Locus 5 (scale 1:2).*

laid sideways (top elev. 955.51 m asl), edge-to-edge across a channel 0.31 m wide, resting at either end on support walls built of small, irregular, flat stones. Several strata were found within the channel: firm sandy soil and sherds from –0.12 to –0.23 m (Locus 02); fine, soft red-brown sand without sherds from –0.23 to –0.37 m (Locus 03); and a hard, light brown silty deposit with sherds from –0.37 to the floor at –0.44 (Locus 04; floor surface at 955.07 m asl). Locus 04, which contained a few very worn small sherds (possibly Byzantine), appears to be the residue of the last period of the drain's use. Wind-blown sand sifted in early in the period of abandonment (Locus 03), followed by soil and sherds washed in after some cover slabs were lost in the vicinity. The ceramic material, first- to seventh-century in date, is typical of surface material found everywhere at the site. The channel floor was built of irregular flat stones set in mud. Sandstone slabs (W 0.25–0.28 m) were set on edge on this floor to form the side walls, with a single course of small, flat stones on the upper edge probably intended to facilitate levelling of the cover slabs or to allow water to escape if the channel was completely filled. There was no sign of mortar, plaster, or water-deposited carbonates within the channel.

The fill outside the channel, to the north, was excavated to –0.54 m (955.00 m asl), below the level of the slab floor. Locus 05 (–0.14 to –0.39 m) consisted of fairly loose soil and rubble containing very small sherds, of which the definers all dated to the first century. Below, Locus 06 (–0.39 to –0.54 m) consisted of a gravelly deposit with cobbles and a large amount of ceramics, with material dateable to the first to early second century. This rested on red sand containing large numbers of ceramics, including a large proportion of fine wares (Locus 07) dating to the first century. These loci should represent backfill placed around the drain immediately after its construction, filled with rubbish containing many burned potsherds. Although no dateable sherds were later than the second century, the construction of the channel could date much later. A worn coin found on the surface 15 m east of the drain (1987.195.01) is possibly Early Islamic in date.

Locus 01 (surface, to –0.14 m)
Bucket 87.121. 21 body, 3 rim, 1 handle.

Locus 02 (firm, sandy soil inside channel, –0.14 to –0.23 m)
Bucket 87.122. 7 body, 1 handle, 1 base. NPFW bowl (Phase 3c, 100–106); Nabataean rosette lamp (1C).

Locus 03 (fine, soft red-brown soil inside channel, –0.23 to –0.40 m)

Locus 04 (hard, light brown silty soil inside channel, on floor, –0.40 to –0.48 m; 955.07 m asl)
Bucket 87.123. 4 body.

Locus 05 (fill north of channel, –0.14 to –0.39 m; fig. 5.87)
Bucket 87.124. 35 body, 2 rim, 1 handle. Very small sherds.
124.1. NFW bowl: very fine, hard, reddish yellow (7.5YR 7/6) fabric. Bikai and Perry 2001: fig. 5.5 (20 BC–AD 80).
124.2. NFW bowl: very fine, hard, light red (10R 6/8) fabric. (1C?).
124.3. NFW bowl: fabric as 124.1. Phase 2c or 3? (1C).
124.4. Cup or bowl: fabric as 124.2, but only 1.5 mm thick. Surface light red (10R 6/6) with dark red (10R 3/6) painted decoration. Probably Phase 3b, see *EZ II Farbtafel* 3–4 (70/80–100).

Locus 06 (silty soil fill with gravel and cobbles, north of channel, –0.39 to –0.48 m; fig. 5.88)
Bucket 87.126. 64 body, 3 rim, 1 handle.
126.1. NFW jug: very fine, hard, pink fabric. *EZ II* fig. 350, mid-1C.
Bucket 87.131. 103 body, 6 rim, 1 handle, 1 base. Many of the sherds appear to have been burned.
131.1. Round-bottomed pan: coarse, sandy, brown (7.5YR 5/4) fabric, burned dark grey (7.5YR 5/0) on exterior. D 0.13 m? Gerber 2008a: fig. 22.12 (2nd half 1C–1st half 2C); Parker 1987: fig. 93.26 (1C).
131.2. Bowl (?): fine, hard, reddish yellow (5YR 6/6) fabric. D 0.09 m. Cf. *EZ II* fig. 139 (chronology unknown).

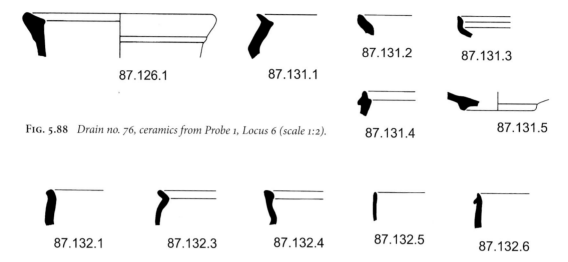

FIG. 5.88 *Drain no. 76, ceramics from Probe 1, Locus 6 (scale 1:2).*

FIG. 5.89 *Drain no. 76, ceramics from Probe 1, Locus 7 (scale 1:2).*

131.3. NFW bowl: slightly sandy, reddish yellow (5YR 6/8) fabric with many white specks, burned dark grey (7.5YR 4/0) on exterior.

131.4. Cooking pot: granular, light reddish brown (5YR 6/4) fabric. Light grey (5YR 7/1) exterior slip.

131.5. NFW bowl (?): slightly sandy, reddish brown (5YR 4/3) fabric. (1C?).

131.6. NPFW bowl body sherd: fine, reddish yellow (5YR 6/6) fabric. Reddish brown (5YR 5/4) slip paint on interior. Very small and worn. Possibly Phase 3c (ea. 2C).

Locus 07 (coarse, red sand fill north of channel, from −0.48 to 0.57 m, 955.00 m asl; fig. 5.89)

Bucket 87.132. 93 body, 9 rim, 1 base. 1 sherd of Nabataean cream ware (1C–ea. 2C). Sherds very small, possibly burned.

132.1. Jar (?): gritty, hard, reddish yellow (5YR 6/8) fabric. Light grey (5YR 7/1) core. D 0.12 m.

132.2. Bowl: fabric as 132.1.

132.3. Pot rim: gritty, yellowish red (5YR 5/8) fabric. D 0.09 m? Cf. *EZ* II fig. 139 (chronology unknown).

132.4. Bowl (?): gritty, reddish brown (5YR 4/3) fabric (burned?).

132.5. NFW bowl: very fine, reddish yellow (5YR 6/8) fabric. Red (10R 5/6) slip paint on exterior and on interior lip. (1–2C).

132.6. Cooking pot: sandy, red (2.5YR 5/6) fabric. Dark grey (2.5YR 4/0) exterior surface (burned?).

132.7. ETSA (?) jug (?) body sherd: very fine, very pale brown (10YR 7/3) fabric. Glossy red (10R 4/8) slip paint on exterior only. (1C?).

132.8. Bowl (?) body sherd: medium fine, pinkish white (4.5YR 8.2) fabric. Splash of light reddish brown (5YR 6/3) paint on exterior.

5.L.2. *Drain no. 76, Probe no. 2*

A second probe (L 1.0 m north/south, 0.50 m east/west) was laid out 8 m east of Probe 1 on the line of the channel to document its continuation downhill in this direction (fig. 4.46). The soil loci are more or less the same as those of Probe 1. Surface clearing of 0.10 m of loose, light brown soil (Locus 01, to 955.05 m asl) showed that no cover slabs remained in place over the channel (W 0.28–0.32 m). The channel was filled with light, sandy brown soil (Locus 02) down to the level of the floor (at 954.81 m asl), which was constructed of irregular flat stones set in clay (fig. 5.90). The channel walls were built of irregular slabs set on edge, topped by a course of fist-sized cobbles that originally supported the cover slabs. The ceramics consisted of small, very worn sherds possibly dating as late as the Byzantine period. The fall from the lip of the basin in Probe

5 to the drain floor at this point is 0.35 m over 12.4 m, or 2.82 percent.

Locus 01 (light brown surface soil to –0.11, 955.05 m asl)

Bucket 87.135. 28 body, 1 rim.

Locus 02 (fill inside channel, 955.04 to 955.81 m asl)

Bucket 87.136. 14 body, 1 rim.

5.L.3. *Drain no. 76, Probe no. 3*

Since the channel identified in Probes 1 and 2 clearly must have been connected to some other collection or feeder conduits, a search was made for surface indications of hydraulic features uphill from the channel. A marl conduit block of the type used in the aqueduct was observed at the surface 9.14 m northwest of Probe 1 (L 0.64 m, W 0.29 m, H 0.21 m, channel W 0.11 m, 0.13 m deep), at the edge of an unpublished excavation carried out by the Department of Antiquities in the 1960s. The north end of the block had been cleared at that time, and it appeared to slope to the south out of a small court in front of a house. A small probe (Probe 3; L 1.20 m, W 1.0 m) was laid out over the conduit block. Excavation of the packed, light brown surface soil to –0.21 m (Locus 01) exposed one heavy sandstone slab (Th 0.05 m) laid directly on the top edges of the conduit (elev. 955.77 m asl). More cover slabs were revealed over a series of conduit blocks sloping downhill to the south on a bearing of 150 degrees. The cover slabs were only as wide as the conduit blocks themselves (W 0.29 m). A stratum of sandy, reddish-brown soil ran up against both sides of the conduit block to its base at –0.49 m (Locus 02, 03). At this point, the floor of the conduit channel is at 955.61 m asl, the base of the block at 955.45 m asl (figs. 5.91–92). The ceramics in all these loci included sherds dating from the first century through possibly the Late Byzantine or Early Islamic period, indicating late deposit of the surrounding fill. The ceramic fragments in the reddish brown sand below the level of the conduit block (Locus 04, to –0.66 m, 955.29 m asl) were very small and not distinctive, but one could be dated to the first century. Given the presence of probably late ceramics in Locus 03, it

Fig. 5.90 *Drain no. 76, view of Probe 2 from north.*

is possible that this conduit was set up in the Early Islamic period.

Locus 01 (surface soil to –0.21 m, 955.79 m asl)

Bucket 87.155. 45 body, 4 rim, 2 handle, 2 base.

Locus 02 (reddish brown soil with small stones, on both sides of conduit, 955.79 to 955.45 m asl)

Bucket 87.156. 26 body, 1 handle.

156.1. Handle: hard, sandy, pink (7.5YR 8/4) fabric with red inclusions, white sand, and bubbles.

Locus 03 (sandy red soil on both sides of channel, –0.29 to –0.46 m; fig. 5.93)

Bucket 87.157. 87 body, 7 rim, 3 handle, 2 base. Numerous animal bone fragments.

FIG. 5.91 *Drain no. 76, view of Probe 3 from north.*

157.1. Nabataean cream ware jar: soft, white (2.5Y 8/2) fabric with white and black specks. D 0.14 m. The shape does not appear in 'Amr 1992 or *EZ* I fig. 579–91, but the fabric is distinctive (1C–ea. 2C).

157.2. Basin: hard, very sandy, reddish yellow (5YR 6/6) fabric with numerous white and grey specks and bubbles. No close parallels noted, but the shape and fabric suggest a Late Byzantine or Early Islamic date; cf. Melkawi, 'Amr, Whitcomb 1994: 456, fig. 8.P (5C–6C?); 'Amr and Schick 2001: fig. 11.36 (650); Kareem 2001: fig. 4.6 (8C–9C).

157.3. Jar: medium hard, slightly sandy, red (2.5YR 5/6) fabric with white specks. Light reddish brown (2.5YR 6/4) core. D 0.10 m. Cf. Gerber 2001b: fig. 1.27 (4C–1st half 5C).

157.4. Cooking pot lid: sandy, dark grey (2.5YR 4/0) fabric.

157.5. Cooking pot: hard, sandy, dark reddish brown (2.5YR 3/4) fabric with numerous grey and white specks. Surfaces dark grey (2.5YR

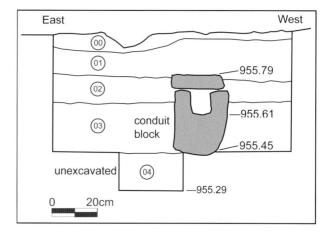

FIG. 5.92 *Drain no. 76, section across Probe 3.*

4/0). Cf. Gerber 2001a: fig. 2C (2C–3C?); 2008: fig. 22.12 (2nd half 1C–1st half 2C, or later).

157.6. Nabataean cream ware jug: fabric as 157.1. 'Amr 1992: fig. 4. (1C–ea. 2C).

157.7. NFW bowl: fine, slightly soft, reddish yellow (7.5YR 6/6) fabric with a few white specks and numerous bubbles. Base D 0.05 m (1C?).

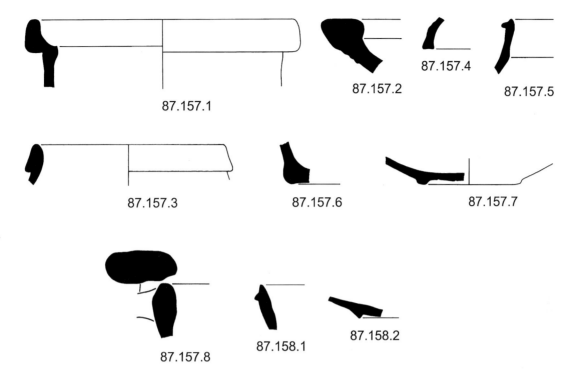

FIG. 5.93 *Drain no. 76, ceramics from Probe 3, Loci 3 and 4 (scale 1:2).*

157.8. Heavy pot or jar (?): hard, sandy, red (2.5YR 5/8) fabric with numerous white specks and bubbles. Exterior surface grey (2.5YR 6/0).

157.9. Nabataean cream ware jug handle: fabric as 157.1. (1C–ea. 2C).

Locus 04 (red sandy soil below level of conduit block, to 955.29 m asl)

Bucket 87.158. 1 rim, 1 base, 33 body. Very small fragments.

158.1. Cooking pot: hard, sandy, dark brown (7.5YR 4/4) fabric with many white sand particles. Dark grey surfaces (7.5YR 4/0).

158.2. NFW bowl: fine, hard, reddish brown (5YR 5/4) fabric. Burned? (1C?).

5.L.4. Drain no. 76, Probe no. 4

Probe 4 (L 0.50 m, W 1.0 m) was laid out 3 m south of Probe 3 to document the continuation of the conduit beyond Probe 3 towards an intersection with the line of the channel found in Probes 1 and 2. The loose, light brown surface soil (Locus 01, to –0.11 m) contained the usual wide range of ceramics. This stratum overlaid a more compact layer of brown soil and cobbles, which incorporated the conduit cover slabs at –0.24 m (Locus 02). Removal of one cover slab (L 0.30 m, W 0.15 m, Th 0.05 m) revealed the conduit channel (W 0.10 m, 0.13 m deep, floor at 955.46 m asl), filled with a fine, light brown silt devoid of artefacts (Locus 03). A few probably first- and second-century sherds were found outside the conduit block just below the cover slabs. The floor of the conduit in Probe 4 is 0.15 m below that in Probe 3, giving a slope of 5 percent over 3 m.

Locus 01 (light brown surface soil to –0.11 m, 955.74 m asl)

Bucket 87.170. 5 rim, 2 base, 3 handle, 55 body.

Locus 02 (compact brown soil, 955.74 to 955.61 m asl)

Bucket 87.171. 19 body.

Locus 03 (light brown silt inside conduit, beneath cover slabs, 955.61 to 955.46 m als)

Bucket 87.172. 3 body.

5.L.5. *Drain no. 76, Probe no. 5*

Probe 5 (L 1.06 m east/west, W 1.85 m north/south) was laid out 3.65 m west of Probe 1 to examine the projected intersection of the drains identified in Probes nos. 1–4. Clearing of the packed, light-brown, pebbly surface soil to -0.27 m (955.50 m asl) exposed a roughly rectangular plastered basin (L 0.86–0.98 m, W 0.61–0.66 m, 0.94 m deep) with an intake in the centre of the north wall and possible outlets in the south and east walls (fig. 4.47–48). The visible parts of the tank walls were built of heavy, fairly well-squared blocks of varying sizes. The fill within the tank was essentially a single deposit of loose, light brown soil containing cobbles, a few stone slabs, and small, worn sherds. It was excavated in three loci: Locus 02 to the level of the base of the drain openings (Locus 02, 955.50–955.29 m asl), Locus 03 below these openings to an arbitrary change at 954.97 m asl, and Locus 04 the fill just above the plastered floor (at 954.83 m asl). The ceramics were a mixture of all periods from the first through the seventh century.

The basin was plastered up to a point roughly 0.52 m above the floor, probably its original height, since the upper edge is quite even at the four corners and corresponds with the solid construction of the tank walls. The plaster dips to 0.44 m above the floor (elev. 955.27 m asl) to accommodate the entry of the drain in the north wall and to 0.36 m (955.19 m asl) to accommodate the possible drain in the south wall, although any plastered transition from wall to channel has been lost. The plaster (Th 0.025–0.03 m; Buckets 87.185–186) was hard, very pale brown (10YR 8/3), heavily tempered with poorly-sorted, rounded sand and pebbles, and contained frequent nodules of lime but no flecks of carbon. The surface had been smoothed but not polished, and it had weathered to a very pale brown (10YR 7/4).

The opening of the drain in the centre of the north wall was roofed and reinforced by the upper stone of a "Pompeian"-type basalt grain mill, broken in half longitudinally and laid on its side to form a short tunnel over the water channel. The channel itself (W 0.22 m) was built of small flat stones. The top edge of the millstone abuts the outside of the tank wall, 0.25 m north of the tank; the passage of the channel through the wall may originally have been roofed with a block or slabs. Although the marl conduit blocks seen in Probes 3 and 4 are not visible at the junction with the tank, the channel in Probe 4 lines up with the opening in the north wall of the tank 3.14 m to the south and should be part of the same conduit. The base of the conduit in Probe 3 is 0.35 m higher than the drain opening at the tank, yielding a slope of 5 percent over 7 m. A smaller (W 0.17 m) opening was built neatly into the centre of the south wall, 0.10 m lower than the north drain, but possibly intended as a drain opening for intake or outflow. There was no time to probe for this feature south of the tank, but within the tank, the plaster dips to accommodate the opening just as it does on the north wall. The west wall was solidly constructed with heavy sandstone blocks and plastered from top to bottom.

At the time of excavation, no opening was visible in the east wall, but the plaster dipped neatly to 0.31 m above the floor at the centre of the wall (955.14 m asl). At this point, a wide, flat stone (W 0.25 m) is built into the wall, and the fill above it appears more irregular than construction elsewhere in the tank. Since the tank lines up with the deep, wide channel revealed in Probes 1 and 2 and has the same orientation, it is likely that in its first phase of use the tank was connected with that channel by an opening in its east wall. The fall from the sill in the east wall of the tank to the floor of the channel in Probe 2 is 0.33 m over 12.40 m (2.66 percent). The possible opening in the south wall may belong to the same phase or may have been added when the opening in the east wall was closed up, to direct outflow to a different cistern or in a different direction. The great disparity in capacity between the small north and south conduits and the east/west channel is puzzling. It is possible that a drain, originally designed to channel large amounts of water from ground level run-off in this part of the settlement, was reworked to channel either household wastewater from the house to the north or to collect clean rain water from the roof and courtyard of that house for clarification in the settling basin, which was then conveyed to a cistern or tank not yet identified farther to the south.

Locus 01 (packed, pebbly, light brown soil, surface to -0.27 m, 955.50 m asl)

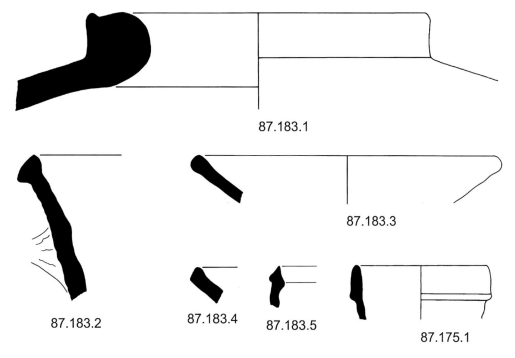

87.183.1

87.183.3

87.183.2

87.183.4

87.183.5

87.175.1

FIG. 5.94 *Drain no. 76, ceramics from Probe 5, Loci 2 and 3 (scale 1:2).*

Bucket 87.176. 18 body, 1 rim, 1 handle, 1 base. Lamp (*EZ* III no. 479 (363)).

Locus 02 (fill in front of drain opening, 955.50 to 955.29 m asl). Very small, worn sherds (fig. 5.94).
Bucket 87.175. 19 body, 3 rim, 4 handle.
175.1. Amphora (?): fine, hard, light red (2.5YR 6/8) fabric. D 0.07 m. Cf. 'Amr and Schick 2001: fig. 3.4 (650).
175.2. Nabataean cream ware jug: soft, fine, chalky, white (2.5Y 8/2) fabric. (1C–ea. 2C).

Locus 03 (pebbly, light brown soil in tank, 955.29 to 954.97 m asl; fig. 5.94)
Bucket 87.183. 49 body, 11 rim, 4 handle, 1 base.
183.1. Dolium: medium soft, fairly fine, olive grey (5Y 5/2) fabric with white sand. D 0.18 m? 'Amr and Schick 2001: fig. 6.11 (650); Kareem 2001: fig. 2.17 (7C); Waliszewski 2001: fig. 2.1 (7C).
183.2. Nabataean cream ware jug: hard, sandy, white (2.5Y 8/2) fabric with white sand inclusions. Shades to reddish yellow (7.5YR 6/6) on interior surface. 'Amr 1992: fig. 1 (1C–ea. 2C).

183.3. Bowl or lid: hard, light red (2.5YR 6/8) fabric with a few white sand inclusions. Shades to weak red (2.5YR 4/2) at outside rim. D 0.16 m.
183.4. Lid (?): hard, slightly sandy, reddish yellow (5YR 7/8) fabric with a few white inclusions.
183.5. Cooking pot: hard, sandy, dark reddish brown (5YR 3/3) fabric.
Bucket 87.186. Hard, very pale brown (10YR 8/3) plaster, heavily tempered with poorly-sorted, rounded sand and pebbles, and containing frequent nodules of lime. No carbon flecks. The surface has been smoothed, but not polished, and has weathered to a very pale brown (10YR 7/4).
Bucket 87.185. Plaster. Very close to 87.186, but the sand and pebbles are well sorted, and the nodules of lime are less frequent.

Locus 04 (pebbly, light brown soil in tank, just above floor, 954.97 to 954.83 m asl)
Bucket 87.184. 27 body, 4 rim, 1 conch shell fragment.

Chapter 6

Catalogue of Registered Artefacts
and Laboratory Analyses

6.A. INTRODUCTION

This chapter presents the finds from the 1986 and 1987 surveys and from the excavations in 1989 — with the exception of the finds from the bath, which will be presented along with that structure in a future volume. A summary analysis of the ceramic wares appears in Section B.1, while the small collection of registered ceramic artefacts is catalogued in B.2. The unregistered ceramic finds have been presented in summary fashion along with the relevant probe reports in Chapter 5. Analyses of the non-ceramic artefacts and catalogues of the registered non-ceramic artefacts follow in Section C, organised by material and/or type (metal, coins, stone, other). Manufactured construction materials (plaster and mortar) are catalogued in Section D. Analysis of soil samples is presented in Section E, and radiocarbon analyses in Section F. The catalogue numbers are constructed from the year of excavation, bucket number, and registered object number from that bucket. Given the limited amount of excavation, only a small number of objects required registration.

6.B. CERAMIC FINDS

6.B.1. *Analysis of Unregistered Ceramic Wares*

The unregistered ceramics have been described and the characteristic sherds illustrated in Chapter 5, with citation of dates and parallels where these could be determined. The typically small size of the potsherds often made identification and determination of rim diameters difficult. The collection is not a large one, but it is in fact very similar to the substantial corpus of ceramics recovered in the excavations carried out at Humayma between 1991 and 2005. Although the ancient coarse wares of southern Jordan are still not completely understood, it does not seem likely that any of these wares, or any other ceramics found at Humayma, were produced at the site (Gerber 2008a). No kiln wasters have been recovered at the site, and the lack of clay, scarcity of fuel and water, and small population make it an unlikely location for ceramic production.

By far the largest portion of the ceramics from the probes described in Chapter 5 can be paralleled at Petra or from sites equally dependent on Petra. These vessels were produced at Petra and exported to Hawara. The wares include painted and unpainted Nabataean fine ware, along with Nabataean storage jars, jars, cooking pots, bowls, juglets, and lamps, and a variety of Late Roman and Byzantine coarse wares and lamps. A smaller percentage of the corpus was imported from Aqaba, such as the so-called Aqaba Ware (Dolinka 2003), Mahesh Ware, amphoras, and large jars. The Nabataean so-called Cream Ware (or Green Ware) was also imported, although the production site has not yet been identified. Other imports from

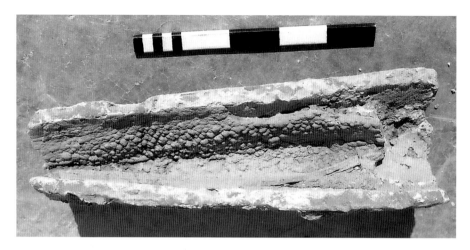

FIG. 6.1   *Tile from Jammam Aqueduct km 5.419 (1986.001.01), top view.*

farther afield include Parthian glazed ware, Eastern Terra Sigillata A and B (Syria?), Roman factory lamps, and possibly Pompeian Red Ware (Italy?). Dolinka's summary of the non-local wares found at Aila (2003: 70–74) is in broad outlines similar to what has been found at Humayma. Holmquist (oral communication, 22 November 2008) has proven through laboratory analysis of ceramic fabrics that cooking pots were imported into Aila from Petra and Khirbet edh-Dharih, and that Aila (Aqaba ware) amphoras were exported to Petra, Khirbet edh-Dharih, and Elusa. Combined with the results at Humayma, these data testify to a lively regional trade in all types of ceramic vessels.

6.B.2. *Catalogue of Registered Ceramic Finds*

1986.001.01. Gutter tile. Jammam Aqueduct, km 5.419. Removed from a series of inverted tiles placed inside the conduit block trough, their ends overlapping. Intact; very ashy, off-white mortar adheres to exterior surface; pillowy, layered sinter deposit on interior to within 0.02–0.03 m of the upper edges. L 0.40 m, W 0.07–0.13 m, H 0.10–0.11 m, wall Th 0.015 m (fig. 6.1).

Heavy tile with parabolic cross-section, tapering markedly from one end to the other, resembling a cover tile used in roofing. Slight ridge around the edges. Hard, light red fabric (10R 6/6) containing much clear quartz sand and black sand and frequent white specks. Chronology uncertain, but probably late third century.

Approximately 70 percent of the conduit was fitted with these tiles, which averaged 0.34 m in length and overlapped 0.05 m at either end, suggesting a rough total of 18,000 tiles. Despite this impressive total, the fact that the tiles vary in length from 0.28–0.40 m suggests they were salvaged from several pre-existing structures rather than purpose-made for the aqueduct. Extensive remains of roof tiles have been found at Hauarra only in the fort, consisting of the typical Roman large, flat pan tiles with flanged edges, and V-section cover tiles tapering from one end to the other. Fragments of cover tiles were found in 207 excavation buckets: 191 in the fort, 14 in the *Vicus* (E125), and 1 in the Late Roman Bath (E077). All the structures in the fort are represented. The few nearly complete cover tiles recovered from the fort seem more rounded and less strongly tapered than the examples under discussion in this section, but the fabric is virtually identical. If the gutter tiles in the aqueduct were in fact roof tiles brought from Hauarra, the fort is the obvious source. The most likely period for this salvage is the last 25 years of the third century, when the fort was abandoned, or perhaps after its final abandonment in the late fourth century.

Like the tiles in the aqueduct, the pan tiles found in the Roman fort for which the original dimensions could be determined, varied in size. The two best-preserved examples measured 0.485 × 0.38 m and 0.30 × 0.132 m. Assuming that the tiles from the aqueduct originally were used as cover tiles along with the flat pan tiles found in the fort, a pan tile and cover tile pair would cover an area ranging from 0.0356 to 0.1659 square metres (depending on dimensions). Placing the pan tiles tightly side-by-side, and allowing ten percent for overlapping at the lower end, 18,000 pairs of tiles would have been sufficient to cover an area between approximately 641 and 2986 square metres. The Praetorium alone had ca. 446.84 m of covered area, so the fort could in theory have been the source of the aqueduct tiles, particularly if most of the pan tiles were at the lower end of the size range.

FIG. 6.2   *Tile from Jammam Aqueduct km 7.529 (1986.002.01), top view.*

Nevertheless, some questions remain. If 18,000 cover tiles were salvaged intact from the fort, what happened to the pan tiles? Only one complete and a few nearly complete pan tiles have been recovered from the entire site of Hauarra, and even the many fragments of pan tiles recorded seem insufficient to account for a hypothetical original count adequate to roof the major buildings in the fort. The one complete tile (1995.0674.01; 0.485 × 0.38 × 0.02–0.045 m), recovered from the fort, weighed 8.43 kg. The fragments of both cover tiles and pan tiles recovered in the fort total 903 kg. Even assuming that all of these tiles were pan tiles (which they were not), 903 kg accounts for only slightly over 100 of the large pan tiles, 466 of the smaller variety. If the cover tiles were in fact salvaged for use in the aqueduct, perhaps the pan tiles were exported for reuse elsewhere, most likely Udhruh, Petra, or Aila.

It remains unclear what effect the tiles were intended to have on the aqueduct, but raising the level of the channel, allowing easier removal of sinter, and preventing leaks are all possibilities. I have not found any parallel for this use of tiles in other Nabataean type aqueducts.

1986.002.01. Gutter tile. Jammam Aqueduct, km 7.529. Removed from a series of inverted tiles placed inside the conduit block trough, their ends overlapping. Portion of narrow end missing; very ashy, off-white mortar adheres to exterior surface; smooth, layered sinter deposit on interior to the upper edges. An evaporation lip and pebbly pattern in the sinter suggests a usual water level of 0.06 m. L 0.39 m, W 0.09–0.14 m, H 0.10–0.11 m, wall Th 0.015 m (fig. 6.2).

Heavy tile with parabolic cross-section, tapering markedly from one end to the other, resembling a cover tile used in roofing. Hard, light red fabric (10R 6/8) containing much clear quartz sand; dark reddish-grey core. Chronology uncertain, but probably late third century.

See discussion of 1986.001.01.

1992.0613. Gutter tile. Jammam Aqueduct, km 7.340. Removed from a series of inverted tiles placed inside the conduit block trough, their ends overlapping. Hard, yellowish red fabric (5YR 5/6, surface), heavily tempered with clear and black sub-angular sand and containing small white specks. Soft, light grey bedding mortar adheres to the exterior, containing numerous lime nodules, voids, and occasional flecks of ash. The interior is nearly filled with layers of concretion formed of long, thick, tightly-packed crystals perpendicular to the walls. The deposit varies greatly in thickness: 0.013, 0.022, 0.023, 0.032 m. Layering is not very marked, but at one point 9 divisions seem to be visible. The pillowy concretions extend up to the top of the tile and left free an irregular channel only 0.01–0.03 m wide. Portion of narrow end missing. L 0.28; W 0.11–0.095; H 0.105; Th 0.015 (fig. 6.3).

Heavy tile with parabolic cross-section, tapering markedly from one end to the other, resembling a cover tile used in roofing. Chronology uncertain, but probably late third century.

See discussion of 1986.001.01.

1987.114.01. Pipe section. Reservoir 63, Probe 5, locus 03. Removed from the buried terracotta pipeline bypassing the reservoir outside the N wall. Broken; part of wider end missing. Remains of fine white sealing mortar at narrow end (figs. 6.4, 5.49)

Heavy, cylindrical pipe section, with slightly swelling body, well-defined, sloping shoulder at narrow end, and heavy rounded rims. L 0.30 m, outside D of rims 0.055 m and 0.085 m, inside D of openings 0.04 and 0.07 m; shoulder inset 0.015 m to rim 0.02 H. Hard, granular red (10R 5/8) fabric with large amount of clear quartz sand temper. Midway along one side of the pipe body, a small hole (D 0.04 m) was broken through the pipe wall, then covered with a sherd from another pipe that was held in place with the same white mortar used to seal the pipe sections. This pipe is similar in shape and dimensions to second-century pipes found at Jabal az-Zuhur, near Petra ('Amr and al-Momani 2001: 270, fig. 24). The Humayma pipeline was laid in the second or third century to service a shrine and some domestic structures in the *vicus* southeast of the reservoir (Oleson et al. 2003: 49–50; 2008).

The hole in the wall of the pipe does not seem large enough to have allowed its use to remove debris blocking the interior. Since nearly all the pipe sections exposed around the reservoir have these holes, they may have been made in order to determine the location of a blockage, which was then removed either by making a larger hole or by taking out a whole pipe section. A soil sample taken from inside this pipe was sent for analysis (pp. 358–59).

FIG. 6.3   *Tile from Jammam Aqueduct km 7.340 (1992.0613.01), view of narrow end.*

1987.114.02. Pipe section. Reservoir 63, Probe 5, locus 03. Removed from the buried terracotta pipeline bypassing the reservoir outside the W wall. Broken; part of wider end missing. Remains of fine, white sealing mortar at narrow end (figs. 6.4, 5.49)

Heavy, cylindrical pipe section, with slightly swelling body, well-defined, sloping shoulder at narrow end, and heavy rounded rims. L 0.30 m, outside D of rims 0.058 m and 0.08 m, inside D of openings 0.04 and 0.07 m; shoulder inset 0.01 m to rim H 0.02. Hard, granular red (2.5YR 5/8) fabric with large amount of clear quartz sand temper. Midway along one side of the pipe body a small hole (D 0.02) was broken through the pipe wall, then covered with a sherd (now lost), which was held in place with the same white mortar used to seal the pipe sections. For date and the function of the hole, see no. 1987.114.01.

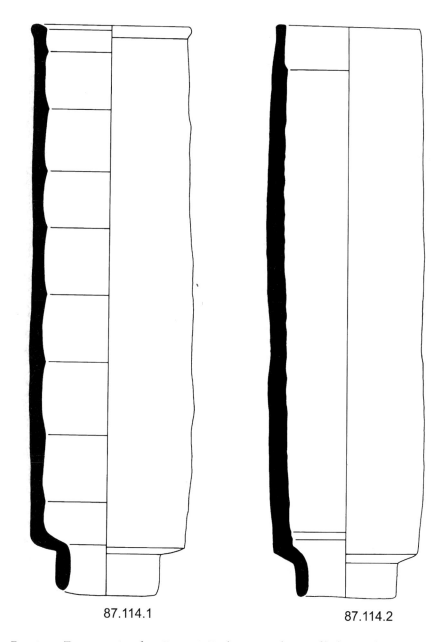

87.114.1   87.114.2

FIG. 6.4   *Terracotta pipes from Reservoir/Pool no. 63, Probe 5, profile drawing (1987.114.01, 02).*

6.C. NON-CERAMIC ARTEFACTS

6.C.1. *Introduction and Analysis*

Given the limited extent of excavation and the small number of registered non-ceramic artefacts, it is not surprising that no particular patterns of material or function emerge. The bronze stopcock housing is an atypical artefact in the Near East.

Although the number of coins recovered was small, all but one could be at least partly identified (a high proportion for Humayma). Five out of six were found in the fort, a chance statistic, because excavation since 1991 has shown a more even balance in coin use between the fort and the community up to the time of the abandonment of the fort around 400. The chronological spread is similar to that of the much larger sample recov-

FIG. 6.5   *Bronze stopcock housing, after cleaning (1987.106.01).*

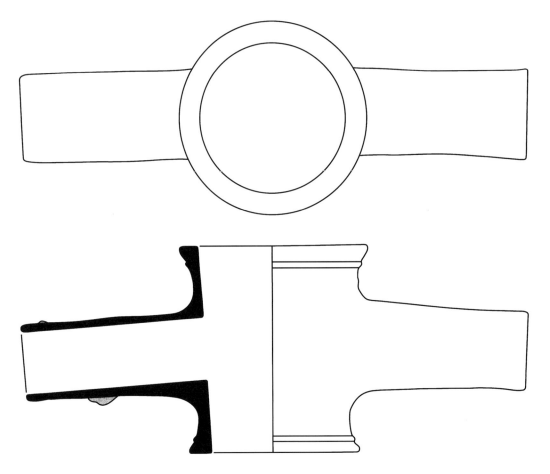

FIG. 6.6   *Bronze stopcock housing, section drawing (1987.106.01).*

ered in the fort since 1991, with most finds from the third and fourth centuries. The presence of a block carrying a possible Nabataean inscription is in accord with the frequent reuse of Nabataean architectural elements in the construction of the fort (Oleson et al. 1999: 416–17), possibly reflecting violence associated with Roman occupation of the site (see Oleson 2003).

6.C.2. *Miscellaneous Metal Objects*

1987.106.01. Bronze stopcock housing. Reservoir 63, Probe 3, Locus 14. Found in its original position, installed inside the niche in the S wall of the reservoir and connected to a lead pipe (106.02) set inside the outflow conduit. Intact, surface corroded and encrusted. Cleaned in 1989, 1995. Valve plug missing. L 0.296 m, H 0.118, outside D of pipes 0.044 and 0.046 m, inside D of pipes 0.036 and 0.036 m, outside D of body 0.111 (top) and 0.10 m (base), inside D of body 0.088 (top) and 0.074 m (base). 3.350 kg. (Figs. 6.5–6)

Large stopcock housing with cylindrical body, tapering inside to accommodate a valve plug. There is a thick, flat rim around the upper and lower openings, and a raised line sets both rims off from the body. Intake and delivery pipes (L 0.105 m) project horizontally from opposite ends of the body. A small casting flaw can be seen at one end of one of the pipes, and the exterior surface has been worked with a rasp, particularly in spiral patterns around the two pipes. The interior of the body has been carefully smoothed to fit the plug tightly, perhaps by working the two parts together with a grinding compound. A thin layer of water-deposited sinter adheres to the interior of both pipes (Th 0.001–0.002 m). The archaeological context suggests a second-century date.

This stopcock, which is precisely one Roman foot in length, was installed to control the flow of water into a lead pipeline leading to the Roman bath building E077 (figs. 5.35–36). It is a typical Roman design frequently seen in the western Mediterranean, although larger than the usual stopcocks found in domestic contexts (Kretzschmer 1960; Fabio and Fassitelli 1990; Hodge 1992: 322–31). One hundred and twenty-two stopcocks were found at Pompeii alone (Jansen

2001: 29), so it is surprising that this seems to be only the third Roman stopcock so far found in the entire Near East. This is also by far the largest stopcock documented from that region. It is possible that a stopcock of similar dimensions was installed on the subterranean reservoir fed by a Roman period aqueduct at Sepphoris, but only the outlet pipe survives (Tsuk 1996: 122; Peleg 2000). Small stopcocks in domestic use were found at Antioch on the Orontes (Stillwell 1941: 5; second to third century) and at Zeugma (Z. Kamash, personal communication, August 2007; Roman?).

A small sample was taken by drilling and submitted to A. Hauptmann (Deutsches Bergbau-Museum) for analysis, to determine the chemical composition of the metal and the type of alloy used (sample no. JD-44/1). The sample was dissolved in a mixture of $HCl + HNO_3$, and the chemical composition was measured by Atomic Absorption Spectroscopy: Cu 65.3%, Pb 27.4%, Sn 6.0%, Zn 430 ppm, As 650 ppm, Sb 550 ppm, Bi 46 ppm, Co 36 ppm, Ni 270 ppm, Fe 770 ppm, Ag 700 ppm.

The object was cast in a heavily leaded lead-tin bronze. The composition is comparable with a group of Etruscan objects (Riederer 1987) and some Hellenistic statuettes (Craddock 1977). The closest parallel, however, is the alloy composing the head of the portrait of Hadrian from Tel Shalem, which showed very similar proportions of the three main metals: Cu 65.5%, Pb 26.5%, Sn 7.6% (Foerster 1986). The torso and arm of this statue, which may have been reused from Hellenistic statues (Gergel 1991), showed a higher copper to lead ratio (71.0% to 20.5% and 69.5% to 22.0%, respectively). The similarity in composition of the metal composing both the stopcock and the portrait of Hadrian reinforces the Roman origin and second-century date for the stopcock. The character of the alloy also suggests a Near Eastern origin for both. The analytical results, however, do not allow determination of the provenance of the metals. The use of local copper ores from Faynan in Wadi 'Arabah is possible but cannot be proven with these data. There is no known lead deposit in the Levant (cf. Hammond 2000: 153 on imported lead ore).
Bibliography: Oleson 1988b: 163, pl. 30; Fabio and Fassitelli 1990: 151–52.

FIG. 6.7   *Lead pipe (1987.106.02), showing plaster seal over seam.*

1987.106.02. Lead pipe. Reservoir 63, Probe 3, Locus 14. Found in its original position, connected to the stopcock (106.01) installed inside the niche in the S wall of the reservoir. Incomplete, one end broken, surface corroded and encrusted. MPL 0.325 m, outside D 0.044–0.055 m, inside D 0.038–0.049 m (figs. 6.7–8)

Section of lead pipe manufactured by rolling up a lead sheet (Th 0.003 m) so that the edges overlapped approximately 0.008 m. The seam is badly discoloured and corroded, as if some sort of solder was poured along it, or possibly plaster. This sealant has now disintegrated, leaving a crumbly, greenish-grey corrosion product. The pipe abutted the downstream pipe of the stopcock and the joint was sealed with a lead sweat joint water-proofed with a layer of plaster wrapped in cloth (fig. 5.36). The heavy, probably woollen, textile has left its impression in the plaster (fig. 6.8). The archaeological context suggests a second-century date.

While this pipe was less neatly finished than the typical Roman pipe with folded and soldered seams (Hodge 1992: 307–15), similar small-diameter rolled pipes have been found at Pompeii (Jansen 2001: 29) and Velia (Fabio and Fassitelli 1990: 52–53).

A small sample was taken by drilling and submitted to A. Hauptmann (Deutsches Bergbau-Museum) for analysis, to determine the chemical composition of the metal (sample no. JD-44/2). The sample was dissolved in a mixture of HCl + HNO_3, and the chemical composition was measured by Atomic Absorption Spectroscopy: Cu 410 ppm, Pb 99.2%, Sn 120 ppm, Zn < 20 ppm, As 13 ppm, Sb 90

FIG. 6.8   *Lead pipe (1987.106.02), impression of textile on plaster sealing.*

ppm, Bi 50 ppm, Cd < 20 ppm, Fe 30 ppm, Ag 90 ppm. The lead sheet was cast from a very pure lead, but the analytical results do not allow determination of the provenance of the metal. In any case, there is no known lead deposit in the Levant (cf. Hammond 2000: 153 on imported lead ore). Bibliography: Oleson 1988b: 163.

6.C.3. *Coins*

1987.042.01. Bronze Antoninianus of Maximian. Reservoir 62, Probe 2, Locus 01. Corroded. D 0.019. Die orientation 6:00. Wt after cleaning 4.05 g. Obv: diademed head of emperor to right. …] MAXIMIANVSPFAVG. Rev: Jupiter standing, leaning on standard? IOVICON]SERVATOR[I. 294–305? (fig. 6.9.b)
Bibliography: Possibly Sutherland and Casson 1967: 640 no. 153a, struck in Antioch, 310–311. Cf. Robertson 1982: 30, nos. 84–89.

FIG. 6.9 *Bronze coins. a) Elagabalus (1987.057.01). b) Maximian (1987.042.01). c) House of Constantine (1987.194.01-02).*

1987.057.01. Bronze coin of Elagabalus, struck at Petra. Reservoir 62, Probe 4, locus 03. Corroded. D 0.02 m. Die orientation 11:00. Wt after cleaning 4.30 g. Obv: head of Elagabalus, to right. MAVPAN]TON[INOC around edge. Rev: founder (of Petra colony), togate, right hand raised, ploughing right with pair of oxen. P(etra) in front of oxen, COLO(ni) in exergue. 221–22 (fig. 6.9.a).
Bibliography: Ben-Dor 1948; Spijkerman 1978: 236–37, no. 56, pl. 18.11.

1987.193.01. Bronze coin. Surface find in fort, 10 m S of S end of Reservoir 62. Broken, one third missing, corroded. D 0.019 m. Die orientation 10:00. Wt after cleaning 2.05 g. Obv: head of bearded emperor with diadem, facing left. Rev: two standing figures? Inscriptions illegible. Probably second half of third century (fig. 6.10.a).

1987.194.01. Bronze coin, House of Constantine. Surface find in fort, 20 m W of SW corner of Res-

ervoir 62. Corroded. D 0.014. Die orientation 5:00. Wt after cleaning 1.35 g. Obv: Bust of emperor to left, with diadem. CONSTANT[.... Rev: Victory striding left, shield in lowered right hand. Fourth century (fig. 6.9.c).

1987.194.02. Bronze coin, House of Constantine. Surface find in fort, 15 m E of SE corner of Reservoir 62. Corroded, broken, one half missing. D 0.013. Die orientation 6:00. Wt after cleaning 1.00 g. Obv: Bust of emperor to right, with diadem.]CONST[.... Rev: standing figure. Fourth century (fig. 6.10.b).

1987.195.01. Bronze coin. Surface find, 15 m E of drain no. 76. Corroded. D 0.012 × 0.014 m. Wt after cleaning 2.33 g. Thick, irregular, dished flan. Surfaces are fairly clear, but no patterns are visible. Possibly Early Islamic? (fig. 6.10.c).

FIG. 6.10   *Bronze coins. a) third-century emperor (1987.193.01). b) House of Constantine (1987.194.01-02). c) Possible early Islamic issue (1987.195.01).*

6.C.4: Inscribed Block

1987.164.01. Inscribed sandstone block. Reservoir 62 intake conduit, Probe 8, Locus 04. Broken; portions of top and front surfaces remain. MPL 0.26 m; MPH 0.12 m; MPW 0.17 m (fig. 6.11).

The block, cut from the local white sandstone, had been reused as part of the wall framing the drain. A recessed margin (W 0.13 m) was carved around the periphery of the block, and the inscription was cut on the raised central portion. Only the top half or third of the first line of the inscription (or possibly the bottom of the last line) survives (MPL 0.21 m; MPH 0.02 m), 8 or 9 letters in all. With such a small portion of the letterforms surviving, it is difficult to determine the language of the inscription. The repetition of rounded or hooked forms, however, resembles more the top edge of a line of Nabataean letters than of a line of Latin or Greek letters (cf. Cantineau 1930–32: II, 15–16, 26, etc.). First century AD?

The block probably belonged to one of the large Nabataean public buildings dismantled or destroyed by the Romans during the occupation of Hawara in 106 (see Oleson 2003). Blocks with this sunken edge appear in Nabataean architecture as part of their adaptation of "Second Style" wall decoration, executed in stone or reproduced in plaster, and examples can be seen at Petra on the façade of the Qasr al-Bint (McKenzie 1990: pl. 71), the niche inside ed-Deir (Glueck 1965: pl. 54b), in a luxurious first-century house on ez-Zantur, and in the painted *triclinium* in Siq al-Barid (Weber and Wenning 1997: pl. 52b, 69b). The building from which the block was taken should date to the earlier first century AD, but of course the inscription might be slightly later. If the inscription is in fact Nabataean, it represents one of the very few

FIG. 6.11 *Inscribed block (1987.164.01).*

monumental public inscription in that language from the settlement centre. In 2007, half of a tomb inscription neatly carved in a *tabula ansata* on a sandstone block was found in a pile of blocks heaped up a year or two earlier, 25 m southeast of the Roman fort (Bevan and Reeves 2010). A monumental Nabataean tomb inscription of the second century AD was found in the vicinity of Humayma by clandestine diggers (Hayajneh 2001), and two tomb stelae roughly inscribed in Nabataean were found in the necropolis west of the site by the Humayma excavation project (Oleson et al. 1993a: 486–87; 1993b: 147–49).

6.D. MANUFACTURED CONSTRUCTION MATERIALS

6.D.1. *Introduction*

"Manufactured construction materials" (abbreviated as MCM) include mortar, plaster, and kiln-fired brick, although in this context we will consider only the first two materials. Mortar can be defined as "any material used in a plastic state which can be towelled, and becomes hard in place, and which is utilised for bedding and jointing" (Cowper 1927: 51). Plaster, on the other hand, can be defined as "any material used in a plastic state

to form a durable finishing coat to the surfaces of walls and ceilings" (Cowper 1927: 29). In situations where the original structural surface is rough or where considerable strength or water-resistance are needed, plasters will be backed with mortar. In the context of Humayma, we also classify the finishing layer of a "mortar" floor as "plaster," in part because many of the "flooring" samples derive from the floor of a basin, which was not intended to bear traffic but simply to water-proof the structure. In addition, the floor surface of a room is usually distinguished from the bedding mortar as a layer of greater fineness and polish. Roofing plaster has been found in several structures at Humayma that will be published in subsequent report volumes.

Only lime-based mortar and plaster will be discussed here, although mortars and plasters composed of mud with a small admixture of lime have been observed at Humayma on structures of all periods represented at the site. Lime plasters tend to be somewhat finer in texture and denser than mortars, because of the more careful selection and sifting of the micro-aggregate (D usually < 6 mm) and the compacting or tooling of the surface. It is difficult to determine where the lime used in the settlement centre of Hawara was prepared. The closest sources of limestone are two small, isolated outcroppings 1.734 and 2.200 km north of the settlement. A small portion of the closer outcropping has been quarried away, and what appears to be a hillside lime kiln survives at the farther outcropping (see p. 99, Ghana Aqueduct km 16.688). Neither working is extensive, and the problem of fuel supply would have been significant. Preparation of a ton of lime in a traditional type hillside kiln requires approximately 250–350 kg of dry wood (Meir et al. 2005: 771) or even a higher proportion, depending on the character of the rock and the fuel (Brown: 1996: 3; Cowper 1927: 9–16; Adam 1994: 65–73). Collection of sufficient fuel from the immediate vicinity of the settlement would have required enormous effort, but might have been possible, particularly if chaff was available from the nearby agricultural fields. The presence of large quantities of carbon flecks in the mortar and plaster at Humayma, along with numerous fragments of carbonised twigs and stems, indicate that brush and stubble formed at least part of the fuel. There are extensive outcroppings of Cretaceous limestone on the al-Shara escarpment above 1300 m, and sinter removed from the aqueducts could also have been burnt for lime. It is probable that a more extensive supply of fuel was available on the escarpment than on the drier desert floor below. Only a century ago, the Turks built a branch line of the Hejaz railroad to Ras en-Naqb in order to exploit the local forests for fuel (Hart 1986a: 51). It is likely that all of the lime for the aqueduct was produced on the escarpment, and it is possible that some or all of the lime for the settlement centre was produced there as well and carried down.

Ground-up ceramic materials (probably derived from pulverised bricks) or certain types of volcanic ash (pozzolana) could be added to mortar and plaster to increase durability and impermeability (Massaza 1988; Bugini 1993; Adam 1994: 73–76; Davidovits 1995), and there is evidence for both practices at Humayma. The crushed ceramic material could have been produced locally, but the source of the possible natural pozzolanas indicated in three samples (see below) remains a puzzle. The micro-aggregate consists of local sands: rounded, wind-blown particles of quartz and granite (figs. 6.13, 6.15).

It was obvious from the very beginning of the survey of hydraulic structures in and around Humayma in 1986 that the collection of data regarding lime-based mortars and plasters should be an integral part of the research. All the hydraulic structures made use of some sort of plaster along the surfaces that were in contact with water, and the built structures usually made use of mortar as well. Close visual inspection indicated that there was significant variation in the hardness, composition, and colour of the plasters used, and great variation in the mortars. This diversity was interesting both from a purely technical point of view and because it seemed possible that the variations depended on function and chronology. In consequence, 50 samples were taken from a broad sample of structures in and around Humayma, later supplemented with eight samples from six other sites in Jordan that were relevant to the cultural periods represented at Humayma. These samples were given a visual inspection with a geologist's lens, and Oleson then wrote the gross physical descriptions that appear in Sections 6.D.2 and 6.D.3. Twenty samples were submitted to Gordon E. Brown (Concrete Consultant) of Keswick Ontario in 1987 (MCM Sample nos. 44, 46–50, 52) and 1990 (MCM Sample nos. 57–70) for physical and chemical analysis (Section 6.D.4). Brown's reports contained some useful colour microphotographs. Unfortunately, the information they display is less apparent in grayscale prints, so only a small sample has been reproduced here.

The MCM samples catalogued below in fact do show variation across time and according to function (see summary analysis in Section 6.D.5). It is still not possible, however, to use the analysis of plaster and mortar alone as the basis for dating the structures in which they occur, and for the moment it is best to consider the information as data supplementing our understanding of the construction and function of the structures in and around Humayma. It cannot yet be determined whether the patterns seen at Humayma can be paralleled at contemporary sites in the region, since until the 1990s there were few attempts to collect large numbers of MCM samples for analysis. Occasionally, there is mention in archaeological reports of the characteristics and assumed dating value of MCM. Bachmann et al. (1921: 54–58), for example, suggest that pink mortar at Petra belongs to the second half of the third century, while grey mortar was produced in the fourth and fifth century. Negev (1986: 66; 1988b: 36) states that the hard grey plaster at Mampsis was typical of the Nabataean period, while the reddish plaster with added terracotta was Byzantine in date. Gregory (1996: 107–10) discusses the use of mortar and plaster at Roman military structures along the frontier, but focuses more on the application of the materials than their composition. Brown (1996: 17–20, 40–41, 51–61) provides analyses of several late Hellenistic and Byzantine samples from Gamla and Tel Hum (Israel) and Late Roman samples from the Dakhleh Oasis and Qasr al-Halaka (Egypt), but the sample is not large enough or geographically close enough to yield useful comparisons with the Humayma material. The careful report on the composition of the plaster and mortar in the synagogue at Khirbet Shema' is a good model for this kind of analysis (Meyers et al. 1976: 32), but the limitation of the sampling to a single structure and its distance from Humayma do not allow application of the results to the data published here. Rababeh (2005) has little to say about plaster and mortar at Petra, but Bellwald and al-Huneidi provide the formulae for modern mortars and plasters used in the consolidation of structures around the *Siq* (2003: 25–32, 105).

More recently, sophisticated analyses of mortars, plasters, and pozzolanic materials from Petra and Umm al-Jimal have been published (Dunn and Rapp 2004; Sha'er 2004), based on a variety of analytical techniques, but particularly on x-ray diffraction and microscopic petrography. The Petra samples are few in number, but geographically and culturally relevant to Humayma. The Umm al-Jimal samples were numerous, but from a very different region.

It is hoped that the publication of the Humayma MCM samples will stimulate collection and analysis of comparable material at other sites in the region. The important characteristics are hardness, fineness, weight, colour, type of micro-aggregate, and the addition of natural pozzolanic materials or crushed terracotta.

6.D.2. *Catalogue and Gross Physical Description of Plaster and Mortar Samples from Humayma*

The catalogue is organised by structure survey number, then by probe locus or bucket number, according to the situation. The descriptions are Oleson's, except those that begin with the phrase "MCM Sample no. xxx", which are based on the report submitted by Brown.

Structure no. 1. Ghana Aqueduct

Chronology: probably late-first century BC or early first century AD.

Km 6.553. Bucket 87.026; mortar between blocks of structure at junction with Jammam branch. Very hard, medium weight, light grey (10YR 7/1) mortar, heavily tempered with well-sorted, rounded quartz sand and small, angular, poorly-sorted, but ubiquitous fragments of pulverised red (2.5YR 5/8) terracotta. Includes frequent bits of charcoal, large lumps of lime, and possibly small fragments of the local sandstone. In April 2001, Oleson examined several more samples from this feature, but none contained fragments of crushed terracotta.

Km 6.553. Bucket no. 87.025; mortar between blocks of structure at junction with Jammam branch. MCM Sample no. 69: well-compacted, dense, medium grey mortar (fig. 6.12). Contains an abundance of crushed red terracotta to 7 mm and powdered and coarse charcoal to 4 mm. Micro-aggregate (magnified 24×): natural multi-coloured aggregate, white opaque and translucent quartz to 7 mm, similar to MCM Sample nos. 66 (Cistern no. 51), 67, and 68 (Cistern no. 64). Similar to sample in Bucket 87.026, but less well-mixed, resulting in patches that are lighter in colour, and lacking ground-up terracotta.

Km 9.144. Mortar from foundation. Bucket 86.012. MCM Sample no. 48: grey mortar containing voids from under-compaction, natural sand grains to 3 mm D, and sporadic aggregate pieces to 10 mm D. Micro-aggregate (magnified 24×): many carbon specks, pale yellow possible products of hydration, and some natural yellow quartz grains.

Fig. 6.12 *MCM Sample no. 69, from structure at junction of Ghana and Jammam aqueducts (Photo: G. E. Brown).*

Fig. 6.13 *MCM Sample no. 50, from off-take tank no. 20 at Ghana aqueduct km 9.597, micro-aggregate (Photo: G. E. Brown).*

Km 9.597. Plaster from off-take cistern (see below, Structure no. 20).

Structure no. 1. Jammam Branch

Chronology: structure probably first century AD, tiles probably added sometime between the third century and the Byzantine period.

Km 0.665. Bucket 86.011; mortar from bedding course. Hard, well-mixed greyish brown (10YR 5/2) mortar, containing much clear, rounded quartz sand, occasional charcoal specks, and very occasional small lumps of lime. MCM Sample no. 70: poorly-compacted, dark grey mortar similar to Sample no. 69 (Ghana Aqueduct km 6.553) but without any crushed terracotta; contains powdered charcoal and coarse charcoal to 1 mm. Micro-aggregate (magnified 24×): natural translucent fine white quartz and coarse dark grey aggregate to 5 mm.

Km 0.993. Bucket 86.027. Mortar packing around conduit block. MCM Sample no. 46: chalky white mortar with chalky white aggregate to 4 mm D. Micro-aggregate (magnified 24×): abundance of translucent natural quartz grains interspersed with light and dark brown possible products of hydration.

Km 1.181. Aqueduct Probe 5 (H87–01–P05). a) Bucket 87.018; plaster lining of settling basin. Very irregular outer surface. Very hard, sandy, off-white plaster, containing frequent specks of carbon and much poorly-sorted, clear, rounded quartz sand. Attached to it is the mortar backing on which it was laid, a soft, grey (2.5YR 5/0) mortar with a few lime inclusions. b) Bucket 87.019; mortar from support wall. Medium soft, friable, light grey (10YR 7/1) mortar containing a moderate amount of well-sorted, rounded sand, frequent large nodules of lime, and occasional large carbon bits.

Km 1.768. Aqueduct Probe 1 (H87–01–P01). Bucket 87.016; mortar sealing around cover slabs over conduit. Hard, fine, white (10YR 8/2) mortar with infrequent particles of rounded quartz sand and frequent badly-sorted lumps of lime. Occasional small flecks of charcoal and frequent large air bubbles.

Km 1.779. Aqueduct Probe 2 (H87–01–P02). Bucket 87.003; mortar from blocks of settling tank. Very crumbly, light grey (10YR 7/1) mortar containing frequent rounded sand grains and occasional pebbles. Infrequent very small nodules of lime and flecks of carbon.

Km 1.951. Aqueduct Probe 3 (H87–01–P3). Bucket 87.020; plaster lining of basin. Medium soft, very pale brown plaster moderately tempered with well-sorted, rounded sand and pebbles. Occasional lime nodules. The seams and bubbles of the outer layer are filled with water-deposited calcium carbonate. Backed by a medium hard, greyish-brown (10YR 5/2) mortar heavily tempered with rounded sand and containing frequent flecks of carbon.

Km 2.494. Aqueduct Probe 4 (H87–01–P4). Bucket 87.017; plaster lining of basin. Soft, light grey (10YR 8/1) mortar moderately tempered with poorly-sorted quartz sand and pebbles, containing large lime nodules and large carbon bits. This material looks like the mortar between the blocks of the tank and is not smoothed like a plaster, but the surface carries water-deposited calcium carbonate.

Structure no. 20. Rock-cut Cistern fed by Ghana Aqueduct at km 9.597

Chronology: probably late first century BC or early first century AD.

Bag 86.010. Plaster lining of off-take Cistern no. 20 (on Ghana aqueduct km. 9.597). MCM Sample no. 50: hard grey plaster containing fine natural sand and natural coarse aggregate to 10 mm D; coarse aggregate is buff coloured. Sandstone bedrock adhering on one side. Micro-aggregate (magnified 24×): appears to contain a small amount of vesicular pozzolanic material and some translucent natural quartz sand of various colours (fig. 6.13).

Structure no. 44. Dam

Chronology: probably late first century BC or first century AD.

Bucket 86.023. MCM Sample no. 47: mortar between blocks of downstream face of dam. Relatively soft, light grey mortar containing natural sand grains to 2 mm D. Micro-aggregate (magnified 24×): abundance of translucent natural quartz grains and various other rock types; minimal pozzolanic additive.

Bucket 87.030. Paving plaster around altar at south end of dam. Very hard, light grey (approximately "white" 5YR 8/1), with a very high proportion of poorly-sorted, round, clear and reddish quartz sand, and occasional specks of carbon.

Bucket 87.032. Plaster on upstream face of dam, from Probe 1 (H87–44–P1). Hard, white (approx. 10YR 8/2) plaster containing much poorly-sorted, rounded red quartz sand and pebbles, occasional lime nodules, and a very few flecks of carbon. The outer 3 mm has been stained a light brown (7.5YR

6/2), and the surface is very carefully smoothed and compacted.

Structure no. 45. Rock-cut cistern

Chronology: uncertain, probably Nabataean.

Bucket 86.008. Plaster laid on rock-cut cistern wall. Light grey plaster heavily tempered with quartz pebbles. MCM Sample no. 45.

Structure no. 51. Rock-cut cistern

Chronology: uncertain, probably Nabataean.

Bucket 86.009. Mortar or plaster from floor of settling basin. Soft, slightly off white (almost 10YR 8/2) mortar, poorly mixed, with much sub-rounded, white and clear quartz sand, and occasional rounded pebbles. Occasional large bubbles and a few lumps of lime. No visible charcoal specks. MCM Sample no. 66: grey mortar. Micro-aggregate (magnified 24×): natural multi-coloured granite; white opaque and translucent quartz to 4 mm.

Structure no. 53. Rock-cut cistern

Chronology: probably late first century BC or first century AD.

Bucket 86.017. Plaster lining of cistern. MCM Sample no. 49: hard, light grey plaster containing large sand particles to 6 mm D (occasionally to 12 mm) and multi-coloured aggregate (red, brown, buff, white). Micro-aggregate (magnified 24×): clear to dark orange, yellow natural quartz sand, translucent and opaque, various other rock types, and some possible products of hydration (fig. 6.14)

Bucket 90.004. Plaster lining of cistern. Very hard, white (10YR 8/1) plaster (Th 0.015) very heavily tempered with rounded, clear quartz sand and sub-angular clear quartz pebbles. No lime nodules or carbon flecks visible. The plaster was laid directly on the bedrock walls. The surface has weathered, exposing the pebbles.

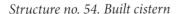

FIG. 6.14 *MCM Sample no. 49, from Cistern no. 53, micro-aggregate (Photo: G. E. Brown).*

FIG. 6.15 *MCM Sample no. 44, from Reservoir no. 62, micro-aggregate (Photo: G. E. Brown).*

Structure no. 54. Built cistern

Chronology: probably mid-first century BC or early first century AD.

Bucket 87.029. Probe 1, Locus 03 (H87–54–P01); mortar from seams on outside of cistern wall. Soft, light grey mortar containing a small amount of well-sorted, rounded quartz sand and occasional carbon flecks. Very well-mixed.

Bucket 87.055. Probe 2 (H87–54–P02); mortar or bedding plaster from wall of settling basin. Hard, light grey (10YR 7/1) mortar or plaster containing much poorly-sorted sand, pebbles, and angular fragments of terracotta. No visible carbon component.

*Structure no. 62. Fort reservoir
and associated conduit*

Chronology: early second century.

Bucket 86.013. MCM Sample no. 44: mortar between blocks in E wall. Chalky white mortar containing grey, green/grey, and brown aggregate to 2 mm D. Micro-aggregate (magnified 24 ×): abundance of opaque, light yellow, natural quartz grains interspersed with multi-coloured rock types (fig. 6.15).

Bucket 86.015. Plaster lining at NE corner. MCM Sample no. 52: very hard brown plaster containing a natural siliceous sand and coarse aggregate of crushed red/brown granite to 11 mm D. Micro-aggregate (magnified 24 ×): no natural quartz sand; a multi-coloured, course-textured pozzolana-like material.

Bucket 87.173a. Mortar between blocks of E wall of reservoir. Soft, light grey (10YR 7/1) mortar containing a small amount of well-sorted, rounded sand and occasional small nodules of lime and flecks of carbon.

Bucket 87.173b. Facing plaster from E wall of reservoir. Crumbly white plaster containing a moderate amount of sand and rounded pebbles, frequent large nodules of lime, and large bubbles. The material has weathered to a very hard surface.

Bucket 87.101. Probe 4, Locus 04 (H87–62–P04); mortar along edge of conduit leading to Reservoir 62. Soft, poorly-compacted, light grey mortar, containing a small amount of poorly-sorted, sub-rounded quartz sand.

Structure no. 63. Nabataean reservoir/pool

Chronology: probably late first century BC or early first century AD.

Bucket 87.110. Plaster lining on south wall, around the exit pipe, laid on in two layers. The outside layer (Th 0.10) is a medium hard, well-compacted white plaster very heavily tempered with well-sorted, rounded quartz sand. There are no carbon flecks or lime nodules. The outer surface is even but has not been brought to a polish, and the outer 1 mm has weathered to a very pale brown (10YR 7/2). The inner layer (Th 0.01) is a softer, light grey (10YR 7/2) mortar, less heavily tempered with poorly-sorted, rounded sand and pebbles, containing frequent medium carbon flecks and lime nodules (fig. 6.16). MCM Sample no. 57A: surface plaster facing S wall, Th 10 mm. A white plaster, not as well-compacted as might be expected of a reservoir lining; surface flat but somewhat eroded and stained brown from use. Adheres to no. 57B. Micro-aggregate (magnified 24×): natural translucent and opaque white to buff quartz, to maximum size of 4 mm; similar to bedding aggregate. MCM Sample no. 57B: bedding mortar adhering to back of Sample no. 57A. Grey bedding mortar 12 mm thick, with a flat but rough surface. Well-compacted, with an abundance of coarse charcoal that has caused the grey colour. Micro-aggregate (magnified 24×): natural translucent and opaque quartz, white to buff, maximum D 5 mm.

Bucket 87.151. North Probe 3, Locus 01 (H87–63–P3). Backing mortar on reservoir wall. Very hard, very pale brown (10YR 7/2) mortar heavily tempered with poorly-sorted, sub-rounded sand and sub-angular pebbles. Occasional very small flecks of carbon and lumps of lime.

Bucket 87.134. North Probe 3, Locus 05 (H87–63–P3). Plaster of pipe join. Very soft, very fine white plaster completely lacking in sand temper or flecks of carbon.

Bucket 87.089. North Probe 3, Locus 13 (H87–63–P3). Mortar or plaster packing around stopcock. Very fine, soft white mortar or plaster containing no sand temper or carbon flecks, but frequent casts left by clumps of straw temper and impressions of wool cloth wrapping on the exterior. Some flecks of calcium carbonate deposit and oxidised lead piping adhere to the material.

Bucket 87.180. Probe 3, Locus 16 (H87–63–P3). Plaster from joint between valve and lead pipe. Very light brown (less than 10YR 8/2), friable, lightweight plaster containing a moderate amount of well-sorted, sub-rounded sand, frequent bubbles, large nodules of lime, and the casts of vegetable temper.

FIG. 6.16 *MCM Sample no. 57, from Reservoir/Pool no. 63. (Photo: G .E. Brown).*

Structure no. 64. Built cistern

Chronology: probably first century AD.

Bucket 87.076. Plaster lining from settling tank. Very hard, very pale brown (10YR 8/3) plaster heavily tempered with poorly-sorted, sub-rounded quartz sand and pebbles. No charcoal flecks or lime nodules visible. Well-compacted, with a smooth outer surface (Th 0.13–0.22). The mortar backing was very heavily tempered with sand and pebbles. MCM Sample no. 68A: plaster lining. Well-compacted, pink to light brown plaster, with a smooth, very hard, polished surface, 12 mm thick. Micro-aggregate (magnified 24×): similar to sample nos. 66 and 67, but with crushed terracotta to 5 mm D; naturally fine sand is absent. MCM Sample no. 67: dense, well-compacted grey mortar backing Sample no. 68. Lacks the fine natural sand noted in Sample no. 66 (Structure no. 51, Bucket 86.009). Contains an abundance of coarse charcoal to 2 mm. Micro-aggregate (magnified 24×): similar to that of Sample no. 66 but larger, to 6 mm D. Although the coarse aggregates are the same as in Sample no. 66, the mortar is distinctly different in colour and aggregate content.

Bucket 87.076. Mortar from roofing arch. MCM sample no. 68B. Greyish white (close to 10YR 8/1) mortar containing a small amount of poorly-sorted quartz sand and pebbles, frequent carbon flecks, lime nodules, and bubbles.

Structure no. 68. Nabataean reservoir

Chronology: probably late first century BC or early first century AD.

Bucket 87.177. Plaster facing inside cistern. Same composition as mortar in spandrel (Bucket 87.178), but better compacted and brought to an even — although not smoothed — surface (Th 0.015). MCM Sample no. 58: light grey plaster, 12 mm thick. Surface irregular and eroded; not well-compacted. Contains an abundance of coarse charcoal to 3 mm, which has caused the grey colour, and occasional coarse aggregate to 7 mm. Abundant micro-cracking; water stained surfaces in cracks. Micro-aggregate (magnified 24 ×): fine-grained natural quartz, white to orange/buff, translucent and opaque.

Bucket 87.178. Mortar from filling walls in spandrel above arches of the main tank. Medium soft, light grey (10YR 8/1) mortar moderately tempered with well-sorted, rounded sand and occasional rounded pebbles. Frequent very small lime nodules, flecks of carbon, and bubbles. MCM Sample no. 59: light grey mortar, coloured by an abundance of coarse charcoal. Some porosity due to under-compaction. Micro-aggregate (magnified 24 ×): natural and crushed grey and brown aggregate to 12 mm (fig. 6.17).

Bucket 87.192. Plaster lining from west wall of settling tank. Hard, white to grey, poorly-mixed plaster or mortar, heavily tempered with poorly-sorted, rounded sand and pebbles. Contains many poorly-sorted, angular fragments of terracotta, and many lime nodules. A very coarse plaster, with many bubbles and fissures.

Bucket 89.077. Probe 2, Locus 04 (H89–68–P02). Mortar between blocks of outside face of east cistern wall. Crumbly white (5Y 8/1) mortar with a very high proportion of well-sorted, rounded sand, occasional chunks of sandstone, lumps of lime, and large flecks of carbon. MCM Sample no. 60: dark grey mortar with abundant coarse charcoal inclusions to 8 mm. Micro-aggregate (magnified 24 ×): natural and crushed grey and brown aggregate to 5 mm; some opaque quartz.

FIG. 6.17   *MCM Sample no. 59, from Reservoir no. 68. (Photo: G. E. Brown).*

Bucket 89.093. Probe 2, Locus 04 (H89–68–P02); mortar between blocks of outside face of east cistern wall. The composition is the same as the sample in Bucket 89.077. These are rounded lumps of mortar (D ca. 0.05–0.07) with a layer of the local sand adhering to them, as if they rolled on the ground during construction.

Structure no. 72. Built cistern

Chronology: probably Late Byzantine or Early Islamic.

Bucket 87.086. Mortar between blocks forming dome. Soft, light grey (10YR 7/2) mortar moderately tempered with well-sorted, rounded quartz sand. Occasional lumps of lime, bubbles, and small carbon flecks.

Bucket 87.179. Probe 1, Locus 03 (H87–72–P01). Plaster lining of cistern. Soft, very pale brown (10YR 8/3) plaster heavily tempered with poorly-sorted, rounded sand and pebbles, and containing occasional small lumps of lime.

Structure no. 76. Settling tank for drain

Chronology: probably Byzantine or Early Islamic.

Bucket 87.186. Probe 5, Locus 03 (H87–76–P05). Plaster lining of settling tank. Hard, very pale brown (10YR 8/3) plaster, heavily tempered with poorly-sorted, rounded sand and pebbles, and containing frequent nodules of lime. No carbon flecks. The surface has been smoothed, but not polished; it has weathered to a very pale brown (10YR 7/4).

Bucket 87.185. Probe 5, Locus 03 (H87–76–P5). Plaster lining of settling tank. Very similar to previous sample, but the sand and pebbles are well sorted, and the nodules of lime are less frequent.

Structure no. E077. Bath

Chronology: Phase I: first century AD, Phase II: mid-second century; Phase III, probably fourth century. The samples presented here probably belong to Phase III.

Although the complete publication of the Bath is being held over for a subsequent volume, presentation of the MCM materials here, in the context of the samples from other structures, makes more sense than presenting them in isolation. The samples are organised by Room designation rather than bucket number (see fig. 4.49).

Room A (*Calidarium*). Bucket 89.096; mortar adhering to flue tile in southeast corner. Medium hard, crumbly white (10YR 8/2) mortar with very high proportion of well-sorted, rounded sand, frequent small carbon bits, and occasional nodules of lime. MCM Sample no. 64: poorly-compacted grey mortar containing powdered charcoal. Micro-aggregate (magnified 24 ×): similar to Sample no. 63B (below), except that sand particles are smaller.

Room A, Locus 3. Bucket 89.013; mortar from flue tile. Gross composition identical to the sample in Bucket 89.096.

Room A, Locus 10. Bucket 89.020; flooring plaster at north side of room. Very hard, pink (5YR 8/3) plaster (Th 0.018 m), heavily tempered with well-sorted, rounded sand particles, and frequent sub-angular particles of yellowish red (5YR 5/8) terracotta. Contains poorly-sorted nodules of incompletely-calcined limestone, occasional small flecks of carbon, and occasional small bubbles in the lower portion. The surface has been carefully polished. The bedding mortar still adheres (Sample no. 63B). MCM Sample no. 63A: hard floor plaster with smooth, flat, well-compacted surface, polished, but worn down so that sand grains are exposed;

Th 0.018–0.020 m. Stained pink/brown colour, possibly by the addition of ground-up terracotta. Some coarse charcoal to 2 mm D. Well-bonded to bedding mortar (sample 63B). Micro-aggregate (magnified 24 ×): same as Sample no. 61 surface plaster but finer, with more brown aggregate and more crushed terracotta. Bedding mortar for plaster floor at north side of room, adhering to back of previous sample. Medium hard, light grey (2.5Y 7/2) mortar (Th 0.03 m) heavily tempered with poorly-sorted, rounded quartz sand and pebbles. Contains frequent charcoal bits and small nodules of lime and incompletely calcined limestone. MCM Sample no. 63B: well-compacted, grey mortar with an irregular surface. Contains powdered charcoal and an abundance of coarse charcoal to 6 mm. Adheres to Sample no. 63A. Micro-aggregate (magnified 24 ×): white, red, and pink natural and crushed opaque quartz, to 7 mm D.

Room B (*Apodyterium*). Bucket 89.061; plaster facing at base of bench. MCM Sample no. 62: pure white, chalky plaster, well-compacted but light in weight and lacking any appreciable amount of micro-aggregate. Minute carbon (charcoal) inclusions. Although this sample resembled a light Plaster of Paris, chemical testing (see below) indicated a lime-based substance. The sample was produced from an impure limestone, resulting in low compressive strength. The magnesium impurities give it the intense white colour that may have stimulated its use.

Room E (*Frigidarium*). Bucket 89.062; plaster lining of basin. Very hard, reddish yellow (5YR 6/6) plaster (Th 0.008 m), heavily tempered with well-sorted, rounded quartz sand and small, sub-rounded particles of a soft, yellowish red (5YR 5/8) terracotta. Contains occasional small pebbles and infrequent, small lime nodules. Surface carefully polished. Adheres to Sample no. 61B. MCM Sample 61A: plaster, very smooth, polished surface, possibly coloured brown with crushed terracotta; Th 5–10 mm. Very well-compacted and dense. Not well bonded to mortar bedding (Sample no. 61B). Micro-aggregate (magnified 24 ×): white translucent and opaque quartz with brown and red brown aggregate and crushed terracotta, to 2 mm D (fig. 6.18).

Room E. Bucket 89.062; mortar bedding for plaster lining of basin. Very hard, heavy, white (10YR 8/2) mortar, heavily tempered with well-sorted, clear quartz sand. Contains infrequent carbon flecks. The surface of this layer (Th 8 mm) was carefully smoothed; adheres to Sample no. 61A. MCM Sample no. 61B: light brown/buff bedding mortar Th 10 to 15 mm, overlying layer of grey mortar (Th 3 mm). Contains some fine charcoal and powdered charcoal. Micro-aggregate of major part of sample (magnified 24 ×): white translucent and opaque quartz, fine grained. The thin layer of dark grey mortar has a flat surface well-bonded to bedding mortar; it contains an abundance of coarse charcoal and powdered charcoal. Micro-aggregate (magnified 24 ×): dark grey with some translucent white quartz, fine grained.

Room E. Bucket 89.127; flooring plaster. Very hard, reddish yellow (5YR 6/6) plaster (Th 0.02), heavily tempered with well-sorted, rounded quartz sand and small, sub-rounded particles of a soft, yellowish red (5YR 5/8) terracotta. The proportion of terracotta temper seems to be less than for the basin lining. Contains numerous bubbles and small lime nodules, and occasional charcoal bits and casts of plant inclusions. MCM Sample no. 65: pink/brown plaster, smooth flat surface (Th 0.019 m) overlying minute remains of a grey mortar bedding. Micro-aggregate (magnified 24 ×): similar to Sample nos. 61 and 63 surface plaster. Bedding mortar adheres to lower surface: very hard, well-compacted, white (10YR 8.2) mortar heavily tempered with well-sorted, clear quartz sand; very infrequent bits of carbon.

Room E. Probe 1, Locus 03 (H89–77–P01). Bucket 89.153; mortar of the sub-flooring. Light grey (10YR 7/1), medium hard mortar containing a moderate amount of well-sorted, rounded sand, frequent small carbon bits, and occasional lime nodules.

6.D.3. *Catalogue and Gross Physical Description of Comparative Plaster and Mortar Samples*

The samples described below were collected opportunistically, although with an interest in Nabataean structures, structures with a hydraulic function,

FIG. 6.18   *MCM Sample no. 61, from Late Roman bath E077. (Photo: G. E. Brown).*

and Roman military structures. For budgetary reasons, Oleson subjected these samples only to visual analysis.

Al-Zar'ah (Kallirrhoe). Bath Complex

Chronology: late first century BC or fourth century AD.

Bucket 90.013; plaster from wall of room or tank. Medium hard to hard white plaster heavily tempered with poorly-sorted, rounded sand and rounded to sub-angular small pebbles. Contains occasional small bubbles, but no visible carbon or terracotta. The surface is well-smoothed and may have been polished. This sample adheres to a bedding plaster of the same colour but containing a higher proportion of larger stones and pebbles, as well as more bubbles.

Wadi Ramm. Temple of Allat, Aqueduct

Chronology: first century.

Bucket 87.043; wall of room north of naos chamber. Very hard white plaster or preliminary wall surfacing, containing some lumps of lime and heavily tempered with well-sorted white and clear quartz sand.

Bucket 87.044; sealing mortar from wall of small cistern with arched roof, adjacent to naos. Crumbly, light grey (10YR 7/1) mortar, heavily tempered with well-sorted, rounded sand. Occasional flecks of carbon. Very uniform colour and texture.

Bucket 87.045; mortar from end of conduit block of aqueduct uphill behind temple. Hard, very light grey mortar, containing infrequent lumps of lime and numerous bubbles, and heavily tempered with small grains of clear quartz sand.

Al-Lejjun. Roman fort

Bucket 90.009; floor plaster from barracks room in Square 11. Medium hard, off-white flooring plaster (Th 0.025) heavily tempered with poorly-sorted, rounded sand and rounded and sub-angular quartz pebbles. The upper surface was carefully smoothed, but was not polished. Chronology: fourth–fifth century.

Bucket 90.010; Bath Building. A) wall plaster from *tepidarium*. Hard off-white to white (10YR 8/2) plaster (Th 0.01) tempered with a moderate amount of rounded sand and — near outer surface — small pebbles, along with sub-angular fragments of red (2.5YR 4/8) terracotta. Contains occasional small carbon flecks and lime nodules. The surface seems to have been polished, and straw temper in the core has left casts. Adheres to the following sample. B) bedding mortar for wall plaster of *tepidarium*. Hard, light grey (10YR 7/1) mortar (Th 0.02–0.03) tempered with a moderate amount of rounded sand and occasional poorly-sorted pebbles. Contains occasional nodules of lime, small specks of carbon, and the casts of a heavy straw temper, but no ground-up terracotta. Chronology: first half of fourth century.

Bucket 90.011; Bath Building, bedding mortar for flue tiles. Hard white (2.5Y 8/2) mortar moderately to heavily tempered with rounded sand and poorly-sorted, rounded pebbles, and a small amount of straw. No carbon flecks or terracotta visible. Chronology: first half of fourth century.

Bucket 90.012; Bath Building, wall mortar of *calidarium*. Medium soft, off-white mortar tempered with a moderate amount of well-sorted, rounded sand and occasional rounded to sub-rounded pebbles. Contains frequent large flecks of carbon. Chronology: first half of fourth century.

Petra. Al-Hubtha Cistern

Chronology: first century BC or AD.

Bucket 90.013; cistern formed by blocking the end of a crevice, near NW entrance to al-Hubtha. Mortar between blocks on inside face of barrier wall. Soft, light grey (10YR 7/2) mortar heavily tempered with well-sorted, rounded sand, containing occasional large carbon specks and frequent small lime nodules.

Qasr Bshir

Chronology: AD 306 (Parker 1986: 53–55).

Bucket 90.014; northeast tower, mortar between blocks of inner face of the upper surviving courses of the wall. Hard, blotchy, white to grey mortar heavily tempered with well-sorted, rounded sand, containing numerous small, hard lime nodules and very frequent large particles of carbon, including whole twigs.

Qasr Mushash

Chronology: seventh–eighth century.

Bag 90.008; mortar between blocks of north precinct wall, east of palace structure. Soft, grey (10YR 6/1) mortar heavily tempered with rounded quartz sand and containing frequent large flecks of carbon and large nodules of incompletely calcined limestone.

Bag 90.016; plaster lining of tank outside north precinct wall. Very hard, very pale brown (10YR 8/3) plaster (Th 0.017), very heavily tempered with poorly-sorted, rounded sand, pebbles, and sub-angular fragments of light red (2.5 YR 6/8) terracotta. No carbon component noted.

6.D.4. *Chemical and Physical Analysis of Mortar and Plaster Samples*

Eight samples of mortar and plaster from Humayma (MCM Sample nos. 44–51) were submitted to Quanta Trace Laboratories of Burnaby B.C. in February 1987 for chemical analysis through plasma emission spectroscopy. Portions of six

Table 6.1   Chemical analysis of MCM by Plasma Emission Spectroscopy.

STRUCTURE NO.:	62	45	01J	44	01G	53	20	01G
STRUCTURE TYPE:	reservoir	cistern	aqueduct	dam	aqueduct	cistern	cistern	aqueduct
MCM TYPE:	mortar	plaster	mortar	mortar	mortar	plaster	plaster	plaster
SAMPLE NO.:	44	45	46	47	48	49	50	51
AMOUNT ANALYZED (G)	0.199	0.200	0.200	0.201	0.201	0.199	0.200	0.199
Majors as oxides (%)								
Silicon (SiO_2)	40.6	32.5	13.0	58.7	44.2	50.4	53.6	50.7
Aluminum (Al_2O_3)	2.44	3.51	0.89	1.3	3.31	5.21	1.8	2.18
Iron (Fe_2O_3)	1.24	1.50	0.95	0.73	2.25	1.37	0.657	3.5
Calcium (CaO)	26.5	30.8	33.3	17.7	21.0	19.3	20.9	19.0
Magnesium (MgO)	3.0	0.8	12.0	2.04	4.08	1.08	2.09	3.8
Sodium (Na_2O)	0.2	0.4	<0.1	1.5	0.3	2.6	0.3	0.1
Potassium (K_2O)	<0.6	0.8	<0.6	0.9	<0.6	1.2	<0.6	<0.6
Barium (BaO)	0.016	0.041	<0.006	0.01	0.023	0.066	0.055	0.014
Manganese (MnO)	0.034	0.069	0.028	0.020	0.038	0.053	0.016	0.035
Phosphorus (P_2O_5)	<0.5	0.5	<0.5	<0.5	<0.5	0.7	0.6	0.6
Strontium (SrO)	0.021	0.056	0.013	0.037	0.058	0.079	0.096	0.053
Titanium (TiO_2)	0.14	0.20	0.062	0.10	0.37	0.16	0.16	0.16
Zirconium (ZrO_2)	0.03	0.02	0.02	0.03	0.04	0.03	0.04	0.04
Loss on Ignition	25.00	28.10	40.40	17.10	23.60	18.40	20.20	21.10
Total Oxides %	99.16	99.23	100.4	100.5	99.9	101.4	101.3	101.3
Total Carbon %C	6.13	7.53	9.13	4.39	5.17	4.31	5.39	4.92
Total Sulphur %S	0.09	0.07	0.07	0.27	0.08	0.13	0.12	0.10

of these samples (Sample nos. 44, 46–50) and a seventh not sent to Quanta Trace (Sample no. 52) were also submitted to Gordon E. Brown (Concrete Consultant) of Keswick Ontario in March 1987 for physical analysis, including gross physical description, specific gravity of aggregate, hardness, and compressive strength, unit weight, absorption, and lime content. In December 1990, a further fourteen samples (reference nos. 57–70) were submitted to Gordon Brown for the same physical analysis. The data resulting from the tests run on this relatively limited and localised group of samples will become more useful as samples from other sites in the region are subjected to testing (Brown 1996: 28–40).

Results of Chemical Analysis
(based on a report by G. Brown)

While it is useful to have a reading of the major chemical elements in these eight samples (Table 6.1), the data do not at this point provide sufficient information for a long discussion or particularly significant deductions. Sample no. 46, the chalky white mortar from the Jammam aqueduct km 0.993, is very low in silicon and aluminium, compared with the other samples, and high in calcium and magnesium, evidently because of the very low proportion of sand temper. Otherwise, there does not seem to be a great deal of correlation among function, chronology, and chemical composition.

Table 6.2   Specific gravity of mechanically extracted aggregate.

SAMPLE NO.	STRUCTURE	SITE NO.	SAMPLE TYPE	SPECIFIC GRAVITY
44	reservoir	62	mortar	2.58
46	aqueduct	01J	mortar	2.41
48	aqueduct	01G	mortar	2.55
49	cistern	53	plaster	2.68
50	cistern	20	plaster	2.41
52	reservoir	62	plaster	2.50
			StD	0.105

Variations in the first five components probably reflect variations in the mix of the mortar or plaster and differential erosion of the cementing material prior to sampling, while variations in the minor elements most likely reflect varying sources for sand and lime.

Results of Physical Analysis
(based on a report by G. Brown)

In general, no outstanding features were noted during examination of these samples. Sample nos. 49, 50, and 52 (and, to a lesser degree nos. 65 and 68) were notably higher in compressive strength, lower in absorption, and higher in unit weight than all other samples, suggesting that a mortar of higher quality was prepared for use in lining cisterns.

The micro-aggregate was extracted and examined in two ways. First, a small sample was dissolved in a 10% solution of HCL acid and examined with a microscope. A second, larger sample was extracted mechanically and was kept for future study by a geologist. Acid was used to clean the aggregate after it was mechanically extracted, and some of the natural carbonates will have dissolved during this process. Observations made on the basis of an examination at 24 × are included in the sample descriptions. The variations in content indicate that the micro-aggregate was obtained from a variety of sources, but that some samples shared a common source. No pumice was detected in any of the samples, but Samples no. 50 and 52 contained possible natural pozzolanic material. The

relatively small deviation in specific gravity among the samples (StDev = 0.105) probably reflects the general absence of lighter, natural pozzolanic additives and the loss of natural carbonates during the cleaning with acid (Table 6.2).

The Moh hardness was measured on the interior of each sample (Table 6.3). A graph developed by Brown (see Brown 1996: 8, fig. 4) was then used to estimate of the compressive strength of the material. There is enormous variation in calculated Moh hardness (Average: 2.37; Median: 2; StDev: 1.13) and compressive strength (Average: 7.94; Median: 7; StDev: 4.194). Nevertheless, the plaster samples are nearly always much harder than the mortar samples, a distinction particularly marked among some of the multiple samples taken from a single structure, such as the Roman Reservoir (no. 62) and the Bath (no. 77). There is no obvious correlation between chronology and hardness. The subjective, tactile evaluation of hardness given above as part of the gross physical description of these samples corresponds fairly well with the measured hardness.

Where sample size permitted, small cubes were cut and tested in compression (Table 6.4). With the exception of Sample no. 63, a good correlation exists between the actual compression measured and the estimated compression.

Unit weight was calculated from the measured bulk specific gravity in a saturated, surface dry condition. Absorption was measured after 24 hours immersion in 20°C water. An excellent inverse correlation exists between unit weight and absorption (Table 6.5). As might be expected from their better

Table 6.3   MOH hardness and estimated compressive strength.

SAMPLE NO.	STRUCTURE	SITE NO.	MATERIAL	MOH HARDNESS	COMPRESSIVE STRENGHTH, MPA
44	reservoir	62	mortar	-1	2.5
46	aqueduct	01J	mortar	2.5	10
47	dam	44	mortar	1+	4
48	aqueduct	01G	mortar	2+	8
49	cistern	53	plaster	3-	12
50	cistern	20	plaster	3-	12
52	reservoir	62	plaster	3	14
57	reservoir	63	plaster, surface	3	–
57			plaster, interior	1.5	5
57			mortar	1.5	5
58	reservoir	68	plaster, surface	2	–
58			plaster, interior	2-	6
59	reservoir	68	mortar	2-	6
60	reservoir	68	mortar	1	3
61	bath	77	plaster, surface	4	–
61			plaster, interior	3-	13
61			mortar, interior	2.5	10
61			thin mortar	1	3
62	bath	77	mortar	1-	3
63	bath	77	plaster, surface	3	–
63			plaster, interior	3-	13
63			mortar, interior	2-	6
64	bath	77	Mortar	1.5	5
65	bath	77	plaster, surface	4.5	–
65			plaster, interior	3-	13
66	cistern	51	Plaster	2	7
67	cistern	64	Mortar	1	3
68	cistern	64	plaster, surface	6-	–
68			plaster, interior	3+	17
69	aqueduct	01G	mortar	2.5	10
70	aqueduct	01J	mortar	2+	8
			StD	1.13	4.19

Table 6.4   Measured compressive strength of MCM samples.

SAMPLE NO.	STRUCTURE	SITE NO.	MATERIAL	CUBE SIZE (MM)	COMPRESSIVE STRENGTH, MPA
59	reservoir	68	mortar	21 x 21	4.6
60	reservoir	68	mortar	25 x 26	2.7
63	bath	77	plaster	19 x 21	20.0
64	bath	77	mortar	21 x 21	6.8

Table 6.5   Unit weight and absorption of MCM samples.

SAMPLE NO.	STRUCTURE	SITE NO.	MATERIAL	UNIT WT. (KG/CUM)	ABSORPTION (%)
44	reservoir	62	mortar	1967	19.9
46	aqueduct	01J	mortar	1875	19.5
47	dam	44	mortar	1930	16.6
48	aqueduct	01G	mortar	1847	27.2
49	cistern	53	plaster	2092	9.8
50	cistern	20	plaster	2124	9.9*
52	reservoir	62	plaster	2169	10.3
57	reservoir	63	plaster	1930	20.2
58	reservoir	68	plaster	1813	30.0
59	reservoir	68	mortar	1643	40.6
60	reservoir	68	mortar	1712	29.6
61	bath	77	plaster	1967	17.3
62	bath	77	plaster	1573	65.6
63	bath	77	plaster	1855	25.5
64	bath	77	mortar	1610	38.8
65	bath	77	plaster	1966	18.5
66	cistern	51	plaster	1832	30.2
67	cistern	64	mortar	1680	38.9
68	cistern	64	plaster	1984	19.5
69	aqueduct	01G	mortar	1956	17.9
70	aqueduct	01J	mortar	1913	23.1
			Average:	1878	25.95
			Median:	1913	21.26
			StD:	163.28	12.81
			Avg. (mortar)	1813.30	27.21
			Median (mortar)	1861.00	25.15
			StD (mortar)	137.78	9.34
			Avg. (plaster)	1936.82	24.69
			Median (plaster)	1966.00	19.85
			StD (plaster)	168.06	15.99

*This unit weight might be slightly higher than actual due to the adherence of traces of sandstone bed-rock to the sample.

compaction and the higher proportion of micro-aggregate, the plaster samples show overall higher unit weight than the mortar samples.

In order to determine the extent of carbonation, all samples were subjected to phenolphthalein and the results recorded. None of these samples, how-ever, reacted to phenolphthalein, indicating that carbonation was complete.

A modification to the ASTM 457 Modified Point Count was used to make estimates of the paste and aggregate content. The method involves sectioning, resin impregnation, polishing, and

Table 6.6   Lime content of MCM samples (by bulk volume).

SAMPLE NO.	STRUCTURE	SITE NO.	MATERIAL	LIME/AGGREGATE RATIO
46	aqueduct	01J	mortar	1:0.7 (142.9%)
47	dam	44	mortar	1:1.4 (71.4%)
48	aqueduct	01G	mortar	1:0.7 (142.9%)
49	cistern	53	plaster	1:1.7 (58.8%)
52	reservoir	62	plaster	1:2.1 (47.6%)

Table 6.7   MCM samples containing crushed terracotta.

Ghana Aqueduct (no. 1)	Mortar from junction with Jammam branch, at km 6.553 (Bucket 87.026, MCM Sample no. 69).
Cistern no. 54	Plaster lining of settling basin (Bucket 87.055).
Cistern no. 64	Plaster lining of settling basin (Bucket 87.076, MCM Sample no. 68A).
Reservoir no. 68	Plaster lining of settling basin (Bucket 87.192).
Roman Bath (no. 77)	Plaster floor of *calidarium* (Bucket 89.020, MCM Sample no. 63A).
Roman Bath (no. 77)	Plaster lining of basin in *frigidarium* (Bucket 89.062, MCM Sample no. 61A).
Roman Bath (no. 77)	Plaster floor of *frigidarium* (Bucket 89.127, MCM Sample no. 65).

Table 6.8   MCM samples possibly containing natural pozzolanas.

Ghana Aqueduct (no. 1)	Plaster from wall of off-take cistern (no. 20) at km 9.597 (Bucket no. 86.010, MCM Sample no. 50).
Nabataean Dam (no. 44)	Mortar from barrier wall (Bucket no. 86.023, MCM Sample no. 47).
Roman Bath (no. 77)	Plaster floor of *frigidarium* (Bucket 89.127, MCM Sample no. 65).

a point count examination with a special stage equipped microscope. The results are given in a bulk volume ratio (Table 6.6). Although the number of samples is small, the higher proportion of lime in the mortar samples reinforces the results indicated by the calculation of unit weight. The mortars are quite rich in lime compared to the formulae given by Vitruvius, who recommends 1 part lime to 2 parts river or sea sand, or 3 parts pozzolana, or 2 parts river or sea sand and 1 part crushed terracotta (Vitruvius 2.5.1; Adam 1994: 74–75; Oleson et al. 2006). The two samples from the aqueduct have very high, identical proportions

of lime, despite their origin in the two different branches, the Jammam branch (sample no. 46) and the Ghana branch (sample no. 48). Although calculated in a different manner, plaster samples from Petra were composed of 37.9% to 64.8% carbonates (Sha'er 2004: 146); mortar samples at Umm al-Jimal contained 70–90% carbonates (Dunn and Rapp 2004: 150).

Sample no. 62, a very light-weight plaster lacking aggregate, resembled Plaster of Paris. The sample, however, reacted to hydrochloric acid, eliminating the possibility that this plaster was based on gypsum. An x-ray diffraction analysis indicated the sample to be Kutnohorite, Ca 0.74 (Mn Mg) 0.26 CO_3, an impure calcium carbonate containing manganese and magnesium. Gypsum mortars have been identified at both Petra and Umm al-Jimal (Dunn and Rapp 2004: 147, 151; Sha'er 2004).

6.D.5. *Summary Analysis of Manufactured Construction Materials*

The MCM samples were collected, examined, and tested in the hope of answering a series of questions. Is there a marked difference between the composition of the mortars and the plasters used in the structures in and around Humayma, or between plasters intended for contact with water and plasters intended as simple structural finish? Is there any evidence for the use of natural or artificial pozzolanic additives in the mortar or plaster? Is there a marked difference between the mortars and plasters used in the Jammam branch of the aqueduct as opposed to the main Ghana branch, perhaps supporting the hypothesis that the Jammam branch was a later addition? Is there a marked difference between the mortars and plasters used in what appear to be Nabataean period (first century BC to second century AD) cisterns, and cisterns or related structures of the Roman and later periods? Finally, how does the range of MCM at Humayma compare with that used at other sites in the region?

It is obvious from the visual descriptions and testing of the MCM from Humayma that there is usually a marked difference in the composition and characteristics of the mortars and the plasters, both within a single structure and among the entire group. The mortars are almost always softer, lighter in weight, and less resistant to compression than the plasters, and the ratio of lime to aggregate is less. The micro-aggregates used in the mortars are more varied in size than those used in the plasters, and the maximum size is greater. In addition, the mortars have been less well mixed, so they tend to contain lumps of lime and large fragments of charcoal from the process of burning the lime.

There does not seem to be any marked difference between the plasters intended for contact with water and those intended to be in contact with the atmosphere alone, except for the occasional addition of crushed terracotta. This artificial pozzolanic additive was found in seven of the samples taken at Humayma, all but one of them plasters intended for contact with water (Table 6.7).

Although the structure at the junction of the two aqueduct branches has been uprooted by vandals, scrambling the original arrangement, the sample with crushed terracotta (no. 69) seemed to have been applied as mortar between two blocks, rather than as a basin lining. Several other samples from that structure, however, showed no terracotta additive, so the situation remains unclear. Since water constantly drained across the plaster floors of the Bath, hydraulic plaster was appropriate there. The samples from the Aqueduct, Cisterns nos. 54 and 64, and Reservoir no. 68 should date to the first century BC or AD, while the second phase of the Bath should date to the fourth century. It is interesting that the plaster and mortar in Reservoir no. 62, inside the Roman fort, made use of crushed red granite micro-aggregate, which closely resembles crushed terracotta but has no hydraulic effect. The Roman engineers would have known the difference between the two materials, and a large deposit of crushed terracotta apparently intended for use in construction was found in a room associated with the *Principia* (Oleson et al. 1999: 418). The reservoir and the terracotta deposit both belong to Phase I of the fort. The wall plaster of the Byzantine Bath at Lejjun also contained crushed terracotta (Bucket 90.010), as did the plaster of a basin at Qasr Mushash (seventh–eighth century, Bucket 90.016). Crushed terracotta was found in mortars at Umm al-Jimal (Dunn and Rapp 2004: 153) and in plasters at Petra (Sha'er 2004).

Possible natural pozzolanic additives (visually similar to volcanic ash, but not subjected to close analysis) were found in three samples (Table 6.8).

Here again the structures belong to the first century BC or AD and to the fourth century. It cannot be determined at present whether the additives in fact are pozzolanic in character or were added intentionally, but in all three structures the plaster and mortar would have been in contact with water. Possible natural pozzolanic materials were identified in the Umm al-Jimal mortars, but without any concomitant evidence for hydraulic reaction within the mortar.

Most of the mortars used in and around Humayma contain significant quantities of bits of carbon, probably deposited by the fire in the lime kiln, and in some structures the mortar ranges in colour from light grey to a very dark grey as the proportion of ash increases. Although certain types of ash can have a pozzolanic effect on mortar, the ash has to contain significant amounts of silica, as with the husks of some grains, particularly rice (Massazza 1998: 487). It is unlikely that sufficient quantities of this sort of material would have been available around Humayma for burning lime. In any case, the darker mortars tend to be softer than the lighter coloured mortars and less well-mixed. Since no ancient author seems to have recognised the potential pozzolanic effect of some plant ashes, its presence in the mortar at Humayma probably reflects carelessness in firing or collecting the lime. Since the plasters tend to contain a very low proportion of ash, the cleaner lime was probably reserved for their production in order to achieve a brighter effect.

The use of crushed terracotta as a pozzolanic additive to mortar is usually associated with Roman technology (Bugini 1993; Davidovits 1995), but the data suggest that some of the Nabataean inhabitants of Hawara had already learned of this Roman innovation prior to the stationing of Roman soldiers at the site in the early second century. This deduction assumes, of course, that the appearance of hydraulic plasters in the non-Roman structures is not the result of Roman period construction or renovation. Nabataean traders or military engineers may have picked up this useful engineering innovation at one of the trading ports of the eastern Mediterranean, where they most likely also found the earlier, Hellenistic system of roofing cisterns with transverse arches. It is clear, however, that the use of crushed terracotta as an additive to mortars and plasters never became common at Hawara. The use of natural pozzolanic ingredients was even more rare and may in fact not have been intentional in the few samples where it was tentatively identified. The well-mixed and compacted lime plasters apparently were sufficiently durable and impermeable to satisfy most local builders, so the simple formula of a plaster rich in lime continued to be used.

It is difficult to discern any major difference between the plaster and mortar used in the Ghana Aqueduct and those used in the Jammam branch and the structure at the junction between the two. Although the number of samples is relatively small, the mortar used in the Jammam branch shows a more pronounced tendency to be poorly mixed, resulting in the appearance of nodules of lime in the mortar. The same relatively subtle difference tends to characterise both the mortars and the plasters used in the sampled structures that can be shown to date to the second century or later. The mortars and plasters from the Roman Reservoir (no. 62), for example, tend to contain lumps of un-mixed lime, bubbles, and poorly-sorted micro-aggregate. The same tendencies can be seen in the mortars and plasters used in the Byzantine Phase III of the Bath no. E077 and in the Late Byzantine or Early Islamic cistern (or granary?) no. 72 and drain complex no. 76. It is possible that builders of the Nabataean cultural period at Hawara burned or slaked their lime more carefully or took more care in the mixing and placing of their mortars and plasters than those of the Roman or later periods. The Nabataeans may also have had cleaner fuels at their disposal, for example, billets of wood rather than shrubs and chaff.

Although the number of samples examined from sites elsewhere in Jordan is small, the results are similar to those outlined above for Humayma. The plasters are harder and finer than the mortars and tend to contain less ash. As at Humayma, the earlier samples from Wadi Ramm, Petra, and possibly al-Zar'ah are better mixed and placed than the later samples and contain less carbon. It remains to be seen whether these results can be duplicated at other ancient sites in Jordan. Brown (1997: 17–20, 40–41, 51–61) provides analyses of several late Hellenistic and Byzantine samples from Gamla and Tel Hum (Israel), and Late Roman samples from Ismint in the Dakhleh Oasis and Qasr al-Halaka (Egypt). The results show that, as at Humayma, plasters are finer, harder, and heavier than mortars. The statistics for hardness, weight, etc. are comparable to those of the Humayma samples, except that the plasters tend to have a much lower lime content than those at Humayma: Gamla (second century BC–first century AD) 1:4.1, 1:4.4 (lime to aggregate

Table 6.9   Origin of soil samples submitted for testing.

Soil Sample 1	Bucket 90.001. Surface of field, 50 m W of Roman Bath (Structure E077).
Soil Sample 2	Bucket 90.002. Surface of field between Lower Church (C101) and Cistern no. 54.
Soil Sample 3	Bucket 90.006. Surface of field 1.5 km N of settlement centre at the N edge of the catchment field for the settlement, south of Cistern no. 45.
Soil Sample 4	Bucket 86.007. Surface of field 1 km E of Farmhouse (A127).
Soil Sample 5	Surface of field 300 m NW of north gate of Fort (B100), on high ground; area plowed in the 1980s.
Soil Sample 6	Surface of field 300 m W of the Fort (B100), on lower ground; alluvial area; area plowed for wheat as late as the early 1990s.
Soil Sample 7	Surface of cultivated field associated with Nabataean Campground (C124); olive and fruit trees; wheat and Bedouin tobacco (hishi) planted as late as the early 1990s; certain amount of alluvium; field fenced for grazing.
Soil Sample 8	Same location as no. 7, but 0.60 m deep, in Nabataean cultural strata.
Soil Sample 9	Surface of field 300 m SW of Farmhouse (A127), cultivated as recently as the 1970s.
Soil Sample 10	Surface of field 300 m SW of Farmhouse (A127), cultivated as recently as the 1970s.
Soil Sample 11	Surface of field 300 m SW of Farmhouse (A127), cultivated as recently as the 1970s.
Soil Sample 12	Surface of recently cultivated field 3.7 km E of Cistern no. 67.

by volume); Ismint (AD 200) 1:2.4; Qasr al-Halaka (AD 200) 1:4.0; Humayma (first and second century) 1:1.7, 1:2.1. More samples are needed before this discrepancy can be interpreted.

6.E.   *Soil Analysis (based on a report by C. Nikolic)*

Four samples of soil (nos. 1–4) from fields in the centre of Humayma and in the immediate vicinity were submitted to Soilcon Laboratories of Richmond B.C. for chemical and physical analysis, and a report was submitted by M.J. Goldstein (18/01/1991). In July 2004, eight more samples (nos. 5–12) were taken and analysed at the excavation house by Christina Nikolic, a trained landscape designer, and a report submitted. Another, non-agricultural sample (no. 13) from inside a pipe excavated in 1987 was been submitted to MB Research in Sidney B.C. in 1989. This discussion has been constructed from those three reports. Some of the sites selected for sampling were under cultivation for grain crops at the time of the sampling, or they showed signs of having been ploughed recently. The sites were also

obvious candidates for agricultural activity in antiquity (Table 6.9). The fields show compaction on the surface from the hard rainfalls in combination with alkaline and slightly saline conditions. Hard, fist-size clumps of soil occasionally were left behind by cultivation, suggesting that they were ploughed while wet. This evidence agrees with the strategy of cultivating only those fields sufficiently watered by run-off water in the winter. In most cases it took the help of a small pick to collect the material even at the shallow depths of 0.10 to 0.15 m tested. The samples represent coarse to medium soil types, with sand being the dominant particle size in all of them. In addition to simple manual and sedimentation tests to determine soil texture, pH value and salinity were tested to find out whether these are limiting factors for agriculture.

The general agricultural potential of the soil is surprisingly high for a desert area. Soils in arid climates are often at the alkaline end of the pH scale, and the neighbourhood of Humayma is no exception. With an average pH of 8, the samples are definitely alkaline, but this is a low level of alkalinity at which plant nutrients are still quite

Table 6.10 Chemical analysis of soil samples.

	No. 1	No. 2	No. 3	No. 4	No. 5	No. 6	No. 7	No. 8	No. 9	No. 10	No. 11	No. 12
CHEMICAL ANALYSES:												
pH	7.95	8.0	8.0	8.0	8.0	8.0	8.0	8.0	8.0	8.0	8.0	8.0
EC (mS/cm)	0.62	0.70	1	0.70								
Dissolved solids (ppm)					400	20	40	100	>2000	30	85	60
Total Carbon (%, organic and carbonate)	3.31	1.68	2.61	2.09								
Total Nitrogen (%)	0.07	0.04	0.02	0.03								
Avail. Phosphorus (ppm)	2	7	<2	<2								
Avail. Potassium (ppm)	650	465	160	160								
Avail. Calcium (ppm)	2600	2000	2450	2050								
Avail. Magnesium (ppm)	295	120	195	165								
CEC (NaOAc) (meg/100g)	17.3	8.8	12.5	8								
Exc Ca (NH4OAc) (meg/100g)	13.8	10.3	12.6	10.7								
Exc Mg (NH4OAc) (meg/100g)	2.7	1.1	1.8	1.6								
Exc Na (NH4OAc) (meg/100g)	0.3	0.2	0.1	0.1								
Exc K (NH4OAc) (meg/100g)	1.8	1.3	0.4	0.5								
ESP (%)	1.7	1.9	0.8	0.6								

well available and toxicity levels of certain metals are not crucial. Most grain plants would perform sufficiently well at a pH of 8. Nevertheless, at this pH level both the process of chemical weathering of rock into soil and the process of creation of humus from organic matter are slowed down considerably. Therefore, in desert conditions we find old, yet thin topsoil layers (the A horizon), often directly above the unweathered parent rock (the C horizon, here: sandstone), with the B horizon missing (which in temperate climates is the layer of decomposed rock that is slowly being broken up physically and chemically and that is at an intermediate stage between rock and topsoil). There is little to no stable organic matter at all, except where accumulated by chance or added artificially.

Electrical conductivity (EC) is a measure of the soluble salts in the soil; Samples 1–4 were subjected to this analysis. In many desert regions salt is the major impediment to agriculture. While an EC of 1 mS/cm is slightly high, salts are not a major problem below an EC of 4. Soils are said to be "saline" at an EC of over 4. The EC would also be lowered by the occasional rainfall that preceded localised sowing, according to the regimen practised in this region. The lack of direct irrigation of the grain crops also avoided the build-up of salt. The salinity of Samples 5–12 was determined in the field laboratory by means of an dissolved solids tester (DiST1 ATC Dissolved Solids Tester, range 10/1990 TD). In plastic containers, one part soil was mixed with two parts local tap water by volume, stirred, and let sit for 15 minutes. Then the dissolved solids were tested in parts per million (ppm), subtracting those solids already present in the water. Two readings were taken per sample in a 15 minute interval. In the context of the Humayma landscape, the dissolved solids should be mostly salts.

Aside from the erroneous reading for Sample 9 (corrected in samples 10 and 11), in this second group only Sample 5, from a field northwest of the Fort, should be classified as moderately saline. The variation in salinity levels in Samples 10 and 11 shows that there can be quite a bit of variation even within the same field. The salinity test readings for Sample 9, taken from the same spot, were off the scale of the testing instrument, probably for some incidental reason, such as recent contamination by animal urine or manure.

The properties of the four soil samples subjected to chemical analysis (nos. 1–4) are very similar and can be discussed together (Table 6.10). In addition to total salts, excess sodium (Na) is a problem in many desert areas. Exchangeable sodium is less than 1 milli-equivalents per 100 grams (meg/100gm) in all the Humayma samples. This figure represents less than a 1/10 of the cation exchange capacity, resulting in an exchangeable sodium percentage (ESP) of less than 2%. This level is good for agriculture. Soil with ESP's over 15 are termed "sodic" and cause major production problems. Cation exchange capacity (CEC) is a measure of the ability of soils to store available nutrients, such as potassium, calcium, and magnesium. The CECs of Samples 1–4 are fairly high for the texture and age of the soil and would be adequate for agriculture.

In terms of plant nutrients, available calcium and magnesium in Samples 1–4 are high, but in balance. Available potassium is also high. Nitrogen and phosphorus, however, are both low. Phosphorus is especially low, reaching a maximum of only 7 ppm, a level that would be a problem for modern as well as ancient farmers. Grain yields would be low at these phosphorus levels. Since most virgin, arid soils would be substantially higher in phosphorus (possibly 20 times higher), it is a reasonable hypothesis that the available phosphorus at Humayma was depleted by agricultural activity. The normal cure for low phosphorus and nitrogen is the addition of organic matter, manures in particular. The present-day farmers at the site do not seem to make intentional use of manure as part of their agricultural regimen, since much of the manure is lost as the animals wander to graze. In addition, the arid climate does not foster incorporation of manure in the soil, since the droppings tend to dry out quickly on the surface, break up, and blow away.

The thick, hard lenses of sheep and goat manure that build up in the occasional Bedouin corrals around modern Humayma are sometimes broken up into blocks and stacked, perhaps for use as fuel. Even these concentrated deposits of manure do not evolve into soil.

The physical properties of the soil samples are more variable (Table 6.11). Sample 1 is loamy in texture and has excellent physical properties, including an available water storage capacity (AWSC) of 13%. Sample 2 is a sandy loam, with an AWSC of only 1.8%. This soil would be very droughty for grain production based on water storage in the soil before sowing. Sample 3 falls between Samples 1 and 2 in water storage capacity. Since soil physical properties are longer-lived than chemical properties, the ancient farmers probably faced the same limited water storage capacities the soils now possess.

Samples 5–12 show a similar range of character. Sample 5 is a loam, similar to Sample 1. Samples 7, 9, 10, and 11 are sandy loams, while Samples 8 and 12 are loamy sands (meaning the sand content is higher in the latter two). These are two closely related, coarse textures where two thirds or more by volume consists of sand, and the remaining third is made up from silt and clay. Sample 6, surface soil from an alluvial plain, is an extreme, as it consists of 100% silt. This type of pure loess soil, although characterised by a high water holding capacity, lacks the porosity and structural component contributed by sand as well as the nutrient holding capacity of clay, and is therefore problematic for agriculture. Sample 5, on the other hand, is a textbook loam from the centre of the soil triangle, a very versatile and well-balanced soil texture of roughly 40% sand, 40% silt and 20% clay. From a purely physical or mineral point of view, this loam would be the best soil type around and highly desirable for agriculture. It must be noted, however, that five out of six samples, including this one, were completely devoid of organic matter and any perceptible soil life. Organic matter and soil life — animals, fungi, bacteria, microbes — are crucial to soil fertility; without these the soil is nearly sterile. Additionally, without water there is no soil life, no matter how much organic matter is present. And finally, a good soil structure — rather

Table 6.11   Particle size and water retention of soil samples.

	No. 1	No. 2	No. 3	No. 4	No. 5	No. 6	No. 7	No. 8	No. 9	No. 10	No. 11	No. 12
Material												
gravel (% by wt)	0.9	6.8	0.8	3.2	0	0	0	0	0	0	0	0
sand (% by wt)	45.8	71.6	64.1	n/a	43	0	70	78	67	65	61	78
silt (% by wt)	33.1	19.0	25.4	n/a	41	100	20	18	20	16	21	13
clay (% by wt)	21.2	9.4	10.4	n/a	16	0	10	4	13	19	18	9
Textural class	Loam	Sandy loam	Sandy loam	n/a	Loam	Loess/ Silt	Sandy loam	Loamy sand	Sandy loam	Sandy loam	Sandy loam	Loamy sand
Water Retention												
1/10 bar (% by vol)	32.6	27.9	28.1	n/a								
1/3 bar (% by vol)	29.6	17.3	19.7	n/a								
15 bar (% by vol)	15.7	15.4	12.9	n/a								
AWSC (% by vol)	13.9	1.8	6.7	n/a								
Bulk Density (kg/m^3)	1530	1827	1666	n/a								
Particle Density (kg/m^3)	2561	2582	2618	n/a								
Total Porosity (% by vol)	40.3	29.3	36.3	n/a								

than texture — is what makes a soil crumbly and coherent, and it is the humus formed from organic matter, combined with clay particles in a stable clay-humus-complex, that acts as the glue that gives soil a structure conducive to plant growth.

Sample 7 stands out as the only one with a notable organic matter content and a rich earthy smell that indicates the presence of fungi. The water used for the sedimentation tests was medium brown coloured in this sample, whereas it appeared almost clear after the 24-hour settlement time in all other samples. Therefore, although not the perfect loam, this soil has much more potential fertility at present than any of the others. This anomalous character is probably directly attributable to the fact that animal manure has been allowed to accumulate in this fenced field in the years immediately preceding the sampling.

Another soil sample (no. 13), recovered from the fill inside a terracotta pipe (1987.114.01) from the pipeline around Reservoir no. 63 (Probe 5, locus 06) was submitted to MB Research of Sidney B.C. for chemical analysis (Table 6.12). The major elements are all higher or very much higher in this sample than in Samples 1–4, probably as a result of its isolation in a buried terracotta pipe section. The calcium and magnesium in particular may have leached from the pipe and the plaster at the joint, while the sodium may have accumulated through alternate soaking and drying cycles. The high levels of phosphorus, potassium, and nitrate may also result from capillary action, along with the absence of cultivation. The pH is close to that of the other samples, while the organic matter is lower, again probably because of isolation in the pipe.

Table 6.12   Chemical analysis of Soil Sample 13.

Major Elements (ppm)		Other Elements (ppm)	
Calcium	24,130.0	Aluminum	102.20
Magnesium	1,076.0	Silicon	21.34
Phosphorus	68.45	Titanium	0.79
Potassium	961.8	Arsenic	<0.03
Nitrate-N	290.05	Beryllium	0.01
Phosphate-P	40.01	Bismuth	<0.05
Sodium	781.0	Cadmium	<0.003
		Lead	34.6
Minor Elements (ppm)		Antimony	<0.04
Iron	0.59	Barium	9.22
Cobalt	0.24	Chromium	0.68
Copper	0.49	Lanthanum	1.52
Manganese	11.18	Molybdenum	0.38
Zinc	0.34	Nickel	0.76
Boron	53.2	Strontium	88.49
		Vanadium	0.8
		Tungsten	3.4
		EC (uS/cm)	5,003.01
		pH	7.358
		Organic Matter (%)	0.7

With the exception of Samples 6 and 13, all of the soils tested would have been suitable for modest agriculture, although the two loamy sands (nos. 8, 12) are marginal. The physical and chemical characteristics of the soil are similar to those of the soils around agricultural fields of Nabataean origin in the Negev (see Bruins 1986: esp. 101–4, 161–71). There is no obvious geographical pattern to the fertility of the Humayma samples, other than the mediocre quality of the soil in the most distant sample (no. 12). Soils with a high sand content are actually easy to work; they do not require deep ploughing, and they drain and ventilate well. On the other hand, their water and nutrient holding capacities are low. They need frequent light watering rather than sporadic deep watering. This is a limiting factor to farming at Humayma, but one that can be overcome with careful water management. The other limit lies in the lack of organic matter. Addition of organic matter, such as manure from confined animals, in combination with protection from the wind and extreme sun, mulching, companion planting, and crop rotation, would result in marked improvement in soil fertility and crop yields. In the long term, these measures would also influence the pH towards a neutral level. Irrigation would be necessary for most crops, but not as much as might be expected, since soils high in organic matter have a naturally high water-holding capacity. The main threat posed to this landscape and its agricultural and ecological potential was overgrazing by flocks of domestic animals on a larger scale than what the natural environment could sustain. Overgrazing has seriously degraded the environment around Humayma over the last century, but we cannot evaluate the intensity of grazing during antiquity.

Table 6.13 Summary of 14C sample information.

Sample no.	Description	Amt. used	IsoTrace no.	Age b.p.	Calibrated age
1	Carbonized wood	197 mg	TO-1150	1,840 ± 30	171 ± 39
2	Humates?	2200 mg	TO-1151	2,390 ± 50	542 ± 117
3	Carbonized twig	183 mg	TO-1590	1,640 ±.60	416 ± 83

6.F. RADIOCARBON ANALYSES

Three samples of carbonised organic material — two from the Jammam aqueduct, one from the furnace in the Roman Bath — were submitted to Isotrace Laboratory at the University of Toronto for radiocarbon analysis, and reports were returned on 3/12/88 (TO-1150 and TO-1151) and 22/12/89 (TO-1590).

Sample nos. 1 and 2 represent the results of the average of four machine-ready targets measured on different occasions and have been corrected for natural, preparation and sputtering fractionation to a base of $d^{13}C = -25$ ‰. The ages from the Isotrace Lab are quoted in uncalibrated radiocarbon years using the Libby ^{14}C mean life of 8033 years. The errors represent 68.3% confidence limits. From the small carbon content of Sample no. 2 (0.17%) it is clear that this material is not carbonised wood. It is most likely made up of compacted humates. Sample no. 3 is the average of two machine-ready targets (normal precision) and has been corrected for natural and sputtering fractionation to a base of $d^{13}C = -25$ ‰. The age from the Isotrace Lab is quoted in uncalibrated radiocarbon years using the Libby ^{14}C mean life of 8033 years. The error represents the 68.3% confidence limit. These results were calibrated with the on-line Cologne Radiocarbon Calibration Package (CalPal).

Sample no. 1 (TO-1150): Carbonised wood. Radiocarbon date: 1840 ± 30 BP. The carbonised twig (L 0.03; Th 0.007) was recovered from Aqueduct Probe no. 2 (H87–01–P2), locus 04: mortar packing along the south face of the discharge conduit of the settling tank at km 1.779 of the Jammam aqueduct. Bucket 87.014.

Radiocarbon calibration data: bidecal smoothed data set.

Probability	Cal Age	68.3% c.i	95.5% c.i.
100%	138 AD	123–224 AD	84–242 AD

All solutions, with a probability greater than 50% for the calibrated age of this radiocarbon date have been calculated from the dendro-calibration data. The 68% and 95% confidence intervals, which are the 1s and 2s limits for a normal distribution, are also given. A probability of 100% means the radiocarbon date intersects the dendro-calibration curve at this age.

CalPal calendric age: AD 171 ± 39.

Sample no. 2 (TO-1151): Humates (?). Radiocarbon date: 2390 ± 50 BP. The carbonised material (probably brush fuel used to burn the lime) was recovered from a matrix of lime mortar packing along the upper edge of a conduit block on the Ghana aqueduct, at km 9.144. Bucket 86.018.

Radiocarbon calibration data: bidecal smoothed data set.

Probability	Cal Age	68.3% c.i.	95.5% c.i.
100%	406 Cal BC	525–398 BC	602–390 BC

All solutions, with a probability greater than 50% for the calibrated age of this radiocarbon date have been calculated from the dendro calibration data. The 68% and 95% confidence intervals, which are the 1 and 2 limits for a normal distribution, are also given. A probability of 100% means the radiocarbon date intersects the dendro calibration curve at this age.

CalPal calendric age: AD 542 ± 117.

Sample no. 3 (TO-1590): Carbonised twig. Radiocarbon date: 1640 ± 60 BP. The twig, which appears to be the twisted stem of a bush of Jointed Saltwood (*Haloxylon articulatum*) was recovered from an ash deposit in the stone packing on the floor of the furnace in the Bath Building: Room C, locus 37. Bucket 89.145.

Radiocarbon calibration data: bidecal smoothed data set.

Probability	Cal Age	68.3% c.i.	95.5% c.i.
100%	412 Cal AD	341–440 AD	248–549 AD

All solutions, with a probability greater than 50% for the calibrated age of this radiocarbon date have been calculated from the dendro calibration data. The 68% and 95% confidence intervals, which are the 1 and 2 limits for a normal distribution, are also given. A probability of 100% means the radiocarbon date intersects the dendro calibration curve at this age.

CalPal calendric age: AD 416 ± 83.

Discussion. Since there was probably continuous activity around the settling basin at Jammam Aqueduct km 1.779, any of the proposed dates or date ranges would work. The date of AD 171 ± 39 is particularly interesting, since it could be used to suggest that some of the alterations or maintenance work on the Jammam branch were carried out by Roman engineers. Perhaps the arrival of a unit of soldiers, and diversion of a portion of the aqueduct discharge to Reservoir 62 in the fort, necessitated the renovation or redesign of portions of the Jammam branch. Sample 2 provides a date that is not impossible, but does not contribute much to the discussion other than the possibility of maintenance during the fifth or sixth century. Sample 3 should date to the last few years of the Bath's existence, and the calibrated age of AD 416 ± 83 fits well with the abandonment of the fort at the end of the fourth or beginning of the fifth century.

Chapter 7

Reconstruction of the Water-Supply System

7.A. INTRODUCTION

At the moment when the founder of Hawara — whether Aretas III or Aretas IV — stood blinking in the desert sun after his vision of a white camel had led him to the site, some characteristics of the landscape must have convinced him that the divine guidance was based on an appreciation of practical human advantages, particularly concerning potential water-supply. Whether divine guidance or human scouting was involved, the advantages of the site are obvious to those who know the desert. Regional patterns of precipitation across the kingdom undoubtedly were common knowledge among the Nabataeans, and a glance at the local vegetation would in any case have provided Aretas with information on the extent and reliability of the rainfall in this particular location. The topography, which figures in the foundation story, would also have attracted the founder's attention, along with the local soils. Aretas saw the al-Shara escarpment towering above the desert to the northeast, an obstacle that caught rainstorms and channelled enormous amounts of run-off water into the Wadi Qalkha, which skirted the eastern boundary of the future settlement. The white sandstone ridges to the east and southeast formed enormous catchments that directed run-off water to large areas of relatively fertile and easily cultivated soil in close proximity to the site. Aretas must have noticed that the surviving portion of the eroded Pleistocene

lake bed immediately north of the future settlement centre provided a large catchment field focused on the location indicated by the vision, but at a slope allowing relatively easy control of the water (cf. Avner 2001–2: 405). Experience at Petra indicated that the identical red and white sandstones exposed around Hawara were sufficiently impermeable to allow the excavation of effective cisterns. Furthermore, an ambitious prince or king eager to enhance his prestige might have found the green smudges high on the escarpment a tantalising promise of spring water to feed an aqueduct. The resources at this site were more than sufficient to support pastoral and agricultural activities, and the location on or near the age-old King's Highway was advantageous. Hawara was well-placed to satisfy the political and economic needs of a society newly energised by contact with Hellenistic culture and involvement in transit trade between Southern Arabia and the Mediterranean. This settlement called "White" had great promise.

The water-supply system of Hawara involved input from precipitation and springs, artificial structures for storing or transporting the water, natural losses, and consumers. Figure 7.1 provides a diagram of the system as it functioned from the arrival of the Roman garrison to the abandonment of the fort around AD 400. In fact, the only Roman period modifications to the Nabataean system were the addition of consumers and the diversion of some of the aqueduct flow to the fort reservoir

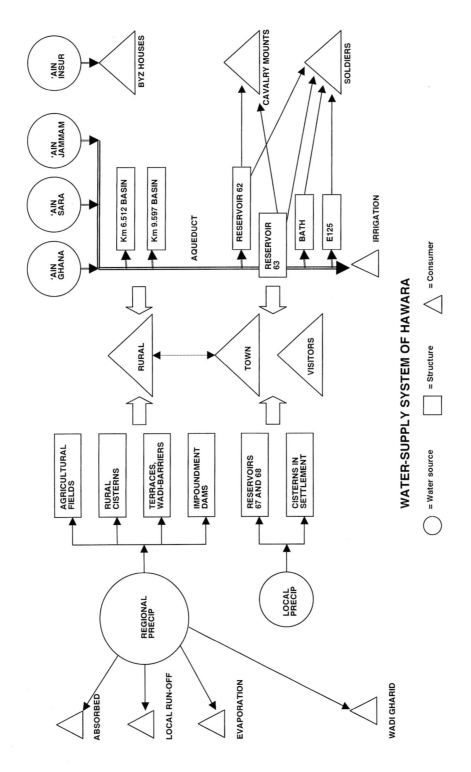

Fɪɢ. 7.1   *Diagram of the water-supply system of ancient Humayma.*

and a Roman bath. The resources, structural elements, and capacity of the water-supply system are presented in this chapter. In order to allow a clearer focus on the situation at Humayma, consideration of the technological and cultural context of the system in the Nabataean and wider Near Eastern world is for the most part reserved for Chapter 8. In order to keep the text less cluttered, the numerous references to structures and their catalogue numbers are not accompanied by illustration numbers. Readers may refer to the catalogue for illustrations as desired.

7.B. INPUT TO THE SYSTEM

7.B.1. *Precipitation and Run-Off*

There have been no functioning springs in the immediate vicinity of Humayma since the Epi-Palaeolithic period, and the local aquifer is too deep (over 250 m) for exploitation by the means available to the Nabataeans (see Section 2.A.3). As a result, input into the water system of Hawara came solely from precipitation and the importation of water from springs on the escarpment. Annual precipitation at the settlement centre in recent decades has been calculated at 80 mm, but the standard deviation is probably close to that same figure, as it is at Quweira, the nearest rainfall measuring station (average annual 87 mm, StD 81.7; see Table 2.2). The figure of 80 mm is, in fact, itself an approximation based on isohyets drawn around rainfall measuring stations in Southern Jordan. Nonetheless, the similarity of the plant life at Humayma and Quweira and anecdotal information from local Bedouin suggest that 80 mm is an accurate estimate. The average annual rainfall probably rises significantly across the foothills of the escarpment, since precipitation at Ras en-Naqb averages 143 mm/year, but for the purposes of this study the figure of 80 mm will be applied to the entire Humayma catchment as defined in Chapter 1. It will also be assumed that the climate in antiquity was essentially the same as that today, since the documentation of any major differences is very subjective and the results approximate (see pp. 34–35). Engineering details of the aqueduct, however, do suggest that the discharge of

the springs that fed it may have been significantly higher in antiquity.

It has been noted above (pp. 31–35) that the potential total precipitation across the Humayma catchment in an average year might be as high as 16.48 mcm and the run-off yield anywhere from 329,600 cum to 2.472 mcm. Even the lower figure represents a significant resource, given the convenience of the catchments, and this amount would have been far more than enough to fill all the ancient water storage structures in the region (Section 7.C). The catchment formed by the Pleistocene lake bed north of the settlement centre, approximately 1 km square, could have delivered somewhere between 1,600 and 12,000 cum/year directly to the public and private reservoirs in the centre of the settlement. There are numerous sites on the west bank of the wadi, within 2 km of the settlement centre, where catchment fields could be prepared with relative ease on extensive slopes of Umm 'Ishrin sandstone or pebbly soil, and at least 34 containment structures were built in this area. The rest of the region is equally well-supplied with potential catchment fields, at least above the basin floor. Only one containment structure, Dam no. 44, occurs in a transitional band of territory 2 to 4.5 km from the settlement centre, and cisterns are more thinly scattered outside the 4.5 km radius. The sloping sandstone hills funnelled run-off water to the agricultural fields at their feet, and the run-off available from a catchment field could be increased by the removal of surface stones or the provision of barriers or channels along the periphery. At this point it is impossible to quantify the result of such intervention, and in any case it has only been possible to provide approximate estimates of the size of the many ancient catchment fields.

7.B.2. *Springs and the Aqueduct*

Although the four springs are located high up on the escarpment and on the periphery of the catchment region, they constituted a potential resource for a properly located settlement on the plain below (fig. 2.7). In theory, the topography would have allowed a gravity flow channel from the springs to reach any point in the region — excepting a small portion at the south end — without having to cross

Table 7.1   Flow of escarpment springs as reported by the Jordan Irrigation Authority.

	MINIMUM FLOW	MAXIMUM FLOW	AVERAGE FLOW
'Ain al-Jammam	0.6 cum/hour	2.0 cum/hour	1.2 cum/hour
'Ain Sara	0.3 cum/hour	2.0 cum/hour	0.75 cum/hour
'Ain al-Ghana	0.0 cum/hour	0.4 cum/hour	0.25 cum/hour
'Ain Abu an-Nusur	0.5 cum/hour	1.42 cum/hour	0.9 cum/hour
TOTALS	1.4 cum/hour	5.82 cum/hour	3.1 cum/hour

the major wadis. Hawara, however, was founded at the one location in the central portion of the catchment region that could be reached without the need for major detours around the head of the Wadi al-Jammam and difficult passages across the main directions of flow down the ridges forming the east rim of the catchment. Hawara is by far the most efficient destination for an aqueduct tapping the three main springs — 'Ain al-Ghana, 'Ain Sara, and 'Ain al-Jammam. Tapping 'Ain al-Ghana, probably the most copious of the four springs in antiquity, for a site east of Hawara's actual location would have required a particularly long detour around Jebel Ghana.

The ratio of straight-line distance to conduit length is a fairly good measure of efficiency for an aqueduct that does not require bridges, inverted siphons, and arcades. An experienced Nabataean aqueduct engineer could have produced such an approximation of the relative efficiency of various routes after a fairly cursory examination of the springs, the escarpment, and the landscape below. Between 'Ain al-Ghana and Hawara the ratio of straight-line distance to conduit length was 71.5 percent (13.5 km straight-line distance, 18.888 km conduit length); between 'Ain al-Jammam and Hawara it was 71.1 percent (14.2 km to 19.961 km). The 'Ain al-Jammam channel could tap 'Ain Sara, too, so that was a bonus. From the junction point of the two channels to Hawara the ratio is even better: 82.7 percent (10.2 km to 12.335 km). The virtually identical efficiency of the two branches of the system is probably coincidental, but it underlines the special advantages of the site selected for Hawara.

The aqueducts serving Petra have not yet been as closely measured as those serving Humayma. A rough measurement taken from a map of the 'Ain Brak aqueduct (Lindner and Hübl 1997: fig. 2), however, indicates a ratio of 76 percent (2.675 km to 3.5 km), reasonably comparative to the statistics at Hawara. Just for comparison, the "efficiency" of the Aqua Marcia at Rome, which made use of numerous bridges and tunnels to keep the average channel slope to 0.27 percent, was only 48.4 percent (91 km of conduit needed for the 44 km distance between Marano Equo and Rome; Hodge 1992: 347; Pace 1983: 125).

It is impossible to reconstruct the yield in antiquity of the three springs tapped by the aqueduct. In 1986, the Jordan Irrigation Authority provided figures for maximum, minimum, and average flow (Table 7.1), but it was not specified when, how frequently, or over how long a period the measurements had been taken.

Further observations were made in the course of the Humayma Survey Project. In June 1986, the discharge of the 'Ain al-Jammam was 0.9 cum/hour; in March 2001, after several years of drought, it was discharging 0.64 cum/hour. In June 1986, 'Ain Sara was supplying sufficient water to maintain a weedy earthen pool approximately 200 cum in volume, but there was no visible overflow. By March 2001, the pool had been lined with concrete, but only a small trickle of water crossed the floor. Two separate springs at 'Ain al-Ghana feed two modern concrete cisterns. In June 1986, the discharge of the upper spring was recorded as 0.6 cum/hour, but in March 2001, the discharge was 0.06

cum/hour. In June 1986, July 1989, and July 2000, the lower spring discharged only a trickle of water, but in March 2001, the yield was measured at 0.32 cum/hour. In late April 2008, the discharge of the lower spring was 0.18 cum/hour, while the upper spring yielded only a trickle. Taking the two springs together, the total observed discharge varies from ca. 0.06 to 0.60 cum/hour. Observations have been made at ʿAin Abu an-Nusur numerous times since June 1986, but the flow has never been more than a trickle. The discharge over the year, however, must be relatively significant, since squatters across the Desert Highway have installed a plastic irrigation pipe to carry the water to a small grove of fruit trees. All four springs support a certain amount of vegetation in their immediate vicinity, particularly ʿAin al-Jammam, which has been harnessed to irrigate a small farm and orchard.

It seems clear from both the figures in Table 7.1 and the observations made since 1986 that the flow of these four springs can vary significantly, and that there has been a significant decline in the discharge of all except ʿAin al-Ghana since the measurements reported by the Jordan Irrigation Authority were taken. Since the flow from ʿAin al-Ghana apparently has increased over that same period, it is possible that blasting during construction of the new Desert Highway bypass around Ras en-Naqb in the late 1970s and its expansion in the late 1990s have damaged the aquifers of the failing springs and redirected some of the flow to ʿAin al-Ghana (unidentified engineer of Condotte Roma, oral communication, May 2000). The three failing springs are very close to the highway, while ʿAin al-Ghana is 2.7 km away. Decreases in annual precipitation and thus in recharge of the aquifers may also be playing a part, along with the extensive exploitation of aquifers by deep wells around Maʿan. There is copious anecdotal evidence that aridity has increased in the Hisma since the later nineteenth century, leading to the disappearance of numerous springs (see Sections 1.B, 2.A.3). It may be significant that in 1910, Musil's informants described the ʿAin al-Ghana as "copious" (Musil 1926: 56–61).

The flow through an aqueduct is limited by the cross-sectional area of the water channel and the least slope along its course. If an aqueduct starts with a steep slope and a full channel, the channel will overflow and probably destroy the aqueduct structure once the slope and thus the speed of flow begin to lessen. The least slope along the Hawara aqueduct system seems to occur in the last few kilometres of its course before reaching the city, where the slope is approximately 1 percent (see discussion in 7.D.1). As a result, it is relatively simple to calculate the maximum possible discharge by means of the Manning formula: $V = 1/n \, r^{2/3} \, s^{1/2}$, where V is velocity of the stream, r is the hydraulic radius (wetted area divided by the wetted perimeter, in metres), n is the roughness coefficient for the conduit wall, and s is the hydraulic gradient (Manning 1891: 161–207; Hauck and Novak 1987: 145–49). In this case, the roughness coefficient is assumed to be 0.015, the standard figure for dressed ashlar or rough cement surfaces. This is a conservative figure, since smooth cement surfaces are rated at 0.010, and Hauck and Novak used 0.0125 for the Nîmes aqueduct (Hauck and Novak 1987: 147). Assuming that the channel is only three-quarters full, since it would have been hazardous to fill completely the channel of such a lightly built structure, the result is a calculated discharge of 5.44 l/sec, or 19.6 cum/ hour. Assuming a roughness coefficient of 0.0125 (smoother), the discharge rises to 6.53 l/sec, or 23.5 cum/hour. A potential maximum discharge of 19.6 cum/hour will be assumed here, but with the understanding that it may seldom or never have been achieved. The least slope along the Jammam branch, between 0.3 and 0.5 percent, occurs over the first 5.9 km. Assuming a slope of 0.5 percent and a full channel, the Jammam aqueduct could have contributed at most 3.8 l/sec or 13.7 cum/hour to the system in its original state, and 1.3 l/sec or 4.5 cum/hour to the system after insertion of gutter tiles in the channel. The fact that the cross-section of the Ghana Aqueduct channel downstream from its junction with the Jammam branch is no larger than above the junction indicates that neither contributing channel was expected to flow at full capacity. The unchanged cross-section also strongly suggests that the engineers who built the branch line believed that the Ghana line had sufficient unused capacity to absorb seasonal surges in flow.

Even taking account of the many variables involved, these figures for potential aqueduct

capacity are far above the total maximum discharge reported by the Irrigation Authority for
the three springs that fed the aqueduct: 4.4 cum/
hour; the average discharge was only 2.2 cum/hour.
Although it seems odd that Nabataean engineers
built an elaborate and expensive aqueduct system
that must have functioned at much less than its safe
maximum capacity, they seem simply to have made
use of a standard design. Nearly identical aqueduct
structures, with conduits of the same dimensions,
were constructed at many other Nabataean sites, so
the engineers at Hawara were simply following the
usual practice. Furthermore, even 4.4 cum/hour
of spring water represents a significant resource
for a small community in a hyper-arid environment. It will be assumed here that the discharge
from the springs has declined significantly since
the aqueduct was constructed, and that the aqueduct normally discharged approximately 10 cum/
hour at Hawara. Calcium carbonate deposits in
the channels are of little use in this calculation,
since they testify to water levels varying from a
few centimetres to the full height of the conduit.
There may, of course, have been seasonal changes
in discharge, so the aqueduct was filled to capacity only at certain seasons or in years following
particularly abundant precipitation on the plain
around Ma'an. It is also possible that 'Ain al-Ghana
was the only spring tapped at first, and that the
branch tapping the other two springs was built
only when the 'Ain al-Ghana discharge fell below
an acceptable minimum at some point after the
original construction period. It is at least possible
that the earthquake of 31/30 BC that caused damage
at Petra (Bikai et al. 2008: 494) caused a temporary or permanent decrease in the flow from that
spring, requiring construction of the riskier 'Ain
al-Jammam branch (M.B. Reeves, personal communication, 28 November 2008). Constructional
details of the 'Ain al-Jammam branch suggest that
there were difficulties obtaining sufficient flow
from that branch in the final period of its use (see
pp. 388–95).

Input into the aqueduct, of course, had to be
somewhat higher than the discharge at Hawara,
given inevitable losses from leakage, absorption
by the stone conduits, and evaporation. In view of
the length of the system, the small cross-section

of the stream, and the numerous joints between
conduit blocks (approximately 28,000), the loss
may have been as much as 25 percent. It is possible the conduits were filled to capacity at the
springs, with the knowledge that the depth of the
stream would soon decrease to a safe level. From
time to time the discharge would also have been
affected by diversion of some of the flow to the
two off-take cisterns at km 6.512 and 9.579, but it
is unlikely the administrators could have found
ways to compensate for the temporary increase in
demand on the system. Most likely, the inhabitants
of Hawara simply tolerated the occasional small
decrease in flow. The Roman garrison also found
it possible to divert a significant quantity of water
to the reservoir and water system in the fort.

Since 'Ain Abu an-Nusur is ca. 37 m higher
than 'Ain al-Jammam and only 1.15 km away across
an easily traversed portion of the escarpment, it
would have been relatively simple to link it to the
'Ain al-Jammam branch of the aqueduct system.
An intensive search of the slopes between and below the two springs, however, failed to reveal any
trace whatsoever of an aqueduct linking them. The
landscape is composed for the most part of earth,
which would have made this branch vulnerable
to damage from landslips, but the same conditions were successfully faced elsewhere along the
al-Jammam branch. If 'Ain Abu an-Nusur was as
prolific a spring in antiquity as it seems to have
been until recently, neglect of the resource is another piece of evidence suggesting that the three
other springs were sufficient by themselves to supply the aqueduct.

7.B.3. *Summary of Input to the System*

The inhabitants of the catchment area around
Hawara had at their disposal between 329,600
cum (run-off at two percent of precipitation) and
2,472,000 cum (run-off at 15 percent of precipitation,) of run-off water, some of it passing directly
by the settlement centre. In addition, the aqueduct
could have provided between 52.8 (at 2.2 cum/
hour) and 470.4 cum/day (at maximum capacity;
240 cum/day is more likely), most of it delivered
directly to the settlement, but with allowances for
rural access to two off-take tanks capable of hold-

Table 7.2   Number, location, and capacities of water harvesting and storage facilities.

	CENTRE	CAP. CUM	PERIPHERY	CAP. CUM	TOTAL NO.	TOTAL CAP. CUM	% CAP.
CLEARED CATCHMENT FIELDS	—	—	3	—	3	—	
TERRACES	—	—	6	—	6	—	
WADI BARRIERS	—	—	3	—	3	—	
BARRIER WALLS	—	—	2	2069.0	2	2069.0	16.7
DAMS	—	—	1	1400.0	1	1400.0	11.3
ENHANCED NATURAL POOLS	—	—	2	45.6	2	45.6	0.4
OFF-TAKE TANKS	—	—	2	85.2	2	85.3	0.7
ROCK-CUT CISTERNS	3	417.2	40	3923.0	43	4340.2	34.9
BUILT CISTERNS	10	1093.8	4	22.5	14	1116.3	9.0
RESERVOIRS	4	2846.8	1	515.9	5	3362.7	27.1
TOTAL	17	4357.8	64	8061.2	81	12,419.0	100.0

ing 44.5 and 40.7 cum. In summary, the total water supply available for exploitation in the course of a year was probably somewhere between 348,872 (run-off at 2 percent of precipitation and aqueduct discharging 2.2 cum/hour) and 2,559,600 cum (run-off at 15 percent and aqueduct discharging 10 cum/hour). The water available from precipitation undoubtedly varied dramatically from year to year in amount and location. The discharge from the aqueduct probably showed less short-term variation than did precipitation patterns, providing a certain predictability and elegance to the water-supply at the settlement. Nevertheless, the key to Hawara's success was the storage of the run-off water captured by its inhabitants.

7.C. *Water Harvesting and Storage Facilities*

The full array of Nabataean techniques for water storage was applied in the settlement and the territory of Hawara: intentional recharge of soil moisture in agricultural fields by means of terraces and wadi barriers, damming of large, natural run-off channels, and direction of run-off to enhanced natural bedrock pools, to cisterns cut in the bedrock or built of blocks, and to built reservoirs. Aqueduct water was also detained in two pools that functioned as large draw-tanks but could also be used for short-term storage. The terminal aqueduct pool in the settlement centre was designed as a flow-through access tank, but it was redesigned as a storage reservoir in the Roman period. The structures catalogued in the survey are tallied in Table 7.2, organised more or less from the more natural to the most artificial structures. There is some overlap in classification (although no duplication of estimates of capacity), and some structures (such as terraces or enhanced natural pools) appear in sets counted as one entry.

The statistics summarised in Table 7.2 reinforce the conclusion that the water-supply system of ancient Humayma was regional in scope. The aqueduct, which brought spring water from the periphery of the catchment area directly to the settlement centre, was a key project for the settlement of Hawara nearly from its start. Although the project was meant at least in part to enhance the prestige of the king and the settlement he established (see pp. 381–83, 439–43), the water was undoubtedly put to more practical use as well. Given the concentration of population in the settlement centre, it is not surprising that four of the five reservoirs were built in the settlement centre and the other within 1 km of it, together constituting 27.1 percent of the system's storage capacity. Since most of the settlement was located on porous sandy soil rather than bedrock, all four of the reservoirs and all but three of the 13 cisterns located within 500 m of Reservoir no. 67 were built of blocks rather than cut in the bedrock. The statistics are reversed in the rest of the catchment, where the remaining reservoir and all but four of the 46 cisterns were cut in bedrock. The four exceptions (Survey nos. 21, 22, 58, 60) are in fact all doubtful examples for one reason or another. Cisterns were the most common type of structure (57 out of 81 catalogued hydraulic sites), and together they had a capacity of 5,456.5 cum, 43.9 percent of the storage capacity of the entire system. Fifteen of these cisterns (Structure nos. 21, 22, 29, 30, 31, 32, 33, 35, 41, 50, 51, 52, 56, 60, 82), with a capacity of 1,462.6 cum, may not have had roofs. If only high-quality water from roofed cisterns (3,993.9 cum) and roofed reservoirs (1456.0 cum) is counted, along with the contents of the four structures fed by the aqueduct (Reservoirs no. 62 and 63, and off-take tanks at km 6.512 and 9.597; 1991.9 cum), these structures held 7441.8 cum of potable water, 59.9 percent of the 12,419.0 cum of stored water available to the inhabitants of the region. It has not yet been proven that Reservoir no. 62 in the Roman fort held flowing rather than stale water, but this seems a likely conclusion (see below).

Of the cisterns outside the settlement centre (defined as more than 500 m from Reservoir no. 67), only three (nos. 58, 59, 60), with a total capacity of 115.8 cum, lie within 1 km of the reservoir. To these can be added the capacity of Reservoir no. 53 (515.9 cum), 1 km distant, for a total of 631.7 cum. Seven cisterns (nos. 18, 19, 45, 48, 50, 51.1, 52), with a capacity of 703.5 cum, are located between 1 and 2 km distance. No cisterns were found between a radius of more than 2 km and less than 4.7 km from the settlement, suggesting a boundary zone in which stored potable water was not needed by either the "urban" or rural populations. The pool behind Dam no. 44, located 3.09 km from the settlement, was open to the air and the water was

probably low in quality. The 35 cisterns more than 4.7 km away from the settlement are fairly evenly scattered in terms of their distance. All except Cistern no. 3, at a distance of 12.5 km, are less than 9.5 km from the settlement. There is no obvious reason for the atypical location of no. 3, but it may be that the nearby isolated patch of soil was particularly suitable for farming or grazing. The isolated dam, barrier walls, and enhanced natural pools are also opportunistic structures, their location determined by special topographical features and special needs.

For reasons of topography and the necessary segregation of settlement activities and agricultural fields, the cleared catchment fields, terraces, and wadi barriers all occur outside the settlement centre. It is impossible to estimate the amount of soil and/or water these structures made available to their owners, but their relative rarity indicates that the labour needed to prepare and maintain them only infrequently justified the effort involved.

7.C.1. *Cleared Catchment Fields, Terraces, and Wadi Barriers*

The geology of the Humayma region provided its inhabitants with an ample supply of effective, natural run-off catchment fields. The slopes composed of Umm 'Ishrin sandstone tend to be fractured and angular, their surfaces carpeted with harder debris left behind by erosion of the main formation (fig. 2.4). The stone, however, absorbs little water, and the debris apparently do not constitute a significant barrier to run-off. Channels were cut in the red bedrock along the edges of some of cistern catchment fields (e.g., nos. 25, 48, 55) and sometimes supplemented along the more gentle slopes by fieldstones set in an earth base (e.g., nos. 25, 50, 52, 55, 59). Although most, if not all, fieldstone and earthen barriers visible at present probably were erected in the last century, as the cisterns were put back into use, their presence is an obvious solution to the problem of directing run-off. It may be that the flat slabs now scattered across some of the catchment fields are the remains of degraded barrier walls erected in antiquity.

The Qa Disi Formation weathers in a very different fashion, resulting in rounded, pillowy slopes joined by natural run-off channels eroded in the soft stone (fig. 2.3). Cisterns associated with these catchments usually made use of a natural channel to direct water towards the intake. Since little surface debris develop as this formation erodes, most of the precipitation runs off, even though the stone may be slightly more absorbent than the Umm 'Ishrin sandstone. Because of the lack of surface debris and the constant sloughing of the granular surface, the catchments were enhanced where necessary with channels cut in the rock rather than with peripheral barrier walls (e.g., fig. 3.83). Large natural or enhanced catchments on both types of stone also served to provide water to agricultural fields located up against or close to the periphery of the two basins north and south of Hawara. There is no direct evidence for these Nabataean fields, but modern Bedouin practices mimic the ancient, and the cisterns located around the periphery of the basins most likely were associated with fields sustained by particularly reliable catchments.

Water was also harvested from catchments consisting largely of sloping fields of soil. Because such catchments absorb more precipitation than bedrock slopes and the run-off usually carries a load of silt, the Nabataeans used them more often to sustain agricultural activities than to fill cisterns. Nevertheless, a particularly large and well-shaped or well-positioned soil catchment field could attract the construction of a cistern (e.g., nos. 54, 58, 65) or even the public reservoirs of Hawara (nos. 53, 67, and 68). Because of the effect of wind and water erosion on these catchments, little evidence survives for any methods used to enhance them. At many sites in the Negev (Evenari, Shanan, and Tadmor 1982: 127–47), surface stones were piled up in neat patterns to expose the soil and enhance the run-off to agricultural fields. Sloping fields with distinct stone piles appear at two sites in the Humayma catchment (Structure nos. 8 and 47) and possible stone piles at another (Structure no. 9). The stone piles at sites 8 and 47 were sufficient in number to have enhanced run-off, but neither appears to be associated with an appropriate adjacent agricultural field. The stones may have been piled up simply to allow cultivation of the sloping fields themselves, but in the absence of any supplementary water-supply, it is difficult to understand how cultivation could have been successful. These features may represent a failed agricultural experiment. The soil exposed by the original clearing has since washed and blown away, exposing another carpet of stones.

Terracing is one of the oldest and most persistent human techniques for conserving water and soil, with examples in the Near East dating as early as the Middle Bronze Age (Levy and Alon 1987: 56). In the arid portions of the Near East, walls were built across a slope to catch soil and water, ultimately accumulating enough soil to allow sufficient storage of run-off water to sustain a crop of grain. Where rainfall was sufficient, terraces could also be used for orchards or vineyards. It is interesting that the number of terraced sites around the Humayma catchment is small and the affected areas modest in size. Only six terraced sites appear in the catalogue (nos. 9, 15, 46, 49, 80, 81). Structures no. 9 and 46 are associated with stone piles, and Structure no. 80 was located in the catchment above Cistern no. 53. Structure no. 15 consists of a single retaining wall 20 m long, while the other sets of walls vary in length from 10 to ca. 120 m. The longer retaining walls were poorly built of unshaped boulders rolled into approximate lines and reinforced with smaller fieldstones. For the most part, these walls have collapsed since their abandonment, and they no longer retain any soil. The walls at Structures no. 15 and 81 were neatly built of sandstone slabs and still retain a significant amount of soil, and a small amount of soil remains behind the rougher walls at Structure no. 80. There is no evidence for dating any of the terraces, but the absence of any signs of recent occupation suggests that they were constructed sometime during the florescence of the ancient site.

A significant feature of the terraces at Humayma is their association with obvious natural catchment fields, such as bowl-shaped valleys or a gully delivering water from Jebel Qalkha. The only exceptions are the terraces at Structure no. 9, which benefited from the higher precipitation on the escarpment, and those at Structure no. 46, which seem to have no special advantage. The small number of terraces and their typical association with catchment fields indicate that this laborious method of collecting soil for water storage and farming provided little advantage over the practice of farming the richer soil around the edges of the plains north and south of the ancient settlement centre.

Wadi barriers function much like terrace walls, but they are constructed on gentle slopes across natural run-off channels to collect soil and water for agricultural activity. Because of its location, this type of structure is vulnerable to total destruction once maintenance has ceased. There may have been barriers across the main wadi drainage system north and south of the settlement, now washed away or covered by silt, but no evidence survives. Only three sets of wadi barriers (one possibly modern, no. 16) have been identified in the Humayma catchment area, all built of rough boulders. Structure no. 79 is just below Reservoir no. 53, which is associated with the terraces of Structure no. 80, and thus perhaps part of a single agricultural and pastoral unit. Like the stone piles, these features, too, may be part of a failed or marginal agricultural experiment.

7.C.2. Barrier Walls and Dam

Large volumes of water can be retained with relatively little investment of labour by constructing a barrier wall across the outlet of a natural reservoir. Two such structures were identified in the Humayma catchment, nos. 27 and 28, built 230 m apart in a formation of Umm 'Ishrin sandstone. Modern walls have obscured the ancient arrangement, but it is likely the barriers consisted of block-built walls (L ca. 8 m, Th <1.0 m) plastered on the interior. Barrier Wall no. 28 blocked off a strikingly regular circular basin below an excellent natural catchment field, creating a reservoir capable of holding approximately 1,069 cum. Barrier Wall no. 27 closes off a more irregular but equally effective formation capable of holding approximately 1,000 cum. Since no spillways were cut in the bedrock, there must have been overflow conduits on the barrier walls themselves. After a short time, water kept in these unroofed reservoirs would have become very poor in quality, so it probably was used for animals. There were two substantial roofed cisterns close by (Structure nos. 25 and 26) that could have provided high-quality water for human consumption.

The fact that there are not more examples of this type of structure around the Humayma catchment area, despite the relative ease of construction and the presence of numerous suitable sites, suggests that poor water quality and exposure of a large pool to evaporation were considered serious problems. That two structures otherwise unparalleled in the Humayma catchment appear in close association indicates that some special circumstance was at work here, perhaps the need to water a particularly large number of animals that grazed on the plains nearby. The two adjacent cisterns can hold a total of approximately 491 cum, already a very significant amount, possibly intended for a tent settlement associated with local herding and agriculture. Perhaps the unroofed reservoirs were used as safety reserve allowing response to periodic spikes in the livestock population.

There is only one large-scale barrier dam in the Humayma catchment region, sturdily built of substantial, carefully shaped blocks facing a core of mortared rubble and provided with a spillway cut in the bedrock beside it. Dam no. 44 (L 9.70 m, W 4.36 m, H 3.65 m) should be early first century AD in date, given the presence of a betyl block at its south end, the red pigmentation of the facing plaster (also seen on the retention dams around the Siq at Petra; Bellwald and al-Huneidi 2003: 61, 71), the coursing of blocks as headers and stretchers (as seen in Pool no. 63 and at Petra), and the numerous Nabataean graffiti carved in the canyon walls around it. As a result, it must have formed part of the overall Nabataean water-supply strategy for the region. It is difficult to say why the dam was located deep in a canyon 3.09 km from the site, particularly since no other containment structures were built within a radius of 2 and 4.7 km from the settlement centre. The characteristics of the locality — enormous bedrock catchment field, deep narrow canyon well-protected from the sun and easy to dam — may have been irresistible, or the wider canyon bed downstream may have been a favoured camping ground. The large pool contained by the dam (1,400 cum) may have been intended for watering flocks of animals that were grazed on the slopes of the Jebel Qalkha above. Naturally eroded pot-holes both above and below the dam supplemented the artificial containment and could have been used as natural watering troughs filled from the pool with buckets. Because of the steep canyon walls, it would have been difficult for animals to drink from the pool itself except when it was completely full.

7.C.3. *Enhanced Natural Pools*

This category includes relatively large natural pools that either show possible signs of enhancement by means of cuttings or are so closely associated with a rock-cut cistern that their use as a supplementary water source would have been inevitable. Structure no. 28 discussed above is in fact a type of enhanced natural pool, but its scale and the use of barrier walls puts it in a different category. The survey identified only two sites with enhanced pot-holes isolated from other hydraulic installations; Structure no. 17 is identified only tentatively as a hydraulic structure, since the natural pot-hole may have been intended to store grain rather than water, and the alterations may be completely modern. Structure no. 19, in contrast, has the patina of age; it consists of a series of seven rounded natural depressions in the floor of a small valley draining Jebel Qalkha. Although there was no attempt at roofing, at least two of the pot-holes carry water-eroded chisel marks suggesting they had been enlarged or regularised. Although the water quality would have been poor, the total capacity of ca. 35 cum represented a significant resource for local livestock for a few months after the winter rains. Natural potholes occur and were undoubtedly used in association with several types of artificial hydraulic structures. Dam no. 44, not far from Structure no. 19, was built across a similar valley, and several potholes remained exposed above and below the resulting pool. These natural pools of water were an obvious and in some ways more convenient source of drinking water for livestock than the dammed pool. The pool downstream from the dam may also have been used as a drinking trough for the animals, filled by emptying buckets onto the spillway. Structure no. 39, a roofed cistern cut into the floor of a shallow wadi, shows a similar symbiotic situation. Once the cistern was full, water was diverted around it over a ledge, where there were two natural pot-holes with a total capacity

of ca. 8.8 cum. Since there seem to be numerous sites along this wadi where a rock-cut cistern could have been located successfully, it is quite possible that this cistern was excavated at this spot with the intention that the natural pools would be used as a supplementary water source.

7.C.4. *Rock-Cut Cisterns*

As noted above, cisterns constituted the backbone of the water system of ancient Humayma, particularly for the supply of high-quality water. Although rock-cut and built cisterns function in precisely the same manner, differences in construction, design, and capacity make it necessary to discuss them as separate classes. Thirty-five rock-cut cisterns appear in the catalogue (pot-holes and some doubtful examples are omitted from this list): nos. 3, 12, 14, 18, 23–26, 29–43, 45, 48, 50–52, 55–57, 59, 61, 82, and 83 (fig. 2.7). Cisterns cut in the bedrock have numerous advantages over those constructed of blocks. Site preparation was simpler and probably easier, since the relatively soft sandstone could be pried out quickly in chunks or excavated as blocks to be used in roofing the tank or applied to other structures. In addition, rock-cut tanks were much more stable than built tanks and immune to buckling because of soil movement, the percolation of water, or the outward force of the roofing arches. They were also most likely easier to waterproof, since there were fewer obvious seams in the tank wall. The drawback, of course, was that this type of cistern could only be located where bedrock was exposed. As a result, only three are found near the settlement centre (nos. 55, 56, 57).

Although theoretically almost any cistern cut into the rock could have been excavated in such a way that a complete or partial bedrock roof was left, only eight of the 25 rock-cut cisterns that are known to have been covered over had roofs formed by bedrock: nos. 3, 12, 26, 38, 40, 48, 55, 61. The rest were roofed with stone slabs carried on built transverse arches: nos. 14, 18, 23–25, 34, 36.1, 36.2, 37, 39, 42, 43, 45, 57, 59, 61, 83. A roof of bedrock would in most cases have been more stable than one carried on arches and would have obviated the need for masons with specialised skills. The effort involved, however, apparently was only occasionally worthwhile and in general restricted to larger capacity structures.

The procedure for cutting a cistern in bedrock and roofing it with arches was relatively simple: a site with suitable catchment field was selected, the surface levelled, the outline of the tank sketched out on the rock, and the whole area excavated to a depth sufficient for the capacity desired. Excavation and removal of blocks or debris was relatively straightforward, along with detection of flaws in the rock. Many useful comparisons can be made with the procedures reconstructed by Bessac (2007) for the excavation of tomb façades and chambers at Petra. The unfinished Cistern no. 52 preserves at one end traces of the trench and wedge system of removing blocks, as in a quarry (Adam 1994: 23–27; Bessac 2007: *passim*). Once excavation of the tanks was complete, imposts were cut into the walls for the arches, the arches were laid over wooden centring, the spandrels filled in with blocking walls, and the walls and arches waterproofed with pebbly plaster. The roofing slabs, which survive in place on Cistern no. 45, were long, roughly-trimmed slabs of stone, laid to bridge the arches, carefully chinked around their edges with pebbles, and then plastered. This final treatment does not survive on no. 45, but it can be seen on Reservoir no. 68 in the settlement centre. Since goats and sheep could easily mount the cistern roof, a tight seal was important to prevent pollution of the water source.

On the other hand, if a bedrock roof was to be left, first an access shaft was excavated at the selected site, no larger than the intake or access hole required for the cistern. This shaft (or, in the case of a few cisterns in cliff faces, a tunnel) could not be enlarged until the excavator had penetrated below the depth required for a self-supporting roof. Once the lower portion of the expanded shaft had reached a sufficient size, several diggers could work simultaneously, but the darkness and still air, along with the need to hoist all debris out through the access hole, would have made the work difficult, slow, and unpleasant. In addition, it is unlikely that the excavation of blocks rather than useless chunks of stone could have been organised under such conditions. During the carving of Cistern no. 26, some of these difficulties may have been ameliorated by the excavation of a stepped side entrance

from the surface, supplementing the central access hole in the roof.

Probably as a result of these factors, the eight cisterns in the Humayma catchment provided with bedrock roofs are either quite small (and thus easy to carve) or quite large (and thus difficult to roof with arches). The minimum capacity in this group is 25.6 cum, the maximum 300 cum, and the average 163.75 cum. Total capacity is 1310.0 cum. The standard deviation of the capacities, however, is large: 98.7. Cisterns nos. 3 and 40 are relatively small, 25.6 and 39.2 cum respectively, while the rest form two clusters around the average and at the high end of the range. The 17 rock-cut cisterns with arch-supported roofs show a different pattern. The minimum capacity in this group is 25.7 cum, the maximum 277.8, and the average 101.6 cum. Total capacity is 1,727.2 cum. The standard deviation in the capacities is smaller than that of the previous group: 72.3. Fifteen of these cisterns are relatively evenly spread along the range from minimum capacity to 171.6 cum, while the two largest have capacities of 237.9 cum (no. 25) and 277.8 cum (no. 24). These statistics suggest that for rock-cut cisterns with a capacity smaller than about 150 cum, arch-supported roofing was more economical or easier to provide and maintain than a bedrock roof. For capacities above 150 cum, the two techniques were more evenly balanced, particularly if one includes in the equation the rock-cut, arch-roofed Reservoir no. 53, and the two built, arch-roofed reservoirs in the settlement centre (nos. 67–68). Presumably the need for the large number of arches involved in roofing larger rock-cut cisterns could tip the scale in favour of a rock-cut roof.

Because most rock-cut cisterns roofed with arches carrying slabs were less than 150 cum in capacity, the most common number of arches used in such roofing was two, three, and five (see Table 7.3). For some unknown reason, Cistern no. 14 was built with long, narrow proportions, so it had eight arch supports, but a capacity of only 111.4 cum. Cistern no. 61 is also atypical in that one half was covered by a bedrock roof, while the rest was roofed with slabs carried on arches. As a result, only two arches were needed for a length of 5.90 m. Other than no. 14, the cisterns with more than five arch supports had capacities well over 150 cum.

Table 7.3   Dimensions and capacities of rock-cut cisterns with arch-supported roofs.

CISTERN NO.	NO. ARCHES	LENGTH	WIDTH	DEPTH	CAPACITY
57	2	4.00	3.95	3.50	55.3
61	2	5.90	5.40	4.30	137.0
83	2	3.94	3.50	3.60	49.6
34	2?	—	3.00	4.00	28.3
39	2?	—	3.00	4.00	28.3
43	2?	3.76	2.80	2.44	25.7
23	3	4.62	4.63	3.83	81.9
37	3	4.95	3.85	2.60	49.6
59	3	5.20	5.00	3.75	97.5
42	3?	6.0	3.0	4.0	72.0
36.1	5	7.40	5.00	3.20	118.4
36.2	5	7.20	2.45	3.50	61.7
45	5	7.90	4.00	3.90	123.2
18	7	10.95	5.70	2.75	171.6
14	8	8.65	3.88	3.32	111.4
25	8	12.42	4.55	4.24	237.9
24	10	11.20	6.20	4.00	277.8
Total					1727.2

Although cisterns cut in the bedrock could be as long as the site and the owner's resources allowed, it appears that there were advantages in keeping the width below 5 m. Beyond this width the arches presumably had to be more carefully constructed, since inaccurately cut voussoirs would be much more prone to wobble, causing the arches to sway or buckle. This effect would have been exaggerated by the fact that the arches are all less than a semicircle in form. Only the largest in this class, Cistern no. 24, with 10 arches, exceeds 6 m in width, presumably because more care was taken with the construction overall.

There also seems to have been some disadvantage in excavating cisterns to a depth greater than 4 m. Technically, it would seem easier to roof a cistern narrower than 5 m but much deeper than 4 m in order to provide a desired capacity, but this solution was not favoured. Perhaps dry cistern tanks more than 4 m deep were viewed as a hazard to humans and animals, or we may simply under-estimate the extra effort involved in removing spoil from a pit deeper than about 4 m. It is interesting that the Nabataeans at Hawara turned away from the bottle-shaped cisterns typical of the Iron Age and their pre-sedentary period, as described by Diodorus (19.94.7–8; see p. 418). Only two possibly cylindrical rock-cut cisterns were noted in the Humayma catchment area (nos. 34 and 39), but neither could be properly documented because of modern roofing. The family-owned, built cisterns in the settlement centre were all cylindrical in shape in order to save construction materials and promote structural stability.

There is great variety in the type of catchment field and the arrangements for guiding water to the rock-cut cisterns. The fields usually consisted of the slopes of adjacent sandstone jebels, and rock-cut channels or walls built of earth and stone guided the water to an intake hole. Occasionally the cisterns were cut into the bed of a small natural drainage route (nos. 37, 39). This, however, was

Table 7.4　Ratio of settling tank volume to volume of rock-cut and built cisterns and reservoirs.

CISTERN NO.	SETTLING TANK CAPACITY (CUM)	CISTERN CAPACITY (CUM)	RATIO OF TANK TO CISTERN	MATERIAL
59	0.77	97.5	0.8 %	bedrock
12	>1.8	>240	0.8 %	bedrock
26	1.7	153	1.1 %	bedrock
83	>0.58	49.6	1.2 %	bedrock
39	0.42	28.3	1.5 %	bedrock
54	2.77	166.0	1.7 %	built
68	10.6	488.4	2.2 %	built
74	>2.5	92.7	>2.7 %	built
70	2.3	78.9	2.9 %	built
55	ca. 10.0	ca. 300	3.3 %	bedrock
38	8.8	255	3.5 %	bedrock
67	<21.4	444.7	<4.8 %	built
64	3.8	43.0	8.8 %	built

generally a hazardous location, since it would have been difficult to divert potentially damaging flood water away from a full cistern during a period of particularly heavy run-off. Where the channels have survived in good condition, they are often associated with cuttings for sluice gates that allowed the operator to divert water away from the cistern intake once the cistern had reached capacity, and thus to avoid possible structural damage and pollution as the water level rose above the roof and settling basin.

Small settling basins, designed to give sediment a chance to settle out of the run-off water before it poured into the cistern, were observed at 10 of the 41 rock-cut cisterns catalogued (nos. 3, 12, 14, 26, 34, 38, 39, 55, 59, 83). It is likely that others have been lost to erosion or obscured by soil. Where possible, the tanks were measured and their capacity compared with that of the cistern served; as expected, the larger cisterns with larger catchment fields presumably subject to sudden heavy run-off had larger settling tanks (Table 7.4). The size of a settling tank most likely was decided on the basis of experience rather than careful calculation, and it would have been easy to enlarge a rock-cut settling tank found to be ineffective.

While the intake channel and entry point into a rock-cut cistern can usually be identified, the access hole through which water was drawn has almost always been lost along with the roof. Even on Cistern no. 45, where nearly all the roofing slabs survive, the original framed hole has disappeared. There are re-built draw holes (ca. 0.8 m square) on the roofs of Cisterns nos. 34, 42, and 43, usually toward one side or end of the tank, but there is no guarantee that these reflect the original arrangements. What seem to be original draw-holes can occasionally be recognised on a cistern with rock-cut roof, such as Cisterns nos. 48 and 55, but even in these cases there has often been some recent re-cutting. At Cisterns nos. 3, 26, 48, and Reservoir no. 53, a shallow trough for watering animals was cut into the rock adjacent to the cistern or several metres away and connected by a runnel.

The ancient inhabitants of the Humayma region apparently did not see any pressing need for steps allowing convenient access to the interior of their cisterns or reservoirs. None of the built cisterns or reservoirs was provided with steps; the one rock-cut reservoir, however, has steps, along with two of the rock-cut cisterns. A flight of 14 steps descends to the floor of Reservoir no. 53. This is the largest and deepest of the rock-cut containment structures, and it is even larger than the two built reservoirs in the settlement centre, so the steps may have had something to do with a special function or activity. It is also possible the steps were designed to facilitate removal of debris during excavation of the tank, along with occasional cleaning and direct access to the water surface. The use of an earth slope as a catchment field possibly necessitated more frequent cleaning than would have been the case with a bedrock catchment. It is interesting that the largest rock-cut reservoirs around Petra, at Beq'ah (al-Muheisen 2009: 106–7) and Siq al-Barid (Bir al-'Arayis; Bikai et al. 2009: 363), were provided with rock-cut steps. At the former, 13 steps provided access to a tank (23 × 10 × 5 m; 1150 cum) roofed with slabs carried on 11 arches. At the latter, 35 steps led down into a completely rock-cut chamber holding 1400 cum). Like Reservoir no. 53, both these reservoirs are in a "suburb."

The peculiar basin or small Cistern no. 50 was provided with three rock-cut steps, but they were hardly needed, since the basin is only 1.05 m deep. There may have been steps into Cistern no. 37 as well, but the situation is not clear.

It was noted above that no cisterns were built or cut in the rock between 2 and 4.7 km distance from the settlement centre. The only correlation between distance and cistern capacity appears to be the restriction of cisterns with a capacity of more than 300 cum to the area within 1 km of Reservoir no. 67.

7.C.5. *Built Cisterns*

All but four of the structures catalogued as built cisterns are located in the settlement centre, within 400 m of Reservoir no. 67. The four exceptions are all peculiar in one way or another. Structure no. 58 is still covered with earth, but the site on the slopes west of the settlement looks suitable for a cistern, which at this spot would probably have had to be built rather than rock-cut. Structure no. 60 is a puzzling structure built in the corner of a quarry cutting, so that two walls and the floor are formed of bedrock, while two walls are built of blocks (cap. ca. 18.3 cum). The interior has been plastered, but no intake channel is preserved, and the built walls

do not seem strong enough to have withstood the pressure of water at any substantial height inside. Structure no. 22 is a small, rectangular, unroofed tank (cap. 3.6 cum) adjacent to the aqueduct 5 km north of the settlement. The interior is not plastered, suggesting that it was used for some purpose other than water supply. Structure no. 21 was constructed of carefully trimmed and laid blocks 5.5 km north of the settlement, a few metres from the Via Nova and the aqueduct. The interior of the unroofed tank (cap. 0.64 cum) was plastered as if to contain water, but no connection with the aqueduct survives. It would not have been worthwhile, however, to fill such a small tank from a run-off field. It is not possible to evaluate the relationship of these structures to the water-supply system of ancient Humayma on the basis of the information available at present.

Ten structures within the settlement centre have been identified as cisterns built of blocks (two of them tentatively; see Table 7.5). As noted in the previous section, three rock-cut cisterns were located on the periphery of the settlement centre (nos. 55–57) as well. All but one of the built cisterns are cylindrical in form. The exception, Cistern no. 65, is the smallest of the group but has been very neatly built on a rectangular plan and roofed with three transverse arches. The rectangular cistern is similar to some of the smaller rock-cut cisterns with arch-supported roofs seen in the Humayma region (e.g., Cistern nos. 57 or 83), but at the small end of the range and quite shallow. Two of the remaining group of nine built cisterns had domed roofs, while seven had slab roofs supported by transverse arches. The two domed structures (Structure nos. 72 and 73) may not have functioned as cisterns. The better preserved example (no. 72) was lined with a very poor plaster and was built at too high an elevation to have been filled easily with run-off water. These two structures, neither of which has been conclusively dated, may have been designed as silos for grain.

The seven remaining cisterns (nos. 54, 64, 66, 69, 70, 71, 74) form a clearly defined type (figs. 2.14, 4.25). Their cylindrical tanks, solidly built of blocks and plastered on the interior, vary in diameter from 3.8 m to possibly as much as 7.4 m and in depth from 4 m to 6.25 m. Transverse segmental arches, between three and six in number, were bedded in the upper reaches of the cylindrical

Table 7.5   Built cisterns in the settlement centre.

Cistern no.	Number of Arches	Length	Width	Diameter	Depth	Capacity (cum)
65	3	4.12	3.87		1.30	20.7
64	3			3.80	4.50	43.0
73	dome			5.50	2.00	73.5
70	4			5.00	4.02	78.9
71	4			5.00	4.25	83.5
72	dome			5.50	3.90	92.7
74	4			5.10	4.54	92.7
54	5			5.80	6.25	166.0
66	6?			7.40	5.00	215.0
69	6?			7.00	5.92	227.8
						1093.8

wall and supported roofing slabs. The willingness of the builders to exceed the depth of 4 m, which served as the limit for most rock-cut cisterns, may reflect both the greater ease with which soil could be excavated as opposed to stone and the increasing difficulty involved in building tanks with a diameter exceeding 6 m. The cylindrical form of these tanks provided a greater volume with less masonry than the rectangular form, and the relative efficiency increased with diameter. The volumetric efficiency of the cylinder and sphere was widely known in the Hellenistic world. It is unlikely that Nabataean cistern diggers had read Euclid's *On the Sphere and Cylinder*, but they had centuries of practical experience at their disposal. They obviously realised that this efficiency does not extend to the rock-cut forms, which will hold 1 cum of water for every 1 cum of stone removed, no matter what the shape. The cylindrical design also helped these structures support the pressure of the surrounding earth, while the absence of corners facilitated water-proofing. Beyond 6 m diameter, the erection of stable roofing arches apparently became much more difficult, and only two examples were found. The approximate upper limit for the arches spanning the rock-cut rectangular cisterns was also 6 m (Table 7.3). The diameter of the two largest cylindrical cisterns (nos. 66 and 69) probably surpasses this figure, but only the two arches

that spanned the central portion of those tanks would have exceeded the calculated approximate limit. Perhaps two wide spans were tolerated if those arches were framed on either side by more stable arches with smaller spans.

It is, of course, also possible that in the settlement centre, where public water sources were available, there was little need for private cisterns of more than 100 cum capacity and thus of a diameter that might exceed 5.5 m. If all ten built cisterns in the settlement centre are taken together, the average capacity is 109.4 cum, with a standard deviation of 70.0, and a total capacity of 1001.1 cum. If the two doubtful structures (nos. 72 and 73) are omitted, along with the small, rectangular Cistern no. 65, the average capacity is 129.6 cum, with a standard deviation of 72.8, and a total capacity of 906.9 cum.

Since the cisterns in the settlement centre received run-off from catchment areas composed largely of soil, it is not surprising that settling tanks have been found in association with five of the built cisterns and with both of the reservoirs fed by run-off (Table 7.4). The exceptions either may not have been cisterns (nos. 72 and 73), or they are still partly covered with ancient or modern fill (nos. 65, 69, 71). Where the volume of the settling tank can be measured, the ratio of settling tank volume to that of the cistern itself varies between 1.7 and 8.8 percent. The

Table 7.6   Dimensions and capacity of reservoirs in Humayma catchment area.

No.	Source	Length	Width	Depth	Capacity	Arches
67	run-off	19.74	7.04	3.50	451.7	16
68	run-off	20.05	7.00	3.83	488.4	16
53	run-off	17.53	6.54	4.50	515.9	15
63	aqueduct	27.60	17.00	1.35	633.4	none
62	aqueduct	29.40	14.20	3.05	1273.3	none
Total					3362.7	

ratio of settling tank to cistern volume falls below this range for four of the seven rock-cut cisterns for which it could be determined (Table 7.4), possibly suggesting that the builders recognised the need to allow the run-off from earthen catchments a longer time to settle. The rock-cut cisterns were nearly all fed by bedrock run-off fields.

7.C.6. *Reservoirs and Pool*

The reservoirs that formed part of the water-supply system of ancient Humayma are a very mixed group in terms of the source of water, construction, and design (Table 7.6). What sets them apart from the cisterns is their greater capacity and, with the exception of no. 53, an obvious association with the public water-supply network. Although Reservoir no. 63 may not have been designed as a storage reservoir, it will be considered with the other reservoirs in this discussion. The smallest reservoir still in its original condition (no. 68) has a capacity almost fifty percent greater than that of the largest cistern (no. 55, ca. 300 cum). The average capacity of the reservoirs (672.5 cum) is nearly seven times that of the average cistern capacity (97.4 cum). Even if the atypical Reservoir no. 62, twice the size of the next largest reservoir, is omitted, the average capacity of the remaining four reservoirs is 552.3 cum. Reservoir no. 62 was built in the early second century inside the Roman fort; the other reservoirs were built to serve Nabataean Hawara. Reservoir no. 53 was cut into the bedrock 1 km west of the settlement, while the rest were built of blocks in the centre itself. Reservoirs nos. 67, 68,

and 53 were fed by run-off from large catchment fields, while nos. 62 and 63 were part of or fed by the aqueduct system.

The characteristics of Reservoirs nos. 67 and 68 help define this class of containment structure and set it apart from that of the cisterns. These two reservoirs were built as a pair in the centre of the settlement site, most likely at the same time or over a short period of time. They were identical in size and design (the dimensions of no. 67 were altered slightly during the modern renovation), only 19 m apart, and oriented at ninety degrees to each other. The central location, size, redundancy, and rectangular form set these reservoirs apart from the cylindrical private cisterns in the settlement centre. The absence of any structural remains above or around them also distinguishes the reservoirs and suggests that they were surrounded by some planned public open space. The provision of large settling basins and arch-supported roofs, the largest such roofs in the Hawara catchment area, indicates that this particular supply of water had to be of sufficient quality for human consumption. Taken together with the early ceramics found in the probes around Reservoir no. 68, these factors leave little doubt that the two reservoirs were part of the public water-supply system constructed at the time of Hawara's foundation. The presence of the enormous, gently sloping catchment field that fed them, stretching for a kilometre to the north, may even have been the deciding factor in locating the settlement at this particular point.

The other royal contribution to the water-supply system was the aqueduct (discussed below).

It is likely that Reservoirs nos. 67 and 68 were constructed before the aqueduct to sustain the new settlement until individual, privately-owned cisterns could be built. It may be that completion of an aqueduct system was also anticipated, particularly if Hawara was founded by Aretas IV rather than Aretas III (see below). There is, however, no hard evidence that the aqueduct was used to fill these two reservoirs. While the aqueduct water probably was considered to be higher in quality than cistern water upon its arrival at the pool/reservoir no. 63, water drawn from the pool and the pool overflow were polluted by bathing and exposure to the air. In any case, it is likely the inhabitants of Hawara would have felt uneasy depending on a spring-fed reservoir alone for their water supply. The flow of water through the 26.5 km of aqueduct channel was very susceptible to interruption by landslips, structural failure, sabotage, or seasonal changes in spring discharge. Reservoirs nos. 67 and 68, in contrast, would have filled completely or partially during every rainy season, as long as the intake channels were maintained and the long-term rainfall trends remained stable. The construction of a pair of reservoirs may have been part of a strategy of storing a two-year supply of water to allow for the significant deviations in average annual precipitation (see pp. 401–4). Finally, any potential deficit in the reservoir supply would have been apparent immediately at the end of the rainy season, allowing the inhabitants to modify their plans for local stock-raising or seasonal transhumance accordingly.

The intake arrangements for Reservoir no. 67 were totally rebuilt in the 1960s, but the structures associated with Reservoir no. 68 survive. A very heavily built intake channel conducted the runoff water into a large settling tank (cap. 10.6 cum) roofed with slabs carried on two transverse arches. Once the level of water in the tank reached 1.35 m, the overflow passed through a carefully built channel into the reservoir proper. The ratio of settling tank to reservoir volume was 2.2 percent. No draw hole is visible in the intact sections of the roofing over the main tank, but there must have been one, probably located adjacent to one of the reservoir walls in proximity to a watering tank for animals and a stand for containers. Fragments of a large stone trough were found near the southwest corner of the reservoir, and a block with sockets for three betyls was reused face down as a roofing slab at the same corner. Although the betyl block may have been reused simply as building material, the connection of basin and relief suggests that the draw hole may have been installed here.

Reservoir no. 53 is the only reservoir that was cut in the bedrock, and it is the only reservoir located outside the settlement centre, 1 km west of Reservoirs nos. 67 and 68. Nevertheless, it has been classified as a reservoir because of its similarity to nos. 67 and 68 in design and scale, and because its capacity is 72 percent greater than that of the largest cistern (no. 55). Some details of the stoneworking possibly indicate that the reservoir was originally one-third smaller, but the evidence is subtle and cannot be verified, so a single phase of development is assumed here. It can no longer be determined whether the structure was a public or private structure, or what factors determined that such a large water source should be located outside the settlement centre, but it is at least possible that this reservoir was meant to serve transhumant groups that camped from time to time on the ridges above Hawara or the flocks pastured on the high ground west and southwest of Hawara by groups that lived for the most part in or around the settlement centre.

Reservoir no. 53 is slightly narrower and shorter than nos. 67 and 68, but it is one metre deeper than no. 68, giving it a slightly greater capacity. Fifteen transverse arches carried a slab roof. No settling tanks survive at either of the two intake channels, but they may have been built of masonry and washed away by subsequent erosion of the soil surrounding the reservoir. A stairway cut in the rock at the southwest end of the reservoir gave access to the interior, descending all the way to the floor. A drinking trough cut in the rock adjacent to the stairway indicates that water was drawn from the tank at this point, but once the water level had fallen two metres, it would have been easier to draw the water out with a rope and container than to descend the stairs and dip it out. It is possible that these stairs, unique among the large containment structures in the Humayma region, were intended primarily to help with the excavation and subsequent occasional cleaning of the large and deep tank. Elsewhere in the Nabataean territory, cistern or reservoir stairs are common, for example at Petra, Mampsis, Ruheiba, Sobata, Qatrana, Ziza, and Bostra.

The two remaining reservoirs, nos. 62 and 63, are quite different from each other and from the three already discussed. The aqueduct fed both and neither was roofed, but no. 63 was designed as a flow-through tank, while the much larger no. 62 was designed as a storage tank that may have had some flow-through capacity. Supplying water to Reservoir no. 63 clearly was the most important function of the aqueduct system serving Hawara. There were two access tanks along the aqueduct out in the countryside, 9.2 km and 12.3 km away from the settlement, but these were both off-take tanks by-passed by the main aqueduct stream. These two tanks were also much smaller (capacities 40.7 cum and 44.5 cum, respectively). In contrast, the aqueduct emptied directly into Reservoir no. 63, built into the exact centre of its north wall. Naturally, since the aqueduct theoretically never stopped flowing, there had to be an overflow spout and a conduit to carry the overflow stream away. Exposure of the aqueduct water to light and air, wind-born soil and impurities, and to pollution by the humans and animals who accessed it at this point completely changed its character, and the overflow may have been considered suitable only for bathing, animal consumption, and irrigation. A large Nabataean structure 100 m south of the reservoir, possibly a bath like its Roman successor, may have absorbed much of the overflow from the Phase I arrangement.

Presumably many of the permanent or occasional inhabitants of Hawara, particularly those with houses or tents in the vicinity of the reservoir, along with travellers passing along the King's Highway would have sought out aqueduct water for drinking. It is not clear, however, how the aqueduct discharge was accessed or made available. Humans could hold containers by hand or on a rope under the intake spout of Reservoir no. 63, presumably the most desirable location for watering, or dip and draw water while standing along the walls. Because of the position of the overflow spout, even when the reservoir was filled to capacity the surface of the pool was ca. 0.5 m below the top of the walls, which would have made it impossible for most animals to drink directly from the reservoir. This arrangement may have been intended to divert livestock to troughs a short distance away filled by containers dipped in the pool. Nevertheless, there would have been numerous opportunities for direct and indirect pollution. Given the high quality of the water delivered to this reservoir, why was there no effort to roof it to keep out pollutants? Evaporation and plant growth would not have been significant problems in this unroofed reservoir, since the water was constantly recharged, but a roofed reservoir would have preserved the quality of the overflow water, allowing it to be directed to other cisterns around the settlement. If Reservoir no. 63 had been only 7 m wide, like Reservoirs nos. 67 and 68, it could have been roofed with transverse arches and slabs. Keeping the same length, but increasing the depth of the tank to ca. 3.8 m and the water depth to 3.28 m would have given the same capacity. At maximum flow (19.6 cum/hour), it would have taken the aqueduct just over 32 hours to fill this reservoir, and — without allowing for any withdrawals from the system — the same amount of time to completely renew the water passing through it.

Given all these factors, it seems likely that the Nabataean Reservoir/Pool no. 63 served some other purpose or some purpose besides the provision of water for drinking and agriculture. One explanation is that of a swimming pool. The depth is sufficient to allow immersion and paddling without exposing anyone but small children to the danger of drowning. There are very striking parallels in the later first century BC at Petra, Jericho, Caesarea, Masada, and Herodium (Bedal 2000a–b, 2001: 37–39, 2007; Schmid 2001b: 387; see Chap. 8), although always in connection with a royal palace and *paradeisos*, or garden. Elitzur (2008) has suggested that the "Solomon's Pool" in Jerusalem mentioned by Josephus (*JW* 5.145) was a swimming pool built by Herod. In addition to its recreational value, this type of pool served as a prestige display, intended by the royal patron to show his power over the desert and the general success of the Nabataean way of life. This was also the era when the Aqua Virgo aqueduct, built to supply Rome in 19 BC, for

FIG. 7.2   *Pipeline along north side of* Via principalis sinistra, *Roman fort, before removal of mortar packing.*

FIG. 7.3   *Pipeline along north side of* Via principalis sinistra, *Roman fort, after removal of mortar packing.*

the first time allowed the extensive use of aqueduct water for ostentatious display in a public bath, gardens, fountains, and a swimming pool (Koloski-Ostrow 2001: 5). Bowersock (oral communication, 2001; cf. Bowersock 1999) has suggested that the pool at Petra might have been used for celebration of the Maioumas festival, a festival of Near Eastern origin involving nude swimmers, celebrated at a number of sites in Asia Minor and the Near East. Although the location may seem an unlikely one to the modern visitor, the Hawara pool may have accommodated the same religious frolics.

No evidence has yet been identified for the presence of a royal garden or palace associated with Reservoir no. 63, but Hawara was a royal foundation, and the striking sight of a pool of fresh water in the centre of the Hisma would have impressed any visitor and reinforced the king's reputation. Since both the intake and overflow streams could be put to use, prestige was not the only purpose of the complexes at Hawara or Petra, but it was an important factor. The Garden and Pool Complex at Petra may date to the early years of the reign of Aretas IV (Bedal 2001; Bedal and Schryver 2007), and given the political importance and wealth of Petra, the Hawara pool is unlikely to have preceded it. In consequence, the aqueduct system and pool at Hawara, if properly interpreted as a prestige project, should be dated to his reign as well. Although the precise date of the original foundation of Hawara remains a puzzle, it is nevertheless possible that the foundation of the town and concomitant construction of Reservoirs 67 and 68 were the accomplishments of Aretas III, while the water-supply system was enhanced with a prestigious aqueduct system and pool/reservoir only during the reign of Aretas IV. Whatever its original date, the arrangements at Reservoir no. 63 underwent several phases of alteration as the Roman engineers changed the character and focus of the aqueduct system at its entry point to the settlement.

Reservoir no. 62, in contrast to no. 63, seems to have been a utilitarian storage reservoir, built inside the northwest corner of the Roman fort as a secure daily and emergency water source. It was fed by a specially built branch conduit tapping the Ghana aqueduct approximately 400 m before its junction with Reservoir no. 63. This branch must

have diverted a significant quantity of water from the aqueduct. At the hypothetical flow of 10 cum/hour and assuming complete diversion of the stream, it would have taken the aqueduct five days and seven hours to fill the fort reservoir, without taking into account the daily requirements of approximately 500 soldiers and possibly as many as 50 or 100 mounts. If we allot 8 l/day for each of the soldiers and 5 l/day for 50 camels, the total requirements are 4.25 cum/day. If the 50 mounts were horses, which require about 36 l/day (Gichon 2000: 543), the total need would jump to 5.8 cum/day, but still only slightly more than 30 minutes of the calculated aqueduct discharge.

Reservoir no. 62 is located at the highest point in the fort, and given the availability of a constantly flowing intake channel, the strategic importance of the pooled water, and the typical Roman concern with healthful water sources, it seems likely that there was some sort of outflow arrangement feeding a pressurised system. Excavations in the fort between 2000 and 2005 exposed sections of pressurised terracotta piping at several locations within the walls serving fountains, latrines, and stables (figs. 7.2–3; Oleson et al. 2003, 2008; Sherwood et al. 2008). The arrangement that connected the reservoir to the pipelines has been lost, but given the need to refresh the reservoir water, it is probable that a certain minimum flow-through was built into the system in addition to the necessary consumption. If the combined consumption and flow-through were sufficient to renew the water, for example, every 20 days, the contents of the reservoir would have remained relatively fresh. Such a practice would have required drawing 63.7 cum from the aqueduct every day, perhaps by diversion during the night of some or all of the total flow by means of a sluice gate, rather than as a twenty-four hour trickle. The drainage system would have carried the overflow from internal water-using installations out the south gate by means of the main drain under the *Via Praetoria* (main north/south road; Oleson et al. 1999: 420), where it could have been channelled into some low-lying fields (fig. 7.4). There was also a drain for run-off water under the east gate (fig. 7.5).

These figures and procedures are all conjectural, but they provide a reasonable scenario for the

FIG. 7.4   *Drain down middle of* Via Praetoria, *20 m north of south gate of Roman fort.*

FIG. 7.5   *Drain down middle of* Via principalis sinistra, *at east gate of Roman fort, looking west.*

alteration of the aqueduct system after the Roman conquest. The reconstructed daily diversion of 63.7 cum from the aqueduct into the fort reservoir represents 26.5 percent of the hypothetical daily aqueduct discharge. If the remaining 176.3 cum were directed entirely to the original Nabataean reservoir no. 63, it could have filled the reservoir in three days and 14 hours or refreshed the pooled water in the same period of time. The overflow arrangements were changed, however, at some point in the second half of the second century, when the occupants of the Roman fort built a bath on top the remains of a substantial Nabataean building 100 m south of the reservoir (E077; see pp. 223–30). The earlier structure may well have been a public bath itself, fed by the outflow channel from the reservoir that passed by it just to the east. The Roman engineers redirected the water supply through a lead pipe laid in the conduit blocks in order to allow the supply to be turned on and off by means of a large stopcock installed in the south wall of the reservoir, just above the level of the interior floor. This system protected the water from diversion and also provided a pressurised system capable of feeding an elevated supply tank or boiler in the bath building. The provision of a reservoir fed by an aqueduct to supply a bath building is typical of Roman North Africa, where climatic conditions are similar to those at Humayma (Wilson 2001). In Israel, the Roman aqueduct at Sepphoris fed a subterranean reservoir that may have served a valve-operated pressurised water system for the town (Tsuk 1996: 122; Peleg 2000; Meyers and Meyers 1997: 536).

There were at least two basins in the Roman bath building, with a total capacity of 757 l, approximately 450 l of which was heated before use. We have no way of knowing how many individuals the bath could accommodate once it was heated for a session, but since bathing involved dipping water out of the basins and sluicing it over the body, an individual might have used at least 6 l of warm water and 8 l of cold water. The cold water was applied before and after the hot or sometimes only after the hot; the hot water ran across the heated floor and provided a warm, humid atmosphere. Processing 75 individuals (in 15 groups of five?) would have used up both tanks of water in the course of an eight-hour day. Even if we allow for topping up the tanks for the sake of freshness and convenience, it is difficult to see how the bath could have consumed more than 1 cum in the course of a session of heated bathing. This is a conservative figure, but nevertheless it is clear that the reservoir was very much larger and the potential flow of the aqueduct — even after diversion of water to the fort reservoir — much more abundant than needed simply to service the bath building. Presumably the pipeline could have fed some other structures in addition to the bath, but, given the relatively small diameter (0.038–0.049 m) and low head of the lead pipe, it could not have accommodated a discharge anywhere near the 406.7 cum/day theoretically available.

Although the situation is still not entirely clear, excavation around Reservoir no. 63 has revealed the presence of a number of conduits and terracotta pipelines that diverted water from the aqueduct immediately before its intersection with the north wall of the reservoir. Unfortunately, the junction of pipelines and aqueduct has been lost (see pp. 279–80), but there presumably was some sort of basin with sluice gates or outlets at staggered heights to regulate the diversion of aqueduct water. Excavation in 1987 revealed the presence of a terracotta pipeline skirting the north and west walls of the reservoir, then setting a course more or less in the direction of the bath building, before being lost to ploughing between 15 m and 19 m south of the reservoir (see pp. 279–80, 288–89). The pipeline, which could not have been pressurised, was constructed of wheel-made terracotta sections (L ca. 0.30 m, inside D ca. 0.04–0.07 m; see pp. 330–31). This pipeline was laid down sometime in the Late Roman period, but other off-take conduits or pipelines may have been built at the time the stopcock was installed. When the Department of Antiquities cleared the interior of the reservoir and consolidated the walls in 2001, their work revealed the remains of a conduit constructed of conduit blocks of the type used in the aqueduct, but laid on earth along the outside of the east reservoir wall. This conduit presumably drew water from the aqueduct, but its chronology and function are uncertain. Since the blocks were not built into the fabric of the wall, the conduit cannot be part of the initial construction phase.

It is unfortunate that the purpose of the terracotta pipeline and its chronological relation to the lead pipeline laid in the original overflow aqueduct cannot be precisely documented. It is likely that the terracotta pipeline post-dates installation of the lead pipeline, since it is founded somewhat higher in the fill, but it cannot be determined from present evidence whether the lead pipeline was still functioning when the terracotta pipeline was laid. It is tempting to associate the terracotta pipeline with the Byzantine renovation of the bath building, but there is no proof of the connection, and in 2000 a similar pipeline was traced up-slope in the direction of the reservoir pipeline from the third-century shrine in Field E125. It is possible that the lead pipeline continued to serve the bath, while some of the extra flow was diverted through the terracotta pipeline to the shrine and domestic structures in E125. In any case, it is difficult to see what advantage there would have been in replacing a valved, pressurised pipeline to the bath building with a constantly flowing, unpressurised pipeline.

One construction detail may provide a hint about the sequence of water use at the reservoir. The limestone splash plate built into the floor of the reservoir below the aqueduct discharge spout carries a depression (0.12 × 0.09 m, 0.04 m deep) eroded into it by the stream falling 1.75 m from the conduit. Since the presence of a pool of water even 0.20 m deep over the stone would have prevented this erosion, it is clear that for significant periods of time the aqueduct emptied into a reservoir that was nearly empty or frequently completely empty. One possible explanation is that the demands of the reservoir in the fort, combined with the off-take by the terracotta pipeline above the Nabataean reservoir, frequently consumed nearly the entire flow of the aqueduct. Such a reduction or intermittent interruption of the flow would have forced the bath to rely on a shallow pool of water allowed to build up in the reservoir in the intervals between bathing. The frequent emptying of the reservoir can best be explained by the presence of diversion pipelines around it, of a low-level outlet with stopcock in the south wall, and the needs of the soldiers in the fort. Ultimately, this arrangement became unworkable, the stopcock was plugged, and the reservoir was used as a dead-end tank occasionally

or intermittently refreshed from the aqueduct. The water pooled in the tank in this last phase of use would have been of very poor quality. Demotion of the limpid Nabataean swimming pool to a shallow bath cistern, then to a stagnant pool, reflects a new set of priorities, post-Nabataean and probably post-Roman. The fort, and thus presumably the off-take channel serving the fort reservoir, went out of use around AD 400, possibly as a result of the earthquake of 363. Once the aqueduct ceased to flow, probably some time in the late sixth or early seventh century to judge from the ceramics around the Nabataean reservoir, that reservoir went out of use as well.

7.D. WATER TRANSPORTATION AND DISTRIBUTION FACILITIES

Several types of structures found in the Humayma catchment area were concerned with the transport or distribution of water; most of these have already been mentioned in passing in the discussion above. The most spectacular is the aqueduct system, which itself involved a number of subsidiary structures, such as settling tanks, off-take tanks, and distribution tanks. In addition, within the settlement centre, several separate distribution systems involved lead and terracotta pipelines and open conduits. Drains were occasionally built to handle unwanted water. Finally, human and animal labour was used to draw and distribute water in containers.

7.D.1. *Aqueduct System*

The design and functioning of the aqueduct system serving ancient Humayma has already been touched upon in several sections above (3.B.2, 7.B.2, and 7.C.6). In short, the system involved three separate springs, one main line 18.888 km long (the Ghana Aqueduct), and a branch line 7.620 km long (the Jammam branch) (fig. 2.7). The branch line joined the main line at km 6.553 km from 'Ain al-Ghana, and the combined flow emptied into Reservoir no. 63. Given the peculiar character of this reservoir, the initial motivation for construction of the aqueduct system may have been primarily a prestige project designed to reflect royal control of the desert, although with significant practical side benefits. The maximum possible discharge from the aqueduct is 19.6 cum/hour, but the typical discharge was probably much less.

Several factors suggest that the Jammam Aqueduct was constructed as a supplement to the Ghana Aqueduct, although possibly not long after the Ghana Aqueduct was completed. Firstly, the Jammam conduit abutted the Ghana conduit at a right angle (at Ghana km 6.553, Jammam km 7.620), making no allowances for the local topography — a theatre-shaped recess in the hillside to which the Ghana branch conforms with a long, unbroken curve (figs. 3.23, 3.26). Approximately the last 200 m of the Jammam branch before the junction seem to have been built (or re-built) to a width of ca. 1.35 m, wider than the dimension of 0.88–0.90 m typical of the rest of this branch and of the Ghana Aqueduct. Contrary to a previous assertion (Eadie and Oleson 1986: 66), this wider dimension does not occur along the escarpment slope as well. In addition, the Jammam branch differs from the rest of the system in some construction details: the presence of at least five small settling basins, the absence of off-take tanks, and the insertion of gutter tiles along much (if not all) of its length. The two rock-cut off-take tanks along the Ghana Aqueduct are very similar to each other in design and capacity and appear both before and after the junction with the Jammam branch, linking the two sections of the Ghana system above and below the junction. These tanks differ in form and function from the settling basins along the Jammam branch. Finally, although ʻAin al-Jammam is only marginally farther away from Humayma than ʻAin Ghana in a direct line (13.8 km, as opposed to 13.1 km), the topography along the Jammam route up to the junction point presented more difficulties, requiring a very steep section down the face of the escarpment. The Jammam branch is actually more "efficient" up to the junction than the Ghana branch (cf. Section 7.B.2): Jammam, straight-line distance of 4.66 km vs. 7.626 km of conduit = 61.1%; Ghana, straight-line distance of 3.36 km vs. 6.553 km of conduit = 51.3%. The greater efficiency, however, is largely a reflection of the use of the very steep and risky short-cut down the al-Shara escarpment.

The initial slope of the Jammam branch is very slight (ca. 0.5 percent), so the maximum possible discharge before installation of the tiles was 13.7 cum/hour, and 4.5 cum/hour after their installation. The conduit blocks of the Ghana Aqueduct and those of the Jammam branch (in their original state) have the same cross-section. The fact that the cross-section of the Ghana Aqueduct channel downstream from its junction with the Jammam branch is no larger than above the junction indicates that neither contributing channel was expected to flow at full capacity, again suggesting that the Jammam branch could have been built to supplement the flow in the original system.

The absolute chronology of the Ghana branch cannot be precisely determined with present information, but it was functioning for certain by the first half of the first century AD. Only a small amount of closely datable ceramic material was found associated with the aqueduct (1st–2nd century AD), none of it in foundation levels. A Nabataean or early Roman jar fragment of the late first century BC or early first century AD was recovered from the mortar packing of the Ghana aqueduct at km 4.480, but this provides only a *terminus post quem*. Ceramics recovered in the foundation levels of Reservoir no. 63, designed as part of the aqueduct system (see Probe H87-63-P02), suggest a date sometime in the first century AD. First- and second-century AD Nabataean and Roman sherds occur in a thin scatter along almost the entire length of the Ghana aqueduct, indicating that the structure was a focus of activity at this time. The absence of any sherd material from the foundation levels of the Ghana Aqueduct suggests that it was constructed not long after intensive occupation of the region had begun (see p. 239, Aqueduct Probe no. 6).

Similar systems elsewhere in the region confirm this dating. Above all, the aqueduct system reflects Nabataean rather than Roman technology, and many features of the system find parallels at Petra and other sites that date to the first century BC or AD (see Chapter 8). As noted above (Section 7.C.6), the main purpose of the original aqueduct system may have been to present the spectacle of a flowing swimming pool (Reservoir/Pool no. 63) in the desert as a sign of the King's technical prowess and control of the environment. The aqueduct and Garden Pool at Petra, built early in the reign of Aretas IV, most likely was the model for the Hawara system, reinforcing a date in the later first century BC or early first century AD (Bedal 2000a–b; 2001: 37–39; 2007; Schmid 2001b: 387). In any case, the Ghana Aqueduct must pre-date construction of the Roman fort at Hawara in the early second century, since a branch line had to be constructed to supply the fort reservoir.

The absolute chronology of the Jammam branch is more debatable. The basic design, dimensions, and materials of the aqueduct structure proper are the same as those of the Ghana Aqueduct, indicating a continuous engineering tradition. Since the details that differ — gutter tiles, settling tanks, and a wider substructure for the last 200 m — can all be later modifications, construction of the Jammam branch may have begun immediately after completion of the Ghana Aqueduct. Alternatively, it may have been constructed 10 or 20 years later, as demand on the system increased or the output of 'Ain al-Ghana declined. Although it is possible that the Jammam branch was built early in the second century to help fill the demands of the fort reservoir, it seems unlikely that the new branch would be so similar in materials, design, and dimensions to the original aqueduct if it had been constructed a century later.

Although materials and some details of construction vary from point to point (especially on the Jammam branch), the general design of the whole aqueduct system is uniform over its entire length. The water was conducted by characteristically Nabataean conduit blocks: long troughs (L ca. 0.95; W ca. 0.35; H ca. 0.36) of marl or sandstone (according to the character of the nearest source) carefully finished to a smooth, level surface at either end and along the top, but usually only roughly finished along the sides and bottom (figs. 3.14, 3.22). A gutter for the water (usually W 0.11 m; 0.12 m deep) was cut down the length of the blocks, which then were placed end-to-end — usually without any cement in the joints or along the inside surface. These conduits were bedded in a foundation of rubble (sometimes mixed with a crumbly mortar) that was framed on either side by heavy pieces of rubble or partly trimmed blocks (figs. 3.28–29). The overall width of the structure, which usually was built directly on the surface of the ground, was ca. 0.90 m. A single course of fist-sized stones was laid in

mortar along the upper edges of the conduit block on either side of the channel to support the roughly trimmed cover slabs (L 0.25–0.40; W 0.20–0.35; Th ca. 0.15; figs. 3.17, 3.29, 3.41). Where the topography demanded it, long support walls or viaducts up to 30 m long and 8 m high supplemented the substructure (Section 3.B.2, Ghana Aqueduct, km 5.942, 6.072, 6.591, 8.534, 10.333; Jammam branch, km 1.808, 2.394, 3.051, 3.300, 3.607, 5.942), along with small slab bridges (Section 3.B.2, Ghana Aqueduct, km 0.890, 4.008, 5.942; Jammam branch, km 1.359, 2.118, 3.051, 5.240, 6.784, 6.884). Across particularly steep bedrock slopes the water channel and bedding for the framing walls sometimes were carved directly in the bedrock (Section 3.B.2, Ghana Aqueduct, km 0.945, 1.366, 4.008, 4.212; Jammam branch, km 1.118, 1.177, 1.402, 6.784).

For several long stretches of the Jammam branch, and perhaps originally for that whole branch line, long, tapering terracotta gutter tiles with a parabolic cross-section were set into mortar within the water channel. The tiles (L ca. 0.30–0.40 m, W ca. 0.13–0.07, ca. H 0.10–0.11 m) resemble typical Mediterranean cover tiles used for roofing. It seems more likely that they were recycled from structures in the Roman fort rather than manufactured specifically for use in the aqueduct (see pp. 328–30, nos. 1986.001.01, 1986.002.01). The tiles fit the conduit channels perfectly, which seems a remarkable coincidence, but they are not uniform in length, which one would expect them to be if they had been manufactured for that function. Calculating on the basis of average length and overlap, approximately 18,000 tiles were used in the aqueduct. The structures in the first phase of the fort — the only complex at Hawara where significant quantities of roof tile fragments have been found — could easily have provided this total. In comparison with 18,000 cover tiles, relatively few fragments of pan tiles have been found in the fort, so it seems likely that the pan tiles were salvaged for export to some other regional site at the same time the cover tiles were recovered for use in the aqueduct. The most appropriate moment for such recycling was the temporary abandonment of the fort during the reign of Diocletian.

It is difficult to reconstruct the function the tiles were intended to serve, since they appear along both steep and gently sloping sections of the Jammam branch, near the springs and near the junction, both on ground that appears stable and on ground that has shifted or eroded. At km 1.768, the interior surface of the tiles has been plastered, while elsewhere the sinter has been deposited directly on the red ceramic. At some points, tiles seem to have been removed by modern vandals (e.g., Jammam km 0.993), revealing conduit block troughs free of calcium carbonate deposit (sinter). Elsewhere (Jammam km 1.779–1.808, 6.228, 6.492, 6.621–6.884), the tiles were removed in antiquity (or possibly never installed) and the conduit blocks carry sinter deposits. I found no examples of tiles installed over existing calcium carbonate deposits. There do not appear to be any parallels for this use of gutter tiles in an aqueduct elsewhere in the Nabataean cultural region. The original early first-century BC northern aqueduct in the Siq at Petra was renovated and a terracotta pipeline installed in the conduit channel in the third quarter of that century (al-Huneidi and Bellwald 2003: 55–60; see Chap. 8.A.1). The last section of the Nabataean aqueduct serving a reservoir at Umm Rattam near Petra was fitted with terracotta pipes that may belong to the Late Roman period of occupation (Lindner, Hübner, Hübl 2000: 554–60). The installation of a lead pipe in the outflow conduit from the Nabataean Reservoir no. 63 in the second century involves a similar concept. These parallels are only approximate, but they indicate that the hydraulic engineers in the region were open to the use of ceramic conduits inside stone conduits.

There are several possible explanations for the installation of the tiles, but none is entirely satisfactory. Since the presence of tiles in a conduit block would have raised the level of the stream of water by anywhere from 0.02–0.05 m, the tiles may have been added along some of the gentle slopes to correct slumping of the channel. This function, however, would not apply to the steeper sections where tiles also appear. Sinter deposits appear in both aqueduct branches. The tiles cannot have been inserted to facilitate removal of sinter, since the concretions adhere more tightly to the tiles than to stone, and the tiles were cemented into position and sometimes plastered over. A more plausible explanation is that the tiles were intended to protect a greatly diminished flow of water by providing a channel that would lessen the wetted structural area, reducing friction and absorption (particularly during periods of low flow), while at the same time providing better protection against leaks. The approximate cross-sectional area of the tile conduits (ca. 0.0036 sq m) is only 32.7 percent of the cross-sectional area of the original conduits (0.011 sq m). The level of the sinter on many of the tiles shows that they were running nearly full at least part of the time, but often were filled to only a fraction of their capacity. Near the spring (Jammam km 0.773), the sinter extends up to the lip of the tile. At km 5.419, a thin layer of sinter reached to within 0.02 m of the lip. At km 7.340, a thick, pillowy deposit nearly filled the entire tile (Chapter 6, cat. no. 1992.0613; fig. 6.3). At km 7.382 and km 7.529, on the other hand, the sinter extended to within 0.02 m of the lip, but a projecting evaporation ridge showed that the water depth was typically around 0.035 m and 0.06 m, respectively. Since the tiles have a parabolic cross-section, the lower water depth reflects either higher stream velocity or much lower stream volume. Since the varying slopes of the sections where measurements of the sinter were taken do not seem to explain the variations in water height, it could be that the installation of the tiles was a response to new and significant seasonal variations in discharge from the 'Ain al-Jammam and 'Ain Sara. If discharge throughout the year was sufficient to fill the tile conduits completely, their installation would not seem to provide much advantage. But if the discharge fell to very low levels during the summer, the seasonal advantage might have been significant.

Another idiosyncrasy of the Jammam branch is the presence of small settling basins (probe reports, Section 5.B.2–5). These basins, which occur at Jammam km 1.181, 1.779, 1.951, 2.259, and 2.494, may contribute to our understanding of the tiles. The basins vary greatly in size, design, and degree of preservation, but they all straddle the aqueduct, allowing the water to pool and drop sediment. Since uncontrolled access for the purpose of drawing water would have polluted the entire aqueduct system, the tanks were all provided with heavy cover slabs that would have been lifted only to clean out sediment. The structure at km 1.779 is the largest and best-preserved (Section 5.B.2). A circular curb wall (D 2.15 m) surrounds a central basin (0.80 m square, 0.60 m deep; cap. 0.384 cum). The aqueduct emptied water into the basins from the upstream side and drew it again from the downstream side. Circular curbs also survive around the basins at km 1.181 (D 1.80 m) and 2.494 (D 1.80 m). The basins vary significantly in volume: km 1.181, 114 l; km 1.779, 341 l; km 1.951, > 51 l; km 2.259, undetermined; km 2.494, > 44 l.

The off-take tanks at km 6.512 and 9.597 of the Ghana Aqueduct are very different in design. They are much larger than the Jammam settling tanks (cap. 44.5 and 40.7 cum, respectively) and are set apart from the aqueduct stream, which was diverted by sluice gates through short channels to fill them. Presumably these tanks were used to make aqueduct water available to groups resident in the countryside. The complete absence of settling tanks from the Ghana Aqueduct and the lower two-thirds of the Jammam branch indicates that the five tanks placed at irregular intervals (1181 m, 598 m, 172 m, 308 m, 235 m) along the first 2.5 km of the Jammam branch were meant to solve some special, localised problem, probably the deposition of sediment. None of the connections between the aqueduct system and the springs survive, so it is not clear how sediment could enter the system. Presumably, if one of the Jammam branch springs was discharging water containing gravel or sand, a settling basin at the source could have solved that problem more effectively. If the sediment was finer, more of it might enter the system and begin to cause problems in the first few kilometres of conduit, where the slope was very gentle. Where the deposit of sinter is rapid and heavy, it is also possible for gravel-like sinter to develop and move along a water channel. Since the parabolic cross-section of the tiles, like that of modern drainage conduits, would have fostered a higher stream velocity and better scouring capacity during low water level than the square cross-section of the stone conduits, the tiles may have been intended in part to help move silt, sand, and gravel to the settling tanks during periods of decreased flow. Perhaps the tiles contributed to the solution of several problems associated with low water level in the stone conduits: scouring of sediments, reduction

in wetted perimeter and friction, and enhanced water-proofing. A multi-purpose solution would help explain the presence of tiles well beyond the first few kilometres of the Jammam branch.

The questions of the speed of formation of sinter in both the Ghana Aqueduct and the Jammam branch, and the methods for dealing with it, cannot be answered with the information available at present. Toward the top edges of conduit blocks or tiles, which presumably the water reached less often, the layer of sinter usually was thin (1–2 mm) and fairly smooth. Along the lower portions of the walls and on the floors of both conduit blocks and tiles, the sinter was thicker (up to Th 0.06–0.08 m) with a surface of rounded bumps that occasionally nearly filled the tile (fig. 6.3). In cross-section, sinter deposits from both branches show alternating bands of light and dark (or white and clear) mineral deposits, probably corresponding to seasonal variations in temperature, although there is little agreement on this cause (Schulz 1986: 264, 268; Gilly 1986: 132; Guendon and Vaudour 1986; Hauck and Novak 1987: 149; Garbrecht and Manderscheid 1992).

Sinter (calcium carbonate deposit, $CaCO_3$) forms when spring water high in dissolved calcium and low in dissolved magnesium leaves a subterranean phreatic system. The decrease in pressure allows the water to release dissolved carbon dioxide, essentially lowering the acidity of the water and allowing the calcium carbonate to precipitate out (Müller 1996). The gradual increase in the water temperature as it is exposed to the air may accelerate this process (Baatz 1978). Since deposits form more quickly where stream flow is slower, the shallow slope of the first few kilometres of the Jammam branch (0.3–0.5 percent; Table 7.7) probably made that area particularly susceptible to the formation of sinter, a process accelerated by the rapid rise in water temperature. The first 3.5 km of the Ghana Aqueduct, in contrast, were generally steeper (0.7–14.9 percent; Table 7.8). The process of sinter formation is complicated, however, and it can take time for the dissolved carbon dioxide to leave the water, delaying the precipitation reaction (see general discussion in Hodge 1992: 227–32).

Both aqueducts carry heavy sinter deposits up to their junction point (Th 0.01–0.09 m), after which the deposits appear to be much thinner (Th ca. 0.002–0.01 m). Either the dissolved calcium had reached a relative equilibrium in the water by this point, or this section of the conduit was cleaned out more often. The former seems more likely, since along the Nîmes aqueduct the thickness of the sinter rings diminishes with distance from the spring (Garbrecht and Manderscheid 1992: 225). It is interesting that conduits along some of the steeper slopes of both aqueducts carry particularly heavy concretions (e.g., Ghana km 3.704, Jammam km 6.228). It is possible the sinter was cleared out of a section of aqueduct only when the deposit became thick enough to force water up and out below the cover slabs. This problem would have become apparent more quickly on gently sloping sections, since on steeper slopes stream velocity was higher and its depth consequently less. In consequence, the gently sloping portions of the system may have been cleaned out more often. At the entrance to the settling tank at Jammam branch km 1.779, the concretion had formed around delicate, hair-like strands of algae that were growing in the channel, almost completely obstructing the flow of water. The algae, which still grow around 'Ain Ghana and 'Ain al-Jammam, most likely infested the channel and tank when cover slabs were removed or allowed to decay during the last years the aqueduct was functioning. Similar deposits were found in the Nîmes aqueduct (Guendon and Vaudour 1986: 147–50).

Unfortunately, the evidence available at present does not allow determination of the typical interval between cleanings and the method of disposing of the sinter. The longest sequence of sinter layers that could be counted was approximately 25, found in a thin layer of sinter attached to a fragment of tile discovered near the Jammam branch at km 7.529. All the thicker samples examined exhibited confused patterns of layering that did not allow precise counting, but the totals appear to be in the same range, around 22–25 rings: Ghana Aqueduct km 3.827 and Jammam Aqueduct km 1.779. The thinnest deposits involve 4 rings. In any case, it is not certain that each layer or pair of light and dark layers represents an annual sequence. If the sinter built up in annual layers only 0.5 mm thick (one-half the rate suggested for European aque-

Table 7.7 GPS elevations and approximate slopes along the Jammam Aqueduct branch.

Distance	Elevation	Interval	Slope
0.000	1418		
0.790	1417		
0.934	1415		
1.118	1415		
1.181	1419		
1.359	1418		
1.779	1413	1779	0.3%
2.259	1411		
2.394	1409		
2.494	1410		
2.681	1413		
2.899	1410	1120	0.3%
3.051	1403		
3.300	1403		
3.607	1417		
3.982	1410		
4.100	1409		
4.267	1407		
4.918	1410		
5.240	1410		
5.818	1415		
5.933	1395	3034	0.5%
6.228	1355	295	13.6%
6.492	1287	264	25.8%
6.521	1256	29	106.9%
6.621	1236	100	20.0%
6.784	1246	163	6.1%
6.884	1243	100	3.0%
6.976	1239	92	4.3%
7.543	1209	567	5.3%
7.620	1201	77	10.4%
Overall:		7.620	2.8%

Table 7.8   GPS elevations and approximate slopes along the Ghana Aqueduct.

Distance	Elevation	Interval	Slope	Distance	Elevation	Interval	Slope
0.000	1414			6.512	1202	440	0.7%
0.890	1405	890	1.0%	6.553	1201	41	2.4%
1.436	1395	546	1.8%	6.858	1191	305	3.3%
1.638	1397			7.070	1187	212	1.9%
1.711	1389	275	2.2%	7.609	1164	539	4.3%
1.916	1359	205	14.6%	8.035	1160	426	0.9%
2.192	1318	276	14.9%	8.534	1154	499	1.2%
2.810	1320			9.144	1151	610	0.5%
2.974	1320			9.597	1151		
3.307	1310	1115	0.7%	10.333	1170		
3.392	1296	85	16.5%	10.881	1163		
3.617	1298			11.107	1148	1963	0.2%
3.972	1272	580	5.9%	11.526	1134	419	3.3%
4.008	1264	36	22.2%	11.902	1107	376	7.2%
4.212	1240	204	11.8%	12.473	1089	571	3.2%
4.350	1225	138	10.9%	13.309	1062	836	3.2%
4.756	1226			13.912	1044	603	3.0%
5.400	1229			13.985	1034	73	13.7%
5.700	1216	1350	0.7%	16.378	1020	2393	0.6%
5.822	1207	122	7.4%	17.154	1014	776	0.8%
5.942	1207			18.888	977	1734	2.1%
6.072	1205	250	0.8%		Overall:	18888	2.3%

ducts, Hodge 1992: 228), a typical conduit block would have been completely obstructed within a century and a conduit tile within about 50 years. Since the aqueduct was in use for at least three centuries, and possibly for six, it is very likely that some sort of cleaning operation took place periodically. Sequences of up to 370 layers have been documented in the roughly contemporary aqueduct serving Nîmes (Gilly 1986: 132), but the large size of the original channel allowed the system to continue functioning despite the neglect. There was much less scope for neglect of the Hawara aqueduct system, and cleaning must have been necessary at least once every 50 years.

Although it is likely that sinter was removed from the aqueduct from time to time, no deposits of discarded calcium carbonate have been recognised along its course. Occasional large pieces of sinter have been pulled from conduit blocks in the modern period and dropped near their original location, but any ancient discards have disappeared. Even if reduced to chips during removal, it seems unlikely that the sinter could have completely weathered away in the intervening millennia, given the apparent stability of the deposits still in position in the channel. The sheets were not large enough for reuse as building materials or decorative veneer, as was the case for sinter from the Roman aqueduct serving Cologne (Hodge 1992: 231–32). Perhaps the sinter fragments were gathered up and burned to produce some of the lime needed for plasters and cementing materials along the aqueduct and in the settlement. The calcium carbonate of which the sinter is composed constitutes the essential ingredient of any raw material burned for lime (Cowper 1927: 10).

There is also little evidence for the methods by which the Nabataean engineers planned and levelled the Hawara aqueduct system. The survey procedures and instruments used by the Romans, and to a lesser extent the Greeks, are well-documented (Hodge 1992: 171–215; Lewis 2001), but Nabataean engineering techniques have been examined in detail only for the rock-cut tombs and built temples of Petra (Rababeh 2005; Bessac 2007). The typically Nabataean use of a ground-level channel meant that careful selection of the routing and accurate measurement of slopes were far more important than engineering works. Where necessary, viaducts were built across gullies, but no major excavation was carried out to avoid detours around hills. A large part of Hawara's aqueduct system was built at a slope greater than 2 percent — a 2 m fall in every 100 m, ten times the usual slope of a Roman aqueduct system (Hodge 1992: 347–48) and presumably relatively easy to achieve. The average slope for the Ghana aqueduct is 2.24 percent, for the Jammam branch 2.85 percent. The last 5.5 km of the Ghana Aqueduct, where it crosses the Pleistocene lake bed north of the settlement centre, had a more gentle slope, approximately 1 percent, which required greater care. The steeper slopes could have been surveyed with simple water levels or plumb bob devices, but the final slope of 1 percent may have required use of the *chorobates*, a larger, table-sized water level with sights (Hodge 1992: 194–208; Adam 1994: 17–19; Lewis 2001: 31–35). This device was widely known and used in the Hellenistic world (*contra* Lewis 2001: 31–35), with which the Nabataeans, of course, were familiar (cf. Schmid 2001a–b), and cuttings on the edges of the outflow channel from Reservoir no. 63 may even represent it (fig. 5.61, inset). These cuttings were well-placed to have served as survey marks, as were two T-shaped marks on either edge of the same conduit 20 m south of the reservoir (Section 5.E.12; fig. 5.61). A less convincing box-like cutting appears on the conduit 15 m south of the reservoir (fig. 5.61, inset). The only other possible survey marks were observed at km 9.144 of the Ghana aqueduct, a lozenge with two sharp ends and rounded sides (L 0.16; W 0.08), and an equal-armed cross (W 0.08;

H 0.08; fig. 3.33). Both marks are oriented side-by-side along the direction of the channel. They seem too inconspicuous and too carefully carved to be *wusum* (recent tribal markers; King 1992). Since all these marks would have been invisible once the covering slabs were put in place, they must have had something to do with the quarrying, positioning, or measurement of the conduit channel. Many more survey marks may be hidden beneath cover slabs, plaster, or drifted fill.

As the field description of the aqueduct system in Section 2.B.2 makes clear, the conduit slope varied significantly from point to point along its course. Since the readings taken with a pocket level during the initial field survey did not form a continuous series, Tables 7.7 and 7.8 summarise the data for slope based on GPS elevation readings taken in 2001. Even these readings were usually subject to a margin of error of ± 4 m, so the elevations recorded along the very gradual slopes do not always decrease with distance from the springs. Although the slope has been calculated only for sets of readings that do decrease, the percentage figures for gentle slopes derived from the GPS figures are liable to be inaccurate in detail. The general impression, however, is accurate and informative. Most of the system was very steep by Roman standards, but there were occasional long, gently sloping sections where the terrain flattened out or the engineers were trying to preserve altitude.

The first 5.933 km of the Jammam branch seem to have the least slope in the entire system that can be well-documented: 0.3–0.5 percent. A slope of 0.2 percent is suggested by GPS elevations for a stretch of the Ghana Aqueduct (km 9.144 to 11.107), but the margin of error is far greater here than for the beginning of the Jammam branch. The engineers clearly were trying to avoid having to drop below the ridge connecting Jebel Jammam and Jebel Ghana, since that would have forced them to build the aqueduct through very steep boulder-strewn terrain in the valleys feeding Wadi al-Jammam. Once clear of this hazard, the channel dropped over the edge of the escarpment and followed a very steep, nearly straight course to its junction with the Ghana Aqueduct. After a difficult and generally steep descent down the flanks of Jebel Ghana, frequently across unstable ground, the Ghana

Aqueduct levelled off to a slope of somewhere around 0.7 percent between km 2.192 and 3.307 as it rounded the base of the jebel. The aqueduct then dropped steeply down the difficult terrain of a projecting ridge to the talus below Jebel Ghana (km 3.307–4.350), where again the slope levelled off as the engineers preserved altitude in order to attain the ridge the aqueduct would follow down to the plain north of Hawara (km 4.350–5.700). Gentle descents also occur between km 9.144 and km 11.107, where the sloping ridge levels off, and along the last 4.9 km of the Ghana Aqueduct, where it crosses the Pleistocene lake bed north of the settlement centre (km 13.985 to km 18.888). The GPS elevations yield a slope of 2.3 percent for the last 1.734 km, but an EDM survey has shown the slope on this section to be close to 1 percent.

Presumably, a rough survey was carried out to establish the course of the aqueduct, most likely working from both the settlement and the spring simultaneously. Actual construction, however, probably proceeded from the spring toward the settlement, so that water could be introduced to check the slope. The foundation area would have been smoothed first, then the framing blocks placed in position on the uphill side of the structure. The conduit blocks could then be positioned on gravel backfill, their precise level of slope checked with a surveying device, and the rest of the framing structure completed. It would seem a wise precaution to leave the conduit un-roofed until each section was given a trial run by temporarily introducing spring water. Whatever the planning and construction procedures, the aqueduct system clearly functioned effectively for several centuries.

7.D.2. *Conduits and Pipes*

The infrastructure for distributing water within the settlement of Hawara is still poorly-known. Since 1998, every season of excavation in the area of the Roman fort and the associated *vicus* has revealed additional terracotta pipelines branching out from the direction of the two reservoirs fed by the aqueduct, and it is likely that many more remain hidden (Oleson et al. 2003; 2008). So far, these pipelines all seem to belong to the Roman or Early Byzantine periods, but they may replace or supplement pipelines or conduits of the Nabataean period. The original open channel carrying the overflow from Reservoir no. 63, for example, was replaced by lead and terracotta pipelines in the second or third century. The aqueduct distribution basin described below may be testimony to a local distribution network that was part of the original Nabataean water-supply system. In any case, it is probably not coincidental that evidence for conduits and pipelines has turned up at Humayma only around the termination of the aqueduct and two aqueduct-fed reservoirs. Without a constantly flowing source of water, the use of conduits and pipes is seldom an efficient solution to the need for water distribution.

Aqueduct Distribution Basin

The remains of what may have been a sandstone basin installed across the Ghana Aqueduct channel were found at km 18.837, 51 m upstream from the junction with Reservoir/Pool no. 63 (fig. 3.40). Although the context was very badly disturbed and only one quarter of the basin has survived, the location and configuration suggest the block was part of a distribution basin. The basin would have had an intake receiving all the aqueduct water and three or four outlets at a lower level, one feeding the continuation of the aqueduct, the others feeding conduit channels or pipelines serving other needs nearby — possibly basins for human use and troughs for animals. The various outlets could have been closed as required by sluice gates or with simple wads of wet cloth. The basin was located close to the edge of a bluff, at a point where the aqueduct suddenly changed direction on the way to the main reservoir, a good position for feeding subsidiary channels. A similar basin still *in situ* in the water system feeding the main cistern at Sobata has high walls pierced by three conduits for the distribution of water, and there are similar arrangements in the water systems in private homes (fig. 8.54). Other such basins were found beneath downspouts in the water-collecting system of the North Church complex at Nessana (Eadie and Oleson 1986: 63–64). A distribution basin identical in function but slightly different in design appears

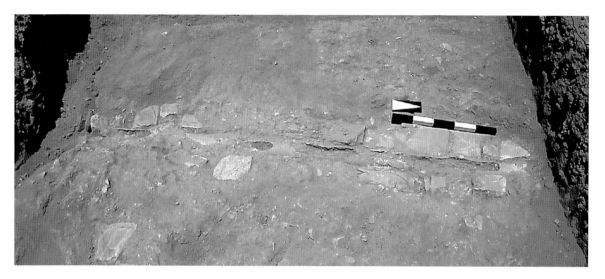

FIG. 7.6 *Terracotta pipeline entering north wall of* Praetorium *of Roman fort.*

toward the end of the 'Ain Brak aqueduct at Petra (cf. Lindner and Hübl 1997; fig. 8.5). The Romans called this sort of arrangement a *castellum aquae* or *dividiculum* (Hodge 1992: 279–91). The more explicit term *castellum divisorium* is a modern construct. This was a structure in which water from a major public source was divided in carefully calculated proportions among conduits serving a variety of public and private purposes.

It is unfortunate that this installation was not found in better condition. It is not certain that the block in fact formed part of a large distribution basin, and it can no longer be determined whether the basin formed part of the original Nabataean water-supply system or was part of the Roman renovation connected with construction of the diversion channel to the reservoir in the fort. As yet, no pipelines or conduit channels have been exposed in the vicinity of the basin.

Pressurised Pipelines in the Roman Fort

During the 2000 excavation season, a stretch of terracotta pipeline was discovered beneath a sidewalk along the north edge of the road leading from the centre of the fort to the east gate, near its intersection with the parade ground (*via principalis sinistra*; Oleson et al. 2003: 42–43; figs. 7.2–7.3). The pipes were wheel-thrown in a coarse, hard, reddish-brown fabric (L ca. 0.31–0.33 m, D 0.09 m) with an inset rim at one end. They were laid in a channel 0.13 m wide formed by unworked limestone rubble, with their inset ends laid to the east, most likely to carry water in that direction. The joints were heavily smeared with a hard white plaster, and the tops and sides of the pipes were carefully encased in the same plaster, which was tooled to a length-wise peak. The pipeline slopes downward to the east across the 5 m excavation square, from an elevation of 960.50 to 960.41 m asl (top surface). Further excavation in 2004 and 2005 located several other ground-level pipelines, one serving some sort of hydraulic feature in the centre of the *Praetorium* courtyard, possibly a fountain, and a branch of this pipeline probably serving a small hypocausted bath or heated room in the northeast corner of the *Praetorium* (fig. 7.6; Oleson et al. 2008). Yet another pipe was found entering the area of a latrine inside the fort, supplied either by an elevated pipe system or filled occasionally with containers carried by porters or donkeys.

The heavy fabric of the pipes and the hard plaster packing around the pipeline by the *Principia* indicate that it was designed to function under pressure. The same may have been true for the other pipelines, but they are less heavily built. The only possible source of water for these conduits is Reservoir no. 62 in the northwest corner of the fort, the floor of which stands at about 960.0 m asl, the upper lip at about 963.0 m asl. The pipelines

FIG. 7.7   *Boy drawing water from Reservoir no. 53 in June 1987.*

serving the *Praetorium* head directly toward the south end of the reservoir but are lost 15 m south of it. Excavation in 2004 and 2005 failed to locate any overflow conduits or tanks associated with the south wall of the reservoir or any pipeline tapping the interior of the reservoir through its south wall. There were, however, platforms built against the southeast and southwest inside corners that may have served pumpers drawing water from the reservoir with *shadufs* to fill basins, now lost, that fed the pipelines (fig. 4.4).

Further excavation is needed to document the extent of these pipelines and their functions. The typical activities carried out within a Roman fort, however, suggest the following applications: filling basins for human and animal consumption, providing water to workshops or a bath, and flushing latrines and street drains.

Conduit and Pipelines around Reservoir no. 63

In its original configuration, Reservoir no. 63 received water directly from the Ghana Aqueduct, and the overflow was conducted to the south in another stretch of aqueduct that may have fed a Nabataean bath and irrigated fields. If this reservoir was in fact a prestige project intended in part for bathing, it is unlikely the outflow was used for drinking. The subsequent changes to the system, involving pressurised and free-flowing pipelines, have been discussed above (Section 7.C.6). Outflow from the reservoir was used to supply a Roman bath, while several pipelines seem to have intercepted the aqueduct flow just upstream from the reservoir to serve household and religious purposes in nearby structures in Field E125 (fig. 5.25).

7.D.3. *Human and Animal Transport*

Until the drought of the late 1990s, Bedouin camping near Humayma visited the site at least once a day to water their flocks and to fill water containers for household use (see Chapter 7.E.5). Cooking-oil containers recycled as buckets were lowered into the cisterns or reservoir on ropes to obtain the water (figs. 4.15, 7.7). Because the tents were often one or two kilometres away, donkeys were usually used to carry the household supply back in large rubber water bags. Since about 2000, most local households have depended on portable galvanised steel cisterns that hold several cubic metres of water and are filled as needed by tanker trucks. Human and animal transport must also have formed an important part of the water distribution system in ancient Humayma. We tend to underestimate the role of water-carriers in ancient water-supply systems, but even in Rome, which had an elaborate water system incorporating pipe connections to some private houses, human water carriers (*aquarii*) remained an important part of the local distribution system (Oleson 1984b: 41–42, 48, 396–97; Habel 1895). At Mampsis, where there was no alternative, animal and human porters may have been used to fill a large public reservoir (Negev 1988a: 186–87). At Masada and some of the other desert fortresses on the West Bank, water was brought by aqueduct to cisterns below the defences, from which donkeys carried it in water bags to the settlement area (Garbrecht and Peleg 1989, 2001; Netzer 2001a).

The fortunate inhabitants of the houses that had their own cisterns could have drawn small amounts of water in pots or leather buckets as needed. Individuals from houses without a cistern would have had to walk a short distance to the central reservoirs nos. 67 and 68 or to basins around Reservoir no. 63 supplied by the aqueduct. Presumably, the farther individuals had to go for water, the more structured the activity became, both in terms of scheduling and of selection of containers. Families living in tents just outside the settlement centre either camped near a "suburban" cistern to which they had rights or carried water back from the public reservoirs in the centre by means of large leather water bags slung over camels or donkeys. There was also a reservoir 1 km west of the centre (no. 53) that may have served the public. If Reservoir no. 53 was intended to serve public needs, its location — although in part enforced by the need for a run-off field — suggests an understandable reluctance to travel more than 500 m for water. It was noted above that no cisterns or reservoirs have been found at a distance between 2 and 4.7 km from the settlement centre, once again emphasising the focus of this regional water-supply system on Hawara.

7.D.4. *Waste Water and Drains*

Very little is known about the disposal of waste water generated by the Humayma water-supply system. It is uncertain how the Ghana Aqueduct terminated in its original phase of use, but any water not diverted to other uses probably was absorbed in irrigating plots of land at the south end of the settlement centre. Even the significant, although intermittent, discharge from the Roman bath fed by Reservoir no. 63 was simply allowed to run out through a small drain in the west wall and down a slope (Section 4.B.4). Since the soil beneath and around the settlement centre is light and sandy, most waste water drawn from cisterns or other water sources by means of containers and used for household or craft activities in the civilian settlement must simply have been poured out on the ground in courtyards or in the passageways between structures. Disposal of waste water in the fort, which was for the most part built over or paved, was effected by built drains under the road (see above). No evidence has been found for the use of cesspits or sink-aways in the civilian settlement at Hawara. The relatively low population density, bright sun, and drying winds fostered the casual disposal of household waste water and human waste. The Bedouin of the region today discard waste water very close to their tents, where it quickly disappears in the sand, briefly refreshing swarms of flies, but not in itself creating unsanitary conditions. Clusters of small shrubs in the wadi beds are used as latrines, and the waste itself is either left to dry in the sun or lightly covered with sand (Dickson 1959: 81). Rapid dehydration of the waste satisfies most aesthetic and sanitary concerns.

Here again the fort was probably an exception. Hygiene and discipline required the presence of latrines in Roman forts (Webster 1985: 259–60), and one was identified in the fort at Hawara in 2004 (Oleson et al. 2008). The very dry climate and scattered grazing also do not foster the hoarding of animal or human waste as fertiliser, an application that can affect strategies for water storage and drainage. Manure dropped thinly on the widely scattered fields or grazing lands simply dries up, is ground to a powder by passing flocks or windblown sand, and is carried away by the wind. There is not enough moisture on the surface to foster the formation or accumulation of humus.

The same casual approach was taken in the civilian settlement with regard to unwanted run-off from precipitation. Hawara was located at the junction of several run-off fields that were harvested to fill cisterns and reservoirs, but the houses were positioned high enough to avoid damage. As a result, there was no need for a constructed run-off drainage system in the settlement area. One possible subterranean drain was found in association with two early Islamic houses north of Reservoir no. 68, but the precise purpose of the feature is not clear (see pp. 220–22, Structure no. 76). A series of stone conduit blocks conducted water from the courtyard of one house to a slab-roofed catching or settling basin in the centre of the unpaved passageway outside. A second conduit entered the basin from the opposite direction. The outflow from the basin was carried away to the east in a substantial slab-built drain (W 0.28–0.32; H 0.34 m), which could be traced downhill for 17.2 m before it was lost (figs. 4.46–48). It is possible that this system was intended to carry off waste water from the houses connected to it, but given the presence of a settling tank, it is more likely that it was designed to guide run-off water from the house roofs or courtyards to a still-undiscovered cistern.

Within the fort, commodious and sturdy drains were provided under the two main roads to channel away precipitation running off the roofs and paved areas. Surface water channelled to the road entered the drains through typically Roman drain covers with rosette-shaped openings (Hodge 1992: 342), while branch drains carried run-off water and waste water from the adjacent barracks, workshops, and stables (fig. 7.4). If the pressurised piped water system in the fort was in fact directed to fountains, the constant run-off may have been channelled beneath the latrine to wash the waste into the same drainage system or into a cesspit. A small drain (W 0.13–0.20 m; H 0.15 m) for surface water exited under the east gate (fig. 7.5), but the main drain (W 0.31–0.36 m, H 0.35 m) ran underneath the centre of the sloping *via praetoria* and out the south gate, following the main slope of the land (fig. 7.4; Oleson et al. 1995: 328–9, fig. 10; 1999: 419–20, fig. 6).

7.E. THE WATER-SUPPLY SYSTEM IN USE: EVOLUTION OF DESIGN, APPLICATIONS, AND SOCIAL CONTROL

7.E.1. *Development of the Physical Infrastructure*

The main lines of the chronology and evolution of the water-supply system serving Nabataean Hawara and the succeeding ancient communities are clear (for relevant chronological data, see Chapters 3, 4, and 5). Permanent occupation of the site would have been impossible without facilities for storing run-off water, and at least one of the reservoirs in the settlement centre (nos. 67 and 68) belongs to the initial period of settlement (see Section 2.B.1). The pair may in fact be contemporaneous, and it is likely that the royal founder built them. At the same time, or soon after, private individuals began to build or excavate cisterns to collect run-off water in the settlement centre and the surrounding hillsides to supplement the public supply and provide further water for humans and livestock. The cylindrical cisterns in the settlement centre may have been built on open ground and used for some time by tent-dwellers before houses were constructed around them. The aqueduct and the reservoir/pool associated with it (Structure no. 63) belong to the end of the first century BC or very beginning of the first century AD. Given the nature of the pool, the whole system was probably in large part a prestige project built by King Aretas IV on the model of his pool complex at Petra. If this king rather than Aretas III founded Hawara, the aqueduct and three reservoirs in the settlement centre are part of a single, very ambitious, regional water-supply system. The aqueduct discharge most likely was used for livestock, craft processes, agricultural irrigation, and bathing. There may have been a bathhouse as well, under the later Roman bath, 100 m south of the aqueduct pool.

The Roman fort was constructed soon after the conquest of the Nabataean kingdom by Trajan in 106, including a reservoir fed by a branch line from the aqueduct. At least some of the overflow from the reservoir served a pressurised water system in the fort. Late in the second century, the free-flowing overflow conduit at the aqueduct pool was replaced by a stopcock and pressurised pipe providing water to a heated bath constructed over the remains of the Nabataean structure to the south. The rest of the aqueduct discharge seems to have been diverted to the *vicus* associated with the fort. At some point in its history, the channel of the Jammam Aqueduct was renovated with tile inserts, probably to correct problems with leakage and to compensate for reduced flow.

Unfortunately, because of the paucity of ceramic finds, very few of the other elements of the water-supply system in the settlement centre and throughout the catchment can be dated with any precision, particularly the many cisterns. Ceramic evidence is similarly poor for the numerous cisterns of the Negev highlands (Kloner 2001–2: 472). Nevertheless, the design and execution of most of the structures and the associated sherd scatters or occasional betyls are Nabataean in character. These factors indicate that the regional system was for the most part complete by the late first century AD, including another reservoir, numerous roofed and unroofed private cisterns, dammed pools, wadi barriers, and a few terraced fields. There is so far no evidence that cisterns were built into the Byzantine churches, as at Petra (Fiema et al. 2001: 70–73), Mampsis (Negev 1988b: 36–38, 57), Nessana (Shereshevski 1991: 59), Oboda (Negev 1997a: 109–13, 129), Sobata (Shereshevski 1991: 79; Tsuk 2002: 73), and other sites in the Nabataean cultural region, indicating that the reservoirs and cisterns in the settlement centre already provided sufficient capacity. The Byzantine foot does not appear to have been used as the module for planning out any of the cisterns or reservoirs in the region (see Section 7.E.2). There is also no indication that cisterns were constructed in the early Islamic period. None have been found in the Abbasid family manor house (Field F103), and the two domed structures in the settlement centre that may belong to this period (Structure nos. 72–73) are more likely silos than cisterns. Renovations of older structures, of course, would have been ongoing.

7.E.2. *Modules Used in Design and Construction*

The Nabataean architects, cistern diggers, and builders who designed and constructed the elements of the Hawara system undoubtedly made use of some sort of standard of linear measurement, but it is difficult to find clear evidence for the use of a specific unit. In contrast, it is easy to demonstrate that the Roman engineers who laid out the fort and its reservoir used the Roman *pes Monetalis* of 0.2959 m (Oleson et al. 1995: 321–30; 2008). A search of the measurements of the surviving structures for patterns can help elucidate the history of the system and the process of construction.

Although Hellenised and on the periphery of the Hellenistic world, the Nabataeans, like the earlier Near Eastern cultures, made use of a system of "natural" measures — the finger, palm, and cubit. The "foot" is a more artificial concept, adopted by the Greek and Roman cultures (Powell 1992: 899). In the few situations where archaeologists have calculated modules for Nabataean structures, they have proposed the use of cubits of various lengths. Bellwald (private communication, March 2002) states that he has documented the use of the "Egyptian-Palestinian cubit" of 0.52 m for parts of the Nabataean period water-supply system of Petra. Schmid (2001c: 169; cf. 2005) has found that a column diameter of 0.60 m was used as the defining module to plan out parts of the complex of the so-called "Soldier Tomb" at Petra, although he does not state that this defining measurement equalled a cubit. Several scholars assert that the "larger Egyptian-Palestinian cubit" of 0.525 m was used in the first century BC in the Qasr al-Bint at Petra and in the first century AD at Khirbet edh-Dharih (Dentzer-Feydy 1990; 1995; Kanellopoulos 2003: 156; Zayadine et al. 2003: 77–79). A cubit of 0.515 m has been identified on the third-century Tomb no. 36 at Palmyra (Schmidt-Colinet 1992: 25–35). The word "cubit" (*'mh*) only occurs once in Nabataean inscriptions, on a tomb façade at Meda'in Salih dating to AD 57/58 (Healey 1993: 147–51, no. H 14): "…And the share of Hagaru has been allotted to the right five cubits (*'myn*) and the share of (Mahmiyyat to the left) five cubits (*'myn*)." Healey suggests that the width of the tomb (façade?) — 5.40 m — may equal the ten cubit total, yielding a cubit of 0.54 m. Rababeh (2005: 98–101) has little to say on this topic.

Powell (1992: 899–900) emphasises the difficulty of documenting the specific length of a

Table 7.9   Application of various modules to selected hydraulic structures.

STRUCTURE	MODULE	THEORETICAL DIMENSIONS	ACTUAL DIMENSIONS
Pool no. 63	cubit of 0.55 m	50 × 30 × 3	50.18 × 30.90 × 3.18
Reservoir no. 68	cubit of 0.50 m	40 × 14 × 7	40.10 × 14.00 × 6.96
	cubit of 0.57 m	36 × 12 × 6	35.18, 12.28, 6.10
Reservoir no. 53	cubit of 0.54 m	32 × 12 × 8	32.46 × 12.11 × 8.33
Cistern no. 54	cubit of 0.57 m	10 (diameter)	10.17
Cistern no. 18	cubit of 0.55 m	20 × 10	19.90 × 10.36
	cubit of 0.52 m	21 × 11	21.05 × 10.96
Off-take tank 6.512	cubit of 0.57 m	20 × 11 × 1.25	19.91 × 10.91 × 1.26
Off-take tank 9.597	cubit of 0.55 m	21 × 8 × 1.5	20.78 × 8.09 × 1.45
	cubit of 0.54 m	21 × 8 × 1.5	21.17 × 8.24 × 1.48
Aqueduct	cubit of 0.47 m	2 (width)	1.9
	Roman foot	3 (width)	3.04
Dam no. 44	cubit of 0.54 m	8 (thickness)	8.07
	Roman foot	15 (thickness)	14.72

cubit, since ancient errors of measurement can be assumed to lie between five and ten percent, and he notes that in Egypt between 2000 BC and 395 AD the length of the cubit varies between 0.50 and 0.54 m. Powell suggests that 0.50 m is a reasonable compromise for the length of a cubit used for measurement at a specific structure, since ancient measurements were often approximate and the "natural" cubit defined by the human forearm varies between 0.44 m and 0.56 m. Allowing a plus/minus variation of five percent suggests that metric dimensions of ancient structures should be searched for reasonable multiples of units between 0.475 m and 0.525 m for a cubit of 0.50 m, and between 0.494 m and 0.546 m for a cubit of 0.52 m. It is obvious that unless the structures measured were planned and constructed with precision, it will be nearly impossible to define the module accurately. It is, of course, also important to determine which design dimensions might have been the determiners of a structure built of blocks: the interior dimensions, the mid-point of the walls, or the exterior.

Measurements should be more straight-forward for a rock-cut cistern or reservoir, since the interior dimensions are the only critical ones.

Unfortunately, the application of units varying between 0.47 m and 0.57 m to some of the more carefully built or rock-cut features of the ancient water-supply system of Hawara does not produce any convincing evidence for the use of a specific, precise cubit. Hypothetical cubits of 0.47, 0.50, 0.52, 0.54, 0.55, and 0.57 m (along with the Roman foot of 0.296 m and Byzantine foot of 0.3089 m) were applied to the main dimensions of reservoirs nos. 63, 68, and 53, cisterns nos. 18 and 54, the aqueduct (width), the aqueduct off-take tanks at km 6.512 and 9.597, and dam no. 44 (thickness; Table 7.9). For built structures, both the outside and inside dimensions were calculated. Each hypothetical cubit produced at least one result that looks reasonable, but no cubit produced equally satisfying results for all the structures. In some cases, two different cubits produce reasonable results. The actual number of modules is given in parentheses, and unless otherwise stated, the measurements are length, width, and depth of the water tank.

Some of these calculated dimensions in cubits and feet are more convincing than others, but on the whole the impression is one of only approximate measurement. Application of the various cubits to the rest of the cisterns in the Humayma catchment that have a distinct architectural form gives similar results. The engineers who designed and built or excavated the reservoirs and cisterns clearly had some kind of cubit in mind, if only an approximate one, and possibly even their own forearms. They also conceived of the interior dimensions of the structures as multiples of the width or depth, or as multiples of a common denominator such as 3 or 4.

Although the Roman foot can be made to fit the width of the aqueduct structure and the thickness of Dam no. 44, these structures are both firmly placed in the Nabataean architectural tradition and cannot be attributed to Roman builders. It is significant, however, that the Roman foot was chosen as the module for the "Great Temple" and the adjacent Garden and Pool Complex at Petra — both clearly Nabataean structures (Kanellopoulos 2003). Reservoir no. 62 in the Roman fort, like the fort walls and interior structures, was planned and constructed by Roman engineers on the basis of the Roman foot (Oleson et al. 1995: 321–30; 2008). The reservoir was laid out as 100 × 50 × 10 Roman feet, and the dimensions were measured off with errors of less than one percent to just over four percent (99.32 × 47.97 × 10.30 RF). A Byzantine foot of 0.3089 m has been documented in use at a number of churches in Syria (Milson 2003), and it was used with margins of error well under one percent in the Church of the Blessed Virgin at Petra (Fiema et al. 2001: 163–64). Although the evidence at Humayma is not as clear as at Petra, the same foot appears to have been used to plan the Lower Church (C101; nave L 19.25 m × W 14.0 m = ca. L 60 × W 45 feet), the church in B100 (nave L > 17.5 m × W 12.25 m = ca. L 60 × W 40 feet), and the church in F102 (nave L 19.3 m × W 9.4 m = ca. 60 × 30 feet). Application of this foot to a selection of built and rock-cut cisterns and reservoirs in and around Humayma did not produce any evidence for its use.

7.E.3. Applications of the Water-Supply and Potential Population

The applications to which water might be put in a small pre-modern settlement in the Jordan desert are varied, but predictable. The highest priority use, of course, was direct human consumption. An average adult accustomed to an active life in this arid environment needs to consume at least 2 l of water per day in order to feel comfortable. Evenari, Shanan, and Tadmor (1982: 148) assume a daily drinking ration of 2 l in winter, rising to 7 l in summer, but the latter figure seems too high. In addition, water is needed for cooking and for washing the body, clothing, and eating utensils. Estimates of the amount of water required in antiquity to satisfy all these basic human needs (including drinking) vary, but 8 l per day is a reasonable figure (Helms 1981: 188–89; 1982: 97–113; de Vries 1987). If we assume that all the run-off water in the reservoirs and cisterns in the habitation centre was intended entirely for human use and that the system was designed with a safety margin of 100% (i.e., that the inhabitants counted on the cisterns being filled only every second year; cf. Shereshevski 1991: 191–93), the 2,284.9 cum stored there could have sustained a population of approximately 390 souls. This figure excludes the aqueduct discharge and Nabataean Pool no. 63, which may have been used for other purposes, the Roman Reservoir no. 62, which is part of an essentially separate system, and the doubtful Structures nos. 72 and 73.

Eleven well-documented possibly domestic cisterns have been found in the settlement centre (nos. 54–57, 64–66, 69–71, 74) with an average capacity of 122.25 cum and a total capacity of 1,344.8 cum. Assuming the 100% safety margin, an average-capacity domestic cistern could support 21 individuals and all eleven together, 230 individuals. These both seem reasonable figures, given all the assumptions made. If only the seven built domestic cisterns in the settlement centre are counted (nos. 54, 64–66, 69–71), all but one of which (no. 54) are associated with domestic structures, the average capacity of 119.27 cum could support 20 individuals. Given the significant size of the domestic structures now visible in the settlement centre, an estimate of 20 individuals per household — assuming the presence of several generations of the family, closely associated clan members, servants or slaves, and visitors — does not seem excessive. Hirschfeld (2003) estimates that 12–13 individuals lived in the houses at Sobata.

The reservoir in the Roman fort was probably refreshed at frequent intervals from the aqueduct, but the through-flow of 63.7 cum/day proposed above (Section 7.C.6) is completely conjectural. If correct, such a through-flow could have supported the individual needs of 7,963 persons, an impossibly large total for either the fort or the town. Although the dimensions of this reservoir (10 × 50 × 100 Roman feet) are too even to suggest that the resulting volume (1,273.3 cum) had been carefully calculated to support a certain anticipated garrison size, the planners must have considered the possibility of withstanding a siege after interdiction of the aqueduct flow. Assuming loss of half the water to evaporation (which can total 3.4 m/year in this region; Natural Resources Authority 1977: Map SW-5) and a siege of the camp lasting no longer than six months, the water stored in a full reservoir could have supported a human garrison numbering approximately 436. This figure corresponds well enough with the size of the camp, which is suitable for an auxiliary cohort of approximately 500 men (cf. Parker 1986: 105; Webster 1985: 145–51). Any mounts present in the fort, of course, would have required a large daily allowance of water as well.

The flow of the aqueduct, which was calculated to have had a theoretical maximum of 19.6 cum/hour, supplemented the stored water. If we assume a real average discharge of about half the theoretical maximum, ca. 10 cum/hour, and diversion of 63.7 cum/day to the fort reservoir, the hypothetical resulting daily discharge of 176.3 cum could have sustained the astonishing figure of 22,038 individuals. The daily discharge, of course, may have been much less, and in fact very little of the discharge may have been used for drinking.

Some of the water available in and near the settlement centre and much of the water in the rural cisterns must have been designated for use by livestock. If we assume that half of the capacity of the two central public reservoirs (Structure nos. 67–68) was designated for consumption by animals, while the cisterns were used for human

consumption, the potential population supported by water stored in the civilian centre falls to 311. As for livestock, camels and donkeys require approximately 5 l/day when eating dry fodder, goats or sheep 3 l/day (Helms 1981: 188–89; 1982: 97–113; de Vries 1987; Evenari, Shanan, Tadmor 1982: 148). If we assume that the herds consisted of 10 percent camels and donkeys, along with 90 percent goats and sheep, we get the figures of approximately 18 camels or donkeys and 183 ovicaprids supported by a 50-percent share of the water in the two public reservoirs (again assuming 100% redundancy). The proportion of donkeys and camels is high by recent standards among the Humayma Bedouin (see Section 7.E.5), but the appearance of inexpensive motor vehicles over the past 20 years has reduced the importance of beasts of burden. There is not sufficient evidence to propose what the ratio of donkeys to camels or of goats to sheep might have been, but it makes no difference to the calculations of consumption. Recent statistics in the Badia region of northern Jordan show that herds average around 13 sheep for each goat, but that there is much variation depending on local conditions (Campbell and Roe 1998: 191). It is reasonable to assume that 90 percent of the 8,061.2 cum of water stored in the reservoir, cisterns, off-take tanks, and dammed pools outside the settlement centre was intended for livestock, since the human population was more thinly scattered in the rural district and since unroofed pools holding poor-quality water constitute 40.5 percent of the total (3,264.0 out of 8,061.2 cum). Assuming both a safety margin of 100 percent (although, in fact, many animals most likely were slaughtered in times of drought because of the problem of finding fodder) and the same proportion of camels, sheep, and goats as in the settlement centre, this water supply could have supported 137 persons, 282 camels or donkeys, and 2,825 ovicaprids. The combined regional total is 448 persons, 300 camels or donkeys, and 3,008 ovicaprids. These figures, of course, represent an absolute minimum, since the output of the aqueduct is ignored, some cisterns may have been missed in the survey, and 100 percent redundancy is assumed.

The combined regional population density for the 234 sq km survey area reconstructed from these calculations is 1.91 persons/sq km, the urban density 311 persons/sq km, and the rural density 0.59 persons/sq km. All of these figures, of course, are highly hypothetical, but they give an idea of the significant carrying capacity of this arid landscape. In fact, it is likely that most of the families and their flocks moved from the rural landscape to the settlement and back again several times in the course of a year. In the National Water Master Plan, Humayma is counted as part of the Wadi al-Yutum catchment, map area ED, an area of 4443 sq km; the specific sub-region is ED11, the Wadi Rumman catchment, with an area of 1416 sq km. The population of this region in 1975 was 3,918, or 3 inhabitants/sq km. The projected population for 2000 was 5,180, or 3.7 inhabitants/sq km. Given the partial economic integration of this region with the rest of Jordan in the later twentieth century and improvements in health care and nutrition, the hypothetical density of 1.91 persons/sq km for the catchment area around ancient Hawara seems quite reasonable.

Although the total maximum amount of stored water in the Hawara water-supply system seems impressive (12,419.0 cum), it constitutes only a tiny fraction of the total amount of run-off theoretically available in the catchment area (between 329,600 and 2,472,000 cum; see pp. 31–34). In fact, in antiquity, as today, the activity "consuming" the largest amount of water in the catchment was agriculture. Although the evidence is now almost entirely lost, there must have been numerous fields in and around the wadi beds and at the foot of appropriate natural run-off catchments that were left in their natural state or provided with low earth or stone barriers to slow the passing streams of water and allow them to soak into the soil. Those fields that received sufficient moisture during the winter rains would have been seeded with wheat or barley and protected from grazing until the crop had been harvested. It is impossible to reconstruct how much water was "consumed" in this fashion around Hawara, but it was many times the volume of the stored water. In the Negev, where the agricultural fields fed by run-off are better preserved, it has been possible to generate some figures on water consumption. Barley (*Hordeum bulbosum*), for example, consumed 2,300 cum/ha (Evenari,

Shanan, Tadmor 1982: 191–205). The minimum amount of precipitation needed to grow wheat without irrigation is somewhere around 250 mm, a consumption of approximately 2,500 cum/ha (Hillel 1982: 148; Allen et al. 1998). If all the water stored artificially in the Humayma catchment had been used for irrigating this type of crop, it would have sufficed for only about 5 ha of fields, a very small proportion of the arable land available around Humayma, and sufficient to sustain only 8 persons (see below).

Although irrigation of grain crops was impractical, it is likely that there was some small-scale hand irrigation of small patches of vegetables and fruit trees in the immediate vicinity of Hawara, both from cisterns and by making use of the aqueduct run-off. The existence of a probable rock-cut wine press 1.7 km west of Hawara (Structure no. 51) indicates the presence of at least one vineyard, which would have required irrigation for at least a portion of the year. The 500 olive trees planted by ʿAli ibn ʿAbd Allâh ibn al-ʾAbbâs (or his son Muhammad; Section 2.B.2) would have required some irrigation as well.

Given the large amount of run-off water available in the Humayma catchment and the potentially large number of fields with good agricultural soil properly located to receive the run-off, it is useful to calculate how much land would have had to be in cultivation to support the hypothetical minimum population of 448 persons. Bruins (1986: 86–95) has used ancient and modern figures for wheat yields in the Negev to calculate the ancient population that could have been supported by local fields there. Assuming that the farmers of Hawara experienced the same average yield of 646 kg of wheat per hectare, that they kept back one-third as seed (215 kg), and that 10 percent of the remaining grain (43 kg) was lost or spoiled, each hectare would have produced 388 kg of wheat for consumption. If we assume that a person required 250 kg of wheat per year to survive (Broshi 1980; Bruins 1986: 175–181), 289 ha of wheat fields would have been required to feed the hypothetical minimum population of 448 persons in the Hawara catchment. As noted above (Section 2.A.3), the "principle of least effort" tends to restrict agriculture to within a radius of 5 km of a traditional Middle Eastern settlement, and the fields recently tilled by the Bedouin are in fact generally within a 5 km radius of Humayma. Because of soil conditions and topography, the northeast and southeast quadrants or such a hypothetical circle have been favoured. Since even one-quarter of the territory within a circle 5 km in diameter equals 1,963 ha, it is clear that even the fields in the immediate vicinity of Hawara could have provided sufficient grain to support a regional population much larger than 448 persons, even allowing for mediocre soil and unpredictable patterns of precipitation.

Craft activities would also have consumed some of Hawara's water supply, but it is impossible to make a close estimate of how much. As with the local hand irrigation, the water could have been drawn from the aqueduct outflow. If pottery was produced locally, water would have been needed for washing the clay. There was undoubtedly some production of leather at the site, but, given the dry climate and local resources, the favoured procedures probably were oil, mineral, or smoke tanning and the production of rawhide. None of these techniques requires as much water as vegetable tanning (Forbes 1966; van Driel-Murray 2008). The production of woollen textiles consumes significant quantities of water in washing the fleeces and dyeing them, as would the occasional production of mudbricks for construction. The remaining technologies likely to have been practised at Hawara, however — iron-working and the production of cosmetics, perfumes, medicines, and pigments — would have required negligible amounts. In summary, craft activities consumed some portion of Hawara's water supply, but they were probably not a significant drain on the resource, particularly since the lower-quality water that flowed through Pool no. 63 would have been acceptable.

Religious rituals are also unlikely to have consumed any significant amount of water. The role of water in Nabataean ritual is unclear, but — as in Roman religious rituals — its main function may simply have been for washing up after a blood sacrifice (Healey 2001: 161–63). The Christian liturgy practised in the churches of Byzantine Hauarra also consumed only small amounts of water. Baptism involved at least partial immersion, but this ceremony only took place once or twice a year. The ritual washing before prayers required by Islam probably consumed more water than the practices of the other religions, but presumably these ablutions simply took the place of some personal washing for the sake of hygiene, resulting in little extra consumption.

The data accumulated by the Humayma survey, along with some new data gathered in 2008, was entered into a computerised water-balance model at the School of Human and Environmental Sciences at the University of Reading (Foote et al., forthcoming). Although many of the assumptions implicit in the modelling were different from those I have described above, the results are in general agreement with my own.

7.E.4. *Sequence of Possible Socio-Economic Systems and Social Control*

Since the presence of a water-supply system is the factor that makes human habitation at Humayma possible, the character of the system and its development over time should have been reflected in the social and economic arrangements of the community. Although any reconstruction of these arrangements remains hypothetical, it is nevertheless useful to provide a brief account of the possibilities.

The desert tribes of the Near East have always oscillated between pastoral and agricultural modes of existence and the various stages in between. Groups dependent entirely on pastoralism undoubtedly passed across the site of Hawara from time to time before the town was founded, trekking from one natural water hole to another or to the springs on the escarpment. Literary accounts of the Nabataeans, pictographs in the Hisma, and the faunal remains excavated at the site show that the raising of sheep, goats, and camels remained an important part of the economy after the foundation of Hawara (Section 2.A.6–7). At the same time, it is clear from the location of Hawara that the site was selected at least in part for its proximity to good agricultural soil appropriately situated for run-off farming. In consequence, the majority of the settlers must have engaged in both pastoral and agricultural activities from the start. These two

FIG. 7.8   *Bedouin flocks grazing in the higher slopes south of Humayma, May 1996.*

activities are complementary in a region where run-off irrigation is practised, since the labour-intensive agricultural activities are very restricted in time (Lancaster and Lancaster 1999: 119–21, 167–237). Many of the year-round, labour-intensive tasks inherent in drought farming in ancient Greece — such as repeated preparatory ploughing, ploughing of fallow fields, weeding, composting, spreading of dung, digging around trees, pruning, and wood chopping — were not part of the scheme (cf. Isager and Skydsgaard 1992: 19–52).

After repairing any earth or stone barriers or channels needed to slow or direct run-off water, the landowners simply waited for rain to fall. Because of the extreme aridity, weeding was unnecessary, and the growth of shrubs might actually have been encouraged to help hold the soil in place, particularly along the margins of fields. Given the light and porous nature of the soil and the danger of losing it to the strong daily northwest winds if the surface is loosened when dry, it is unlikely that

the fields were dug over or ploughed in preparation for the rainy season. Significant precipitation might occur any time between November and March. If a field was judged to have received sufficient run-off to bring a crop to maturity, the surface crust was most likely broken with a light plough or harrow, possibly at the time of seeding. Sheep and goats might also have been herded to moistened fields before planting in order to graze down the weeds nourished by the water, deposit manure, and break up the surface with their hooves. After seeding, the farmers simply kept their flocks out of these fields until after the harvest in May or June, when they could be turned in to eat the stubble left by the harvest (figs. 7.8–9).

Since the modern Bedouin tend to live farther away from their fields, often in New Humayma, the whole plant is often plucked from the soil at harvest, bagged, and taken elsewhere for threshing and storage of the straw. When a small combine is available from the farming cooperative, the grain

FIG. 7.9   *Bedouin flocks grazing on stubble near Humayma after the harvest, July 1989.*

is harvested mechanically and the stubble left for grazing. During the same period, while the fields are off limits, good grazing can be found in the rocky hills around the central soil basin, sustained by the same rains that had moistened the planted fields. During the dry months after the harvest, once the stubble has been consumed and natural pasturage is poor, families and flocks can migrate to the highlands north of the escarpment. The relatively marginal importance of tree crops and vineyards at ancient Humayma also freed up farmers to work as pastoralists for a large part of the year.

This agricultural regime is very seasonal in character, and for much of its history a significant portion of the population of Hawara must have occupied the site only during the times for planting and harvesting. As a result of the need for mobility and despite the amenity of a public water supply, many families associated with Hawara probably never built homes at the settlement centre, but while residing there simply lived in tents set up around and among the growing number of private cisterns and associated houses. This process has

been documented at Petra in the first century BC and the first and second centuries AD (Stucky et al. 1996: 47–50, 88–89), and it continues today in the region in small towns such as Jafr (fig. 7.10; cf. Köhler-Rollefson 1987; Lancaster and Lancaster 1999: 254–71). Many scholars have noted the oscillation of the Bedouin between nomadic and settled lifestyles in antiquity (e.g., Young 2001: 133, 268 n. 239; Graf 1989a: 360–61).

Although the difficult environment necessarily enforced strong ties between the small desert community and the complementary resources of the surrounding region, Hawara must also have accommodated activities appropriate to a proto-urban community. Hawara was the only significant habitation centre along the King's Highway between Petra and Aila, and numerous merchants and travellers, most likely moving in caravans of pack animals, had to pass through it on their way north or south. To judge from the accounts of nineteenth-century visitors, a camel caravan could easily reach the settlement from Petra in two days, from Aila in a day and a half, and from Wadi Ramm in one day (see pp. 9–14). Although

FIG. 7.10 *Bedouin tents among houses at Jafr, July 1998.*

much larger habitation centres were within reach, travellers will have stopped for water, and they may have required the services of saddlers, drovers, and guides. Pliny (*HN* 12.65) describes the payments required from the caravans travelling the incense road from Arabia Felix to Gaza.

> All along the route they keep on paying, at one place for water, at another for fodder or the charges for lodging at the stopping places, and the various customs fees, so that the expenses amount to 688 denarii per camel before they reach the Mediterranean coast.

The temples and other public structures of pre-Roman Hawara required skilled stonecutters who may also have worked on the aqueduct system and the reservoirs, cisterns, and dams scattered in and around Hawara. Since most, if not all, ceramics used at Hawara were imported from Petra and Aqaba (Section 6.B.1), there may not have been any need for local potters in the pre-Roman period. Given the parallels elsewhere in the Near East and

the Mediterranean world (de Ligt 1993; Graf 2000; 2001), it is likely that throughout its history Hawara served as the site of a market or fair that at regular intervals attracted the regional population and through local or itinerant merchants supplied it with ceramics, clothing, metal or wood implements, jewellery, animals, slaves, and supplementary foods, such as salt, dried fish, and dates. The earliest historical testimony of the Nabataeans describes them in attendance at just such a rural market (Diodorus 19.95), held at some distance from Petra (de Ligt 1993: 70, n. 65). The term used (πανήγυρις) has the overtones of a religious festival accompanied by commercial activity, and the religious element may have been important at Hawara as well. The presence of a Roman garrison would also have fostered the establishment of periodic markets, as at Dura Europos (de Ligt 1993: 127). Markets for buying manufactured goods and selling livestock and produce remain important among the Bedouin (Lancaster and Lancaster 1999: *passim*).

How would this lively community have been planned and administered? As a royal foundation,

Hawara benefited early on from royal munificence, which probably provided the two public run-off reservoirs, the aqueduct system, and a pool for bathing or display. Presumably, the royal house maintained some interest in the settlement, which was most likely intended as a focus for sedentarization of the local tribes (see Chapter 2), but no evidence survives. Schmid (2001c: 191; cf. Glueck 1965: 138, 512–13; Hackl et al. 2003: 217–18) has suggested that the *r's 'yn l'aban* ("Master of the Spring of La'aban") attested in a late first-century BC Nabataean inscription found near Khirbet edh-Dharih was an official equivalent to a Roman *curator aquarum*. If that is the case, such a royal official may also have regulated exploitation of the 'Ain Jammam and 'Ain Ghana. The local sheikhs probably worked out among themselves problems involving land and water rights and public order at Hawara proper, referring only intractable problems to the king at public audiences (cf. Strabo 16.4.21, 26). The overflow from Pool no. 63, for example, could have been divided among various fields south of the settlement by timed diversions from the outflow channel. Several documents in the late first- to early second-century Babatha archive and other papyri from the Cave of Letters document the leasing of garden plots with irrigation systems and associated water rights measured by time (e.g., *P. Yadin* no. 7, 44–46; Yadin et al. 2002). This type of traditional system is documented in detail by an inscription of the Roman period at Lamasba in Tunisia (*CIL* 8.18587; Shaw 1982). The system remains in use today in the desert Near East (Lancaster and Lancaster 1999: 147–50).

Surprisingly to western eyes, no rural or urban boundary markers survive even from Roman Hauarra (see Graf 2000; 2001), and only two proprietary inscriptions exist — indicating ownership of funerary monuments rather than any water works (Hayajneh 2001; Bevan and Reeves 2010). The *wasm* (tribal brand) associated with Dam no. 44 may be recent in date. Presumably, individuals or families owned the cisterns they constructed, and they probably exercised some rights over the run-off field that fed them. Such ownership would have been public knowledge to the relatively small and homogeneous regional population in antiquity, as it is today, although a *wasm* mark or simple personal

naming inscription may also have made the claim overt. Elsewhere, expressions of ownership could be more explicit. A Nabataean inscription next to a large cistern at Jebel Ratama (22 km southeast of Humayma) provides both the name of the builder (Shaba, son of Eleh) and a date in the 41st year of Aretas IV (AD 32; Sartre 1993: 169). In a Thamudic inscription at Wadi Ramm, two individuals claim to have "collected rain water at Diwah," probably in a cistern or modified field. This inscription, too, is undoubtedly an indication of ownership (Farès-Drappeau 1995). An early first-century BC Nabataean inscription outside the Siq at Petra also mentions construction and ownership of a cistern (Dalman 1912: 99–101; Hackl et al. 2003: 219–20). Either the inscriptional evidence for ownership of water systems has been lost around Hawara, or owners were reluctant to express themselves in formal inscriptions (see Oleson 2003a: 358–59).

In Islamic law, water that comes from God — seas, lakes and marshes, rivers, water flowing underground, and wells dug by an unknown person — is free for all to use. Water that has been made more productive by human hands, particularly by containment in a well, cistern, reservoir, pipe, channel, or jar can be owned (Lancaster and Lancaster 1999: 129–33; Wilkinson 1977: 97–121). Owned water may be taken by anyone to allow the survival of men and animals, but not for the sake of profit. Rainwater and spring water that appear on private property belong to the owner of the property, and run-off water captured in a cistern belongs to the owner of the cistern (Lancaster and Lancaster 1999: 143–44). Various tribes owned the springs around Wadi Musa in the early twentieth century, but this probably was a side effect of ownership of the land (Canaan 1929: 198). It is likely that these rules codify long-standing practices in the desert regions of the Nabataean kingdom.

The Nabataean inhabitants of Hawara most likely felt that their gods (or god, cf. Healey 2001: 84–85) had a role to play in filling their reservoirs and protecting their contents. Betyls ("Dushara Block" images; Healey 2001: 155) of greater or lesser elaboration can be seen carved on the walls of four rock-cut cisterns in the region around Hawara (Structure nos. 14, 26, 37, 48), on the cliff wall near Dam no. 44, and on a slab reused (?) near the draw hole of Reservoir no. 68 in the settlement centre. The images on three of the cisterns are simple outlines of a block with spreading foot (nos. 14, 26, 37), while at Cistern no. 48 a carefully carved frame surrounds a niche containing three blocks or a taller central block framed by two altars (fig. 3.89). The relief at Reservoir no. 68 carries three recessed block images below an arched roof (fig 4.22), while the block at Dam no. 44 is so wide and thick (H 0.60 m, W 1.90 m, Th 0.50 m) that it probably served as an altar or base that held betyls inset into the five cuttings in its upper surface (fig. 3.104). The greater elaboration of the representations of divinity at the reservoir and dam can be explained by the greater expense and public character of those structures, while the niche by Cistern no. 48 may be part of a shrine complex including the cistern, the distinctive cave, and numerous graffiti.

Although Dushara does not seem to have been specifically connected with storms or water, as a source of blessings he undoubtedly was thought to have the power to bestow or protect a good supply of water (Healey 2001: 93). In any case, it has recently been shown that these aniconic images can represent a variety of deities (Wenning 2001: 79). Whatever their precise meaning, betyls and dedicatory inscriptions to the god Dushara appear in association with Nabataean water-works and springs at Petra (Wenning 2001: 82; Parr 1962), and at sites such as 'Ain Shellaleh at Iram/Ramm (Savignac 1932: 581–82), Hegra (Wenning, personal communication 2002), and Oboda (Glueck 1959: 223–24; 1965: pl. 210). Given the crucial social importance of the water supply, it might seem curious to the modern observer that betylic images of the gods are not found more often in association with the hydraulic structures in and around Hawara. Loss of a portion of the images can be expected, but the survival of only six across with the whole water-supply system of Hawara indicates that representations of the deity were not considered essential. More than 500 such niches have been recorded at Petra (Wenning 2001: 79), but nearly always in association with torrents or aqueducts rather than cisterns (R. Wenning, personal communication November 2002). As a result, it seems likely that the Nabataeans felt that running water had some particular association with the gods.

Perhaps the presence of an image was not generally felt to be critical to divine protection once the water had been "captured." The absence of betyls in association with the Hawara aqueduct system clearly differs from the practice at Petra, but it may be the result of geology: the lack of smooth bedrock cliffs along much of its course.

No evidence survives for any community planning or collaboration in the development of the Nabataean water-supply system beyond the presumed initial provision of the aqueduct and Reservoirs 63, 67 and 68. Families built cisterns for their own use when and where they were needed, close to the settlement or around the edges of the catchment. The Roman garrison that arrived early in the second century naturally approached the provision of water from a different perspective. The location for the fort was selected as much on the basis of military considerations as on water supply. The fort required a large, relatively level piece of property close to the settlement centre and the main north–south land route, with a view of the route south towards the Wadi al-Yutum and north to a signal station at the former Nabataean caravanserai or fort 6.5 km north of Hauarra. Self-sufficiency in water was crucial to the security of the garrison, so there had to be significant water-storage capacity within the walls. Since the selection of a location suitable for the collection of run-off water would have left the fort open to observation and attack from higher ground, the fort was forced to depend on water diverted from the Nabataean aqueduct. The extreme vulnerability of this water source was mitigated by feeding the water into a holding reservoir within the walls that fed an internal system of pressurised terracotta pipes. It was suggested above that a constant flow through this system refreshed the reservoir water at least every three weeks. If the flow from the aqueduct were cut off, the garrison could survive approximately six months on the stored water.

Although rights of access and methods of sharing the water carried to Hawara by the aqueduct most likely had been decided by local sheikhs or imposed by royal fiat not long after the system was completed, it is unlikely the Roman commander consulted or compensated any local authority regarding the diversion of aqueduct water to the fort.

Even apart from the unbalanced relationship between victor and vanquished, the aqueduct system was most likely still considered royal property in AD 106 and, in consequence, within the control of the new provincial administrators. It is no coincidence that the arrangements for distributing the reduced overflow from the aqueduct pool soon changed as well. The simple overflow conduit of typically Nabataean design was replaced by a pressurised lead pipe system regulated by a stopcock installed behind a locked grating at the south end of the pool. Since the pipe conducted water to a typical Roman military bath building, it seems likely that the new political authority had claimed ownership of the entire aqueduct discharge. By at least the third century, any remaining flow was diverted through pressurised terracotta pipes to the *vicus* south of the fort. Once the aqueduct pool had become essentially a closed tank, it is unlikely that the proprietors of the bath building would have allowed its continued use for bathing.

Since we do not yet know the use to which the original inhabitants of Hawara had put the overflow from the aqueduct pool, it is impossible to judge how the change in administration of the aqueduct after AD 106 affected the civilians. If the Nabataean structure beneath the Roman bath had been a Nabataean bath in the first century, it was now, of course, derelict. Given the size of the fort in relation to the second-century bath, it seems unlikely that civilians could have been accommodated in it alongside the soldiers. The loss of bathing privileges would not have been a disaster for Hawara, but the loss of a small but constant flow of water to fields of vegetables or orchards downstream from the pool would have had some sort of impact. We can no longer document that event, but it did not affect the viability of the civilian settlement, which continued to thrive during the Roman and Byzantine periods.

7.E.5. *Modern Ethnographic Data for Water Use at Humayma (Based on a report by Judith D. Mitchell)*

Some of the practices for the administration of water for Hawara reconstructed above can be paralleled in the practices of modern Bedouin, both at Humayma and elsewhere. Although the modern parallels are more likely to be the result of common sense and practicality than of direct inheritance from antiquity, it can still be useful to examine some of the data. In July 1992, Mitchell interviewed a number of family members of the local Bedouin employed on the Humayma Excavation Project concerning their use of the renovated ancient cisterns on the site and their application of the water to human and animal needs. The procedures were approved by the Human Research Ethics Board of the University of Victoria. This presentation of the results has been adapted from a report submitted to Oleson in 1994. The catalogue numbers used in Chapters 3 and 4 have been added to any local names for the cisterns. Eight informants were interviewed between 7 and 21 July 1992. All informants identified themselves as members of the Huweitat tribe and from the Bedul lineage. Seven of these informants were interviewed personally through an interpreter. One informant submitted a written response to the questionnaire.

Informant no. 1

Family Name: Muasi. Head of household: Salameh. Number of people in household: 10. This informant stated that at present his family used the cistern catalogued here as Reservoir 67. He claimed that it was purchased by the family during the Ottoman rule, approximately three hundred years ago, and had been used by them as a water source ever since. He reported that the cistern had been cleaned out at the time of the British mandate and that, according to tradition, the work had cost 120 gold guineas, 6 large tins of ghee (clarified butter), 200 cups of dried yogurt, and 200 cups of wheat flour. Retaining walls were also built at a cost of 3,000 guineas. He referred to the measurements of the cleaned area in terms of "arm stretches" (fathoms?), with one arm stretch equalling approximately 1.5 m. The length was equal to 7 arm stretches, the circumference was equal to 19 arm stretches, and the total depth of the cleaned area was equal to seven times the height of an adult. (None of these dimensions correspond with the dimensions of Reservoir no. 67, but the informant clearly intended this structure.) A total of 10 family members in the household use the water, which is collected daily by anyone able to do so. Access to the cistern is allowed to immediate kin, consisting of the informant, his sons and their families, the informant's brother, the brother's two wives and fourteen children, and to his brother's grandchildren. The informant stated this to be a little over fifty people. The time of collection varies daily, but generally occurs between 5:00 a.m. and 6:30 p.m. In winter, a total of seven 25-litre jerry cans are taken daily for human consumption, and in summer ten 25-litre cans of water are withdrawn daily. Traditionally, the water was transported in goatskin bags carried by donkeys, but in the late 1980s the switch was made to jerry cans transported by pick-up trucks.

In "the old days," once the water reached the household it was kept in goatskin containers placed on grassy herbs strewn on the floor. These containers were then covered with more grass to keep the water cool. At present, plastic jerry cans are covered with wet burlap to assist the cooling process through evaporation. There are no restrictions as to who can use the water in the informant's household. It is consumed by drinking, body washing (10 litres per person per day), and washing clothes, for which three jerry cans are set aside each day. Children's clothes are washed every day, whereas adult clothing is washed every second day.

The informant added that in "the old days" people came from Kerak and Tafila to trade and sell their agricultural products. A goat was killed to feed these guests, and they were provided with water as well. He stated that fig trees used to grow around the cisterns but that they died in a drought "around seven years ago" (1985?). Oleson did not see any fig trees at this location upon his first visit in 1981, but shadows possibly produced by trees in the appropriate location can be seen on British air force aerial photographs taken in 1937–38. The "old men" in the community remember the trees well and have eaten from them.

The informant stated that his household owned approximately 200 sheep and 97 goats. Some of these animals are brought to the cistern to be watered, while others are watered at home. The scheduled watering takes place daily from noon to 1:00 p.m. He stated that when it is hot, the flock consumes 2.5 cum of water. Often sheets of plastic

are transported in a pick-up truck so that they can be improvised to hold pumped water. The water is then dumped into the animal troughs at home. The sheep are watered first and then the goats. The informant reported that the cistern had been used that very year until it went dry in mid-June. His family is now buying water from Quweira. Water purchased by the tank is subsidised by the government. A tank of water can be bought for 2 JD if a certificate can be produced as proof that the household owns sheep; if not, the tank costs 6 JD. One tank of water lasts his household approximately four days. When the truck arrives with the tank of water, it is emptied into four cement pools near his house. He added that about eight years ago, water began to be piped from al-Mureighah to New Humayma. Each household has bought a pipe and the water is metered. To qualify for piped water, one must possess a dwelling structure or a storage hut to facilitate the installation of a water outlet.

Informant no. 2

Family Name: Muasi. Head of household: Salem. Number of people in Household: 18. This informant is the brother of Informant no. 1. He uses Reservoir no. 67 as well. He confirmed that the reservoir was bought by the family during Ottoman rule 300 years ago and that it has been used since the Turks had been there. He also mentioned the fig trees that used to be around the cistern. He stated that the cistern had been cleaned in Ottoman times and that the family had cleaned it in recent times as well.

In his household, anyone who is capable of it collects the water, daily or every second day, depending on the needs of the family. He estimated that 3 to 4 cum of water are taken for human consumption each time. The water is transported either in jerry cans, which are carried by a pick-up truck, or in a water tank drawn by his tractor. The informant stated that once the water reaches the house, it is stored in the cement pools mentioned by Informant no. 1, jerry cans, and buckets. He mentioned that his brother's household and his own were the only households that have rightful access to the cistern water.

There are no restrictions as to who uses the household water. The informant estimated that most of the household water is used for washing clothes and for personal washing. The rest is designated for cooking and drinking. This informant owns 100 sheep, 10 goats, and 2 camels. He employs a shepherd who is also responsible for watering the animals; they are watered daily around noon. He stated that the total water consumed daily by the animals is one cubic metre. Sheep are watered first, next the goats, and the camels last. This informant stated that piped water was also available to his household at New Humayma and that household members were using it at present because Reservoir no. 67 was dry.

Informant no. 3

Family Name: Jdailat, Head of household: Ali. Number of People in Household: 7. This informant claimed to own 60–70 dunams and a cistern in the hilly area of Hdeibet al-Khadem just northwest of the Humayma site. This cistern is most likely Cistern no. 59. The informant described the cistern as being ancient. He claimed that it was given to the family a long time ago and that family members have cleaned and restored it.

The informant stated that the water is generally obtained on a daily basis, but sometimes only every other day. He reported that when there is water in the cistern, 10 to 15 25-litre jerry cans are taken each time by anyone in the family and that it was not any particular person's duty to do this. In the past, water was transported from the cistern to the household in goatskin bags, but at present jerry cans are used to transport the water. Sometimes the water is transported in a portable metal tank and then transferred to jerry cans at the household, and at times the water is just left in the tank. Pick-up trucks and tractors are used to convey the jerry cans and tanks, respectively.

The informant stated that the only other household that has rightful access to his cistern is that of his cousin. The informant mentioned that there were no restrictions placed on who used the water in his household and that the bulk of the water is used for washing clothes and bathing. The rest is used for cooking and drinking.

The animals are generally watered daily at the cistern between noon and 1:00 p.m., but because of the present drought, he is now bringing water to them at the household. The total consumption of all the animals is one cubic metre of water per day. The informant claimed that the hierarchical watering of the sheep, then goats and lastly, the camels, was the natural way arranged by the animals and not a watering order contrived by man. He stated that he had no piped water of his own due to the fact that he is a nomad with no set place of residence. At present, his brother and friends were supplying his household with piped water because there was no water in his cistern.

Informant no. 4

Family Name: Hasassin. Head of household: Suleiman 'Audeh. Number of People in Household: 6. This informant stated that the members of his household presently resided in the town of New Humayma and used piped water, which they paid for by meter rating. His father used a cistern, but the informant was unable to identify which one this was at the Humayma site. The informant stated that his father's family cleaned the cistern and they had used it from the 1950s onwards. At that time, they owned and resided on the land in close proximity to the cistern.

The informant stated that water was collected from the cistern by any member of the household on a daily basis in the summer and every two days in the winter. He did not know how much was taken each time. Special black rubber water bags were used to contain the water, and these bags were transported from the cistern to the household by way of donkey. Once at the household, the water would either remain in the bags or be transferred into barrels. There were no restrictions placed on who was able to use the water in the household. The bulk of the water was used for washing bodies and clothes. Water was only fetched from the cistern and conveyed to the household for human consumption. His father's household contained six members and his father's cousin's household had nine people. Both these households had rightful access to the cistern water.

His father had 60–70 sheep and goats in all. These animals were taken to the cistern for watering on a daily basis at noon. On very cold winter days, the animals were watered every other day. Both his father's animals and the animals of his father's cousin could be watered at noon simultaneously. He was not able to recollect how much water was consumed by the animals daily. The informant stated that goats were watered first and then the sheep. He claimed that if you tried to stop the goats from watering you would stop the sheep, because sheep tend to follow the goats as a natural course of events.

Informant no. 5

Family Name: al-Jaramyeh. Head of Household: Mohammad Hamad. Number of People in Household: 21. This informant asserted family claims to Cisterns 54, 57, 65, 66, 71, and 73. The last is no longer in use. He stated that he owned 76 dunams at the Humayma site, and that this land had been in the family since before his grandfather's time. He stated that Cistern no. 66 had been cleared by his family in 1951, when they had been able to afford to do so. At that time, they lived in close proximity to the cistern and had built small troughs to hold winter water for the animals and themselves. The informant stated that before 1951, water had been brought to the household from Beidha by camels. This toponym is applied ambiguously to a locality north and northeast of Humayma, but the source of the water is not clear.

Cistern water was obtained daily by the women and the sons of his household. The water was transported to the household by camels and donkeys that carried a total of 22 20-litre jerry cans on each trip. At the household, the water was transferred into barrels for storage.

Only the informant's household and that of his father have rightful access to the cistern water. Occasionally, they will allow others to use the cisterns for water as a special favour. Within the informant's household, there are no restrictions as to who can use the water. The main consumption of this water is associated with eating and drinking.

This informant stated that his household owned 40 sheep, 35 goats, 8 camels, and 8 don-keys. At this point in the interview, the informant became impatient with the questioning and would only state that the animals were watered daily at noon. He added that camels were watered first, goats second, then sheep and donkeys.

Informant no. 6

Family Name: al-Jaramyeh. Heads of household: ʿUtaiqa and Abdula. Number of people in household: 2. This informant claimed to own Cistern no. 55. At present, this cistern is being used to water only the animals of her household and her brothers' animals.

Small metal tanks and jerry cans are kept at her household and are filled with water brought from either al-Mureighah or Quweira by tanker. The informant stated that water was ordered by phone as needed. A tank of water from the government cost 2.20 JD, whereas a tank from a private source cost 10 JD.

The informant stated that her household owned 40 sheep, 25 goats, and 2 donkeys. These animals are watered daily at mid-day. They consume approximately as much water as can be contained in 11 jerry cans. She stated that sometimes the animals were watered at the household and not at the cistern. The informant stated that there was no special order for watering the animals.

Informant no. 7

Family Name: al-Muwasa. Head of household: Mohammad Abdula. Number of People in Household: 14. This was a written response to the questionnaire.

The informant described his family's cistern as ancient and identified it as the "Mdeisi cistern" in Old Humayma. The location of this cistern on the Humayma site could not be identified. The informant wrote that the cistern has been used since 1850, when it was first cleaned out. It is now cleaned out regularly every year. Water collection from the cistern is a joint effort by all members of the household. It is done daily in the summer and on alternate days in the winter. The amount of water taken daily amounts to 120 litres, and this is transported in three large goatskin bags, carried either by camels, donkeys, or mules. When the water reaches the household, it is transferred to other bags.

The informant stated that his cousins also use this cistern and that travellers are always allowed access to water and food. There are no restrictions on who uses the water in his household. The water is consumed by activities such as drinking, cooking, washing clothes, and twice weekly bathing by household members.

The informant stated that his household owns 150 goats, 100 sheep, 20 camels, 2 horses, and 5 donkeys. With the exception of the camels, all the animals are taken to the cistern daily between noon and 1:30 p.m. The camels are watered once every four days. According to this informant, on a daily basis 1–2 litres of water are consumed by each goat, 3 litres by each sheep, 15 litres by each donkey, 5 litres by each horse and 75 litres by each camel. The informant indicated that sheep were watered first, goats next, then donkeys and horses, and lastly camels.

Informant no. 8

Family Name: Musa. Head of household: Abdula Issa. Number of People in Household: 13. This informant described his family's cistern as being located at Jebel Humayma. He stated that the cistern was cleaned a long time ago by his father's grandfather and is now cleaned regularly when it becomes too full of silt.

The water is collected for human use daily in jerry cans and large water bags, and every two days for the sheep and goats. He estimated that the household population used an amount of water equivalent to two large barrels (total ca. 300 l?). This water is transported from the cistern by donkey and is emptied into a metal tank at the household. There are no restrictions on who is allowed to use the water in the household. He stated that five other households of his cousins have access to the cistern. The water is used mostly for bathing and washing clothes, but also for drinking.

This informant states that his household owns 5 sheep, 4 goats and 2 donkeys. Water is brought to the house for the goats and sheep by anyone in the household. The animals are watered twice daily, at noon and in the evening. The informant stated that each sheep consumes 2 litres of water per day and each goat, 1 litre. He stated that there is no hierarchical order for animal watering, that the animals all drank together.

Field Observations at Cistern no. 55

The only cistern that was being used during the researcher's time at the Humayma site was Cistern 55. On 15 July 1992, at approximately 11:00 a.m., the researcher positioned herself near the cistern to observe at what time Informant no. 6 would arrive to water her herds of sheep and goats and what procedures she would follow. By 11:30 a.m., Informant no. 6 and her herds were observed in the open area northeast of the escarpment into which Cistern no. 55 was cut. At 12:05 p.m., she arrived at the cistern, followed by one very young goat, and acknowledged the researcher's greeting. The elderly informant picked up a metal bucket, which was lying near the cistern, then struggled up the incline to the alcove containing the cistern opening. As she lowered the bucket through the opening on a rope, it banged continuously against the rock walls of the cistern until reaching the water level. She hauled the water up and poured it down an improvised metal chute into a trough made from leather skins; the young goat stood on the ground below her and bleated for its mother.

Within several minutes, the informant's young granddaughter arrived with the rest of the goats and sheep, the goats being well in the lead. There was a general push by the animals for the watering trough and they consumed the water as quickly as it could be hauled from the cistern and poured down the chute. In the meantime, the informant's grandson climbed the escarpment with several of his friends and took over the water drawing. The researcher was encouraged by the men to come and take a turn. It was strenuous work, as it was necessary to swing the bucket in pendulum fashion while lowering it, in order to find the pool of water for dipping. At this point in the season, the water did not lie directly beneath the cistern opening but rather to the west of its aperture. The informant became nervous that the researcher would fall into the cistern and asked her to cease drawing water.

She also warned the researcher against drinking the water, as it was not healthy for humans. At 12:40 p.m. the young men left, leaving the informant and her granddaughter to complete the daily watering of the sheep and goats.

Interpretation of the Survey

Recurrent patterns appeared in the information given by these informants with regard to water resources and its collection and usage. In all instances there was a proprietary attitude towards the cistern water, and there was a clear link between kinship and access to the water held in specific cisterns. The household of Informant no. 6 was the only household that used their cistern water only for animals and obtained water for human consumption from other sources. Informant no. 1 mentioned that guests had been provided with water from his household cistern in the past. Informant no. 7 stated that travellers were always allowed access to water. None of the informants stated or implied that access to the individual cisterns was allowed to anyone who wished it. Each informant knew exactly who had access to the water in his or her own cistern. Claims by Informants no. 1 and no. 2 of their exclusive right to the use of Reservoir no. 67 may be exaggerated, since the excavation team has observed many different individuals drawing water from this source. All but one informant specifically mentioned that their immediate families, or ancestors, had cleaned their cisterns or restored them. In all but two instances, water collection for human consumption did not appear to be the specific job of any particular person in the household.

Jerry cans appeared to be the most commonly used containers for transporting water from the cistern to the household. One informant still continued to use goatskin bags for this purpose. Collection of the water by a tanker truck was also mentioned by two informants. Three of the informants stated that their water containers were at present being transported to the household either by pick-up truck or tractor. They mentioned however, that donkeys had been used for this purpose until four years ago. Four of the informants described the water as being conveyed to their households by camel, donkey, or mule.

The amount of water consumed by humans and animals varied from household to household. However, seven of the eight informants claimed to know the exact amount of cistern water that was consumed daily by the humans living in their households. Seven of the informants also claimed to know the amount of cistern water consumed daily by their animals. Information revealed that in seven households there were no restrictions placed on who used the water. It appears from the information obtained that, as a general rule, water is collected for human use on a daily basis. In most instances the informants stated that the bulk of the water was used for bathing and washing clothes.

Although the number of animals varied from household to household, one fact remained clear. The animals of all eight informants were watered daily at mid-day, between noon and 1:30 p.m., regardless of whether this activity took place at the cistern or at the household. The mid-day watering of herds by Informant no. 6 at Cistern no. 55 was confirmed by field observation. The only animals that were reported as not requiring daily watering were the camels belonging to Informant no. 7. Informant no. 8 watered his animals in the evenings as well as at noon.

There was no consensus among the informants as to whether the animals followed a hierarchical watering order. Two informants stated that there was no set order. Four informants stated that sheep were watered first. Five of the informants listed the goats as having second place for watering. Informant no. 4 was adamant that the goats must be watered first, because he stated that sheep are naturally prone to follow the goats. Informant no. 5 stated that the order was camels, then goats, then sheep. The claim by Informant no. 4 that goats take priority for watering is supported by the literature. Goats and sheep are herded together in arid areas, primarily because each species exploits different vegetation in the environment. They are also herded together because goats tend to move along rather quickly as they browse, causing the sheep to follow along, thereby avoiding the overgrazing of an area (Hopkins 1993: 204–7; Campbell and Roe 1998). During the investigator's field observation at Cistern 55, it did not appear to be coincidental that Informant no. 6 came ahead of the herd with a young goat in the lead. Sheep do tend to follow goats and herders make good use of this trait.

It is not surprising that close kinship and access rights to the water of specific cisterns are linked among the Bedouin in the Humayma region. In most instances, the household cistern is located on land that is owned by the informant's family. Because of the cost of importing tanks of water, either from Quweira or al-Mureighah, it seems practical that each household would safeguard the preciously collected winter rainwater. Kinship rights to well water have been documented for various semi-nomadic tribes throughout the world (Barfield 1993; Lancaster and Lancaster 1999: 129–66). The situation around Humayma, however, is somewhat different in that proprietary claims are linked to rain-harvested water held in cisterns, rather than to ground-fed well water. It is interesting to note that even when access to piped water is needed by the Bedouin of New Humayma who lack water outlets themselves, it is to close family kin that they turn for provision of this service.

Chapter 8

The Hawara Water-Supply System
in the Context of the Ancient Near East

8.A. A SURVEY OF NABATAEAN, ROMAN, AND BYZANTINE WATER-SUPPLY SYSTEMS IN THE SOUTHERN NABATAEAN REGION

The archaeological and textual evidence presented in the previous chapters provides a remarkably detailed and, very likely, nearly complete picture of the water-supply system that served ancient Hawara. Where clarification or explanation was needed, I cited examples of hydraulic structures at other ancient sites, but I did not attempt a thorough review of archaeological parallels. This chapter is reserved for a more detailed examination of the techniques and structures that constituted Nabataean hydraulic technology, in particular as they are seen working within coordinated urban and/or rural water-supply systems. I will review some of the well-preserved systems that served a variety of settlements both large and small within the southern Nabataean cultural region, noting their similarities and differences with the Hawara system, their output or capacities, and their relation to topography, climate, and settlement size. These settlements for the most part were Nabataean creations that — like those at Hawara — continued to flourish to some degree during the Roman, Byzantine, and Early Islamic cultural periods. This typical site history also allows some analysis of the development of these water-supply systems across time. In the end, we are very well-provided with material

evidence for Nabataean hydraulic technology, but the general absence of corresponding textual evidence means that we remain less well-informed about related questions of ownership, legal rights, social meaning, and finances. Nevertheless, some relevant papyri, inscriptions, and literary sources have survived and will be discussed below.

Petra, the cultural and political capital of Nabataea, is only 45 km northwest of Humayma in a direct line, so it is natural that the history and culture of Hawara should reflect developments and events in that centre. In consequence, it is particularly important to note the details of the water-supply system for Petra as a possible model for the Hawara system. Evidence from Nabataean sites farther away and in somewhat different topographical and climatic situations, such as the settlements in the Negev, will be presented more selectively.

8.A.1. *The Water-Supply System of Petra*

The bibliography concerned with Petra is enormous, and nearly all of it, whether archaeological or historical in character, makes some reference to the water-supply system or elements of it. The most useful recent surveys of the site and its structures, often including some discussion of the water-supply system, include the following: Frösén and Fiema 2002; Markoe 2003; McKenzie 1990; Schmid and Kolb 2000; Stucky et al. 1996; Weber and Wenning

1997; Wenning 1987: 197–304; Zayadine, Larché, and Dentzer-Feydy 2003. The long survey in Brünnow and Domaszewski (1904–9: 1, pp. 137–428) contains information that is still useful. The main aspects of the water-supply system are best explained by Bellwald and al-Huneidi 2003 and Bellwald 2007, but much useful information is presented by the following authors: Akasheh 2002; Bedal and Schryver 2007; Bellwald 2007; Dalman 1908: 37–41; 1912: 15–18; Gunsam 1989; Lindner and Hübl 1997; Lindner 1984; 1987a; 1987b; 2003; al-Muheisen 1983; 1990; Parr 1967. Ortloff 2005 must be used with great caution. Z. al-Muheisen 2009, which contains useful photographs and descriptions of the Petra water-supply system, only came to my attention when this book was already in press.

Petra: Historical Background

The southeastern portion of the Nabataean kingdom — Arabia Petraea — was proverbially a rocky desert in which human ingenuity was needed to supplement or preserve the few sources of water. Herodotus (3.6–7) reports that the Persians crossed the region by caching amphoras of water at strategic points. He also reports (3.9), with scepticism, that the "king of the Arabians" filled reservoirs cut in the ground (δεξαμενὰς ὀρύξασθαι) deep in the desert by means of three long pipelines (ὀχετοί) made of sewn ox hides. Strabo reports that Arabia Petraea was sandy and barren, with little vegetation and "water obtained by digging" (ὀρυκτὰ ὕδατα). This term could apply to the excavation both of wells and of cisterns filled by run-off. The long description of the early Nabataean way of life in Diodorus (19.94.2–10), probably taken from the late fourth- or early third-century BC historian Hieronymus of Cardia (Hackl et al. 2003: 449–50, 452, 464–65), reports the same challenges and technologies in fuller form.

> [The Nabataeans] live in the open air, claiming as native land a wilderness that has neither rivers nor abundant springs from which it is possible for a hostile enemy to obtain water. It is their custom not to plant grain, nor set out any fruit-bearing tree, use wine, or construct any house;

and if anyone is found acting contrary to this, death is his penalty … Some of them raise camels, others sheep, pasturing them in the desert. While there are many Arabian tribes that use the desert as pasture, the Nabataeans far surpass the others in wealth although they are not much more than ten thousand in number, for not a few of them are accustomed to bring down to the sea frankincense and myrrh and the most valuable kinds of spices, which they procure from those who convey them from what is called Arabia Eudaemon. They are exceptionally fond of freedom. Whenever a strong force of enemies comes near, they take refuge in the desert, using this in place of a fortress. For the desert lacks water and cannot be crossed by others, but to them alone it furnishes safety, since they have prepared cisterns dug into the earth (ἀγγεῖα κατὰ γῆς ὀρύκτα) and lined with plaster … As the earth in some places is … of soft stone, they make great excavations in it, the mouths of which they make very small, but by constantly increasing the width as they dig deeper, they finally make them of such a size that each side can be one *plethron* long [27 m; sic!]. After filling these cisterns with rain water, they close the openings, making them even with the rest of the ground, and they leave signs that are known to them but are unrecognisable to others (Geer 1954: 87–89).

Diodorus has either mistaken or exaggerated the dimensions of the cisterns. He provides similar information in an earlier book (2.48.1–6), although he uses the word φρέατα there rather than ἀγγεῖα. For Byzantine Greek authors, φρέαρ can mean "cistern" as often as "well."

> For in the waterless region (ἄνυδρος χώρα), as it is called, (the Nabataeans) have prepared cisterns (φρέατα) at convenient intervals and have kept the knowledge of them hidden from the peoples of all other nations, and so they retreat in a body into this region out of danger. For since they

themselves know about the places of hidden water and open them up, they have for their use drinking water in abundance (δαψιλῆ ποτά) (Oldfather 1935: 41–44).

Although the issue is complex and disputed, the association of the name "Nabataean" with excavated cisterns and hydraulic engineering may be reflected in Old South Arabic (Sabaic), where the verb *nbt* signifies "to dig down for water" (Graf in Gibb 1986–2002, s.v. "Nabat"). On the other hand, Uranius reports that in Arabic the root *Nabates* can also be construed as the unrelated term "bastard" (Bowersock 2003: 25).

In this hostile landscape, Petra stands out as the one place with an ample supply of water, provided both by the abundant springs and by the run-off from precipitation that is significantly higher than elsewhere in the region (150–200 mm/year; fig. 2.9). Strabo, using the eyewitness account of his friend Athenodorus (see Graf 2009), alludes to the special character of the site (16.4.21).

> The metropolis of the Nabataeans is called Petra, "The Rock," because it occupies a site that is mainly smooth and level but is fenced in all around by rock, the outside being precipitous and sheer. Within, there are abundant springs, used for both domestic purposes and for irrigating gardens (ἐπὶ χωρίου … πηγὰς ἀφθόνους ἔχοντος εἴς τε ὑδρείαν καὶ κηπείαν). Outside the circuit of the rock most of the territory is desert … (Jones 1917–32: vol. 7, pp. 351–53).

Most of these "gardens," except for the king's *paradeisos* (see below), probably were intended to produce food, since the pleasure gardens associated with private tomb complexes, such as the Turkamaniya Tomb, seem to have been supplied from adjacent cisterns filled by run-off. Many of the tomb inscriptions mention both cisterns and *triclinia*, but the longest survives on the Turkamaniya Tomb (Browning 1982: 233; Cantineau 1930–32: vol. 2, pp. 3–5).

> This tomb and the large and small chambers inside, and the graves made as loculi, and the courtyard in front of the tomb,

and the porticoes and the dwelling places within it, and the gardens and the triclinium, the water cisterns (*shwt*), the terrace and the walls, and the remainder of the whole property which is in these places, is the consecrated and inviolable property of Dusares …

Several of the Petra papyri mention fields that produced wine, wheat, and orchard fruits, but these seem to have been in the hinterland rather than the town centre (Koenen 1996: 181, 183–85).

Pliny the Elder's observations about Petra are similar to those of Strabo, but he seems to confuse the springs with the Wadi Musa.

> Next are the Nabataeans, inhabiting a town named Petra. It lies in a deep valley a little less than two miles wide, with a river flowing down the middle (*amne interfluente*). Inaccessible mountains surround it (*HN* 6.144).

The strongest of these springs, now called 'Ain Musa, the "Spring of Moses," is traditionally associated with the spring Moses created at God's command to quench the thirst of the People of Israel as they made their way through Edom during the Exodus (Numbers 20: 8, 11–12).

> The Lord spoke to Moses and said, "Take a staff, and then with Aaron your brother assemble all the community, and in front of them all, speak to the rock and it will yield its water. Thus you will produce water for the community out of the rock, for them and their beasts to drink." … Moses raised his hand and struck the rock twice with his staff. Water gushed out in abundance and they all drank, men and beasts … Such were the waters of Meribah, where the people disputed with the Lord and through which his holiness was upheld.

Although the connection remains in the realm of folklore, the combination of abundant spring water and surrounding rocky desert certainly is reminiscent of Petra.

FIG. 8.1 *Map of Petra with indication of water-supply systems (after Bellwald 2007: 317, with permission). 1: as-Siq aqueduct (from 'Ain Musa). 2: North Khubtha aqueduct (from 'Ain Musa). 3: 'Ain Brak aqueduct. 4: 'Ain Debdebah aqueduct. 5: 'Ain Abu Ullayqa aqueduct.*

Petra: Springs and the Aqueduct Systems

The water-supply system of Petra, like that of Ha-wara, depended for the most part on spring-fed aqueducts and pipelines, along with built or rock-cut cisterns filled by run-off from precipitation.

Unlike Hawara, however, the settlement centre proper contained relatively few run-off cisterns and depended for the most part on aqueduct water. The system also involved terraces and wadi barri-ers intended to slow run-off so it could soak into the soil, as well as a few dams. In fact, unlike most

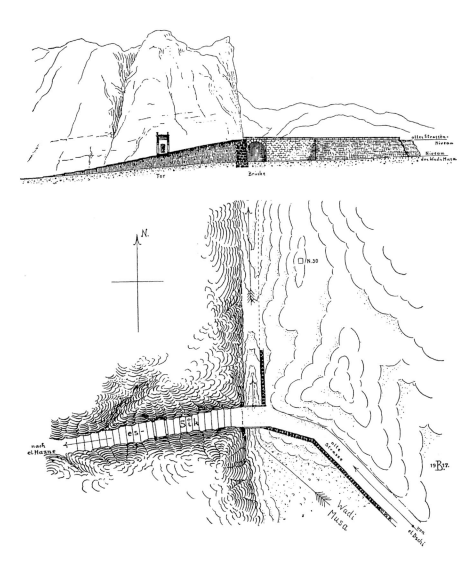

FIG. 8.2   *Tunnel and remains of dam at entrance to Siq. Petra. (Bachmann et al. 1921: 63).*

Nabataean settlements, a combination of topography and precipitation patterns meant that Petra occasionally had problems with too much water (al-Muheisen and Tarrier 1996; Akasheh 2002). During winter storms, the Khubtha, Jilf, Madrass, and Qantara massifs that frame the winding Siq quickly generate enormous quantities of run-off. Much of this enters the Siq, which then can turn into a deep, raging torrent. In addition, the Wadi Musa, which drains much of the mountain towering above the settlement centre, found its natural outlet through the Siq, across the centre of the habitation area, then down to the Wadi Arabah through the Wadi Siyyagh (fig. 8.1).

A coordinated effort was made to solve this problem in the second half of the first century BC (Bellwald and al-Huneidi 2003), so that the entrance to the city could be regularised and monumentalised, and several aqueducts and pipelines could be installed in the Siq to serve the growing settlement centre. First, a dam was constructed across the entrance to the Siq to divert the Wadi Musa water through an impressive rock-cut tunnel (L 88 m, W 6 m) into the Wadi Mudhlim (fig. 8.2). This narrow gorge fed the Wadi Mataha, which rejoined the Wadi Musa in the city centre, safely past the Siq. An inscription dates some work on the dam and tunnel to the reign of either Malichus II

FIG. 8.3   *Detention dam (in background) and bridge for southern aqueduct in Siq. Petra.*

(39/40–70) or Rabbel II (70–106), but the original project must date to the third quarter of the first century BC (Parr 1967; Bellwald and al-Huneidi 2003: 45–47). Secondly, numerous detention dams and associated "stilling basins" were constructed across the major natural run-off channels leading into the Siq from both sides. These barriers were provided with openings (D 0.14 m) near the base, so that the water behind them would be released slowly, spreading the run-off over many hours, and thus avoiding dangerous peak flow (fig. 8.3). Artificial, reedy ponds were also constructed to further delay the flow into the paved Siq (Bellwald and al-Huneidi 2003: fig. 125). The calculation of peak run-off and of the corresponding capacity of the detention structures was very accurate, and the reconstructed system now functions effectively to protect visitors and the archaeological remains (Bellwald and al-Huneidi 2003: 69–75; Bellwald 2004).

The output from at least four springs was brought to various parts of the Petra centre, at an altitude of ca. 900 m, by means of rock-cut and built aqueduct channels, sometimes supplemented with terracotta pipelines: 'Ain Musa (5.5 km east of Petra), 'Ain Brak (3.2 km southeast of Petra), 'Ain Debdebah (5 km north of Petra), and 'Ain Abu Ullayqa (1.2 km north of the centre). As at Hawara, the springs issue from the seam between the layer of Cenomanian limestone at the top of the steep slope towering above Petra and Wadi Musa and the supporting Cambrian sandstone, at an altitude of 1,300–1,400 m (fig. 8.1). Since all these springs are fairly close to the settlement centre, most of the aqueduct courses were very steep, averaging 10 percent (al-Muheisen 1983: 125), but some stretches resembled the precipitous fall of the 'Ain Jammam aqueduct down the Jebel Ghana. Given their greater length and the differences in topography, the average slope for the Ghana aqueduct at Hawara is only 2.24 percent and for the Jammam branch 2.85 percent. The springs to the north and south of Petra apparently served those respective parts of the settlement centre, while the three aqueduct channels fed by the 'Ain Musa discharged directly in the centre, two of them following routes from the Zurraba reservoir through the Siq, the third circling around Jebel Khubtha. The probable route of the path from 'Ain Musa (elev. ca. 1,325 m) to the Zurraba reservoir (elev. 1,050 m) is roughly 3.36 km, for a slope of 8.2 percent. From the reservoir, the path through the Siq to the settlement centre (elev. ca. 880 m) is approximately 3.9 km, for an average slope of 4.4 percent. The course of the North Khubtha aqueduct is roughly 3.14 km, with a fall of ca. 125 m, for an average slope of 4 percent. All these slopes are higher than those of the Hawara system, reflecting the steeper topography around Petra. The combined discharge of the springs in the early 1980s was approximately 574 cum/day: 'Ain Musa 544 cum/day, 'Ain Brak 20 cum/day, 'Ain Debdebah 10 cum/day.

The 'Ain Siyyagh in the Wadi Siyyagh well below the settlement centre has a yield of 90 cum/day (al-Muheisen 1983: 145–46). This last spring fed a conduit of stone blocks, very similar to those of the Hawara aqueducts, that led the water 12 km down the wadi to a reservoir in the Nabataean and Roman settlement at Qasr Umm Rattam (al-Muheisen 1983; Lindner, Hübner, Hübl 2000; Lindner 2005: 46). Lindner calculates a slope of 5 percent for this conduit and notes the presence of five arched bridges, both rock-cut and masonry conduit channels, and the use of terracotta pipes. Although there is no room to discuss them here, there were at least two other spring-fed aqueduct systems in the environs of Petra, serving es-Sabra (Lindner 1982, 2005: 33–43) and es-Sadeh (Lindner, Farajat, Zeitler 1988; Lindner, Farajat, Knauf, Zeitler 1990; Lindner 2003, 2005: 43–44).

Little has been published about the 'Ain Abu Ullayqa conduit, but it originated at the spring in the lower Wadi Turkmaniyya and apparently delivered its water via an open gravity-flow channel and a parallel terracotta pipeline down the Wadi Abu Ullayqa to the Qasr al-Bint (Bellwald and al-Huneidi 2003: 56; Bellwald 2007: 320). Bellwald dates this aqueduct to the late first century BC.

Only a few short descriptions of the 'Ain Debdebah aqueduct have been published (al-Muheisen 1983: 52–56, 166; 2007: 482–84; Bellwald 2007: 320). The spring is above the village of the Amarin Bedouin (aerial view in Kennedy and Bewley 2004: 144), and the system supplied the northwest portion of the city. The channel seems to have consisted for the most part of stone gutter blocks (L 0.70–0.80, W 0.40, H 0.40 m) with cover slabs, frequently supported on block-built viaducts 1.6 m wide, up to 10 m long, and 5 m high. Where possible, the channel was cut in the bedrock. Bellwald indicates that, like the 'Ain Brak system, the 'Ain Debdebah system employed both a gravity-flow channel and a pressurised pipeline with "decompression basins" (Bellwald 2007: 320; Bellwald and al-Huneidi 2003: 55–56; Dalman 1912: 10). Pressure reduction towers, such as those seen in the water system at Pompeii (Larsen 1982) but on a smaller scale, could have performed this function. Al-Muheisen found terracotta pipe sections with strongly flaring terminations set in a channel cut in bedrock and encased in a thick layer of mortar. At one point, the 'Ain Debdebah conduit detoured around a rock-cut cistern (al-Muheisen 1983: 166; 2007: 483), which it filled from two off-takes. Al-Muheisen claims that the overflow was diverted back into the aqueduct again downstream. While such an arrangement would have allowed unattended filling of the cistern, it also raises the possibility of pollution of the main stream. It is more likely that the tank served as an access tank filled by the aqueduct, but that the overflow was simply dumped to avoid polluting the spring source. Al-Muheisen also assumes that branch lines from the aqueduct served the Mughur al-Mataha area, although he did not observe any in situ. According to local Bedouin, 50 years ago the conduit could be traced down to a block-built cistern (9 × 6 × >1.2 m; cap. >64.8 cum) in front of the Qasr al-Bint. The cistern overflow was directed towards the temple in a channel. Bellwald (2007: 320) interprets the use of recycled blocks in the construction of this system to indicate a foundation or renovation late in the first century BC or AD.

The 'Ain Brak aqueduct has been surveyed by several scholars or groups, but only brief discussions have been published (Dalman 1908: 40–41; al-Muheisen 1983: 38–51; 1990: 207–8; Lindner and Hübl 1997; Bellwald 2007: 318–20). Bellwald dates this aqueduct to the late first century BC. Today, the spring issues from a crevice beneath a projecting

FIG. 8.4 *'Ain Brak (next to tree) and pool, in 2005. Petra.*

limestone shelf, at an elevation of about 1,300 m (fig. 8.4). The situation closely resembles that of the 'Ain Jammam at Hawara (figs. 3.2–4). The original arrangements for protection or reception of the spring water have been destroyed or obscured by fill, but a line of roughly-cut conduit blocks heading toward Petra can be seen at one point. The ancient structures on the hillside below the spring have been dated to the first or second century (Lindner and Hübl 1997: 62). 'Ain Brak is about 3.2 km southeast of the settlement centre as the crow flies, and the course (which Lindner, surprisingly, did not measure) can be calculated from maps as roughly 4.2 km. The "efficiency" of the conduit, the ratio of the straight-line distance to constructed length, may be around 76.2 percent, slightly better than that of the Ghana Aqueduct at Hawara (71.5 percent). Bellwald (2007: 319) states that the spring served both a conduit and a pipeline, which frequently followed very different courses, and

that the pipeline included "decompression tanks" below steep stretches, but he does not provide any documentation. Once again, pressure reduction towers such as those seen in the water system at Pompeii could have performed this function (Larsen 1982).

The conduit blocks can be followed down a very steep slope to al-Qantara, where the course levelled off, but then crossed two depressions on massive masonry viaducts (one of them L 14.30, H 7.0, W 1.05 m). Although much of the channel is cut in bedrock in this area, the occasional sandstone conduit blocks are similar in dimensions to those at Hawara (L 0.45, W 0.25 m; channel W 0.10 m, varying depth). The conduit is then associated with and probably filled a rock-cut tank with one masonry wall (9.35 × 7.40 × >3 m; cap. >207.6 cum). Dalman states that the aqueduct passed through the tank, entering through a channel cut in the rock and exiting across the opposite wall. Lindner interprets it as both a settling and storage tank. Since the presence of a large unroofed tank along an aqueduct brings danger of pollution, it is possible that both Dalman and Lindner misinterpreted the tank's overflow conduit as the continuation of the aqueduct. Since the tank is much larger than needed for clearing the water, it would make more sense if the aqueduct filled but bypassed the tank, allowing access to the water in this locality. This was the arrangement for the two draw tanks along the 'Ain Ghana Aqueduct at Hawara.

The aqueduct subsequently enters the very dissected landscape of Zibb 'Atuf, where viaducts and possibly one arched bridge carried the channel over clefts in the rock. Lindner assumed incorrectly that the aqueduct filled several reservoirs in this area, one of them serving the Lion Fountain. In fact, the cisterns in this area were all filled by run-off (Bellwald 2007: 319–20). The channel continued further along the Zibb 'Atuf to an earth ridge leading to the ez-Zantur hill. A wide foundation wall can be seen here, which probably carried a pressurised terracotta pipeline across the depression to a monolithic stone junction box at the highest point in this part of the city. This structure was fashioned out of a block of sandstone ca. 1 m square; a deep circular basin was carved into the centre, and three slots ca. 0.10–0.15 m deep through three sides of the block allowed the entry and exit of water (fig. 8.5). The stone gutter blocks of the 'Ain Brak aqueduct discharged water into a monolithic catch-basin with a long spout that funnelled water into the basin through a slot 0.15 m wide; the slots that discharged water into gutter blocks on one side of the basin and a terracotta pipeline on the other are much narrower. Conduit blocks remain in position here and there on the ridge, leading in and out of several rock-cut clearing basins. A pipeline in one of these two branch conduits served the villa overlooking the south city wall (Kolb and Keller 2002), the other the Pool and Garden Complex overlooking the colonnaded street (discussed below; Bellwald 2007: 319–20). This junction basin is similar in basic design and materials to the junction basin set up near the end of the Hawara Aqueduct (fig. 3.40).

In antiquity, as today, 'Ain Musa was probably by far the most abundant of the regional springs,

FIG. 8.5   *Distribution basin near termination of 'Ain Brak aqueduct. Petra (Photo U. Bellwald).*

issuing from the ground ca. 5.5 km east–southeast of the ancient settlement centre. The rapid modern development of the settlement of Wadi Musa/Elji has destroyed or obscured most of the evidence for the Nabataean aqueducts and other hydraulic installations that made use of the water, but the early travellers provide some information (collected in Brünnow and Domaszewski 1904–9: 1, pp. 428–31). The spring burst from the rock at the narrow entrance to Wadi Musa. Burckhardt saw "no ruins near the spring," but at least some of the water was carried down the wadi in "an artificial channel." Brünnow and Domaszewski mention several "Wasserleitungstürme" below the spring, but as Dalman comments (1908: 37; 1912: 8), these are more likely reservoir towers for nineteenth-century penstock mills (mentioned by Burckhardt). By the early nineteenth century, the spring water issued from a vault built into the rock and passed by a pavement where invalids passed the night

FIG. 8.6   *Zurraba reservoir, looking south. Petra.*

FIG. 8.7   *Zurraba reservoir, looking north. Petra.*

FIG. 8.8   *Zurraba reservoir, staircase. Petra.*

in the hope of a cure (Dalman 1912: 8). In 1928, visitors noted the overhang with a small dry stone shelter to one side of a large boulder and massive door jambs supporting a lintel (Chatelard and de Tarragon 2006: 135). The rivulets fed by the spring trickled down the slope, where some water was diverted to irrigate crops on numerous terraces. From this point on, until the reservoir at Zurraba 1.3 km above the entrance to the Siq, the course of the ʿAin Musa aqueduct was already covered or destroyed even in the nineteenth century. Yellow marl conduit blocks similar to those used in the Hawara aqueducts can be seen here and there in road embankments above the modern town, but there is no guarantee that they formed part of the ʿAin Musa system. Just above the Zurraba reservoir the conduit channel has been carved in the sandstone bedrock.

The Zurraba reservoir must have played an important part in the Petra aqueduct system, since all three main aqueducts or pipelines served by ʿAin Musa appear to have run through or by it and it is located on the crest between the Wadi Musa and Wadi Mudhlim watersheds (figs. 8.6–7). The precise function of the reservoir, however, is unclear, since the arrangements for intake and discharge have not been preserved, or at least are not visible at present. Brünnow and Domaszewski (1904–9: 1, p. 431) and some modern commentators (e.g.,

Ortloff 2005: 97–98) mention one reservoir, while Dalman (1908: 37) describes two. Gunsam (1989: 320–22) and al-Muheisen (1983: 17–23, 109–10) accept the presence of two reservoirs; al-Muheisen gives their volumes as 1,080 cum (north) and 1,440 cum (south). At present, there is a large rectangular cutting in the sandstone hillside (ca. 52 × 18 m), the southern half of which is occupied by a well-preserved reservoir built of sandstone blocks set in mortar (interior ca. 26 × 15 × >2.5 m; cap. >975 cum). It is unclear whether a second reservoir occupied the north end of the platform, but Dalman and others assume its presence on the basis of wall stubs and a rock-cut conduit that led to the cylindrical shaft for a penstock mill, partly built and partly cut in the rock near the northeast end of the platform. The mill may be a modern addition and, in any case, it could only have functioned in a free run-off situation. The whole east wall and part of the north and south walls of the surviving southern reservoir were cut into the bedrock, while the rest was constructed of neat limestone blocks facing a core of large rubble and mortar. A staircase built of the same materials descends from the southwest corner along the north wall to the reservoir floor (fig. 8.8). This reservoir resembles the Hawara aqueduct Pool no. 63 in scale and the Dam no. 44 in the method of construction, but its chronology has not been documented. The two

FIG. 8.9 *Earliest (northern) Siq aqueduct (upper channel) and later addition (lower channel), upstream from entrance to the Siq. Upper channel later reused for southern Siq aqueduct. Petra.*

parallels at Hawara are both Nabataean in origin. As far as can be determined from early photographs (Brünnow and Domaszewski 1904–9: 1, figs. 232, 229; Parr 1967; Bellwald and al-Huneidi 2003: fig. 71), the construction of the Nabataean diversion dam across the entrance to the Siq used a similar construction technique.

The absence of a roof suggests that water either flowed through the reservoir or was frequently drawn down by means of a valved pipe near the floor or by dipping. No pipe outlet is visible in the walls, but the staircase would have facilitated dipping with jars. One possible explanation for the design is that this was a dead-end reservoir, served by a short branch line from the 'Ain Musa aqueduct, and intended to provide for a settlement outside the main centre. Two such draw pools (although much smaller) occur along the 'Ain Ghana aqueduct at Hawara (km 6.512, 9.597). It is also possible that the reservoir served as both a settling and

division tank supplying the two conduit systems that passed through the Siq and the North Khubtha aqueduct that detoured around it. The reservoir seems much too large for a settling tank, but perhaps the spring water threw a significant amount of sediment or calcium carbonate pebbles; the staircase would have facilitated periodic cleaning. Ortloff (2005: 97–98) assumes the reservoir was filled by both run-off and spring water and that it served as a holding tank to supplement the spring flow when necessary. Given the care taken to isolate the draw cisterns along the Hawara aqueduct, it seems unlikely that the engineers at Petra allowed both the mixing of run-off and spring water and the reintroduction of this mix into the main aqueduct system after storage in an open tank. Bellwald (2007: 316) assumes that the reservoir stored water for the mill and the adjacent pottery workshop. In the apparent absence of pipes through the cistern wall, use of the Zurraba reservoir as a combination

FIG. 8.10 *Earliest aqueduct channel, inside the Siq, with later pipeline. Petra.*

of settling and overflow-division tank seems most probable.

Research by Bellwald has provided convincing archaeological evidence for the chronology and design of the conduits and pipelines fed by ʿAin Musa, particularly those that followed the Siq (Bellwald and al-Huneidi 2003). The earliest conduit can be traced along the north side of the Wadi Musa nearly from the present entrance gate. It was cut into the bedrock where possible, but was carried across areas of loose debris on viaducts faced with stone blocks, some pierced with openings for drainage of ground water (fig. 8.9). The channel crossed two larger side wadis on arched bridges. It entered the Siq at the original level of the Wadi Musa and followed the northern side (on the right hand while descending to the settlement centre). There was apparently no diversion dam at this time, so the conduit and adjacent road pavement must have suffered frequent damage from floods. In the Siq, the construction techniques were the same as upstream, consisting in part of a bench flume constructed of blocks, with a plastered channel and cover slabs, and partially of an inset channel carved in the bedrock, waterproofed with plaster, and roofed with slabs (fig. 8.10; Bellwald and al-Huneidi 2003: 35–40, 45). The plaster was hydraulic in character, a mixture of lime and finely crushed ceramics. The channel has a constant width of 0.34 m and averages 0.34 m in depth; the gradient varies significantly at the various points where it can be documented: 12.25, 3.6, 14.5, and 3.25 percent. The conduit was carried across the side wadis on small slab bridges, arched bridges, and buried in the debris of the slope in a cocoon of blocks and mortar. Only one rock-cut settling tank has been documented along this early channel.

Bellwald dates this conduit to the early first century BC, justifiably associating it with the development of permanent residential architecture in the settlement centre. The continuation of the channel into the settlement centre was found in 2004 and dated to ca. 100 BC (Graf et al. 2005: 428–32). The archaeological data suggest that the

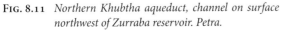

FIG. 8.11 *Northern Khubtha aqueduct, channel on surface northwest of Zurraba reservoir. Petra.*

FIG. 8.12 *Northern Khubtha aqueduct, channel cut into cliff face in Wadi Sh'ib Qays. Petra.*

system was destroyed by flood action around 50 BC and that the whole infrastructure of the Siq was renovated dramatically during the second half of the century (Bellwald and al-Huneidi 2003: 39–40, 52; Bellwald 2007: 315–16). This project, which may have taken decades to complete, involved construction of the diversion dam, tunnel, and bridge at the entrance to the Siq, two aqueduct lines through it, and massive amounts of fill supporting a carefully paved road. The expanded water supply was intended to service both a growing population and royal prestige structures, while the pavement was needed to facilitate trade and the movement of construction materials. Bellwald has made the appealing suggestion that the Northern Khubtha aqueduct, which begins at the Zurraba reservoir

and detours around the Siq into the city, was a replacement system intended to provide a reliable supply of water during the lengthy renovation of the system in the Siq (Bellwald and al-Huneidi 2003: 55).

The Northern Khubtha aqueduct, which fortunately has been well-preserved, itself involves some significant engineering accomplishments (Dalman 1908: 39–40; al-Muheisen 1983: 129–31; Lindner 1987b: 196; Gunsam 1989). Like the first aqueduct through the Siq, it consisted of a gravity-flow channel, for the most part cut in the bedrock (0.30 × 0.30 m to 0.40 × 0.40 m) and covered with slabs. The winding course is ca. 4.5 km long, from Zurraba to a reservoir below the Palace Tomb, descending 125 m (from ca. 1,050 to 925 m asl)

FIG. 8.13 *Northern Khubtha aqueduct, arched bridge. Petra.*

for an overall slope of 2.8 percent, very similar to that of the Hawara aqueducts. The first portion of the aqueduct was cut across gentle slopes and consisted of a rock-cut conduit lined with plaster and framed by blocks that carried cover slabs (fig. 8.11). After reaching the steep-walled Wadi Sh'ib Qays, the conduit was cut into the wadi walls (fig. 8.12). At one point in this area, the conduit passes close to a collection of rock-cut ritual niches and betyls, where an associated inscription may mention the engineer who designed the system (Milik and Starcky 1975: 126–28): *dkrwn tb* / [...] *br nhshtb* / *bny' nm qdm* / *dwshr* "In commemoration of [... son of] Nahashtab, the engineer, before Dushara." A stonecutter's or engineer's inscription also appears on an aqueduct channel cut across the theatre at Petra: *dkyr hwrw*, "*hwrw* was remembered" (Knauf 1997).

A short distance beyond the inscription, the conduit is carried over the deep, narrow Sheb Kes gorge on a single arch (fig. 8.13: W 1.30 m; span 5–6 m), the only surviving arch of the many that originally served the Petra aqueduct system. On the arch, the water travelled through roughly-cut

sandstone gutter blocks (channel: W ca. 0.032, deep 0.20 m) built into the fabric (fig. 8.14). Another arch (now lost) carried the aqueduct over the Wadi al-Mudhlim, after which it followed a winding course cut into the side of the Jebel Khubtha above the Wadi al-Mataha and into the settlement centre. At several points, the bedrock shelf was supplemented with cut blocks set in mortar, and steps were cut into the rock to allow access for construction and maintenance. Another arch carried the channel over the Wadi al-Khubtha and a large rock-cut channel (0.60–0.80 × 0.50–0.60 m) that served a separate run-off water system from the Jebel Khubtha. Next to the Palace Tomb, the water apparently cascaded 10 m into a rock-cut cistern (fig. 8.15; cap. 300 cum). Given its modest capacity, this tank probably served both as a drop-basin accommodating the need for a sudden decline in elevation and as a distribution tank for one or more conduits leading water into the settlement. Bellwald (2007: 316) mentions the presence of three draw basins "in front of" the reception tank. The drop itself, essentially an artificial waterfall, may have been at least in part designed as a spectacu-

FIG. 8.14 *Northern Khubtha aqueduct, conduit on arched bridge. Petra.*

FIG. 8.15 *Northern Khubtha aqueduct, terminal cistern by Palace Tomb. Petra.*

FIG. 8.16 *Bench supporting pipeline along north wall of Siq. Petra.*

lar display of the Nabataean control of the desert environment.

While the Northern Khubtha system, along with numerous run-off cisterns and reservoirs, presumably supplied the needs of the settlement centre, the water-supply system through the Siq was completely renovated in conjunction with the construction of a paved road in the third quarter of the first century BC. The information below is derived almost entirely from Bellwald and al-Huneidi 2003. A pipeline was laid in the original aqueduct channel along the north (right-hand) wall, and a new aqueduct channel was carved and built along the south wall; both were fed from the vicinity of the Zurraba reservoir with 'Ain Musa water. Bellwald has determined that the south conduit was part of the last phase of the project.

The first phase of the renovated northern channel consisted of a pressurised pipeline made up of heavy, wheel-turned terracotta pipe sections with male/female joints that were sealed with mortar (figs. 8.10, 8.16; Bellwald and al-Huneidi 2003: 55–60). The pipes (L 0.40, inner D 0.14–0.18 m) have a markedly concave exterior surface, reflecting increased thickness at the joints. Similarities between this system and the sophisticated long-distance pipe systems serving the Hellenistic city of

Pergamon suggests to Bellwald that the engineers supervising the renovation came from Asia Minor. While the influence of Hellenistic technology is likely for this system and for some aspects of cistern design (Section 8.B.2), there is no pressing need to hypothesise the actual presence of Greek engineers, since the Nabataeans themselves had wide exposure to the Hellenistic world (Oleson 1995; Schmid 2001a–b) and were expert potters.

Where possible, particularly in the lower portion of the Siq, the pipeline was laid in the rock-cut channel of the original aqueduct. In the upper portion of the Siq, a bench was built to accommodate the pipes just above the level of the road, protected on the exterior face with stone slabs (fig. 8.16). Between the entrance to the Siq and the Zurraba reservoir, a new, narrower channel was cut in the rock below the original aqueduct channel, probably reflecting the greater flexibility in elevation allowed with a closed, pressurised system. The pipes were set in a bed of dark grey mortar and fixed in position with large curved sherds from broken pipes, positioned upright in the mortar. The pipe joints were sealed with mortar, and the entire pipeline was originally enveloped in mortar, which often rose to the top of the cutting, presumably to increase the pressure capacity of the pipes.

Fig. 8.17 *Bridge and division tank feeding two pipelines along north wall of Siq. (Reconstruction by U. Bellwald).*

The same procedure was used in a smaller-scale Roman system in the fort at Hawara (Oleson et al. 2003: 42–43; fig. 7.2). Several narrow (0.58 m) arches supported bridges carrying the pipeline over crevices in the Jebel Khubtha.

Bellwald calculates the capacity of the original pipe system at 56 litres/second, or 4,838.4 cum/day, which is almost nine times the recent discharge of the 'Ain Musa (544 cum/day). Ortloff's account (2005: 98–99) is full of archaeological errors and misinterpretations, but after suggesting a capacity of 90 cum/hour (2,160 cum/day) and an impossible loss of 50 percent by leakage he rightly notes that the resulting figure is still well above the spring discharge. Either the pipeline did not run full, or — given the careful attention to reinforcement of the pipes — after leaving the Siq the water was delivered to an elevated discharge tank, thus forcing the pipe to run full. Bellwald (2007: 316) suggests that the relatively steep slope alone kept the pipeline full and that it was not intended to serve an elevated reservoir. He locates the termination of the lower pipeline at a reservoir and nymphaeum at the eastern end of the colonnaded street, later moved to the Roman nymphaeum farther down the street. Ceramic finds suggest that this pipeline system was completed during the third quarter of the first century BC. Evidence was found for various renovations and repairs to the system, but after the disastrous earthquake of 363, the system seems to have been left to decay.

One early but undated renovation, approximately 125 m before the end of the Siq, involved interruption of the closed pipeline by a division tank made of stone blocks (fig. 8.17; Bellwald and al-Huneidi 2003: 86–87). Water discharged into the tank, and if the water level reached a high enough level, it began to fill a second pipeline set into a new cutting in the side of the Siq (fig. 8.18). This new pipeline had a lower slope than the original one on the pavement, allowing it to fill a new reservoir in the developing area across from the theatre, around 15 m above the level in the original pipeline. In a second phase of renovation, the priority of supply

FIG. 8.18 *Elevated pipeline along north wall of Siq. Petra.*

was reversed, the upper pipeline filling before the lower. At a still later date, the original pipeline system became occluded with calcium carbonate deposits and the upper third of each pipe was neatly broken open to allow removal of some of the sinter (fig. 8.16). After this operation, of course, the pipes functioned as an open system, with less capacity than the closed pipeline.

The final addition to this water-supply complex, the open channel aqueduct cut into the south wall of the Siq, can be dated by ceramic evidence to between 20 and 70 AD (Bellwald and al-Huneidi 2003: 55, 60–68). This system reused the channel cut for the first conduit from the area of the Zurraba reservoir as far as the new bridge at the entrance to the Siq. From this point on, the channel took a new route, along the southern (left-hand) side of the Siq, cut into the bedrock 1.5 m above the paving wherever possible and supplemented with a built bench where necessary. The conduit channel, lined with hydraulic plaster, averages 0.34 m wide × 0.18 m deep and follows a constant slope of 4.9 percent (fig. 8.19). The naturally sinuous course may have helped to slow the flow, avoiding erosion of the structures and loss through splashing. Stone cover slabs were preserved at several points (fig. 8.20). Bellwald estimates the capacity at 160 l/second

(13,824 cum/day). Once again, the maximum capacity of the system seems to have been well above the likely average discharge of the spring.

This aqueduct crossed various crevices or small side wadis on slab bridges that allowed run-off water to pass underneath, very similar to those seen on the Jammam aqueduct at Hawara. One of these bridges made use of a mortar conduit; a coin struck between 378 and 388 indicates that this feature belongs to a repair after the earthquake of 363. At least seven settling tanks (0.60 × 0.60 × 0.60 m) were cut into the bedrock or built into the supporting bench at irregular intervals along its course in the Siq and lined with plaster (fig. 8.21). Evidence was found for cover slabs with a central hole to allow the removal of debris. As with the Jammam Aqueduct at Hawara, there is no obvious motive for the presence or absence of the basins at particular locations, and their spacing varies from 80 to 180 m. Four smaller basins, two cut in the bedrock and two built of masonry, appear next to the conduit (fig. 8.22). Like the two much larger access basins along the Ghana Aqueduct at Hawara, they served as drinking basins, providing access to the water without allowing pollution of the main supply. They were located on the street side of the conduit channel and connected to the flowing water by a hole or

FIG. 8.19   *Rock-cut conduit channel along south wall of Siq. Petra.*

FIG. 8.20   *Cover slabs over rock-cut conduit channel along south wall of Siq. Petra.*

pipe (D 0.20 m) that allowed water to fill the basin. This aqueduct initially supplied the court in front of the Khazneh tomb with water, but after the earthquake of 363 it was extended into the settlement centre (Bellwald 2007: 316).

Petra: Terraces and Wadi Barriers

The hillsides around Petra that are composed of soil rather than bedrock frequently have been terraced by means of stone walls running across the slope, and the wider, less steep run-off channels were blocked by low barrier walls across the direction of flow. The objective of this technique, which was very widespread in the ancient Mediterranean world and adjacent areas from at least the Chalcolithic period onward (e.g., Levy and Alon 1987), was to trap soil and water and to provide a level surface for the cultivation of crops. Since the small plots created by these structures soak up water from a large run-off area, they effectively multiply the local rainfall many times over. Although such features are very difficult to date, many of the terraces and barrages around Petra are associated with settlements dating from the Iron Age through the Byzantine period; most, however, seem to belong to the period of Nabataean florescence (Lindner et al. 1996; Lavento et al. 2007b: 148). Some of the terraces have been repaired for reuse in the modern period. A large number of reused ancient terraces are fed by the 'Ain Debdebah, north of Petra (Kennedy and Bewley 2004: 144–45).

Although terraces and barriers represent a spectacular alteration of the landscape for hydrological reasons, and the resulting agricultural production undoubtedly was of significant importance to the inhabitants of Petra, they have in general generated only casual mention (e.g., Burckhardt in Brünnow and Domaszewski 1904–9: 1, p. 429; al-Muheisen 1983: 147; 1990: 209–10; Lindner 1987a: 149–52; 2005: 49; 'Amr et al. 1998: 504, 516, 532, 539; Tholbecq 2001: 403–4). An exception is the careful evaluation of the arrangements for run-off farm-

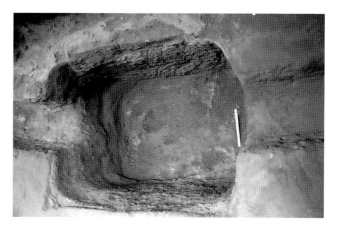

FIG. 8.21 *Settling tank in rock-cut conduit channel along south wall of Siq. Petra (Photo: U. Bellwald).*

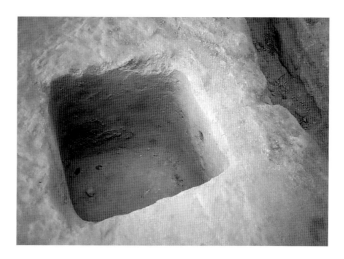

FIG. 8.22 *Drinking basin supplied by rock-cut conduit channel along south wall of Siq. Petra.*

ing on the slopes of Jebel Haroun (Lavento et al. 2007b; Huotari in Frösén and Fiema 2002: 229–33). An intensive archaeological survey of this jebel identified 391 barrages and terraces in an area of only 4 sq km. Most of the walls are fairly simple constructions, one block thick and 0.2–0.3 m high. In the areas where intense flow was expected, the barriers consisted of heavy facing walls with a rubble core. They were sometimes provided with stepped overflow channels, similar to those seen at Phaino and in the Negev. The complex of run-off fields seems to show the influence of central planning, and it may represent a collaborative response to the needs of the growing city of Petra in the first century AD. Although the local precipitation is not by itself sufficient to support agriculture, the fields

that benefited from the collection of run-off might
have allowed even the cultivation of vines and olive
trees, along with grain. The preliminary survey
for the Petra Siq Project found 136 terraces and
143 wadi barriers (Bellwald and al-Huneidi 2003:
5), indicating the scope of this approach to land
use even close to the settlement centre. In striking
contrast, terraces and barriers are uncommon in
the landscape around Hawara.

Petra: Containment Dams

Containment dams differ from detention dams,
terraces, and wadi barriers in that their purpose
is to hold pools of water that can be accessed
through dipping, occasional overflow, or a pressurised pipeline. In the Petra area, the typical
containment dam was a high masonry wall with
a mortared core, built across the downstream
opening of a natural cleft in the bedrock. The wall
was sometimes built into a vertical cutting in the
wall of the cleft — today often the only evidence
for a wall that has been swept away — but in most
cases the walls of the cleft were left unaltered.
Given the relative simplicity of the arrangement,
these small containment dams were very common
around Petra, and they are mentioned in most
reviews of the water system (esp. al-Muheisen
1983: 47–101, 104–7; Lindner 1987a). A 10 m high
cutting in the wall of a gorge near the base of Umm
Biyara may represent the remains of a very high
containment dam, but most were much smaller
in scale. Several small containment dams appear
around the edge of the Jebel Khubtha, one of them
creating a pool of ca. 300 cum that was plastered
to prevent leakage (Gunsam 1989: 325). Many of
the dams across the wadis and clefts leading into
the Siq and in the watersheds that feed them were
in fact detention dams, intended simply to delay
peak flow by allowing the water to escape slowly
through a pipe near the base of the wall (fig. 8.3).
The opening in the large detention dam above the
Wadi Farasa complex may have held some sort of
fitting, perhaps a stopcock designed to preserve
the detained water once the threat of flood had
passed (fig. 8.23). Otherwise, these constructions
resemble containment dams. In the absence of a
comprehensive published catalogue, it is not pos-

FIG. 8.23 *Drain hole in detention dam in the Wadi Farasa,
detail. Petra.*

sible to discern any patterns in the distribution and
possible use of this type of structure.

Since open pools were subject to evaporation
and pollution, their water was most likely used for
animals and for small-scale irrigation. When it was
desired to preserve the quality of the water, the
walls of the cleft could be regularised and provided
with impost cuttings to support cross arches and a
slab roof. A large cistern or reservoir of this type
with at least 10 cross arches can be seen near the
top of Jebel Khubtha (fig. 8.24). Lindner estimates
its capacity at more than 650 cum (Lindner and
Gunsam 2002: 231). The spillway was partly cut in
the bedrock to avoid erosion of the barrier wall; a
similar arrangement was used for Dam no. 44 at
Hawara.

FIG. 8.24 *Dammed cleft cistern with arch-supported roof (fallen), Jebel Khubtha. Petra.*

Petra: Reservoirs and Cisterns

In the catalogue of hydraulic structures at Hawara, water containment structures that were significantly larger than the typical cistern and that appeared to be state-owned or public in character were classified as reservoirs. The resulting group of five structures (Structure nos. 53, 62, 63, 67, 68) varied in capacity from 451.65 to 1,273.3 cum; the three smallest were roofed with cross-arches and slabs. The situation at Petra is less clear-cut. There are unroofed reservoirs that obviously were state-controlled or served a public function: for example, the Zurraba reservoir (cap. 1,440 cum; figs. 8.6–7), the catch basin and distribution tank (?) for the North Khubtha conduit (cap. 300 cum; fig. 8.15), the garden pool served by the 'Ain Brak conduit (cap. 2,100 cum; figs. 8.26–27), and the arch-roofed, rock-cut reservoir near the summit of Jebel Haroun (cap. >650 cum; fig. 8.25), which probably was associated with a sanctuary. On the other hand, there are some large cisterns at Petra with capacities beyond the threshold for reservoirs at Hawara, but which are likely to have been privately owned.

At the site of Shammasa, north of the settlement centre, a rock-cut cistern (13.5 × 10 × 4.8 m; cap. 648 cum) roofed with 11 cross-arches and provided with a rock-cut staircase, is associated with a wine press and villa (Lindner and Gunsam 2002). The roofed cleft cistern on Jebel Khubtha noted above is even larger. As at Hawara, the largest reservoirs at Petra are built of blocks and unroofed, while the others were cut in the bedrock and roofed with cross-arches carrying slabs of stone.

The only reservoir at Petra that has been carefully excavated and published is the large pool in the Pool and Garden Complex in the settlement centre, fed by the 'Ain Brak aqueduct (figs. 8.26–27; Bedal 2001; 2002; Bedal and Schryver 2007). The aqueduct discharged into a rock-cut holding tank above the complex, possibly feeding an intermittent or continuous waterfall that supplied a large pool (43.20 × 23.70 × 2.5 m; cap. 2,559.6 cum) with a central island pavilion (14 × 10 m). Although the complex was set into an enormous cutting in the bedrock, the pool itself was built of heavy masonry blocks and provided with access steps in the northeast corner. On the basis of Vitruvius (*De arch.*

FIG. 8.25 *Cistern below Tomb of Aaron, Jebel Haroun, interior view, Petra.*

FIG. 8.26 *Pool and Garden Complex, view from above. Petra.*

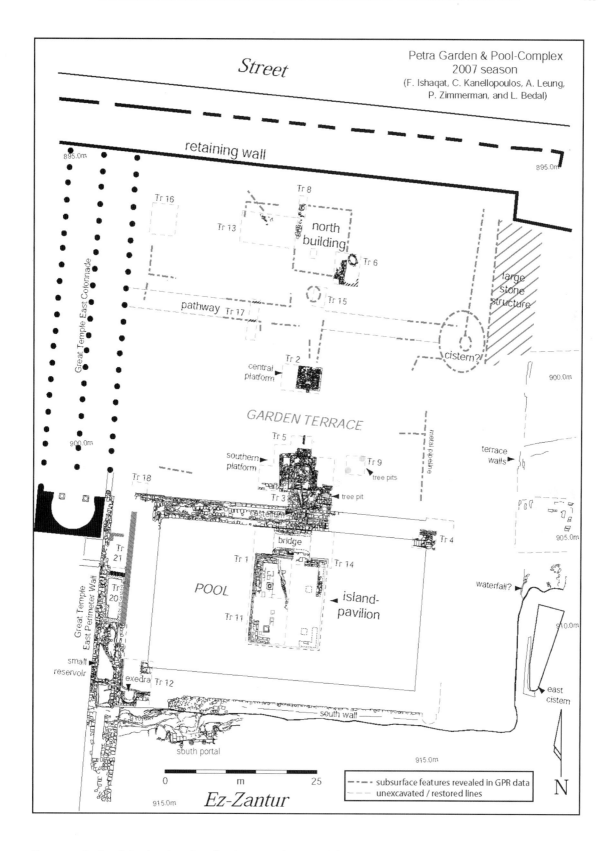

FIG. 8.27 *Pool and Garden Complex, plan (courtesy of L.-A. Bedal). Petra.*

FIG. 8.28 *Rock-cut cistern with arch-supported roof (lost), above Wadi Abu Ullayqa. Petra.*

FIG. 8.29 *Rock-cut cistern with arch-supported roof, below Snake Monument. Petra.*

FIG. 8.30 *Rock-cut bottle-shaped cistern on Umm Biyara. Petra.*

6.3.10), the island structure has been identified as a "Cyzicene oecus," a pleasure-pavilion overlooking the garden below, but with the added allure of being surrounded by water. Gutter blocks and terracotta pipelines carried the overflow from the pool to a large garden adjacent on the north and various structures therein. The initial phase of this complex belongs to the reign of Aretas IV (9 BC–40 AD). The location and spectacular design of this structure sets it apart from the utilitarian structures of Petra's water-supply system. The monarch was very likely imitating the palatial structures and associated waterworks of the Herods and other royal gardens in the Near East (Bedal 2001; 2002). A case has been made in Chapter 7 that the pool at the end of the Hawara aqueduct was also meant as a prestige statement.

Numerous rain-fed cisterns designed to preserve water for later use were cut into the bedrock of the hills above and below Petra. They are mentioned by all the publications that concern the water-supply of the Petra area, but only al-Muheisen has attempted a partial survey (1983: 111–17). In the absence of a comprehensive catalogue, only a sample of the material can be presented here. Unlike the

reservoirs, which required functioning aqueducts, the cisterns have often been put back in use by the Bedouin. Where the site made it possible, cisterns were cut completely in the bedrock, like caves, and the water led to the intake opening in gutters carved in the catchment area above. Some of these, such as the Bir al-'Arayis (Cistern of the Brides), excavated in a cliff-face just outside Siq al-Barid (cap. 1400 cum), could be very large and were provided with staircases to access the water (Bikai et al. 2009: 363). Others, such as a group near the ed-Deir tomb, were more modest in capacity (25–50 cum?). The tanks were generally lined with plaster: a thick, pebbly base coat topped by a finer, polished plaster. The most visible cisterns, although not necessarily the most numerous, were those cut down into a relatively flat area of bedrock and provided with block-built cross-arches holding a slab roof (fig. 8.28). Most often, the roof has fallen and been removed, and only the imposts cut in the bedrock remain to indicate the method of roofing. As at Hawara, the use of cross-arches was usually limited to spans of 5 or 6 m, but there are exceptions (see p. 377). Access stairs cut in the bedrock can be seen in some of these cisterns, and al-Muheisen asserts that all of

them had steps in order to facilitate periodic cleaning. If this is the case, it sets the Petra cisterns apart
from those at most other Nabataean sites. Gutters
cut in the rock or fieldstone walls guided water to
the intake, which usually was a rock-cut channel.
The few cisterns with surviving block-built roofs
show the use of reinforced draw-holes to access
the water, as at Hawara (fig. 8.29). It is unlikely that
any of the aqueduct systems serving Petra provided
spur lines to fill these small cisterns (Bellwald 2007:
320–21). Although Diodorus specifies the bottle-
shaped cisterns as typically Nabataean, they do
not seem to be common at Petra. The numerous
examples on Umm al-Biyara may be Edomite in
origin (fig. 8.30).

There are apparently only a few block-built
cisterns in the settlement centre, although this is
nearly the only place in the region where bedrock
is not easily accessible. In this area, the fountains
and reservoirs served by the aqueduct system seem
to have provided running water for drinking and
other purposes. There is, however, a large block-
built tank near the nymphaeum, which itself has
a masonry pool. The run-off cisterns themselves
served a variety of needs, depending on location.
Many of the cisterns most visible today are found in
the necropolis areas, where they apparently served
the needs of religious rituals and ceremonial meals
in the attached *triclinia* and irrigated the gardens
that sometimes formed part of larger tomb complexes. The Garden tomb complex in the Wadi
Farasa provides the best-documented example (figs.
8.31–32; Schmid 2002: figs. 35–36; 2007). Cisterns in
some residential areas, for example at ath-Thughra,
were most likely used for household purposes,
while isolated cisterns in grazing areas may have
been intended mainly for sustaining herds of animals. Al-Muheisen (1983: 142–46) measured many
of the cisterns in and around Petra and calculates
a total capacity of 8,300 cum. This figure may be
only a portion of the original amount, since the
cisterns around the much smaller settlement of
Hawara held 5,456.5 cum. Nevertheless, the ample
supply of aqueduct water to the Petra centre may
explain the smaller figure. Cisterns along the trade
routes leading down to the Wadi 'Arabah were most
likely intended to service caravan traffic (Bellwald
2007: 321–23).

Fig. 8.31 *Rock-cut detention cistern with built barrier wall,
Wadi Farasa Garden Complex. Petra.*

Comparison of the Water-Supply Systems of Petra and Hawara

Although the final study remains to be written, it
is clear that by the end of the first century BC, and
possibly more than a century earlier, the settlement
or city of Petra enjoyed the use of a sophisticated
and adaptable water-supply system. The regional
springs were harnessed to supply at least six and
possibly as many as nine separate conduits or pipelines, following a variety of routes, using a variety
of techniques, and supplying drinking water to
various parts of the settlement. The multiplicity
of channels and routes may have been intended
as insurance in the event of natural disasters or
enemy action. In addition, there were numerous
reservoirs and large or small cisterns in and around

FIG. 8.32 *Rock-cut, roofed cistern fed by detention cistern, Wadi Farasa Garden Complex. Petra.*

Petra filled by run-off water. They served a variety of functions but could also have been thought of as supplying redundancy in the event of the disruption of the aqueducts. Finally, terraces and wadi barriers enhanced local agriculture.

The very concept of a long-distance conduit fed by a spring, as seen at Petra, undoubtedly provided both the inspiration and the engineering skills allowing construction of the Hawara aqueduct system sometime in the first century BC. Although they are different in many details of execution, the same aqueduct technology was applied at both sites, with the exception of long-distance pipelines, which are absent at Hawara. While local pipelines were used within the settlement of Hawara, some of them apparently under pressure, the much longer distance to be travelled, the lower average slope, and the much lower output of the available springs probably were all factors that made use of a pipeline unfeasible outside the settlement centre.

It is possible, however, that the occasional use of pipes within stone gutter blocks at Petra inspired the use of tiles in the gutter blocks of the Jammam aqueduct to solve some sort of supply problem.

Although the Hawara conduits were cut into the bedrock where possible, the local conditions meant that at least 95 percent of the course consisted of stone gutter blocks cut from the most easily available local stones. Gutter blocks of the same design appear where necessary in the Petra system, but in general the channels there were somewhat larger to accommodate the greater flow of the springs. In all the cases where the capacity of the conduits or pipelines serving Petra has been calculated, the potential maximum flow seems far in excess of the probable available spring flow, even for any single one of the three lines served by the 'Ain Musa. The calculated capacity of the north and south conduits in the Siq alone, for example, is 34 times the recent discharge of the 'Ain Musa. A disparity between probable input and maximum possible discharge was noted for the Hawara aqueduct system as well, although only at a factor of 4.5. Several explanations are possible: the excess capacity gave the engineers greater leeway for error when calculating slopes, particularly for situations where the slope was constantly changing; the excess capacity was meant to allow for the formation of sinter in the channels and pipes over decades without the need for cleaning; in the 'Ain Musa system, a distribution basin at the Zurraba reservoir allowed the entire flow from the spring to be directed to any one of the three conduits or pipelines at different times of the day or as special needs in various parts of the city became apparent. Intentional over-engineering by individuals uncertain about flow rates, slopes, and levels is probably the most likely solution.

There are other parallels between the Petra and Hawara aqueduct systems. Both make use of occasional settling tanks within the flow regime, and both supplied draw tanks or drinking tanks isolated from the flow by branch lines. Large stone junction or division basins have been found at both sites, and both systems fed reservoirs or pools that made the water directly available or serviced local pipe systems. It seems very likely that the pool into which the Hawara aqueduct system discharged was modelled on the Garden and Pool Complex in Petra.

This comparison, however, has the remarkable implication that the major motive for the construction of the long Hawara aqueduct was royal or cultural prestige, the dramatic proof of the Nabataean ability to control the desert. The intended audience may have been the caravans travelling the King's Highway, particularly those heading north through Hawara towards Petra. It is obvious that many of the monuments in the Siq were meant to impress visitors arriving by that entrance: the arched entrance, water basins, betyls, inscriptions, bas reliefs of camel caravans, and the spectacular al-Khazneh tomb facade. Once inside the city, visitors may have gaped as well at waterfalls at the termination of the 'Ain Brak and North Khubtha conduits and at the *paradeisos* associated with the Garden Pool. Although compromised in quality, the overflow from both the Petra Garden Pool and the Hawara aqueduct pool would have been suitable for agricultural or industrial purposes. The Lion Fountain in the Wadi Farasa complex must also have made a striking impression when run-off from the winter rains burst through the animal's mouth.

The basic technology of the reservoirs and cisterns at Hawara also resembles or is modelled on the equivalent structures at Petra, although accommodation is once again made for the differences in topography. Some cisterns were cut entirely in the bedrock, while others were cut down into a levelled rock surface and provided with slab roofs carried on cross-arches. For reasons that are not clear, only one cistern and one reservoir at Hawara were provided with stairs into the pool (Structure nos. 37 and 50). If stairs were designed to facilitate periodic cleaning of a cistern, as al-Muheisen assumes for Petra, one might expect them to be more common at Hawara, where even the rock-cut cisterns can be associated with earthen run-off fields and the air is full of blown sand and soil. Although the observation is not based on hard statistics, settling basins associated with cistern intakes seem to me to be less common at Petra than at Hawara, where they are routinely provided. Perhaps there was simply a different approach at each site to the problem of cleaning the tanks.

A more striking anomaly is the appearance of built reservoirs and cisterns with arch-supported roofs in the settlement centre of Hawara, for which there do not seem to be parallels in Nabataean Petra. Only one small example has been found so far, in the Roman baths associated with the "Great Temple" (Joukowsky 2007: 88–98; 2009: 292–96). A rock-cut cistern with slab roof supported by cross-arches, holding 390 cum, was found nearby under the "Great Temple" platform (Joukowsky 2009: 292–95). Cisterns and reservoirs had to be built rather than rock-cut in the Hawara centre because the bedrock was out of reach there, and it is no particular surprise to see the usual rectangular design constructed entirely of blocks. What is surprising is the appearance of seven built domestic cisterns with the typical arch-supported roof, but with a circular plan. I have found only two partial parallels for this design, at Oboda and Nessana (see below; Negev 1997a: 103; Shereshevski 1991: 59–60). The design certainly makes sense, since the cylindrical shape not only provides more volume in proportion to the amount of masonry than rectangular plans, but it is also easier to plaster and better able to resist any pressure from the surrounding soil. Did an innovative engineer responding to the local situation possibly develop the design at Hawara?

Another anomaly at Hawara is the rarity of agricultural terraces and wadi barriers. Agricultural terraces appear here and there where the topography and pedology are appropriate, but for the most part the best soil in the region lies in the two depressions north and south of the settlement centre, below the bedrock jebels. In these areas, one would expect wadi barriers rather than terraces, but even here such structures are relatively rare. Not all the barriers visible at present were catalogued, because of difficulties of definition and dating, but, even so, little attempt seems to have been made to detain the flow in the numerous wadis. Perhaps their flow was too violent or too intermittent to be of use. Agriculture undoubtedly was practised around Hawara, but most likely near the foot of sandstone ridges or jebels, and possibly the fields were furnished in antiquity, as today, with earthen barrier walls and conduits rather than with constructions of stone. Earthen features naturally were more likely to disappear over time, and in the Negev built stone spillways for such barrier walls have been found associated with the faint traces of the lost earthen barriers (Evenari et al. 1982: 118).

8.A.2. *The Water-Supply Systems around 'Udhruh and Ma'an*

The high, rolling plain east of Petra and north of Humayma, framed on the west and south by the al-Shara mountain system, contains the evidence for numerous ancient settlements and roads, most of them dating from the Iron Age through the Early Islamic period. The most striking site at present, thanks to the presence of a Roman legionary fort constructed in the early second century and rebuilt around 300 (Kennedy 2008), is 'Udhruh (probably ancient Augustopolis). There are, however, numerous smaller civilian and military settlements scattered here and there, in particular Sadaqa and Ma'an (Parker 1986: 87–104; Kennedy 2004: 178–91). Given their proximity, it is important to note whether the patterns and structures of water-supply in this very different landscape vary from those at Petra and Humayma.

The water-supply system of the fort at 'Udhruh has not yet been excavated, but the region to the east and south contains numerous agricultural establishments. Abudanh (2007) has surveyed three sites that made use of large reservoirs to irrigate adjacent fields. The reservoirs (Birkat 'Udhruh, 50 × 50 m; Birkat al-Fiqiyy, 33 × 40 m; Jebel at-Tahuna, 26 × 24 m, 10 × 5 m) were built of stone blocks set in mortar and plastered on the interior. Birkat 'Udhruh was provided with a settling tank in the intake channel. The first two reservoirs were probably supplied by nearby springs, but no conduits have survived. A *qanat* system feeding spring water in from the west supplied the two reservoirs at Jebel at-Tahuna. In southern Jordan, *qanats* (subterranean aqueducts with frequent access shafts designed to allow excavation and periodic cleaning) have been found only in the region between 'Udhruh and Ma'an, but they appear at eight sites in northern Jordan, where conditions are more propitious (Lightfoot 1997; Lancaster and Lancaster 1999: 155–57). All these sites seem to have been in use from the first century AD through the Early Islamic period. Another *qanat* system can be seen below the fort at 'Udhruh, but it seems to carry water eastward, away from the fort. The topography around Petra was unsuited to *qanats*. The numerous spring-fed reservoirs at that site

may have been used in part to irrigate plants, but the scale and design of fields in the Petra centre was probably very different from that on the high plains to the east. While the reservoir in the Roman fort at Hauarra resembles the reservoirs near 'Udhruh in construction technique, it was filled by a spring-fed aqueduct, since the landscape around Humayma is also unsuited to the construction of *qanats*. Run-off from the Hawara aqueduct pool may have been used for incidental irrigation, but the practice of agriculture in the Hisma required a different strategy than artificial irrigation with stored water.

The same contrast can be drawn with several poorly-known Late Roman or Early Islamic agricultural sites just east of Ma'an: al-Hammam, Khirbet Samra, and al-Mutrab (Brünnow and Domaszewski 1904–9: 2, pp. 3–7; Parker 1986: 100–4; Kennedy 2004: 184–86; Kennedy and Bewley 2004: 60–61). At al-Hammam, there is a reservoir ca. 60.5 m square, associated with a large courtyard structure, an aqueduct, and ancient field boundaries. Early travellers reported that the aqueduct was fed by a spring at Basta, 21 km to the west. The aqueduct continued on to al-Mutrab, where it fed another large reservoir.

Abudanh (2007: 494) has also documented large areas of fields with stone piles, particularly east and southeast of Basta and Ayl. These occur on gently sloping hills and may be the result of clearing for agriculture, rather than for the enhancement of run-off.

A number of small sites in this region are mentioned in the Byzantine papyri from Petra (Frösén, Arjava, Lehtinen 2002: nos. 2, 3, 7–10; Frösén 2004). Inventory no. 83 records a dispute between two householders at Zadakathon (Sadaqa) around AD 574. One householder had constructed a channel across the other householder's property in order to conduct water from a spring owned by the other party. Even at this late date, many of the names in the papyri, such as Obodianos and Dusarios, are Nabataean in character, just as the hydraulic technology must have been. *PPetra* III no. 25 records a "well-watered field" (γεωργία ἐπίρρυτος) near Augustopolis/'Udhruh (Arjava et al. 2007: 279–88).

FIG. 8.33 *Aqueduct, settling tank, and reservoir, view from northeast. Phaino.*

8.A.3. *The Water-Supply System of Phaino (Faynan), Toloha (Qasr et-Telah), and the Evidence of the Nahal Hever Papyri*

Another important water-supply system in the region of Arabia Petraea can be found at Faynan, the ancient mining settlement of Phaino, 35 km north of Petra in the Wadi Arabah (elev. 250 m). Exploitation of the mineral deposits was carried out in the Chalcolithic period and Bronze Age, then from the first century BC to the fifth century AD (Barker et al. 2007: 227–70). Although the function of the settlement was very different from that of Hawara and much of the water-supply was intended for use in processing ore, there are some similarities in topography and in soil and water resources. The survey catalogued the following "hydraulic structures" (counts are in parentheses): aqueduct bridge (2), aqueduct channel (6), water-mill (2), reservoir (2), channel (rock-cut channels associated with parallel walls, 5), parallel walls

(for channelling water, 63), barrage (2), catchment structure (5), cistern (8), diversion wall (1), sluice (intentional gap in a field wall, 42), spillway (a sluice with steps or terraces below, 82) (Barker et al. 2007: 98). Only a sample of these structures can be considered here.

A spring-fed aqueduct of very Roman design, involving a masonry channel with wide plastered conduit and a 12-arched arcade carrying the conduit over a wadi tributary, fed a large reservoir (33 × 30 × 4 m; cap. >3,000 cum) built of large blocks set in mortar (fig. 8.33; Barker et al. 2007: 124–26, 315–18). The water entered the reservoir through a settling tank, indicating that it carried a significant load of sediment. A branch of the aqueduct continued along one wall of the reservoir and fed the cylindrical reservoir of a penstock mill that has been dated anywhere from Byzantine to modern (Barker et al. 2007: 163, 317–18). There are numerous terraces on the hillsides above the settlement centre, presumably intended for agricultural ex-

FIG. 8.34 *Dam or Barrier wall adjacent to settlement. Phaino.*

ploitation, and a barrage or barrier wall (L ca. 65 m; cap. ca. 12,500 cum) adjacent to the settlement (fig. 8.34). The latter was most likely designed either to impound water for industrial use or to impound noxious sediments resulting from the mineral processing (Barker et al. 2007: 127, 162–64, 335–43). Some areas of stone piles were observed, but these represent either burial sites or simple field clearing, rather than a stratagem to increase runoff (Barker et al. 2007: 164–66).

The most prominent surviving remains of the water-supply system of Phaino are the numerous field boundaries built of water-worn boulders, barrier walls with spillways, and earthen, stone-framed water conduits built on and just above the wide, braided plane of the Wadi Faynan (fig. 8.35). The survey recognised 85 simple field systems, 10 complex field systems, 6 side terraces, and 1 possible field system (Barker et al. 2007: 98, 141–74). An area of approximately 253.2 ha was prepared

for agriculture in this manner during the Roman and Byzantine occupation, and more has probably disappeared through continued erosion of the run-off area. Six separate systems have been recorded, involving over 946 individual fields. By far the largest complex of contiguous fields (WF4) involved 785 fields in an area of 209.3 ha (Barker et al. 2007: 143). One procedure was to construct barrier walls with one or two facing walls of boulders on the wadi floor. These delayed the flowing water so it could soak into the soil and diverted some of the water to adjacent fields. The boundary stones delimiting the fields forced much of the water to pool and infiltrate the soil. An alternate procedure involved using barriers on the wadi floor upstream from the field to divert some of the flow into earthen channels running along the left bank. Since these channels had a gentler slope than the wadi, they could water fields located above the precarious wadi floor. Some of these field systems

Fig. 8.35 *View of run-off fields by Wadi Faynan. Phaino.*

date to the Early Bronze Age, but judging from the ceramics left by manuring, most probably were in use from the Nabataean through Byzantine periods. The extent of the Nabataean contribution is not clear, but at least some of the fields in WF4 yielded Nabataean ceramics (Barker et al. 2007: 141, 250, 292–93, 298–301). Barker calculates that these field systems could have produced enough food to sustain 300 persons, that the population of the settlement centre in the Roman/Byzantine period was approximately 600 and the total regional population 1,500–1,700 (Barker et al. 2007: 415). There are close parallels between this approach to run-off farming and the practices seen in the contemporary sites in the Negev (see 8.A.6) and in Libya (Barker et al. 1996: vol. 1 pp. 191–225).

In the context of this chapter, the remarkably elaborate irrigation system at Phaino is useful primarily for revealing techniques that could have been applied at Hawara to make use of the flow of the wadis that pass by the site, but which apparently were not. In particular, south of Hawara the Wadi Qalkha becomes a braided plain not unlike that of the Wadi Faynan. A portion of this plain at present is very sandy and useless for agriculture, but part of it is composed of loessial soil. It is possible that a system similar to what can still be seen at Phaino once existed, but it has now been lost to erosion or covered by encroaching sand. It could also be that, given the general absence of boulders in the wadi beds around Hawara (a result of the local geology), the field boundaries were made of earth and consequently have been lost.

Earthen field boundaries of the Nabataean period survive in remarkable condition at the site of Qasr et-Telah, ancient Toloha, 25 km north of Phaino in the Wadi Arabah (fig. 8.36; Kennedy 2004: 214–15; Kennedy and Bewley 2004: 142–43). At this site, however, the fields were constructed to the side of the alluvial fan fed by a wadi and, consequently, protected from flood damage. A spring-fed conduit may have irrigated them. Similar fields survive on either side of a braided wadi bed at the "Gardens of Petra," a run-off farming area at the point where the Wadis fed by Wadi Musa debouch into the Wadi Arabah. All in all, if such fields had existed around Hawara, one would expect at least some evidence to have survived beyond the occasional wadi barrier constructed of boulders that one sees today.

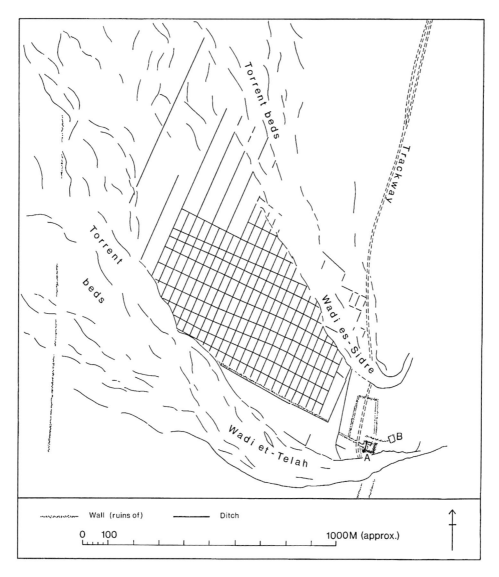

FIG. 8.36 *Plan of ancient fields, Qasr et-Telah. A = castellum, B = reservoir (adapted from Kennedy and Riley 1990: 207, fig. 158).*

Some of the Hebrew, Nabataean-Aramaic, and Greek papyri found in the Cave of Letters at Nahal Hever in 1960–61 refer to irrigation practices at sites on the lower slopes of the Wadi Arabah in the first and second century AD, probably involving fields very similar to those at Toloha and Phaino (Yadin et al. 2002: 6–7). *P. Yadin* 2 and 3 are Nabataean-Aramaic contracts for the sale of irrigated palm groves, dated to the twenty-eighth year of Rabbel II (97/98). The plantation was located in "Galgala' which is in Mahoz 'Eglatain;" Moaza was probably a village located in the district of the village of Zoar,

most likely Zoara, 25 km north of Toloha (Yadin et al. 202: 9, 217–18). Although the name of the locality means "wheel" and suggests the presence of mechanical water-lifting wheels for irrigation (Oleson 1984b: 8, 100–1), no such device is mentioned in these documents. Both documents seem to refer to the same property, which is surrounded by fields belonging to other individuals.

At several points *P. Yadin* 2 specifies details of the irrigation arrangements (Yadin et al. 2002: 201–31):

...a plantation of date palms which is in Galgala', which is in Mahoz 'Eglatain, including irrigation ditches and assigned watering periods; as is proper (lines 3–4, 22).

...including garden and spring, and water... and assigned watering periods... (lines 6–7, 27).

P. Yadin 3 is very similar in content, but adds a few details (Yadin et al. 2002: 233–44):

...a date palm plantation belonging to 'Abi-'adan , called *GH.*, which is in Galgala', which is in Mahoz 'Eglatain, including irrigation ditches and assigned water periods; half of one hour on the first day of the week, every single week and forever... (lines 3, 24–25).

A Jewish-Aramaic deed of gift of a palm grove at Mahoz 'Eglatain, dated 120, was preserved in the Babatha archive (*P. Yadin* 7; Yadin et al. 2002: 73–108). The district Galgala' is not named, but otherwise the arrangements are the same. A Greek papyrus from a different archive in the cave, dated to 129, mentions another date orchard at Mahoza, "with the water [allowance], once a week on the fourth day, for one half hour" (Cotton 1995: 183–203, lines 8–9, 27–28).

Clearly, the plantations depended on a source of flowing water, probably the spring that is mentioned in *P. Yadin* 2.6. Although the spring is listed as part of the property, it is unlikely to have been located on it, since the owner benefits from only a small share of the water. This water apparently was conducted to the fields in irrigation ditches, which must have been in part communal property, since access was guaranteed. The flow in the main channel was probably diverted to adjacent properties for the specified amount of time by removing a low earthen barrier or by lifting the plank in a simple sluice gate built of stone blocks. This approach to water sharing was widespread in the ancient world and remains in use today in the Middle East and elsewhere (Shaw 1982; Oleson 1984b: 37–8; Trousset 1986; Lancaster and Lancaster 1999: 147–66). It is likely that the water was divided among the plots at Toloha in a similar manner. Since the area around

the plantation was called Galgala', at least one owner may have had the right to use a compartmented wheel to lift the water. Alternatively, the spring may have discharged into a cistern, from which water was lifted to the communal irrigation channel by such a wheel. This may have been the arrangement at Toloha, where a large masonry reservoir (cap. ca. 4,500 cum) had some function within the water-supply system (Glueck 1934–35: 11–14). Although the overflow from the aqueduct pool at Hawara probably was less copious, it may have been apportioned in a similar manner among fields south of the settlement.

P. Yadin 3, a Nabataean-Aramaic loan contract secured by property, mentions "gardens and springs" associated with a palm plantation and vineyard at "*RMWN*, which is in Moab." This site may be the modern Khirbet Umm Rummane, just north of the Wadi al-Hasa (Yadin et al. 2002: 170–200). The document is dated to the twenty-third year of Rabbel II (92/93). *P. Yadin* 42 and *P. Yadin* 44, early second-century lease agreements in Aramaic and Hebrew regarding properties near 'Ein Gedi, describe the irrigated fields as "white land" (*ha efer ha lavan*) (Yadin et al. 2002: 45, 50, 144). This is a Mishnaic term for "cropland," and it probably arose from the markedly lighter colour of the silty soil in fields irrigated by spring or run-off water. Ancient and modern fields in the Nabataean cultural region fed by run-off water can still be identified by this means today (e.g., fig. 1.2).

8.A.4. *The Water-Supply System of the Sanctuary and Settlement at Wadi Ramm*

The well-known temple of Allat at Iram, modern Ramm, was built on a slope of scree at the foot of the precipitous cliffs characteristic of Wadi Ramm. The ancient name of the site might be Aramaua, mentioned by Ptolemy (*Geography* 6.7.27), but the connection with the "many-columned city of Iram" mentioned in the *Quran* (89: 5–7) is not certain (Dudley and Reeves 1997: 82–3). The site is tucked back into a recess in the west wall of the main wadi, framed by smaller wadis that climb into the cliffs to the north and south (fig. 8.37; Savignac 1932; 1933; 1934; Savignac and Horsfield 1935; Dudley and Reeves 1997; 2007; Tholbecq 1998; Taylor

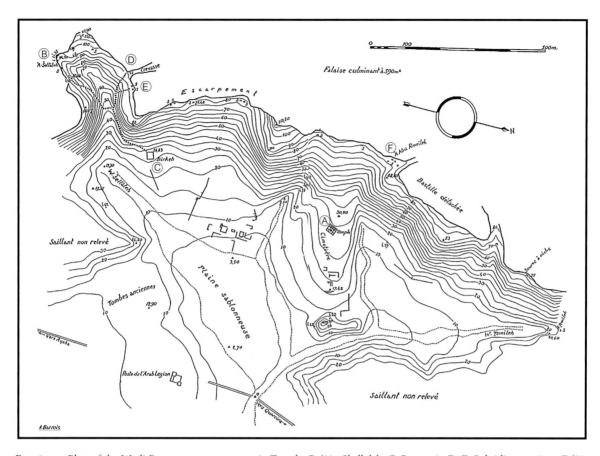

FIG. 8.37 *Plan of the Wadi Ramm sanctuary area. A, Temple. B, 'Ain Shellaleh. C, Reservoir. D–E, Subsidiary springs. F, 'Ain Abu Rumayleh (adapted from Savignac 1934: pl. 35).*

2001: 128–30; Kennedy and Bewley 2004: 132–33). Hawara lies 43 km to the north, but otherwise there were no other Nabataean settlements of any size in the Hisma. The Nabataean caravan city of Hegra, modern Meda'in Salih, is distant 440 km to the southeast. The precise character of the sanctuary at Wadi Ramm and any associated settlement is still not entirely clear (Tholbecq 1998; Dudley and Reeves 1997; 2007; Perry and Jones 2006). The temple (elev. ca. 980 m asl) was constructed in several stages from the first century BC through the late first or early second century AD (Tholbecq 1998; fig. 8.37, A). At one corner of the adyton there is a small cistern (1.6 × 1.6 × 1.8 m; cap. 4.6 cum) built of blocks and lined with hydraulic plaster. The roofing slabs were supported by one small cross-arch.

Several springs flow from strata around the edges of the recessed valley where the temple is located, but only the largest, 'Ain Shellaleh in the west-facing wall of the south wadi (elev. ca. 1,050 m), preserves significant traces of structures and inscriptions (fig. 8.37, B). Savignac found the stubs of block-built walls, a conduit of stone gutter blocks, and numerous betyls and rock-cut inscriptions (fig. 8.38; Savignac 1933; 1934). There was also a stone slab carrying an inscription in honour of Rabbel II: "Rabbel the king, king of Nabataea, who brought life and deliverance to his people." It has been suggested that this honorific phrase, which is applied to many of the Nabataean kings, refers to their involvement in the construction of water-supply systems (Negev 1963: 117; 1977: 639–40).

As at 'Ain Jammam, the walls line up approximately with the overhang above the mouth of the spring, as if to create a protected space. An aqueduct built of gutter blocks similar to those at Hawara carried the spring water approximately 475 m downhill to the mouth of the small valley, where it discharged into a reservoir built of neat

FIG. 8.38 *View of 'Ain Shellaleh, 1987, Wadi Ramm.*

FIG. 8.39 *View of reservoir fed by 'Ain Shellaleh aqueduct, Wadi Ramm.*

FIG. 8.40 *View of 'Ain Shellaleh aqueduct, Wadi Ramm.*

sandstone blocks (figs. 8.37, C, 8.39; interior ca. 24 × 24 m; elev. ca. 980 m). Tholbecq mentions two reservoirs fed by this aqueduct, but he does not specify the location of the second (Tholbecq 1998: 252). The course of the aqueduct weaves down the slope below the spring among the large tumbled boulders, supported where necessary on walls of neatly coursed blocks (fig. 8.40). At one point, the conduit makes an abrupt 90-degree turn on a steep slope. Unfortunately, the junction does not survive; perhaps it consisted of a block-built junction box designed to absorb the force of the descending water and restrict splashing. The slope varies dramatically, from approximately five to ten percent near the top and bottom to as high as 40 percent at the steepest point. Two shorter, less steep branch lines brought water from two less productive springs across the wadi from the 'Ain Shellaleh, joining the main conduit just after it crossed the wadi bed (figs. 8.37, D, E). Unfortunately, as at Hawara, the junction point has been lost. Savignac's detailed map of the area (1934: pl. 35) does not show it, but a conduit continues on from the reservoir at the foot of Wadi Shellaleh to the temple. The gutter blocks have been

preserved in position only intermittently, but they document the presence of an aqueduct during at least one phase of the temple use. The slope was very gentle; the total length of the channel back to the spring would have been ca. 1.5 km. Yet another steep conduit brought water to the temple area from the 'Ain Abu Rumayleh at the foot of the cliff directly above the temple (Dudley and Reeves 1997: 105–6; fig. 8.37, F). Although at least one of these conduits should have provided water to the temple cistern, they may also have continued on to the bath and settlement farther down the slope.

In both design and construction techniques, the aqueduct and reservoir at Wadi Ramm closely resemble the aqueduct and associated pool at Hawara. Although the interior has not been excavated, the visible upper courses of the reservoir consist largely of header blocks of sandstone, set end-on into the wall, as at Hawara. The aqueduct was built of sandstone gutter blocks of varying lengths and outside dimensions, but with relatively constant channel dimensions (W ca. 10 m, depth 0.12 m), similar to those at Hawara. The most crisply carved blocks have the typically Nabataean

neat diagonal trimming on the exterior, while
others were only roughly-trimmed with a
punch. The variation in finish may reflect the
need for frequent repair of the channel, which
crossed a very difficult, unstable rock slope.
The gutter blocks were set in a bed of mortar
and small cobbles, framed with blocks of the
local granite.

Although the aqueduct system, like some
of the inscriptions at 'Ain Shellaleh, was probably a royal project, there is a small amount
of evidence for private ownership of smaller
water-supply structures at Wadi Ramm and
elsewhere nearby. A Dedanite inscription in
Wadi Ramm records the efforts of two individuals who built some sort of structure that
"collected rain water at Diwah," most likely a cistern (Farès-Drappeau 1995). Farès-Drappeau
and Zayadine found a large number of small-
scale dams during a survey of Wadi Ramm,
designed to trap water in bedrock gullies (2004:
370). The names of North Arabian tribes were
carved in the rock near most of these structures,
indicating their owners. There are also dams
scattered here and there in the jebels on the
route between Hawara and Wadi Ramm; one
of them, at Jebel Ratama, had a more expansive
inscription: "Belonging to Shaba', son of Eleh,
(this dam) was built in the year 41 of Aretas,
king of Nabataea, who loves his people. Yaqqa"
(fig. 8.41; Kirkbride and Harding 1947: 19–20; Sartre
1993: 169, no. 136). The father's name is written in
Greek nearby: ΗΛΕΟΣ. The pool formed by the
dam (W 4 m, H 3 m) was 25 m long and roofed with
slabs carried on 23 cross-arches. Nearby, at Jebel
Haraza, a neat rock-cut channel guided runoff water
to a gully dammed by a carefully built masonry wall
(Jobling 1983–84: 266–67, fig. 22).

At Muqawwar (or Mughur) near the end of the
Wadi Hafir, opposite Wadi Ramm, run-off water
cascades off the al-Shara escarpment into a very
large circular pool, natural in origin but enhanced
to increase its capacity (Corbett 2009: 344, fig. 7).
There are hundreds of graffiti in the area depicting
wild and domesticated animals, including cattle
(Jobling 1989a; 1989b). The impression is similar to
that of the large natural basin blocked by a barrier
wall at Structure no. 28 near Hawara.

FIG. 8.41 *Dammed cleft cistern at Jebel Ratama (Photo: J. Starcky,
from Milik 1958: pl. XVIII.a),*

The water-supply system of Wadi Ramm and
the structures in the region around it show some
striking parallels with the system serving Hawara.
The construction of the aqueduct is very similar, as
are the contribution of several branch lines to the
main conduit, and the conduction of at least some
of the water to a reservoir. Although as yet not
well-documented, there were numerous cisterns
and small dams in the region, as around Hawara,
providing privately owned water. Given the proximity of the two sites, it is quite possible that there
were social, religious, or political bonds between
them. In fact, Wadi Ramm may be the site of the
oracular shrine referred to in the foundation story
of Hawara, the oracle that told Obodas to "seek a
place called 'white.'" Hydraulic engineers probably
moved freely about the region.

8.A.5. *Miscellaneous Small-Scale Water-Supply Systems in Arabia Petraea*

Before turning to the water-supply systems of the Nabataean cities in the Negev, which is a markedly different landscape from that of Arabia Petraea, it is useful to consider details of some smaller Nabataean and Roman systems in the desert parts of Jordan and Saudi Arabia.

The Nabataean city of Hegra (or Egra), known above all for its splendidly-preserved rock-cut tomb facades (Wenning 1987: 119–22; Taylor 2001: 153–64), also encompassed habitation areas, agricultural fields, and a water-supply system. There are springs in the area, and some crops are grown there today through irrigation from fossil ground water. Unfortunately, the region has only recently been opened up to archaeological excavation and survey, so little has been published about the water-supply system. Courbon (2008) reports the presence of a large number of ancient wells (depth 18 m) in the necropolis and settlement areas, but he does not mention conduits or cisterns. Nehmé et al. (2006: 65–74, 94–96) outline the agricultural potential of the site, the water resources, and the possible use of the 131 wells scattered around the site for irrigation of local plots by the Nabataeans. At least one stone conduit block was found at the site. Nehmé provides a plan of a run-off system in the Jebel Ithlib that involved rock-cut collection and transport channels, rock-cut cisterns and settling tanks, and a large natural rock basin to which the water was conveyed. Wenning (personal communication, November 2002) indicates that several niches with betyls can be seen "in connection with water channels," and Healey (1993: 11) mentions the Jebel Ithlib water channels as well. Parr (1997) mentions "ample supplies" of run-off water available from "wells and cisterns."

Although Hegra lies 440 km south of Hawara, they were connected by an active trade route. The topography of the two sites is similar and the amount of precipitation is approximately the same, but it appears that there are fewer rock-cut cisterns at Hegra than at Hawara. The presence of ground water at a depth of only 18 m probably fostered a water-supply system dependent on wells rather than aqueducts and cisterns. Since the wells are

very wide, up to 7 m in diameter, Nehmé (2006: 68–69) suggests that they served as a type of cistern fed by the percolation of water from the surrounding porous earth and rock. The rest of the water-supply system is very similar to what existed at Hawara. Terraced wadis and fenced fields fed by run-off that date to the Nabataean period (and possibly earlier) have been found at Qurayya, a site 275 km to the north of Hegra (Parr et al. 1968–69: 220–41).

The Romans built a series of watchtowers and strong points along the course of the Via Nova Traiana, particularly in the descent through the Wadi Yutum to Aqaba. Some of these sites are named on the Peutinger Table (fig. 2.13). Quweira, the site of a small fort, is 19 km west of the entrance to Wadi Ramm, 18 km south–southeast of Humayma, near the mouth of the Wadi Yutum (Parker 1986: 105–8; Kennedy 2004: 198–99). The *castellum* (32.5 × 32.5 m inside measurements), which had four projecting corner towers, was built in the second century on top of a Nabataean structure. The garrison was probably meant to protect the roads, control a viewpoint on top of the adjacent jebel, and provide a secure watering station. Jaussen (1903: 101, 107) reported that the water from a spring at the foot of Jebel Quweira flowed into an adjacent rock-cut basin, then was brought in a *canal* 200 m to a reservoir (32 × 18 × >2 m; cap. >1,152 cum) adjacent to the fort (fig. 8.42). The reservoir was rebuilt in the Turkish period, and the entrance channel in the northeast corner and staircase in the southwest corner seem to date to that period or to the later British occupation of the adjacent police compound. Parker states that the reservoir was cut in the sandstone bedrock, but this detail, which cannot be verified because of recent cementing of the interior, seems unlikely in view of the local topography. The juxtaposition of Roman fort and spring-fed pool is reminiscent of Roman Hauarra, but in its present state the site provides no further information.

On the left bank of the Wadi Yutum, 18 km south of Quweira, the Romans built another *castellum* (44 × 33 m) adjacent to a Nabataean structure, possibly a caravanserai. The site, ancient Praesidium, is now called Khirbet al-Khalde (Parker 1986: 108–9; Kennedy 2004: 199–202). It is 33 km south of Hawara, precisely the 23 Roman

FIG. 8.42 *Reservoir by Roman fort, looking southwest, Quweira.*

FIG. 8.43 *General view of Khirbet al-Khalde: castellum (left foreground), possible caravanserai (right foreground), and area of spring.*

miles indicated in the Peutinger Table between "Praesidium" and "Hauarra." There is a cistern (ca. 6.4 m square) in the first courtyard within the fort and remains of a hypocausted bath or banqueting room in the second. A pipeline connected the cistern with a spring 800 m southeast and 250 m higher in a rocky gully above a steep slope of scree (fig. 8.43). The pipes, made of a hard, sandy, white fabric, with male and female joints, were set in a bed of mortar and small cobbles framed by blocks of stone (fig. 8.44). No cover slabs were observed, but they may have been supplied to protect the ceramic pipes. The conduit followed a straight line towards the spring until reaching the rocky gully, where it is now lost. At one point, the conduit passes by or over a structure ca. 6 m square that may be a cistern.

Since the relatively light pipes could not have taken a pressure of 25 atmospheres, the pipeline must have run partly empty but at high velocity, given the slope (31 percent). The use of terracotta pipes, of course, is typical of the Nabataean and Roman period structures at Hauarra, but they were not used down steep slopes. This approach is, however, seen in several of the aqueduct systems at Petra, and in that serving the Roman fort at Qasr Umm Rattam, below Petra.

Although much farther afield, 100 km north of Petra, the Nabataean and Roman period sanctuary and habitation site of Khirbet edh-Dharih provides some information of interest concerning water-supply systems (Kennedy and Bewley 2004: 128–29). The site is tucked into the Wadi La'aban, which opens on the south slope of the Wadi Hasa opposite the Nabataean sanctuary of Khirbet et-Tannur. The sites are 6.5 km apart, but each can be seen from the other, probably one motivation for choosing this spot for the Khirbet edh-Dharih temple. Another motive was the presence of the 'Ain Shedam 6 km to the southeast and at a slightly higher elevation (Villeneuve 1986). Water was brought from the spring to the settlement in a conduit very similar to the Hawara aqueduct. Although now mostly destroyed, the structure was built of stone gutter blocks (H 0.32 m, W 0.54 m, L 0.55–0.63 m) with a large channel (W 0.29 m, depth 0.15 m; fig. 8.45). Most of the blocks have been pulled out of their original position in recent times to serve a penstock mill.

FIG. 8.44 *Support structure for pipeline from spring (pipes lost), Khirbet al-Khalde.*

This spring seems to have had regional importance, since an inscription at the Khirbet et-Tannur temple, dated 8/7 BC, mentions "Netir'el son of Zayd'eh, Master of the Spring of La'aban" (*r's 'yn l'aban*) (Glueck 1965: 512–13). This place name is still preserved in the name of the wadi and a spring near Khirbet edh-Dharih. It is not clear what the duties of a "Master of the Spring" might have involved, but the office may have had something to do with the administration of the discharge. A very similar term, *rb 'yn* ("Head of the Spring"), appears in inscriptions concerning the Efqa spring at Palmyra, along with many details about tasks and achievements. The Head or *Curator* of the Efqa spring took care of the practical infrastructure, while a separate figure, *'pkl dy msb 'yn,* "Priest of the Idol of the Spring," was in charge of religious observances (Placentini 2001–2). Wenning (2009) has proposed that the representation of a leaf-covered divinity at Khirbet et-Tannur (Glueck 1965:

FIG. 8.45 *Conduit blocks below temple, Khirbet edh-Dharih.*

pls. 31–33; Markoe 2003: fig. 4) is a personification of 'Ain La'aban rather than "Atargatis," and that similar sculptures at Petra may represent 'Ain Musa and 'Ain Brak.

8.A.6. *Nabataean, Roman, and Byzantine Water-Supply Systems in the Negev*

The early stages of the Nabataean occupation of the Negev, now part of Israel and the Palestinian Entity, are still obscure, but the Nabataeans seem to have established trade routes across the region by the late fourth century BC, and these routes attracted watchtowers and settlements by the second half of the third century BC (Wenning 1987: 137–39). The caravan routes led west from Petra towards the shore of the Mediterranean Sea, mainly to emporia at ancient Gaza and Pelusium (El-Arish) (Meshel and Safrir 1974, 1975; Glucker 1987: 86–93; Johnson 1987; Finkelstein 1990). Incense and other high-value commodities imported from the Arabian peninsula and the Indian subcontinent were carried along this "incense road" and contributed

to the development of six main settlement centres with a total population possibly as high as 20,000: Oboda, Sobata, Nessana, Mampsis, Elusa, and Ruheiba (Elliot 1982: 103–14; Rubin 1989; 1996; Shereshevski 1991: 200–14; Rosen 2000; fig 2.1). Sobata was not located on the main road, but it must have reflected to an extent the regional increase in population and prosperity. To support their human and animal populations in a very arid environment, sophisticated water-supply systems were developed, many of which provide interesting parallels or contrasts with the system that supplied Hawara. The average annual precipitation around these settlements varies from 50–150 mm (Mayerson 1967; Evenari et al. 1982: 32). Although the caravan trade contributed to the prosperity of these settlements, additional support came from a remarkably intensive system of agriculture based on run-off water. By the early Byzantine period, these techniques even supported an extensive export trade in the famous white wine shipped from Gaza but apparently produced around Ruheiba and Elusa (Mayerson 1985; Glucker 1987: 93). There were also numerous isolated fortlets, watchtowers, and farms throughout the region, most of which preserve some evidence for water-supply systems. Early aerial photographs of some of the sites and views of the landscape appear in Wiegand (1920).

There are several problems in evaluating the relevance of this archaeological evidence to the system at Hawara and Nabataean hydraulic technology in general. Most important is the question of chronology. The region remained well-populated and prosperous from at least the first century BC through the seventh century AD (Shereshevski 1991; Gutwein 1981), and it is often not clear to which period various water-supply structures belong. One extreme and unlikely proposal is that all these structures belong to the Late Byzantine period (Nevo 1991). On the other hand, some of the wadi barrages and terraces go back to the Chalcolithic (Levy and Alon 1987), and wells appear as early as the Neolithic (Avner 2001/2). Despite the chronological uncertainty, most of the structures appear to be Nabataean in design or inspiration, even if somewhat later in date. The best discussions of the water-supply systems typical of the Negev appear in Mayerson 1961, 1967; Kloner 1973, 2001–2; Evenari et al. 1982; Hillel 1982; Bruins 1986; Shereshevski 1991; Rosen 2000; Avner 2001/2; Tsuk 2002; Oleson 2003b.

A second problem is that although the Negev is largely a desert, in many areas the soil is generally more extensive and better in quality than that around Hawara or in the rest of Arabia Petraea. In addition, there are varying calculations of the amount of run-off generated by the hills, which are generally not smooth bedrock but often have a covering of soil and small stones (Evenari et al. 1982: 126–47). Finally, only small portions of the important sites of Elusa and Ruheiba have been excavated, and their water-supply systems remain poorly documented. The structures at Oboda and Sobata, in contrast, were cleared rather than excavated archaeologically and have been insensitively restored for tourism. The site of Nessana suffered from Turkish, British, and Israeli military occupation and some intrusive restoration. The varying archaeological condition of the settlement centres naturally affects interpretation of the ancient water-supply systems.

The Water-Supply System of Oboda

The early history of Oboda (also termed Eboda in the ancient sources; modern Avdat) is obscure, but there probably was a settlement of some sort at least by the second half of the third century BC serving the Petra–Gaza road. The history, monuments, and water-supply system of the site have been discussed by numerous authors (see esp. Evenari et al. 1982; Hillel 1982; Wenning 1987: 159–72; Shereshevski 1991: 36–48 and *passim*; Negev 1993d; 1997a; 1997b). The site was probably named after a deified king Obodas, who according to Uranius was buried there (*FgrH* III.C, no. 675.24). The identity of this Obodas is in doubt, as it is with the Obodas to whom Uranius says the oracular message to found Hawara was given. This Obodas may have been either Obodas II (62/1–60/59 BC; Negev 1997a: 236) or Obodas III (30–9 BC; Wenning 1987: 160). In any case, it is likely that some degree of urbanisation and the creation of permanent structures took place only at this time and that there was a concomitant increase in the harvesting of run-off water for drinking and agriculture. In consequence, it is possible that the water-supply systems at Hawara and Oboda evolved contemporaneously. Oboda is slightly lower in elevation than Hawara (610 m asl), but the figures for annual precipitation (68.8 mm) and evaporation (3031.3 mm) are very similar (Evenari et al. 1982: 34, Table 4), so the two sites provide an interesting comparison. There was some sort of destruction at Oboda around AD 40–50 and possibly a hiatus in urban activities until the second or third century (Wenning 1987: 167–63; Negev 1997b). There was a great deal of building during the Late Roman and Byzantine periods, but the decline in political and economic importance of the Levant in the seventh and eighth centuries resulted in the decline and abandonment of Oboda and all the other settlements in the Negev (Rosen 2000).

The most spectacular aspect of the exploitation of water in and around Oboda was the development of enormous agricultural fields designed to make use of run-off water (fig. 8.46). From aerial photographs, Kedar calculated the area of arable land at 685 ha (reported in Negev 1988b: 5). Hundreds of low walls constructed of five to seven courses of boulders were built across wide, gently

FIG. 8.46 *Stepped fields in the wadis around Oboda.*

FIG. 8.47 *Hillside catchment channels in the wadis around Oboda (Evenari et al. 1982: fig. 65).*

sloping wadis to hold back soil and delay the flow of run-off water so that it could infiltrate the soil (Evenari et al. 1982: 95–119, 179–190). The walls are typically 0.60–0.80 m high, 6–20 m long, and spaced 12–15 m apart. Walls of this type form an attractive habitat for the natural desert vegetation, which reinforces and protects the barrier, while the fields themselves were used for a wide variety of Mediterranean food crops (Evenari et al. 1982: 191–219). Many of the walls were provided with stepped spillways, as at Jebel Haroun near Petra and at Phaino. Identical arrangements are found around Sobata and Nessana as well. There are remarkable parallels between this approach to run-off farming and that seen in contemporary sites in Libya (Barker et al. 1996: vol. 1, pp. 191–225), but these are likely to be the result of parallel development rather than shared ideas.

The water flowing across the terraced fields consisted not only of wadi flow but also of run-off from adjacent slopes. In a sample of approximately 100 wadi-barrier complexes ("farms") around Oboda and other Negev sites, the ratio between the area of the agricultural fields and that of the adjacent catchment fields varied from 1:17 to 1:30, with an average of around 1:20. Experimental farms at Oboda and Sobata have shown that approximately 15–20 percent of the annual precipitation arrives at the fields as run-off, raising the effective annual precipitation from ca. 70–100 mm to 300–500 mm (Evenari et al. 1982: 104–9, 127–47), sufficient for a wide variety of crops. Inscribed stone troughs have been found in association with the field system in the Nahal Avdat (Wadi Ramliya) near Oboda, some of them asserting ownership (Evenari et al. 1982: 119, fig. 80; Wenning 1987: 169; Negev 1986: 107). Negev translates the longest as follows: "This dam (which was built) by … the sons of …/ (and his associates) the sons of Saruta for the offering of sacrifices / to Dushara the God of Gaia in the year 18 (?) of the King Rabbel King of the Nabataeans who brought life and deliverance to his people." The date is AD 88/89. Unfortunately, there is dispute regarding the reading of the word "dam" (MDR?): other interpretations are "channels," "measure," and "irrigated land" (Wenning 1987: 169). The implications, however, all involve privately owned, enhanced, agricultural land.

The catchment fields themselves usually were modified to enhance, control, and direct the run-off water. One method was to dig channels across the slope of the hillside at a relatively low gradient, thus salvaging run-off that might otherwise be lost below the cultivated area, or directing the water to a specific field or field group and simultaneously dividing the run-off into manageable amounts. The outside edges of these channels, which could extend for hundreds of metres, were reinforced with fieldstones (fig. 8.47). Another spectacular method of enhancing both the run-off of water and the transportation of soil to the fields was the removal of surface stones across large areas of a catchment. In order to minimise effort, the stones were moved to uniform piles on the slope itself; these form patterns of random or orderly mounds (D 1–5 m, H 0.20–1.0 m; see fig. 8.51), long single or double lines (W 2–3 m, H 0.15–0.25 m) oriented down-slope toward the fields, or alternating lines and mounds. The areas treated in this manner could be very large — more than 2,500 ha at Oboda, 250 ha at Sobata — or a more modest 2–3 ha at rural farms (Kedar 1957a; 1957b; Mayerson 1959; Evenari et al. 1982: 126–47). The local Arab term for the mounds, *teleilat al-anab* ("grape mounds"), led many scholars in the nineteenth and early twentieth century to propose that the mounds originally were piled up around grape vines in order somehow to harvest the dew or run-off water (e.g., Mayerson 1959; 1960; 1961). In fact, the heaps cannot have functioned in this manner, and excavation has not found any traces of vine roots or stalks. Controlled experimentation in the Negev, however, has shown that removal of surface stones to nearby heaps can increase run-off by removing the small barriers to flow and by facilitating crusting over of the exposed soil during the early stages of rainfall. The degree of slope has an effect, as does the intensity of the rainfall. It is striking to note that the resulting enhancement works more effectively with the light rains of a drought year, when enhancement would be particularly important, than with heavy rainfall: an enhancement to 40 cum/ha as opposed to 10–20 cum/ha (Kedar 1964; Evenari et al. 1982: 127–47). Miller (1977: 438) estimates the labour requirements for this clearing and calculates a return of 1 cum of runoff/year/man-day of work, which seems a good return. An obvious corollary of slope enhancement is that the individual who performed or commissioned the work somehow owned the resulting run-off.

Slope enhancement, particularly the use of hillside channels, was also used to fill cisterns cut into the limestone bedrock near the foot of slopes, both on the acropolis of Oboda and in the surrounding countryside (fig. 8.48; Evenari et al. 1982: 148–72). The cisterns were often cut into the side of a hill, in a naturally waterproof layer of chalk below a stratum of limestone that served as a roof; central pillars might be left for support in particularly large cisterns, along with access stairs. Around Oboda, the floor area is usually ca. 36 sq m and the height ca. 4–6 m, providing a capacity of ca. 144–216 cum; this figure is significantly larger than the average capacity of cisterns around Hawara (97.4 cum) or in Sobata (46.2 cum). The Oboda average may be larger because the human population was greater and the flocks larger in size, or the chalk into which the cisterns were carved may simply have been easier to excavate than the sandstone around Hawara. Although the chronology is uncertain, there were cisterns on the acropolis of Oboda, below the churches, and apparently below most of the private homes as well (Evenari et al. 1982: 166; Negev 1997a: 27, 78, 103, 109–13, 129). One of the cisterns on the acropolis approximately resembles the cylindrical cisterns built of blocks in the Hawara centre, but the parallel is not striking: it was "rounded in shape, with a diameter of 6–7 m," 3 m deep, with a capacity of 300 cum. The roof was made of slabs supported on cross-arches. The cistern apparently was cut in the rock, but "lined" with walls (Negev 1997a: 103). Negev suggests that it was designed to supply water to the nearby Nabataean temple.

Unlike the situation at Hawara, the aquifers in the Negev were sometimes close enough to the surface to allow the successful excavation of wells for water supply, although many of the wells are in fact very deep. A Late Roman bathhouse was constructed in the Wadi Zin northwest of the acropolis

FIG. 8.48 *Draw-hole of cistern cut in the bedrock in Nahal Zin, near Oboda.*

of Oboda to make use of the water brought up from a deep well. Some sort of animal-driven, geared water-lifting device was probably installed at the top (Hillel 1982: 171–74; Evenari et al. 1982: 156; Negev 1997a: 171–76). The wadi bed is composed of chalk and limestone and holds water only during winter storms. The engineers, however, noticed that a spring flowed from the foot of a 100 m drop along the wadi, 3 km downstream from Oboda, above a layer of impermeable stone. Apparently they were confident enough in their ability to tap the same aquifer closer to the town that they undertook excavation of a circular well shaft 3–4 m in diameter through 70 m of hard stone. The well was cleared in 1954 to its solid floor and once again provided water at the level of the downstream spring.

Despite the similarities in climate and cultural development, the water-supply system serving ancient Oboda seems quite different from that at Hawara. The creation of fields at Oboda through the terracing of wadis and the removal of surface stones on hillsides to enhance run-off can be documented at Hawara, but on a very much smaller scale. The slopes on which stone piles are found at Hawara do not seem associated with fields suitable for agriculture, so their presence is puzzling. There simply may have been enough suitable bedrock slopes in the vicinity of Hawara that it was not necessary to enhance soil slopes. Furthermore, the intensive agriculture in the Negev, particularly the production of wine, has been seen as an exten-

FIG. 8.49 *Terraced fields and stone piles (far right) in Wadi Lavan, Sobata.*

sion of the needs of the adjacent Mediterranean economy (Rosen 2000). Arabia Petraea was too distant to be affected to the same extent, and food production very likely was intended for local consumption.

The Water-Supply System of Sobata

Ancient Sobata (also Sobeita, modern Shivta, Isbeita) is located 17.5 km northwest of Oboda but seems to have developed apart from the regional trade routes. The site lies at 340 m asl, in an area of Irano-Turanian steppe vegetation, with an annual precipitation of 90–100 mm, conditions slightly more propitious than those at Hawara (Kedar 1957a: 178). Given the intense agricultural development of the surrounding area, it probably served as a residential centre for the farmers and as a market centre for the nomadic pastoral population (Groh 1997: 90). The settlement occupied an area of 8 ha, approximately the same as Oboda (8.5 ha; Shereshevski 1991: 204). Despite the superb preservation of the architecture, there has been little stratigraphic excavation, so the history of the site has been recreated on the basis of inscriptions, coins, unstratified ceramics, and architectural styles. A Nabataean phase of the late first century BC and

early first century AD has been tentatively identified, but most of the visible remains belong to the Byzantine period (late fifth to seventh centuries) (Kedar 1957a, 1957b; Gutwein 1981: 89–93; Evenari et al. 1982: *passim*; Hillel 1982: *passim*; Segal 1983; Wenning 1987: 155–56; Shereshevski 1991: 61–82 and *passim*; Negev 1993e; Tsuk 2002; Hirschfeld 2003). The settlement appears to have grown as clusters of houses organised in a casual manner, perhaps along convenient routes of passage. The open areas were gradually filled with structures, leaving only lanes and a few open squares. This type of development, which resembles what can be seen at Hawara (Blétry-Sébé 1990), follows a different set of rules than grid planning, perhaps based on tribal organisation (Whitcomb 1996; Gawlikowski 1997).

As at Oboda, the most spectacular aspect of Sobata's water-supply system involved the construction of low terraced fields in and alongside the wadis that pass by the settlement centre, in particular the Wadi Lavan (fig. 8.49). Kedar has calculated an area of 494 ha of cultivated fields in the region controlled by Sobata: 284.7 ha of fields in the wadi floors, formed by low barrage walls, and 209.7 ha of "fenced-in" field systems, generally built up the slopes above the wadis and served by

FIG. 8.50 *Stepped spillway at terraced field in Wadi Lavan, Sobata.*

FIG. 8.51 *Catchment fields with stone piles, Sobata.*

FIG. 8.52 *Southern reservoir in settlement centre, Sobata.*

flood water diverted from the wadi. These fields are within 4–6 km of the settlement centre, in accord with the "principle of least effort" as seen at Hawara (see p. 35; Simmons 1981; Beaumont et al. 1976: 164–65; Wagstaff 1985: 52–53). Allowing for 100 mm of precipitation and the proportion of run-off as 10–15 percent, there would have been between 4,900 and 7,300 cum of water available for these fields and for other uses. Kedar identified 83 separate fenced-in field systems, varying from 0.09 to over 10 ha in size, with the mean in the range of 1 to 1.5 ha. He calculates a ratio of field size to catchment size of 1:12 (Kedar 1957a; 1957b). Most of the walls were supplied with stepped central spillways to allow passage of the water (fig. 8.50), while wooden sluice gates set in stone grooves allowed diversion of the main flow into several separate fields in sequence (Evenari et al. 1982: 95–119, esp. 104). As at Oboda, the slopes around these fields were often enhanced by removal of the surface stones into long lines or separate piles (fig. 8.51). On other slopes, the run-off was increased and compartmentalised by the use of long hillside conduits, some of them up to 1.5 km long, 3 m wide,

2.5 m deep, reinforced on the down-slope side with stones (Kedar 1957a: 183).

Another major feature of the water-supply system was a ground-level, earthen water conduit 2.5 km long that diverted the run-off water from 25 ha of the Wadi Qorhah to the settlement centre (Kedar 1957a: 184; Tsuk 2002: 77–79). The channel, descending from 420 to 350 m asl (for a slope of 2.8 percent), was about 2 m wide and 0.40 m deep, faced with blocks on one or both sides depending on the topography. Close to the settlement it was 1 m wide and 0.70 m deep. At one point, the aqueduct passed across a valley on a low earthen viaduct reinforced with stones (L 30 × W 4.7 × H 1.0 m). At two points, there were distribution boxes with sluice gates; one outside the city allowed diversion of water to fields, the other, on the edge of the settlement, had three gates allowing diversion to the reservoir and cisterns in the centre, or to the cistern beneath the northern church.

Two large, open reservoirs in the southern portion of the habitation area also formed part of the water-supply system (fig. 8.52). They are adjacent and form irregular trapezoids in plan, which sug-

Fig. 8.53 *Conduit leading to southern reservoir, Sobata.*

gests they may have originated as stone quarries (Tsuk 2002: 74–75). The bedrock walls have been lined with small stones set in mortar; a flight of steps leads down into one of them. Their areas (486 and 324 sq m), combined with a reconstructed average depth of 2.5 m, indicate a combined capacity of 2,025 cum. The reservoirs may have been filled in part with run-off from house roofs and streets in this part of town, but the resulting water would have been poor in quality and the amount of run-off probably insufficient to fill them. Several channels that serve the reservoirs may have carried water from the aqueduct; they run beneath and predate the Byzantine houses in this part of town (fig. 8.53). Four sixth-century ostraka found in spoil from the cistern in a private house near the reservoirs were receipts to individuals for compulsory labour. Two of them specifically mention public pools, probably the reservoirs themselves (Youtie 1936; Tsuk 2002: 75–76). The documents date to October, the month before winter rains might begin, when water levels would have been lowest — the best time for cleaning or maintenance.

> (No. 1): To Flavius Garmus, son of Zacharius: you have finished one work unit for the cistern (κιστέρνα)…

> (No. 3): To father Iohannes, son of Victor, husband, greetings. You have finished one work unit in the cistern (κιστέρνα).

Κιστέρνα, borrowed from Latin *cisterna*, seems an odd word to designate a reservoir (usually λάκκος), but this usage is common in Byzantine texts. Public *corvée* labour would not have been expended on private cisterns. The name Γάρμος is the Greek equivalent of Nabataean Garmu, well-attested in the Negev, Sinai, and Egypt (Negev 1991: no. 242; Youtie 1936: 457). This cultural continuity, seen also in the Byzantine papyri from Petra (Frösén, Arjava, Lehtinen 2002: 9–10; Frösén 2004), Sobata, and Nessana (Kraemer 1958), reminds us that the hydraulic technology of the Byzantine period can have its roots in the Nabataean accomplishments as well.

In his survey of the portion of Sobata that has been cleared of debris, Tsuk found 57 cistern draw holes, providing access to cisterns of varying shapes and sizes cut into the sandstone bedrock (Tsuk 2002: 67–74). The cisterns were circular or square in plan with flat bedrock ceilings; in two examples, the bedrock was supplemented or supported by slabs carried on cross-arches. Nearly all the houses at the site were roofed with slabs carried on cross-arches (Segal 1983). The plaster, pink on a grey bedding layer, was 0.015–0.004 m thick. The draw holes, which also provided access for cleaning, were built up above the pavement and finished off with a monolithic well-head slab and cover stone (fig. 8.54). The circular openings in the well-heads were 0.33–0.40 m diameter. The cisterns were filled with run-off from the roof of the structure in which they were located, carried to the draw hole in large channels carefully constructed of blocks of stone (from 0.10 × 0.10 m to 0.40 × 0.40 m) and buried 1–2 m below the pavement.

Of the 57 cisterns recorded by Tsuk, 40 were located in the courtyards of private homes, 5 in rooms within houses, 6 in churches or church yards, 2 in streets, and 4 outside the settlement centre. Clearly, domestic cisterns were an important part of the water-supply system for Byzantine Sobata, as they were for Nabataean Hawara. Most of the cisterns were partly filled with sediment or debris, but the original average depth was around 2.5 m. The volume of 28 cisterns was measured: 3 held less than 20 cum, 8 held 20–25 cum, 15 held 40–70 cum, and two held 130–170 cum. The average capacity was 46.2 cum, the total was 1292.7 cum. Three of the 13 domestic cisterns in the habitation centre at Hawara had capacities larger than 200 cum, bringing the average at that site up to 116.2 cum, with a large standard deviation (84.2 cum). The average area of the 170 residential units at Sobata is 400 sq m, which at 50 percent capture would yield 21 cum of run-off from the annual precipitation of 90 mm. Assuming 13 persons per unit, this amount allows 4.2 l/day per person (Tsuk 2002: 77). Since this ration would have been barely enough to sustain life, some cisterns may have been topped

FIG. 8.54 *Monolithic settling and distribution basin by domestic cistern draw hole, Sobata.*

up with aqueduct water, and the water in the reservoirs may have been used for washing, watering domestic animals, and industrial purposes. If each unit somehow received enough water to fill the average-sized cistern (46.2 cum), the ration would be 9.7 l/day, which is sufficient for a human's various needs. On the basis of the occupation area, Hirschfeld (2003: 402–4) restores a population of around 2,200.

Six cisterns were found in association with the three churches at Sobata, but only the large cistern (162.5 cum) in the courtyard in front of the Northern Church was part of the church construction project; the other five pre-dated the construction of the churches but were kept in use. The Northern Church cistern may have been intended for public use. Water was fed into the two cisterns

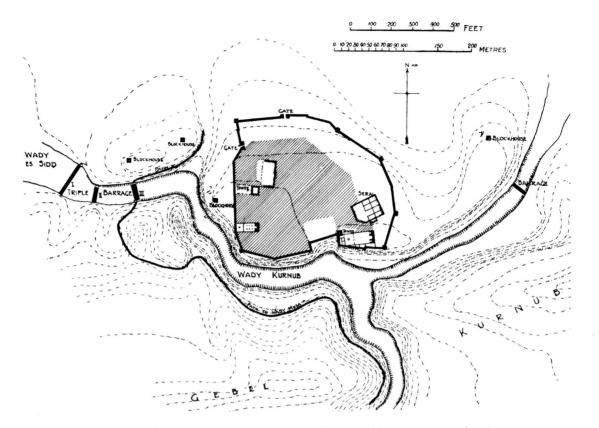

FIG. 8.55 *Mampsis, plan of settlement and immediate vicinity (Woolley and Lawrence 1914–15: fig. 55).*

in the courtyard in front of the Southern Church through a cylindrical monolithic distribution basin (D 0.5 m, depth 0.49 m), which may have served as well as a settling tank: water entered the basin through one hole and could be directed into either of the adjacent cisterns through two holes slightly lower in the wall (Tsuk 2002). This arrangement appears in some of the domestic water systems at Sobata (fig. 8.54), and the same principle was used to direct aqueduct flow at Hawara and Petra.

The basic arrangement of the water-supply system at Sobata is very similar to that of Oboda: reliance on enhanced run-off fields and wadi flow to irrigate terraced fields on and near the wadi floors and the use of run-off to fill public and private cisterns. Because of differences in geology, however, Sobata lacks the major public well seen at Oboda. On the other hand, the engineers at Sobata constructed a ground-level aqueduct to bring in water from a separate catchment area to supplement the local run-off and help fill public

reservoirs and possibly private cisterns as well. The better preservation and more complete excavation of Sobata have provided more information on the capacity of the water-supply system than work at the other Negev sites.

The Water-Supply System of Mampsis

The Nabataean settlement of Mampsis (also Kurnub, modern Mamshit) was founded in the second half of the first century BC, but any early architectural remains have been destroyed or covered by later occupation (Evenari et al. 1982: 110–14; Wenning 1987: 145–52; Negev 1988a; 1988b; 1993b; 1997d; Shereshevski 1991: 20–36). The early history of the site is not clear, but, as at Sobata, it is likely that there was more or less continuous occupation and some Nabataean cultural continuity from the foundation of the settlement through the Roman occupation in the second century and into the Byzantine period. The settlement centre may have

FIG. 8.56 *View of wadi and dams, Mampsis.*

been destroyed in the mid-sixth century by early Arab invaders (Negev 1990). Mampsis is located on the northern, less direct of the two caravan routes from Petra to Gaza at the junction with the route to Jerusalem. In area it is the smallest of the settlements of Nabataean origin in the Negev (4.2 ha), half the size of Oboda (Shereshevski 1991: 204), perhaps because of the lack of agricultural potential and consequent focus on activities involving the caravan road (fig. 8.55).

The site lies at an altitude of 470 m and the annual precipitation is approximately 100 mm, so climatic conditions are similar to those at Oboda and Sobata. There is less available agricultural soil, however, so only a relatively small area (10–12 ha) of the Wadi Kurnub was farmed, 2 km south of the habitation centre. Here, a low barrier wall diverted some of the wadi flow at a narrow point in the wadi to a channel (W 9–5 m, L 400 m) built of stones that carried the water to a series of 14 wide, low terraces. The barrier walls were provided with stepped spillways. Run-off was guided to fields from the

surrounding slopes by means of hillside channels (Evenari et al. 1982: 110). From aerial photographs, Kedar calculated the presence of 43 ha of arable land around Mampsis, but this is still by far the smallest amount among the ancient cities in the Negev. Given the poor agricultural opportunities, it is likely the inhabitants of Mampsis depended to a large extent on the grazing of herds, horse breeding, caravan activities, and, in the Roman and Byzantine periods, military service (Negev 1990). Nevertheless, the human and animal population in the settlement centre required significant quantities of water, more than could be supplied by a very small spring near the foot of the acropolis (Negev 1988a: 6). There is a small well of uncertain date in this same location.

The most spectacular feature of the water-supply system at Mampsis is a series of three large impoundment dams built across the Wadi Mamshit beginning 300 m upstream from the acropolis (fig. 8.56; Woolley and Lawrence in Negev 1988a: 17–18, 1993b; Shereshevski 1991: 33). The downstream face of the lowest dam (L 24 m, H 11 m) is strongly battered, but the upper surface is nevertheless very wide (W 7.8 m). The core of the dam is composed of boulders set in mortar, faced with neat blocks set end-on in mortar (fig. 8.57); the upper surface, perhaps used as a road crossing, consists of layers of flint cobbles set in a very hard mortar. The second dam (L 20 m; W at crest 5 m), built in the same design and with the same materials, is located 50 m upstream. There is yet a third barrier 35 m further upstream (L 53 m; W at crest 3.4 m) that seems to have had vertical faces. Given the relatively lighter construction of the third barrier, it may have been intended to slow the arrival of silt and to increase the average depth of the pool above the second dam. Negev estimates the volume of the two pools at 10,000 cum. As with Dam no. 44 at Hawara, the pools behind each dam are now completely filled with silt; frequent clearing would have been necessary to keep them functional in antiquity. Negev alludes to a "second system" further west, with a capacity of 1,600 cum, and Woolley and Lawrence report another, smaller dam in the wadi just east of the acropolis (L 20 m; H 3 m; fig. 8.55). Kloner calculates the capacity of all these systems at 13,000–15,000 cum and dates the three main dams to the second or third century (Negev 1988a: 6, 18). A Roman origin for the dams visible today is possible, since the Nabataean period dams in Arabia Petraea do not seem to have had battered faces.

Since the water impounded by these dams lay approximately 10 m below and several hundred metres away from the lowest portion of the town, 25 m below the highest structures, it was not conveniently accessible to the inhabitants of Mampsis. Negev proposes that some of the water was transported up the hill by donkeys or human porters for immediate use or for storage in cisterns and the reservoir associated with the public bath (Negev 1988a: 125, 187; 1988b: 57).

Cisterns have been found in all the houses excavated so far and in the atria of the two Byzantine churches. All the cisterns were cut in the bedrock, the fissures filled with stones set in mortar, and the inside waterproofed with a grey plaster. They could be either rectangular or circular in plan, and all but one were roofed with slabs carried by two to four cross-arches springing from imposts cut in

FIG. 8.57   *Detail of second dam above settlement, Mampsis.*

FIG. 8.58   *Domed cistern in West Church, Mampsis (Photo: E. De Bruijn).*

the bedrock. The exception, in the atrium of the West Church (D 3.5 m, Depth 3.0 m, cap. 30 cum), was circular in plan, with bedrock walls carrying a dome with a central draw hole constructed of stones and tiles set in mortar. This domed cistern is one of only two partial parallels for the domed room in Structure no. 72 at Hawara (fig. 8.58; see Nessana, below). The cistern probably received some run-off water from the roof and courtyard, but there was also a block-built intake channel connecting the settling tank with a hole in the city wall, 14 m south. Water-carriers could have filled the cistern without having to enter the city (Negev 1988b: 57). The cistern in the East Church (5.5–5.75 × 4.3–4.05 × 3.5 m deep; cap. 82 cum) was cut in the bedrock, lined with plaster, and roofed with slabs carried on four cross-arches. The arrangements for filling it suggest only the collection of run-off from the roof (Negev 1988b: 36–38).

The cistern in Building XI was cylindrical (D 3.1 m, deep 3.6 m; cap. ca. 100 cum), excavated in the rock and lined with plaster over a layer of small stones. The capping stone (0.6 × 0.7 m) had a square recess for the cover, surrounding a circular draw hole (D 0.4 m) (Negev 1988a: 94–95), an arrangement seen frequently at Hawara and Petra (fig. 8.29). The cistern in Building XII was cut into the bedrock below one of the corner rooms (ca. 4 × 3.50 × 6 m deep; Negev 1988a: 125 gives the capacity as 140 cum). Water collected from the roof and courtyard flowed through a plastered settling tank (1.5 × 1.2 × 0.6 m deep) into a plastered channel that passed through the adjacent wall into the cistern. Negev suggests that another opening in the cistern, adjacent to the outside wall of the house, allowed the deposit of water into the cistern by water carriers through an opening in the street wall (now lost). According to Negev (1988a: 73), the two cisterns serving the large Building I had to be located in the little piazza in front of the entrance door; both were cut in the bedrock and lined with grey plaster. The larger (3.5 × 6.5 × 2.5 m deep; cap. 57 cum) was roofed with slabs carried on three cross-arches; the depth of the other cistern (3.5 × 3 m) could not be measured. These cisterns were fed by run-off from the streets and the roof of Building I.

The Late Roman bath, which resembles in design and scale the bath at Hawara (Oleson 1990a), was fed by water lifted from the only reservoir at Mampsis (Negev 1988a: 167–90). The reservoir, 15 m below the high point of the acropolis and adjacent to the east city wall, was built of mortared masonry facing mortared rubble and plastered

(17.5–18 × 10.28–11.3 × 3 m deep; cap. 550 cum; fig. 8.59). A flight of stairs was built into the west corner, while the other three corners were rounded off with cobbles set in mortar. Four piers spaced equally along the two long walls, corresponding with four free-standing piers along the central line, carried eight cross-arches. The arches were spaced too far apart (2.4–2.8 m) to have carried stone roofing slabs, so the roofing probably consisted of planks or beams carrying a light sunshade of reeds or palm fronds. According to Negev, in its first phase the reservoir was filled by water-carriers pouring water into a plastered masonry tank (1.5 × 1.3 × 1 m deep; cap. 1.95 cum) adjacent to the southeast corner. An overflow spout dumped the water into the reservoir, which was reinforced at this point by a stone slab (0.9 × 1.15 m) set into and projecting slightly above the floor plaster, as in the aqueduct Pool no. 63 at Hawara. In Negev's second phase, after construction of the city wall around AD 300, a conduit was built to connect the filling tank with a small opening in the wall 12 m to the east, so that water carriers could fill the reservoir without entering the city. A second conduit, probably filled by means of a *shaduf*, led water from the northwest corner of the reservoir to the bath.

The character of the excavation of Mampsis makes it difficult to evaluate the water-supply system with confidence. Most of the structures seem to date from the second to the fourth century, but the Nabataeans were present from at least the late first century BC, and many of the arrangements are similar to those at other Nabataean sites. The dams seem more Roman than Nabataean in design, but the cisterns and reservoir are similar to what was built in and around Hawara. The purpose of the large pools of water in the wadi, however, remains in my opinion unsolved. Negev assumes that water bearers (presumably using donkeys or camels with large water bags) carried water from the pools to fill the reservoir and to supplement "insufficient" run-off in the cisterns. This method of filling is feasible and was apparently used to fill very large reservoirs at Masada and the fortresses in the Jordan valley (Garbrecht and Peleg 1989; Netzer 2001a, 2002: 361–62; Patrich 2002: 348). The conduits connecting the reservoir and the cistern in the West Church certainly suggest this sort of

FIG. 8.59 *Settling tank and reservoir, Mampsis.*

arrangement. In order to ensure that the water was drinkable, however, it would have had to be drawn from the wadi pools within a few weeks of each major flood. If local livestock customarily accessed these pools directly from the banks of the wadi, even recently trapped water would probably have been poor in quality (for modern parallels, see Lancaster and Lancaster 1999: 132). The dammed wadi and large dammed pools at Hawara would not have been as vulnerable to pollution, because they were surrounded by bedrock. Furthermore, the roofed and courtyard areas of all the structures with cisterns, except for Building XI, were extensive enough to fill the cisterns with the calculated 100 mm of annual precipitation. The reservoir, too, could have been filled easily with run-off from the upper part of the town. The use of run-off water would explain the provision of settling tanks at the reservoir and some of the cisterns, a feature that would not be necessary with water delivered by porters. Whatever the arrangements were, the

settlement of Mampsis flourished for centuries in a very demanding environment.

Elements of the Water-Supply Systems of Elusa, Ruheibeh, and Nessana

The Nabataean settlement of Elusa (also Halusa) was founded in the late third or second century BC as an important stopping point on the Petra–Gaza road (Wenning 1987: 141–44; Negev 1993a; 1997c; Shereshevski 1991: 82–93). Its main period of prosperity, however, extended from the fourth through the seventh centuries, when Elusa was the chief city of the Negev. With an inhabited area of 39 ha, it is more than twice as large as the runner-up (Nessana, 17 ha); estimates of the population vary between 4,000 and 20,000 (Shereshevski 1991: 201, 204). Although many structures have been preserved beneath the sand, excavation has been spotty, and the water-supply system is poorly understood. Since the sandy soil of the region did not allow the collection of run-off water, water was collected from wells 8 m deep in the Wadi Bsor. This water was somehow conveyed to open reservoirs outside the habitation area; one of these reservoirs, built of mortared masonry, measures 10 × 5 × 2 m deep (cap. 100 cum). There was a terracotta drainpipe at the base of one wall of this reservoir, and Negev claims that lead and terracotta pipes supplied reservoir water to a bath and private houses (Negev 1993a: 380).

Ruheibeh (ancient Betomola-chon?), 11 km southwest of Elusa, was located on a route connecting that city with Nessana and the road to Pelusium (Shereshevski 1991: 94–102; Tsafrir et al. 1988). The history of Ruheibeh parallels that of Elusa, although it was only a quarter the size and less important. The water-supply system is poorly-known, but seems to have been similar to that of Elusa. A very deep well (60 m; fig. 8.60) was cut into the limestone bedrock and apparently supplied water to a nearby bath and an irregular, round

reservoir built of blocks (18.5 × 22.5 × 4.5 m deep; cap. ca. 1,414 cum) just outside the south city gate (fig. 8.61). The effort involved in lifting the water would have been too much for humans, and most likely a geared, animal-driven water-lifting device was installed over the well in antiquity. A flight of stairs descends into the cistern along one wall. Although only a few houses have been probed, they

FIG. 8.60 *Well outside south city gate, Ruheibeh.*

FIG. 8.61 *Reservoir outside south city gate, Ruheibeh.*

FIG. 8.62 *Well shaft at north end of acropolis, Nessana.*

were all supplied with a cistern cut in the bedrock, with a bedrock roof. It seems likely that they were filled with run-off from roofs and streets.

Artefacts show that Nessana (Nizzana, 'Auja al-Hafir), a major stopping point on the Petra–Pelusium road, was occupied sometime in the third century BC and that the Nabataean settlement flourished during the first century BC and first century AD. There is little evidence for occupation at Nessana from the early second through the fourth quarter of the fourth century. At the end of this period, a fort was built on the acropolis, later followed by several churches, and by the seventh century Nessana had grown into the second largest settlement of Nabataean origin in the Negev (17 ha; Mayerson 1961; Wenning 1987: 156–58; Evenari et al. 1982: 120–34; Shereshevski 1991: 49–60; Negev 1993c; 1997e; Urman 2004: 113–16). Extensive construction in the Byzantine period has obscured the Nabataean remains on the acropolis, while extensive stone robbing and construction by the

Turks resulted in the loss of much of the lower town. The lower town seems to have depended on the water from several wells, along with run-off cisterns, while the upper town depended mainly on cisterns filled by run-off.

The wells in the wadi floor were approximately 15 m deep. There was one well at the north end of the acropolis, constructed as part of an extension in the early seventh century. A square masonry shaft 15 m deep provided access to a circular rock-cut well shaft (D 3 m) that must have descended another 35 m to the aquifer (fig. 8.62; Colt 1962: 19). Given the size and depth of the shaft, it is likely that a *saqiya*-driven bucket chain was used to raise the water. There were two cisterns in the North Church complex. A deep, bottle-shaped cistern (D 2.6 m, depth 10.5 m; cap. 55.7 cum) cut into the bedrock may be pre-Byzantine in date. A second cistern of the same shape (D 4.70, depth uncertain) was built of mortared cobbles, with a corbelled vault of small, flat stones framing a central draw hole. This domed cistern is one of only two partial parallels for the domed room in Structure no. 72 at Hawara (see Mampsis, above). There was a large, rock-cut cistern below the courtyard in the Byzantine fort, rectangular in shape, with seven cross-arches supporting the roofing slabs (L 10.83 × 3.75 × 3.60 m deep; cap. 146.2 cum). A small tank with a capacity of only 1.9 cum in the South Church was also interpreted as a cistern. Ceramic and stone downspouts carried the run-off from roofs to the various cisterns (Colt 1962: 27–28). Given the small amount of storage capacity, it is not surprising that the deep well had to be added in the early seventh century.

There were "dozens" of farms in the neighbourhood of Nessana employing the same techniques of run-off farming seen at Oboda, Sobata, and Mampsis (Urman 2004: 102–13). Their presence is not surprising, since Nessana is only 30 km west of Sobata and located on the same watercourse, the Wadi Laban. Well-defined, fenced areas employed wadi barriers with stepped spillways, hillside collection channels, and earthen conduits with sluice gates. Ceramics reveal that these sites were occupied from the fifth to the late eighth century. The same dates were determined for a cluster of farms at Nahal Mitnan, 25 km south of Nessana, subjected to a careful analysis of ancient agricultural potential by Bruins (1986).

A deposit of sixth- and seventh-century papyri at Nessana has provided some useful documentation of the agricultural practices at these run-off farms (Kraemer 1958; Mayerson 1961; Evenari et al. 1982: 120–27). Even at this late date, the documents refer to persons with Nabataean names, as do the documents found at Sobata and Petra. The crops mentioned include barley, wheat, vetch (?), figs, grapes, olives, dates, and almonds. *P.Ness.* 82 provides virtually unparalleled information about the yield of grain crops in the region: an increase of 6.8–7.2-fold for wheat, 8.0–8.7-fold for barley. These results were evaluated as satisfactory to good by twentieth-century Bedouin farmers in the region. Wheat represented 78.9 percent of the crops sown, barley 15.8 percent, *aracus* (vetch?) 5.3 percent (Mayerson 1961: 17–21). The ratio of wheat to barley is the reverse of what has been documented through plant remains at Humayma, perhaps because of the poorer soil in the vicinity

of that site. The sixth-century *P.Ness.* 31 describes the division of buildings and agricultural land, with careful definition of boundaries and the location of the "water channel" (ὑδραγόγιον, lines 17, 31; Kraemer 1958: 95–101). *P.Ness.* 32, a sixth-century cession of land, allots a half share of a fig orchard, a quarter share of the cistern (ὑδηρὸς λάκκος) located in it, and the right of access to the water conduits (ὑδραγωγεῖα, lines 10–11, 18; Kramer 1958: 102–3).

Comparison of the Water-Supply Systems of the Negev Settlements with Hawara

Many details of the water-supply systems of the settlements of Nabataean origin in the Negev seem familiar to one who has studied the systems at Hawara, but the overall impression is different. The Negev was a frontier area during the florescence of the Nabataean kingdom, on the outskirts of the Nabataean cultural region and close to the alluring cultures and economies of the Mediterranean. While the regional water-supply system of Hawara, like those of Petra and Wadi Ramm, was essentially designed and completed during the first century BC and first century AD, the systems serving the Negev settlements are for the most part Byzantine in date and dependent on direct contact with the Mediterranean cultures (Finkelstein 1988; 1990; Haiman 1995; Rubin 1996). Nevertheless, there is little in the technology that is essentially new, and the differences are for the most part due to a larger economy and population, to an intense focus on agriculture, and to some differences in geology and pedology.

In the Negev, as in Arabia Petraea, rural and "urban" cisterns were an important part of the water-supply system. Because of the geology, the most common design was a regular or irregular tank carved in soft bedrock, with a natural roof formed by a stratum of harder stone (Kloner 2001–2). This technique was obviously easier to execute and more durable than installing a roof of stone slabs supported on arches over a rock-cut or built tank. The slab roof supported by cross-arches on block-built walls appears on cisterns in the Negev, and it was ubiquitous for roofing houses. The first-century cistern at Bor Nekarot on the

"Incense Road" looks particularly similar to the type of built reservoir with arch-supported roof seen at Hawara, perhaps because of its early date (Frank 1934: 273, pl. 59A; Glueck 1953: 13; T. Gini, personal communication, October 2008). It had three cross-arches and a slab roof (fig. 8.63). Another such cistern, once again apparently built of blocks, with nine cross-arches survives near the road at Mezad Mahmal (4.75 × 8.10 × > 2m; cap. 77 cum; Meshel and Tsafrir 1975: 11–12, pls. 2b, 2c), and a third existed at Horvat Bor. Where cisterns are associated with houses, they usually appear beneath the courtyard, as at Hawara.

Reservoirs, usually unroofed because of their size, formed part of most of the Negev water systems; they were occasionally built but more often cut in the bedrock. There seems to have been a light roof over the reservoir at Mampsis, which served a bath. The other reservoirs served the human and animal population, although the quality of the water customarily must have been poor. The water was collected from run-off, lifted from wells, carried in from dammed pools by porters or draft animals, and, in only one case (Sobata), filled at least in part by an aqueduct that carried in run-off from a separate catchment. At Hawara, Petra, and Wadi Ramm, in contrast, the largest reservoirs were filled entirely by spring-fed aqueducts. In fact, the only long aqueduct in the Negev with engineering features such as a built viaduct and distribution tanks was that at Sobata. Nothing has been found that resembles the long channels built of stone gutter blocks set in mortar and framed with stones found in Arabia Petraea. Springs existed in the Negev, but inconveniently below or distant from the site of the larger Nabataean settlements along the caravan routes. The very deep wells at Oboda, Elusa, and Nessana represent the typical regional solution to this problem. Water channels made of stone gutter blocks very similar to those used at Hawara can be seen in use in all the Negev settlements, but only to carry water relatively short

FIG. 8.63 *Nabataean cistern roofed with slabs carried on cross-arches, Bor Nekarot (Photo: Tsvika Tsuk).*

distances within a house, along a street, or between a reservoir and a bath. The stone distribution basins also appear in these same circumstances. The use of terracotta pipelines to distribute water has been proposed for several sites, but they have not yet been documented.

The most spectacular difference in the water-supply systems of the two regions, however, is the presence of large areas of cultivated land in large and small wadis, formed and protected by low walls, and provided with run-off water from large catchment fields, often enhanced by the removal of surface stones or the cutting of channels. The numerous hillside terraces at Petra are similar in character, but much less extensive. Only a very few possible examples can now be found at Hawara. As noted above, the concentration on this type of farming in the Negev was made possible both by the presence of better soil in that region and by easier access to the Mediterranean market.

8.B. THE HELLENISTIC AND ROMAN CONTRIBUTION TO NABATAEAN HYDRAULIC TECHNOLOGY

The well-known passage from Hieronymus of Cardia preserved in Diodorus (19.94.2–10), quoted at the beginning of this chapter, describes Nabataeans living a spare, largely nomadic lifestyle. An equally famous passage in Strabo (16.4.26 [Jones 1917–32: vol. 6, pp. 367–69]), probably based on the eyewitness account of his friend Athenodorus, describes a more prosperous and sophisticated Nabataean culture.

> The Nabataeans are a sensible people, and they are so much inclined to acquire possessions that they publicly fine anyone who has diminished his possessions and also confer honours on anyone who has increased them. Since they have but few slaves, they are served by their kinsfolk for the most part, or by one another…, or even by their kings. They prepare common meals together in groups of thirteen persons, and they have two girl-singers for each banquet. The king holds many drinking-bouts in magnificent style, but no one drinks more than eleven cups of wine, each time using a different golden cup. The king…often renders an account of his kingship in the popular assembly; and sometimes his mode of life is examined. Their homes, through the use of stone, are costly; but on account of peace, the cities are not walled. Most of the country is well supplied with fruits except the olive; they use sesame oil instead. The sheep are white-fleeced and the oxen are large, but the country produces no horses. Camels afford the service they require instead of horses… Some items are imported completely from other countries, but others only in part, especially in the case of native products, such as gold and silver and most of the aromatics, whereas copper and iron, purple garments, styrax, crocus, costaria, embossed metalwork, paintings, and moulded images are not produced locally.

The contrast between the hedonistic, settled Nabataeans described by Strabo and the lean, foxy nomads described by Diodorus has provoked frequent comment (Negev 1977: 523–35; Bowersock 1983: 120; Schmid 2001a: 415–18; 2001b; Hackl et al. 2003: 439–53, 615–17; Bowersock 2003; Parr 2003).

Most see the contrast as evidence for the changes that overtook Nabataean society between the third and first century BC: monarchy (although remarkably populist in tone), a sort of settled urbanism with elaborate stone houses, agriculture (including fruit trees and vineyards), herds of animals (including carefully-bred and well-fed cattle), and luxurious possessions associated with sophisticated manufacture and long-distance trade. Others see the contrast as an historian's unlikely reconstruction or as the depiction of the differences between rural and urban Nabataean culture (Knauf 1990; Patrich 1990: 48–49). The technology of water supply, unfortunately, is not mentioned.

How were these materialistic winebibbers and flute girls, their homes, flocks, and fields supplied with water in an environment just as arid in the first century BC as it had been in the third and only slightly less arid than it is today? Increased consumption of water is implicit in many of the changes. The commensurate increase in production came both from the more intensive application of traditional water-harvesting techniques that originated as early as the Neolithic and from the introduction of new techniques from the Hellenistic and Roman world. There is no space here to deal with the contentious topics of where the Nabataeans "came from" or why they so enthusiastically embraced a settled life around 100 BC. The Nabataeans probably moved into Edom in the fifth century BC, and they certainly were a recognisable group occupying Petra by the time they came into conflict with Antiochus the One-Eyed in 312 BC (Diodorus 19.94–95; Bowersock 1983: 12–27; Graf 1992b). The Nabataean culture experienced sedentarization and monumentalisation at Petra and many other major sites around 100 BC, most likely as a result of economic and political factors (see esp. Schmid 2001b). The sedentarization and the employment of more sophisticated water-supply systems undoubtedly went hand in hand.

8.B.1. *Pre-Nabataean Water-Supply Systems in the Nabataean Cultural Region*

Although meagre in amount and very localised in occurrence, precipitation does fall reliably in the deserts of Arabia Petraea and the Negev every

year when averaged out over the
large catchment areas individual
Nabataean tribal groups and
settlements controlled. This
chapter has made it clear that
the secret to survival was the
knowledge of how to harvest this
precipitation. The most obvious
techniques had been discovered
by the Early Bronze Age (Philip
2001: 173–74), possibly even
during the Neolithic, and had
been put to work in many of
the arid areas later occupied by
the Nabataeans, providing them
with a ready-made, appropriate
technology (Oleson 1995; 2001b).
The terracing of hillsides is the
most spectacular and visible of

FIG. 8.64   *Interior of plastered bottle cistern, as-ʿSela.*

these early methods: heavy stone walls built across
the slope of a hill captured both run-off water and
the particles of earth it carried (Hopkins 1997:
27–28). This type of structure is notoriously difficult
to date, but the terraces around Tall al-Handaquq
northwest of Amman (Mabry 1989) and some at
Wadi Faynan (Barker et al. 2007: 115) should date
to the Early Bronze Age. Low wadi barriers were a
variation on this technique, and some apparently
were constructed as early as the Chalcolithic (Levy
and Alon 1987). By the seventh century BC the technique is well-documented (Stager 1976). There is
evidence for wells and channel irrigation in the Negev during the Neolithic (Levi and Alon 1987), for
Neolithic period wells at Beidha and Wadi Dobai,
and there is widespread evidence for wells during
the Bronze Age, e.g., at Tell es-Saʾidiyeh (Miller
1980; 1988; Oleson 1992: 885–87; 2001: 604–5). Surprisingly large containment dams designed to trap
and hold a pool of water appear in the Near East as
early as the Early Bronze Age, as at Tell Handaquq
(Mabry 1989), Ai, Arad (Tsuk 2001–2), Tell Jalul,
and Jawa (Philip 2001; Helms 1981; 1982; Oleson
2001: 608). Natural catch basins in the sandstone
bedrock around Petra were dammed for use by the
Edomites (Lindner et al. 1996: 146), as they were
later on around Nabataean Hawara.

From the Early Bronze Age onward, cisterns
were the standard method for storing water to

FIG. 8.65   *Stone conduit blocks, Late Bronze Age palace,*
Ugarit.

be used for drinking (Miller 1980; Oleson 1992b; 887–88; 2001b: 605–8). The capture, de-siltation, and entry of water were controlled, and the stored water was protected from evaporation and pollution. Hand in hand with advances in cistern design, the archaeological record shows progress in the creation of plasters resistant to the percolation and erosive effect of the water. By the Iron Age, the Edomites had settled on the rock-cut bottle cistern fed by run-off as the technique most appropriate to their needs. This type of cistern is well-illustrated by examples at the Edomite settlement on Umm Biyara at Petra (fig. 8.30) and as-Sela' (fig. 8.64; Horsfield and Horsfield 1938; Wenning 1987: 256–57). The design remained in use among the early Nabataeans and is described by Diodorus in a passage quoted above (19.94.7). The Edomite and similar Nabataean cisterns are usually three to four metres in greatest diameter. Their interiors were lined with a hard, sandy, white plaster.

Naturally, there is little direct physical evidence at the pre-Nabataean sites in this region for the type of earthen water channel seen at the Nabataean settlements in the Negev. Nevertheless, indirect evidence, such as channels, has been cited for several Neolithic and Bronze Age sites in the Negev and Wadi Arabah (Levi and Alon 1987; Miller 1980; 1988; Oleson 1992b). Block-built water channels lined with plaster have been found in a Late Bronze Age context at Tell es-Sa'idiyeh, served by a well, and this kind of arrangement was common during the Iron Age. It is more difficult to date the invention of the monolithic gutter block for conducting water, the kind of blocks frequently used in Nabataean aqueduct systems. This simple but effective system certainly appeared by the Late Bronze Age in the Eastern Mediterranean, since examples have been found in the palaces at Ugarit (fig. 8.65; Calvet and Geyer 1987) and in several of the palaces and houses on Crete (Shaw: 1973: 126–34, 200). An Iron Age II rock-cut cistern of 800 cum at Tel Beth-Shemesh was fed by a series of conduit blocks of this type (oral communication by S. Bunimovitz, Z. Lederman, 20 November 2008). Because gutter blocks are obvious candidates for reuse, it is likely that they have disappeared from many early contexts. In any case, they were common throughout the Mediterranean and the Near East by the fifth century BC, often associated with stone basins like those seen at many Nabataean sites (e.g., Lang 1968: fig. 32; Wycherly 1978: 56–57, 248–50). Although the Nabataeans probably found gutter blocks in use when they arrived in this region, there were no local precedents for the long aqueducts their engineers constructed with such blocks in the first century BC and AD.

These were the techniques available to the early Nabataeans as they moved into the southern desert and Edom. Judging from the rapidity with which they occupied their new territory, they undoubtedly already knew or quickly learned the appropriate methods of harvesting the scanty desert precipitation. But in the course of the first century BC, and possibly as early as the second century BC, new techniques appeared, probably first in response to a growing population and more frequent transit through the desert, then in response to the shift to an economy based more on agriculture and trade. Since many of these techniques remained in use through the Byzantine period throughout the area occupied by Nabataean communities — from the Hauran on the north to the Hejaz on the south, and west across the Negev to the Mediterranean coast — it is very difficult to document the precise time and place of their introduction. Nevertheless, the excavations at Petra and Hawara suggest that the first century BC was a period of particularly rapid innovation and that Nabataean needs governed the process. Shaw (1984) has noted in the context of the Maghrib that rural systems of water management in that region were part of long-term traditions, while the urban systems were Roman imports. The same can be said of the Nabataean cultural region, in that new techniques for water supply begin to appear as the Nabataeans founded and monumentalised settlement centres, all of them based on Hellenistic and Roman accomplishments.

8.B.2. The Influence of Hellenistic and Roman Water-Supply Systems on the Nabataeans

The Nabataeans were deeply involved with the Hellenistic world, including Egypt and the Red Sea, from at least the later fourth century BC, when Antigonus the One-Eyed threatened Petra.

Greco-Roman historians, such as Diodorus and Josephus, report mainly the political and military interaction (Bowersock 1983: 12–58), but inscriptions and numismatic evidence also attest to the presence of Nabataean merchants in the Aegean in the second and first centuries BC and in Italy by the mid-first century BC (Wenning 1987: 22–24; Roche 1996; Meshorer 1975: 3; Graf and Sidebotham 2003; Ripa 1989). Inscriptions in Nabataean, Greek, or Latin mentioning Nabataeans at the following sites can be dated earlier than the reign of Aretas IV (9 BC–AD 39/40): Rhodes (second half of the 2nd century BC), Tinos (second half of the 2nd century BC), Priene (129 BC), Puteoli (ca. 50 BC), Rome (58–30 BC), and Tel esh-Shuqafiya (77 and 35 BC; Fiema and Jones 1990). A coin of Aretas III was found at Antiochia, as well as Nabataean ceramics (Wenning 1987: 23). Prior to the overthrow of the Nabataean kingdom by the Romans in 106, there is inscriptional and historical evidence for the activity of Nabataean merchants and political envoys at the port cities of Gaza, Sidon, Beirut, Salamis in Cyprus, Rhodes, Cos, Miletus, Priene, Delos, Rheneia, Tinos, Athens, Puteoli, Ostia, and Rome (Graf and Sidebotham 2003: 71). A coin of Aretas IV even turned up in excavations at Aventicum in Switzerland, although, naturally, it may have reached the site at second or third hand (Meshorer 1975: 3). Since many of the sites mentioned contained sanctuaries, it is possible that many of these Nabataeans were involved in trading incense and medicines based on balsam and bitumen (Roche 1996: 96).

These Nabataean kings and princes, soldiers, military engineers, merchants, and possibly priests inevitably brought back to their homeland vivid impressions of the rich Hellenistic world, along with new ideas that transformed Nabataean material culture and strongly affected Nabataean society (see esp. Schmid 2001a; 2001b; 2007). The first phase of Nabataean painted ceramics closely reflects Hellenistic types, and the famous tomb façades of Petra find their most likely models in Alexandrian and Rhodian designs (Schmid 2000: 111–31; 2003). King Malichus I (59/58–30 BC) built an elaborate banquet hall at Beidha, whose architectural design and sculptural decoration formed a sophisticated programme borrowed from Alexandrian models and intended to link the royal house with Dionysus and Alexander the Great (Bikai et al. 2008).

Among the new ideas flooding into the Nabataean cultural region were designs for water-supply systems and installations. These new techniques included cisterns roofed with slabs of stone carried on cross-arches, large reservoirs, sometimes intended as much for display as for use, aqueducts many kilometres long, pipelines with pressure reduction towers, small-scale amenities such as junction or division basins for conduits, and stop-cocks for lead pipes. A more quixotic influence was the provision of a bas-relief of a lion through whose mouth water flowed to impress and refresh the onlooker. The Lion Fountain at Petra (first century AD?; Bellwald 2007: 319) bears a striking resemblance to the late third-century BC leopard fountain at the palace at ʿIraq al-Amir (ancient Tyros; Lapp: 1993). Spectacular water display was a feature of this palace.

Arch-Roofed Cisterns

Along with the carved gutter block for conducting water, the arch-roofed cistern is a characteristic and essential part of Nabataean water-supply systems in Arabia Petraea. This structure consists of a block-built rectangular box or cylinder, or a rock-cut rectangular box, with cross-arches that sprang from imposts set into the wall or from supporting piers (figs. 3.58, 3.86–88, 4.17–20, 4.25). The arches were more often segmental than a complete semi-circle. The extrados of each arch was framed with blocks that were built up to form a level surface equal in height to the exterior cistern wall. Stone slabs were laid to bridge the intervals between the arches, their seams were waterproofed to keep out pollution, and arrangements were made for admitting and drawing water. The same design was used for roofing houses throughout the Nabataean cultural region, but particularly in the Negev and the Hauran. The elegant simplicity and structural stability of this type of roof ensured its spread throughout the Middle East and its survival into the Early Islamic period. Many of these cisterns and some of the houses have been renovated and remain in use today.

FIG. 8.66 *Theatre Cistern, Delos, first half of third century* BC.

The date of the introduction of this type of cistern to Nabataea cannot be precisely documented, but the early first century BC seems likely on the basis of arrangements at Petra. The design clearly originated somewhere in the Hellenistic world. The vault appeared in tomb architecture in Thrace as early as the fifth century BC, and by the mid-fourth century BC, the tomb design had spread to Macedonia and was described by Plato (Hellmann 2002: 269–77; Plato, *Laws* 947d–e). During the late fourth and the third century BC, use of the arch and vault was applied to gateways, foundations, bridges, and *cryptoportici* throughout the Greek world. The earliest known example of a cistern roofed with slabs of stone carried on cross-arches seems to be the large Theatre Cistern on Delos, built in the first half of the third century BC (fig. 8.66; Vallois 1966: 265–68; Hellmann 2002: 274). The cistern (22.5 × 6.5 × ca. 6 m deep; cap. ca. 877.5 cum) was built of granite blocks backed by rubble in an enormous trench cut in the fissured bedrock. The eight semi-circular arches spring from projecting wall stubs six courses high, keyed into the cistern wall. The entire extrados of each arch was framed by a neat

block wall, also keyed into the cistern wall, which rose to the level of the cistern wall. Large granite slabs bridged the ca. 2.5 m gaps between these walls. A conduit of gutter blocks gathered run-off from the auditorium of the theatre and conducted it directly into the cistern without passing through a settling tank. Five or six well-heads (H 0.58 m, inside D 0.265 m) assembled from marble blocks provided access to the water (fig. 8.67).

The high support walls around the arches of the Theatre Cistern give the structure a more monumental appearance than the impression conveyed by the Nabataean arch-roofed cisterns. The design, however, continued to evolve, and some second-century BC examples in the Granite Palaestra (Delorme 1961: 40; Vallois 1966: 268–69; Hellmann 2002: 274) and the House of the Poseidoniasts are virtually identical to the smaller Nabataean version: the arch imposts are set into the walls rather than set out on antae, the extrados of each arch reaches to the level of the top of the cistern wall, the distance between the arches is usually close to the thickness of the arches, the arches are often segmental rather than a full semicircle,

FIG. 8.67 *Theatre Cistern, Delos, well-heads for draw holes.*

FIG. 8.68 *Cistern in Clubhouse of the Poseidoniasts, Delos.*

FIG. 8.69 *Cistern in the Granite Monument, Delos.*

and settling tanks are sometimes employed (figs. 8.68–69). Cisterns of this type appear in most of the second- and early first-century BC houses on Delos (Chamonard 1924: 323–56). Stone gutter blocks were also very common.

While this roofing design occurs on cisterns elsewhere in the Hellenistic world, as at Telmessus (Orlandos 1966–68: 248), Delos preserves by far the largest number of examples and may be unique among the Aegean islands in making use of the design (Vallois 1966: 267). The reasons for its use there are most likely the low annual rainfall on a small island (ca. 400 mm), the meagre aquifers, and the absence of large timbers that could be used to roof the cisterns, in combination with the high population density fostered by uniquely intense religious and commercial activities. The roofing design does occur in non-hydraulic structures in the Hellenistic world, particularly in fortifications, and also in oracular chambers, as beneath the early Hellenistic Temple of Apollo at Clarus (fig. 8.70; Bean 1967: 190–96, pls. 46, 48). In fact, the late third-century BC technical author Philon of Byzantium carefully

describes the method in his *Paraskeuastika* (*Design of Fortifications*), Book 7 of his *Mechanike Syntaxis* (*Compendium of Technology*, Garlan 1974: 302–3, "p. 87.11–18"). The text is somewhat corrupt, but the meaning is clear enough.

But if there is a lack of timber, the granary must be constructed in the following manner. As soon as the foundation walls have been laid, a half circle must be laid out, with a radius half the width of the foundation and the same height. On this measure, arches must be built of blocks along both walls, three cubits apart (ca. 1.32 m). The arches should be (1 cubit thick?) (ca. 0.88 m). If two (impost?) blocks are laid on the foundation, the arches can be built 1 cubit thick (0.44 m) but (the impost blocks) should project 2 cubits (0.88 m). These arches should be constructed of the largest possible cut blocks or rough stones so as to be able to support the weight (of the superstructure). Once the arches have been

FIG. 8.70   *Room roofed with cross-arches supporting stone slabs, Temple of Apollo, Clarus.*

FIG. 8.71   *Subterranean room with cross-arches supporting stone slab roof, Nekromanteion, Epirus (Photo: B. Burke).*

FIG. 8.72 *Detail of cross-arches supporting stone slab roof, Nekromanteion, Epirus (Photo: T. van Damme).*

erected, the walls of the room are built on the foundation. The space between the extrados of the arches and the side walls must be filled with cut blocks until the level upper surface reaches to the top of the arch. Then the strongest possible beams must be laid over the spaces between the arches, and on the beams reeds, which are very carefully plastered… But if one does not build in this way, one can construct the whole room as a vault, so that there is no need for beams.

A particularly good example of this type of roof construction can be seen in the third-century BC Nekyomanteion (or Nekromanteion) in Epirus, which used to be thought of as an oracular sanctuary, but now has been reinterpreted as a small military establishment or fortified farm (Baatz 1979; Dakaris 1996; Wiseman 1998). The subterranean room (15 × 4.25 m) was built into a cutting in the bedrock, with 15 carefully built semicircular arches supporting the roof (figs. 8.71–72).

Philon's comment that this design was appropriate for situations in which it was difficult to obtain timber for long rafters applies to both Delos and Arabia Petraea. It seems very likely that either a Nabataean merchant brought this design back from Delos, or a Nabataean military engineer no-

ticed the design in use in Asia Minor and realised — as did some Greek engineer before him — that it was a perfect solution for desert regions that required cisterns for storage of water. In Greece, this type of roofing seems to have remained a rare solution for extreme circumstances, since it is rare outside of Delos. Most Greek cisterns were completely cut in the bedrock or roofed with large slabs, sometimes supported on medial pillars (Brinker 1990). We cannot yet determine whether the Nabataeans first put the design to use for roofing cisterns or houses, but by at least the mid-first century BC it had been applied to both types of structure.

Decorative Pools

The atypical, somewhat impractical design of the pool at the end of the Hawara aqueduct (Structure no. 63) has been discussed above. On the basis of parallels with the Pool and Garden Complex at Petra, it was suggested that the pool was used as a showpiece indicating to visitors the Nabataean control over their desert environment. The pool may have accommodated swimmers and may have been surrounded by a garden. Both pools may even have been used for the celebration of the Maioumas festival, a festival of Near Eastern origin involving nude swimmers and celebrated at a number of sites in Asia Minor and the Near East (Bowersock, oral communication 2001, cf. Bowersock 1999). Very striking parallels can be drawn between these two Nabataean pools and structures of the later first century BC at Jericho, Masada, the Herodium, Jerusalem, and Caesarea (fig. 8.73; Bedal 2000a–b; 2001: 37–39; 2007; Elitzur 2008; Geva 1993; Netzer 2001b; Schmid 2001b: 387; Wilkinson 1974: 39–45; see discussion in Chapter 7.C.6). The use of aqueduct water for ostentatious display appears in Rome in the same period, when the completion of the Aqua Virgo aqueduct for the first time allowed construction of lavish public baths, gardens, fountains, and a swimming pool (Koloski-Ostrow 2001: 5). A Nabataean king (Aretas IV?) may have constructed the Petra pool as part of a royal competition with the Hellenising

FIG. 8.73 *Double reservoir at Birketein, near Jerash.*

luxuries of the Hasmonean kings and Herod the Great. As a royal showpiece in the southern desert, Hawara received one of these prestigious pools as well, possibly accompanied by a garden.

The decorative pool at Hawara resembles the parallels cited above only in a general fashion. The technology used for the pool at Petra bears the closest resemblance, as is reasonable, but the two structures differ in details. Nevertheless, both these pools were inspired by the general idea of a spectacular pool and garden in an unexpected location, an idea current in the late Hellenistic world. In contrast, it is interesting that an arrangement similar to that at Hawara appears toward the beginning of the imperial aqueduct that served Tigava Municipium in modern Algeria (Leveau and Paillet 1976: 169–70, fig. 95), but in fact is unrelated in function. The pool, trapezoidal in plan (8.70/8.90 × 11.90/13.65 m; depth 1.30–1.70 m), was built across the line of the aqueduct in a poor concrete. The floor of the exit channel was only 0.45 m above the basin floor, so the water depth in the basin cannot have been much more than 1 m, giving a capacity of ca. 112 cum. A second exit channel would have

allowed complete drainage of the tank, which must have served as a settling tank. A nearby wadi may have been the source of water, and sedimentation consequently would have been a problem.

Aqueducts

Intensified exploitation of spring water certainly was part of the developed Nabataean repertoire of water-supply techniques, since the Nabataeans constructed very ambitious conduits and pipelines to carry the water to some settlement centres in the southern part of the kingdom. The most notable examples can be seen at Petra, where spring-fed water conduits ranged around 4 km in length but could extend for up to 12 km, and at Hawara, where the main branch ran for 18.9 km and was served by a branch line 7.6 km long. The Hawara and Petra aqueducts are by far the longest aqueducts built by Nabataean engineers, and their construction was probably stimulated not only by the high population at Petra and the extreme aridity at Hawara, but also by the royal desire for prestige displays at both sites. Apart from the sanctuary at Wadi Ramm (1.5

km) and the small settlement of Sobata (2.5 km), the Nabataeans elsewhere made use of only short, local conduits. Since the scale of the systems at Petra and its technological "colony" Hawara is so out of character, we must ask whether the engineers working at these two sites were inspired by earlier regional accomplishments in aqueduct design.

The Bronze and Iron Age cultures of Transjordan do not appear to have constructed long aqueducts, so we must look farther afield for possible models. There are, in fact, numerous aqueducts associated with the fortresses and palaces of the Hasmonean kings on the west slopes of the Wadi Arabah, at Jericho, Qumran, Alexandreion, Dok, Kypros, and Hyrkania. The individual systems extend from 1 km to 10 km in length and like the Nabataean systems, they can incorporate settling basins, support walls, rock-cut channels, viaducts, arched bridges, cisterns, and pools (see the articles in Amit et al. 2002; Dierx and Garbrecht 2001). The water source was usually a spring, but in some cases wadis were dammed to trap and elevate occasional run-off water to feed the conduits. Portions of the elaborate water-supply system of Jerusalem are as early as the Iron Age, but the construction of the long-distance aqueducts connecting the spring-fed Pools of Solomon with the city only began in the Hasmonean period (Mazar in Dierx and Garbrecht 2001: 165–94; Mazar 2002). This system was also designed on a much larger scale than the Nabataean systems, and it involved mortared and rock-cut channels, viaducts, arched bridges, and socketed stone pipe sections.

Although similar in general principle, these systems were nearly all designed to handle larger volumes of water and, as a result, the conduits were constructed of mortared rubble with a plastered surface, rather than cut in long narrow blocks of stone. It may have been the general concept of these systems — the provision of spring water to an arid location some kilometres away — that inspired the Nabataean kings and their engineers, rather than the details of their execution. In fact, the borrowing of the idea of a large-scale system, instead of just details of the technique, may explain the dogged insistence of Nabataean engineers on using conduit blocks rather than plastered concrete channels to conduct the water. If instructed by an ambitious

king to build a conduit 4 km or 19 km long, the local engineers may have been tempted simply to apply the techniques of short-distance conduction on a larger scale. Where the volume of water to be conveyed was relatively small, these conduits worked well, and the problem of slope could be solved easily. In the rugged landscape of Arabia Petraea, long stretches of these aqueducts could also be carved in bedrock.

One detail of the aqueduct system of Petra is not paralleled in the Hasmonean water systems: the use of terracotta pipelines for long-distance water transport. Short sections of terracotta piping do appear in the Hasmonean palace at Jericho, often as part of a pressurised system (Netzer 2001b: 27, 31, 33), but outside the palace area the water flowed in mortared conduits. Terracotta pipes were added to the systems serving Cypros and Jerusalem in the early Islamic or Ottoman periods, but they seem to be absent from the Hellenistic and Roman systems in this area. Short pipelines composed of socketed terracotta sections were in use in Mesopotamia and the Aegean from the second millennium BC onward (Connan 1999: 35; Shaw 1973: 198–201), and they are common throughout the region from the sixth century BC on (Tölle-Kastenbein 1994; Jansen 2000: 106–110). At Priene, a terracotta pipeline is associated with a stone basin serving as a distribution tank that resembles those used in Nabataean systems (Jansen 2000: 109, fig. 4; Fahlbusch 2006: 121). There do not, however, appear to be any long-distance terracotta pipelines that date to the Hellenistic period in the area of Nabataean cultural influence or the immediately surrounding region. It is possible that a Nabataean engineer picked up the idea at a major city in the Aegean region, such as Pergamon or Athens. Since the thickly-settled acropolis of Pergamon was waterless, the water-supply system depended on the storage of run-off water in rock-cut cisterns and the delivery of water through terracotta pipes in a sophisticated pressurised system. The Madrag Aqueduct, built by Eumenes II (197–159 BC), was the most spectacular (Garbrecht 1987). Three parallel adjacent terracotta pipelines brought spring water 45 km to a collection basin on the edge of a valley, 3 km distant from and 35 m higher than the acropolis. A heavy lead pipe reinforced by stone brackets then carried the water across the valley to the acropolis, descending at one point to 200 m below the hydraulic gradient, which resulted in a pressure of 20 atmospheres. Several other Hellenistic and Roman aqueducts at Pergamon also involved terracotta pipelines.

It is at present impossible to determine how the Nabataean engineers at Petra hit upon the idea of using pipelines to carry some of their aqueduct water into the city. Similar pipelines in the Hellenistic cities were spectacular in design, but the pipes themselves were hidden in the ground. Nabataean merchants or military engineers may have seen such pipelines under construction, seen the pipes in production at a pottery workshop, or had the principles explained to them by Greek engineers. In contrast, the pressure-reducing towers associated with some pressurised pipelines, such as the possibly Hellenistic example at Methymna on Lesbos (Koldewey 1890: 18; cf. Buchholz 1976: 57–58), were conspicuous and would have elicited questions from any visiting Nabataean hydraulic engineer. Such a process would explain how Nabataean engineers apparently learned how to install pressure-reducing towers on the 'Ain Brak and 'Ain Debdebah systems at Petra — if in fact these poorly-documented structures existed. On the other hand, as conjectured for the open gutter blocks, the Nabataean engineers at Petra may simply have decided or been ordered to adapt pipes designed for short-distance water management to a long, spring-fed water-supply system. The main difference would have been the scale of the undertaking, since the pipelines at Petra were only rarely pressurised. In any case, the authorities in charge of the water supply soon realised that the spring water at Petra deposited calcium carbonate at a rate that made maintenance an urgent problem for pipelines.

The Roman Contribution

It is striking testimony to the appropriateness and thoroughness of the Nabataean water-supply systems at Petra and Hawara that no substantial changes were made to those systems after the Roman conquest, despite the continued prosperity of both towns. At Hauarra, the Romans simply appropriated some of the flow from the Nabataean aqueduct to fill a new reservoir within the fort.

The method of distribution of the water obtained from the aqueduct, however, did change, with the addition of terracotta pipelines and a stopcock with lead pipeline to the aqueduct pool and the creation of a terracotta pipeline system within the fort. The absence of cisterns beneath the five Byzantine churches at Hauarra indicates that the Nabataean system continued to supply sufficient water into that period as well. In the Negev settlements the pattern was slightly different. There was a vast expansion of the area of terraced or stepped fields fed by run-off water and of rain-fed cisterns concomitant with an expansion of population and market economy, but the techniques remained Nabataean in character. In the northern part of the Nabataean kingdom, where the environment was less marginal, the Romans introduced their typical imperial suite of hydraulic structures: aqueducts, monumental baths and fountains, and drains. Philadelphia (Amman), Gerasa (Jarash), Gadara (Umm Qeis), Abila (Quwayliba), and Bostra (Busra) are good examples (see Freeman 2001:427–45; Oleson 2001b; Butler 1914).

While the Hellenistic cities of the Eastern Mediterranean and the Roman occupiers apparently had little to teach the desert Nabataeans about aqueducts other than scale, some Roman period aqueduct systems in the region reveal interesting parallels with the Nabataean systems at Petra and Hawara. These parallels are more likely to be the result of similarities in materials, scale, and hydrological conditions than the influence of Nabataean technology, but they do point out the lasting value of the Nabataean achievement.

The major supply of water to the late third-century Roman legionary fort of Betthorus (Lejjun) came from a spring up a wadi bed to the west (De Vries 1987). The spring water pooled behind a dam built of gravel faced with ashlar blocks (L 80 m, W 12 m). The pool rose high enough to enter a conduit built of mortared rubble (inside W 0.24, depth 0.25–0.30 m) that carried the water 360 m to a reservoir inside the fortifications. At one point, a rectangular tank was built across the conduit (W 0.80, L 0.57 m) to catch sediment, extending 0.60 m below the level of the aqueduct floor (fig. 8.74). The principle is the same as that seen on the Jammam branch of the Hawara aqueduct.

FIG. 8.74 *Settling tank in aqueduct serving Roman fort at Betthorus (Lejjun).*

A whole series of such settling tanks can be seen along the course of the spring-fed aqueduct at Panias-Caesarea Philippi (Banias), built in the first century AD (Hartal 2002). Where possible, the 3 km long channel (W 0.43, depth 0.50 m) was cut in the limestone bedrock, lined with plaster, and covered with stone slabs. The six settling tanks were all uniform in size and configuration: rectangular basins with rounded corners, cut in the rock or partly built directly across the channel (0.65 × 0.85 m), their floors 0.30 m below the floor of the channel (fig 8.75). Unlike the Hawara aqueducts, there were also 20 distribution tanks along the course of this aqueduct, providing water to terracotta pipelines that served neighbourhoods down the hill. The aqueduct water entered four of these basins through short sections of lead pipe that possibly served as *calices* regulating the maximum flow (cf. Frontinus, *Aq.* 1.36). The first-century aqueduct serving Hippos (Susita) made use of settling tanks very similar to those at Panias (Meshel et al. 1996: fig. AL-18, AL-19).

Some of the other techniques applied in the Nabataean aqueducts also found continued use

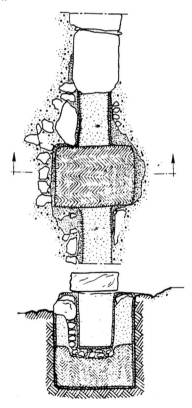

FIG. 8.75 *Settling tank in the aqueduct serving Panias (Banias) (Hartal 2002: fig. 8.1).*

during the Roman period. For example, long channels made up of stone gutter blocks were built during the Roman period at Emmaus (Hirschfeld 1978) and Kourion (Last 1975). At Kourion this was supplemented with a pipeline, as at Petra, and the system included settling tanks and distribution basins.

8.C. CONCLUSIONS

Judging from the data presented in this volume, Hawara was a cultural and technological colony of Petra. Hawara was most likely a political dependent of some sort as well, although we know little about the political relationships among the towns and cities of the Nabataean kingdom and between those settlements and Petra. Petra provides the closest and apparently earliest parallels for all aspects of the water-supply system. The system at Petra had more capacity than the system at Hawara, was more complex and extensive, and, in all but one respect, the structures that composed it were more monumental. The Ghana aqueduct remains the exception, as it is the longest known Nabataean aqueduct channel. The neighbouring water-supply system at Iram constitutes the one other close parallel to the arrangements at Hawara. The parallels at other sites are less close, since Nabataean engineers naturally responded to local variations in climate, topography, geology, and population when designing or executing water-supply systems.

The data supplied above provide a great deal of information about the physical structures that supplied the Nabataeans with water and their interrelationships. Nevertheless, many questions remain concerning the social and religious structures that governed the creation and use of the physical framework. The inscriptions, papyri, and literary texts quoted in the previous chapters can help us conjecture how Nabataean society created and managed these water-supply systems, and modern anthropological data from the region provide an alluring but unverifiable set of models. Numerous questions remain to be answered, and this presentation of the remains of the water-supply system of Hawara presents data that other scholars can build on, along with the suggestion of possible answers or useful lines of inquiry.

Bibliography

Abudanh, F.
2007　The Water-Supply Systems in the Region of Udhruh. *SHAJ* 9: 485–96.

Adam, J.-P.
1994　*Roman Building Materials and Techniques*. London: Batsford.

Aharoni, Y.
1963　Tamar and the Roads to Elath. *IEJ* 13: 30–42.

Akasheh, T. S.
2002　Ancient and Modern Watershed Management in Petra. *NEA* 65.4: 220–24.

Allen, J. H., and Greenough, J. B.
1931　*New Latin Grammar*. 4th ed. Boston: Ginn.

Allen, R. G; Pereira, L. S.; Raes, D.; and Smith M.
1998　*Crop evapotranspiration - Guidelines for computing crop water requirements*. FAO Irrigation and drainage paper 56. Rome: Food and Agriculture Organization of the United Nations.

Allen, W. S.
1978　*Vox Latina: The Pronunciation of Classical Latin*. 2nd ed. Cambridge: Cambridge University Press.

Alt, A.
1921　*Die griechischen Inschriften der Palaestina Tertia westlich der Araba*. Berlin: Walter de Gruyter.
1936　Der südliche Endabschnitt der römischen Strasse von Bostra nach Aila. *ZDPV* 59: 92–111.

Amit, D.; Patrich, J.; and Hirschfeld, Y. (eds.)
2002　*The Aqueducts of Israel*. JRA Supplement 46. Portsmouth RI: JRA.

ʿAmr, K.
1992　Islamic or Nabataean? The Case of a First to Early Second Century AD Cream Ware. *SHAJ* 4: 221–25.
2004　Beyond the Roman Annexation: The Continuity of the Nabataean Pottery Tradition. *SHAJ* 8: 237–45.

ʿAmr, K., and al-Momani, A.
1999　The Discovery of Two Additional Pottery Kilns at az-Zurraba/Wadi Musa. *ADAJ* 43: 175–94.
2001　Preliminary Report on the Archaeological component of the Wadi Musa Water Supply and Wastewater Project (1998–2000). *ADAJ* 45: 253–85.

'Amr, K.; al-Momani, A.; Farajat, S.; and Falahat, H.
1998   Archaeological Survey of the Wadi Musa
       Water Supply and Wastewater Project
       Area. *ADAJ* 42: 503–48.

'Amr, K., and Schick, R.
2001   The Pottery from Humeima: The Closed
       Corpus from the Lower Church. Pp.
       107–27 in Villeneuve and Watson 2001.

Arden-Close, C. F.
1941   Sir Aurel Stein's Explorations of the Ro-
       man Frontiers in Iraq and Trans-Jordan.
       PEQ 73: 18–21.

Aresvik, O.
1976   *The Agricultural Development of Jordan*,
       New York: Praeger.

Arjava, A.; Buchholz, M.; and Gagos, T. (eds.)
2007   *Petra Papyri*, III. Amman: ACOR.

Assemanus, J. S.
1719–28 *Bibliotheca orientalis Clementino-
         Vaticana*. Vatican City.

Augé, C., and de Bellefonds, P. L. (eds.)
1994   *Leon de Laborde, Pétra Retrouvée. Voyage
       de l'Arabie Pétrée, 1828*. Paris: Pygmalion.

Avi-Yonah, M.
1973   Palaestina. *RE*, Supp. XIII: 321–454.

Avner, U.
2001–2   Ancient Water Management in the
         Southern Negev. *ARAM* 13/14: 403–21.

Avni, G.
2007   From Standing Stones to Open Mosques
       in the Negev Desert: The Archaeology of
       Religious Transformation on the Fringes.
       NEA 70.3: 124–38.

Baatz, D.
1978   Temperatur und Sinterbildung. *Das Rhei-
       nische Landesmuseum Bonn* 6: 90.
1979   Teile hellenistischer Geschütze aus
       Griechenland. *AA* 1979: 68–75.

Bachmann, W.; Watzinger, C.; and Wiegand, T.
1921   *Petra*. Berlin: Vereinigung Wissenschaftli-
       cher Verleger.

Bailey, C.
1980   The Negev in the Nineteenth Century:
       Reconstructing History from Bedouin
       oral Traditions. *Asian and African Studies*
       14: 35–80.

al-Bakri, Abu 'Ubayd
1945–51   *Mu'jam ma Ista'jama min Asma' al-
          Buldan wa al-Mawadi'*. Cairo.

al-Balâdhurî
1978   *Ansâb al-Ashraf*, pt. 3, 'Abd al-'Aziz al-
       Dûrî, ed., Wiesbaden: Franz Steiner.

Barker, G.; Gilbertson, D.; Jones, B.;
and Mattingly, D. (eds.)
1996   *Farming the Desert*. 2 vols. London: Soci-
       ety for Libyan Studies.

Barker, G.; Gilbertson, D.; and Mattingly, D. (eds.)
2007   *Archaeology and Desertification: The
       Wadi Faynan Landscape Survey, Southern
       Jordan*. Oxford: Oxbow Books.

Bartlett, J. R.
1989   *Edom and the Edomites*. Sheffield: Shef-
       field Academic Press.

Bean, G. E.
1967   *Aegean Turkey: An Archaeological Guide*.
       London: Earnest Benn.

Beaumont, P.; Blake, G. H.; and Wagstaff, J. M.
1976   *The Middle East: A Geographical Study*.
       London: John Wiley & Sons.

Bedal, L.-A.
1999   A Paradeisos in Petra: New Light on the
       'Lower Market'. *ADAJ* 43: 227–39.
2000a *The Petra Pool Complex: A Hellenistic
       Paradeisos in the Nabataean Capital*. PhD
       diss., University of Pennsylvania.
2000b Paradise Found: Petra's Urban Oasis.
       Expedition 42.2: 23–36.

2001 A Pool Complex in Petra's City Center. *BASOR* 324: 23–41.

2002 Desert Oasis: Water Consumption and Display in the Nabataean Capital. *NEA* 65.4: 225–34.

Bedal, L.-A., and Schryver, J. G.
2007 Nabataean Landscape and Power: Evidence from the Petra Garden and Pool Complex. Pp. 375–83 in Levy et al. 2007.

Bellwald, U.
2004 Streets and Hydraulics: The Petra National Trusts Siq Project in Petra 1996–1999. The Archaeological Results. Pp. 73–94 in H.-D. Bienert and J. Häser (eds.), *Men of Dikes and Canals: The Archaeology of Water in the Middle East.* Rahden: Marie Leidorf.

2007 The Hydraulic Infrastructure of Petra: A Model for Water Strategies in Arid Land. *SHAJ* 9: 315–24.

Bellwald, U.; al-Huneidi, M.; Salihi, A.; Keller, D.; Naser, R; and al-Eisawi, D.
2003 *The Petra Siq: Nabataean Hydrology Uncovered.* Amman: Petra National Trust.

Bender, F.
1974 *Geology of Jordan.* Berlin: Borntraeger.

Ben-Dor, S.
1948 Petra Colonia. *Berytus* 9: 41–43.

Benzinger, I.
1898 Auara. *RE* II.2: col. 2264.

Bessac, J.-C.
2007 *Le travail de la pierre à Pétra. Technique et économie de la taille rupestre .* Paris: Editions Recherche sur les Civilizations.

Bevan, G., and Reeves, M. B.
2010 A New Nabataean Inscription from the Site of Humayma, Ancient Hawara. *Journal of Semitic Studies* 55: 497–507.

Bienert, H.-D.; Lamprichts, R.; and Vieweger, D.
2000 Ba'ja — The Archaeology of a Landscape, 9000 Years of Human Occupation: A Preliminary Report on the 1999 Field Season. *ADAJ* 44: 119–48.

Bienkowski, P.
2001 The Persian Period. Pp. 347–66 in MacDonald et al. 2001.

Bikai, P. M.
2003 Beidha al-Amti. *ACOR Newsletter* 15.2: 1–3.
2009 Introductory Speech. *SHAJ* 10: 23–26.

Bikai, P. M.; Kanellopoulos, C.; and Saunders, S. L.
2008 Beidha in Jordan: A Dionysian Hall in a Nabataean Landscape. *AJA* 112: 465–507.
2009 Bayda Documentation Report. *SHAJ* 10: 363–68.

Bikai, P. M., and Perry, M.
2001 Petra North Ridge Tombs 1 and 2: Preliminary Report. *BASOR* 324: 59–78.

Billerbeck, M.
2006 *Stephani Byzantini Ethnika*, vol. 1: *A–Γ.* Berlin: De Gruyter.

Bisheh, G.; Farajat, S.; Palumbo, G.; and Waheeb, M.
1993 Archaeological Rescue Survey of the Ras an-Naqab-Aqaba Highway Alignment, 1992. *ADAJ* 37: 119–33.

Blétry-Sébé, S.
1990 Habitat et urbanisme sur le site de Humeima. Recherches préliminaires. *ADAJ* 34: 313–19.

Bowersock, G.
1971 Report on Provincia Arabia. *JRS* 61: 219–42.
1983 *Roman Arabia.* Cambridge ,MA: Harvard University.
1984 Nabataeans and Romans in the Wadi Sirhan. Pp. 133–36 in A. M. Abdalla et al., eds., *Studies in the History of Arabia*, vol. II. Riyadh: King Saud University.

1988   The Three Arabias in Ptolemy's Geogra-
        phy. Pp. 47–53 in P.-L. Gatier, B. Helly
        and J.-P. Rey-Coquais, eds., *Geographie
        Historique au Proche-Orient (Syrie, Phé-
        nicie, Romaines, Byzantines): Actes de la
        Table Ronde de Velbonne, 16–18 Septem-
        bre 1985*. Paris: CNRS.
1991   The Babatha Papyri, Masada, and Rome.
        JRA 4: 336–44.
1997a   Jacoby's Fragments and Two Greek His-
        torians of Pre-Islamic Arabia. Pp. 173–85
        in G. W. Most, ed., *Collecting Fragments*.
        Göttingen: Vandenhoeck & Ruprecht.
1997b   Nabataeans on the Capitoline.
        Hyperboreus 3: 347–52.
1999   Maioumas. P. 553 in G. W. Bowersock, P.
        Brown, and O. Grabar, eds., *Late Antiq-
        uity: A Guide to the Postclassical World*.
        Cambridge, MA: Harvard University.
2003   The Nabataeans in Historical Context. Pp.
        19–25 in Markoe 2003.

Braemer, F.
1990   Formes d'irrigation dans le Hawran (Sy-
        rie du sud). Pp. 453-74 in B. Geyer, ed.,
        *Techniques et Pratiques Hydro-Agricoles
        Traditionnelles en Domaine Irrigué*, vol.
        II, Paris: Paul Geuthner.

Brinker, W.
1990   Wasserspeicherung in Zisternen. Ein
        Beitrag zur Frage der Wasserversorgung
        früher Städte. *Mitteilungen, Leichtweiss-
        Institut für Wasserbau* 109: 1–155.

Broshi, M.
1980   The Population of Western Palestine in
        the Roman-Byzantine Period. *BASOR*
        236: 1–10.

Brown, G. E.
1990   The Testing of Concretes, Mortars,
        Plasters, and Stuccos. *Archeomaterials* 4:
        185–91.
1996   *Analyses and History of Cement*. Keswick:
        Gordon E. Brown Consultants.

Browning, I.
1982   *Petra*. Rev. ed. London: Chatto & Windus.

Bruins, H. J.
1986   *Desert Environment and Agriculture in the
        Central negev and Kadesh-Barnea during
        Historical Times*. Ph.D. diss. Agricultural
        University of Wageningen. Nijkerk: MID-
        BAR Foundation.
1990a   The Impact of Man and Climate on the
        Central Negev and Northeastern Sinai
        Deserts during the Late Holocene. Pp.
        87–99 in S. Bottema, G. Entjes-Nieborg,
        W. van Zeist, eds., *Man's Role in the Shap-
        ing of the Eastern Mediterranean Land-
        scape*. Rotterdam: Balkema.
1990b   Ancient Agricultural Terraces at Nahal
        Mitran. *Atiqot* 10: 22–28.

Brünnow, R. E.
1909   Über Musils Forschungsreisen. *Wiener
        Zeitschrift für die Kunde des Morgenlan-
        des* 23: 18–32.

Brünnow, R. E., and Domaszewski, A. von
1904–9 *Die Provincia Arabia*. 3 vols.
        Strassburg: Trübner.

Buchholz, H.-G.
1976   *Methymna: Archäologische Beiträge zur
        Topographie und Geschichte von Nord-
        Lesbos*. Mainz am Rhein: Philipp von
        Zabern.

Bugini, R.
1993   Investigation of the Characteristics and
        Properties of 'Cocciopesto' from the An-
        cient Roman Period. Pp. 386–93 in M.-J.
        Thiel, ed., *Conservation of Stone   and
        Other Materials, vol. 1: Causes of Disor-
        ders and diagnosis*. New York: Spon.

Butler, H. C.
1914   *Ancient Architecture in Syria*. Section A,
        Southern Syria, pt. 4, *Bosra*. Leiden: Brill.

Calvet, Y., and Geyer, B.
1987   Pp. 129–56 in M. Yon, ed., *Le centre de la ville. Ras Shamra-Ougarit*, III. Paris: Éditions Recherche sur les Civilisations.

Campbell, D., and Roe, A.
1998   Results of a Preliminary Survey of Livestock Owners. Pp. 189–96 in R. Dutton et al., eds., *Arid Land Resources and their Management: Jordan's Desert Margin*. London: Kegan Paul.

Canaan, T.
1929   Studies in the Topography and Folklore of Petra. *Journal of the Palestine Oriental Society* 9: 136–218.

Cansdale, G.
1970   *Animals of the Bible Lands*. London: Paternoster Press.

Cantineau, J.
1930–32   *Le Nabatéen*. 2 vols. Paris: Ernest Leroux.

Casson, L.
1989   *The Periplus Maris Erythraei*. Princeton: Princeton University.

Chamonard, J.
1924   *Exploration archéologique de Délos,* VIII: *Le Quartier du théâtre,* III: *Construction et technique—Appendice*. Paris: École Française d'Athènes.

Chatelard, G., and de Tarragon, J.-M.
2006   *The Empire and the Kingdom: Jordan as seen by the École biblique et archéologique français de Jérusalem (1893–1935)*. Amman: Centre Culturel Français.

Clermont-Ganneau, M. I.
1906   L'Édit byzantin de Bersabée. *RBib* 1906: 412–32.

Clutton-Brock, J.
1971   The Primary Food Animals of the Jericho Tell from the Proto-Neolithic to the Byzantine Period. *Levant* 3: 41–55.

Cobb, P.
2001   *White Banners: Contention in 'Abbasid Syria, 750–880*. Albany, NY: SUNY.

Colt, H. D. (ed.)
1962   *Excavations at Nessana (Auja Hafir, Palestine)*. London: British School of Archaeology in Jerusalem.

Connan, J.
1999   Use and Trade of Bitumen in Antiquity and Prehistory. *Philosophical Transactions of the Royal Society, London, Ser. B* 354: 33–50.

Cook, R. J.
2004   *An Archaeological Examination of Towers in Arabia in their Social, Economic and Geographical Context: Field Survey and Excavation of Purported Roman Military Towers near the Fort at al-Humayma (ancient Hawara), Jordan*. M.A. thesis, University of Victoria.

Corbett, G. J.
2009   A Landscape/GIS Perspective on the Thamudic Inscriptions and Rock Drawings of the Wadi Hafir, Southern Jordan. *SHAJ* 10: 339–46.

Cordova, C. R.
2007   *Millennial Landscape Change in Jordan: Geoarchaeology and Cultural Ecology*. Tucson: University of Arizona.

Cotton, H. M.
1995   The Archive of Salome Komaise Daughter of Levi: Another Archive from the 'Cave of Letters'. *ZPE* 105: 171–208.

Courbon, P.
2008   Les puits nabatéens de Mada'in Salih (Arabie Saoudite). *AAE* 19: 48–70.

Cowper, A. D.
1927   *Lime and Lime Mortars*. London: HM Stationery Office.

Craddock, P. T.
1977 The Composition of the Copper Alloys used by the Greek, Etruscan and Roman Civilizations. Part II. *JAS* 4: 103–23.

Crowfoot, J. W.
1937 *Churches at Bosra and Samaria-Sebaste.* British School of Archaeology in Jerusalem Supplementary Papers, 4. Jerusalem: British School of Archaeology.

al-Daire, M.
2004 Water Management in Trans-Jordan Byzantine Architecture with Respect to Excavated Monuments in the City of Gadara/Umm Qais. Pp. 219–29 in H.-D. Bienert and J. Häser, eds., *Men of Dikes and Canals: The Archaeology of Water in the Middle East.* Rahden: Marie Leidorf.

Dakaris, S.
1996 *The Nekyomanteion of the Acheron.* 2nd ed. Athens: Ministry of Culture.

Dalman G.
1908 *Petra und seine Felsheiligtümer.* Leipzig: Hinrichs.
1912 *Neue Petra-Forschungen und der heilige Felsen von Jerusalem.* Leipzig: Hinrichs.

Daniel, R. W.
2001 P.Petra Inv. 10 and its Arabic. Pp. 331–41 in *Atti del XXII Congresso Internazionale di Papirologia.* Florence: Istituto Papirologico G.Vitelli.

Davidovits, F.
1995 *Les mortiers de pouzzolanes artificielles chez Vitruve: evolution et historique architecturale.* M.A. Thesis, Université Paris X—Nanterre.

de Ligt, L.
1993 *Fairs and Markets in the Roman Empire.* Amsterdam: Gieben.

Delorme, J.
1961 *Exploration Archéologique de Délos, XXV: Les Palestres.* Paris: De Boccard.

Dentzer-Feydy, J.
1990 Khirbet edh-Dharih: Architectural Decoration of the Temple. *Aram* 2: 229–34.
1995 Remarques sur la métrologie et le projet architectural de quelques monuments d'époque hellénistique et romaine en Transjordanie. *SHAJ* 5: 161–71.

de Vries, B.
1987 The el-Lejjun Water System. Pp. 399–428 in Parker 1987.

Dickson, H. R. P.
1959 *The Arab of the Desert: A Glimpse into the Badawin Life in Kuwait and Saudi Arabia.* 3rd ed. London: Allen & Unwin.

Dierx, W., and Garbrecht, G. (eds.)
2001 *Wasser im Heiligen Land. Biblische Zeugnisse und archäologische Forschungen.* Cologne: Frontinus-Gesellschaft.

Dilke, O. A. W.
1971 *The Roman Land Surveyors. An Introduction to the Agrimensores.* Newton Abbot, UK: David & Charles.

Dirven, L.
1999 *The Palmyrenes of Dura-Europos. A Study in Religious Interaction in Roman Syria.* Leiden: Brill.

Di Segni, L.
2004 The Beersheba Tax Edict Reconsidered in the Light of a Newly Discovered Fragment. *Scripta Classica Israelica* 23: 131–58.

Dolinka, B. J.
2003 *Nabataean Aila (Aqaba, Jordan) from a Ceramic Perspective.* BAR International Series S1116. Oxford: Archaeopress.

Doughty, C. M.
1936 *Travels in Arabia Deserta*. 3rd ed. 2 vols. London: Jonathan Cape.

Drack, W.
1997 *Zur Geschichte des Wasserhahns: Die rö-mischen Wasser-Armaturen und mittelal-terlichen Hahnen aus der Schweiz und dem Fürstentum Liechtenstein*, with a supple-ment by O. A. Baumgärtel. Zürich: Rohr.

Driel-Murray, C. van
2008 Tanning and Leather. Pp. 483–95 in J. P. Oleson, ed., *Oxford Handbook of Engi-neering and Technology in the Classical World*. New York: Oxford University.

Dudley, D., and Reeves, M. B.
1997 The Wadi Ramm Recovery Project: Preliminary Report of the 1996 Season. *Echos de monde classique* 16: 81–106.
2007 Luxury in the Desert: A Nabataean Pala-tial Residence at Wadi Ramm. Pp. 401–8 in Levy et al. 2007.

Dunn, E., and Rapp, G.
2004 Characterization of Mortars and Poz-zolanic Materials from Umm al-Jimal. *Studies in Conservation* 49: 145–60.

al-Dûrî, 'A., and al-Mutallabî, 'A. (eds.)
1971 *Akhbâr al-Dawla al-'Abbâsiya*, Beirut: Dâr al-Talî'a.

Eadie, J.
1984 Humayma 1983: The Regional Survey. *ADAJ* 28: 211–24.
1985 Artifacts of Annexation: Trajan's Grand Strategy and Arabia. Pp. 407–23 in J. W. Eadie and J. Ober, eds., *The Craft of the Ancient Historian: Essays in Honor of Chester G. Starr*. New York: University Press of America.
1986 The Evolution of the Roman Frontier in Arabia. Pp. 243–52 in D. Kennedy and P. Freedman, *The Defence of the Roman and Byzantine East*. British Archaeological Reports 297. Oxford: BAR.

1989 Strategies of Economic Development in the Roman East: The Red Sea Trade revisited. Pp. 113–120 in D. French and C. S. Lightfoot, eds., *The Eastern Frontier of the Roman Empire*. British Archaeo-logical Reports International Series S553. Oxford: BAR.

Eadie, J.; Graf, D.; and Oleson, J. P.
1989 Humayma. Pp. 270–74 in D. Homès-Fredericq and J. B. Hennessy, eds., *Archaeology of Jordan, II: Field Reports*. Leuven: Peeters.

Eadie, J., and Oleson, J. P.
1986 The Water-Supply Systems of Nabataean and Roman Humayma. *BASOR* 262: 49–76.

Edelman, D. V.
1995 Edom: A Historical Geography. Pp. 1–11 in D. V. Edelman, ed., *You Shall Not Abhore an Edomite for He is Your Brother: Edom and Seir in History and Tradition*. Atlanta: Scholars.

al-Eisawi, D. M.
1985 Vegetation in Jordan. *SHAJ* 2: 45–57.

Elitzur, Y.
2008 The Siloam Pool—'Solomon's Pool'—was a Swimming Pool. *PEQ* 140: 17–25.

Elliot, J. D.
1982 *The Elusa Oikoumene. A Geographical Analysis of an Ancient Desert Ecosystem Based on Archaeological, Environmental, Ethnographic, and Historical Data*. M.A. Thesis, Mississippi State University.

Emery-Barbier, A.
1995 Pollen Analysis: Environmental and Cli-matic Implications. Pp. 375–84 in Henry 1995.

Evenari, M.; Shanan, L.; and Tadmor, N.
1982 *The Negev: Challenge of a Desert*, 2nd ed. Cambridge, MA: Harvard University.

Fabio, E., and Fassitelli, L.
1990   *Roma: Tubi e valvole*. Milan: Petrolieri d'Italia.

Fahlbusch, H.
1982   *Vergleich antiker griechischer und römischer Wasserversorgungsanlagen*. Mitteilungen des Leichtweiss-Institut für Wasserbau der Technischen Universität Braunschweig, 73.
2006   Wasserwirtschaftliche Anlagen des antiken Priene. Pp. 65–84 in S. Mols and E. Moormann, eds., *Omni Pede Stare: Saggi architettonici e circumvesuviani in memoriam Jos de Waele*. Naples: Electa.

Fall, P. L.
1990   Deforestation in Southern Jordan: Evidence from Fossil Hyrax Middens. Pp. 271–81 in S. Bottema, G. Entjes-Nieborg and W. van Zeist, eds., *Man's Role in the Shaping of the Eastern Mediterranean Landscape*. Rotterdam: Balkema.

Farès-Drappeau, S.
1995   L'inscription de type dédanite de Abu ad-Diba'/Wadi Ramm. Une nouvelle lecture. *ADAJ* 39: 493–97.

Farès-Drappeau, S., and Zayadine, F.
2004   Archaeological and Epigraphical Survey at Wadi Ramm/Iram. *ADAJ* 48: 357–71.

Farrand, W.
1984   Hydrologic resources and their management around the Nabatean Town of Humayma, Jordan. P. 506 in *1984 GSA Meetings, Abstr, with Programs V. 16*, No. 6.

Fiema, Z.
1991   Economics, Administration and Demography of Late Roman and Byzantine Southern Transjordan. Ph.D. diss., University of Utah.
2002   Late antique Petra and its Hinterland: Recent Research and New Interpretations. Pp. 191–252 in J. Humphrey, ed. *The Roman and Byzantine Near East*, 3. JRA Supplement 49. Portsmouth, RI: JRA.
2003   Roman Petra (A.D. 106–363). A Neglected Subject. *ZDPV* 119: 38–58.

Fiema, Z., and Jones, R. N.
1990   The Nabataean King-List Revised. *ADAJ* 34: 239–48.

Fiema, Z.; Kanellopoulos, C.; Waliszewski, T.; and Schick, R.
2001   *The Petra Church*. Amman: American Center of Oriental Research.

Finkelstein, I.
1988   Arabian Trade and Socio-Political Conditions in the Negev in the Twelfth–Eleventh Centuries B.C.E. *JNES* 47: 241–52.
1990   Processes of Sedentarization in the History of Sinai and the Negev. *BASOR* 279: 67–88.

Finnegan, M.
1978   Faunal Remains from Bad edh-Dhra, 1975. *AASOR* 1978: 51–54.

Flannery, K.
1982   Early Pig Domestication in the Fertile Crescent: A Retrospective Look. Pp. 163–87 in T. C. Young, P. Smith, and P. Mortensen, eds., *Hilly Flanks: Essays on the Prehistory of Southwest Asia*. Chicago: Oriental Institute.

Foerster, G.
1986   A Cuirassed Bronze Statue of Hadrian. 'Atiqot (English Series) 17: 139–60.

Foote, R.
1999   Frescoes and Carved Ivory from the Abbasid Family Homestead at Humeima. *JRA* 12: 423–28.
2007   From Residence to Revolutionary Headquarters: The Early Islamic Qasr and Mosque Complex at al-Humayma and its 8th-century Context. Pp. 457–66 in Levy et al. 2007.

Foote, R.; Wade, A.; el- Bastawesy, M.; Oleson, J. P.; and Mithen, S.

forthcoming A Millennium of Rainfall, Settlement and Water Management at Humayma, southern Jordan, 100 BC–900 AD. In S. Mithen and E. Black, eds., *Water, Life & Civilisation: Cimate, Environment and Society in the Jordan Valley.* Cambridge: Cambridge University/UNESCO.

Forbes, R. J.

1966 Leather in Antiquity. *Studies in Ancient Technology* 5: 1–79.

Frank, F. von

1934 Explorations in Eastern Palestine, I. *AASOR* 14: 1–113.

Frazer, J. G.

1913 *Pausanias's Description of Greece. Translated with a Commentary.* 6 vols. London: Macmillan.

Freeman, P.

2001 Roman Jordan. Pp. 427–60 in MacDonald et al. 2001.

Freeman, P. and Kennedy, D. (eds.)

1986 *The Defence of the Roman and Byzantine East.* BAR International Series 297. Oxford: BAR.

Frösén, J.

2001 The First Five Years of the Petra Papyri. Pp. 487–93 in *Atti del XXII Congresso Internazionale di Papirologia.* Florence: Istituto Papirologico G.Vitelli.

2004 Archaeological Information from the Petra Papyri. *SHAJ* 8: 141–44.

Frösén, J.; Arjava, A.; and Lehtinen, M. (eds.)

2002 *The Petra Papyri I.* Amman: American Center of Oriental Research.

Frösén, J., and Fiema, Z.

2002 *Petra: A City Forgotten and Rediscovered.* Helsinki: Helsinki University.

Garbrecht, G.

1984 Geschichtliche Talsperren im östlichen Mittelmeerraum. *Mitteilungen des Leichtweiss-Institut für Wasserbau* 82: 1–21.

1987 Die Wasserversorgung des antiken Pergamon. Pp. 11–48 in *Die Wasserversorgung antiker Städte,* 2. Mainz am Rhein: Philipp von Zabern.

1987–91 *Historische Talsperren,* 2 vols. Stuttgart: Wittwer.

Garbrecht, G., and Manderscheid, H.

1992 'Etiam fonte novo antoninano.' L'acquedotto Antoniniano alle Terme di Caracalla. *Archeologia Classica* 44: 193–234.

Garbrecht, G., and Peleg, Y.

1989 Die Wasservorsorgung geschichtlicher Wüstenfestungen am Jordantal. *Antike Welt* 20.2: 2–20.

2001 Die Wasservorsorgung geschichtlicher Wüstenfestungen am Jordantal. Pp. 222–39 in Dierx and Garbrecht 2001.

Garlan, Y.

1974 *Recherches de poliorcétique grecque. BEFAR* no. 223. Paris: De Boccard.

Gawlikowski, M.

1997 The Oriental City and the Advent of Islam. Pp. 339–50 in G. Wilhelm, ed., *Die Orientalische Stadt: Kontinuität, Wandel, Bruch.* Saarbrück: SDV.

Geer, R. M.

1954 *Diodorus of Sicily.* Vol. 10. Cambridge MA: Harvard University.

Gerber, Y.

1994 Nabataean Coarse Ware Pottery. Pp. 286–92 in R. A. Stucky, Y. Gerber, B. Kolb, and S. G. Schmid, Swiss-Liechtenstein Excavations at ez-Zantur in Petra 1993: The Fifth Campaign. *ADAJ* 38: 271–92.

1997 The Nabataean Coarse Ware Pottery: A Sequence from the End of the Second Century BC to the Beginning of the Second Century AD. *SHAJ* 6: 407–11.

1998 Coarse Ware Pottery from Room 6. Pp. 272–74 in B. Kolb, D. Keller and Y. Gerber, Swiss-Liechtenstein Excavations of az-Zantur in Petra, 1997. *ADAJ* 42: 259–77.

2000 Observations on the 1999 Pottery. Pp. 409–11 in J. Frösén et al., The 1999 Finnish Jabal Harun Project: A Preliminary Report. *ADAJ* 44: 395–424.

2001a A Glimpse of the Recent Excavations on ez-Zantur/Petra: The Late Roman Pottery and its Prototypes in the 2nd and 3rd Centuries AD. Pp. 7–12 in Villeneuve and Watson 2001.

2001b Selected Ceramic Deposits. Pp. 359–66 in Fiema et al. 2001.

2001c Report on the Pottery. Pp. 427–32 in H. Merklein, R. Wenning and Y. Gerber, The Veneration Place of Isis at Wadi as-Siyyagh, Petra: New Research. *SHAJ* 7: 421–32.

2001d Observations on the 'Post-Byzantine' Pottery at Jabal Harun. Pp. 378–79 in J. Frösén et al., The 1998–2000 Finnish Harun Project: Specialized Reports. *ADAJ* 45: 377–424.

2002 Byzantine and Early Islamic Ceramics from Jabal Harûn. Pp. 201–9 in Frösen and Fiema 2002.

2008a Preliminary Characterization of the Humayma Ceramics. Pp. 334–41 in J. P. Oleson et al. 2008.

2008b The Byzantine and Early Islamic Pottery from Jabal Harun. Pp. 287–310 in Z. T. Fiema and J. Frösén, eds., *Petra – The Mountain of Aaron: The Finnish Archaeological Project in Jordan, Vol. I: The Church and the Chapel.* Helsinki: Societas Scientiarum Fennica.

Gergel, R. A.
1991 The Tel Shalem Hadrian Reconsidered. *AJA* 95: 231–51.

Geva, H.
1993 Water Supply (Jerusalem). *NEAEHL* 2: 746–47.

Gibb, H. A. R.
1986–2002 *Encyclopedia of Islam.* 2nd ed. Leiden: Brill.

Gichon, M.
2000 The Siege of Masada. Pp. 542–54 in Y. Le Bohec, ed. *Les Légions de Rome sous le Haut-Empire.* Lyon: De Boccard.

Gilly, J.-C.
2001 Étude géochemique des incrustations de l'aqueduc romain conduisant les eaux d'Uzès à Nîmes. *Méditerranée* 1–2: 131–39–150.

Glucker, C. A. M.
1987 *The City of Gaza in the Roman and Byzantine Periods.* British Archaeological Reports International Series S325. Oxford: BAR.

Glueck, N.
1934–35 Explorations in Eastern Palestine, II. *AASOR* 15.
1953 Explorations in Eastern Palestine. *BASOR* 131: 6–15.
1959 *Rivers in the Desert: A History of the Negev.* New York: Farrar, Straus and Cudahy.
1965 *Deities and Dolphins: The Story of the Nabataeans.* New York: Farrar, Straus and Giroux.

Graf, D.
1978 The Saracens and the Defense of the Arabian Frontier. *BASOR* 229: 1–26.
1979 A Preliminary Report on a Survey of Nabatean-Roman Military Sites in Southern Jordan. *ADAJ* 23: 121–27.
1983 The Nabateans and the Hisma: In the Footsteps of Glueck and Beyond. Pp. 647–64 in C. L. Meyers and M. O'Connor, eds., *The Word of the Lord Shall Go Forth: Essays in Honor of David Noel Freedman.* Winona Lake: Eisenbrauns.
1989a Rome and the Saracens: Reassessing the Nomadic Menace. Pp. 341–400 in T. Fahd, ed., *L'Arabie préislamique et son environnement historique et culturel.* Leiden: Brill.

1989b Zenobia and the Arabs. Pp. 143–67 in D. French and C. S. Lightfoot, eds., *The Eastern Frontier of the Roman Empire.* British Archaeological Reports International Series S553. Oxford: BAR.

1992a God of Humamya. Pp. 67–76 in Z. J. Kapera, ed., *Intertestamental Essays in Honour of Józef Tadeusz Milik.* Kraków: Enigma.

1992b Nabataeans. Pp. 970–73 in *ABD* 4.

1993a The Via Nova Traiana between Petra and Aqaba. *Syria* 70: 262–63.

1993b The Persian Royal Road System in Syria-Palestine. *Transeuphratène* 6: 149–44.

1995 The *Via Nova Traiana* in Arabia Petraea. Pp. 241–67 in J. H. Humphrey, ed., *The Roman and Byzantine Near East: Some Recent Archaeological Research.* JRA Supplement 14. Ann Arbor, MI: JRA.

1997 The *via militaris* in Arabia. *DOP* 51: 271–81.

2000 Town and Countryside in Roman Arabia during Late Antiquity. Pp. 219–40 in T. Burns and J. Eadie, eds. *Urban Centers and Rural Contexts in Late Antiquity.* East Lansing, MI: Michigan State University.

2001 First Millennium AD: Roman and Byzantine Periods Landscape Archaeology and Settlement Patterns. *SHAJ* 7: 469–80.

2009 Athendorus of Tarsus and Nabataea: The Date and Circumstances of his Visit to Petra. *SHAJ* 10: 67–74.

Graf, D.; Bedal, L.-A.; Schmid, S. G.;
and Sidebotham, S. E.
  2005 The Hellenistic Petra Project. Excavations in the Civic Center, Preliminary Report of the First Season, 2004. *ADAJ* 49: 417–41.

Graf, D., and Sidebotham, S. E.
  2003 Nabataean Trade. Pp. 67–73 in Markoe 2003.

Grawehr, M.
  2006 Die Lampen der Grabungen auf ez-Zantur in Petra. Pp. 261–398 in Keller and Grawehr 2006.

Gregory, S.
  1996 *Roman Military Architecture on the Eastern Frontier, A.D. 200–600,* 3 vols. Amsterdam: Hakkert.

Gregory, S., and Kennedy, D.
  1985 *Sir Aurel Stein's Limes Report: The Full Text.* 2 vols. British Archaeological Reports International Series, 272. Oxford: BAR.

Groh, D. E.
  1997 Subeita. *EANA* 5: 89–90.

Guendon, J.-L., and Vaudour, J.
  2001 Les concretions de l'aqueduc de Nîmes: observations et hypothèses. *Méditerranée* 1–2: 140–150.

Gunsam, E.
  1989 Die nördliche Hubta-Wasserleitung in Petra. Pp. 319–30 in M. Lindner, ed., *Petra und das Königreich der Nabatäer.* 5th ed., Bad Windsheim: Delp.

Gutwein, K. C.
  1981 *Third Palestine: A Regional Study in Byzantine Urbanization.* Washington, DC: University Press of America.

Habel, P.
  1895 *Aquarii. RE* II.1: 311–13.

Hackl, U.; Jenni, H.; and Schneider, C.
  2003 *Quellen zur Geschichte der Nabatäer.* Göttingen: Vandenhoeck & Ruprecht.

Haiman, M.
  1995 Agriculture and Nomad-State Relations in the Negev Desert in the Byzantine and Early Islamic Periods. *BASOR* 297: 29–53.

Hajjar, Y.
  1990 Divinités oraculaires et rites divinatoires en Syrie et en Phénicie à l'époque gréco-romaine. *ANRW* 2.18.4: 2236–2320.

Hammond, P. C.
2000 Nabataean Metallurgy. Pp. 145–56 in L. Stager, J. Greene and M. Coogan, eds., *The Archaeology of Jordan and Beyond: Essays in Honor of James A. Sauer.* Winona Lake, IN: Eisenbrauns.

Hart, S.
1986a Some preliminary thoughts on settlement in southern Edom. *Levant* 18: 51–58.
1986b Nabataeans and Romans in Southern Jordan. Pp. 337–42 in Freeman and Kennedy 1986.

Hartal, M.
2002 The Aqueduct to Banias. Pp. 89–104 in Amit et al. 2002.

Hartmann, R.
1913 Materialien zur historischen Topographie der Palaestina tertia. *ZDPV* 36: 100–13, 180–98.

Hassan, F. A.
1995 Late Quaternary Geology and Geomorphology of the Area in the Vicinity of Ras en Naqb. Pp. 23–31 in Henry 1995.

Hauck, G. F. W., and Novak, R. A.
1987 Interaction of Flow and Incrustation in the Roman Aqueduct of Nîmes. *Journal of Hydraulic Engineering* 113.2: 141–57.

Hayajneh, H.
2001 Marcus Ulpius Su'aidu in einem Bruchstück einer nabatäischen Inschrift aus Süd-Jordanien. *ZDPV* 117: 171–85.

Hayes, J. W.
1985 *Atlante delle forme ceramiche, I: Ceramica fine romana nel bacino mediterraneo (medio e tardo impero).* Encyclopedia dell'arte antica, classica e orientale. Rome: Istituto della Enciclopedia Italiana.

Healey, J. F.
1993 *The Nabataean Tomb Inscriptions of Mada'in Salih.* Oxford: Oxford University.

2001 *The Religion of the Nabataeans: A Conspectus.* Leiden: Brill.

Heinrichs, K., and Fitzner, B.
2000 Lithotypes of Rock-Carved Monuments in Petra/Jordan: Classification and Petrographical Properties. *ADAJ* 44: 283–312.

Heinzel, H.; Fitter, R.; and Parslow, P.
1979 *The Birds of Britain and Europe.* London: Collins.

Hellmann, M.-C.
2002 *L'Architecture grecque, 1: Les principes de la construction.* Paris: Picard.

Helms, S.
1981 *Jawa.* London: Methuen.
1982 Paleo-Beduin and Transmigrant Urbanism. *SHAJ* 1: 97–113.

Henry, D. O.
1982 The Prehistory of Southern Jordan and relationships with the Levant. *JFA* 9:4: 417–44.
1985 Late Pleistocene Environment and Paleolithic Adaptations in Southern Jordan. *SHAJ* 2: 67–77.
1987 Topographic Influences on Epipaleolithic Land-use Patterns in Southern Jordan. *SHAJ* 3: 21–27.
1992 Seasonal Movements of Fourth Millennium Pastoral Nomads in Wadi Hisma. *SHAJ* 4: 137–41.
1996 Middle Paleolithic Behavioral Organization: 1993 Excavation of Tor Faraj, Southern Jordan. *JFA* 23: 31–53.

Henry, D. O. (ed.)
1995 *Prehistoric Cultural Ecology and Evolution: Insights from southern Jordan.* New York: Plenum.

Henry, D. O.; Hassan, F. A.; Jones, M.; and Henry, K. C.
1981 An Investigation of the Pre-History and Palaeoenvironments of Southern Jordan (1979 Field Season). *ADAJ* 25: 113–146.

1983 An Investigation of the Prehistory of
      Southern Jordan. *PEQ* 115: 1–24.

Herr, L., and Najjar, M.
2001 The Iron Age. Pp. 323–46 in MacDonald
      et al. 2001.

Hill, B. H.
1964 *The Springs: Peirene, Sacred Spring,
      Glauke. Corinth*, Vol. I pt. 6. Princeton:
      American School of Classical Studies.

Hillel, D.
1982 *Negev: Land, Water, and Life in a Desert
      Environment*. New York: Praeger.

Hirschfeld, Y.
1978 A Hydraulic Installation in the Water-
      Supply System of Emmaus-Nicopolis. *IEJ*
      28: 86–92.
2003 Social Aspects of the Late-Antique Vil-
      lage of Shivta. *JRA* 16: 394–408.

Hodge, A. T.
1992 *Roman Aqueducts and Water Supply*.
      London: Duckworth.

Hopkins, D. C.
1993 Pastoralists in Late Bronze Age Palestine:
      Which Way Did They Go. *BA* 56: 200–11.
1997 Agriculture. *EANE* 1: 22–30.

Horsfield, G, and Horsfield, A.
1938 Sela-Petra, The rock of Edom and Na-
      batene. *QDAP* 7: 1–42.

Isaac, B.
1990 *The Limits of Empire: The Roman Army in
      the East*. Oxford: Oxford University.
1992 The Babatha Archive: A Review Article.
      IEJ 42: 62–75.
1998 *The Near East under Roman Rule: Selected
      Papers*. Leiden: Brill.

Isager, S., and Skydsgaard, J. E.
1992 *Ancient Greek Agriculture: An Introduc-
      tion*. London: Routledge.

Jacoby, F.
1958 *Fragmente der griechischen Historiker*, vol.
      III.C. Leiden: Brill.

Jansen, G. C. M.
2000 Urban Water Transportation and Distri-
      bution. Pp. 103–26 in Wikander 2000.
2001 Water Pipe Systems in the Houses of
      Pompeii: Distribution and Use. Pp. 27–40
      Koloski-Ostrow 2001.

Jaussen A.
1903 Voyage du Sinai. *RBib* 12: 100–14.

Jobling, W. L.
1981 Preliminary Report on the Archaeologi-
      cal Survey Between Ma'an and 'Aqaba,
      January–February 1980. *ADAJ* 25:
      105–12.
1983a The 1982 Archaeological and Epigraphic
      Survey of the 'Aqaba-Ma'an Area of
      Southern Jordan. *ADAJ* 27: 185–96.
1983b Prospection archéologique et épigraphi-
      que dans la région de 'Aqaba-Ma'an. *Syria*
      60: 317–23.
1983–84 The 'Aqaba-Ma'an Archaeological and
      Epigraphic Survey, 1980–82. *Archiv für
      Orientforschung* 29/30: 264–70.
1984 The 'Aqaba-Ma'an Archaeological and
      Epigraphic Survey, 1980–84. *Trasus* 2:2:
      34–54.
1986a Prospection archéologique et épigra-
      phique dans la region d'Aqaba-Ma'an,
      1984–85. *Syria* 63: 405–15.
1986b North Arabian (-Thamudic) Inscriptions
      and Rock Art from the 'Aqaba-Ma'an
      Area of Southern Jordan. *ADAJ* 30:
      261–83.
1989a 'Aqaba-Ma'an Archaeological and Epi-
      graphic Survey. Pp. 16–24 in D. Homès-
      Fredericq and J. B. Hennessy, eds.,
      Archaeology of Jordan: II.1. Field Reports,
      Leuven: Peeters.
1989b Report of the Eighth Season of the
      'Aqaba-Ma'an Archaeological and Epi-
      graphical Survey (January–February
      1988). *Liber Annuus* 39: 253–55.

Jobling, L.; Bannigan, M.; and Morgan, R.
1997   Aqaba-Ma'an Survey. P. 500 in P. Bikai
       and V. Egan, eds., Archaeology in Jordan.
       AJA 101: 493–535.

Johnson, D. J.
1987   *Nabataean trade: Intensification and
       culture change.* Ph.D. diss. University of
       Utah.
1990   Nabataean Piriform Unguentaria. *ARAM*
       2: 235–48.

Jones, H. L.
1917–32 *The Geography of Strabo.* 8 vols.
         Cambridge, MA: Harvard University.

Joukowsky, M. S.
2007   Exciting Developments: The Brown Uni-
       versity 2006 Petra Great Temple Excava-
       tions. *ADAJ* 51: 81–102.
2009   Surprises at the Petra Great Temple: A
       Retrospective. *SHAJ* 10: 291–323.

Kaegi, W. E.
1992   *Byzantium and the early Islamic Conquests.*
       Cambridge: Cambridge University.

Kaimio, M.
2000   P.Petra inv. 83: A Settlement of Dispute.
       Pp. 719–24 in *Atti del XXII Congresso
       Internazionale di Papirologia.* Florence:
       Istituto Papirologico G.Vitelli.

Kanellopoulos, C.
2003   The Layout of the Garden and Pool Com-
       plex in Petra, A Metrological Analysis.
       ADAJ 47: 149–57.

Kareem, J.
2001   The Pottery from the First Season of Ex-
       cavations at Khirbet Nakhil. Pp. 77–93 in
       Villeneuve and Watson 2001.

Kedar, Y.
1957a Ancient agriculture at Shivtah in the
       Negev. *IEJ* 7: 178–89.
1957b Water and soil from the desert: Some
       ancient agricultural achievements in the

Central Negev. *Geographical Journal* 123:
179–86.
1964   More about the Teleilat El-Anab in the
       Negeb. *BASOR* 176: 47–49.

Keller, D., and Grawehr, M.
2006   *Petra: ez Zantur III. Teil 1, D. Keller, Die
       Gläser aus Petra, Teil 2, M. Grawehr, Die
       Lampen der Grabungen auf ez Zantur
       in Petra.* Mainz am Rhein: Philipp von
       Zabern.

Kennedy, D. L.
1982   *Archaeological Explorations on the Roman
       Frontier in North-East Jordan: The Roman
       and Byzantine Military Installations and
       Road Network on the Ground and from
       the Air.* British Archaeological Reports
       International Series, S134. Oxford: BAR.
2004   *The Roman Army in Jordan.* 2nd edition.
       London: Council for British Research in
       the Levant.
2008   *Castra Legionis VI Ferrata*: A Building
       Inscription for the Legionary Fortress at
       Udruh near Petra. *JRA* 21: 301–18.

Kennedy, D. L., and Bewley, R.
2004   *Ancient Jordan from the Air.* London:
       Oxbow Books.

Kennedy, D. L., and Riley, D.
1990   *Rome's Desert Frontier from the Air,*
       Austin, TX: University of Texas.

King, G.
1988   Wadi Judayid Epigraphic Survey: A Pre-
       liminary Report. *ADAJ* 32: 307–17.
1992   *Wasm* (Camel Brand). *ABD* 6: 880–82.

Kirk, A.
1998   A Synthesis of Climatic Data with Spe-
       cific Interest in the Precipitation Record.
       Pp. 47–66 in R. W. Dutton, J. I. Clarke
       and A. Battikhi, eds., *Arid Land Resources
       and their Management: Jordan's Desert
       Margin.* London: Kegan Paul.

Kirk, G. E.
1938 Archaeological Exploration in the Southern Desert. *PEQ* 70: 211–35.

Kirkbride, A. S., and Harding, L.
1947 Hasma. *PEQ* 79: 7–26.

Kirwan, L.
1984 Where to Search for the Ancient Port of Leuke Kome. Pp. 55–61 in A. M. Abdalla et al., eds., *Studies in the History of Arabia*. Riyadh.

Klein, R. G.
1995 The Tor Hamar Fauna. Pp. 405–16 in Henry 1995.

Kloner, A.
1973 Dams and Reservoirs in the North-Eastern Mountains of the Negev. *Eretz Israel* 11: 248–57.
2001–2 Water Cisterns and Reservoirs in Idumea, Judaea and Nabatea during the Hellenistic and Roman Periods. *ARAM* 13/14: 461–85.

Knauf, E. A.
1990 Dushara and Shai' al-Qaum. *Aram* 2: 175–83.
1997 Eine nabatäische Inschrift von der oberen Wasserleitung am Theaterberg (Gevel el-Madbah), Petra. *ZDPV* 113: 68–69.

Koenen, L.
1996 The Carbonized Archive from Petra. *JRA* 9: 177–88.
2001 Preliminary Observations on Legal Matters in P.Petra 10. Pp. 727–42 in *Atti del XXII Congresso Internazionale di Papirologia*. Florence: Istituto Papirologico G.Vitelli.

Köhler-Rollefson, I.
1987 Ethnoarchaeological Research into the Origins of Pastoralism. *ADAJ* 31: 535–42.

Kolb, B., and Keller, D.
2002 Swiss-Liechtenstein Excavation at az-Zantur/Petra: The Twelfth Season. *ADAJ* 46: 279–93.

Koldewey, R.
1890 *Die antiken Baureste der Insel Lesbos*. Berlin: Reimer.

Koloski-Ostrow, A. O.
2001 *Water Use and Hydraulics in the Roman City*. Dubuque, IA: Kendall/Hunt.

Kraemer, C. J.
1958 *Excavations at Nessana*, III: *Non-Literary Papyri*. Princeton: Princeton University.

Kretschmer, F.
1960 La robinetterie romaine. *Revue archéologique de l'Est et du Centre-Est* 89–113.

Laborde, L. de
1830 *Voyage de l'Arabie Pétrée*. Paris: Girard.
1836 *Journey through Arabia Petraea, to Mount Sinai, the Excavated City of Petra, the Edom of the Prophecies*. London: John Murray.

Lancaster, W., and Lancaster, F.
1999 *People, Land and Water in the Arab Middle East. Environments and Landscapes in the Bilâd ash-Shâm*. Amsterdam: Harwood Academic.

Lang, M.
1968 *Waterworks in the Athenian Agora*. Princeton: American School of Classical Studies at Athens.

Lapp, P. W.
1993 'Iraq el-Emir. *NEAEHL* 3: 646–49.

Larsen, J. D.
1982 The Water Towers in Pompeii. *Analecta Romana Instituti Danici* 11: 41–67.

Last, J. S.
1975　Kourion: The Ancient Water Supply. *Proceedings of the American Philosophical Society* 119.1: 39–72.

Lavento, M.; Kouki, P.; Eklund. A.; Erving, A.; Hertell, E.; Junnilainen, H.; Silvonen, S.; and Ynnilä, H.
2007a　The Finnish Jabal Harun Project Survey. Preliminary Report of the 2005 Season. *ADAJ* 51: 289–302.

Lavento, M.; Kouki, P.; Silvonen, S.; Ynnilä, H.; and Huotari, M.
2007b　Terrace Cultivation in the Jabal Harun Area and its Relationship to the City of Petra in Southern Jordan. *SHAJ* 9: 145–56.

Lawrence, T. E.
1927　*Revolt in the Desert*. London: Jonathan Cape.

Lehtinen, M.
2001　Preliminary remarks on the prosopography of the Petra papyri. Pp. 787–94 in *Atti del XXII Congresso Internazionale di Papirologia*. Florence: Istituto Papirologico G.Vitelli.

Leveau, P., and Paillet, J.-L.
1976　*L'Alimentation en eau de Caesarea de Mauretanie et l'aqueduc de Cherchell*. Paris: Éditions L'Harmattan.

Levy, T. E., and Alon, D.
1987　Settlement Patterns along the Nahal Beersheva-Lower Nahal Besor: Models of Subsistence in the Northern Negev. Pp. 45–138 in T. E. Levy, ed., *Shiqmim*, I, British Archaeological Reports International Series, S356. Oxford: BAR.

Levy, T. E.; Daviau, P. M. M.; Younker, R. W.; and Shaer, M. (eds.)
2007　*Crossing Jordan: North American Contributions to the Archaeology of Jordan*. London: Equinox.

Lewis, B.
1960　Abbasids. pp. 15–23 in *Encyclopedia of Islam*, vol. I. Leiden: Brill.

Lewis, M. J. T.
2001　*Surveying Instruments of Greek and Rome*. Cambridge: Cambridge University.

Lewis, N. (ed.)
1989　*The Documents from the Bar Kokhba Period in the Cave of the Letters, Greek Papyri*. Jerusalem: Israel Exploration Society.

Lightfoot, D. R
1997　Qanats in the Levant: Hydraulic Technology at the Periphery of Early Empires. *Technology and Culture* 38: 432–51.

Lindner, M.
1976　Die zweite archäologische Expedition der Naturhistorischen Gesellschaft nach Petra (1976). *Natur und Mensch. Jahresmitteilungen der Naturhistorischen Gesellschaft Nürnberg* 1976: 83–91.
1982　An Archaeological Survey of the Theater Mount and Catchwater Regulation System at Sabra, South of Petra, 1980. *ADAJ* 26: 231–42.
1984　New Explorations of the Deir-Plateau (Petra) 1982/1983. *ADAJ* 28: 163–81.
1987a　Nabatäische Talsperren. Pp. 147–74 in G. Garbrecht, ed., *Historische Talsperren*, 1. Stuttgart: Wittwer.
1987b　Petra. Pp. 196–201 in G. Gläser, *Die Wasserversorgung antiker Städte*. Mainz am Rhein: Philipp von Zabern.
2003　Hydraulic Engineering and Site Significance in Nabataean-Roman Southern Jordan: Ba'ja, as-Sadah, Sabra, Umm Ratam. *ADAJ* 47: 183–94.
2005　Water Supply and Water Management at Ancient Sabra (Jordan). *PEQ* 137: 33–52.

Lindner, M.; Farajat, S.; and Zeitler, J.
1988　Es-Sadeh: An Important Edomite-Nabataean Site in Southern Jordan. *ADAJ* 32: 75–99.

Lindner, M.; Farajat, S.; Knauf, E. A.;
and Zeitler, J.
1990   Es-Sadeh—A Lithic–Early Bronze–Iron
       II (Edomite)–Nabataean Site in Southern
       Jordan. Report on the Second Explorato-
       ry Campaign, 1988. *ADAJ* 34: 193–237.

Lindner, M., and Gunsam, E.
2002   A Fortified Suburb of Ancient Petra:
       Shammasa. *ADAJ* 46: 225–41.

Lindner, M., and Hübl, H.
1997   Where Pharao's Daughter Got Her Drink-
       ing Water From. The '*En Brak* Conduit to
       Petra. *ZDPV* 113: 51–67.

Lindner, M.; Hübner, U.; and Hübl, J.
2000   Nabataean and Roman Presence between
       Petra and Wadi Arabah: Survey Expedi-
       tion 1997/98, Umm Ratam. *ADAJ* 44:
       535–67.

Lindner, M.; Knauf, E.A.; Zeitler, J.; and Hübl, H.
1996   Jabal al Qseir: A Fortified Iron II
       (Edomite) Mountain Stronghold in
       Southern Jordan, its Pottery and its His-
       torical Context. *ADAJ* 40: 137–66.

Lloyd, J. W.
1969   *The Hydrogeology of the Southern Desert
       of Jordan*. UNDP/FAO 212, Technical
       Report, no. 1. Rome: FAO.

Mabry, J.
1989   Investigations at Tell el-Handaquq, Jor-
       dan (1987–88). *ADAJ* 33: 59–95.

MacDonald, B.
1992   Archaeology of Edom. *ABD* 2: 295–301.
2001   Climate: Changes in Jordan through
       Time. Pp. 595–602 in MacDonald et al.
       2001.

MacDonald, B.; Adams, R.; and Bienkowski, P.
2001   *The Archaeology of Jordan*. Sheffield:
       Sheffield Academic.

Macumber, P. G.
2001   Evolving Landscape and Environment
       of Jordan. Pp. 1–30 in MacDonald et al.
       2001.

Manning, R.
1891   On the Flow of Water in Open Channels
       and Pipes. *Transactions of the Institute of
       Civil Engineers in Ireland* 20: 161–207.

Markoe, G. (ed.)
2003   *Petra Rediscovered: Lost City of the Naba-
       taeans*. New York: Abrams.

Massazza, F.
1998   Pozzolana and Pozzolanic Cements. Pp.
       470–635 in P. C. Hewlett, ed., *Lea's Chem-
       istry of Cement and Concrete*, 4th ed. New
       York: Elsevier.

Maughan, W. C.
1874   *The Alps of Arabia: Travels in Egypt, Sinai,
       Arabia and the Holy Land*. 2nd ed.
       London: King.

Mayerson, P.
1959   Ancient Agricultural Remains in the
       Central Negeb: The Teleilat El-Anab.
       BASOR 153: 19–31.
1960   The Ancient Agricultural Remains of the
       Central Negeb: Methodology and Dating
       Criteria. *BASOR* 160: 27–37.
1961   *The Ancient Agricultural Regime of
       Nessana and the Negev*. Jerusalem: Colt
       Archaeological Institute.
1967   A Note on Demography and Land Use in
       the Ancient Negeb. *BASOR* 185: 39–43.
1985   The Wine and Vineyards of Gaza in the
       Byzantine Period. *BASOR* 257: 75–80.
1986   The Beersheba Edict. *ZPE* 64: 141–48.

Mazar, A.
2002   A Survey of the Aqueducts to Jerusalem.
       Pp. 210–43 in Amit et al. 2002.

McKenzie, J.
1990   *The Architecture of Petra*. Oxford: Oxford
       University.

McKenzie, J.; Reyes, A.; and Gibson, S.
2002   Khirbat at-Tannur in the ASOR Nelson
        Glueck Archive and the Reconstruction
        of the Temple. *ADAJ* 46: 451–76.

Meir, I. A.; Freidin, C.; and Gilead, I.
2005   Analysis of Byzantine Mortars from the
        Negev Desert, Israel, and Subsequent En-
        vironmental and Economic Implications.
        JAS 32: 767–73.

Melkawi, A.; 'Amr, K.; and Whitcomb, D. S.
1994   The Excavation of Two Seventh Century
        Pottery Kilns at Aqaba. *ADAJ* 38: 447–68.

Meshel, Z.; Henning, F.; Tsuk, T.; and Peleg, Y.
1996   *The Water-Supply System of Susita.* Tel
        Aviv: Institute of Archaeology.

Meshel, Z., and Tsafrir, Y.
1974   The Nabataean Road from 'Avdat to Sha'ar
        Ramon. *PEQ* 106: 103–118.
1975   The Nabataean Road from 'Avdat to Sha'ar
        Ramon. *PEQ* 107: 3–21.

Meshorer, Y.
1975   *Nabataean Coins.* Qedem 3. Jerusalem:
        Hebrew University.

Meyers, C. L., and Meyers, E. M.
1997   Sepphoris. *EANE* 4: 527–36.

Meyers, E. M.; Kraabel, A. T.; and Strange, J. F.
1976   *Ancient Synagogue Excavations at Khirbet
        Shema', Upper Galilee, Israel, 1970–1972.*
        AASOR 42.

Milik, J. T.
1958   Nouvelles inscriptions nabatéennes. *Syria*
        35: 227–51.

Milik, J. T., and Starky, J.
1975   Inscriptions récemment découvertes à
        Pétra. *ADAJ* 20: 111–30.

Millar, F.
1993   *The Roman Near East, 31 B.C.–A.D. 337.*
        Cambridge, MA: Harvard University.

Miller, K.
1887–88   *Die Peutingersche Tafel.* Ravensburg:
          Otto Maier.

Miller, D. H.
1977   *Water at the Surface of the Earth: An
        Introduction to Ecosystem Hydrodynamics.*
        New York: Academic.

Miller, R.
1980   Water Use in Syria and Palestine from
        the Neolithic to the Bronze Age. *World
        Archaeology* 11: 331–41.
1988   The Water System (Tell es-Sa'idiyeh).
        Levant 20: 84–88.

Milson, D.
2003   The Syrian *technites* Markianos Kyris
        (†425 C.E.). *ZDPV* 119: 15–20.

Mitchell, J.
1993   The Bidul Bedouin of Humayma: Ties of
        Kinship and Water. Unpublished report.

Morris, E. J.
1842   *Notes of a Tour through Turkey, Greece,
        Egypt, Arabia Petraea, to the Holy Land.* 2
        vols. Philadelphia: Carey & Hart.

al-Muheisen, Z.
1983   *L'alimentation en eau de Pétra.* PhD Dis-
        sertation, Paris, Sorbonne.
1990   Maîtrise de l'eau et agriculture en naba-
        tène: L'exemple de Pétra. *Aram* 2: 205–20.
1992   Modes d'Installations agricoles naba-
        téennes dans la region de Petra et le wadi
        Arabah. *SHAJ* 4: 215–19.
2007   Water Engineering and Irrigation System
        of the Nabataeans: A Regional Vision.
        ADAJ 51: 471–86.
2009   *The Water Engineering and Irrigation
        System of the Nabataeans.* Irbid: Yarmouk
        University.

al-Muheisen, Z., and Tarrier, D.
1996   Menace des eaux et mesures preventatives
        à Pétra à l'époque nabatéenne. *Syria* 73:
        197–204.

2001–2   Water in the Nabataean Period.
          ARAM 13/14: 515–24.

Müller, C.
1901   *Claudii Ptolemaei Geographia*. Vol. I.2.
        Paris: Firmin-Didot.

Müller, W.
1996   Bildung von Sinterablagerungen in
        Wassersystemen. Pp. 185–89 in N. de
        Haan and C. M. Jansen, *Cura Aquarum in
        Campania*. Leiden: BABESCH.

Munro, N.; Morgan, R.; and Jobling, W.
1997   Optical Dating and Landscape Chronol-
        ogy at ad-Disa, Southern Jordan, and its
        Potential. *SHAJ* 6: 97–103.

Musil, A.
1907–8   *Arabia Petraea*, II: *Edom. Topogra-
          phischer Reisebericht*. 2 vols. Vienna:
          Alfred Hölder.
1926   *The Northern Hegaz*. 2 vols. New York:
        American Geographical Society.

National Atlas
1984   *National Atlas of Jordan, I: Climate and
        Agroclimatology*. Amman: Jordan Nation-
        al Geographic Centre.

Natural Resources Authority, Amman
1977   *National Water Master Plan of Jordan*.
        Amman: Natural Resources Authority, in
        cooperation with the German Agency for
        Technical Cooperation, Federal Republic
        of Germany.

Negev, A.
1963   Nabataean Inscriptions from ʿAvdat
        (Oboda). *IEJ* 13: 113–24.
1977   The Nabataeans and the Provincia Ara-
        bia. *ANRW* II.8: 520–686.
1986   *Nabataean Archaeology Today*. New York:
        New York University.
1988a   *The Architecture of Mampsis, Final Report,
        Vol. I: The Middle and Late Nabatean
        Periods*. Qedem 26. Jerusalem: Hebrew
        University.

1988b   *The Architecture of Mampsis, Final Report,
        Vol. II: The Late Roman and Byzantine
        Periods*. Qedem 27. Jerusalem: Hebrew
        University.
1990   Mampsis: The End of a Nabataean Town.
        Aram 2: 337–65.
1991   *Personal Names in the Nabataean Realm*.
        Qedem, 32. Jerusalem: Hebrew Univer-
        sity.
1993a   Elusa. *NEAEHL* 4: 379–83.
1993b   Kurnub. *NEAEHL* 3: 882–93.
1993c   Nessana. *NEAEHL* 3: 1145–49.
1993d   Oboda. *NEAEHL* 3: 1155–65.
1993e   Sobata. *NEAEHL* 4: 1404–10.
1997a   *The* Architecture *of Oboda: Final Report*.
        Qedem 36. Jerusalem: Hebrew University.
1997b   Avdat. *EANE* 1: 236–38.
1997c   Halusa. *EANE* 2: 465–66.
1997d   Kurnub. *EANE* 3: 312–14.
1997e   Nessana. *EANE* 4: 129–30.

Nehmé, L.; Arnoux, T.; Bessaac, J.-C.; Braun, J.-P.;
Dentzer, J.-M.; Kermorvant, A.; Sachet, I.;
and Tholbecq, L.
2006   Mission archéologique de Madaʾin Salih
        (Arabie Saoudite): Recherches menées
        de 2001 à 2003 dans l'ancienne Hijra des
        Nabatéens (1). *AAE* 17: 41–124.

Nehmé, L., and Villeneuve, F.
1999   *Pétra: Métropole de l'Arabie antique*. Paris:
        Seuil.

Netzer, E.
2001a   Das Wasserversorgungssystem von
        Masada. Pp. 195–204 in Dierx and
        Garbrecht 2001.
2001b   *Hasmonean and Herodian Palaces at
        Jericho. Final Reports of the 1973–1987
        Excavations*, vol. I: *Stratigraphy and
        Architecture*. Jerusalem: University of
        Jerusalem.
2002   The aqueducts and water-supply of
        Masada. Pp. 353–64 in Amit et al. 2002.

Nevo, Y. D.
1991   *Pagans and Herders: A Re-Examination
        of the Negev Runoff Cultivation Systems*

in the Byzantine and Early Arab Periods.
Midreshet Ben-Gurion: IPS.

Nobbe, C. F. A.
1913 *Claudii Ptolemaei Geographia.* Vol. 2.
      Leipzig: Holtze.

Ohannessian-Charpin, A.
1992 Discours et territoires: Deux récits de
      fondation pour la tribu des Bdoul. *SHAJ*
      4: 403–7.

Oldfather, C. H.
1935 *Diodorus of Sicily.* Vol. 2. Cambridge,
      MA: Harvard University.

Oleson, J. P.
1984a Survey and Excavation at the Nabataean
       and Roman City of Humayma (Jordan).
       EMC 28: 235–48
1984b *Greek and Roman Mechanical Water-Lift-
       ing Devices: The History of a Technology.*
       Toronto: Toronto University.
1986   The Humayma Hydraulic Survey: Prelim-
       inary Report of the 1986 Season. *ADAJ*
       30: 253–60.
1987a The Humayma Hydraulic Survey: Pre-
       liminary Report of the 1986 Season. *EMC*
       31: 263–72.
1987b Technology and Society in Ancient
       Edom. *Transactions of the Royal Society of
       Canada* Ser. 5, vol. 2: 163–74.
1988a Nabataean and Roman Water Use in
       Edom: The Humayma Hydraulic Survey,
       1987. *EMC* 32: 117–29
1988b The Humayma Hydraulic Survey: Prelim-
       inary Report of the 1987 Season. *ADAJ*
       32: 157–69
1989   Exploration du système hydraulique de
       Humayma (1986–87). *RBib* 96: 243–48
1990a The Humeima Hydraulic Survey: Prelimi-
       nary Report of the 1989 Season. *ADAJ* 34:
       285–311.
1990b The Humeima Hydraulic Survey, 1989.
       EMC 9: 145–63.
1991a Aqueducts, Cisterns, and the Strategy
       of Water Supply at Nabataean and Ro-
       man Auara (Jordan). Pp. 45–62 in A. T.

Hodge, ed., *Future Currents in Aqueduct
Studies.* Leeds: Francis Cairns.
1991b Eine nabatäische Talsperre in der Nähe
       von Humeima (das antike Auara) in
       Jordanien. Pp. 65–71 in G. Garbrecht, ed.,
       Historische Talsperren, 2. Stuttgart:
       Wittwer.
1992a The Water–Supply System of Ancient
       Auara: Preliminary Results of the Humei-
       ma Hydraulic Survey. *SHAJ* 4: 269–76.
1992b Water Works. *ABD* 6: 883–93.
1992c The Humeima Excavation Project: Pre-
       liminary Report of the 1991 Season. *EMC*
       11: 137–69.
1992d Hellenistic and Roman Elements in
       Nabataean Hydraulic Technology. Pp.
       473–97 in G. Argoud et al., eds., *L'Eau
       et les hommes en Méditerranée et en Mer
       Noire dans l'antiquité.* Athens: Centre de
       Recherches Néo-Helléniques.
1993a The Humeima Excavation Project,
       Jordan: Preliminary Report of the 1992
       Season. *EMC* 12: 123–58.
1993b Humeima Hydraulic Survey, 1989. *Syria*
       70: 248–54.
1994a The Humeima Excavation Project,
       Jordan: Preliminary Report of the 1993
       Season. *EMC* 13: 141–79.
1994b Un poste-clé: el-Humeima. *Le monde de
       la Bible* 88: 38–39.
1995   The Origins and Design of Nabataean
       Water-Supply Systems. *SHAJ* 5: 707–19.
1996   Surface Water Management at an An-
       cient Site in Jordan's Southern Desert.
       Pp. 141–56 in *Acts, 16th Congress of the
       International Commission on Irrigation
       and Drainage, Cairo, 1966.* Cairo.
1997a Landscape and Cityscape in the Hisma:
       The Resources of Ancient al-Humayma.
       SHAJ 6: 175–88.
1997b Humeima. *EANE* 3: 121–22.
2000   Irrigation. Pp. 183–215 in Wikander
       2000.
2001a King, Emperor, Priest, and Caliph:
       Cultural Change at Hawara (Ancient al-
       Humayma) in the First Millennium AD.
       SHAJ 7: 569–80.

2001b Water-Supply in Jordan. Pp. 603–14 in MacDonald et al. 2001.

2003a 'Romanization' at Hawara (Humayma)? The Character of 'Roman' Culture at a Desert Fortress. *SHAJ* 8: 353–60.

2003b Nabataean Water Supply. Pp. 39–42, 55–60 in R. Rosenthal-Heginbottom, ed., *The Nabataeans in the Negev*. Haifa: Reuden and Edith Hecht Museum.

2007a Nabataean Water Supply, Irrigation, and Agriculture. Pp. 217–49 in Politis 2007.

2007b Nabataean Water Supply Systems: Appropriateness, Design, and Evolution. *SHAJ* 9: 167–74.

2007c From Nabataean King to Abbasid Caliph: The Enduring Attraction of Hawara/ al-Humayma, a Multi-Cultural Site in Arabia Petraea. Pp. 447–56 in Levy et al. 2007.

2009 Trajan's Engineers and the Roman Fort at Humayma (ancient Hauarra, Jordan). *SHAJ* 10: 535–48.

Oleson, J. P.; 'Amr, K.; Foote, R.; Logan, J.; Reeves, M. B.; and Schick, R.
1999 Preliminary Report of the Al-Humayma Excavation Project, 1995, 1996, 1998. *ADAJ* 43: 411–50.

Oleson, J. P.; 'Amr, K.; Schick, R.; and Foote, R.
1995 Preliminary Report of the Humeima Excavation Project, 1993. *ADAJ* 39: 317–54.

Oleson, J. P.; 'Amr, K.; Schick, R.; Foote, R.; and Somogyi-Csizmazia, J.
1993 The Humeima Excavation Project, Jordan: Preliminary Report of the 1991–1992 Seasons. *ADAJ* 37: 461–502.

Oleson, J. P.; Baker, G.; de Bruijn, E.; Foote, R.; Logan, J.; Reeves, M. B.; and Sherwood, A. N.
2003 Preliminary Report of the Al-Humayma Excavation Project, 2000, 2002. *ADAJ* 47: 411–50.

Oleson, J. P.; Bottalico, L.; Brandon, C.; Cucitore, R.; Gotti, E.; and Hohlfelder, R. L.
2006 Reproducing a Roman maritime structure with Vitruvian pozzolanic concrete. *JRA* 19: 31–52.

Oleson, J. P., and Foote, R.
1997 Humeima. Pp. 518–20 in P. Bikai and V. Egan, eds., Archaeology in Jordan. *AJA* 101: 493–535.

Oleson, J. P.; Reeves, M. B.; Baker, G.; de Bruijn, E.; Gerber, Y.; Nikolic, M.; and Sherwood, A. N.
2008 Preliminary Report on Excavations at al-Humayma, Ancient Hawara, 2004 and 2005. *ADAJ* 52: 309–42.

Oleson, J. P.; Reeves, M. B.; and Fisher, B.
2002 New Dedicatory Inscriptions from Humayma (Ancient Hawara), Jordan. *ZPE* 140: 103–21.

Olszewski, D. I.
2001 The Palaeolithic Period, Including the Epipalaeolithic. Pp. 31–66 in MacDonald et al. 2001.

Oppenheim, M. F. von
1943 *Die Beduinen*, II: *Die Beduinenstämme in Palästina, Transjordanien, Sinai, Hedjaz.* Leipzig: Harrassowitz.

Orlandos, A. K.
1966–68 *Les matériaux de construction et la technique architecturale des anciens Grecs.* 2 vols. Paris: De Boccard.

Ortloff, C. R.
2005 The Water Supply and Distribution System of the Nabataean City of Petra (Jordan), 300 BC–AD 300. *CAJ* 15.1: 93–109.

Osborn, G., and Duford, J. M.
1981 Geomorphological Processes in the Inselberg Region of South-Western Jordan. *PEQ* 113: 1–17.

Pace, P.
1983 *Gli acquedotti di Roma*. Rome: S. Eligio.

Palmer, C.
2001 Traditional Agriculture. Pp. 621–29 in MacDonald et al. 2001.

Parker, S. T.
1976 Archaeological Survey of the Limes Arabicus: A Preliminary Report. *ADAJ* 21: 19–31.
1986 *Romans and Saracens: A History of the Arabian Frontier*. American Schools of Oriental Research, Dissertation Series, 6. Winona Lake, IN: Eisenbrauns.
2009 The Roman frontier in southern Arabia: A Synthesis of Recent Research. Pp. 143–52 in W. S. Hanson, ed., *The Army and Frontiers of Rome*. JRA Supplement 74. Portsmouth, RI: JRA.

Parker, S. T. (ed.)
1987 *The Roman Frontier in Central Jordan. Interim Report on the Limes Arabicus Project, 1980–1985*. British Archaeological Reports International Series, S340. Oxford: BAR.

Parr, P.
1962 A Nabataean Sanctuary near Petra: A Preliminary Notice. *ADAJ* 6/7: 21–24.
1967 La date du barrage du Siq à Pétra. *RBib* 74: 45–49.
1978 Pottery, People and Politics. Pp. 202–9 in R. Moorey and P. Parr, eds., *Archaeology in the Levant: Essays for Kathleen Kenyon*. Warminster: Aris & Phillips.
1997 Meda'in Saleh. *EANE* 3: 446–47.
2003 The Origins and Emergence of the Nabataeans. Pp. 27–36 in Markoe 2003.

Parr, P.; Harding, G. L.; and Dayton, J. E.
1968–69 Preliminary Survey in N.W. Arabia. *Bulletin of the Institute of Archaeology, University of London* 6/7: 21–24.

Patrich, J.
1990 *The Formation of Nabataean Art. Prohibition of a Graven Image among the Nabataeans*. Leiden: Brill.
2002 The aqueducts of Hyrcania-Kastellon. Pp. 336–52 in Amit et al. 2002.

Peacock, D. P. S., and Williams, D. F.
1986 *Amphorae and the Roman Economy*. London: Longman.

Peake, F. G.
1958 *A History of Jordan and its Tribes*. Coral Gables, FL: University of Miami.

Peleg, Y.
2000 The Characteristics of Water Distribution in Roman Towns. Pp. 241–46 in G. Jansen, ed., *Cura Aquarum in Sicilia*. Leiden: BABESCH.

Perry, M. A., and Jones, G. L.
2006 The 2005 Wadi Ramm GPR Survey. *ADAJ* 50: 157–67.

Philip, G.
2001 The Early Bronze I–III Ages. Pp. 165–232 in MacDonald et al. 2001.

Placentini, D.
2001–2 Palmyra's Springs in the Epigraphic Sources. *ARAM* 13/14: 525–34.

Politis, K. D. (ed.)
2007 *The World of the Nabataeans*, vol. 2. Stuttgart: Steiner.

Pollard, N.
2000 *Soldiers, Cities, and Civilians in Roman Syria*. Ann Arbor, MI: University of Michigan.

Powell, M. A.
1992 Weights and Measures. *ABD* 6: 897–908.

Rababeh, S. M.
2005 *How Petra was Built*. British Archaeological Reports International Series, S1460. Oxford: Archaeopress.

Rabba, I.
1991   *The Geology of the al Quwayra Area (Map Sheet no. 3049 I)*. Geological Mapping Division, Bulletin 16. Amman: Geology Directorate, Geological Mapping Division.

Reeves, M. B.
1996   *The Roman Bathhouse at Humeima*. M.A. Thesis, University of Victoria.
2009   Landscapes of Divine Power at Humayma. *SHAJ* 10: 325–38.

Reeves, M. B.; Babbitt, I.; Cummer, K.; Karas, B. V.; Seymour, V.; and Shelton, A.
2010   Preliminary Report on Excavations in the Nabataean Town and Roman Vicus at Humayma (Ancient Hawara), 2008. *SHAJ* 53: 229–63.

Reeves, M. B., and Oleson, J. P.
1997   Baths of the Hisma Desert. *Balnearia* 5.1: 2–4.

Riederer, J.
1987   *Archäologie und Chemie*. Berlin: Staatliche Museen.

Ripa, C.
1989   Il tesoro di Porto Giulio. *Il Subacqueo* 17.194 (July): 49–53.

Robertson, A.
1982   *Roman Imperial Coins in the Hunter Coin Cabinet, V: Diocletian (Reform) to Zeno*. Oxford: Oxford University.

Roche, M.-J.
1996   Remarques sur les Nabatéens en Méditerranée. *Semitica* 45: 73–99.

Ron, Z.
1966   Agricultural Terraces in the Judean Mountains. *IEJ* 16: 33–49.

Rosen, S. A.
2000   The Decline of Desert Agriculture: A View from the Classical Period Negev.

Pp. 45–62 in G. Barker and D. Gilbertson, eds., *Archaeology of Drylands: Living at the Margin*. London: Routledge.

Rubin, R.
1988   Water Conservation Methods in Israel's Negev Desert in Late Antiquity. *Journal of Historical Geography* 14: 229–44.
1989   The Debate over Climatic Changes in the Negev, Fourth–Seventh Centuries C.E. *PEQ* 121: 71–78.
1996   Urbanization, Settlement and Agriculture in the Negev Desert—The Impact of the Roman-Byzantine Empire on the Frontier. *ZDPV* 112: 49–60.

Russell, K. W.
1993   Ethnohistory of the Bedul Bedouin. *ADAJ* 37: 15–35.

Salameen, Z.
2005   Nabataean Winepresses from Bayda, Southern Jordan. *ARAM* 17: 115–27.

Salameh, E., and Bannayan, H.
1993   *Water Resources of Jordan: Present Status and Future Potential*. Amman: F. Ebert Stiftung.

Sartre, M.
1993   *Inscriptions de la Jordanie, 4: Pétra et la Nabatène méridionale, du Wadi Hasa au Golfe*. Inscriptions greques et latines de la Syrie, 21. Paris: Geuthner.
2005   *The Middle East under Rome*. Cambridge, MA: Harvard University.

Savignac, M. R.
1932   Notes de voyage. Le sanctuaire d'Allat à Iram. *RBib* 41: 581–97.
1933   Le sanctuaire d'Allat à Iram (1). *RBib* 42: 405–22.
1934   Le sanctuaire d'Allat à Iram (suite). *RBib* 43: 572–91.

Savignac, M. R., and Horsfield, G.
1935   Le temple de Ramm. *RBib* 44: 245–78.

Schick, R.

1994 The Settlement Pattern of Southern Jordan: The Nature of the Evidence. Pp. 133–54 in G. R. D. King and A. Cameron, eds. *The Byzantine and Early Islamic Near East*. Princeton, NJ: Darwin.

1995a *The Christian Communities of Palestine from Byzantine to Islamic Rule: A Historical and Archaeological Study*. Princeton, NJ: Darwin.

1995b Christianity at Humeima, Jordan. *Liber Annuus* 45: 319–42.

2001 Christianity in Southern Jordan in the Byzantine and Early Islamic Periods. *SHAJ* 7: 581–84.

2007 Al-Humayma and the Abbasid Family. *SHAJ* 9: 345–55.

Schmid, S.

1997 Nabataean Fine Ware Pottery and the Destruction of Petra in the Late First and Early Second Century AD. *SHAJ* 6: 413–20.

2000 *Petra, ez Zantur II: Ergebnisse der Schweizerisch-Liechtensteinischen Ausgrabungen, Teil II: Die Feinkeramik der Nabatäer. Typologie, Chronologie und kulturhistorische Hintergründe*. Mainz am Rhein: Philipp von Zabern.

2001a The 'Hellenisation' of the Nabataeans: A New Approach. *SHAJ* 7: 407–19.

2001b The Nabataeans: Travellers between Lifestyles. Pp. 367–426 in MacDonald et al. 2001.

2001c The International Wadi Farasa Project (IWFP) between Microcosm and Macroplanning—A First Synthesis. *PEQ* 133: 159–97.

2002 The International Wadi Farasa Project (IWFP), Preliminary Report on the 2001 Season. *ADAJ* 46: 257–77.

2003 Nabataean Pottery. Pp. 75–81 in Markoe 2003.

2007 Nabataean Funerary Complexes: Their Relation with the Luxury Architecture of the Hellenistic and Roman Mediterranean. *SHAJ* 9: 205–19.

Schmidt-Colinet, A.; al-As'ad, K.; and Müting-Zimmer, C.

1992 *Das Tempel-Grab Nr. 36 in Palmyra*. Mainz am Rhein: Philipp von Zabern.

Schulz, H. D.

1986 Schichtungen im Kalksinter der römischen Wasserleitungen nach Köln. Eine Hilfe zur relativen Datierung. Pp. 263–68 in K. Grewe, *Atlas der römischen Wasserleitungen nach Köln*. Bonn: Habelt.

Seeck, O. (ed.)

1876 *Notitia dignitatum. Accedunt notitia urbis Constantinopolitanae et latercula provinciarum*. Berlin: Weidmann.

Segal, A.

1983 *The Byzantine City of Shivta (Esbeita), Negev Desert, Israel*. British Archaeological Reports International Series, S179. Oxford: BAR.

Sha'er, M.

2004 Nabataean Mortars Used for Hydraulic Construction. Pp. 143–46 in H.-D. Bienert and J. Häser, eds., *Men of Dykes and Canals: The Archaeology of Water in the Middle East*. Rahden: Marie Leidorf.

Shahîd, I.

1984 *Rome and the Arabs. A Prolegomenon to the Study of Byzantium and the Arabs*. Washington, DC: Dumbarton Oaks.

Shaw, B. D.

1982 Lamasba: An Ancient Irrigation Community. *Antiquités Africaines* 18: 61–103.

1984 Water and Society in the Ancient Maghrib: Technology, Property and Development. *Antiquités Africaines* 20: 121–73.

Shaw, J. W.

1973 *Minoan Architecture: Materials and Techniques*. Rome: Istituto Poligrafico dello Stato.

Shehadeh, N.
1985   The Climate of Jordan in the Past and
        Present. *SHAJ* 2: 25–37.

Shereshevski, J.
1991   *Byzantine Urban Settlements in the Negev
        Desert.* Be'er Sheva: Ben-Gurion Univer-
        sity of the Negev Press.

Sherwood, A. N.; Oleson, J. P.; De Bruijn, E.;
and Nikolic, M.
2008   Preliminary Report of the Humayma
        Excavation Project, 2002, 2004–2005:
        The Roman Fort, Part II: Latrine, Plaster
        Bins/Basins, Hydraulic Probes, Weapon-
        Platform/*Ascensus* and Defensive Ditch.
        Mouseion 8: 159–83.

Shmeis, A. A., and Waheeb, M.
2002   Recent Discoveries at the Baptism Site:
        The Pottery. *ADAJ* 46: 561–81.

Simmons, A.
1981   A Paleo-subsistence Model for Early Neo-
        lithic Occupation of the Western Negev
        Desert. *BASOR* 242: 31–49.

Sourdel, D.
1971   Al-Humayma. P. 574 in *Encyclopedia of
        Islam*, vol. 3. Leiden: Brill.

Speidel, M. P.
1977   The Roman Army in Arabia. *ANRW* II.8:
        688–730.
1979   A Tile Stamp of Cohors I Thracum Mil-
        liaria from Hebron in Palestine. *ZPE* 29:
        171–72.

Spijkerman, A.
1978   *The Coins of the Decapolis and Provincia
        Arabia.* M. Piccirillo ed. Jerusalem: Fran-
        ciscan Printing.

Stager, L.
1976   Farming in the Judean Desert during the
        Iron Age. *BASOR* 221: 145–58.

Starcky, J.
1965   Pétra et la Nabatène. Pp. 886–1017 in
        Dictionnaire de la Bible, Supplément,
        Paris: Letouzey et Ané.

Stein, Sir A.
1940   Surveys on the Roman Frontier in 'Iraq
        and Trans-Jordan. *Geographical Journal*
        95: 428–38.
1982   The South of Transjordan. in Kennedy
        1982: 259–97.

Stillwell, R. (ed.)
1941   *Antioch-on-the-Orontes*, III: *The Exca-
        vations, 1937–1939.* Princeton, NJ:
        Princeton University.

Stucky, R. A; Schmid, S. G; and Kolb, B.
1996   *Petra: Az-Zantur*, I. Ergebnisse der
        Schweizerisch-Liechtensteinischen Aus-
        grabungen 1988–1992. Mainz am Rhein:
        Philipp von Zabern.

Sutherland, C. H. V., and Carson, R. A. G.
1967   *Roman Imperial Coinage*, VI: *From Dio-
        cletian's Reform (A.D. 294) to the Death of
        Maximinus (A.D. 313).* London: Spink.

al-Tabarî, Abû Ja'far Muhammad ibn Jarîr
1879–1901   *Ta'rîkh al-Rusul wa al-Mulûk.*
        M. J. de Goeje et al., eds. Leiden: Brill.

Taylor, J.
2001   *Petra and the Lost Kingdom of the Naba-
        taeans.* London: I.B. Tauris.

Teixidor, J.
1984   *Un port romain du désert: Palmyre et son
        commerce d'Auguste á Caracalla.* Paris:
        Librarie Adrien-Maisonneuve.

al-Theeb, S.
2002   New Nabataean Inscriptions from
        Qa' al-Mu' atadel. Pp. 297–306 in J. F.
        Healey and V. Porter, eds., *Studies on Ara-
        bia in Honour of Professor G. Rex Smith.*
        Oxford: Oxford University.

Tholbecq, L.
1998 The Nabataeo-Roman Site of Wadi
      Ramm (Iram): A New Appraisal. *ADAJ*
      42: 241–54.
2001 The Hinterland of Petra from the
      Edomite to the Islamic Periods: The Jabal
      ash-Sharah Survey (1996–1997). *SHAJ* 7:
      399–405.

Tholbecq, L., and Durand, C.
2005 A Nabataean Rock-Cut Sanctuary in Pe-
      tra: Preliminary Report on Three Excava-
      tion Seasons at the 'Obodas Chapel', Jabal
      Numayr (2002–2004). *ADAJ* 49: 299–311.

Thomsen, P.
1906 Untersuchungen zur älteren Palästinalite-
      ratur. *ZDPV* 29: 101–32.

Tölle-Kastenbein, R.
1991 Entlüftung antiker Wasserleitungsrohre.
      AA 1991: 25–30.
1994 *Das archaische Wasserleitungsnetz für
      Athen.* Mainz am Rhein: Philipp von
      Zabern.

Trousset, P.
1986 Les oasis présahariennes dans l'antiquité:
      Portage de l'eau et division du temps.
      Antiquités Africaines 22: 163–93.

Tsafrir, Y.
1988 *Excavations at Rehovot-in-the-Negev,* I:
      The Northern Church. Qedem 25.
      Jerusalem: Hebrew University.

Tsuk, T.
1996 *Piscina Mirabilis* in Campania, Italy, and
      Sepphoris, Israel: Comparison between
      Two Large, Ancient Reservoirs. Pp.
      117–23 in N. de Haan and C. M. Jansen,
      eds., *Cura Aquarum in Campania.*
      Leiden: BABESCH.
2001–2 Urban Water Reservoirs in the Land
      of the Bible during the Bronze Age and
      the Iron Age (3000–568 B.C.). *ARAM*
      13–14: 377–401.

2002 The Water-Supply System of Shivta in the
      Byzantine Period. Pp. 65–80 in C. Oleg,
      Y. Peleg and T. Tsuk, eds., *Cura Aquarum
      in Israel.* Siegburg: DWhG.

Tushingham, A. D.
1985 *Excavations in Jerusalem 1961–1967,* vol.
      1. Toronto: Royal Ontario Museum.

Urman, D.
2004 Nessana Excavations 1987–1995. Pp.
      1–118 in D. Urman, ed., *Nessana:
      Excavations and Studies,* I. Beer-Sheva:
      Ben-Gurion University of the Negev.

Vallois, R.
1966 *L'Architecture hellénique et hellénistique a
      Délos jusqu'a l'éviction des Déliens (166 Av.
      J.-C.),* 1: *Les monuments.* BEFAR no 157.
      Paris: De Boccard.

Villeneuve, F.
1986 Khirbet edh-Dharih (1985). *RBib* 93:
      247–52.
1990 The Pottery from the Oil Factory at
      Khirbet edh-Dahrih (2nd Century A.C.).
      A Contribution to the Study of the Mate-
      rial Culture of the Nabataeans. *ARAM* 2:
      367–84.

Villeneuve, F., and Watson, P. M. (eds.)
2001 *La céramique byzantine et proto-islamique
      en Syrie-Jordanie (IVe–VIIe siècles apr.
      J.-C.). Actes du colloque tenu à Amman
      les 3 et 4 décembre 1994.* Beirut: Institut
      français d'archéologie du Proche-Orient.

Wagstaff, J. M.
1985 *The Evolution of the Middle Eastern Land-
      scapes. An Outline to A.D. 1840.* London:
      Croom-Helm.

Waheeb, M.
1996 'Ain al-Jammam. Pp. 514–16 in P. Bikai
      and V. Egan, eds., Archaeology in Jordan.
      AJA 100: 507–35.

Waheeb, M., and Fino, N.
1997   ʼAyn el-Jammam: A Neolithic Site near Ras
        en-Naqb, Southern Jordan. Pp. 215–19 in
        H. G. Gebel, Z. Kafafi and G. Rollefson,
        eds., *The Prehistory of Jordan*, II: *Perspec-
        tives from 1997*. Berlin: Ex Oriente.

Waliszewski, T.
2001   Céramique Byzantine et proto-islamique
        de Khirbet edh-Dharih (Jordanie du
        Sud). Pp. 95–106 in Villeneuve and
        Watson 2001.

Watson, P.
2001   The Byzantine Period. Pp. 461–502 in
        MacDonald et al. 2001.

Weber, T., and Wenning, R. (eds.)
1997   *Petra: Antike Felsstadt zwischen arabischer
        Tradition und griechischer Norm*. Mainz
        am Rhein: Philipp von Zabern.

Webster, G.
1985   *The Roman Imperial Army of the First and
        Second Centuries A.D.* 3rd ed. Totowa, NJ:
        Barnes & Noble.

Wenning, R.
1987   *Die Nabatäer: Denkmäler und Geschichte*.
        Göttingen: Vandenhoeck & Ruprecht.
1993   Eine neuerstellte Liste der nabatäischen
        Dynastie. *Boreas* 16: 25–38.
2001   The Betyls of Petra. *BASOR* 324: 71–95.
2007   The Nabataeans in History. Pp. 25–44 in
        Politis 2007.
2009   The Message of the Khirbat at-Tannur
        Reliefs. *SHAJ* 10: 577–84.

West, J. M. I.
1974   Uranius. *Harvard Studies in Classical
        Philology* 78: 282–84.

Whitcomb, D.
1996   Urbanism in Arabia. *AAE* 7: 38–51.
2001   Ceramic Production at Aqaba in the
        Early Islamic Period. Pp. 297–303 in
        Villeneuve and Watson 2001.

Wiegand, T.
1920   *Sinai*. Berlin and Leipzig: de Gruyter.

Wikander, Ö. (ed.)
2000   *Handbook of Ancient Water Technology*.
        Leiden: Brill.

Wilkinson, J.
1974   Ancient Jerusalem: Its Water Supply and
        Population. *PEQ* 106: 33–51.
1977   *Water and Tribal Settlement in South-East
        Arabia. A Study of the Aflaj of Oman*.
        Oxford: Oxford University.

Wilson, A.
2001   Urban Water Storage, Distribution, and
        Usage. Pp. 83–96 in Koloski-Ostrow
        2001.

Wiseman, J.
1998   Rethinking the 'Halls of Hades'. *Archaeol-
        ogy Magazine* 51.3: 12.

Woolley, C. L., and Lawrence, T. E.
1914–15 The Wilderness of Zin. *Palestine Ex-
        ploration Fund, Annual*.

Wycherly, R. E.
1978   *The Stones of Athens*. Princeton, NJ:
        Princeton University.

Yadin, Y.; Greenfield, J. C.; Yardeni, A.;
and Levine, B. A.
2002   *The Documents from the Bar Kokhba
        Period in the Cave of Letters: Hebrew,
        Aramic, and Nabataean-Aramaic Papyri*.
        Jerusalem: Israel Exploration Society.

al-Yaʻqûbî, Ahmad ibn Abî Yaʻqûb.
1892   *Kitâb al-Buldân*. M. J. de Goeje, ed.
        Leiden: Brill.

Young, G. K.
2001   *Rome's Eastern Trade: International com-
        merce and imperial policy, 31 B.C.–A.D.
        305*. London: Routledge.

Youtie, H. C.
1936   Ostraca from Sbeitah. *AJA* 40: 452–59.

Zayadine, F.
1994   Ayla-ʾAqaba in the Light of Recent Exca-
       vations. *ADAJ* 38: 485–505.

Zayadine, F.; Larché, F.; and Dentzer-Feydy, J.
2003   *Qasr al-Bint de Pétra. L'Architecture, le
       Décor, la Chronologie et les Dieux*. Paris:
       Éditions Recherches sur les Civilisations.

Zohary, M.
1962   *Plant Life of Palestine, Israel and Jordan*.
       New York: Ronald.
1982   *Plants of the Bible*. Cambridge:
       Cambridge University.

Index